C000180379

SCOTS ME LAW

SCOTS MERCANTILE LAW

BY

ENID A. MARSHALL

M.A., LL.B., Ph.D., Associate R.I.C.S., A.C.I.Arb., F.R.S.A., Solicitor

Reader in Business Law at the University of Stirling

THIRD EDITION

W. GREEN/Sweet & Maxwell
EDINBURGH
1997

First published in 1983
Second edition 1992
Third edition 1997

© 1997
W. GREEN & SON LTD

ISBN 0 414 01214 3

No natural forests were destroyed to make this product;
only farmed timber was used and replanted.

A CIP catalogue reference for this book is available from the British Library.

All rights reserved. United Kingdom statutory material in this publication is acknowledged as Crown copyright.

No part of this publication may be reproduced or transmitted in any form or by any means, or stored in any retrieval system of any nature without prior written permission, except for permitted fair dealing under the Copyright, Designs and Patents Act 1988, or in accordance with the terms of a licence issued by the Copyright Licensing Agency in respect of photocopying and/or reprographic reproduction. Applications for permission for other use of copyright material including permission to reproduce extracts in other published works shall be made to the publishers. Full acknowledgment of author, publisher and source must be given.

Typeset by LBJ Typesetting Ltd of Kingsclere
Printed and bound in Great Britain by the Headway Press, Reading

PREFACE TO THIRD EDITION

THE author's aim continues to be, as in the earlier editions, to produce a readable students' textbook on the major topics of mercantile, commercial or business law as studied at Scottish universities and colleges. It is hoped that the book will be especially helpful to those who are part-time students or for any other reason have little time or facility to consult primary sources in a law library.

No previous knowledge of law is assumed. To assist beginners, statutory language, if complex, has been explained in words of few syllables, the text has been illustrated with brief accounts of, and quotations from decided cases, there are virtually no footnotes, and all the Latin maxims have been provided with translations.

Each chapter ends with a short list of "*Further Reading*," selected mainly from the growing number of recently published works on Scots law. The letter "E" is prefixed to titles which deal with English law and only incidentally (or not at all expressly) with Scots law.

As regards statutory matter, important updating has been necessary especially in the chapters on sale of goods and bankruptcy, as a result of the significant amendments made by the Sale and Supply of Goods Act 1994, the Sale of Goods (Amendment) Act 1995 and the Bankruptcy (Scotland) Act 1993. Account has also been taken of some recent subordinate legislation, including the Commercial Agents (Council Directive) Regulations in the chapter on agency, the Deregulation (Bills of Exchange) Order 1996 in the chapter on bills of exchange, cheques and promissory notes and the Unfair Terms in Consumer Contracts Regulations 1994 in the chapter on arbitration.

Many recent cases, in summary form, have been incorporated in the text for illustrative purposes, particularly in the chapters on agency, bankruptcy and arbitration. Most important perhaps is the change to the common law of Scotland on cautionary obligations made by the decision of the House of Lords in *Smith v. Bank of*

Scotland—not the first time that the House of Lords has overturned a long-established rule in Scots law upheld by both the Outer and the Inner Houses of the Court of Session.

I express my gratitude to Greens for their patience, guidance and helpfulness in the production of this third edition.

I have tried to state the law as at the end of August 1997.

November 11, 1997 ENID A. MARSHALL

ACKNOWLEDGMENTS

THE author gratefully acknowledges the supreme debt owed to the works of greater learning listed in the "*Further Reading*" at the end of each chapter. In particular, the following have been referred to for more than one chapter:

Gloag and Henderson, *Introduction to the Law of Scotland*, The Late W. A. Wilson and Angelo Forte (editors) (10th ed., 1995, W. Green/Sweet & Maxwell).

Gloag and Irvine, *Law of Rights in Security, Heritable and Moveable, including Cautionary Obligations* (1897, William Green & Sons).

Scots Mercantile Law Statutes (annual reprint from *The Parliament House Book*) (W. Green).

The Laws of Scotland: Stair Memorial Encyclopaedia, Robert Black (General ed. from 1988) (Butterworths/The Law Society of Scotland).

David M. Walker, *Principles of Scottish Private Law* (4th ed., 1988–89, Clarendon Press, Oxford).

W. A. Wilson, *The Scottish Law of Debt* (2nd ed., 1991, W. Green/Sweet & Maxwell).

E.A.M.

ACKNOWLEDGMENTS

CONTENTS

PAGE

Preface to Third Edition v

Acknowledgments vii

Table of Cases xi

Table of Statutes xxix

1. Agency 1
2. Partnership 75
3. Companies 126
4. Sale of Goods 195
5. Consumer Credit 289
6. Bills of Exchange, Cheques and Promissory Notes . 380
7. Rights in Security over Moveables 465
8. Cautionary Obligations 517
9. Bankruptcy 565
10. Arbitration 673

Index 741

TABLE OF CASES

Para.

Accountant in Bankruptcy *v.* Allans of Gillcock Ltd, 1991 S.L.T. 765 (O.H.) 9–142, 9–402
Adams *v.* Great North of Scotland Railway Co. (1890) 18 R. (H.L.) 1; (1889) 16 R. 843 .... 10–136, 10–179, 10–187, 10–188, 10–196
Ahmed's Trustee *v.* Ahmed (No. 2), 1993 S.L.T. 651 (O.H.) 9–35
Aird & Coghill *v.* Pullan & Adams (1904) 7 F. 258; 12 S.L.T. 603 4–219
Aitchison *v.* Cooper, 1982 S.L.T. (Sh.Ct.) 41 4–333
Aitchison *v.* Rizza 1985 S.C.C.R. 297 5–371
Aitken's Trs. *v.* Bank of Scotland, 1944 S.C. 270; 1945 S.L.T. 84 .... 8–08, 8–65, 8–108
Albyn Housing Society Ltd *v.* Taylor Woodrow Homes Ltd, 1985 S.C. 104 10–52
Allan *v.* Gronmeyer (1891) 18 R. 784 2–145
Allan *v.* Millar, 1932 S.C. 620; 1932 S.L.T. 436 4–35
Allan, Buckley Allan & Milne *v.* Pattison (1893) 21 R. 195; 1 S.L.T. 334 9–483
Allen *v.* Gold Reefs of West Africa Ltd [1900] 1 Ch. 656 (C.A.) 3–272
Aluminium Industrie Vaassen B.V. *v.* Romalpa Aluminium Ltd [1976] 1 W.L.R. 676 (C.A.); [1976] 2 All E.R. 552 .... 4–154, 7–179
Amag Ltd *v.* Jessop, 1989 S.C.C.R. 186; 1989 C.L.Y. 4935 4–343
Ammon *v.* Tod, 1912 S.C. 306; 1912 1 S.L.T. 118 7–64
Anderson *v.* Croall & Sons Ltd (1903) 6 F. 153; 11 S.L.T. 453 .... 1–05, 1–45, 1–169, 4–324
Anderson *v.* McCall (1866) 4 M. 765 7–90
Anderson's Tr. *v.* Fleming (1871) 9 M. 718 7–148
Anderston Foundry Co. *v.* Law (1869) 7 M. 836 7–41
Apollo Leasing Ltd *v.* Scott, 1984 S.L.T. (Sh.Ct.) 90 5–57
Archivent Sales & Development Ltd *v.* Strathclyde Regional Council, 1985 S.L.T. 154 (O.H.) 4–172
Armour *v.* Duff & Co., 1912 S.C. 120; 1911 2 S.L.T. 394 1–146
Armour *v.* Thyssen Edelstahlwerke A.G., 1990 S.L.T. 891 (H.L.) 4–154, 7–179
Arnot *v.* Stevenson (1698) Mor. 6017 1–99
Ashbury Railway Carriage and Iron Co. Ltd *v.* Riche (1875) L.R. 7 H.L. 653 .... 1–24, 3–222
Ashington Piggeries Ltd *v.* Christopher Hill Ltd *and* Christopher Hill Ltd *v.* Norsildmel [1972] A.C. 441; [1971] 2 W.L.R. 1051; [1971] 1 All E.R. 847 .... 4–76, 4–78
Automotive Financial Services Ltd *v.* Henderson, 1992 S.L.T. (Sh.Ct.) 5–302
Aviemore Station Hotel Co. Ltd *v.* Scott (1904) 12 S.L.T. 494 (O.H.) 10–141
Ayr County Council *v.* Wyllie, 1935 S.C. 836; 1935 S.L.T. 544 8–64

B.O.C.M. Silcock Ltd *v.* Hunter, 1976 S.L.T. 217 8–42
Baker *v.* Barclays Bank Ltd [1955] 1 W.L.R. 822; [1955] 2 All E.R. 571 6–224
Balcraig House's Trustee *v.* Roosevelt Property Services Ltd, 1994 S.L.T. 1133 (O.H.) 9–67

Para.
Ballantyne v. Durant, 1983 S.L.T. (Sh.Ct.) 38 4–25
Bank of Baroda Ltd v. Punjab National Bank Ltd [1944] A.C. 176; [1944] 2 All E.R. 83 .... 6–105, 6–179
Bank of Scotland v. Faulds (1870) 7 S.L.R. 619 .... 9–47, 9–481
Bank of Scotland v. Liquidators of Hutchison, Main & Co. Ltd, 1914 S.C. (H.L.) 1; 1913 S.C. 255; 1914 1 S.L.T. 111; 1912 2 S.L.T. 416 7–19
Bank of Scotland v. Mackay, 1991 S.L.T. 163 (O.H.) 9–137
Bank of Scotland v. Reid (1886) 2 Sh.Ct. Rep. 376 .... 6–102, 6–170
Bankers Trust International Ltd v. Todd Shipyards Corporation (The Halcyon Isle) [1981] A.C. 221; [1980] 3 W.L.R. 400; [1980] 3 All E.R. 197 7–71
Barclays Bank plc v. O'Brien [1994] 1 A.C. 180 8–52
Barnetson v. Petersen Brothers (1902) 5 F. 86; 10 S.L.T. 345 .... 1–17, 1–69, 1–87
Barnton Hotel Co. Ltd v. Cook (1899) 1 F. 1190; 7 S.L.T. 131 7–131
Barry, Ostlere & Shepherd Ltd v. Edinburgh Cork Importing Co., 1909 S.C. 1113; 1909 1 S.L.T. 540 1–86
Bartsch v. Poole & Co. (1895) 23 R. 328; 3 S.L.T. 205 6–89
Beattie v. Macgregor (1883) 10 R. 1094 10–66
Beauforte (Jon) (London) Ltd, *Re* [1953] Ch. 131; [1953] 2 W.L.R. 465; [1953] 1 All E.R. 634 3–225
Bell v. Andrews (1885) 12 R. 961 7–47
Bennets v. Bennet (1903) 5 F. 376; 10 S.L.T. 609 10–57
Bennett v. Inveresk Paper Co. (1891) 18 R. 975 1–160
Bernstein v. Pamson Motors (Golders Green) Ltd [1987] 2 All E.R. 220 4–222
Berry v. Taylor, 1993 S.L.T. 718 (O.H.) 9–277
Berry's Trustee v. Berry, 1994 G.W.D. 29–1735 9–263
Bird v. Brown (1850) 4 Ex. 786; 154 E.R. 1433 1–25
Birkmyr v. Darnell, 1 Smith's Leading Cases (10th ed.) 287 8–21
Black v. Cornelius (1879) 6 R. 581 .... 1–88, 1–111
Black v. Laidlaw (1844) 6 D. 1254 .... 1–89, 10–42
Black v. John Williams & Co. (Wishaw) Ltd, 1924 S.C. (H.L.) 22; 1923 S.C. 510; 1924 S.L.T. 58; 1923 S.L.T. 311 10–161
Blaikies v. Aberdeen Railway Co. (1852) 1 Paterson's App. 119; 15 D. (H.L.) 20 10–69
Bonar v. McDonald (1850) 7 Bell's App. 379; 13 D.(H.L.) 26; (1847) 9 D. 1537 8–146
Border Harvesters Ltd v. Edwards Engineering (Perth) Ltd, 1985 S.L.T. 128 (O.H.) 4–78
Bowman v. Secular Society Ltd [1917] A.C. 406 3–137
Boyter v. Thomson, 1995 S.C. (H.L.) 15 4–91
Brebner v. Henderson, 1925 S.C. 643; 1925 S.L.T. 473 .... 1–151, 6–27
Brenan v. Campbell's Trs. (1898) 25 R. 423; 5 S.L.T. 275 1–173
British Bata Shoe Co. Ltd v. Double M. Shah Ltd, 1980 S.C. 311 (O.H.); 1981 S.L.T. (Notes) 14 (O.H.) 1–93
British Linen Co. v. Monteith (1858) 20 D. 557 8–130
British Linen Co. Bank v. Carruthers and Ferguson (1883) 10 R. 923 .... 1–179, 6–101
British Motor Body Co. Ltd v. Thomas Shaw (Dundee) Ltd, 1914 S.C. 922; 1914 2 S.L.T. 131 4–288
British Westinghouse Electric and Manufacturing Co. Ltd v. Provost of Aberdeen (1906) 14 S.L.T. 391 (O.H.) 10–124
Brown v. Middlemas of Kelso Ltd, 1994 S.L.T. 1352 9–404
Brown v. Sommerville (1844) 6 D. 1267 7–136

Para.
Brown (B.S.) & Son Ltd *v.* Craiks Ltd, 1970 S.C. (H.L.) 51 4–107
Brown Brothers *v.* Carron Co. (1898) 6 S.L.T. 231 (O.H.) 4–142
Brown's Trustee *v.* Brown, 1995 S.L.T. (Sh.Ct.) 2 9–264
Bryan *v.* Butters Brothers & Co. (1892) 19 R. 490 2–57
Bryce *v.* Ehrmann (1904) 7 F. 5; 12 S.L.T. 378 4–147
Brysson *v.* Mitchell (1823) 2 S. 382 10–96
Buchan *v.* Melville (1902) 4 F. 620; 9 S.L.T. 459 10–132
Buchanan *v.* Main (1900) 3 F. 215; 8 S.L.T. 297 8–97
Buchanan & Carswell *v.* Eugene Ltd, 1936 S.C. 160; 1936 S.L.T. 93 4–103
Buchanan-Jardine *v.* Hamilink, 1983 S.L.T. 149 4–89
Bugle Press Ltd, *Re* [1961] Ch. 270 (C.A.); [1960] 3 W.L.R. 956; [1960] 3 All E.R. 791 3–163
Buie *v.* Lady Gordon (1827) 5 S. 464; (1831) 9 S. 923 1–97
Burrell *v.* Harding's Executrix, 1931 S.L.T. 76 (O.H.) 4–222

Calder & Co. *v.* Cruikshank's Tr. (1889) 17 R. 74 8–141
Caldwell *v.* Hamilton, 1919 S.C. (H.L.) 100; 1918 S.C. 677; 1919 2 S.L.T. 154; 1918 2 S.L.T. 41 .... 9–14, 9–70
Caldwell *v.* Keith Bros. (Environmental Services) Ltd, 1990 G.W.D. 10–555 (O.H.) 8–66
Caledonian Banking Co. *v.* Kennedy's Trs. (1870) 8 M. 862 .... 8–78, 8–131
Callman *v.* Bell (1793) Mor. 6255 7–169
Cameron *v.* Nicol, 1930 S.C. 1; 1929 S.L.T. 653 10–19
Campbell *v.* Anderson (1829) 3 W. & S. 384; (1826) 5 S. 86 1–189
Campbell and Beck *v.* Macfarlane (1862) 24 D. 1097 9–467
Campbell *v.* McCreath, 1975 S.C. 81 2–60
Cantiere San Rocco S.A. *v.* Clyde Shipbuilding and Engineering Co. Ltd, 1923 S.C. (H.L.) 105; 1923 S.L.T. 624 4–282
Capital and Counties Bank Ltd *v.* Gordon [1903] A.C. 240 .... 6–209, 6–222
Carabine *v.* Carabine, 1949 S.C. 521; 1949 S.L.T. 429 2–146
Carter *v.* Johnstone (1886) 13 R. 698 9–55
Charteris *v.* Clydesdale Banking Co. (1882) 19 S.L.R. 602 (O.H.) 6–124
Christie *v.* Ruxton (1862) 24 D. 1182 7–162
Ciceri *v.* Hunter & Co. (1904) 12 S.L.T. 293 (O.H.) 2–58
Clark *v.* Bowring & Co., 1908 S.C. 1168; 16 S.L.T. 326 7–72
Clark *v.* G. R. & W. Jamieson, 1909 S.C. 132, 16 S.L.T. 450 2–24
Clark *v.* Watson, 1982 S.L.T. 450 (O.H.) 2–158
Clark *v.* West Calder Oil Co. Ltd (1882) 9 R. 1017 7–16
Clark's Trustee, Noter, 1993 S.L.T. 667 (O.H.) 9–178
Clark Taylor & Co. *v.* Quality Site Development (Edinburgh) Ltd, 1981 S.C. 111; 1981 S.L.T. 308 4–154
Clayton's Case (1816) 1 Mer. 572; 35 E.R. 781 .... 8–106, 8–113, 8–115
Clydebank District Council *v.* Clink, 1977 S.C. 147; 1977 S.L.T. 190 10–78
Clydesdale Bank Ltd *v.* Walker & Bain, 1926 S.C. 72; 1925 S.L.T. 676 7–69
Clydesdale Bank plc *v.* Davidson, 1994 S.L.T. 225 9–365
Clydesdale Banking Co. *v.* Paul (1877) 4 R. 626 6–219
Clydesdale Banking Co. *v.* Royal Bank of Scotland (1876) 3 R. 586 .... 6–219—6–222
Cochrane *v.* Guthrie (1861) 23 D. 865 10–112
Cohen (George), Sons & Co. Ltd *v.* Jamieson & Paterson, 1963 S.C. 289 (O.H.); 1963 S.L.T. 35 4–310
Commissioners of Taxation *v.* English, Scottish and Australian Bank Ltd [1920] A.C. 683 6–158

Para.
Constant *v.* Christensen, 1912 S.C. 1371 (O.H.); 1912 2 S.L.T. 62 7–70
Cooper & Co. *v.* Jessop Brothers (1906) 8 F. 714; 13 S.L.T. 977 10–120
Copland *v.* Brogan, 1916 S.C. 277; 1916 1 S.L.T. 13 .... 1–05, 1–10, 1–114
Costello *v.* Lowe, 1990 S.C.C.R. 90; 1990 C.L.Y. 5786 4–343
Couston, Thomson & Co. *v.* Chapman (1872) 10 M. (H.L.) 74; (1871) 9 M. 675 4–314
Cowdenbeath Coal Co. Ltd *v.* Clydesdale Bank Ltd (1895) 22 R. 682; 3 S.L.T. 41 .... 4–261, 9–57
Cox *v.* Hickman (1860) 8 H.L.C. 268; 11 E.R. 431 .... 2–27, 2–28
Cox Brothers *v.* Binning and Son (1867) 6 M. 161 10–181
Craig (A.F.) & Co. Ltd *v.* Blackater, 1923 S.C. 472; 1923 S.L.T. 240 .... 1–143, 1–163
Crawford *v.* Muir (*see* Muir *v.* Crawford)
Crawford *v.* Paterson (1858) 20 D. 488 10–97
Crawford Brothers *v.* Commissioners of Northern Lighthouses, 1925 S.C. (H.L.) 22; 1925 S.L.T. 341 10–142
Crerar *v.* Bank of Scotland, 1922 S.C. (H.L.) 137; 1921 S.C. 736; 1922 S.L.T. 335; 1921 2 S.L.T. 112 7–116
Cromarty Leasing Ltd *v.* Turnbull, 1988 S.L.T. (Sh.Ct.) 62 .... 1–14, 1–155
Crookston *v.* Lindsay, Crookston & Co. Ltd, 1922 S.L.T. 62 (O.H.) 3–274
Crudens *v.* Tayside Health Board, 1979 S.C. 142 .... 10–24, 10–33
Cruttwell *v.* Lye (1810) 17 Ves.Jun.335; 34 E.R. 129 2–191
Cumming *v.* Quartzag Ltd, 1980 S.C. 276 1–23
Cumming's Trustee *v.* Glenrinnes Farms Ltd, 1995 S.L.T. 904 (O.H.) 9–250
Cunningham *v.* Lee (1874) 2 R. 83 .... 1–40, 1–124
Currie *v.* McKnight (1896) 24 R. (H.L.) 1; 4 S.L.T. 161 7–67
Cuthill *v.* Strachan (1894) 21 R. 549; 1 S.L.T. 527 8–114

D.H.N. Food Distributors Ltd *v.* Tower Hamlets London Borough Council [1976] 1 W.L.R. 852 (C.A.); [1976] 3 All E.R. 462 .... 3–144, 3–161
Daimler Co. Ltd *v.* Continental Tyre and Rubber Co. (Great Britain) Ltd [1916] 2 A.C. 307 3–150
Davidson *v.* Barclays Bank Ltd [1940] 1 All E.R. 316 6–173
Davies *v.* Directloans Ltd [1986] 1 W.L.R. 823 .... 5–312, 5–313
Derry *v.* Peek (1889) 14 App.Cas. 337 3–08
Deutz Engines Ltd *v.* Terex Ltd, 1984 S.L.T. 273 (O.H.) 4–154
Devaynes *v.* Noble (1816) 1 Mer. 529; 35 E.R. 767 8–113
Dick *v.* Cochrane & Fleming, 1935 S.L.T. 432 (O.H.) 4–221
Dickie *v.* Mitchell (1874) 1 R. 1030 2–148
Dickie *v.* Singh, 1974 S.L.T. 129 (O.H.) 6–225
Dickson *v.* Clydesdale Bank Ltd, 1937 S.L.T. 585 (O.H.) 6–104
Dickson *v.* Grant (1870) 8 M. 566 10–139
Dickson *v.* National Bank of Scotland Ltd, 1917 S.C. (H.L.) 50; 1917 1 S.L.T. 318; 1916 S.C. 589; 1916 1 S.L.T. 307 2–153
Dickson *v.* Nicholson (1855) 17 D. 1011 1–192
Digby Brown & Co. *v.* Lyall, 1995 S.L.T. 932 (O.H.) 1–148
Distillers Co. Ltd *v.* Russell's Tr. (1889) 16 R. 479 7–183
Dobie *v.* Mitchell (1854) 17 D. 97 9–24
Doig *v.* Lawrie (1903) 5 F. 295; 10 S.L.T. 523 8–124
Donald *v.* Shiell's Executrix, 1937 S.C. 52; 1937 S.L.T. 70 10–203

Para.

Douglas & Co. *v.* Stiven (1900) 2 F. 575; 7 S.L.T. 361.................. 10–123
Drummond *v.* Cairns (1852) 14 D. 611.................................. 1–134
Drummond *v.* Muirhead & Guthrie Smith (1900) 2 F. 585; 7 S.L.T. 401.... 7–165
Drybrough & Co. Ltd *v.* Brown, 1989 S.C.L.R. 279................ 9–114, 9–136
Dumbarton Steamboat Co. Ltd *v.* MacFarlane (1899) 1 F. 993; 7 S.L.T. 75... 2–198
Duncan *v.* Lodijensky (1904) 6 F. 408; 11 S.L.T. 684.................... 7–55
Dundee Corporation *v.* Marr, 1971 S.C. 96; *sub nom.* Ditchburn Organisation (Sales) Ltd *v.* Dundee Corporation, 1971 S.L.T. 218....... 7–48, 7–49
Dunlop Pneumatic Tyre Co. Ltd *v.* Dunlop Motor Co. Ltd, 1907 S.C. (H.L.) 15; (1906) 8 F. 1146; (1907) 15 S.L.T. 362; (1906) 14 S.L.T. 284.. 3–202
Dunmore (Earl of) *v.* McInturner (1829) 7 S. 595........................ 10–81
Dunmore (Earl of) *v.* McInturner (1835) 13 S. 356..................... 10–160

Eadie *v.* MacBean's Curator Bonis (1885) 12 R. 660...................... 2–141
Edinburgh Albert Buildings Co. Ltd *v.* General Guarantee Corporation Ltd, 1917 S.C. 239; 1917 1 S.L.T. 54.................................... 7–50
Edinburgh (Assessor for) *v.* Caira and Crolla, 1928 S.C. 398; 1928 S.L.T. 280.. 2–195
Edinburgh (Magistrates of) *v.* Lownie (1903) 5 F. 711; 10 S.L.T. 752..... 10–129
Electric Construction Co. Ltd *v.* Hurry & Young (1897) 24 R. 312; 4 S.L.T. 287.. 4–219
Eley *v.* Positive Government Security Life Assurance Co. Ltd (1876) 1 Ex.D. 88 (C.A.)... 3–280
Elliott *v.* Director General of Fair Trading [1980] 1 W.L.R. 977 (D.C.); [1980] I.C.R. 629... 5–102
Emerald Stainless Steel Ltd *v.* South Side Distribution Ltd, 1983 S.L.T. 162 (O.H.).. 4–154
ERDC Construction Ltd *v.* H.M. Love & Co. (No. 2), 1997 S.L.T. 175.... 10–144
Ewart *v.* Latta (1865) 3 M. (H.L.) 36; 4 Macq. 983...................... 8–100
Ewing *v.* Buttercup Margarine Co. Ltd [1917] 2 Ch. 1 (C.A.)............. 3–202
Express Engineering Works Ltd, *Re* [1920] 1 Ch. 466 (C.A.).............. 3–164

Fairlie Yacht Slip Ltd *v.* Lumsden, 1977 S.L.T. (Notes) 41............... 10–13
Farrans *v.* Roxburgh County Council, 1969 S.L.T. 35 (O.H.)............... 10–24
Farrans (Construction) Ltd *v.* Dunfermline District Council, 1988 S.L.T. 466.. 10–175, 10–176
Fearn *v.* Gordon & Craig (1893) 20 R. 352............................... 1–106
Fenwick *v.* Macdonald, Fraser & Co. Ltd (1904) 6 F. 850; 12 S.L.T. 227.... 1–43, 4–316
Ferguson *v.* Mackay, 1985 S.L.T. 94 (O.H.).............................. 2–115
Ferguson *v.* Wilson (1904) 6 F. 779; 12 S.L.T. 117....................... 2–131
Ferguson and Lillie *v.* Stephen (1864) 2 M. 804................... 1–18, 1–174
Ferguson and Stuart *v.* Grant (1856) 18 D. 536........................... 7–175
Ferrier *v.* Alison (1845) 4 Bell's App. 161; (1843) 5 D. 456............. 10–173
Ferrier *v.* Dods (1865) 3 M. 561........................... 1–44, 1–162, 4–324
Findlay (Liquidator of Scottish Workmen's Assurance Co. Ltd) *v.* Waddell, 1910 S.C. 670; 1910 1 S.L.T. 315.......................... 7–140, 7–144
Fitzmaurice *v.* Bayley (1856) 6 El. & Bl. 868; 119 E.R. 1087.............. 1–27

Para.
Flynn *v.* Scott, 1949 S.C. 442 (O.H.).............................. 4–53, 4–222
Ford *v.* Guild, 1990 S.L.T. 502.............................. 4–343
Ford Credit plc *v.* Normand, 1994 S.L.T. 318.............................. 5–166
Forsyth *v.* Hare and Co. (1834) 13 S. 42.............................. 2–32, 2–33
Fortune *v.* Young, 1918 S.C. 1; 1917 2 S.L.T. 150.............................. 2–62, 8–39, 8–48
Fraser *v.* Frisby's (1830) 8 S. 982.............................. 7–29
Free Church of Scotland *v.* MacKnight's Trs., 1916 S.C. 349; 1916 1 S.L.T. 84.............................. 1–115
French *v.* Cameron (1893) 20 R. 966.............................. 8–54
Frost *v.* Aylesbury Dairy Co. Ltd [1905] 1 K.B. 608 (C.A.).............................. 4–105

Galbraith & Moorhead *v.* Arethusa Ship Co. Ltd (1896) 23 R. 1011; 4 S.L.T. 78.............................. 1–181
Gallagher *v.* Shilcock [1949] 2 K.B. 765; [1949] 1 All E.R. 921.............................. 4–274
Garnett *v.* McKewan (1872) L.R. 8 Ex 10.............................. 6–166
Garpel Haematite Co. Ltd (Liquidator of the) *v.* Andrew (1866) 4 M. 617... 7–161
Gavin's Tr. *v.* Fraser, 1920 S.C. 674; 1920 2 S.L.T. 221.............................. 4–22, 4–30
Gemmell *v.* Annandale & Son Ltd (1899) 36 S.L.R. 658.............................. 1–102
George *v.* Duncan, 1991 G.W.D. 39–2354 (Sh.Ct.).............................. 1–93
Gibb *v.* Cunningham & Robertson, 1925 S.L.T. 608 (O.H.).............................. 1–158
Gibbons *v.* Westminster Bank Ltd [1939] 2 K.B. 882; [1939] 3 All E.R. 577.............................. 6–172
Gibson *v.* Fotheringham, 1914 S.C. 987; 1914 2 S.L.T. 78.............................. 10–18, 10–102
Gibson and Stewart *v.* Brown and Co. (1876) 3 R. 328.............................. 7–193
Gilfillan *v.* Brown (1833) 11 S. 548.............................. 10–42
Gilford Motor Co. Ltd *v.* Horne [1933] Ch. 935 (C.A.).............................. 3–159
Gilmour *v.* Clark (1853) 15 D. 478.............................. 1–75, 1–105
Gladstone *v.* McCallum (1896) 23 R. 783; 4 S.L.T. 41.............................. 7–130, 7–133
Glasgow (City of) District Council *v.* Excess Insurance Co. Ltd, 1986 S.L.T. 585 (O.H.).............................. 8–154, 8–156
Glasgow (City of) District Council *v.* Excess Insurance Co. Ltd (No. 2), 1990 S.L.T. 225 (O.H.).............................. 8–154, 8–156
Glendinning *v.* Hope & Co., 1911 S.C. (H.L.) 73; 1911 2 S.L.T. 161.............................. 1–39, 7–153
Glengarnock Iron and Steel Co. Ltd *v.* Cooper & Co. (1895) 22 R. 672; 3 S.L.T. 36.............................. 4–197, 4–199
Glickman *v.* Linda, 1950 S.C. 18 (O.H.); 1950 S.L.T. 19.............................. 6–124, 6–149
Glynwed Distribution Ltd *v.* S. Koronka & Co., 1977 S.C. 1; 1977 S.L.T. 65.............................. 4–46
Godley *v.* Perry [1960] 1 W.L.R. 9; 1960 1 All E.R. 36.............................. 4–115
Goodall *v.* Bilsland, 1909 S.C. 1152; 1909 1 S.L.T. 376.............................. 1–25, 1–89
Goodwins, Jardine & Co. Ltd *v.* Brand & Son (1905) 7 F. 995; 13 S.L.T. 329.............................. 10–72
Gordon *v.* British and Foreign Metaline Co. (1886) 14 R. 75.............................. 2–39, 2–69
Gordon *v.* Kerr (1898) 25 R. 570; 5 S.L.T. 329.............................. 6–240
Gordon (William S.) & Co. Ltd *v.* Mrs. Mary Thomson Partnership, 1985 S.L.T. 122.............................. 2–137
Gosforth (The) S. en S. 1985 Nr. 91.............................. 4–122
Gourlay *v.* Mackie (1887) 14 R. 403.............................. 7–95, 7–100
Gourlay's Trustee *v.* Gourlay, 1995 S.L.T. (Sh.Ct.) 7.............................. 9–309
Govan Rope and Sail Co. Ltd *v.* Weir & Co. (1897) 24 R. 368; 4 S.L.T. 245.............................. 4–293

Para.
Gowans (Cockburn's Tr.) *v.* Bowe & Sons, 1910 2 S.L.T. 17 (O.H.)....... 4–139, 4–247
Graham *v.* Graham's Trs. (1904) 6 F. 1015; 12 S.L.T. 262............... 2–196
Graham *v.* Mill (1904) 6 F. 886; 12 S.L.T. 222......................... 10–87
Graham & Co. *v.* United Turkey Red Co. Ltd, 1922 S.C. 533; 1922 S.L.T. 406.. 1–75, 1–107, 1–120
Graham (Thomas) & Sons Ltd *v.* Glenrothes Development Corporation, 1967 S.C. 284; 1968 S.L.T. 2.. 4–171
Grand Empire Theatres Ltd (Liquidator of) *v.* Snodgrass, 1932 S.C. (H.L.) 73; 1932 S.L.T. 311.. 7–163
Gray *v.* Graham (1855) 2 Macq 435; 18 D. (H.L.) 52; *sub nom.* Gray *v.* Wardrop's Trs. (1851) 13 D. 963.. 7–164
Gray *v.* Weir (1891) 19 R. 25.. 7–58
Great Western Railway Co. *v.* London and County Banking Co. Ltd [1901] A.C. 414.. 6–156
Greenwood *v.* Martins Bank Ltd [1933] A.C. 51.................. 6–25, 6–177
Grierson, Oldham & Co. Ltd *v.* Forbes, Maxwell & Co. Ltd (1895) 22 R. 812; 3 S.L.T. 65.. 2–93, 3–140
Griffiths *v.* Peter Conway Ltd [1939] 1 All E.R. 685.............. 4–108, 4–109
Guild *v.* Young (1884) 22 S.L.R. 520 (O.H.).......................... 7–102
Gunac Ltd *v.* Inverclyde District Council, 1982 S.L.T. 387............... 10–13

Hadley *v.* Baxendale (1854) 9 Ex. 341; 156 E.R. 145.................... 4–281
Haley (John L.) Ltd *v.* Dumfries and Galloway Regional Council, 1985 S.L.T. 109.. 10–13
Halliburton Manufacturing and Service Ltd *v.* Bingham Blades & Partners, 1984 S.L.T. 388 (O.H.).. 10–168
Halliday *v.* Duke of Hamilton's Trs. (1903) 5 F. 800; 11 S.L.T. 65........ 10–137
Halyburtons *v.* Graham (1735) Mor. 2073............................ 8–116
Hamilton *v.* Forrester (1825) 3 S. 572.............................. 1–101
Hamilton *v.* Western Bank of Scotland (1856) 19 D. 152........... 7–112, 7–185
Hamilton & Co. *v.* Freeth (1889) 16 R. 1022..................... 8–81, 8–104
Hamilton of Provenhall's Creditors (Ranking of) (1781) Mor. 6253....... 7–158, 7–160
Hamlyn & Co. *v.* Talisker Distillery (1894) 21 R. (H.L.) 21; 2 S.L.T. 12..... 10–166
Harmer & Co. *v.* Gibb, 1911 S.C. 1341; 1911 2 S.L.T. 211................. 8–71
Hart *v.* Frame (1839) McL. & R. 595; (1836) 14 S. 914................. 1–115
Hart (Chris) (Business Sales) Ltd *v.* Currie, 1992 S.L.T. 544............. 1–133
Harvie's Trs. *v.* Bank of Scotland (1885) 12 R. 1141........... 8–72—8–74, 8–81
Haworth & Co. *v.* Sickness and Accident Assurance Association Ltd (1891) 18 R. 563.. 8–145
Hayman *v.* American Cotton Oil Co. (1907) 45 S.L.R. 207; 15 S.L.T. 606.. 1–19, 1–93
Hayman & Son *v.* McLintock, 1907 S.C. 936; 15 S.L.T. 63....... 4–124, 7–83, 7–91
Heddle's Executrix *v.* Marwick & Hourston's Tr. (1888) 15 R. 698.......... 2–77
Henderson *v.* Paul (1867) 5 M. 628.................................. 10–146
Henderson *v.* Skinner, 1990 S.L.T. (Sh.Ct.) 24.......................... 8–96
Henshaw (Charles) & Sons Ltd *v.* Antlerport Ltd, 1995 G.W.D. 24–1315 (O.H.).. 4–221
Hepburn *v.* Law, 1914 S.C. 918; 1914 1 S.L.T. 228................. 4–29, 7–25
Heritable Securities Investment Association Ltd *v.* Wingate & Co.'s Tr. (1880) 7 R. 1094.. 7–27

Para.

Heyman *v.* Darwins Ltd [1942] A.C. 356; [1942] 1 All E.R. 337. 10–76
Hickman *v.* Kent or Romney Marsh Sheep-Breeders Association [1915] 1 Ch. 881. 3–278
Holmes Oil Co. Ltd *v.* Pumpherston Oil Co. Ltd (1891) 18 R. (H.L.) 52; (1890) 17 R. 624. .... 10–151, 10–189, 10–196
Hood *v.* Stewart (1890) 17 R. 749. 6–63
Horsburgh *v.* Ramsay & Co. (1885) 12 R. 1171. 9–55
Horsefall *v.* Virtue & Co. (1826) 5 S. 36. 9–482
Hosie *v.* Waddell (1866) 3 S.L.R. 16. 2–90
Hostess Mobile Catering *v.* Archibald Scott Ltd, 1981 S.L.T. (Notes) 125 (O.H.). 4–249
Howard (Stanley) (Construction) Ltd *v.* Davis, 1988 S.L.T. (Sh.Ct.) 30. 10–168
Hughes *v.* Assessor for Stirling (1892) 19 R. 840. .... 2–190, 2–194
Hunter *v.* Albancode Group plc, 1989 G.W.D. 39–1843 (Sh.Ct.). 4–219
Hyslop *v.* Shirlaw (1905) 7 F. 875; 13 S.L.T. 209. 4–222

Incorporated Glasgow Dental Hospital *v.* Lord Advocate, 1927 S.C. 400; 1927 S.L.T. 270. 3–241
Inglis *v.* Robertson & Baxter (1898) 25 R. (H.L.) 70; (1897) 24 R. 758; *sub nom.* Irvine and Ors.: Robertson *v.* Baxter, and Inglis, *claimants* (1898) 6 S.L.T. 130; (1896) 4 S.L.T. 366. 7–88
Inland Revenue Commissioners *v.* MacDonald, 1988 S.L.T. (Sh.Ct.) 7. 9–211
International Sponge Importers Ltd *v.* Watt & Sons, 1911 S.C. (H.L.) 57; 1911 1 S.L.T. 414. 1–93
Introductions Ltd *v.* National Provincial Bank Ltd [1970] Ch. 199 (C.A.); [1969] 2 W.L.R. 791; [1969] 1 All E.R. 887. 3–227
Inverclyde (Mearns) Housing Society Ltd *v.* Lawrence Construction Co. Ltd, 1989 S.L.T. 815 (O.H.). 10–168
Irving *v.* Burns, 1915 S.C. 260; 1915 1 S.L.T. 2. .... 1–170, 8–26

Jack *v.* Black, 1911 S.C. 691; 1911 1 S.L.T. 124. 7–58
Jacobs *v.* Scott & Co. (1899) 2 F. (H.L.) 70; 7 S.L.T. 5. 4–102
Jaffrey and Ors., Partners of the Stirling Banking Co. (Stein's Creditors) *v.* Allan, Stewart & Co. (1790) 3 Pat. 191. 4–252
Jenkins *v.* Lombard North Central PLC (1984) 1 W.L.R. 307 (D.C.). 5–155
Johnson *v.* Lamb, 1981 S.L.T. 300 (O.H.). 10–130, 10–154, 10–206
Johnston *v.* Little, 1960 S.L.T. 129 (O.H.). 1–148
Johnston *v.* Robertson (1861) 23 D. 646. 7–192
Johnston *v.* Young (1890) 18 R.(J.) 6. 7–57
Johnstone *v.* Spencer & Co., 1908 S.C. 1015; 16 S.L.T. 182. 10–12
Johnstone (C. & A.) *v.* Duthie (1892) 19 R. 624. 8–139
Jones *v.* Lipman [1962] 1 W.L.R. 832; [1962] 1 All E.R. 442. 3–160
Jones & Co.'s Tr. *v.* Allan (1901) 4 F. 374; 9 S.L.T. 349. .... 4–29, 7–24

Keighley, Maxsted & Co. *v.* Durant [1901] A.C. 240. 1–26
Kelner *v.* Baxter (1866) L.R. 2 C.P. 174. 3–15
Kennedy *v.* Glass (1890) 17 R. 1085. 1–131

Para.
Ketley (A.) Ltd *v.* Scott [1981] I.C.R. 241 ... 5–313
King *v.* British Linen Co. (1899) 1 F. 928; 7 S.L.T. 58 ... 6–170, 6–172
King *v.* T. Tunnock Ltd, 1996 S.C.L.R. 742 ... 1–49
Kinloch, Campbell & Co. *v.* Cowan (1890) 27 S.L.R. 870 ... 6–44
Kintore (Earl of) *v.* Union Bank of Scotland (1863) 1 M. (H.L.) 11; (1861) 24 D. 59 ... 10–10
Kirkintilloch Equitable Co-operative Society Ltd *v.* Livingstone, 1972 S.C. 111; 1972 S.L.T. 154 ... 2–67
Kirkwood & Sons *v.* Clydesdale Bank Ltd, 1908 S.C. 20; 15 S.L.T. 413 ... 6–103, 6–167, 6–170
Knox & Robb *v.* Scottish Garden Suburb Co. Ltd, 1913 S.C. 872; 1913 1 S.L.T. 401 ... 1–88

Laidlaw (James) and Sons Ltd *v.* Griffin, 1968 S.L.T. 278 ... 1–164
Laing (Sir James) & Sons Ltd *v.* Barclay, Curle & Co. Ltd, 1908 S.C. (H.L.) 1; 1908 S.C. 82; (1907) 15 S.L.T. 644; (1907) 15 S.L.T. 482 ... 4–134
Laurie *v.* Denny's Tr. (1853) 15 D. 404 ... 7–140
Law *v.* Humphrey (1875) 3 R. 1192 ... 6–52, 6–54
Lawson's Executors *v.* Watson, 1907 S.C. 1353 ... 6–20
Life Association of Scotland *v.* Caledonian Heritable Security Co. Ltd in Liquidation (1886) 13 R. 750 ... 3–223
Life Association of Scotland *v.* Douglas (1886) 13 R. 910 ... 1–188
Littlejohn *v.* Black (1855) 18 D. 207 ... 7–119
Liverpool Victoria Legal Friendly Society *v.* Houston (1900) 3 F. 42; 8 S.L.T. 230 ... 1–129
Livesey *v.* Purdom & Sons (1894) 21 R. 911; 2 S.L.T. 86 ... 1–152
Lloyds Bank Ltd *v.* E. B. Savory & Co. [1933] A.C. 201 ... 6–215
Lloyds Bank Ltd *v.* Morrison & Son, 1927 S.C. 571; 1927 S.L.T. 415 ... 3–54
Lockhart *v.* Moodie & Co. (1877) 4 R. 859 ... 1–26
Logan (David) & Son Ltd and Liquidator *v.* Schuldt (1903) 10 S.L.T. 598 (O.H.) ... 1–165
London Joint Stock Bank Ltd *v.* Macmillan and Arthur [1918] A.C. 777 ... 6–164, 6–176
London, Leith, Edinburgh and Glasgow Shipping Co. *v.* Ferguson (1850) 13 D. 51 ... 1–201
London Scottish Transport Ltd *v.* Tyres (Scotland) Ltd, 1957 S.L.T. (Sh.Ct.) 48 ... 4–249
Lord Advocate *v.* Chung, 1995 S.C. 32 ... 1–14
Lord Advocate *v.* Maritime Fruit Carriers Co. Ltd, 1983 S.L.T. 357 (O.H.) ... 8–08
Lorne Stewart plc *v.* Mowlem Scotland Ltd, 1995 G.W.D. 3–112 (O.H.) ... 10–53
Lothian *v.* Jenolite Ltd, 1969 S.C. 111; 1970 S.L.T. 31 ... 1–119
Louson *v.* Craik (1842) 4 D. 1452 ... 7–135
Lovat (Lord) *v.* Fraser of Phopachy (1738) Mor. 625 ... 10–205
Lumsden *v.* Gordon (1728) Mor. 14567 ... 10–42
Lujo Properties Ltd *v.* Green, 1997 S.L.T. 225 (O.H.) ... 2–154

McArthur (W. & A.) Ltd, Liquidator of *v.* Gulf Line Ltd, 1909 S.C. 732; 1909 1 S.L.T. 279 ... 3–273

Para.

Macaura *v.* Northern Assurance Co. Ltd [1925] A.C. 619 3–143
McCallum *v.* Mason, 1956 S.C. 50; 1956 S.L.T. 50 .... 4–80, 4–104
McCowan *v.* Wright (1853) 15 D. 494 9–49
Macdonald *v.* Clark, 1927 S.N. 6 (O.H.) 4–47
McDonald *v.* Provan (of Scotland Street) Ltd, 1960 S.L.T. 231 (O.H.) 4–69
Macdonald (Logan's Tr.) *v.* David Logan & Son Ltd (1903) 11 S.L.T. 32 and 369 9–48
McDougall (D. & J.) Ltd *v.* Argyll and Bute District Council, 1987 S.L.T. 7 (O.H.) 10–24
McDowall & Neilson's Tr. *v.* J. B. Snowball Co. Ltd (1904) 7 F. 35 .... 4–196, 4–261
MacFadyen's Trustee *v*, MacFadyen, 1994 S.L.T. 1245 9–38
McGown *v.* Henderson, 1914 S.C. 839; 1914 2 S.L.T. 66 2–112
McGregor (John G.) (Contractors) Ltd *v.* Grampian Regional Council, 1991 S.L.T. 136 10–176
McGregor (John G.) (Contractors) Ltd *v.* Grampian Regional Council, 1991 S.C. (H.L.) 1; 1991 S.L.T. 365 (H.L.) 10–13
Macintyre Brothers *v.* Smith, 1913 S.C. 129; 1913 1 S.L.T. 148 10–148
Mackay *v.* Parochial Board of Barry (1883) 10 R. 1046 .... 10–65, 10–67, 10–135
Mackay & Son *v.* Leven Police Commissioners (1893) 20 R. 1093; 1 S.L.T. 173 10–69
McKenzie *v.* Campbell (1894) 21 R. 904; 2 S.L.T. 85 1–191
Mackenzie *v.* Cormack, 1950 S.C. 183; 1950 S.L.T. 139 .... 1–05, 1–42, 1–45, 1–139, 1–153, 4–324, 7–152
Mackenzie *v.* Girvan (1840) 3 D. 318; *affirmed* (1843) 2 Bell's App. 43 10–198
Mackenzie (William) (Carpenters) Ltd (in receivership) *v.* Mowat, 1991 S.L.T. (Sh.Ct.) 48 1–89
Mackinnon's Tr. *v.* Bank of Scotland, 1915 S.C. 411; 1915 1 S.L.T. 182 8–74
McLaren *v.* Aikman, 1939 S.C. 222; 1939 S.L.T. 267 .... 10–157, 10–200
McLean *v.* Clydesdale Bank Ltd (1883) 11 R. (H.L.) 1; 10 R. 719 6–03
MacLeod *v.* Kerr, 1965 S.C. 253; 1965 S.L.T. 358 4–160
McMahon's Trustee *v.* McMahon, 1997 S.L.T. 1090 9–310
McMartin *v.* Hannay (1872) 10 M. 411 1–66
McMeekin *v.* Easton (1889) 16 R. 363 1–155
McMillan & Son Ltd *v.* Rowan & Co. (1903) 5 F. 317; 10 S.L.T. 542 10–122
MacNab *v.* Alexanders of Greenock Ltd, 1971 S.L.T. 121 4–338
McNeill & Son *v.* Innes, Chambers & Co., 1917 S.C. 540; 1917 2 S.L.T. 5 6–120
McNiven *v.* Peffers (1868) 7 M. 181 2–120
McPherson *v.* Wright (1885) 12 R. 942 6–90
McPherson's Trs. *v.* Watt (1877) 5 R.(H.L.) 9 1–123
Macrae *v.* Leith, 1913 S.C. 901; 1913 1 S.L.T. 273 .... 1–41, 1–67, 7–154
McRobert *v.* Lindsay (1898) 5 S.L.T. 317 .... 6–03, 6–120
McTaggart *v.* MacEachern's J.F., 1949 S.C. 503 6–226
Mactavish's Judicial Factor *v.* Michael's Trs., 1912 S.C. 425; 1912 1 S.L.T. 134 6–79
Main *v.* Fleming's Trs. (1881) 8 R. 880 9–25
Mair *v.* Wood, 1948 S.C. 83; 1948 S.L.T. 326 .... 2–17, 2–33, 2–40, 2–70
Marfani & Co. Ltd *v.* Midland Bank Ltd [1968] 1 W.L.R. 956 (C.A.); [1968] 2 All E.R. 573 6–216
Marshall & Co. *v.* Pennycook, 1908 S.C. 276; 15 S.L.T. 581 8–96
Marshall, Fleming & Co. Ltd, Petrs., 1938 S.C. 873 (O.H.); 1938 S.L.T. 527 3–197
Marshall Wilson Dean & Turnbull *v.* Feymac Properties Ltd, 1996 G.W.D. 22–1247 1–134

Para.
Martini & Co. *v.* Steel & Craig (1878) 6 R. 342 6–75
Martin *v.* Martin's Trustee, 1994 S.L.T. 261 (O.H.) 9–160
Matheson's Trustee *v.* Matheson, 1992 S.L.T. 685 (O.H.) 9–37
Matthews *v.* Auld & Guild (1873) 1 R. 1224 1–157
Mauritzen (Charles) Ltd *v.* Baltic Shipping Co., 1948 S.C. 646 (O.H.); 1948 S.L.T. 300 10–76
Mechan & Sons Ltd *v.* Bow, McLachlan & Co. Ltd, 1910 S.C. 758; 1910 1 S.L.T. 406 4–218
Mechan & Sons Ltd *v.* North Eastern Railway Co., 1911 S.C. 1348; 1911 2 S.L.T. 244 .... 4–264, 4–267
Mechans Ltd *v.* Highland Marine Charters Ltd, 1964 S.C. 48; 1964 S.L.T. 27 4–213
Meikle & Wilson *v.* Pollard (1880) 8 R. 69 .... 7–142, 7–144
Mein (Landale and Co.'s Tr.) *v.* Bogle and Co. (1828) 6 S. 360 7–180
Melrose *v.* Hastie (1851) 13 D. 880 7–182
Mendok B.V. *v.* Cumberland Maritime Corporation, 1989 S.L.T. 192 (O.H.) 10–169
Merry and Cunninghame *v.* Brown (1863) 1 M. (H.L.) 14; (1860) 22 D. 1148 10–112
Metsoja *v.* H. Norman Pitt & Co. Ltd [1990] C.C.L.R. 12; [1990] C.L.Y. 620 5–166
Millar *v.* Mitchell (1860) 22 D. 833 1–147
Millars of Falkirk Ltd *v.* Turpie, 1976 S.L.T. (Notes) 66 .... 4–95, 4–183
Miller *v.* Hutcheson & Dixon (1881) 8 R. 489 .... 7–124, 7–152
Miller *v.* MacLeod, 1973 S.C. 172; 1974 S.L.T. 99 2–78
Miller *v.* McNair (1852) 14 D. 955 7–151
Miller *v.* Thorburn (1861) 23 D. 359 2–76
Miller & Co. *v.* Potter, Wilson & Co. (1875) 3 R. 105 7–36
Miller & Son *v.* Oliver & Boyd (1903) 6 F. 77; 11 S.L.T. 381 .... 10–192, 10–202
Miller & Son *v.* Oliver & Boyd (1906) 8 F. 390; 13 S.L.T. 789 .... 10–55, 10–183
Miln's Judicial Factor *v.* Spence's Trs., 1927 S.L.T. 425 (O.H.) 7–174
Milne *v.* Harris, James & Co. (1803) Mor. 8493 1–86
Milne *v.* Ritchie (1882) 10 R. 365 1–117
Minhas's Tr. *v.* Bank of Scotland, 1990 S.L.T. 23 (O.H.) 9–271
Mitchell *v.* Cable (1848) 10 D. 1297 10–178
Mitchell & Baxter *v.* Cheyne (1891) 19 R. 324 6–170
Mitchell-Gill *v.* Buchan, 1921 S.C. 390; 1921 1 S.L.T. 197 .... 10–13, 10–170, 10–179
Montgomery (Thomas) & Sons *v.* Gallacher, 1982 S.L.T. 138 (O.H.) 9–58
Moore *v.* McCosh (1903) 5 F. 946; 11 S.L.T. 112 10–58
Moorgate Services *v.* Kabir, *The Times*, April 25, 1995; [1995] C.L.Y. 722 5–197
Morgan *v.* Smart (1872) 10 M. 610 .... 8–98, 8–148
Morisons *v.* Thomson's Trs. (1880) 8 R. 147 10–190
Morrison *v.* Statter (1885) 12 R. 1152 1–35
Morrisson *v.* Robertson, 1908 S.C. 332; 15 S.L.T. 697 .... 4–155, 4–161
Muir *v.* Crawford (1875) 2 R. (H.L.) 148; *affirming* Crawford *v.* Muir (1873) 1 R. 91 8–109
Muir *v.* Rankin (1905) 13 S.L.T. 60 (O.H.) 4–258
Mumford *v.* Bank of Scotland; *see* Smith *v.* Bank of Scotland
Munro *v.* Liquidator of Balnagown Estates Co. Ltd, 1949 S.C. 49; 1949 S.L.T. 85 .... 4–37, 4–140
Munro *v.* Stein, 1961 S.C. 362 (O.H.) 2–102

Para.
Munro & Co. *v.* Bennet & Son, 1911 S.C. 337; 1911 1 S.L.T. 120.......... 4–219
Murie McDougall Ltd *v.* Sinclair, 1994 S.L.T. (Sh.Ct.) 74.......... 5–291, 5–297

Napier (N.G.) Ltd *v.* Crosbie, 1964 S.C. 129; 1964 S.L.T. 185............. 8–144
Nash *v.* Inman [1908] 2 K.B. 1 (C.A.).. 4–33
National Bank of Scotland Ltd *v.* Campbell (1892) 19 R. 885.............. 8–42
National Bank of Scotland Ltd *v.* Forbes (1858) 21 D. 79................. 7–111
National Westminster Bank Ltd *v.* Halesowen Presswork & Assemblies Ltd [1972] A.C. 785; [1972] 2 W.L.R. 455; [1972] 1 All E.R. 641......... 6–166
National Westminster Bank plc *v.* Elrick (W.J.) & Co., 1991 S.L.T. 709 (O.H.).. 9–139
Neill *v.* Dobson, Molle & Co. Ltd (1902) 4 F. 625; 9 S.L.T. 451...... 6–77, 6–78, 6–120
Neilson *v.* Mossend Iron Co. (1886) 13 R. (H.L.) 50..................... 2–111
Nelmes & Co. *v.* Ewing (1883) 11 R. 193.................................. 7–56
Nelson *v.* William Chalmers & Co. Ltd, 1913 S.C. 441; 1913 1 S.L.T. 190.... 4–309
New British Iron Co., *Re, ex parte* Beckwith [1898] 1 Ch. 324............. 3–281
Nicol's Trustees *v.* Nicol, 1996 G.W.D. 10–531.......................... 9–364
Nicol's Trs. *v.* Sutherland, 1951 S.C. (H.L.) 21; 1951 S.L.T. 201........... 6–129
Nicolsons *v.* Burt (1882) 10 R. 121.. 8–147
Nivison *v.* Howat (1883) 11 R. 182.. 10–16
Nordic Travel Ltd *v.* Scotprint Ltd, 1980 S.C. 1; 1980 S.L.T. 189........... 9–14, 9–50, 9–53
North British Railway Co. *v.* Newburgh and North Fife Railway Co., 1911 S.C. 710; 1911 1 S.L.T. 266.................................... 10–68
North of Scotland Banking Co. *v.* Fleming (1882) 10 R. 217............... 8–64
North Wales Motor Auctions Ltd *v.* Secretary of State for Trade [1981] C.C.L.R. 1.. 5–130

Obers *v.* Paton's Trs. (1897) 24 R. 719; 4 S.L.T. 350..................... 9–26
Ogilvie & Son *v.* Taylor (1887) 14 R. 399......................... 9–464, 9–469
O'Neill *v.* Scottish Joint Negotiating Committee for Teaching Staff, 1987 S.L.T. 648 (O.H.).. 10–13

Parke *v.* Daily News Ltd [1962] Ch. 927; [1962] 3 W.L.R. 566; [1962] 2 All E.R. 929.. 3–226
Parker *v.* Brown & Co. (1878) 5 R. 979.................................... 7–138
Paterson *v.* Bonar (1844) 6 D. 987... 8–58
Paterson Brothers *v.* Gladstone (1891) 18 R. 403.................. 2–64, 6–24
Patmore & Co. *v.* B. Cannon & Co. Ltd (1892) 19 R. 1004............... 1–199
Paton & Sons *v.* David Payne & Co. Ltd (1897) 35 S.L.R. 112 (H.L.)...... 4–63, 4–306
Paton's Tr. *v.* Finlayson, 1923 S.C. 872; 1923 S.L.T. 593............ 4–37, 4–247, 7–133, 7–145
Pattison *v.* Halliday, 1991 S.L.T. 645 (O.H.)............................. 9–400
Pattison's Tr. *v.* Liston (1893) 20 R. 806; 1 S.L.T. 56............... 7–80, 7–82
Paul *v.* Henderson (1867) 5 M. 613................................ 10–85, 10–88

Para.

Paul *v.* Meikle (1868) 7 M. 235 7–160
Peden *v.* Graham (1907) 15 S.L.T. 143 (O.H.) 1–89
Peebles & Co. *v.* John L. Kerr Ltd (1902) 9 S.L.T. 372 (O.H.) 4–133
Penson and Robertson, *Petrs.*, 6 June 1820, F.C. 7–49
Percy *v.* Meikle, 25 Nov. 1808, F.C. 10–48
Phillips (Godfrey) Ltd *v.* Italian Bank Ltd, 1934 S.L.T. 78 (O.H.) 6–193
Pillans Brothers *v.* Pillans (1908) 16 S.L.T. 611 (O.H.) 2–122
Pini & Co. *v.* Smith & Co. (1895) 22 R. 699 .... 4–198, 4–221
Pollich *v.* Heatley, 1910 S.C. 469; 1910 1 S.L.T. 203 10–204
Pollok *v.* Paterson, 10 Dec. 1811, F.C. 1–195
Powell *v.* Lloyds Bowmaker Ltd, 1996 S.L.T. (Sh.Ct.) 117 5–184
Preist *v.* Last [1903] 2 K.B. 148 (C.A.) 4–105
Premier Briquette Co. Ltd *v.* Gray, 1922 S.C. 329; 1922 S.L.T. 230 1–178
Presslie *v.* Cochrane McGregor Group Ltd, 1996 S.C. 289 10–168
Price & Pierce Ltd *v.* Bank of Scotland, 1912 S.C. (H.L.) 19; 1910 S.C. 1095; 1911 2 S.L.T. 469; 1910 2 S.L.T. 126 7–92
Pulsometer Engineering Co. Ltd *v.* Gracie (1887) 14 R. 316 7–47

R. *v.* Registrar of Joint Stock Companies, *ex parte* More [1931] 2 K.B. 197 (C.A.) 3–133
Raphael *v.* Wilcon Homes Northern Ltd, 1994 S.C.L.R. 940 10–168
Rayfield *v.* Hands [1960] Ch. 1; [1958] 2 W.L.R. 851; [1958] 2 All E.R. 194 3–282
Readers (The) Digest Association *v.* Pirie, 1973 S.L.T. 170 (High Court of Justiciary) 4–348
Reardon Smith Line Ltd *v.* Hansen-Tangen [1976] 1 W.L.R. 989 (H.L.); [1976] 3 All E.R. 570 4–77
Rederi Aktiebolaget Nordstjernan *v.* Salvesen & Co. (1903) 6 F. 64; 10 S.L.T. 543; *affirmed* (1905) 7 F (H.L.) 101; 13 S.L.T. 2 1–05
Redpath Dorman Long Ltd *v.* Tarmac Construction Ltd, 1982 S.C. 14 (O.H.) 10–53
Rennet *v.* Mathieson (1903) 5 F. 591; 10 S.L.T. 765 4–29
Rhind's Tr. *v.* Robertson & Baxter (1891) 18 R. 623 7–89
Rhodes *v.* Forwood (1876) 1 App.Cas. 256 1–200
Richardson *v.* Harvey (1853) 15 D. 628 8–138
Riverford Finance Ltd *v.* Kelly, 1991 S.L.T. 300 (O.H.) 1–89
Roberts *v.* Wallace (1842) 5 D. 6 7–29
Roberts & Co. *v.* Yule (1896) 23 R. 855; 4 S.L.T. 53 4–81
Roberts & Cooper Ltd *v.* Christian Salvesen & Co. Ltd, 1918 S.C. 794; 1918 2 S.L.T. 160 4–49
Robertson *v.* Boyd and Winans (1885) 12 R. 419 10–17
Robertson *v.* British Linen Co. (1890) 18 R. 1225 (O.H.) 3–54
Robertson *v.* Hall's Tr. (1896) 24 R. 120; 4 S.L.T. 139 4–28
Robertson *v.* Ross (1887) 15 R. 67 7–143
Robertson (J. M. & J. H.) *v.* Beatson, McLeod & Co. Ltd, 1908 S.C. 921; 16 S.L.T. 157 1–90
Robertson (J. P.) Ltd *v.* Stewart, 1928 S.N. 31 (O.H.) 4–187
Robertson's Tr. *v.* Royal Bank of Scotland (1890) 18 R. 12 7–156
Robinson *v.* Middleton (1859) 21 D. 1089 1–137
Robinson *v.* Somerville & Russell, 1997 G.W.D. 11–477 9–268
Ronaldson *v.* Drummond & Reid (1881) 8 R. 956 1–127

Para.
Ross & Co. *v.* Plano Manufacturing Co. (1903) 11 S.L.T. 7 (O.H.)........ 4–146
Ross & Duncan *v.* Baxter & Co. (1885) 13 R. 185........................ 7–134
Rover Group Ltd *v.* Sumner [1995] C.C.L.R. 1; [1996] C.L.Y. 104......... 5–166
Roxburgh *v.* Dinardo, 1981 S.L.T. 291 (O.H.).................... 2–141, 10–11
Royal Bank of Scotland Ltd *v.* Brown, 1982 S.C. 89.............. 8–154, 8–155
Royal Bank of Scotland *v.* Greenshields, 1914 S.C. 259.................. 8–52
Royal Bank of Scotland Ltd *v.* Skinner, 1931 S.L.T. 382 (O.H.)............ 1–85
Royal Bank of Scotland plc *v.* Forbes, 1988 S.L.T. 73 (O.H.)....... 9–131, 9–138
Royal Bank of Scotland plc *v.* J. & J. Messenger, 1991 S.L.T. 492 (O.H.).. 9–116, 9–399
Royal Bank of Scotland *v.* Law, 1996 S.L.T. 83.......................... 1–116
Runciman *v.* Craigie (1831) 9 S. 629.................................. 10–104

St. Johnstone Football Club Ltd *v.* Scottish Football Association, 1965 S.L.T. 171 (O.H.)... 3–266
Sales Lease Ltd *v.* Minty, 1993 S.L.T. (Sh.Ct.) 52....................... 9–133
Salmon's Tr. *v.* Salmon, 1989 S.L.T. (Sh.Ct.) 49......................... 9–308
Salomon *v.* Salomon & Co. Ltd [1897] A.C. 22........... 3–128, 3–138, 3–139, 3–142, 3–144
Sanderson & Son *v.* Armour & Co. Ltd, 1922 S.C. (H.L.) 117; 1921 S.C. 18; 1922 S.L.T. 285; 1920 2 S.L.T. 348................. 10–04, 10–65, 10–74
Scholfield *v.* Earl of Londesborough [1896] A.C. 514...................... 6–134
Scott *v.* Carluke Local Authority (1879) 6 R. 616........................ 10–134
Scott *v.* Gerrard, 1916 S.C. 793; 1916 2 S.L.T. 42....................... 10–138
Scott *v.* Mitchell (1866) 4 M. 551...................................... 8–77
Scott *v.* Young, 1909 1 S.L.T. 47 (O.H.)................................ 8–103
Scott (James) Ltd *v.* Apollo Engineering Ltd, 1993 G.W.D. 29–1796 (O.H.)... 10–70
Scott (James) & Sons Ltd *v.* Del Sel, 1923 S.C. (H.L.) 37; 1922 S.C. 592; 1923 S.L.T. 204; 1922 S.L.T. 468.......................... 10–75, 10–76
Scott Lithgow Ltd *v.* Secretary of State for Defence, 1988 S.L.T. 697...... 10–125
Scottish & Newcastle Breweries Ltd *v.* Blair, 1967 S.L.T. 72 (O.H.)........ 3–207
Scottish & Newcastle Breweries Ltd *v.* Edinburgh District Council, 1979 S.L.T. (Notes) 11 (O.H.).. 7–47
Scottish & Newcastle Breweries plc *v.* Mann, 1989 S.C.L.R. 118 (Sh.Ct.)..... 9–130
Scottish & Newcastle plc, *Petrs.*, 1992 S.C.L.R. 540 (O.H.)................ 9–178
Scottish Housing Association Ltd, *Petrs.*, 1947 S.C. 17; 1947 S.L.T. 6....... 3–241
Scottish Metropolitan Property plc *v.* Christie, 1987 S.L.T. (Sh.Ct.) 18...... 8–38
Scottish Provincial Assurance Co. *v.* Pringle (1858) 20 D. 465............. 8–59
Scottish Transit Trust Ltd *v.* Scottish Land Cultivators Ltd, 1955 S.C. 254; 1955 S.L.T. 417....................................... 4–29, 7–26
Scottish Union and National Insurance Co. *v.* Scottish National Insurance Co. Ltd, 1909 S.C. 318; (1908) 16 S.L.T. 671...................... 3–202
Secretary of State for the Environment *v.* Grahame House Investments Ltd, 1985 S.C. 201.. 10–143
Sellar *v.* Highland Railway Co., 1919 S.C. (H.L.) 19; 1918 S.C. 838; 1919 1 S.L.T. 149; 1918 2 S.L.T. 6.................................... 10–128
Shanks & McEwan (Contractors) Ltd *v.* Mifflin Construction Ltd, 1993 S.L.T. 1124 (O.H.).. 10–24
Sharpe *v.* Carswell, 1910 S.C. 391; 1910 1 S.L.T. 80...................... 2–22
Shaw, Macfarlane & Co. *v.* Waddell & Son (1900) 2 F. 1070; 8 S.L.T. 89..... 4–62, 4–230

Para.
Short's Tr. *v.* Chung, 1991 S.L.T. 472 9–34
Sibbald *v.* Gibson (1852) 15 D. 217 .... 1–139, 7–150
Simpson *v.* Brown (1888) 15 R. 716 6–123
Simpson *v.* Fleming (1860) 22 D. 679 8–60
Simpson *v.* Kidstons, Watson, Turnbull & Co., 1913 1 S.L.T. 74 (O.H.) 1–115
Sinclair *v.* Edinburgh Parish Council, 1909 S.C. 1353; 1909 2 S.L.T. 189 9–71
Sinclair, Moorhead & Co. *v.* Wallace & Co. (1880) 7 R. 874 1–84
Skinner *v.* Henderson (1865) 3 M. 867 7–171
Slater *v.* Finning Ltd, 1996 S.L.T. 912 (H.L.) 4–108
Smart *v.* Wilkinson, 1928 S.C. 383 7–194
Smith *v.* Bank of Scotland; Mumford *v.* Bank of Scotland, 1997 S.C. (H.L.) 111; 1996 S.L.T. 392; 1994 S.L.T. 1288 8–52
Smith *v.* Liverpool and London and Globe Insurance Co. (1887) 14 R. 931 10–100
Smith *v.* McBride & Smith (1888) 16 R. 36 2–199
Smith *v.* Scott & Best (1881) 18 S.L.R. 355 .... 1–11, 1–12
Smith, Stone & Knight Ltd *v.* Birmingham Corporation [1939] 4 All E.R. 116 3–161
Smithy's Place Ltd *v.* Blackadder & McMonagle, 1991 S.L.T. 790 (O.H.) 8–93
Snaddon *v.* London, Edinburgh and Glasgow Assurance Co. Ltd (1902) 5 F. 182; 10 S.L.T. 410 .... 8–55, 8–125
Sneddon *v.* Durant, 1982 S.L.T. (Sh.Ct.) 39 4–25
Solicitors' Estate Agency (Glasgow) Ltd *v.* MacIver, 1992 S.C.L.R. 804 1–63
Sommerville *v.* Aaronson (1898) 25 R. 524; 5 S.L.T. 310 .... 6–85, 6–87, 6–120
Southern Foundries (1926) Ltd *v.* Shirlaw [1940] A.C. 701; [1940] 2 All E.R. 445 3–275
Standard Chartered Bank Ltd *v.* Walker [1982] 1 W.L.R. 1410 (C.A.) 8–08
Stark's Trs. *v.* Stark, 1948 S.C. 41; 1948 S.L.T. 158 4–38
"State of California" S.S. Co. Ltd *v.* Moore (1895) 22 R. 562; 2 S.L.T. 579 1–202
Stephen *v.* Skinner (1863) 2 M 287 1–89
Stevenson *v.* Adair (1872) 10 M. 919 8–11
Stevenson *v.* Duncan (1842) 5 D. 167 1–136
Stevenson (Hugh) and Sons Ltd *v.* Aktiengesellschaft für Cartonnagen-Industrie [1918] A.C. 239 .... 2–140, 2–160
Stevenson's Tr. *v.* Campbell & Sons (1896) 23 R. 711; 3 S.L.T. 330 8–21
Stewart *v.* Buchanan (1903) 6 F. 15; 11 S.L.T. 347 2–19
Stewart *v.* Jarvie, 1938 S.C. 309; 1938 S.L.T. 383 9–292
Stewart *v.* North (1893) 20 R. 260 2–121
Stewart *v.* Shannessy (1900) 2 F. 1288; 8 S.L.T. 162 1–150
Stewart *v.* Williamson, 1910 S.C. (H.L.) 47; 1909 S.C. 1254; 1910 1 S.L.T. 326; 1909 2 S.L.T. 125 10–20
Stewart, Moir and Muir *v.* Brown (1871) 9 M. 763 8–140
Stirling Park & Co. *v.* Digby Brown & Co., 1996 S.L.T. (Sh.Ct.) 17 1–152
Stiven *v.* Watson (1874) 1 R. 412 1–113
Stiven (Watson's Tr.) *v.* Cowan (1878) 15 S.L.R. 422 .... 7–28, 7–85
Stone & Rolfe Ltd *v.* Kimber Coal Co. Ltd, 1926 S.C. (H.L.) 45; 1926 S.L.T. 419 1–145
Strachan *v.* McDougle (1835) 13 S. 954 7–94
Strachan (W.M.) & Co. Ltd *v.* John Marshall & Co., 1910 2 S.L.T. 108 (O.H.) 4–221
Strickland *v.* Neilson and MacIntosh (1869) 7 M. 400 .... 1–71, 1–87
Strong *v.* Philips & Co. (1878) 5 R. 770 7–147
Struthers *v.* Dykes (1847) 9 D. 1437 8–61

Para.

Tai Hing Cotton Mill Ltd, *v.* Liu Chong Hing Bank Ltd [1986] A.C. 80 (P.C.) 6–175
Tancred, Arrol & Co. *v.* Steel Co. of Scotland Ltd (1890) 17 R. (H.L.) 31; (1887) 15 R. 215 10–110
Taylor (Liquidator of Neil Middleton and Co. Ltd), *Petr.,* 1976 S.L.T. (Sh.Ct.) 82 3–145
Taylor Woodrow Construction (Scotland) Ltd *v.* Sears Investment Trust Ltd, 1992 S.L.T. 609 10–105
Teheran-Europe Co. Ltd *v.* S. T. Belton (Tractors) Ltd [1968] 2 Q.B. 545; [1968] 3 W.L.R. 205; [1968] 2 All E.R. 886 1–147
Tesco Supermarkets Ltd *v.* Nattrass [1972] A.C. 153; [1971] 2 W.L.R. 1166; [1971] 2 All E.R. 127 4–341
Thom's Executrix *v.* Russel & Aitken, 1983 S.L.T. 335 (O.H.) 2–158
Thomson, *Petr.* (1893) 1 S.L.T. 59 .... 2–141, 2–147
Thomson *v.* Bell (1850) 12 D. 1184 6–124
Thomson *v.* J. Sears & Co. (Trueform Boot Co.) Ltd, 1926 S.L.T. 221 (O.H.) 4–105
Thomson *v.* Thomson, 1962 S.C. (H.L.) 28; 1961 S.C. 255; 1962 S.L.T. 109; 1961 S.L.T. 353 2–138
Thomson & Balfour *v.* Boag & Son, 1936 S.C. 2; 1936 S.L.T. 2 2–79
Thomson & Co. *v.* Pattison, Elder & Co. (1895) 22 R. 432; 2 S.L.T. 546 2–68
Thomson & Gillespie *v.* Victoria Eighty Club (1905) 43 S.L.R. 628 (O.H.); 13 S.L.T. 399 1–155
Thow's Tr. *v.* Young, 1910 S.C. 588; 1910 1 S.L.T. 134 8–101
Tinnevelly Sugar Refining Co. Ltd *v.* Mirrlees, Watson & Yaryan Co. Ltd (1894) 21 R. 1009; 2 S.L.T. 149 .... 1–14, 1–154, 3–15
Tomlinson *v.* Liquidators of Scottish Amalgamated Silks Ltd, 1935 S.C. (H.L.) 1; 1934 S.C. 85; 1935 S.L.T. 297; 1934 S.L.T. 101 1–135
Tournier *v.* National Provincial and Union Bank of England [1924] 1 K.B. 461 (C.A.) 6–162
Tower Cabinet Co. Ltd *v.* Ingram [1949] 2 K.B. 397; 1949 1 All E.R. 1033 2–88
Trans Barwil Agencies (U.K.) Ltd *v.* John S. Braid & Co. Ltd, 1988 S.C. 222 (O.H.); 1989 S.L.T. 73 (O.H.) 1–127
Trego *v.* Hunt [1896] A.C. 7 2–192
Trojan Plant Hire Co. Ltd *v.* Durafencing (Northern) Ltd, 1974 S.L.T. (Sh.Ct.) 3 1–12
Turnbull *v.* Wilsons and Clyde Coal Co. Ltd, 1935 S.C. 580; 1935 S.L.T. 309 10–12
Tyler *v.* Logan (1904) 7 F. 123; 12 S.L.T. 466 1–116

Union Club Ltd (Liquidator of the) *v.* Edinburgh Life Assurance Co. (1906) 8 F. 1143; 14 S.L.T. 314 7–96
United Creameries Co. Ltd *v.* Boyd & Co., 1912 S.C. 617; 1912 1 S.L.T. 297 10–121
United Dominions Trust Ltd *v.* Kirkwood [1966] 2 Q.B. 431 (C.A.); [1966] 2 W.L.R. 1083; [1966] 1 All E.R. 968 6–154
United Dominions Trust Ltd *v.* Taylor, 1980 S.L.T. (Sh.Ct.) 28 5–209

Varley *v.* Whipp [1900] 1 Q.B. 513 4–74

Para.

Veitch *v.* National Bank of Scotland Ltd, 1907 S.C. 554; 14 S.L.T. 800...... 8–73

Waddell *v.* Hutton, 1911 S.C. 575; 1911 1 S.L.T. 223...................... 7–114
Walker *v.* Somerville (1837) 16 S. 217.................................. 1–182
Walker, Fraser & Steele *v.* Fraser's Trs., 1910 S.C. 222; 1909 2 S.L.T. 453.... 1–132
Ward (R.V.) Ltd *v.* Bignall [1967] 1 Q.B. 534 (C.A.); [1967] 2 All E.R. 449.. 4–274
Waverley Vintners Ltd *v.* Matthew, 1991 G.W.D. 19–1130 (Sh.Ct.)........ 9–398
Wemyss *v.* Ardrossan Harbour Co. (1893) 20 R. 500.................... 10–59
Whatlings (Foundations) Ltd *v.* Shanks & McEwan (Contractors) Ltd, 1989 S.L.T. 857.. 10–79
Whatmough's Tr. *v.* British Linen Bank, 1934 S.C. (H.L.) 51; 1932 S.C. 525; 1934 S.L.T. 392; 1932 S.L.T. 386........................... 9–53, 9–55
Whittaker's Trustee *v.* Whittaker, 1993 S.C.L.R. 718 (Sh.Ct.)............ 9–401
Widenmeyer *v.* Burn, Stewart & Co. Ltd, 1967 S.C. 85; 1967 S.L.T. 129..... 4–24
Wight Civil Engineering Ltd *v.* Parker, 1994 S.L.T. 140 (O.H.)............. 1–89
Wilkie *v.* Scottish Aviation Ltd, 1956 S.C. 198; 1956 S.L.T. (Notes) 25...... 10–149
Williamson *v.* Foulds, 1927 S.N. 164 (O.H.)............................ 8–81
Wilson (John) & Son Ltd *v.* Inland Revenue (1895) 23 R. 18; 3 S.L.T. 121... 3–141
Wink *v.* Mortimer (1849) 11 D. 995..................................... 1–195
Wolifson *v.* Harrison, 1977 S.C. 384; 1978 S.L.T. 95..................... 7–79
Wood *v.* Odessa Waterworks Co. (1889) 42 Ch.D. 636..................... 3–279
Woodburn *v.* Andrew Motherwell Ltd, 1917 S.C. 533; 1917 1 S.L.T. 345... 4–135, 4–144
Woodfield Finance Trust (Glasgow) Ltd *v.* Morgan, 1958 S.L.T. (Sh.Ct.) 14.. 8–128
Woods *v.* Martins Bank Ltd [1959] 1 Q.B. 55; [1958] 1 W.L.R. 1018; [1958] 3 All E.R. 166.. 6–157
Woolfson *v.* Strathclyde Regional Council, 1978 S.C. (H.L.) 90; 1977 S.C. 84; 1978 S.L.T. 159; 1977 S.L.T. 60.................... 3–144, 3–145, 3–161
Wormell *v.* R.H.M. Agriculture (East) Ltd [1986] 1 W.L.R. 336........... 4–37
Wright *v.* Tennent Caledonian Breweries Ltd, 1991 S.L.T. 823............ 9–403
Wylie, Stewart & Marshall *v.* Jervis, 1913 1 S.L.T. 465 (O.H.)............. 9–46

Yangtsze Insurance Association Ltd *v.* Lukmanjee [1918] A.C. 585........ 4–200
Young *v.* Clydesdale Bank Ltd (1889) 17 R. 231.......................... 8–52
Young *v.* Welsh (1833) 12 S. 233....................................... 7–52
Yuille *v.* Lawrie (1823) 2 S. 155....................................... 7–61

Zemhunt (Holdings) Ltd *v.* Control Securities plc, 1991 S.L.T. 653......... 4–49

TABLE OF STATUTES

Para.

1621 Bankruptcy Act (c.18) 9–05, 9–07, 9–09, 9–27
1681 Bills of Exchange Act (c.20) .. 6–08, 6–119, 6–124
1693 Judicatories Act (c.34) .. 10–184
1695 Cautioners Act (c.5) 8–151
1696 Bankruptcy Act (c.5) ..... 7–95, 7–102, 9–05, 9–07, 9–09, 9–40, 9–51, 9–53, 9–55, 9–57, , 9–59, 9–63, 9–118
Blank Bonds and Trusts Act (c.25) 7–104
Inland Bills Act (c.36) ... 6–08, 6–119, 6–124
1772 Bankrupts Act (12 Geo. 3 c.47) 9–06
Bills of Exchange (Scotland) Act (12 Geo. 3 c.72) 6–119, 6–124, 6–135
1782 Act (23 Geo. III, c.18) 9–06
1845 Lands Clauses Consolidation (Scotland) Act (8 & 9 Vict., c.19) .. 10–02, 10–170
Railways Clauses (Consolidation) (Scotland) Act (8 & 9 Vict., c.33) 10–02
1856 Joint Stock Companies Act (19 & 20 Vict., c.47) 3–03
Mercantile Law Amendment Act Scotland (19 & 20 Vict., c.60) 4–07, 8–04, 8–27, 8–41
s.6 .... 8–26, 8–40, 8–42
s.7 8–132
s.8 .... 8–84, 8–86, 8–87
s.9 8–148
Bankruptcy (Scotland) Act (19 & 20 Vict., c.79) 9–06

Para.

1862 Companies Act (25 & 26 Vict., c.89) 3–138
1865 Law of Partnership Act (28 & 29 Vict., c.86) 2–20
1872 Pawnbrokers Act (35 & 36 Vict., c.93) 5–11, 5–265, 7–77
1876 Appellate Jurisdiction Act (39 & 40 Vict., c.59)
s.3 10–13
Crossed Cheques Act (39 & 40 Vict., c.81) 6–204
1878 Innkeepers Act (41 & 42 Vict., c.48) 4–156
1880 Hypothec Abolition (Scotland) Act (43 Vict., c.12) 7–45, 7–60
Married Women's Policies of Assurance (Scotland) Act (43 & 44 Vict., c.26) 9–32
1882 Bills of Exchange Act (45 & 46) Vict., c.61) ... 5–283, 6–01, 6–03, 6–101, 6–120, 6–147, 6–155, 6–180, 6–231
s.2 .... 6–04, 6–20, 6–40, 6–41, 6–45, 6–51, 6–152
ss.3–72 6–04
s.3(1),(2) 6–16
(3) 6–20
(4) 6–19
s.4(1) 6–17
(2) 6–18
s.6(1),(2) 6–21
s.7(1)–(3) 6–35
s.8(1)–(5) 6–36
s.9(1)–(3) 6–33
s.10(1) 6–28
(2) 6–31
s.11 6–28
s.12 6–29
s.13(1) 6–30
(2) 6–19

	Para.
1882 Bills of Exchange Act—cont.	
s.14	6–32
s.15	6–117, 6–136
s.16	6–109, 6–112
(1)	6–22
s.17(1),(2)	6–37
s.18	6–38
s.19(1),(2)	6–39
s.20	6–44
(1),(2)	6–43
s.21	6–235
(1)	6–41, 6–146
(2),(3)	6–41
s.23	6–22, 6–24, 6–42
s.24	6–25, 6–197, 6–201
s.25	6–26
s.26(1),(2)	6–27
s.27(1)	6–52
(2)	6–55
(3)	6–53
s.28(1),(2)	6–56
s.29(1)	6–48, 6–68
(2)	6–57
(3)	6–59
s.30(1)	6–54
(2)	6–61
s.31(1)–(3)	6–62
(4)	6–63
s.32(1)–(5)	6–64
s.33	6–65
s.34	6–66
(1)	6–36
s.35	6–67
s.36	6–68
s.38(1)	6–46
(2)	6–47
(3)	6–60
ss.39, 40	6–71
s.41(1)	6–72
(2)	6–73
(3)	6–74
s.42	6–75
s.43(2)	6–80
s.44	6–76
(1)	6–39
s.45	6–77, 6–78, 6–120, 6–180
s.46(1),(2)	6–79
s.47(2)	6–80
s.48	6–81, 6–126

	Para.
1882 Bills of Exchange Act—cont.	
s.49	6–82
s.50(1),(2)	6–83
s.51(1),(2)	6–18, 6–84
(4)	6–88
(6)	6–87, 6–88
(7)	6–89
(9)	6–91
s.52(1)	6–77, 6–106
(2),(3)	6–106
(4)	6–95
s.53(1)	6–14
(2)	1–170, 6–14, 6–99, 6–100, 6–102—105, 6–165, 6–167, 6–170, 6–183
s.54	6–25, 6–107
s.55(1)	6–108
(2)	6–111
s.56	6–114
s.57	6–118
(1)	6–174
s.58	6–116
s.59(1)	6–127
(2),(3)	6–128
s.60	6–203—6–205
s.61	6–130
s.62(1),(2)	6–131
s.63(1)–(3)	6–132
s.64(1),(2)	6–133
s.65(1),(3),(4)	6–138
s.66(1),(2)	6–139
s.67(1)	6–136, 6–139
s.67(4)	6–140
s.68(1)	6–141
(3)–(6)	6–141
s.69	6–143
s.71(1),(2),(4)–(6)	6–144
s.72	6–146
(1)–(3),(5)	6–146
ss.73–82	6–04
s.73	6–04, 6–10, 6–147
s.74(1),(3)	6–180
s.75	6–102, 6–170
s.75A	6–99, 6–170
s.76(1)	6–186
(2)	6–187
s.77(1)–(4)	6–188
s.77(5)	6–190
s.77(6)	6–189

Para.

1882 Bills of Exchange Act—
cont.
s.78 6–191
s.79(1) 6–190
(2) 6–183, 6–191
s.80 .... 6–204, 6–205
s.81 6–194
s.81A 6–195, 6–204
s.82 .... 6–155, 6–156, 6–208—211, 6–213, 6–215, 6–220, 6–221, 6–222, 6–224
s.83–89 6–04
s.83(1) 6–225
(2) 6–228
(3) 6–229
(4) 6–230
s.84 6–235
s.85(1),(2) 6–236
s.86 6–237
(1),(2) 6–238
(3) 6–239
s.87(1) 6–240
(2),(3) 6–241
s.88 6–242
s.89 6–04
(1) 6–231
(2)–(4) 6–232
s.90 .... 6–04, 6–50
s.91 6–04
(1),(2) 6–23
s.92 .... 6–04, 6–32
s.94 6–85
s.97(2) 6–03
s.98 .... 6–77, 6–84, 6–119, 6–120, 6–149, 6–234
s.100 .... 6–54, 6–129
Sched. 1 6–85
1884 Revenue Act (47 & 48 Vict., c.62) 9–71
1887 Merchandise Marks Act (50 & 51 Vict., c.28) .. 4–336
1889 Judicial Factors (Scotland) Act (52 & 53 Vict., c.39)—
s.11A 9–19, 9–29, 9–42, 9–60, 9–281
Factors Act (52 & 53 Vict., c.45) 4–156, 7–84
s.1(4) 4–165
ss.2, 5 4–170

Para.

1889 Arbitration Act (52 & 53 Vict., c.49) .. 10–04, 10–123
1890 Factors (Scotland) Act (53 & 54 Vict., c.40) 4–156, 7–84
s.1 .... 4–165, 4–170
Partnership Act (53 & 54 Vict., c.49) .. 2–01—2–161, 2–168
s.1(1) 2–12, 2–13
(2) 2–13
s.2 .... 2–20, 2–101
s.3 .... 2–29, 9–340
s.4(1) 2–30
(2) 2–31, 2–37, 3–166
s.5 ... 1–17, 2–54, 2–55, 2–56, 2–62, 3–177
s.6 2–61
s.7 .... 2–62, 8–49
s.8 2–63
s.9 .... 2–37, 2–52
s.10 .... 2–65, 2–67, 2–70
s.11 2–71
s.12 .... 2–66, 2–67
s.13 2–72
s.14(1) 2–88, 2–89
(2) 2–91
s.15 .... 2–59, 2–60
s.16 2–59
s.17(1) 2–73
(2) 2–81
(3) 2–81
s.18 .... 2–94, 8–132
s.19 2–97
s.20(1) 2–41, 2–98, 2–99
(3) 2–101
s.21 2–102
s.22 .... 2–42, 2–103
s.24 2–104
(5) 3–177
(7) 3–175, 3–180
s.25 2–105
s.26(1),(2) 2–108
s.27(1) 2–109, 2–110
(2) 2–109
s.28 .... 2–113, 2–114
s.29 .... 2–113, 2–116, 2–117
s.30 .... 2–113, 2–118
s.31(1),(2) 2–125
s.32 .... 2–09, 2–16, 2–108, 2–134, 2–135

Para.

1890 Partnership Act—*cont.*
s.33 .... 2–32, 2–134, 2–136—138
(1) 3–180
s.34 ...... 2–134, 2–139—140
s.35 ...... 2–09, 2–134, 2–141
(f) 10–11
s.36 2–150
s.36(1) 1–176, 2–84, 2–88
(2) 1–176, 2–85
(3) 2–86, 2–87, 2–88
s.37 .... 2–142, 2–150
s.38 ...... 2–142, 2–151—154
s.39 .... 2–142, 2–143, 2–146, 2–155
s.40 .... 2–142, 2–156
s.41 2–132
s.42 ...... 2–142, 2–156—159
(1) 2–157, 2–158
(2) 2–159
s.44 .... 2–142, 2–161
s.45 2–12
s.46 2–04
Directors' Liability Act (53 & 54 Vict., c.64) 3–08
1891 Law Agents and Notaries Public (Scotland) Act (54 & 55 Vict., c.30) 7–65
Stamp Act (54 & 55 Vict., c.39) 3–141
1893 Sale of Goods Act (56 & 57 Vict., c.71) .. 4–01, 4–02, 4–05, 4–09, 4–11, 4–12, 4–15, 4–16, 4–51, 4–57, 4–93, 4–115, 4–253, 7–20, 7–26, 7–179
s.8 4–46
ss.12–15 4–358
s.12 .... 4–64, 4–65
(1)–(3) 4–69
s.13 .... 4–72, 4–74, 4–76
s.14 4–84
(1) 4–76, 4–103, 4–104, 4–107, 4–115
(2) ... 4–76, 4–104, 4–107, 4–115
s.15 4–115
s.16 7–91
s.18 4–135
s.25(2) 4–171
s.61(4) 4–28, 7–23, 7–25, 7–26

Para.

1894 Arbitration (Scotland) Act (57 & 58 Vict., c.13) ...... 10–03, 10–106, 10–107—124
s.1 ... 10–113, 10–123, 10–124
s.2 ... 10–114, 10–122, 10–124
s.3 ... 10–115, 10–120, 10–122
s.4 10–116
s.6 10–117
Heritable Securities (Scotland) Act (57 & 58 Vict., c.44) 7–12
Merchant Shipping Act (57 & 58 Vict., c.60) 7–75
ss.31, 33, 37, Sched. 1 ... 7–75
1900 Moneylenders Act (63 & 64 Vict., c.51) 5–11, 5–15, 5–16, 5–307, 6–154
1906 Bills of Exchange (Crossed Cheques) Act (6 Edw. 7, c.17) 6–211, 6–221
s.1 .... 6–209, 6–210
Prevention of Corruption Act (6 Edw. 7, c.34) .. 1–04, 1–128
Workmen's Compensation Act (6 Edw. 7, c.58) .. 2–22, 2–24, 10–12, 10–170
1907 Limited Partnerships Act (7 Edw. 7, c.24) ..... 2–01, 2–11, 2–162—176, 3–173
s.4(2),(3) 2–163
s.5 2–164
s.6(1) 2–170
(2) 2–171
(3) 2–172
(5) 2–175
s.7 2–168
s.8 .... 2–164, 2–165
s.9(1) 2–166
s.10 2–167
s.15 2–164
s.16(1) 2–167
1908 Agricultural Holdings (Scotland) Act (8 Edw. 7, c.64) 10–20, 10–170

Para.

1913 Bankruptcy (Scotland) Act (3 & 4 Geo. 5, c.20) 9–07, 9–08, 9–291, 9–357, 9–393, 9–426
s.5 9–59
s.10 .... 9–291, 9–293
s.104 9–293
1914 Trading with the Enemy Act (4 & 5 Geo. 5, c.87) 3–149, 3–150
1916 Prevention of Corruption Act (6 & 7 Geo. 5, c.64) 1–04, 1–128
1917 Bills of Exchange (Time of Noting) Act (7 & 8 Geo. 5 c.48) 6–88
1921 Trusts (Scotland) Act (11 & 12 Geo. 5, c.58) .. 9–463
s.4 10–42
1924 Conveyancing (Scotland) Act (14 & 15 Geo. 5, c.27)—
s.27 7–158
1925 Workmen's Compensation Act (15 & 16 Geo. 5, c.84) 10–12, 10–170
1927 Auctions (Bidding Agreements) Act (17 & 18 Geo. 5, c.12) .... 4–12, 4–327—329
s.1(1),(2) 4–327
s.3 4–329
Moneylenders Act (17 & 18 Geo. 5, c.21) 5–11, 5–15, 5–16, 5–307, 7–77
1935 Law Reform (Married Women and Tortfeasors) Act (25 & 26 Geo. 5, c.30)—
s.3 6–25
1939 Trading with the Enemy Act (2 & 3 Geo. 6, c.89) 3–149
1947 Companies Act (10 & 11 Geo. 6, c.47)—
s.115 9–59

Para.

1949 Agricultural Holdings (Scotland) Act (12, 13 & 14 Geo. 6, c.75) 10–170
1950 Arbitration Act (14 Geo. 6, c.27) 10–04, 10–05
s.4(1) 10–04
s.6 10–123
1953 Merchandise Marks Act (1 & 2 Eliz. 2, c.48) 4–336
1957 Cheques Act (5 & 6 Eliz. 2, c.36) 5–224, 6–01, 6–04, 6–147, 6–152, 6–155, 6–213
s.1 6–205
s.4 ..... 6–155, 6–213, 6–216, 6–223
(1) ... 6–211, 6–212, 6–217
(2) 6–211
(3) 6–213
s.6(1) 6–152
1960 Pawnbrokers Act (8 & 9 Eliz. 2, c.24) .. 5–11, 5–265, 7–77
1961 Consumer Protection Act (9 & 10 Eliz. 2, c.40) 4–373
Mock Auctions Act (9 & 10 Eliz. 2, c.47) ..... 4–12, 4–330—333
s.1(1) 4–330
(3) 4–331
s.3(2) 4–332
Trusts (Scotland) Act (9 & 10 Eliz. 2, c.57) .. 9–463
1964 Hire-Purchase Act (c.53) 5–28, 5–385
s.27 5–388
(1) 5–386
s.29(2) 5–387
Trading Stamps Act (c.71) ... 4–12, 4–334—335
s.2(1),(2) 4–335
s.3(1) 4–335
1965 Hire-Purchase Act (c.66) 5–16, 5–384
Hire-Purchase (Scotland) Act (c.67) 5–11, 5–16, 5–384

Para.

1968 Trade Descriptions Act (c.29) .... 4–12, 4–83, 4–336—341, 4–353, 5–10
s.1(1) 4–337
s.2(1) 4–338
s.3(1) 4–339
(2) 4–339
s.11 4–385
s.24(1) 4–341
s.35 4–336
Civil Aviation Act (c.61)—
s.16 7–76
1969 Decimal Currency Act (c.19) 6–34
Age of Majority (Scotland) Act (c.39)—
s.1(1),(2) 5–171
Auctions (Bidding Agreements) Act (c.56) .... 4–12, 4–327—329
ss.1(1), 2(1), 3(1),(2) ... 4–328
s.4 4–329
1970 Conveyancing and Feudal Reform (Scotland) Act (c.35) 7–09, 7–12, 7–188
1971 Consumer Protection Act (c.15) 4–373
Powers of Attorney Act (c.27) 1–04
Unsolicited Goods and Services Act (c.30) 4–344—348
s.1(1),(2) 4–345
s.2(1) 4–346, 4–348
s.3A 4–347
s.6 4–344
Tribunals and Inquiries Act (c.62) 5–34
Banking and Financial Dealings Act (c.80) .. 6–32
1972 Trade Descriptions Act (c.34) 4–342
Administration of Justice (Scotland) Act (c.59)—
s.3 ..... 10–03, 10–13, 10–77, 10–79, 10–144, 10–170, 10–177

Para.

1972 Companies (Floating Charges and Receivers) (Scotland) Act (c.67) 3–09
European Communities Act (c.68)—
s.9(1) 3–218, 3–228
1973 Supply of Goods (Implied Terms) Act (c.13) 4–01, 4–11, 4–16, 4–50, 4–51, 4–64, 4–72, 4–84, 4–90, 4–93, 4–95
Fair Trading Act (c.41) ... 4–349—355, 5–31
ss.1(1), 2(1) 4–349
s.13 4–351
s.17(1),(2) 4–352
ss.22, 23 4–350
ss.34, 35 4–353
s.124(1) 4–355
(3) 4–354
s.125 5–36
(1) 4–355
Prescription and Limitation (Scotland) Act (c.52) 4–372, 6–125, 6–135, 8–151, 8–154, 8–155
s.6 .... 8–152, 8–153
Sched. 1 8–152
Sched. 2 .... 8–153, 8–155
1974 Consumer Credit Act (c.39) ... 4–11, 4–50, 4–84, 4–169, 4–349, 5–01—389, 6–49, 7–14, 7–77
s.1 .... 5–02, 5–32
s.2 5–33
s.3 5–34
s.4 5–35
s.5 5–36
s.6 5–37
s.7 5–38
ss.8–20 5–41
s.8(1) 5–47
(2) 5–46, 5–50, 5–77, 5–78, 5–85
s.9(1) 5–48
(3) 5–71, 5–77
(4) 5–48, 5–71, 5–78
s.10(1)(a) 5–66
(b) 5–67, 5–73

Para.

1974 Consumer Credit Act—
cont.
s.10(2) 5–69, 5–74
(3)(b) 5–70
(i) 5–78
(ii) 5–75
(iii) 5–76
s.11(1) 5–81, 5–82
(a) ... 5–90, 5–93, 5–95
(b) 5–85, 5–90, 5–93, 5–96, 5–98
(c) 5–86
(2) 5–82
(3) 5–83, 5–85, 5–98
s.12 ... 5–45, 5–90, 5–92, 5–94
(a),(b) 5–182
(c) 5–93, 5–98, 5–182
s.13 .... 5–45, 5–91
s.14(1) ... 5–99, 5–100, 5–102
(2) 5–99
(4) 5–101
s.15(1) 5–51, 5–57
s.16 ... 5–45, 5–58—60, 5–123
s.17(1) 5–105
(3),(4) 5–106
s.18(1) 5–108
(2) 5–112
(3) 5–113
s.19 5–117
s.20(1) 5–49, 5–50
s.21 5–123
s.22 5–124
(2) 5–128
s.23 5–127
s.24 5–128
s.25 .... 5–129, 5–130
s.26 .... 5–131, 5–178
s.27 5–132
s.28 5–133
s.29 5–134
ss.30, 31 5–135
s.32 5–138
s.33 5–139
s.34 5–140
s.35 5–141
s.36 .... 5–143, 5–147
s.37 .... 5–02, 5–144
s.38 .... 5–02, 5–144
s.39 5–147
s.40 ...... 5–57, 5–148, 5–149
s.41 5–149

Para.

1974 Consumer Credit Act—
cont.
s.42 5–151
ss.43–47 5–153
s.43 5–154
(1) .. 5–154, 5–155, 5–157
(2)–(4) 5–157
(2)(c) 5–158
(5) 5–159
s.44 .... 5–160, 5–165
ss.45, 46 5–165
s.46(1) 5–166
s.47(1),(2) 5–165
ss.48–51 5–153
s.48 ..... 5–167, 5–168, 5–345
s.49(1)–(3) 5–169
s.50 5–171
s.51 5–173
ss.52–54 5–153
s.52 5–174
s.53 .... 5–04, 5–177
s.54 5–178
s.55 .... 5–181, 5–204
s.56 ..... 5–203, 5–204, 5–351
s.56(1) 5–182
(b) 5–184
(2) 5–184
(4) 5–185
s.60 ..... 5–186, 5–188, 5–190
s.61(1) 5–190
s.62 .... 5–191, 5–194
(1),(2) 5–191
(3) 5–194
s.63 .... 5–191, 5–194
(1),(2) 5–191
(4) 5–193
(5) 5–194
s.64 .... 5–195, 5–198, 5–199, 5–294
s.65 .... 5–189, 5–292
s.67 5–197
s.68 5–198
s.69 5–199
ss.70–73 5–202
s.74 .... 5–203, 5–205
(2) 5–104
s.75 .... 5–207, 5–210
s.76 5–211
ss.77–80 5–214
s.77 5–215
(1) 5–381

Para.

1974 Consumer Credit Act—
cont.
s.78 5–217
s.79 5–218
s.80 5–219
s.81 5–220
s.82 5–222
s.83 5–224
s.84 5–225
s.85 5–226
s.86 . . . . . 5–227, 5–295, 5–296
s.87 . . . . . 5–232, 5–235
s.88 . . . . . 5–234, 5–235
s.89 5–236
s.90 . . . . . 5–237, 5–239, 5–240
s.91 . . . . . 5–237, 5–240
s.92 5–241
s.93 5–242
s.93A 5–243
s.94 . . . . . 5–244, 5–245
s.95 5–245
s.96 5–246
s.97 5–247
s.98 5–249
s.99 . . . . . 5–250, 5–251
s.100 5–251
s.101 . . . . . 5–252, 5–253
s.103 5–254
s.104 . . . . . 5–255, 7–51
s.105 . . . . . 5–259, 5–292
s.106 5–259
ss.107–109 5–260
s.110 5–262
s.111 . . . . . 5–261, 5–292
s.112 5–263
s.113 5–264
s.114 5–268
(3) 5–265
ss.114–122 . . . . . 5–265, 7–77
s.116 5–271
s.117 5–272
s.118 5–273
s.119 5–274
s.120 5–275
s.121 . . . . . 5–263, 5–277
s.122 5–278
s.123 . . . . . 5–280—283, 5–292
s.124 . . . . . 5–282, 5–292
s.125 . . . . . 5–283, 6–49, 6–58
s.126 5–284
s.127 5–294

Para.

1974 Consumer Credit Act—
cont.
s.128 5–296
s.129 5–297
s.130 5–300
s.131 5–301
s.132 5–302
s.133 5–303
s.135 5–290
s.136 . . . . . 5–291, 5–297
ss.137–140 . . . . . 5–58, 5–309, 5–310
s.137 5–308
s.138 5–311
s.139 . . . 5–287, 5–289, 5–313, 5–314, 5–380, 9–289
s.140 5–58
s.141 5–288
s.145 . . . . . 5–26, 5–40, 5–320, 5–324, 5–349
(5) 5–329
(6) 5–332
(7) 5–335
(8) 5–337
s.146 . . . . 5–320, 5–323, 5–328
(6) 5–331, 5–334, 5–336
s.147 5–341
s.148 5–342
s.149 5–343
s.150 . . . . . 5–342, 5–343
ss.151–154 5–344
ss.153, 154 5–345
s.155 5–346
s.156 . . . . . 5–347, 5–348
s.157 . . . . . 5–351, 5–352
s.158 . . . . 5–353, 5–355—357, 5–359
s.159 . . . . 5–353, 5–359, 5–361
s.160 . . . . 5–355, 5–358, 5–361
(5) 5–361
s.161 5–364
s.162 . . . . . 5–368, 5–371
s.163 5–369
s.164 5–370
s.165 5–373
s.166 . . . . . 5–374, 5–375
s.167 5–376
(2) 5–165
s.168 5–378
s.169 5–379

Para.

1974 Consumer Credit Act—*cont.*
s.171 5–380
s.172 5–381
s.173 5–383
s.181 . . . . 5–46, 5–107
s.182 5–03
ss.184, 187(1),(5) 5–96
s.187(1) 5–98
s.188 5–42
s.189 . . . . 5–25, 5–26, 5–40
(1) 5–45, 5–47, 5–49, 5–53, 5–54, 5–58, 5–93, 5–117, 5–123, 5–156, 5–173, 5–197, 5–203, 5–214, 5–256, 5–257, 5–266, 5–287, 5–309, 5–338, 7–77
s.192(3)(b) 5–384
Sched. 1 . . . . 5–38, 5–376
Sched. 2 . . . . 5–26, 5–42, 5–50, 5–56, 5–72, 5–84, 5–98, 5–114, 5–115, 5–120
Sched. 4 5–385
Sched. 5 5–384

1975 Arbitration Act (c.3) 10–05
s.1(1) 10–05

1976 Solicitors (Scotland) Act (c.6)—
s.20 1–152
Insolvency Act (c.60)—
s.1(1), Sched. 1 9–426

1977 Unfair Contract Terms Act (c.50) . . . . . 4–11, 4–50, 4–51, 4–356—359, 5–10, 10–37
s.20(1)(a) 4–71
ss.20(2), 24, 25 4–82
Sched. 2 4–82

1978 Interpretation Act (c.30) . . 5–338
Consumer Safety Act (c.38) 4–373

1979 Land Registration (Scotland) Act (c.33) . . 7–09, 7–12
Banking Act (c.37) 6–153
ss.2, 3 6–153
s.38(1) 5–203
Sched. 2 6–153

Para.

1979 Estate Agents Act (c.38) . . 1–04, 1–55, 1–56—64, 1–65
s.1 1–58
ss.3, 4, 6–8 1–60
ss.9, 10, 11 1–61
ss.13–17 1–62
ss.18–23 1–63
ss.24–26 1–64
Arbitration Act (c.42) . . . 10–04
Sale of Goods Act (c.54) . . . 4–01—324, 4–326, 4–358, 4–363, 7–20, 7–179
s.1(1) 4–15
(2) 4–16
s.2(1) 4–19, 4–44
(3) 4–20
(4)–(6) 4–19
s.3 4–31
s.4(1) 4–35
s.5 4–38
s.6 4–41
s.7 4–42
s.8 4–45
s.9 4–48
ss.10–15 4–50
s.10 . . . . 4–54, 4–306
(1),(2) 4–59, 4–306
s.11(2),(3) 4–55
(5) 4–56, 4–57, 4–58
ss.12–15 . . . . 4–54, 4–57
s.12 . . . 4–54, 4–64, 4–65, 4–71
(1)–(5) 4–67
(3)–(5) 4–70
(1) 4–66, 4–68
(2) 4–66, 4–68
(3) 4–68
(4) 4–66
(5) 4–66
(5A) 4–66
ss.13, 14 4–114
s.13 . . 4–78, 4–80, 4–82, 4–83, 4–88
(1) 4–78, 4–79
(1A) 4–79
(2) 4–79
(3) 4–72
s.14 . . . . 4–05, 4–84, 4–86, 4–87, 4–96

Para.

1979 Sale of Goods Act—*cont.*
s.14(1) 4–86
(2) 4–05, 4–25, 4–92, 4–96
(2A) 4–05, 4–96
(2B) 4–05, 4–96
(2C) 4–05, 4–96
(3) 4–97, 4–98, 4–108
(4) 4–110
(5) 4–90, 4–91
(6) 4–92, 4–93, 4–97
s.15 4–86
(1) 4–111
(2) 4–112
(3) 4–113
s.15B ... 4–116, 4–294, 4–301, 4–304
(1) 4–116, 4–304, 4–305
(2) 4–116, 4–305, 4–306
ss.16–20B 4–08
s.16 .... 4–121, 4–122, 4–123, 4–124, 4–125
s.17 .... 4–131, 4–154
(1),(2) 7–21, 7–179
s.18 ..... 4–21, 4–121, 4–132, 4–136, 7–179
s.18, Rule 1 ..... 4–137—140
Rule 2 ..... 4–141—142
Rule 3 ..... 4–143—144
Rule 4 ..... 4–145—147
Rule 5 ..... 4–148—152
s.19 4–153
(1) 4–153, 4–154
(2) 4–153
s.20 4–42
(1)–(3) 4–120
s.20A ... 4–121, 4–125, 4–126, 4–175
(1) 4–126, 4–127
(2) 4–125, 4–127, 4–130
(3) 4–127
(5) 4–128
(6) 4–129
s.20B ... 4–121, 4–130, 4–175
(1) 4–130
ss.21–26 4–239
s.21(1) 4–155, 4–158
(2) 4–156
s.22 4–157

Para.

1979 Sale of Goods Act—*cont.*
s.23 4–159
s.24 ..... 4–162, 4–166, 4–167
(1),(2) 4–169
s.25 ..... 4–162, 4–166, 4–168
(1) 4–168, 4–169, 4–170, 4–171, 4–172
(2) 4–169
s.26 4–164
ss.27, 28 4–173
s.29 4–176
(1) 4–177
(2) 4–178
(3) 4–179
(4) 4–180
(5) 4–181
(6) 4–182
s.30 .... 4–183, 4–185
(1) 4–186, 4–187
(2) 4–189
(2D) 4–186, 4–189
(3) 4–189
(4) 4–225
(5) 4–184
s.31(1) 4–190
(2) 4–191
s.32(1) 4–192
(2) 4–193
(3) ... 4–194, 4–196, 4–197
s.33 4–201
s.34 4–204
s.35 .... 4–206, 4–336
(1) 4–207, 4–208
(2) 4–208, 4–209
(3) 4–209
(4) 4–210
(6) 4–216, 4–217
(7) 4–223
s.35A 4–226
(1) 4–226
(2) 4–226
(3) 4–227
(4) 4–228
s.36 4–211
s.37(1),(2) 4–229
s.38(1) 4–232
(2) 4–233
s.39(1) 4–234, 4–268
(2) 4–235
s.40 ...... 4–234, 4–275—277
s.41(1) 4–241
(2) 4–243

Para.

1979 Sale of Goods Act—*cont.*
s.42 4–244
s.43(1) 4–245
(2) 4–246
s.44 4–251
s.45 . . . . 4–253, 4–254
s.46 4–253
(1)–(3) 4–265
(4) 4–266
s.47(1) 4–237, 4–239
(2) 4–238
s.48(1) 4–240, 4–269
(2) 4–240, 4–270
(3) 4–272, 4–274
(4) 4–273, 4–274
s.49(1) 4–142, 4–287
(2) 4–287
(3) 4–280, 4–289
s.50(1) 4–290
(2) 4–291
(3) 4–292
s.51 4–301
(1) 4–296
(2) 4–297
(3) 4–298
s.52 4–301
(1) 4–299, 4–300
(3) 4–299
(4) 4–280, 4–299
s.53 . . . . 4–295, 4–299
s.53A 4–301
(1) 4–307
(2) 4–307
s.54 . . . . 4–280, 4–281
s.55(1) 4–51
(2) 4–51
s.57 4–312
(1) 4–313
(2) 4–315
(3) 4–318
(4) 4–321
(5) 4–322
(6) 4–319
s.58 4–310
s.61(1) 4–36, 4–37, 4–39, 4–55, 4–89, 4–100, 4–126, 4–165, 4–175
(2) 4–56, 4–57, 4–58
(4) 4–242, 9–15
(5) 4–138
s.62(2) 4–09, 4–283
(4) 4–27, 4–28, 7–22

Para.

1979 Sale of Goods Act—*cont.*
s.63(1) 4–71, 4–82
Sched. 1 4–16
para. 3 4–65
Sched. 2,
paras 21, 22 4–82
para. 21 4–71
1980 Bail, etc. (Scotland) Act (c.4) 9–369
Companies Act (c.22) 3–08
s.1(2) 3–55
s.2(1) 3–77
Solicitors (Scotland) Act (c.46)—
s.30 1–152
s.62 7–65
Law Reform (Miscellaneous Provisions) (Scotland) Act (c.55)—
s.14 2–143
s.17 . . . . 10–03, 10–106, 10–125—126
(4) 10–117
Married Women's Policies of Assurance (Scotland) (Amendment) Act (c.56) 9–32
1981 Matrimonial Homes (Family Protection) (Scotland) Act (c.59) 9–311
s.1(1) 8–52
Companies Act (c.62) . . . 2–177, 2–183
1982 Civil Aviation Act (c.16)—
s.86 7–76
Civil Jurisdiction and Judgments Act (c.27)—
Sched. 12 5–288
Supply of Goods and Services Act (c.29) 4–02, 4–12, 4–25
ss.11A–11L 4–26
s.11A(1),(2),(3) 4–26
1984 Law Reform (Husband and Wife) (Scotland) Act (c.15) 1–98, 1–99, 1–100
s.7 1–98

Para.

1984 Mental Health (Scotland) Act (c.36)—
s.1 1–196
s.125(1) 9–91
1985 Companies Act (c.6) . . . . 2–179, 3–04—282, 7–10
s.1(1) 3–130
(2)(a) 3–46
(b) 3–52
(c) 3–61
(3) 3–63, 3–72, 3–113, 3–209
(3A) 3–130
(4) 3–55, 3–56, 3–80
s.2(1) 3–210, 3–216
(2) 3–210
(3) 3–242
(5) 3–244, 3–258
(6) 3–130, 3–258
(7) 3–196
s.3 . . . . . 3–74, 3–198
(1) 3–50, 3–57, 3–64, 3–80, 3–81, 3–131
s.4 . . . . . 3–239, 3–257
s.7 3–264
(1) 3–58, 3–65, 3–130
(2) 3–244
(3) 3–263
s.8 3–264
(1),(2) 3–51, 3–131
(4) 3–59, 3–64, 3–131
s.9 . . . . . 3–267, 3–268
(1) 3–40, 3–196
s.10 . . . . . 3–129, 3–211
(1) 3–74
(2),(3),(6) 3–131
s.11 . . . . . 3–32, 3–74, 3–246
s.12(1) 3–132
(3) 3–131, 3–132
s.13(1) 3–75
(3),(4) 3–134, 3–166
(6) 3–75
(7) 3–75, 3–136
s.14(1) 3–276, 3–277
s.16 . . . . . 3–68, 3–243, 3–269
s.17 3–257
s.22(1),(2) 3–261
s.23 3–126
s.24 3–151
s.25(1) 3–82, 3–199
(2) 3–83, 3–199

Para.

1985 Companies Act—*cont.*
s.26(1),(2) 3–201
s.27(1),(4) 3–82, 3–83
s.28(1) 3–203
(2) 3–204
s.29(2) 3–201
s.30 3–83
(2),(3) 3–60
s.32(1),(3) 3–204
s.34 3–83
s.35 . . . . 3–228, 3–229, 3–231, 3–233
(1) 3–229
(2) 3–230
(3) 1–24, 3–232
s.35A . . . 3–228, 3–233, 3–234
(1),(2),(3) 3–234
(4) 3–235
(5) 3–236
s.35B 3–228, 3–237
s.36C 1–146, 3–15, 5–37
s.37 6–23
ss.43–48 3–114
s.43 . . . . . 3–76, 3–114
(1) 3–115, 3–116
(2) 3–116
(3) 3–117
s.45 3–115
s.47(1),(5) 3–118
s.48 3–114
s.49 . . . . . 3–67, 3–113
s.50 3–67
ss.51, 52 3–67
ss.53–55 3–114
s.53(1) . . . 3–119, 3–120, 3–122
(2) 3–119
s.54(1),(2),(5),(6) 3–121
s.55 3–114
(1),(3) 3–122
s.80(1),(4) 3–94
s.80A 3–112
(1),(2) 3–94
s.84(1) 3–96
s.89(1),(4) 3–95
s.91(1) 3–95
s.99(1),(2) 3–97
s.101(1) 3–98
s.102(1) 3–99
s.103(1) 3–100
s.104(1),(2),(4) 3–101
s.106 3–102

Para.

1985 Companies Act—*cont.*
s.108(1) 3–100
s.117(1),(3) 3–85
(2) 3–32, 3–85
s.118 .... 3–74, 3–246
(1) 3–32
s.121 ... 3–248, 3–249, 3–251, 3–265
s.121(2) 3–20
s.125 3–254
s.127 .... 3–255, 3–269
s.135 .... 3–252, 3–265
s.142(1) 3–103
s.146 3–104
s.150(1) 3–105
ss.151–158 3–126
ss.151(1), 155(1) 3–106
ss.162(1),(2), 171(1) ... 3–107
s.227(1) 3–153
s.252 3–112
s.258 .... 3–127, 3–153
s.264(1),(3) 3–108
s.282 3–86
s.283(2),(4) 3–156
s.286 3–90
s.287 3–211
s.288(1) 3–215
s.292(1) 3–87
s.293(1)–(3) 3–88
s.303 3–41
(1) 3–40
(2) 3–41
s.309(1),(2) 3–25
s.324(1) 3–157
ss.330–342 3–89
s.330(2),(3),(4) 3–89
s.331(6),(7) 3–89
s.332–338 3–89
s.346 3–89
s.348–351 .... 3–205—207
s.351(1) 3–214
s.353(1) 3–215
s.366A 3–112
s.368 3–38
s.369(4) 3–112
s.372(1),(2) 3–109
s.378(3) 3–112
s.379 3–41
s.379A(1),(2) 3–112
s.381A 3–111
s.383(1) 3–215

Para.

1985 Companies Act—*cont.*
s.386 3–112
s.425 3–192
s.428–430F 3–162
s.433(1) 3–154
s.442 3–155
ss.462–466 3–181
s.665 2–172
s.711 3–212
(1) 3–135
s.716 .... 2–15, 3–178
s.723A 3–215
s.736 .... 3–126, 3–127
(1) 3–124, 3–152
Sched. 10A 3–127
Sched. 13,
para. 4 3–157
Business Names Act (c.7) .... 2–01, 2–11, 2–177—185, 3–04, 3–07, 3–208
s.1(1) 2–179
(2) 2–180
s.2(1) 2–181
(4) 2–182
s.4(1) ... 2–184, 2–185, 2–188
(2) 2–187, 2–188
(3) 2–184
(6) 2–188
s.5(1) 2–188
s.7 .... 2–182, 2–188
Company Securities (Insider Dealing) Act (c.8) 3–04, 3–06
Companies Consolidation (Consequential Provisions) Act (c.9)—
s.31(2) 2–183, 3–04
Enduring Powers of Attorney Act (c.29) 1–196
Insolvency Act (c.65) 3–06, 3–07
Bankruptcy (Scotland) Act (c.66) .... 4–242, 7–95, 9–02—475, 9–423, 9–426, 9–451, 9–453, 9–471, 9–478
s.1 .... 9–79, 9–84
s.1A 9–85
(1) 9–80
(2) .. 9–81, 9–168, 9–213, 9–243

Para.

1985 Bankruptcy (Scotland) Act—*cont.*
s.1A(3) 9–82
(4) 9–83
s.1B 9–85
s.1C 9–86
s.2 .... 9–89, 9–166
(2) 9–94
(3) 9–88, 9–90
(4) 9–166, 9–175
(5) 9–95
(7) 9–180
s.3 9–444
(1) 9–96, 9–235
(2) 9–97
(3), (4) 9–98
(5) 9–96
(6) 9–99
(7) 9–100
s.4 .... 9–101, 9–236
ss.5–11 9–102
s.5(2) 9–103
(2B) 9–105
(3) 9–107
(4) 9–108
(6) 9–111
(6A) .. 9–112, 9–113, 9–179
(9) 9–113, 9–114
(10) 9–114
s.6(1) 2–171, 9–115
(2) 9–117
(5) 9–116
s.7 9–01
(1) 9–118
s.8(1) 9–109
(3) 9–110
s.9(1),(4),(5) 9–119
s.10(1),(2),(5) 9–122
(3) 9–123
(4) 9–124
s.11(1),(5) 9–125
s.12(1) 9–127
(1A) 9–128, 9–443
(2) 9–129, 9–400
(3) .. 9–132, 9–135, 9–136, 9–140
(3A) 9–132
(4) .. 9–141, 9–326, 9–400, 9–403, 9–404
s.13 9–167
(1) 9–81, 9–168

Para.

1985 Bankruptcy (Scotland) Act—*cont.*
s.13(2) 9–169
(3) 9–169
(4) 9–169
(5) 9–170
(6) 9–170, 9–171
s.14(1) 9–143
(2) 9–144
(4) 9–145
(5) 9–143
s.15(1) 9–120, 9–146
(2) 9–146
(3) 9–147, 9–148
(4) 9–147, 9–150
(5) 9–148
(6) 9–149, 9–447
(8),(9) 9–269
s.16 .... 9–150, 9–311
(1) 9–152
(2) 9–153
(3) 9–154
(4) 9–155, 9–158, 9–160, 9–403
s.17 9–150
(1) 9–155, 9–157, 9–158, 9–160
(2) 9–159
(3) 9–161
(4),(5) 9–163
(7) 9–162
(8) 9–156
s.18 9–173
(1),(4) 9–174, 9–177
(2) 9–175
(3) 9–176, 9–177
(5) 9–177
s.19 9–179
(1) 9–179
(2) 9–179
(4) 9–181, 9–182
s.20 9–183
(1) 9–184
(2) 9–226
(3) 9–186
(4) 9–187
s.20A 9–188
s.21 .... 9–188, 9–189
(1) 9–190
(1A) 9–190
(2) 9–191
(3) 9–192

Para.

1985 Bankruptcy (Scotland) Act—*cont.*
s.21A 9–188, 9–189
(1) 9–193
(2) 9–194
(3) 9–194
(4) 9–195
(5) 9–195
(6) 9–196, 9–198
(7) 9–197
(8) 9–198
s.21B 9–199
(1) 9–199, 9–443
(2) 9–199, 9–430, 9–443
s.22 .... 9–331, 9–333
(1) 9–209, 9–330
(2),(3) 9–200
(5) 9–201
(8) 9–202
s.23(1) 9–203, 9–330
(2) 9–203
(3) 9–204, 9–206
(4) 9–350, 9–351
(5) 9–205, 9–350
s.23A ... 9–128, 9–194, 9–199, 9–209, 9–217, 9–438
(1) 9–439
(2) 9–440
(4) 9–430, 9–441
(5),(6),(7) 9–442
s.24(1) 9–206
(2) .. 9–171, 9–207, 9–385
(3) 9–208, 9–212
(3A) 9–209, 4–430
(3B) 9–443
(4) .. 9–210, 9–440, 9–443
(4A) 9–210, 9–443
(5) 9–210, 9–430
s.25 .... 9–216, 9–431
(1) .. 9–216, 9–217, 9–218, 9–431, 9–443
(2) 9–219
(2A) 9–217, 9–431, 9–443
(3) 9–218
(4) 9–218, 9–219
(6) 9–220
s.25A 9–249
(3) 9–430
s.26 .... 9–221, 9–355
(1) 9–222

Para.

1985 Bankruptcy (Scotland) Act—*cont.*
s.26(2) 9–223
(3) 9–224
(4) 9–225
(5) 9–226
s.26A 9–221, 9–230
(1) 9–230
(3) 9–231, 9–232
(4) 9–232
(5) 9–233
(7) 9–234
s.27 9–221
(1),(2) 9–227
(3),(4),(4A) 9–228
(6) 229
s.28 .... 9–238, 9–432
(1) 9–239
(1A) 9–240
(2) 9–240
(3) 9–241
(5) 9–249, 9–430
(6) 9–247
(7) 9–248
s.29 .... 9–238, 9–433
(1)(a) 9–242
(b) 9–244
(2),(3),(4) 9–244
(5) 9–246
(6) 9–245, 9–246
(8) 9–249, 9–430
s.30 9–434
(1),(2) 9–212
(3),(4) 9–213
s.31 9–270
(1) .. 6–170, 9–250, 9–253
(2) 9–254
(3) 9–255
(4) 9–256
(5) 9–257
(8) 9–250
s.32 9–276
(1) 9–260, 9–263
(2) .. 9–261, 9–263, 9–264, 9–265
(3) 9–262
(4) 9–265
(5) 9–266
(6) 9–267, 9–268
(7) 9–258
(8) 6–170. 9–270

Para.

1985 Bankruptcy (Scotland) Act—*cont.*
s.32(9) .. 6–170, 9–269, 9–270, 9–271
s.33(1) 9–272, 9–440
(2) 9–275
(3) 9–276
s.34 .... 9–17, 9–27, 9–33, 9–279, 9–340
(1) 9–28
(2) 9–29
(3) 9–30
(4) 9–31, 9–34
(7) 9–32
(8) 9–19
(9) 9–33
s.35 9–281
(1) 9–281
(2) 9–282
s.36 ...... 7–95, 7–100, 9–40, 9–41, 9–51, 9–59, 9–60, 9–64, 9–66, 9–280
(1) 9–60
(2) 9–62
(3) 9–61
(4) 9–64
(5) 9–65
(6) 9–42
(7) 9–66
s.36A 9–283, 9–286
(1) 9–283
(2) 9–284
(3) 9–284
s.36B 9–283
(1) 9–285
(7) 9–286
s.36C 9–283
s.37 9–292
(1),(2),(4),(6),(8) .. 9–292
s.38 7–172
(1) 7–172, 9–295
(2) 7–172, 9–296
(4) ... 7–172, 7–174, 9–297
s.39 9–444
(1) 9–298
(2) 9–300, 9–435
(3) 9–301
(4) 9–302
(6) 9–299
s.39(8) 9–303

Para.

1985 Bankruptcy (Scotland) Act—*cont.*
s.40 ..... 9–307, 9–308, 9–309
(1) 9–305
(2) .. 9–305, 9–306, 9–308
(4) 9–304, 9–305
s.41(1) 9–311
s.42(1) 9–312
(2),(3) 9–313
(4) 9–314
s.43 9–315
s.44 .... 9–317, 9–436
(1),(2),(3) 9–319
s.45 .... 9–317, 9–436
(1) 9–320
(3) 9–321
(4) 9–322
s.46 9–317
(1) 9–323
(2) 9–324
(4) 9–325
s.47 9–317
(1) 9–326
(3) 9–327
(5) 9–328
(6) 9–329
s.48 9–331
(2) 9–331
(3) 9–332
(5) 9–334
(7) 9–333
s.49(1),(2) 9–335
(4) 9–336
(6) 9–337
s.51 7–174
(1) 9–338
(2) 9–339
(3) 9–340
(5) 9–341
(6)(b) 7–174
(7) 9–342
s.52 9–343
(1) 9–344
(2) .. 9–319, 9–320, 9–345
(2A) 9–345
(4) 9–346
(5) 9–347
(9) 9–348
s.53 ..... 9–349, 9–375, 9–437
(1) 9–350
(2),(2A) 9–351

Para.
1985 Bankruptcy (Scotland) Act—*cont.*
s.53(3) 9–352
(6) 9–353
(7) 9–354
(8) 9–355
(10) 9–356
s.54 .... 9–358, 9–365, 9–369, 9–400
(1),(2) 9–358
(3) 9–359, 9–401
(4) 9–361
(5) 9–362
(6) 9–363
(7) 9–366
(8) 9–367
(9) 9–368
s.55(1),(2) 9–369
s.56 9–370
s.57 9–379
(1) 9–380
(2) 9–381
(3),(4),(4A) 9–382
(5) 9–383
s.58 9–389
(1),(2) 9–390
(3) 9–391
s.58A 9–379, 9–384
(1) 9–384
(4) 9–386
(6) 9–387
(7) 9–388
ss.60–78 9–392
s.60(1) 8–107
s.61 .... 9–287, 9–288
(1) 9–287
(2) 9–287, 9–288
(3) 9–287
(4),(5) 9–288
(6) 9–289
s.63 .... 9–74, 9–392, 9–393, 9–396, 9–397, 9–399, 9–401, 9–402, 9–403, 9–406
(1) 9–394, 9–398, 9–399, 9–401, 9–402, 9–405
(2) 9–395, 9–406
(3) 9–396, 9–399
s.64 9–369
s.65 .... 9–392, 10–42
(1) 9–405

Para.
1985 Bankruptcy (Scotland) Act—*cont.*
s.65(2) 9–406
s.66 .... 9–392, 9–407
s.69A 9–375, 9–385
s.70 .... 9–392, 9–424
(3) 9–425
s.73(1) .. 9–112, 9–134, 9–425
s.74 9–38
s.75(1) 9–291
(2) 2–172, 9–15, 9–27, 9–59
Sched. 2 ...... 9–101, 9–209, 9–210, 9–214, 9–392, 9–426, 9–427, 9–428, 9–429, 9–431, 9–434, 9–435, 9–436, 9–448
Sched. 2A 9–128, 9–209, 9–217, 9–392, 9–438, 9–441, 9–443, 9–444, 9–448
Sched. 3 .... 9–339, 9–346
Sched. 4 9–370
Sched. 5 .... 9–458, 4–472
Sched. 6 ...... 9–215, 9–392, 9–407, 9–408
Sched. 7 .... 9–59, 9–291
Sched. 8 .... 2–174, 9–15, 9–27
Law Reform (Miscellaneous Provisions) (Scotland) Act (c.73) 9–311
s.10 2–130
s.11 ...... 1–179, 6–99, 6–170
1986 Consumer Safety (Amendment) Act (c.29) 4–373
Insolvency Act (c.45) 3–06, 3–09, 7–10, 9–11, 9–364
ss.1, 8 3–192
s.77(2) 3–69
s.84(1) 3–40
s.110 3–192
s.122(1)(g) 9–250
s.144 7–173
ss.165–167 3–192
s.388(2) 9–462
ss.390–398 9–91
s.390(1)–(4) 9–91
s.392(2) 9–93
s.426(4) 9–250

Para.

1986 Company Directors Disqualification Act (c.46) ... 3–06, 3–07, 9–91, 9–364
Financial Services Act (c.60) 3–06, 3–07, 3–93
s.172 3–162
Sched. 12 3–162
1987 Debtors (Scotland) Act (c.18)—
s.16 9–273
s.108(1) 5–243, 5–297
Sched. 6 .... 5–243, 5–297
Sched. 8 4–277
Banking Act (c.22) 6–153
ss.3, 67, Sched. 3 6–153
Housing (Scotland) Act (c.26) 5–60
Consumer Protection Act (c.43) .... 4–12, 4–342, 4–360—389, 5–10
s.1(1) 4–361, 4–362
(2) 4–363, 4–365
s.2 4–372
(1) 4–364
(4) 4–366
(5) 4–364
(6) 4–366
s.3(1),(2) 4–368
s.5(1) 4–368
(2) 4–369
(3) 4–370
(4) 4–371
s.6(6) 4–372
s.10 4–374
(1) 4–374
(2) 4–376
(7) 4–375
s.11 4–378
(1) 4–378
(2) 4–379
s.12 4–379
s.13(1),(4) 4–380
s.14(1),(2),(6) 4–381
s.15(1),(2) 4–381
s.17(1) 4–382
s.18(1) 4–383
s.19(1) 4–377
s.20(1),(6) 4–386
s.21 4–387
s.25(1),(2) 4–388
s.26(1) 4–389

Para.

1987 Consumer Protection Act —*cont.*
s.41 4–379
s.45(1),(5) 4–363
s.46(5) 4–374
s.48(2) 4–342
Sched. 1 4–372
1988 Consumer Arbitration Agreements Act (c.21) 10–03, 10–37
Court of Session Act (c.36)—
s.40(1) 10–13
1989 Companies Act (c.40) 1–24, 3–06, 3–07, 3–08, 3–77, 3–110, 3–228, 7–10
s.21(1),(2) 3–127
ss.108–110 3–218
s.108 1–24
s.110(2) 3–239
s.113(1),(2) 3–111, 3–112
s.115(1) 3–94
s.129(1) 3–126
s.130(4) 1–154, 3–15
s.136 3–211
s.143 3–215
s.144(1) 3–124
s.145 3–38
Sched. 19 3–38
1990 Law Reform (Miscellaneous Provisions) (Scotland) Act (c.40) 10–08
ss.66, 66(1),(4), Sched. 7 10–06
ss.71, 75(3)(b) 1–196
1991 Property Misdescriptions Act (c.29) 1–55, 1–65
ss.1, 2, 3 1–65
Sched. 1–65
Age of Legal Capacity (Scotland) Act (c.50) 10–41
s.1(1) 4–34, 8–46
(3)(d) 5–171
s.2(1) 1–13, 4–34
s.3(1) 8–46, 4–34
(2) 4–34
(3) 4–34
(5) 4–34
s.4 4–34
s.10, Sched. 2 4–31

Para.

1991 Agricultural Holdings (Scotland) Act (c.55) 10–02
1992 Cheques Act (c.32)—
s.1(1) 6–195
ss.1(2), 2 6–204
s.3 6–211
Tribunals and Inquiries Act (c.53) 5–34
1993 Bankruptcy (Scotland) Act (c.6) 9–03, 9–77, 9–104, 9–451, 9–467
s.1(1) 9–77, 9–80, 9–81, 9–82, 9–83, 9–85, 9–86
s.2 . . 9–89, 9–90, 9–94, 9–166, 9–180
s.2(2) 9–87
s.4 . . . . 9–132, 9–140
s.5 . . . . . . 9–188, 9–199, 9–430
s.6 9–438
(1) . . . 9–194, 9–199, 9–209, 9–430
(2) 9–209, 9–392
s.7 . . . . 9–199, 9–430
s.8 . . . . 9–375, 9–385
Sched. 1,
para. 1 . . 9–96, 9–99, 9–100
para. 2 . . . . 9–81, 9–167, 9–168, 9–169, 9–170, 9–171
para. 3 9–145
para. 4 9–149
para. 5 9–155
para. 7 9–179
para. 8 9–183
para. 9 9–188
para. 10 9–188
para. 11 . . . . . 9–204, 9–205
para. 12 . . . . . 9–171, 9–206, 9–430
para. 13 9–216
para. 14 9–221
para. 15 9–221
para. 17 . . . . . 9–238, 9–430
para. 18 9–238
para. 20 9–323
para. 21 . . . . . 9–320, 9–343
para. 22 9–349
para. 24 . . . . . 9–379, 9–382
para. 25 . . . . . 9–389, 9–390, 9–391

Para.

1993 Bankruptcy (Scotland) Act—*cont.*
Sched. 1—*cont.*
para. 26 9–379
para. 30 . . . . . 9–209, 9–210, 9–426
para. 31 9–370
para. 32 . . . . . 9–458, 9–472
Criminal Justice Act (c.36)—
Pt. V 3–06
1994 Sale of Goods (Amendment) Act (c.32) 4–04
s.1 4–157
Sale and Supply of Goods Act (c.35) 4–03, 4–11, 4–12, 4–26, 4–50, 4–58, 4–79, 4–84, 4–86, 4–87, 4–92, 4–113, 4–183, 4–186, 4–189, 4–203, 4–204, 4–206, 4–207, 4–208, 4–209, 4–210, 4–213, 4–216, 4–217, 4–223, 4–225, 4–226, 4–294, 4–301
s.1(1) 4–05
s.10 4–59
Sched. 2,
para. 5(8) 5–51
1995 Requirements of Writing (Scotland) Act (c.7) 7–104, 10–43, 10–46
s.1(1) 8–43, 10–46
(2) 8–43, 10–46
(3) 8–43
(4) 8–43
s.2(1) 8–43
s.3(1) . . . 8–43, 10–47, 10–101
(7) 8–43
s.7(7) 2–61
s.11 6–129
(3) 8–43
s.14(2),(3) 8–27, 8–40
(6) 8–40
Sched. 2 2–61
Sched. 5 8–27

Para.

1995 Merchant Shipping Act (c.21)—
s.16 7–75
Sched. 1, paras. 7–13 7–75
Pensions Act (c.26)—
s.95(2) 9–283
Sale of Goods (Amendment) Act (c.28) 4–08, 4–11, 4–121, 4–125, 4–126, 4–130, 4–150, 4–175, 7–91
s.2 .... 4–37, 4–39

Para.

1996 Arbitration Act (c.23) ... 10–04
s.5(1) 10–49
s.9(4) 10–05
s.15(3) 10–123
s.86(2) 10–05
ss.89–91 .... 10–03, 10–37
s.89(1) 10–37
s.90 10–37
s.91 10–37
s.107 10–03
(2) 10–37
(4) 10–05
s.108(3) 10–03
s.109(4) 10–05
Sched. 4 ...... 10–03, 10–05, 10–37

Chapter 1

AGENCY

	Para.
Introduction	1–01
(a) Agency and Mandate	1–09
Mandatory's Duty to Exercise Reasonable Care	1–10
(b) Agency and Subcontract	1–11
I Capacity	1–13
II Constitution of the Relationship	1–15
(a) Express Appointment	1–16
(b) Implied Appointment	1–17
(c) Holding Out	1–19
(d) Ratification	1–20
(e) *Negotiorum Gestio*	1–28
III Categories of Agent	1–31
General Agents and Special Agents	1–32
Mercantile Agents	1–36
Auctioneers	1–42
Del Credere Agents	1–46
Commercial Agents	1–47
(a) General	1–49
(b) Rights and Obligations	1–50
(c) Remuneration	1–51
(d) Conclusion and Termination	1–52
Property Agents	1–53
Estate Agents	1–54
Estate Agents Act 1979	1–56
(a) Orders by Director General of Fair Trading	1–60
(b) Information, entry and inspection	1–61
(c) Clients' money and accounts	1–62
(d) Regulation of other aspects of estate agency work	1–63
(e) Supervision and enforcement	1–64
Property Misdescriptions Act 1991	1–65
House and Estate Factors	1–66
Shipmasters	1–68
Solicitors	1–72
IV Agent's Authority	1–73
(a) As between Principal and Agent	1–74
(b) As between Principal and Third Party	1–76
(i) Express Authority	1–80
(ii) Implied Authority	1–81
(iii) Ostensible or Apparent Authority	1–91
(iv) Presumed Authority	1–94
V Duties of Agent to Principal	1–103
(a) Instructions	1–104
(b) Delegation	1–108
(c) Skill and Care	1–112
(d) Accounting	1–116
(e) Relief	1–117
(f) Fiduciary Duty	1–118
(i) Agent Transacting with Principal	1–122
(ii) Agent Receiving Benefit from Third Party	1–126
(iii) Agent in Possession of Confidential Information	1–129
VI Rights of Agent Against Principal	1–130
(a) Remuneration	1–131
(b) Reimbursement of Expenses	1–134
(c) Relief	1–136
(d) Lien	1–138
VII Third Party's Rights and Liabilities	1–142
(a) Agent Naming his Principal	1–145
(b) Agent Contracting "as Agent" for Unnamed Principal	1–156
(c) Agent Contracting Ostensibly as Principal	1–159
(d) Breach of Warranty of Authority	1–166
VIII Termination of the Relationship	1–171
(a) Completion of Transaction or Expiry of Time	1–172
(b) Mutual Agreement	1–175
(c) Revocation by Principal	1–177
(d) Renunciation by Agent	1–183
(e) Frustration	1–185
(i) Death of Principal or Agent	1–187
(ii) Bankruptcy of Principal or Agent	1–191
(iii) Insanity of Principal or Agent	1–195
(iv) Discontinuance of Principal's Business	1–198

INTRODUCTION

1–01 The law of agency is that part of the law of contract which is specially concerned with the situation where a person, instead of acting personally, engages another person to act on his behalf. The first person is the "principal", and the person who acts for him is the "agent", but these are general terms and it should be recognised that the principles of the law of agency extend to cases where the parties, though they stand in the legal position of principal and agent towards one another, are not commonly referred to as "principal" and "agent"; for example, a partner is an agent for his firm, a director is an agent for his company and a person employed in a managerial position (*e.g.* a shop manager) is an agent of his employer.

1–02 There is no general statutory definition of the term "agency". It may be used to denote the *relationship* between principal and agent. Agency may therefore be described as the relationship which exists where one party, the principal, authorises another party, the agent, to act on his behalf in a transaction with a third party. Alternatively, the term "agency" may be used to denote the *contract* out of which such a relationship arises. Agency is then regarded as one of the particular contracts (just as the contract of carriage or the contract of insurance is a particular contract), and may be described as a contract by which one party, the principal, authorises another party, the agent, to act on his behalf in a transaction with a third party.

1–03 Agency involves three parties and two contracts. The three parties are the principal (on whose behalf the transaction is being entered into), the agent (who acts for the principal in the transaction), and the third party (the person with whom the agent transacts on his principal's behalf). The two contracts involved are the contract between the principal and the agent (by which their relationship to one another is governed) and the contract between the agent and the third party (entered into on the principal's behalf by his agent). The purpose of agency is to bring the principal into a contractual relationship with the third party.

1–04 The law of agency in Scotland, as in England, is for the most part common law, to be found in decided cases and in authorita tive writings. Statutory inroads on the common law have been relatively minor: examples are the Prevention of Corruption Acts of 1906 and 1916, equally applicable to both legal systems, the Powers of Attorney Act 1971, only one section of which is applicable to Scotland, the Estate Agents Act 1979 (see 1–56 *et seq.*, below) and the Commercial Agents (Council Directive) Regulations 1993 (see 1–47 *et seq.*, below).

The influence of English law in this branch of Scots law is strong. **1–05**
English cases are often relied on where no Scottish cases are available. A typical instance of this approach is:

"In the absence of Scottish decisions the pursuers rely upon . . . cases in English law. . . . Those decisions no doubt are not binding upon us, but on a mercantile question like the present it is desirable that as far as possible the same rule should be applied in both countries" (*per* Lord Moncreiff in *Rederi Aktiebolaget Nordstjernan v. Salvesen & Co.* (1903) 6 F. 64, at p. 76).

The English influence is particularly strong where there is "a whole series of English cases" (as on the question of warranty of authority in *Anderson v. Croall & Sons Ltd* (1903) 6 F. 153, *per* Lord Stormonth-Darling (Ordinary) at p. 156), and where the relationship of the parties concerned is seen as being the same in the two countries and the English law is already "completely settled" (*e.g.* in the relationship at a public auction among seller, buyer and auctioneer in *Mackenzie v. Cormack*, 1950 S.C. 183, *per* Lord Mackay, at p. 191).

On the other hand, English authorities have been occasionally **1–06**
rejected (as in *Copland v. Brogan*, 1916 S.C. 277 (see 1–10, below), in which the standard of care required of an agent who was acting gratuitously was held to be that supported by a statement in Bell's *Principles*, in preference to that supported by English authorities.

The subject-matter of this chapter is dealt with below under **1–07**
these headings:

I. Capacity;
II. Constitution of the relationship;
III. Categories of agent;
IV. Agent's authority;
V. Duties of agent to principal;
VI. Rights of agent against principal;
VII. Third party's rights and liabilities; and
VIII. Termination of the relationship.

As a preliminary, it is appropriate to note the distinction **1–08**
between:

(a) agency and mandate; and between
(b) agency and subcontract.

(a) Agency and Mandate

1–09 The distinction between agency and mandate now is that agency is onerous (*i.e.* the agent receives a commission or other reward for his services), whereas mandate is gratuitous.

The following definitions of the two terms bring out the distinction:

"Agency is a bilateral onerous consensual contract whereby one party, the principal, authorizes another, the agent, to execute business on his behalf for reward" (David M. Walker, *Principles of Scottish Private Law* (4th ed.), Vol. II, p. 215).

"Mandate is a bilateral gratuitous consensual contract by which one empowers another to act in some respect on his behalf" (*ibid.*, p. 213).

In mandate, the terms "mandant" and "mandatory" correspond to "principal" and "agent" respectively.

The term "mandate" points to the derivation of our law of agency from the *mandatum* ("agency") of Roman law.

In early writings (*e.g.* in Bell's *Commentaries*), as in early reported cases, the term "mandate" was used in a wider sense—denoting the onerous as well as the gratuitous relationship.

Mandatory's Duty to Exercise Reasonable Care

1–10 Although acting gratuitously, a mandatory is under a duty to exercise reasonable care. This duty was considered in *Copland v. Brogan*, 1916 S.C. 277:

B., a carriage-hirer, had been in the habit of acting gratuitously as a messenger for C., a schoolmaster.

On one occasion C. asked B. to cash three cheques for him at a bank in a neighbouring town and bring back the cash to him.

B. received the cash at the bank, but failed to pay it over to C. There was no evidence as to how the loss had occurred.

Held that B. was liable to pay C., since B. had failed to exercise reasonable care, which was taken, in accordance with a statement in Bell's *Principles*, to mean "such care as a man of common prudence generally exercises about his own property of like description".

Lord Justice-Clerk Scott Dickson said (at p. 282): "Now, the packet having gone astray while it was in the defender's custody, the *onus*,[1] in my opinion, rests on him to explain how this happened or at least to show that he exercised the necessary reasonable care. . . . There is enough to shew that the defender, in executing his commission, did not exercise the care which a prudent man would have taken with regard to a valuable packet of this kind."

(b) **Agency and Subcontract**

An agent may be an employee or he may be an independent contractor; *e.g.* a manager or purchasing officer, engaged full-time in his company's business, is most likely to be both an agent and an employee, whereas an estate agent, working in his own premises and for several different clients, is most likely to be an independent contractor. In some situations it is difficult to ascertain whether the agent is an employee or an independent contractor. The importance of the distinction lies in the different legal consequences which flow from the different relationships. An illustration is *Smith v. Scott & Best* (1881) 18 S.L.R. 355: **1–11**

S. & B., contractors for certain waterworks including the construction of a bridge over the Esk, were approached by Cameron who agreed to do that part of the work for £40 less than the schedule price.

Cameron obtained stones from Smith, but later deserted the work and disappeared, leaving Smith unpaid.

S. & B. declined to pay Smith, on the ground that they had already paid Cameron for all the work done and material supplied by him.

Held that as S. & B. had taken no steps to prevent Cameron from being considered their foreman and as a belief to that effect had become current in the district, there was no subcontract, and so S. & B. were liable to pay Smith for the stones supplied by Smith to Cameron.

If there had been a subcontract, Cameron would have been an independent contractor, not an employee, and Smith could then have looked only to Cameron for payment.

---

[1] "burden" (of proof).

The question of whether an agent is an employee or an independent contractor is decided by a consideration of all the circumstances.

1–12 A case which may be contrasted with *Smith v. Scott & Best* is *Trojan Plant Hire Co. Ltd v. Durafencing (Northern) Ltd*, 1974 S.L.T. (Sh.Ct.) 3:

McAlpine Ltd, the principal building contractor on a site at Dundee, engaged D. Ltd for certain fencing work. D. Ltd instructed Arkle, a contractor who had a work force at his disposal, to carry out the fencing work.

Arkle, using one of D. Ltd's vans, hired plant for the fencing work from T. Ltd, and the question arose of whether D. Ltd was liable to T. Ltd for the hire charges.

Held that D. Ltd was not liable to T. Ltd because there was not sufficient evidence that D. Ltd had authorised Arkle to hire the plant.

The effect of the decision was to place Arkle in the position of an independent contractor, to whom alone T. Ltd could look for payment.

I CAPACITY

1–13 Both principal and agent must have the legal capacity necessary for their respective roles; a principal can in general authorise another person to do anything which the principal himself could do, but cannot enlarge his own capacity by appointing an agent (*e.g.* if the principal is under 16 years of age his capacity to contract is limited, by the Age of Legal Capacity (Scotland) Act 1991 (s. 2(1)), to transactions of a kind commonly entered into by persons of his age and circumstances and on terms which are not unreasonable; he cannot free himself from these limitations merely by authorising an agent of full age to carry out a transaction on his behalf).

1–14 Similarly, a principal who has no legal capacity at all or who is in the eyes of the law non-existent cannot even appoint an agent. A limited company which has not yet been registered is an instance of a non-existent principal:

Tinnevelly Sugar Refining Co. Ltd v. Mirrlees, Watson & Yaryan Co. Ltd (1894) 21 R. 1009: On July 11, 1890, Darley & Butler, purporting to act on behalf of T. Ltd, which was registered on July 29, 1890, entered into a contract with M. Ltd for the supply by M. Ltd of machinery to the new company.

T. Ltd brought an action of damages against M. Ltd on the ground that the machinery supplied was defective and had caused great loss to T. Ltd.

Held that T. Ltd had no title to sue M. Ltd, since Darley & Butler could not have acted as agents for T. Ltd before it was in existence.

Lord President J.P.B. Robertson said (at p. 1014): "Where there is no principal there can be no agent; there having been no Tinnevelly Company at the date of this contract, Darley & Butler were not agents of that company in entering into the contract."

A club also has no legal personality and so its office-bearers cannot escape liability for contracts made for the club by putting forward the defence that they were only the agents of the club (*Cromarty Leasing Ltd v. Turnbull*, 1988 S.L.T. (Sh.Ct.) 62). See also 1–155, below.

Similarly, there can be no agent if the supposed principal is dead:

Lord Advocate v. Chung, 1995 S.C. 32: C. undertook, in a letter prepared by the Inland Revenue, to pay £20,000 in respect of his deceased father's tax liabilities for restaurant profits. The offer was made by C. "as the personal representative of" his father.

Held that the relationship of principal and agent could not be created after the death of the father; "personal representative" was purely descriptive and did not indicate agency.

C. was therefore liable personally for his undertaking to the Inland Revenue.

II CONSTITUTION OF THE RELATIONSHIP

The relationship of principal and agent may be constituted by: **1–15**

(a) express appointment;
(b) implied appointment;
(c) holding out;
(d) ratification; or
(e) *negotiorum gestio* ("management of affairs").

(a) **Express Appointment**

The express appointment of an agent may take any form. There **1–16** may be a formal writing, *e.g.* a factory and commission or (properly a term of English law) a power of attorney, both of which are deeds granted by a person who is entrusting the management of his affairs to another because he is himself going abroad or will for some other reason be unable to act for himself. Alternatively, the writing appointing the agent may be informal, *e.g.* letters of mandate. An express appointment may also be merely oral, and there is no restriction on the method by which such an oral appointment may be proved.

(b) **Implied Appointment**

1–17 The relationship of principal and agent is often created by implication. For example, by section 5 of the Partnership Act 1890, every partner is an agent of the firm and his other partners for the purpose of the business of the partnership, and it is equally clear that by the common law relating to companies a director is impliedly an agent of the company. Other instances of implied appointment occur where a person is made manager of a business or is in some other way placed in a supervisory or responsible position. The master of a ship is impliedly the agent of the owners, as may be illustrated by *Barnetson v. Petersen Brothers* (1902) 5 F. 86:

A steamship owned by P. Brothers had been chartered to G., who appointed B. as shipbroker at Methil.

B., having made disbursements and rendered services in accordance with G.'s instructions, brought an action against P. Brothers for outlays and commission.

P. Brothers pleaded that they were not liable because B. had been employed by G.

Held that, as the master of the ship had accepted B.'s services as shipbroker and as P. Brothers had got the benefit of these services, P. Brothers were directly liable to B. for his disbursements and services.

1–18 An implied agency may be terminated by lapse of time and material change of circumstances; actual notice is not necessary to terminate the relationship. An instance is *Ferguson and Lillie v. Stephen* (1864) 2 M. 804:

F. & L., tailors in Glasgow, supplied clothes to S. for himself and his two sons, from 1853 to 1857 when the family lived in Glasgow. Accounts were rendered to and paid by S.

In 1861, when S. had been residing for some years in Dundee and his sons, then 27 and 17 years of age respectively, were resident in Edinburgh, the sons placed an extravagant order for a large quantity of clothes with F. & L., and these goods were delivered to the sons' Edinburgh address.

Held that S. was not liable to pay for these goods.

Lord Justice-Clerk Inglis said (at p. 807): "It is not possible to give effect to the plea of implied agency or mandate, or to say that the supplying of these things was authorised by the father; the dealings which he had authorised had been long before, were different in kind, and the goods were sent to his own house, not to a different place."

(c) **Holding Out**

Agency may be inferred where one party has held out another as his agent and so justified a third party in believing that the second party is in fact the appointed agent for the first party. The principle operating in such a situation is personal bar by holding out. (In English law agency constituted in this way is termed "agency by estoppel".) Any private arrangement between the first and second parties does not defeat the right of the third party to rely on the existence of the agency relationship: **1–19**

Hayman v. American Cotton Oil Co. (1907) 45 S.L.R. 207: A. & Co., an American firm of oil merchants, in newspaper advertisements and in letters to prospective customers, represented McN. & Co., a Glasgow firm, as their exclusive agents for the sale of their cotton-seed oils in Scotland.

F. & Co., also of Glasgow, bought oil from McN. & Co. and paid for it before delivery.

McN. & Co. became bankrupt, and there were competing claims to the oil which had been shipped from America to Glasgow. A. & Co. contended that McN. & Co. had been merely buyers and distributors of their products, while F. & Co. contended that McN. & Co. had been acting as A. & Co.'s agents.

Held that A. & Co., having held out McN. & Co. as their ordinary agents, were barred from maintaining that McN. & Co. had been their agents only in the special and limited sense of being distributing agents.

Lord Justice-Clerk J.H.A. Macdonald said (at p. 212): "McNairn & Company were held out as being the American Company's agents in quite distinct terms, and without any qualification whatever. . . . It is unnecessary to consider any question as to whether as between themselves the company and McNairn & Company had some special arrangements whereby, although the latter were held out as agents, and only as agents, the position of McNairn & Company to the Oil Company was of a special nature, and did not put McNairn & Company in a position of ordinary agents. Of that the customers could know nothing."

(d) **Ratification**

1–20 Where a person has acted on behalf of another without having authority to do so, the party for whom the act was done may later ratify the act. The effect of the ratification is retrospective, *i.e.* the act becomes as valid and binding as it would have been if the person who did the act had then had the proper authority.

1–21 Ratification may be express, or it may be implied by conduct of the principal.

1–22 For agency to be created by ratification, the following conditions must be fulfilled:

1–23 (i) The principal must have been in existence, not merely at the time of the ratification, but also at the time when the unauthorised act was done. Thus contracts made on behalf of a company before its incorporation cannot be ratified by the company once it has come into existence; a new contract (which may be on the same terms) is required. A futile attempt to ratify occurred in *Cumming v. Quartzag Ltd*, 1980 S.C. 276:

C., a landowner, entered into an agreement with Milne, designed as contracting for and on behalf of a company to be incorporated, for quarrying to be done on C.'s land.

The agreement had been made in January 1965, but the company, Q. Ltd, was not incorporated until June 1965.

In October 1976 Q. Ltd requested an agreement for further quarrying, but C. refused and raised an action to have Q. Ltd interdicted from continuing and extending the quarrying operations.

Held that the agreement of January 1965 could not have been ratified by Q. Ltd's subsequent actings; no benefit could be conferred on Q. Ltd since it was not in existence when the agreement was made.

1–24 (ii) The act being ratified must be one which the principal was originally capable of authorising. Thus in company law the general principle of the common law was that a contract which was *ultra vires* ("beyond the powers") of the directors but *intra vires* ("within the powers") of the company itself could be ratified by the company, whereas a contract which was *ultra vires* of the company could not be ratified; even unanimous consent of the shareholders would not suffice (*Ashbury Railway Carriage and Iron Co. Ltd v. Riche* (1875) L.R. 7 H.L. 653). This aspect of the *ultra vires* doctrine in company law was finally abolished by the Companies Act 1989: a contract *ultra vires* of the company may now be ratified by a special resolution of the company (Companies Act 1985, s. 35(3), as substituted by Companies Act 1989, s. 108).

(iii) Ratification must be timeous: if the validity of an act **1–25**
depends upon its being done within a certain time, ratification must follow within that time. For example, an unauthorised stoppage *in transitu* ("in transit") of goods on behalf of an unpaid seller could be ratified by the unpaid seller only so long as the goods were in transit: it would be too late to ratify once the goods had been delivered to the buyer at their destination, and if the buyer were bankrupt the goods would form part of the sequestrated estate (*Bird v. Brown* (1850) 4 Ex. 786; 154 E.R. 1433). Another instance is *Goodall v. Bilsland*, 1909 S.C. 1152:

G., a wine and spirit merchant, applied to a licensing court for renewal of his public-house certificate.

The Vigilance Society, formed to promote temperance, employed Kyle as its agent to lodge objections to the granting of the renewal at the licensing court. The renewal was granted.

Kyle then, without consulting the society, lodged an appeal to the licensing appeal court, and was successful in this appeal.

Held that G. was entitled to have the licensing appeal court's decision set aside because (1) Kyle's authority was limited to the application to the licensing court, no mention being made of an appeal to the licensing appeal court, (2) Kyle's actings could not be ratified after the lapse of the 10 days allowed for appeal, and (3) the proceedings in the licensing appeal court had therefore been null and void.

(iv) The agent must probably have professed to be acting on **1–26**
behalf of an identifiable principal who later ratifies the agent's act and must not have been contracting in his own name with the mere expectation that his action would be ratified. This condition may be expressed as the rule that an undisclosed principal cannot ratify.

The authority for this point is the English case *Keighley, Maxsted & Co. v. Durant* [1901] A.C. 240:

Roberts, a corn merchant at Wakefield, was authorised by K. & Co. to buy wheat on a joint account for himself and them at a certain price.

Having failed to buy at the authorised price, Roberts, without authority from K. & Co., made a contract with D., a corn merchant in London, to buy wheat from him at a higher price. Roberts made this contract in his own name, but intended it to be on a joint account for himself and K. & Co. That intention was not disclosed to D.

The next day, K. & Co.'s manager agreed with Roberts to take the wheat on a joint account.

Roberts and K. & Co. failed to take delivery of the wheat. D. resold it at a loss and sued for damages.

Held that as Roberts had not professed at the time of making the contract to be acting for K. & Co., D. was not entitled to sue K. & Co. on the contract.

There is no clear Scottish authority on the point and the earlier Scottish case of *Lockhart v. Moodie & Co.* (1877) 4 R. 859 suggests that Scots law may differ from English law in this respect. The facts of the *Lockhart* case are closely similar to those of the *Keighley Maxsted* case:

M. & Co. and Mackenzie had entered into a joint adventure for the purchase, bleaching and resale of 10,000 spindles of yarn. M. & Co. authorised Mackenzie to purchase the yarn at a price not exceeding 1s. 11d. per spindle.

Mackenzie purchased the yarn at 1s. 11¼ d. in his own name from L. and granted bills of exchange for the price without disclosing to L. the existence of the joint adventure.

Mackenzie having become bankrupt, L. brought an action against M. & Co. for the price.

Held that M. & Co. were liable to L. for the price to the extent to which they had authorised Mackenzie to pay for the yarn.

The view that the *Lockhart* case, though apparently never referred to since it was decided, is still good law in Scotland is favoured by Sheriff Robin G. McEwan, who states (*The Laws of Scotland: Stair Memorial Encyclopedia*, Vol. I, para. 625): "There seems to be no good reason why the undisclosed principal should not be liable at least up to the sum he authorised the agent to negotiate."

On the other hand most writers, including Gloag on *Contract* (2nd ed., p. 143), state without reserve that on the authority of the *Keighley Maxsted* case the rule that an undisclosed principal cannot ratify would be followed in Scotland.

(v) The principal must at the time of ratification be aware of all **1–27** the material facts, unless his words or conduct can be interpreted as an unqualified adoption of the agent's acts, whatever they were.

The authority for this statement is the English case *Fitzmaurice v. Bayley* (1856) 6 El. & Bl. 868; 119 E.R. 1087:

B. employed Reardon as his agent to make an agreement with F. for the purchase of F.'s house, Hamilton Lodge. F. also held certain stables at a different address, but B. did not authorise Reardon to purchase the stables.

However, Reardon in fact obtained from F. a written agreement for the purchase of both the house and the stables.

B. said: "What he has done for me I know not; but of course I must support him in all he has done for me."

Held that this amounted to ratification by B. of Reardon's agreement, whatever it might have been, and that B. was therefore bound to purchase the stables.

(e) *Negotiorum Gestio*

Agency may arise out of *negotiorum gestio*, which is one of the **1–28** forms of unjust enrichment. The term used in English law for this type of agency is "agency of necessity". It exists where in an emergency one person without authority takes action on behalf of another whose interests are at stake and with whom it is impossible to communicate.

The courts do not readily extend the principle of *negotiorum* **1–29** *gestio* to new situations, and the improvement in communications in modern times also restricts the instances of this type of agency.

Well-recognised examples can occur where the carrier of perish- **1–30** able goods finds it necessary to sell or otherwise dispose of the goods without having obtained the owner's authority, and where the master of a ship, in order to raise sufficient money to complete his voyage, grants security over the ship or cargo by a bond of bottomry or a bond of respondentia respectively (see 7–34 *et seq.*, below).

III CATEGORIES OF AGENT

1–31 Agents are appointed in many different circumstances, and their authority often depends, not only on the instructions actually given (which may have been very brief), but also on the category to which the agent belongs.

General Agents and Special Agents

1–32 The major classification of agents is into general agents and special agents.

1–33 A general agent is one who has authority to act for his principal in all the principal's affairs or in all his affairs of a particular kind, *e.g.* the master of a ship or a solicitor. A special agent has authority to act for his principal in a particular transaction only.

1–34 Third parties dealing with a general agent are entitled to assume that the agent has all the authority which an agent of that type normally has by trade or professional usage, whereas third parties dealing with a special agent must satisfy themselves as to the exact extent of the agent's authority, since anything done by the special agent beyond his actual instructions will not be binding on the principal.

1–35 The distinction between general and special agents was considered in *Morrison v. Statter* (1885) 12 R. 1152:

Calder, head shepherd on S.'s farm, on one occasion bought sheep from M. without instructions from S.

Held that as Calder had had no particular authority and as there had been no general course of conduct by S. from which authority could have been inferred, S. was not liable to M.

Lord Young said (at p. 1154): "Where you have a particular agent employed by a principal, to perform a particular piece of business for him, he must act within the instructions given for the particular occasion, and does not bind his principal if he acts otherwise. If you have a general agent, employed generally in his master's or his principal's affairs, or in a particular department, he is assumed to have all the authority which is necessary to enable him to serve his master as such general agent, or general agent in a particular department."

Mercantile Agents

Mercantile agents may be factors or brokers. Both are employed to buy and sell goods, and have authority to act in accordance with the custom of the particular market on which they deal. **1–36**

A factor differs from a broker in that he has possession of his principal's goods and in that he has authority to sell in his own name. A factor, on account of his possession of the goods, has a lien on them for what is due to him by his principal, whereas a broker, having no possession, has no lien. **1–37**

There are special classes of both factors and brokers: auctioneers are a special class of factors, and special classes of brokers are stockbrokers, shipbrokers ("middlemen" between shipowners and persons who wish to have goods shipped, and between sellers and buyers of ships), and insurance brokers (who are intermediaries between insurance companies and persons wishing to take out insurance). **1–38**

In order to decide whether a mercantile agent is a factor or broker, one must look to the substance of the transaction being undertaken, not solely at the agent's designation. For example, in *Glendinning v. Hope & Co.*, 1911 S.C.(H.L.) 73, a stockbroker was held to have had the legal position of a factor and so to be entitled to a factor's lien: **1–39**

On August 19, G. instructed H. & Co., stockbrokers, to purchase for him 100 shares in a certain mining company. The shares were duly purchased, and G., on August 26, paid the price for them to H. & Co.

On September 1, G. instructed H. & Co. to purchase a further 200 shares for him in the same company. G. then became dissatisfied with H. & Co.'s services and arranged for another firm of stockbrokers to act for him in this second transaction.

H. & Co. claimed that G. was indebted to them in respect of the second purchase, and declined to deliver to G. the transfer of the 100 shares already paid for.

G. brought an action for delivery of the transfer.

Held that H. & Co. were entitled to retain the transfer until payment of the second transaction had been made.

Lord Kinnear said (at p. 79): "For the balance which may arise on his general account the factor has a right of retention or lien over all the goods and effects of the principal which, coming into his hands in his character of factor, may be in his actual or civil possession at the time when the demand against him is made. . . . The conditions upon which the right depends in the case of a mercantile factor are exactly those which govern the relation of a stockbroker and his client. The factor's general right to retention depends upon two considerations—first, that he is required to make payments or undertake liabilities for his principal; and secondly, that the goods and effects belonging to his principal come into his possession and control in the ordinary course of his employment. But that is exactly the position of the stockbroker who buys with a liability to pay the vendor and receives a transfer for delivery to his client."

1–40 A similar explanation of the distinction between factor and broker was given by Lord President Inglis in *Cunningham v. Lee* (1874) 2 R. 83 (1–124, below), a case in which a law-agent who had bought shares in his own name for a client was held not to have been entitled to appropriate the shares to himself when the client failed to pay for them. Lord President Inglis said (at p. 87):

"I should be inclined to say that Lee occupied the position of a factor rather than of a broker. Certain distinctions between the offices of broker and factor lead me to this conclusion. Thus a broker buys and sells, not in his own name, but in the name of his principal, whereas a factor buys in his own name. Again, a broker has no possession of the subject, no control over it, no power of disposal. The factor has such powers and a consequent lien over the subjects. In these respects Lee was rather a factor than a broker."

1–41 A factor who is a mercantile agent is distinct from a factor who manages an estate (see *Macrae v. Leith*, 1913 S.C. 901, 1–67, below).

Auctioneers

1–42 Auctioneers are agents who sell other persons' heritable or moveable property by public auction. The auction need not take place in the auctioneer's saleroom; thus, in *Mackenzie v. Cormack*, 1950 S.C. 183, the circumstance that the auction of the furniture of a castle took place in the castle was held not to affect the legal principle involved.

1–43 On many occasions an auctioneer will be selling on behalf of an exposer whose name he does not disclose, but where the exposer is named, the auctioneer incurs no liability to a person who, claiming to be a purchaser, brings an action for implement or damages (*Fenwick v. Macdonald, Fraser & Co. Ltd* (1904) 6 F. 850, *per* Lord Kyllachy (Ordinary)).

Where the exposer's name has not been disclosed at the sale, but **1–44** is made known to the purchaser at a later date, the purchaser, if he returns the subject purchased as faulty to the exposer, is regarded as having elected to sue the exposer and is no longer entitled to sue the auctioneer (*Ferrier v. Dods* (1865) 3 M. 561 (1–162, below)).

English cases on auction sales are taken as authoritative in **1–45** Scotland: this is supported by *dicta* ("remarks") in *Anderson v. Croall & Sons Ltd* (1903) 6 F. 153, in which an auctioneer, like any other agent, was held to be liable in damages for breach of warranty of authority (see 1–169, below), and *Mackenzie v. Cormack*, 1950 S.C. 183, in which an auctioneer, like any other mercantile factor, was held to have a lien over the price for his charges and commission and so to have a title to sue the successful bidder for the price.

Del Credere Agents

A *del credere* agent is a mercantile agent who for an extra **1–46** commission undertakes to indemnify the principal if the third party with whom the agent deals fails to pay what is due. The phrase "*del credere*" is Italian. A *del credere* agent guarantees the solvency of the third party; an ordinary agent undertakes no such liability. (The function of *del credere* agents has been largely taken over in modern practice by "confirming houses", which guarantee the transactions of parties who pay them a commission.)

Commercial Agents

The category of commercial agents has been established through **1–47** European influence. The EEC Council Directive on the Co-ordination of the Laws of the Member States Relating to Self-Employed Commercial Agents (Dir. 86/653) was adopted in 1986 and implemented in Great Britain by the Commercial Agents (Council Directive) Regulations 1993 (S.I. 1993 No. 3053), which came into force on January 1, 1994.

The general effect of the regulations is to give greater and **1–48** more specific protection to "commercial agents", as defined in the regulations, than they would otherwise have at common law.

The regulations are arranged under four main headings:

(a) general;
(b) rights and obligations;
(c) remuneration; and
(d) conclusion and termination of the agency contract.

(a) *General*

1–49 The regulations govern the relations between commercial agents and their principals and apply to the activities of commercial agents in Great Britain (reg. 1(3)). The regulations do not extend to Northern Ireland (reg. 1(5)).

The definition of "commercial agent" is therefore crucial: "commercial agent" means "a self-employed intermediary who has continuing authority to negotiate the sale or purchase of goods on behalf of another person (the 'principal'), or to negotiate and conclude the sale or purchase of goods on behalf of and in the name of that principal". The following persons, however, are excluded: officers of a company or association, partners and insolvency practitioners.

Further, the regulations do not apply to commercial agents whose activities are unpaid, to commercial agents when they operate on commodity exchanges or in the commodity market or to Crown Agents for Overseas Governments and Administrations.

The Schedule to the regulations enlarges on their scope. In particular a distinction is made between primary and secondary activities of commercial agents. The regulations do not apply to commercial agents whose activities are to be considered secondary (reg. 2(3)(4)).

The purpose of the arrangement between commercial agent and principal is considered to be primary if the business of the principal is the sale or purchase of goods of a particular kind and the goods are such that transactions are normally individually negotiated and concluded on a commercial basis with one transaction likely to lead to further transactions, so that it is in the commercial interests of the principal in developing the market in those goods to appoint a representative who will devote effort, skill and expenditure to such development.

The Schedule then lists five situations where the commercial agent's activities would be primary:

(i) the principal is the manufacturer, importer or distributor of the goods;

(ii) the goods are specifically identified with the principal in the market rather than with any other person;

(iii) the agent devotes substantially the whole of his time to representative activities (whether for one principal or for a number of principals whose interests are not conflicting);

(iv) the goods are not normally available other than by means of the agent;

(v) the arrangement is described as one of commercial agency.

The absence of any of these five situations would be an indication that the activities would not be primary.

Indications that commercial agency is not involved at all or is secondary are that:

(i) promotional material is supplied direct to potential customers;

(ii) persons are granted agencies without reference to existing agents in a particular area or in relation to a particular group;

(iii) customers normally select the goods for themselves and merely place their orders through the agent.

The activities of mail order catalogue agents for consumer goods and consumer credit agents are presumed, unless the contrary is established, not to be within the definition of commercial agency.

A practical illustration of a commercial agent is given in *King v. T. Tunnock Ltd*, 1996 S.C.L.R. 742, in which Sheriff Reeves stated (at p. 743): "The facts point clearly to the conclusion that the pursuer was a commercial agent and that the definition in regulation 2(1) of the Commercial Agents (Council Directive) Regulations 1993 is an exact description of the relationship between the parties".

The facts were that for many years K. operated a business, which he had taken over from his father, supplying bakery products at wholesale prices to retail outlets. He handled only the products of T. Ltd but he was not employed by them. He hired a van from them, although from May 1993 he had not been required to pay for it. The van was maintained by T. Ltd and garaged in their premises, K. paying only for his petrol. K. was supplied with T. Ltd's uniform overalls. He took the stock he required each morning from T. Ltd's premises and delivered it to his customers. Goods were sold at prices fixed by T. Ltd, and K. kept a record of the sales in a receipt book supplied by T. Ltd. Customers paid K. in cash or by cheques made payable to T. Ltd or by monthly credit account paid directly to T. Ltd. K. was paid commission on his sales figures.

(b) *Rights and Obligations*

1–50 In performing his activities a commercial agent must look after the interests of his principal and act dutifully and in good faith (reg. 3(1)).

This general statement is then enlarged on: in particular, a commercial agent must:

(i) make proper efforts to negotiate and, where appropriate, conclude the transactions which he is instructed to take care of;

(ii) communicate to his principal all the necessary information available to him;

(iii) comply with reasonable instructions given by his principal (reg. 3(2)).

Likewise, in relation to the duties of a principal to his commercial agent, there is a general statement that the principal must act dutifully and in good faith, and in particular the principal must:

(i) provide his commercial agent with the necessary documentation relating to the goods concerned;

(ii) obtain for his commercial agent the information necessary for the performance of the agency contract, and in particular notify his commercial agent within a reasonable period once he anticipates that the volume of commercial transactions will be significantly lower than that which the commercial agent could normally have expected (reg. 4(2)).

A principal must also inform his commercial agent within a reasonable period of his acceptance or refusal of, and of any non-execution by him of, a commercial transaction which the commercial agent has procured for him (reg. 4(3)).

The parties are not permitted to derogate from these duties (reg. 5(1)).

(c) *Remuneration*

1–51 The first rule stated under this heading relates to the situation where there is no agreement as to remuneration between the parties. It is that a commercial agent is entitled to the remuneration which commercial agents appointed for the goods concerned are customarily allowed in the place where he carries on his activities and, if there is no such customary practice, a commercial agent is entitled to reasonable remuneration taking into account all the aspects of the transaction (reg. 6(1)).

A commercial agent must be paid in some way (see reg. 2(2), above). Normally, but not necessarily always (reg. 6(3)), his remuneration takes the form of commission, and the regulations make specific provisions for this:

A commercial agent is entitled to commission on commercial transactions concluded during the period covered by the agency contract:

(i) where the transaction has been concluded as a result of his action; or

(ii) where the transaction is concluded with a third party whom he has previously acquired as a customer for transactions of the same kind (reg. 7(1)).

A commercial agent is also entitled to commission on transactions concluded during the period covered by the agency contract where he has an exclusive right to a specific geographical area or to a specific group of customers and where the transaction has been entered into with a customer belonging to that area or group (reg. 7(2)).

If an agency contract has terminated, the commercial agent will still be entitled to commission if:

(i) the transaction in question is mainly attributable to his efforts during the period covered by the agency contract and if the transaction was entered into within a reasonable period after that contract terminated; or

(ii) the order of the third party (referred to in regulation 7(1), above) reached the principal or the commercial agent before the agency contract terminated (reg. 8).

Where a commercial agent has been replaced, an apportionment of commission will be necessary if it is equitable because of the circumstances for the commission to be shared between the previous and the new commercial agent (reg. 9(1)); this may involve a refund to the principal (reg. 9(2)).

A distinction is made between the date when commission is due and the date when it is to be paid.

Commission becomes due as soon as, and to the extent that, one of the following circumstances occurs:

(i) the principal has executed the transaction; or

(ii) the principal should, according to his agreement with the third party, have executed the transaction; or

(iii) the third party has executed the transaction (reg. 10(1)).

In addition, for the protection of the commercial agent, it is provided that commission becomes due *at the latest* when the third party has executed his part of the transaction or should have done so if the principal had executed his part of the transaction as he should have. Any agreement to derogate from this provision to the detriment of the commercial agent is void (reg. 10(2)(4)).

Commission must be paid not later than the last day of the month following the quarter in which it became due and any agreement to derogate from this provision to the detriment of the commercial agent is void (reg. 10(3)(4)).

The right to commission can be extinguished only if and to the extent that:

(i) it is established that the contract between the third party and the principal will not be executed; and

(ii) that fact is due to a reason for which the principal is not to blame (reg. 11(1)).

Any agreement to derogate from this provision is void (reg. 11(3)).

Any commission which the commercial agent has already received must be refunded if the right to it is extinguished (reg. 11(2)).

The final regulation in this Part relates to the periodic supply of information as to commission due and the right of inspection of the principal's books. The principal must supply his commercial agent with a statement of the commission due, not later than the last day of the month following the quarter in which the commission has become due, and the statement must set out the main components used in calculating the amount of the commission (reg. 12(1)). A commercial agent is entitled to demand that he be provided with all the information (and in particular an extract from the books) which is available to his principal and which he needs in order to check the amount of the commission due to him. Any agreement to derogate from these provisions is void (reg. 12(1)–(3)).

(d) *Conclusion and Termination of the Agency Contract*

The commercial agent and the principal are each entitled to receive from the other, on request, a signed written document setting out the terms of the agency contract (reg. 13(1)), and any purported waiver of this right is void (reg. 13(2)). **1–52**

An agency contract for a fixed period which continues to be performed by both parties after that period has expired is deemed to be converted into an agency contract for an indefinite period (reg. 14).

Where an agency contract is concluded for an indefinite period either party may terminate it by notice (reg. 15(1)). The period of notice must be:

(i) one month for the first year of the contract;

(ii) two months for the second year commenced;

(iii) three months for the third year commenced and for the subsequent years.

The parties are not permitted to agree on any shorter periods of notice.

If the parties agree on longer periods of notice, the period of notice to be observed by the principal must not be shorter than that to be observed by the commercial agent (reg. 15(3)).

Unless otherwise agreed by the parties, the end of the period of notice must coincide with the end of a calendar month (reg. 15(4)).

Immediate termination may be resorted to:

(i) because of the failure of one party to carry out all or part of his obligations under the agency contract; or

(ii) where exceptional circumstances arise (reg. 16).

The following regulation relates to the entitlement of a commercial agent to indemnity or compensation on termination of the agency contract. The commercial agent has one year after termination in which to notify his principal that he intends to pursue his entitlement to indemnity or compensation; otherwise he loses his entitlement (reg. 17(9)). Except where the agency contract otherwise provides, the commercial agent is entitled to be compensated rather than indemnified (reg. 17(2)). Indemnity may therefore be excluded by the agency contract, but if it is included, then it is governed by regulation 17 and cannot be derogated from to the detriment of the commercial agent before the agency contract expires (reg. 19). There is no provision for compensation to be excluded by the agency contract: it is governed by regulation 17 and cannot be derogated from to the detriment of the commercial agent before the agency contract expires (reg. 19).

Subject to these provisions, the commercial agent is entitled to an indemnity if and to the extent that:

(i) he has brought the principal new customers or has significantly increased the volume of business with existing customers and the principal continues to derive substantial benefits from the business with such customers; and

(ii) the payment of the indemnity is equitable considering all the circumstances and, in particular, the commission lost by the commercial agent on the business transacted with such customers (reg. 17(3)).

The amount of the indemnity must not exceed a figure equivalent to an indemnity for one year calculated from the commercial agent's average annual remuneration over the preceding five years (reg. 17(4)).

The grant of an indemnity does not prevent the commercial agent from seeking damages (reg. 17(5)).

The commercial agent is entitled to compensation for the damage he suffers as a result of the termination of his relations with his principal (reg. 17(6)). Such damage is deemed to occur particularly when the termination takes place in either or both of the following:

(i) circumstances which deprive the commercial agent of the commission which proper performance of the agency contract would have procured for him whilst providing his principal with substantial benefits linked to the activities of the commercial agent; or

(ii) circumstances which have not enabled the commercial agent to write off the costs and expenses which he had incurred in the performance of the agency contract on the advice of his principal (reg. 17(7)).

Entitlement to indemnity or compensation for damage also arise where the agency contract is terminated by the death of the commercial agent (reg. 17(8)).

Indemnity or compensation, however, is not payable where:

(i) the principal has terminated the agency contract because of default of the commercial agent which would justify immediate termination of the agency contract; or

(ii) the commercial agent has himself terminated the agency contract unless the termination is justified by circumstances attributable to the principal, or on grounds of the age, infirmity or illness of the commercial agent with the result that he cannot reasonably be required to continue his activities; or

(iii) the commercial agent, with the agreement of his principal, assigns his rights and duties under the agency contract to another person (reg. 18).

A restraint of trade clause is valid only if and to the extent that:

(i) it is in writing; and

(ii) it relates only to the geographical area or the group of customers and the geographical area entrusted to the commercial agent and to the kind of goods covered by his agency under the contract (reg. 20(1)).

A restraint of trade clause is valid for not more than two years after the termination of the agency contract (reg. 20(2)).

Property Agents

Agents whose work relates to heritable property include estate agents and house and estate factors. **1–53**

Estate Agents

Estate agents, whose main function is to find purchasers for houses and other heritable property which their clients wish to sell, have been less prominent in Scotland than in England: much of the work which would in England have been done by estate agents was in Scotland done by solicitors. **1–54**

Estate agency work is to some extent regulated by the Estate Agents Act 1979, and the Property Misdescriptions Act 1991. **1–55**

Estate Agents Act 1979

This Act was the culmination of many attempts in Parliament to produce legislation which would protect members of the public from the activities of dishonest persons who, without any qualifications, could set up in business as "estate agents". Most of these attempts at legislation sought to introduce a system of registration for estate agents. The system which finally found sufficient support to enable the Act of 1979 to be passed, however, is not a system **1–56** requiring registration of estate agents, but a licensing system operated by the Director General of Fair Trading and designed to guarantee certain minimum standards. Any person remains free to adopt the title of "estate agent", and set up in business as such.

1–57 The Act is basically within the field of consumer-protection legislation, though, by amendments made to the Bill at a late stage in its passage through Parliament, the Act extends to dealings with commercial as well as residential property and so protects many persons other than consumers.

1–58 The Act does not define "estate agent"; the central definition is that of "estate agency work", *i.e.* things done by any person in the course of a business (including a business in which he is an employee) on instructions received from another person ("the client") who wishes to dispose of or acquire an interest in land—

(a) in order to introduce the client to a third person who wishes to acquire or dispose of such an interest; and

(b) in order, after the introduction, to secure the disposal or acquisition of that interest.

The Act expressly provides that it does not apply to things done by a practising solicitor in the course of his profession (s. 1).

1–59 The leading provisions of the Act are as follows:

(a) *Orders by Director General of Fair Trading*

1–60 Power is conferred on the Director General of Fair Trading by section 3 to make an order prohibiting a person from doing any estate agency work at all or from doing estate agency work of a specified description. Before making any such order the Director must be satisfied that the person is unfit on one or other of several grounds which include convictions for fraud, dishonesty or violence, discrimination in the course of estate agency work, failure to comply with certain provisions of the Act and engaging in practices declared by an order made by the Secretary of State for Trade and Industry to be undesirable (see the Estate Agents (Undesirable Practices) (No. 2) Order 1991 (S.I. 1991 No. 1032)).

The Director has also power to give a warning order where a person has failed to comply with certain provisions of the Act; the person concerned is then not considered as unfit to practise unless he fails to comply with the warning order (s. 4).

There are provisions dealing with revocation and variation of orders and with appeals (ss. 6 and 7).

Particulars of all orders, including warning orders, are entered on a register kept by the Director and open to public inspection on payment of a prescribed fee (s. 8).

(b) *Information, entry and inspection*

The Director in discharging his functions under the Act may compel persons to furnish information to him (s. 9), but he is prohibited from disclosing such information without the consent of the person to whom it relates (s. 10). **1–61**

Where there is reasonable cause to suspect that an offence has been committed, a duly authorised officer has power to enter premises and require documents to be produced to him (s. 11).

(c) *Clients' money and accounts*

The Act declares that clients' money received by any person engaged in estate agency work in Scotland is held by him as agent for the person who is entitled to call for it (s. 13). **1–62**

Clients' money must be kept in a "client account" (s. 14).

Accounts regulations may require an estate agent to account for the interest on any clients' money (s. 15), and the relevant regulations (Estate Agents (Accounts) Regulations 1981 (S.I. 1981 No. 1520)) do so require.

Clients' money must be protected by indemnity insurance, so that in the event of the estate agent failing to account for it a claim may be made against the insurance company (s. 16[2]). Application may be made to the Director for exemption from this provision (s. 17[2]).

(d) *Regulation of other aspects of estate agency work*

Details must be disclosed to the client of his prospective liabilities, including the remuneration which will become payable to the estate agent (Estate Agents (Provision of Information) Regulations 1991 (S.I. 1991 No. 859)); failure to comply could result in the estate agent being unable to enforce the contract (s. 18). **1–63**

There is an illustration of the application of section 18 in the case *Solicitors' Estate Agency (Glasgow) Ltd v. MacIver*, 1992 S.C.L.R. 804: M. had instructed the pursuers, who were estate

---

[2] These sections are not yet in force.

agents, to advertise and market property at 30 Forth Road, Bearsden. The pursuers included the property in their block advertisements in the *Glasgow Herald,* and in charging M. his proportionate share of these advertisements did not disclose or give him credit for an 18 per cent discount allowed to themselves by the newspaper.

The discount was held to be "remuneration" which the pursuers were bound to disclose under section 18.

The sheriff (Fitzsimons), with whom the Inner House of the Court of Session agreed, held that because of the prejudice suffered by M. the commission would be reduced from £1,239.01 to £921.52; the contract was, however, enforceable.

Pre-contract deposits (which in England may, within prescribed limits, be required from prospective purchasers (s. 19[2])) are prohibited in Scotland (s. 20).

Any personal interest which the estate agent has in the property must be disclosed to the client (s. 21).

Regulations may be made by statutory instrument to ensure minimum standards of competence for persons engaged in estate agency work; by this means there might come to be a prescribed degree of practical experience and a prescribed professional or academic qualification for persons engaged in such work (s. 22[2]).

An undischarged bankrupt must not engage in estate agency work except as an employee (s. 23).

(e) *Supervision and enforcement*

1–64 The Director and his staff count as a "tribunal", and so come under the supervision of the Council on Tribunals (s. 24).

The working and enforcement of the Act are under the general superintendence of the Director (s. 25).

The enforcement authorities, other than the Director, are the local weights and measures authorities (s. 26).

Property Misdescriptions Act 1991

1–65 This Act, also within the consumer-protection field, provides that where a person carrying on an estate agency business or a property development business makes a false or misleading statement about

[2] These sections are not yet in force.

a prescribed matter in the course of his business, he is guilty of an offence and liable to an unlimited fine. If the making of the statement is due to the act or default of an employee, the employee is similarly liable, and proceedings may be taken against him, whether or not proceedings are also taken against his employer.

The commission of an offence under the Act does not affect the validity of any contract.

"Estate agency business" has the same meaning as in the Estate Agents Act 1979, but there is no exception here for things done by a practising solicitor in the course of his profession.

"Property development business" is business concerned wholly or substantially with the development of land for the purpose of, or with a view to, disposing of an interest in land and buildings constructed or renovated in the course of the business (s. 1).

In proceedings against a person for an offence it is a defence for him to show that he took all reasonable steps and exercised all due diligence to avoid committing the offence (s. 2).

The enforcement authorities are the local weights and measures authorities (s. 3 and Sched.).

House and Estate Factors

House and estate factors are appointed by the owner of houses or **1–66**
an estate to manage the property on the owner's behalf.

Usually the houses which the house factor manages will have been let by the owner to different tenants. The house factor does not himself have implied authority to grant new leases, but he has implied authority to receive notice from tenants as to defects in the property:

McMartin v. Hannay (1872) 10 M. 411: H. was the owner of a Glasgow tenement of 12 houses, access to which was by one common stair. H. managed the property through a factor.

McM. claimed damages from H. for the death of his seven-year-old daughter, Tiny, who had fallen through a gap in the railing on the common stair when visiting the premises.

Notice of the gap had been given at the factor's office many months before the accident.

Held that H. was liable in damages though he had no personal knowledge of the defect.

A factor managing property has no lien on leases or other **1–67**
documents which he holds for the owner of the property, as was

decided in *Macrae v. Leith*, 1913 S.C. 901, in which M., the heritable creditor in possession of an estate, was held entitled to a court order against L., who claimed to be the factor of the estate, for delivery of the leases and other estate documents in L.'s possession. An estate factor was distinguished from a mercantile factor:

"There is a common enough use of the expression 'factor's lien', but the use is, I think, confined to cases of mercantile agency, and has not been extended beyond that. It was because in mercantile agency, goods are often bought and sold, shipped and received, advances made thereon, and responsibilities undertaken thereanent that the lien was given to mercantile agents over what could be turned into money, such as goods, claims, bills, and so on, and I do not think it has ever in practice been held that this factor's lien could or should extend to an estate manager, who is called in Scotland a factor, but who in England would be called a land-agent" (*per* Lord Johnston at p. 906).

Shipmasters

1–68 The master of a ship is the agent of the shipowner or the charterer in the navigation and management of the ship.

1–69 Where a master has, to the benefit of the shipowner, accepted the services of a shipbroker, the shipowner is liable to pay the shipbroker (see *Barnetson v. Petersen Brothers* (1902) 5 F. 86 (1–17, above)).

1–70 As *negotiorum gestor* ("manager of affairs") a master may grant security over the ship or cargo by a bond of bottomry or a bond of respondentia respectively (see 1–30, above).

1–71 The master does not have authority to make unnecessary alterations in the charterparty entered into by the shipowner:

Strickland v. Neilson and MacIntosh (1869) 7 M. 400: The ship "Tornado", owned by N. & M., had been chartered to carry passengers and cargo from Liverpool to two ports in New Zealand—Auckland and Wellington.

On the arrival of the ship at Auckland, the master, because of difficulties with the crew, arranged with S. & Co., the charterers' agents at Auckland, that the passengers and cargo would be taken on to Wellington in other vessels. The master drew bills of exchange on N. & M. to meet the expense of this operation which was undertaken by S. & Co.

N. & M. refused to accept the bills.

Held that as the deviation from the charterparty had not been necessary for the safety of the ship, it had not been within the master's authority, and that N. & M. were therefore not liable for the expenses incurred by S. & Co.

Solicitors

Solicitors, formerly called "law-agents", are agents employed by their clients for the conduct of legal business. The extent of their authority depends on the nature of the work which is entrusted to them, and is considered in the next part of this chapter (1–89, below). **1–72**

IV AGENT'S AUTHORITY

Questions as to the scope of an agent's authority may arise in two situations: **1–73**

(a) as between the principal and the agent; and
(b) as between the principal and the third party.

(a) As between Principal and Agent

In this situation, questions as to the scope of the agent's authority are resolved by interpretation of the contract, whether express or implied, which established the agency relationship between the parties. **1–74**

If the agent has acted beyond the scope of the agency, he is liable in damages for breach of contract (*cf. Gilmour v. Clark* (1853) 15 D. 478 (1–105, below)), and he will not be entitled to the commission agreed on for the period during which he has been in breach of his contract (*cf. Graham & Co. v. United Turkey Red Co. Ltd*, 1922 S.C. 533 (1–107, below)). **1–75**

(b) As between Principal and Third Party

In this situation the scope of the agent's authority is of central importance in the attainment of the object of agency—the creation of a legal relationship between the principal and the third party—and questions are not resolved solely by a consideration of the terms of the contract between principal and agent. **1–76**

1–77 The agent's authority emanates from his principal in one or other of two ways—by contract or by operation of law.

1–78 The following terms are used to describe the nature of the agent's authority in different circumstances:

(i) express authority;
(ii) implied authority;
(iii) ostensible or apparent authority; and
(iv) presumed authority.

The term "actual authority" is used to cover both (i) and (ii); the authority in both these cases arises out of contract. In (iii) and (iv), on the other hand, the law is not concerned with whether or not there was actual authority; the circumstances are such that authority is deemed to exist, *i.e.* the authority arises by operation of law.

1–79 It is not always easy to identify in a reported case which category of authority is in question. In particular, the dividing line between implied authority (authority which actually exists) and ostensible (or apparent) authority (authority which does not exist) is not clearly drawn in Scottish cases or in pre-twentieth century English cases. For the end result (though not as regards the evidence which must be brought before the court) the distinction is insignificant: the actions in question are generally brought by the third party against the principal with the object of establishing that the principal is bound by the agent's actings and so is liable to the third party; in such an action the third party is equally satisfied with the court's decision whether the court has held that the principal is bound because the agent was acting within his implied authority or within his ostensible (or apparent) authority.

(i) *Express Authority*

1–80 The contract between the principal and the agent may expressly define the scope of the agent's authority. This is essential where the agent appointed is a special agent, as distinct from a general agent. The third party may not, at the time of negotiating with the agent, know the agent's express authority, but he is entitled to found on the express authority, when he comes to know of it, as establishing the contractual relationship between himself and the principal.

(ii) *Implied Authority*

1–81 It is common for the agent's authority not to be expressed in detail in his appointment, but to be left to be implied from the mere fact of the appointment coupled with the surrounding circumstances.

An agent has implied authority to do whatever is incidental to, or ordinarily necessary for, the completion of the transaction committed to him. If he belongs to a recognised profession, he impliedly has the authority usually conferred on members of that profession. Similarly, implied authority may be defined by custom and usage of trade. **1–82**

The nature of implied authority and the circumstances in which it exists may be illustrated as follows: **1–83**

1. A general agent has no implied authority to borrow money: **1–84**

Sinclair, Moorhead & Co. v. Wallace & Co. (1880) 7 R. 874: S. & Co., produce merchants in Glasgow, had an important branch in Dundee. Low was general manager of the Dundee branch, but was not a partner in the firm.

Low borrowed money, saying that it was required by S. & Co. for their business.

Later Low absconded, leaving large deficiencies.

Held that the firm of S. & Co. was not liable for the loan.

Lord Young (at p. 877) referred to Low as having had "all the general powers which an agent managing a mercantile business can have. He had power to buy and sell, accept bills, and open a bank account—in short, general powers such as a general manager in his position is in use to have."

However, of the power to borrow money in name of the principals, Lord Young said: "That is a very important power, and when it is intended to be given it would be well that it should be given expressly, and within certain limits. I apprehend that such is the practice. No prudent money-lender would be likely to lend money to an agent without seeing his authority to borrow, and satisfying himself that the demand is within the prescribed limits. Here we have nothing of that sort."

2. An agent who has authority to open a bank account for his principal does not have implied authority to create an overdraft on the account: **1–85**

Royal Bank of Scotland v. Skinner, 1931 S.L.T. 382 (O.H.): S., a solicitor, opened a bank account for his client Mrs Cameron, who had a drapery business. The account was headed with the solicitor's name followed by the words "for Mrs Duncan Cameron".

After a few years the account fell gradually into debit, Mrs Cameron became bankrupt, and the bank raised an action against S. for payment of the outstanding principal sum and interest.

Held that S. was not liable.

This was not a case in which the agent could be made liable for breach of warranty of authority (see 1–166, below).

Lord Mackay (Ordinary) said (at p. 387): "The fact that a principal permits his agent to open an account with a credit does not involve that he is willing to let him draw upon it under his general agency so as to create indefinite debits. . . . A person who purports to contract as agent on behalf of an alleged principal is liable on an implied warranty of his authority *only* if the other party relied on the existence of the authority. . . . Now the bank do not, and could not, say that they so relied."

1–86 3. A salesman has implied authority to take orders on behalf of his principal:

Barry, Ostlere & Shepherd Ltd v. Edinburgh Cork Importing Co., 1909 S.C. 1113: B. Ltd, manufacturers of floorcloth and linoleum, negotiated with Lawrie, the manager or salesman of cork merchants, for the supply of cork shavings to B. Ltd.

Delivery was not made, the price of cork shavings had risen, and B. Ltd brought an action of damages for breach of contract against the cork merchants.

The cork merchants claimed that they had not intended Lawrie to make a final bargain.

Held that a contract had been formed, since the pursuers were entitled to assume that a person in Lawrie's position had authority to conclude the bargain.

Reference was made to the earlier case of *Milne v. Harris, James & Co.* (1803) Mor. 8493, in which an order for a quantity of tea given in Edinburgh to a travelling agent of a London firm was binding on the London firm, with the result that that firm was liable in damages for failure to deliver the tea. This case was the authority for the statement in Bell's *Commentaries* (Vol. I, p. 515): "In general, it appears that a riding or travelling agent has not only authority to receive payment for his principal of the moneys due to him, but to take orders by which the principal shall be bound as much as if he himself had accepted and bound the contract."

1–87 4. The master of a ship has implied authority to accept the services of a shipbroker (*Barnetson v. Petersen Brothers* (1902) 5 F. 86 (1–17, above)), but not to deviate unnecessarily from the charterparty (*Strickland v. Neilson and MacIntosh* (1869) 7 M. 400 (1–71, above)).

5. An architect has in certain circumstances implied authority to employ a surveyor. Two contrasting cases illustrate the circumstances in which such an implied authority exists: **1–88**

(a) *Black v. Cornelius* (1879) 6 R. 581: C. engaged Deas as his architect in connection with certain houses and shops which C. was about to erect on a site in Edinburgh.

Deas had the plans measured by B., a surveyor.

The buildings were not proceeded with, and B. claimed fees from C.

C. resisted payment on the ground that he had not employed B., and further, that he had made an express agreement with Deas, by which Deas's fee was to include the surveyor's work.

Held that C. was liable to pay B.

"An architect employed in the ordinary way has authority to employ a surveyor, and . . . the surveyor, if not otherwise paid, has a good claim against the person who employs the architect" (*per* Lord Ormidale at p. 582).

(b) *Knox & Robb v. Scottish Garden Suburb Co. Ltd*, 1913 S.C. 872: K. & R., alleging that they had done surveying work on the instructions of the architect of a building company, claimed payment for their work from the building company.

Held that, as the building plans were in this case only proposals which had not been finally approved, the architect had had no implied authority to employ surveyors.

6. A solicitor's implied authority depends on the character of the work entrusted to him. **1–89**

If the solicitor is instructed to bring an action in court, he has implied authority to take any incidental step in procedure and, on the authority of *Riverford Finance Ltd v. Kelly*, 1991 S.L.T. 300 (O.H.), even to appeal from the sheriff court to the Court of Session:

In a sheriff court action by K. against R. Ltd, R. Ltd's solicitor failed to attend the court, and K. obtained a decree by default.

R. Ltd's solicitor then, it was alleged, marked an appeal to the sheriff principal, but did not attend the court for the hearing of the appeal. The appeal was therefore refused.

It was alleged that R. Ltd's solicitor then marked an appeal for the Court of Session, naming Edinburgh solicitors to act in that appeal.

The Edinburgh solicitors stated to the Court of Session that they were not prepared to act and, as a result, the appeal was abandoned for want of insistence.

R. Ltd then raised an action of reduction of the sheriff court decree, alleging that they had not been informed by their solicitor that decree had passed against them until after the abandonment of the appeal to the Court of Session. It was argued by counsel for R. Ltd that as R. Ltd had given no authority to their solicitor to appeal to the Court of Session the proceedings were null, and ought to be reduced because by appealing and then not insisting in the appeal R. Ltd's solicitor had deprived R. Ltd of any remedy other than reduction.

Held, by Lord Morton of Shuna (Ordinary), that a solicitor does not require any special authority to mark an appeal from the sheriff court to the Court of Session. The action of reduction was therefore dismissed.

Counsel for R. Ltd had founded on *Goodall v. Bilsland*, 1909 S.C. 1152 (1–25, above), as authority for the proposition that a solicitor requires a specific mandate from his client before he can mark an appeal to the Court of Session from the sheriff court, but that case turned on the limited wording of the particular mandate which the agent had obtained.

On the other hand, there is in *Stephen v. Skinner* (1863) 2 M. 287 authority for the proposition that a solicitor has no implied authority to defend proceedings in the Court of Session if an appeal is made from a sheriff court by the other party:

Stephen claimed to be ranked as a creditor in the sequestration of a Stornoway merchant, but the trustee in the sequestration rejected his claim.

Stephen instructed a Stornoway firm of solicitors to appeal to the sheriff against this rejection. The action was successful.

The trustee then appealed to the Court of Session, and the Stornoway solicitors instructed Skinner, an Edinburgh solicitor, to protect Stephen's interests in the appeal. The Court of Session decided the appeal in the trustee's favour, and found Stephen liable in expenses.

Held that Stephen was not liable to pay to the Stornoway solicitors the expenses incurred in the Court of Session proceedings, since he had not authorised these proceedings.

A solicitor instructed to bring an action on behalf of his client has implied authority to compromise or abandon the action. This is supported by *William Mackenzie (Carpenters) Ltd (in receivership) v. Mowat*, 1991 S.L.T. (Sh.Ct.) 48:

W. Ltd appealed against a decision allowing a new diet of proof on the ground that at the original diet M.'s solicitor had indicated that he had been instructed to consent to decree. The case had been continued on the procedure roll for settlement, but later M. denied that he had instructed his solicitor to consent to decree.

Held appeal allowed.

Sheriff Principal R. D. Ireland said (at p. 49): "A solicitor acting as a procurator has implied authority to compromise or abandon the action in court (*Stair Memorial Encyclopaedia*, Vol. 1, p. 253); and a principal is bound by the act of his agent acting within his ostensible authority (Gloag, *Contract* (2nd ed.), p. 147). In the present case the defender is therefore bound by the act of his solicitor whether or not he has given actual authority to him to consent to decree."

The law on a solicitor's authority when acting in the Court of Session was described as "unclear" by Temporary Judge H. J. Aronson in *Wight Civil Engineering Ltd v. Parker*, 1994 S.L.T. 140 (O.H.):

W. sought payment from P. of sums allegedly due under a contract for works plus interest on a sum already paid on the ground that it was paid late.

W. concluded in the alternative for payment of a sum offered by P.'s solicitors in settlement of the action on the basis that they had implied authority to bind P.

Proof before answer was allowed.

A solicitor instructed to bring an action in court has no implied authority to submit the question to arbitration instead of to the court. Thus in *Black v. Laidlaw* (1844) 6 D. 1254 B. was held not to be barred from proceeding with an action of count and reckoning where his solicitor, without his authority, had entered into a reference on his behalf with the other party to the action.

A solicitor has no implied authority to receive payment of money lent by his client:

Peden v. Graham (1907) 15 S.L.T. 143 (O.H.): P. obtained a loan of £100 through a solicitor, Aitken. P. paid interest on the loan, and also two repayments of £20 each of the capital, to Aitken.

Aitken embezzled the £40, and subsequently became bankrupt and mentally deranged.

Held that the loss fell on P., since Aitken had had no authority to receive repayment of the capital on behalf of his client.

1–90 7. An agent may have implied authority to employ a solicitor, but this will depend on circumstances such as the nature of the work and the category of agent appointed. For instance, in *J.M. & J.H. Robertson v. Beatson, McLeod & Co. Ltd*, 1908 S.C. 921, a chartered accountant appointed to carry through an amalgamation of two limited companies was held not to have had implied authority to employ a solicitor to prepare a certain deed; the result was that the solicitor was not entitled to claim payment of his account from the principal.

(iii) *Ostensible or Apparent Authority*

1–91 This is authority which the agent has not actually had conferred on him either expressly or impliedly, but which is deemed to exist on the principle of personal bar by holding out. There is a binding relationship between the principal and the third party because the principal has held out the agent as having the necessary authority.

1–92 Such authority can arise where the principal has withdrawn an agent's actual authority without giving proper notice to third parties of the withdrawal. It may also arise where the principal has made some private arrangement with his agent, limiting the agent's usual authority and has not notified third parties of these special limitations: a third party is justified in believing that the agent has the ordinary powers of an agent of the category to which he belongs.

1–93 The following three cases illustrate ostensible authority:

(1) *Hayman v. American Cotton Oil Co.* (1907) 45 S.L.R. 207: See 1–19, above.

(2) *George v. Duncan*, 1991 G.W.D. 39–2354 (Sh.Ct.): When damage to a taxi was repaired by G. on the instructions of the taxi-driver, the owner of the taxi was held liable to G. for the repairs on the ground that by allowing the taxi-driver to display her firm's sign on the vehicle she had included him in the class of ostensible agents who had authority to bind her in a question with G.

(3) *International Sponge Importers Ltd v. Watt & Sons*, 1911 S.C. (H.L.) 57: Cohen, a commercial traveller for a sponge importing company, was in the habit of selling to saddlers, parcels of sponges which he was allowed to carry with him and hand over to

purchasers. He had no authority to receive payment except by crossed cheques in favour of the company.

Occasionally W. & Sons, saddlers in Edinburgh, had paid for sponges by cheque in favour of Cohen, and the company knew of this but did not object. On one occasion W. & Sons paid £120 in cash to Cohen.

Cohen was shown to have been acting dishonestly, and the company sought to recover the irregular payments from W. & Sons.

Held that W. & Sons were not liable, since, in the circumstances, they had had no reason to believe that Cohen was not entitled to receive payment by those methods.

Contrast *British Bata Shoe Co. Ltd v. Double M. Shah Ltd*, 1980 S.C. 311 (O.H.): S. Ltd obtained several consignments of goods from B. Ltd. Kreager, B. Ltd's cashier, without actual authority, regularly received payment for the goods from S. Ltd by cheques on which, at Kreager's request, the payee's name was left blank.

Kreager embezzled the money, was convicted, and became bankrupt.

B. Ltd sued S. Ltd for the price of the goods. S. Ltd, relying on *International Sponge Importers Ltd v. Watt & Sons*, argued that Kreager had had ostensible authority to receive the cheques.

Held that B. Ltd was entitled to succeed: there was no evidence that B. Ltd had known of the payments made to Kreager, and so B. Ltd had not represented to S. Ltd that Kreager had been acting on B. Ltd's behalf in receiving payment.

This case is a good illustration of the point that the representation which gives rise to ostensible authority must be a representation made by the principal to the third party: a representation made by the agent alone is not enough.

Moreover, the circumstances in this case, especially Kreager's odd request for cheques with the payee's name left blank, were sufficiently suspicious to cast upon S. Ltd a duty of inquiry.

(iv) *Presumed Authority*

Presumed authority is authority which the law presumes the principal would have granted if he had been consulted in advance. **1–94**

In *negotiorum gestio* (see 1–28, above) the agent's authority is presumed authority. **1–95**

1–96 Such authority also arises out of a *praepositura* ("superintendence") in a household or a business.

1–97 Formerly in a household a wife was presumed to be *praeposita negotiis domesticis* ("placed in charge of domestic affairs") and so to have authority to order necessaries for which her husband was liable to pay.

The question whether items were necessaries or luxuries was decided according to all the family circumstances. For example, in *Buie v. Lady Gordon* (1827) 5 S. 464; (1831) 9 S. 923, a list including expensive food and drink and charges for chaises supplied to Lady Gordon had to be revised because, while the Lord Ordinary had taken account of the husband's rank and fortune, he had failed to take account also of the husband's embarrassed circumstances.

A wife's presumed authority could be terminated by the husband. Express notice to the individual supplier or the recording of letters of inhibition in the Register of Inhibitions and Adjudications in Edinburgh terminated the authority, but a newspaper advertisement had no legal effect unless the supplier was proved to have been aware of it.

1–98 The Scottish Law Commission (*Outdated Rules in the Law of Husband and Wife*, Scot. Law Com. No. 76 (1983)) recommended the abolition of the common law rules on a wife's *praepositura* on the ground that they were outdated, discriminatory and unnecessary. That recommendation was enacted by section 7 of the Law Reform (Husband and Wife) (Scotland) Act 1984, which provides that for the purpose of deciding a husband's liability for obligations incurred by his wife, a married woman is no longer presumed as a matter of law to have been placed by her husband in charge of his domestic affairs. The formal letters of inhibition associated with the wife's *praepositura* were also abolished.

The ordinary rules of the law of agency now apply: if the husband has expressly or impliedly given his wife authority to act on his behalf or if he has held out his wife to third parties as having his authority, then he will, as any other principal, be liable to third parties.

1–99 The former *praepositura* rules did not apply where a third party had been relying solely on the wife's own credit. An instance was *Arnot v. Stevenson* (1698) Mor. 6017:

S.'s wife bound her son as apprentice to A., an apothecary, and paid part of the fee for the apprenticeship.

A. brought an action against S. for 100 merks, the balance of the fee not paid, and for damages on the ground that the son had run away from his apprenticeship after two years.

Held that S. was not liable, since S.'s wife had not been acting as agent of her husband in relation to the apprenticeship.

The 1984 Act has not affected such situations: if a wife has contracted as principal, she alone is liable.

The Act has also not affected a husband's obligation to reimburse anyone who has provided his wife with necessaries when she was entitled to, but was not receiving, aliment from him. **1–100**

The person who is in charge of a household may be someone other than the wife of the householder. The ordinary rules of the law of agency apply here also: an early instance is *Hamilton v. Forrester* (1825) 3 S. 572, where the eldest daughter of the householder, who was a widower, was held not to be personally liable for the necessaries ordered for the family. **1–101**

In a business the person who is *praepositus negotiis* ("placed in charge of affairs") has presumed authority to conduct the business on behalf of the owner of the business. An instance is: **1–102**

Gemmell v. Annandale & Son Ltd (1899) 36 S.L.R. 658: G., a rag-merchant, brought an action against A. Ltd for the price of rags supplied to A. Ltd.

A. Ltd claimed that, when G. had been in prison, the price had been paid to, and a receipt granted by, G.'s father as *praepositus negotiis*.

Held that payment to G.'s father in that capacity was good payment in a question between G. and A. Ltd

V DUTIES OF AGENT TO PRINCIPAL

The duties of an agent to his principal may be considered under the following headings: **1–103**

(a) instructions;
(b) delegation;
(c) skill and care;
(d) accounting;
(e) relief; and
(f) fiduciary duty.

(a) Instructions

1–104 The agent must perform what he has been instructed to do, and in doing so must act in accordance with the authority conferred on him, or with the customs and usages of the trade, business or profession. If the instructions are express, they must be complied with. Where there are no instructions, express or implied by custom or usage of trade, the agent must act to the best of his judgment.

1–105 There is an instance of an agent's failure to comply with express instructions in *Gilmour v. Clark* (1853) 15 D. 478: G., a merchant in Edinburgh, instructed C., a carter there, to cart a bale of goods to Leith to be put on board "The Earl of Zetland" bound for Orkney.

C.'s servant put the goods on board "The Magnet" instead, and that ship was lost.

Held that C. was liable to G. for the value of the goods.

1–106 Express instructions are not necessarily detailed instructions; for example, a solicitor instructed to make up a purchaser's title to heritable property or to prepare a conveyance is in breach of his duty to his client if he fails, without first obtaining the client's dispensation, to make a search for incumbrances (*Fearn v. Gordon & Craig* (1893) 20 R. 352).

1–107 An agent who fails to comply with the stipulations in his contract of appointment loses his right to claim the agreed commission for the period during which he is in breach:

Graham & Co. v. United Turkey Red Co. Ltd, 1922 S.C. 533: A contract entered into in February 1914 between G. & Co. as agents and U. Ltd as principal prohibited G. & Co. from selling cotton goods supplied by parties other than U. Ltd.

From July 10, 1916, G. & Co. regularly sold goods in contravention of that term.

In November 1917, G. & Co. brought an action of accounting against U. Ltd for the whole period of the agency.

Held that G. & Co. were entitled to an accounting only for the period prior to July 10, 1916.

Lord Ormidale said (at p. 550): "Having ceased to perform the stipulated services in terms of their contract they forfeited the right to call for commissions—the reward stipulated in the contract for these services—the one being the direct counterpart of the other."

(b) Delegation

The general presumption in agency is that the agent must act personally. The maxim applicable is *delegatus non potest delegare* ("an agent cannot delegate"). **1–108**

Delegation may, however, be expressly permitted, or may be impliedly authorised by custom or usage of trade. It may also be later ratified by the principal, or may be justified by necessity. **1–109**

Where there is permissible delegation, the principal is liable to pay for the sub-agent's services. **1–110**

Black v. Cornelius (1879) 6 R. 581 (1–88, above) is authority for the architect's right to delegate to a surveyor. **1–111**

(c) Skill and Care

An agent must exercise due skill and care. If a professional man, he must show the degree of knowledge, skill and care expected of a reasonably competent and careful member of the profession. **1–112**

A case in which an agent, acting as a mutual friend and not as a member of any particular profession, was held not to have exercised reasonable care is *Stiven v. Watson* (1874) 1 R. 412: **1–113**

S., a merchant in Dundee, purchased a quantity of yarn from Annan & Co., Pitscottie Mills, Fife. Annan & Co. failed to deliver all the quantity purchased, and S. threatened to take legal proceedings to compel delivery.

W. proposed an arrangement, which was agreed to, by which Annan & Co. were to forward a quantity of tow belonging to them and then lying at Dundee to Dairsie station and to grant a delivery-order for it in favour of W.

W. received the delivery-order, but failed to intimate it to the station-master at Dairsie. The result was that when the tow arrived at the station, it was removed by Annan & Co.

A few days later Annan & Co. became bankrupt.

S. never received the balance of the yarn, and he brought an action against W. for damages.

Held that (i) W. was liable for the damage caused by his failure to intimate the delivery-order; and (ii) W.'s plea that no damage had been suffered because the transaction would have been reducible under the Bankruptcy Act 1696 could not be sustained because there was no certainty that the retention of the tow would not have persuaded Annan & Co. to deliver the yarn.

1–114 Similarly, in *Copland v. Brogan*, 1916 S.C. 277 (1–10, above), an agent, though acting gratuitously, was held liable for failure to exercise reasonable care.

1–115 Professional persons, provided they show reasonable knowledge and skill and act with reasonable care, are not liable for errors of judgment. Solicitors have thus been held liable to clients for having founded on the wrong section of a statute (*Hart v. Frame* (1839) McL. & R. 595; (1836) 14 S. 914), and for having delayed bringing an action against a local authority until the action was barred by the Public Authorities Protection Act 1893 (*Simpson v. Kidstons, Watson, Turnbull & Co.*, 1913 1 S.L.T. 74 (O.H.)), but not for failure to reclaim income tax on behalf of a religious body through ignorance of English practice and of an English House of Lords decision in which an earlier Scottish case had been disapproved (*Free Church of Scotland v. MacKnight's Trustees*, 1916 S.C. 349).

(d) **Accounting**

1–116 An agent must keep accounts and make good any deficiency which he cannot explain, even though no dishonesty on his part is proved.

Tyler v. Logan (1904) 7 F. 123: T. owned a number of branch establishments for the sale of boots. He appointed L. as manager of his branch in Dundee.

At a stock-taking conducted by T., there was a deficiency of about £62 at the Dundee branch, and T. brought an action against L. for payment of that amount.

There was no evidence of dishonesty or negligence on L.'s part, but no explanation of the deficiency.

Held that T. was entitled to payment.

No liability to account arises until the agent has received his principal's funds. This is illustrated by *The Royal Bank of Scotland plc v. Law*, 1996 S.L.T. 83:

A solicitor was instructed by his client to sell the client's house. Missives were concluded which provided for payment of the price at the date of entry.

Three days before the date of entry an arrestment was served on the solicitor on the dependence of an action of payment which had been brought against the client by a bank.

The solicitor did not have funds until the purchaser paid the price at the date of entry.

The bank brought an action of furthcoming against the solicitor arguing that the arrestment had attached the solicitor's obligation to account to his client.

Held that the arrestment was ineffectual, because the solicitor had had no funds of his client at the relevant time and was therefore not under any obligation to account.

(e) **Relief**

If a principal is held liable on a transaction entered into by an agent exceeding his authority, or for a default by an agent, he is entitled to relief from the agent. **1–117**

Milne v. Ritchie (1882) 10 R. 365: A house was being built for D. M., who was D.'s architect, had authority limited to £1,465 to enter into a contract for the mason-work.

M. accepted an offer from R. to execute the mason-work for £1,646.

R. raised an action against D. for payment of £1,646, and was successful.

D. then raised an action for relief against M., and was successful.

(Subsequently M. brought an action against R. for reduction of the acceptance of the offer, alleging that he had been induced to sign it by fraudulent misrepresentations of R.

Held that M. had a title to sue.)

(f) **Fiduciary Duty**

The relationship of agency is of a fiduciary character: the principal ought to be able to rely on the agent's giving him full benefit of his services in accordance with the contract of agency. **1–118**

The agent's fiduciary duty is restricted to what he does in the course of the agency: in outside matters the agent is entitled to further his own interests or those of other principals; restraints would require to be expressly provided for in the contract of agency or to arise by necessary implication from it. The comparatively recent case of *Lothian v. Jenolite Ltd*, 1969 S.C. 111, is a warning against stating the agent's fiduciary duty in over-wide terms: **1–119**

J. Ltd, an English company, entered into an agreement with L., by which L. was to sell certain of J. Ltd's products in Scotland and receive a commission on sales. The contract was to last for four years from July 1964, but in November 1965 J. Ltd terminated it.

L. claimed damages for breach of contract. J. Ltd alleged in defence that L. had without their consent bought and resold products supplied by a competitor of theirs and had instructed his staff to sell these products in place of J. Ltd's products, and was therefore in material breach of contract.

Held that it was not an implied condition of L.'s contract with J. Ltd that L. should not, without J. Ltd's consent, sell a competitor's products.

Lord Walker said (at p. 124): "The defenders had not stipulated that the pursuer should be their full-time agent, or that he should sell their goods exclusively, or that his freedom to carry on his own business should be restricted in their interests. . . .

" . . . The rule that the agent must act with a single eye to the interests of his principal . . . is, I think, limited to what the agent does in the course of his agency. Here what he did as agent and what he did as an individual were quite separate from one another. . . . If the defenders intended to impose a restriction on the pursuer's freedom to trade, they should have contracted with him to that effect."

1–120 For an agency in which there was a restriction prohibiting the agent from selling goods supplied by parties other than the principal, see *Graham & Co. v. United Turkey Red Co. Ltd*, 1922 S.C. 533 (1–107, above).

1–121 Three important aspects of the agent's fiduciary duty relate to situations where:

(i) the agent transacts with his principal;
(ii) the agent receives a benefit from the third party; and
(iii) the agent is in possession of confidential information.

(i) *Agent Transacting with Principal*

1–122 Where an agent, instead of fulfilling the essential purpose of the agency, *i.e.* the establishment of a legal relationship between the principal and a third party, transacts with himself in his individual capacity, a conflict is likely to arise between the personal interest of the agent and his duties to his principal. In such a situation, the agent should disclose the circumstances to the principal.

1–123 Thus, if the agent is instructed to sell property for his principal, he must not secretly purchase it himself:

McPherson's Trustees v. Watt (1877) 5 R. (H.L.) 9: W., an advocate in Aberdeen, bought for his brother, Dr W. of Darlington, four houses in Aberdeen from McP.'s trustees.

W. was also the law-agent for the trustees.

Before the contract had been made, W. had arranged with his brother, without the knowledge of the trustees, to take over two of the houses himself on paying one-half of the price.

Held that, because W. had not disclosed to the trustees the fact that he was purchasing partly for himself, the transaction was invalid on account of W.'s confidential relationship to the trustees.

Lord Blackburn said (at p. 20): "The writer or attorney must stand towards his client in a position in which there has been, or rather in which there is, confidence more or less reposed in the attorney by his client. . . .

" . . . I think the law both in England and Scotland is that in such cases we do not inquire whether it was a good bargain or a bad bargain before we set it aside. The mere fact that the agent was in circumstances which made it his duty to give his client advice puts him in such a position that, being the purchaser himself, he cannot give disinterested advice—his own interests coming in contact with his client's, that mere fact authorises the client to set aside the contract, if he chooses so to do."

A further illustration is *Cunningham v. Lee* (1874) 2 R. 83: **1–124**

L., a solicitor, had been instructed to buy certain shares for his client, Kirk. L. did so, but Kirk failed to pay the price on the settling day. Instead of then selling the shares, which had fallen considerably in value, L. retained them and some weeks later, when they had risen again, sold them without loss.

Held, on Kirk's sequestration, that L. was not entitled to claim the difference between the price at which the shares had been bought and the market price on the settling day.

Lord President Inglis said (at p. 87): "No agent can buy the property of his principal in any case, except when he is specially authorised to do so. But here there was no authority or consent. Lee obviously took the course which he did in the belief he was entitled to do so. . . . But . . . his actings were quite against the settled rule of law."

Similarly, an agent whose instructions are to buy goods for his **1–125**
principal must not, without the principal's knowledge, buy from himself; the principal is entitled to repudiate any such offer.

(ii) *Agent Receiving Benefit from Third Party*

1–126 An agent must not take a secret profit for himself beyond the commission or other remuneration allowed him by his principal. With the principal's consent, express or implied by usage of trade (*e.g.* tips or shared commission in some situations), the agent may receive benefits additional to the remuneration stipulated for in the contract of agency itself.

1–127 An agent who receives a discount or donation from the third party must credit the principal with the amount:

Ronaldson v. Drummond & Reid (1881) 8 R. 956: Hill, a solicitor acting for Gray's trustees, engaged Dowell, an auctioneer, to sell furniture.

Dowell paid to Hill a portion of the commission charged by him, describing the sum as a "donation" directly out of his own pocket.

Held that Hill was bound to credit Gray's trustees with that amount.

Similarly, in *Trans Barwil Agencies (U.K.) Ltd v. John S. Braid & Co. Ltd*, 1988 S.C. 222 (O.H.), a principal was held entitled to an accounting where the agent had received what was described as a "windfall":

T. Ltd employed B. Ltd to act as their agents in relation to shipments of whisky from the U.K. to Iraq. In transacting with B. Ltd, T. Ltd used a wrong arithmetical conversion rate from Jordanian dinars to sterling, despite B. Ltd's seeking to persuade them otherwise. This resulted in T. Ltd's claiming from B. Ltd only about 42 per cent of the sum which they should have claimed.

When T. Ltd realised their mistake, they issued supplementary invoices, but B. Ltd refused to pay more than the previous invoices.

The shippers used by B. Ltd were charged by them at a rate in line with the correct arithmetical conversion rate, and T. Ltd sued B. Ltd for the balance, contending that it was a secret profit.

Lord McCluskey (Ordinary) said (at p. 227): "The relation of principal and agent is a fiduciary one. It does not matter if the secret profit results from dishonesty, negligence or mistake; it must be accounted for. . . . All the agent is entitled to is the known, agreed remuneration. If there should be a windfall, however arising, the agent must account to the principal for it because the principal is entitled to the benefit of it."

1–128 The consequences of an agent's receiving a secret profit are that the agent must surrender the secret profit to the principal, he loses his right to his lawful remuneration on the transaction and is liable to be dismissed, and the principal may recover damages from the third party for bribing the agent and may refuse to implement the contract with the third party. There are also penalties imposed on the offer and receipt of secret commissions under the Prevention of Corruption Acts of 1906 and 1916.

(iii) *Agent in Possession of Confidential Information*

An agent must treat as confidential all information relating to his principal's business which comes to his knowledge as a result of the agency. An obvious instance is the solicitor's duty of confidentiality concerning his client's affairs. Another instance is *Liverpool Victoria Legal Friendly Society v. Houston* (1900) 3 F. 42: **1–129**

H. had been an agent of a friendly society for about four years, during which time he had had the opportunity of seeing lists of persons insured with the society.

After having been dismissed by the society, H. offered lists of such persons to officials of a rival society.

Held that the lists contained confidential information acquired by H. in the course of his agency and that he was not entitled to make use of them to the detriment of his former principal. H. was also held liable in damages for the loss of business which the society had sustained as a result of having its members canvassed by the agents of the rival society.

VI RIGHTS OF AGENT AGAINST PRINCIPAL

The rights of an agent against his principal are considered below under these headings: **1–130**

(a) remuneration;
(b) reimbursement of expenses;
(c) relief; and
(d) lien.

(a) **Remuneration**

The principal is bound to pay the agreed commission or other remuneration. If there is no express provision, then the remuneration will be the amount which is customary in the particular branch **1–131** of agency: there may be a scale of fees, as for some professions. If there is neither an express provision as to the amount nor a professional custom, the amount will be *quantum meruit* ("as much as he has earned").

Kennedy v. Glass (1890) 17 R. 1085: G. was a dealer in old building material and old machinery.

K., an architect, had on several occasions introduced G. to persons who had old material for sale and for this, K. had been paid a commission by G.

In 1883 K. introduced G. to a sugar refining company with a view to a proposed sale of machinery and plant by the company.

Negotiations were protracted, but in 1888 G. finally entered into a contract with the company for the purchase of the machinery and plant at the price of £7,250.

G. subsequently failed to carry out the contract. K. claimed that there had been an oral arrangement between himself and G. by which he was to receive £250 as commission. G. contended that he had only arranged to give K. £50 if anything came of the transaction.

There was evidence to show that throughout the negotiations K. had acted as G.'s representative and had taken a great deal of trouble in promoting the transaction.

Held that although K. was not a professional broker he was entitled to £50 commission, *i.e.* to commission on a *quantum meruit* basis.

1–132 Difficulty can arise in deciding whether the agent has earned his commission. Has he done what the contract of agency required him to do in order to earn the commission? Is the result obtained by the principal fairly attributable to the agent's activities? An illustration is *Walker, Fraser & Steele v. Fraser's Trustees*, 1910 S.C. 222:

F., the owner of the estate of Balfunning, employed W. F. & S., estate agents, to sell it at a minimum price of £38,000.

In 1903 Scott applied to W. F. & S. for information regarding the estate of Dalnair, and in reply W. F. & S. sent particulars also of a few other estates including Balfunning. Negotiations were then broken off for a time.

In 1906 Scott applied to W. F. & S. for particulars of Balfunning, and was urged by them to make an offer for it, but did not do so.

In October 1907 Scott advertised in the *Glasgow Herald* for property of the general description which he desired, and the following month received from F. a letter about Balfunning. Negotiations followed which resulted in a sale of that property to Scott at £31,000.

W. F. & S. sued F. for £310 commission.

Held that, as W. F. & S.'s exertions had to a material degree contributed to the sale to Scott, W. F. & S. were entitled to the commission.

Lord Dundas said (at p. 229): "Actual introduction of the purchaser to the seller is not a necessary element in a case of this sort; it is enough if the agents introduce the purchaser to the estate, and by their efforts contribute in a substantial degree to the sale. A careful consideration of the evidence leads me to hold that the pursuers have sufficiently complied with the test indicated."

There have been numerous English cases on estate agents' commission, the question most frequently being as to the interpretation of the words used in the agreement between prospective seller and estate agent. A Scottish example is *Chris Hart (Business Sales) Ltd v. Currie*, 1992 S.L.T. 544: **1–133**

C. instructed H. Ltd to sell his public house, the Toll Bar, Cambuslang. Commission was to be payable "upon completion of a concluded contract for the sale of the premises".

An offer received was conditional upon the licence being transferred to the purchaser. In the event the licence was not transferred and the missives fell.

Held that the terms of the agency were clear that commission was payable: there had been completion of a concluded contract, although no implement or settlement had ensued.

Lord Mayfield said (at p. 546): "The overriding consideration in determining the issue in each case is to have regard to the terms of the particular contract. I do not consider that references to English cases are helpful because as I understand it the purchase and sale of property proceeds by various stages not applicable in Scotland."

(b) Reimbursement of Expenses

The agent has a right to be reimbursed by the principal for all expenses properly incurred in the performance of the agency. **1–134**

Drummond v. Cairns (1852) 14 D. 611: D. instructed C., a stockbroker, to purchase 100 shares of the East India Railway Company. The price was 20/6d per share, and the settling day was May 28.

C. duly intimated the transaction to D., but when the settling day arrived D. was not prepared to pay the price.

On June 10, C. sold the shares at 9/4d each.

Held that D. was liable to reumburse C. for the difference between the two prices.

A more recent illustration is *Marshall Wilson Dean & Turnbull v. Feymac Properties Ltd*, 1996 G.W.D. 22–1247:

M., solicitors, had been instructed by F. to sell property, but before settlement could take place, F required to produce building warrants and completion certificates for work which had been carried out by F.'s tenants. F. stated to M. that these documents were about to be issued, and relying on that statement M. granted a letter of obligation, binding themselves to produce them to the purchaser.

No documents were produced and the purchaser brought an action for their delivery against M.

In order to settle that action M. had to instruct certain works at a cost of £12,500 before the certificates were eventually issued.

M. then sued F. for repayment of their costs and expenditure.

Held that M. succeeded: F. had authorised M. to give an undertaking to the purchaser: it had been an implied term of F.'s contract of agency with M. that F. was not knowingly to give to M. inaccurate information material to the completion of the transaction, and F. had been in breach of that implied term.

1–135 The agent has no right of reimbursement if the expenses have not been properly incurred:

Tomlinson v. Liquidators of Scottish Amalgamated Silks Ltd, 1935 S.C. (H.L.) 1; 1934 S.C. 85: The articles of association of S. Ltd provided for the indemnification of any director against all costs, losses and expenses which he might incur by reason of any act done by him as director.

S. Ltd went into voluntary liquidation, and T., who had been a promoter and director, was tried for alleged fraud, the charges being that he had issued a fraudulent prospectus and had fraudulently misapplied funds of the company.

T. was acquitted, and then lodged a claim in the liquidation for the expenses, amounting to over £11,000, incurred by him in his defence. The liquidators rejected the claim.

Held that T. was not entitled to his expenses either under the indemnity clause in the articles or at common law, since expenses incurred in defending himself against an allegation that he did something which he did not in fact do and which it was not his duty to do, were not expenses incurred by him as a director or as an agent of the company in the discharge of his duties.

(c) **Relief**

The principal must relieve the agent of all liabilities incurred by the **1–136** agent and arising out of the proper performance of the agent's duties.

Stevenson v. Duncan (1842) 5 D. 167: D. instructed stockbrokers to sell 20 shares of the London, Leith, Edinburgh and Glasgow Shipping Co. on his behalf. D. did not in fact hold such shares.

The stockbrokers purported to sell the shares to Cullen.

In an action brought by Cullen against the stockbrokers, Cullen was found entitled to £83 damages. The stockbrokers raised an action of relief against D.

Held that D. was bound to relieve them.

An agent who had not acted properly in the execution of the **1–137** agency was held not entitled to relief in *Robinson v. Middleton* (1859) 21 D. 1089:

M., a wood-merchant in Strathmiglo, engaged R., an agent in London, to effect a sale of wood.

R. sold the wood to Perry who was acting for a firm in Melbourne, Australia. Perry arranged with R. that he (Perry) should incur no liability, but this arrangement was not communicated to M.

The price took the form of a bill of exchange drawn by Perry on the Melbourne firm, which, by the time the cargo arrived in Melbourne, was insolvent.

A bank which had discounted the bill sold the cargo but the price obtained fell short of the amount of the bill by about £1,000. R. paid the deficiency to the bank, and then claimed relief from M.

Held that as R. had, without M.'s knowledge or consent, transacted with Perry so as to release him from his liability as drawer of the bill, R. was not entitled to recover from M.

(d) **Lien**

A mercantile agent has a general lien over any of the principal's **1–138** property in his possession, *i.e.* he has a right in security over that property until he is paid his commission or other remuneration and has been relieved of debts incurred by him in the execution of the agency.

1–139 An illustration of a factor's general lien is *Sibbald v. Gibson* (1852) 15 D. 217:

S., corn factor in Leith, employed G. & Co., corn merchants in Glasgow, for several transactions during the years 1850–51.

In December 1850, S. had instructed G. & Co. to purchase for him a large quantity of oats, which were placed in G. & Co.'s store and later distributed from there in small parcels to S.'s customers.

S. and G. & Co. disagreed as to the rate of commission which was due to G. & Co. on these transactions.

In September 1851, S. sent a quantity of beans to G. & Co. for sale, and in remitting the proceeds of the sale G. & Co. deducted an amount for the higher rate of commission which G. & Co. claimed on the oats transactions.

Held that G. & Co. were entitled to retain their commission on the earlier transactions from the proceeds of the sale of the later transactions.

See also *Mackenzie v. Cormack*, 1950 S.C. 183 (1–153, below), as to an auctioneer's lien over the goods being sold and over the price paid to him by the successful bidder.

1–140 A solicitor also has a general lien (see 7–157, below).

1–141 Agents other than mercantile agents and members of some professions have only a special lien: for example, accountants have probably only a special lien (see 7–140, below).

VII THIRD PARTY'S RIGHTS AND LIABILITIES

1–142 As the essential function of agency is to establish a legal relationship between the principal and a third party, the rights and liabilities of the third party are of central importance in the topic of agency.

1–143 These rights and liabilities are affected by the way in which the agent contracts with the third party. A concise statement of the main rules applied is to be found in the opinion of Lord Anderson in *A.F. Craig & Co. Ltd v. Blackater*, 1923 S.C. 472, at p. 486:

"If A contracts as agent of a disclosed principal, A cannot competently sue or be sued with reference to the contract. Again, if A contracts for an undisclosed principal, A may sue and is liable to be sued as a principal, the third party having no knowledge that he is anything but a principal. If, however, A contracts for an undisclosed principal who is subsequently disclosed to the third party, the latter may sue either agent or principal. He cannot, however, sue both. If an action is raised against the third party he may insist that it be at the instance of the disclosed principal."

Four situations are given further consideration below; these are: **1–144**

(a) where the agent names his principal;
(b) where the agent states that he is an agent but does not give the name of his principal;
(c) where the agent does not disclose the agency at all, with the result that the third party believes that the agent is himself a principal; and
(d) where the agent has no authority, with the result that no binding relationship is established between principal and third party and the agent incurs liability to the third party for breach of warranty of authority.

(a) Agent Naming his Principal

The general rule is that where the principal is named, the contract takes legal effect as if the two parties to it had been the principal and the third party; the agent is regarded as having dropped out of the situation: he cannot sue on the contract nor is he liable to be sued. An illustration is *Stone & Rolfe Ltd v. Kimber Coal Co. Ltd*, 1926 S.C. (H.L.) 45: **1–145**

A ship owned by S. Ltd was chartered to the Atlantic Baltic Co., Copenhagen, to carry a cargo of coal from Grangemouth to Denmark.

The charterparty had been negotiated in Glasgow by G. & Co. for the owner and by K. Ltd for the charterers. The document, a printed form with blanks filled in before signature, had an additional manuscript clause: "Freight and demurrage (if any in loading) to be paid in Glasgow by K. Ltd". The signature on behalf of the charterer was:

"For the Atlantic Baltic Co., Copenhagen.
J.B. Jamieson of K. Ltd."

S. Ltd brought an action against K. Ltd for demurrage incurred at Grangemouth.

Held that K. Ltd was not liable because (i) the form of signature showed that K. Ltd had signed as agent only and (ii) the manuscript clause was not sufficient to rebut the inference drawn from the form of the signature.

1–146 The same general rule applies where the principal's name is not actually given but can be ascertained by the third party:

Armour v. Duff & Co., 1912 S.C. 120: A. received from D. & Co., who carried on business as "steamship owners and brokers", the following order: "Please supply the s.s. 'Silvia' with the following stores to be put on board at Port-Glasgow. . . . "

A. delivered the goods, and rendered an account to D. & Co., whom he believed to be the owners of the vessel. D. & Co. were not, and had never been, the owners, and they refused to pay the account.

Held that, as A. could, by examining the Register of Shipping, have discovered who the owners of the "Silvia" were, D. & Co. were not liable since they had been acting as agents for a disclosed principal.

1–147 The same general rule applies even where the principal is a foreign principal. This point was unsettled in England until the decision of the Court of Appeal in *Teheran-Europe Co. Ltd v. S. T. Belton (Tractors) Ltd* [1968] 2 Q.B. 545, but in Scotland was established more than a century earlier by *Millar v. Mitchell* (1860) 22 D. 833, a decision of the whole Court of Session.

Mitchell & Co. of Leith, acting as agents for C. of Hamburg, entered into a contract with Millar of Musselburgh for the supply of a quantity of bones to be shipped from Denmark in March and April 1854.

The bones were not shipped in accordance with these terms, and Millar brought an action for damages against Mitchell & Co. for the loss sustained as a result.

Held (by a majority of the whole court) that (i) there was no *praesumptio juris* ("presumption of law") that an agent acting for a named foreign principal incurred personal liability, and (ii) the evidence in this case did not establish that Mitchell & Co. had undertaken personal liability.

1–148 Where in a conveyancing transaction a solicitor signs a letter of obligation he does not necessarily incur personal liability even although his signature is unqualified. The terms of the letter may be such as to exclude such liability. This was the case in *Digby Brown & Co. v. Lyall*, 1995 S.L.T. 932 (O.H.):

Boyd Lyall & Co., a firm of solicitors, granted to D. & Co., another firm of solicitors, a letter of obligation relating to the delivery of a discharge of a standard security. The signature was unqualified, but in the body of the letter the obligation was undertaken "on behalf of our above-named clients".

Held that D. & Co. were not entitled to enforce the letter of obligation: the quoted words were not a mere narrative, and in the context "on behalf of" meant "as agents for".

A contrasting case is *Johnston v. Little*, 1960 S.L.T. 129 (O.H.):

A seller's solicitor granted a letter of obligation in what was regarded as the normal or standard form relating to the delivery of certain writs. There was no qualification either in the signature or in the body of the letter.

The purchaser's solicitor raised an action for implement against the seller's solicitor.

Held that the undertaking in the letter of obligation was an inter-solicitor transaction and that personal liability attached to the seller's solicitor, although his principal was disclosed.

There are four main exceptions to the general rule: **1–149**

(i) The agent may voluntarily undertake personal liability. An **1–150**
illustration is *Stewart v. Shannessy* (1900) 2 F. 1288:

Shannessy was appointed sales manager for a cycle company and also for a tyre company, with authority to appoint travellers at the expense of the respective companies.

Shannessy wrote a letter, on paper headed with the name of the cycle company, to Stewart, appointing Stewart as representative for the two companies on stated terms as to salary and commission. The letter was signed "J.J. Shannessy".

Stewart raised an action against Shannessy for payment of commission. Shannessy maintained that Stewart's only claim was against the two companies.

Held that Shannessy was personally liable, since he had signed the letter in his own name without qualification and without indicating that he did not intend to bind himself as principal.

Similarly, in *Brebner v. Henderson*, 1925 S.C. 643, a director and **1–151**
the secretary of a limited company were held to have undertaken personal liability by signing a promissory note which read: " . . . we promise to pay . . . ". The signatures took the form:

"JAS. R. GORDON, Director
ALEX HENDERSON, Secretary
The Fraserburgh Empire Limited."

The reasoning was that the word "we" referred prima facie ("until the contrary was proved") to the individuals who signed the note, and that the words which followed the signatures were merely descriptive of the positions held by the signatories and did not have the effect of exempting them from personal liability.

1–152 (ii) The agent may incur personal liability by custom of trade.

The case of *Livesey v. Purdom & Sons* (1894) 21 R. 911 was an unsuccessful attempt by an English solicitor, L., to make Scottish solicitors, P. & Sons, liable to pay for an action raised in the English courts, on P. & Sons' instructions, for a named client of P. & Sons. L. relied on the custom in England by which a solicitor employing another solicitor on behalf of a client was liable for the costs of an action, unless he expressly stipulated to the contrary. The court held that L. had failed to prove that that custom extended to the situation where the solicitor conducting the action was employed by a Scots law-agent.

(Since the Solicitors (Scotland) Act 1976 (s. 20) a solicitor employing another solicitor on the business of a client, *whether or not he discloses the client*, has been liable to that other for fees and outlays unless he disclaims liability when the employment takes place. See now the consolidating Solicitors (Scotland) Act 1980 (s. 30).)

In *Stirling Park & Co. v. Digby Brown & Co.*, 1996 S.L.T. (Sh.Ct.) 17 there was held to be a custom of trade making a solicitor, acting for a named client, personally liable for a sheriff officer's fees and expenses:

D. & Co., a firm of solicitors, acted for the successful party in an action for recovery of a debt. S. & Co., a firm of sheriff officers, served a charge on the debtor and carried out a poinding.

D. & Co. paid the sheriff officers their fees and expenses for serving the charge, but did not pay them for carrying out the poinding on the ground that they were acting as agents for a disclosed principal.

Held that S. & Co. had established, in an action brought by them against D. & Co., the existence of a custom, which was certain, uniform, notorious and reasonable, making the solicitors personally liable for the sheriff officers' fees and expenses.

(iii) An agent who can show that he has some interest of his own in the transaction entered into on his principal's behalf with the third party has a title to sue the third party; an instance is *Mackenzie v. Cormack*, 1950 S.C. 183: **1–153**

M., an auctioneer, acting on the instructions of Knight, the owner of Keiss castle, conducted a sale of the furnishings of the castle in the castle.

C. was the successful bidder for a carpet, but, alleging that the carpet had not been delivered to him, refused to pay the price at which it had been knocked down to him.

M. brought an action against C. for the price, and C. pleaded that M., being an agent for a disclosed principal, had no title to sue.

Held that as M. was a mercantile agent with a lien over the price for his charges and commission he had a title to sue C. for the price.

(iv) If the principal is not a legal person, the agent is personally liable to the third party. **1–154**

A familiar example is the contract made by persons acting on behalf of a company not yet registered: the "agents" are personally liable "subject to any agreement to the contrary" (Companies Act 1985, s. 36C introduced by the Companies Act 1989, s. 130(4)). The words "subject to any agreement to the contrary" enable novation to take place when the new company is registered. Contrast *Tinnevelly Sugar Refining Co. Ltd v. Mirrlees, Watson & Yaryan Co. Ltd* (1894) 21 R. 1009 (1–14, above).

The legal position is the same where the principal is a church congregation (*McMeekin v. Easton* (1889) 16 R. 363, in which a minister and two other persons who had signed a promissory note on behalf of a church were held personally liable for payment of the note), or where the principal is a club (*Thomson & Gillespie v. Victoria Eighty Club* (1905) 43 S.L.R. 628 (O.H.), in which the members of the committee, but not the club itself or its ordinary members, were held liable to pay for liquor supplied to the club, and *Cromarty Leasing Ltd v. Turnbull*, 1988 S.L.T. (Sh.Ct) 62, in which Sheriff A.B. Wilkinson held that a defence of agency was irrelevant in an action against the chairman and treasurer of a club for payments due to C. Ltd which had leased equipment to the club). **1–155**

(b) **Agent Contracting "as Agent" for Unnamed Principal**

1–156 Where the agent contracts "as agent" without naming his principal, the same general rule applies as to the situation under (a), above: the third party is made aware that the person with whom he is dealing is only acting on behalf of another person, and so the third party cannot be regarded as having relied on the agent's credit.

1–157 A consequence of the general rule is that if the principal sues the third party on the contract, the third party cannot plead compensation of a debt due to him by the agent:

Matthews v. Auld & Guild (1873) 1 R. 1224: M. instructed Henderson, a stockbroker in Dundee, to sell certain securities and purchase other securities for him.

Henderson employed A. & G., stockbrokers in Glasgow, to carry out the transaction. He did not disclose M.'s name to A. & G., but represented throughout that he was acting for a client.

On completion of the transaction, a balance of about £83 remained in the hands of A. & G.

Shortly afterwards, Henderson absconded, leaving a large balance due by him to A. & G.

A. & G. sought to retain the £83 in their hands against the much larger debt due by Henderson to them.

Held that A. & G. were not entitled to plead compensation, since they had known that Henderson was acting for a client, although the client's name had not been disclosed.

1–158 An agent who has contracted as agent without naming his principal incurs personal liability if he declines to name his principal when requested to do so by the third party:

Gibb v. Cunningham & Robertson, 1925 S.L.T. 608 (O.H.): G. entered into negotiations with C. & R., a firm of solicitors, for the sale to them of 1,000 shares in G.'s family company and of G.'s house. The correspondence showed that C. & R. were acting for others (in fact for the other directors in respect of the shares and for the company itself in respect of the house), but the missives in which the price of £5,000 was agreed did not name any principals.

C. & R. failed to pay the full price, and they were asked to state to G. the names of the principals for whom they had been acting. C. & R. made no answer to the inquiry.

Held that G. was entitled to sue C. & R. for implement of the bargain or, failing implement, for damages.

(c) Agent Contracting Ostensibly as Principal

In this third situation, the third party is unaware of the existence of any principal behind the agent, and looks only to the agent for performance of the contract. **1–159**

The principal may disclose himself, and he has then a title to sue the third party. **1–160**

Bennett v. Inveresk Paper Co. (1891) 18 R. 975: B., a newspaper proprietor in Sydney, Australia, through Poulter & Sons, his London agents, entered into a contract with I. Co. for the supply of paper which was to be shipped to him in Australia. At the time of the making of the contract, the I. Co. did not know of B.

The paper was duly paid for, but on arrival at Sydney was found, owing to bad packing, to be damaged and spoiled.

B. brought an action of damages for breach of contract against I. Co.

Held that B. had a sufficient title to sue the action.

When the third party discovers the identity of the principal, he must elect whether to sue the principal or to sue the agent: he cannot sue both. Election, once made, is final. **1–161**

The best known case on the third party's right of election is *Ferrier v. Dods* (1865) 3 M. 561. In this case the third party was held to have elected to sue the principal. **1–162**

D., an auctioneer, advertised a sale by auction of certain horses, all warranted good workers. At the sale F. bought a mare for £27.

A few days later, F. informed D. that the mare was utterly unsound and unfit for work. D. admitted F.'s right to return the mare if unsound, but he requested F. to return her direct to her former owner, Bathgate, whose name had not been disclosed at the auction.

F., having returned the mare to Bathgate, brought an action both against D. and against Bathgate.

Held that F., by returning the mare to Bathgate, had elected to sue Bathgate, the principal, and the action as against D., the agent, was dismissed.

A case in which the third party was held to have elected to sue the agent was *A.F. Craig & Co. Ltd v. Blackater*, 1923 S.C. 472: **1–163**

C. Ltd supplied two marine boilers to B., shipowners, at a price of £5,900. The full price was not paid, and C. Ltd brought an action against B. for the unpaid balance.

B., averring that the boilers had been disconform to contract, brought a counter-action for over £9,000 as damages for breach of contract.

The two actions were conjoined, and in the course of the proof it transpired that B. were not the registered owners, but only the managing owners, of the ship in question, and that the registered owners were the Cadeby Steamship Co. Ltd.

C. Ltd, as defenders in the counter-action, then pleaded that B. had no title to sue, and had sustained no loss through any breach of contract on C. Ltd's part.

Held that, by prosecuting their own action to decree, C. Ltd had elected to treat B. as their debtors in the contract, and, therefore, that B. were entitled to counter-claim for damages.

Lord Anderson, explaining the third party's right of election, said (at p. 486): "When the two actions were raised the principals were undisclosed. It was only during the course of the proof of the conjoined actions that it was casually divulged that the Cadeby Steamship Co. were the principals in the contract. When this fact became known to Messrs Craig they were, in my opinion, put to their election. They had to determine whether or not they would proceed to decree against Messrs Blackater or against their true debtors the Cadeby Co. . . . There would have been no difficulty, by our procedure, in substituting the one party for the other in both actions. . . . But no proposal to this effect was made by Messrs Craig. They elected to continue the action in which they were pursuers against the agents, but in the counter-action they declined to submit themselves to a decree for damages in respect of their breach of contract. . . . This is plainly inequitable; it is, moreover, a result which is against all legal principle and which is supported by no decided case."

1–164 This case was followed in *James Laidlaw and Sons Ltd v. Griffin*, 1968 S.L.T. 278.

L. Ltd, building contractors, entered into a contract with G. for certain structural work at the G. Hotel, which was owned by G. Ltd. In making the contract G. was acting as agent for G. Ltd, of which he was a director, but the agency was not then made known to L. Ltd.

The contract provided that L. Ltd was to be responsible for all damage to "property of employer", and that "employer" denoted G.

L. Ltd came to know that G. had been acting on behalf of G. Ltd.

L. Ltd raised an action against G. for payment of sums certified as due for works executed under the contract, and G. counterclaimed on the ground that L. Ltd had caused serious damage to the hotel. L. Ltd argued that the only damage claimable under the contract was damage to G.'s property and the hotel did not belong to G., but to G. Ltd.

Held that, as L. Ltd had elected to sue G. as agent for G. Ltd, G., in his capacity as agent for G. Ltd, was entitled to counterclaim for the damage to the hotel.

For the purposes of election, the sustaining of a claim in a sequestration has the same effect as judgment in an action: **1–165**

David Logan & Son Ltd and Liquidator v. Schuldt (1903) 10 S.L.T. 598 (O.H.): Gans & Sell, steamship brokers in Glasgow, as agents of S., entered into two charterparties with L. for the conveyance of two cargoes of coal from Methil to the continent.

L. sued S. for payment.

S., however, averred that he had paid Gans & Sell, and that L. had claimed in the sequestration of Gans & Sell and been paid a dividend.

Held that L. had elected to sue the agents by receiving a dividend in the agents' sequestration.

(d) Breach of Warranty of Authority

Where an agent, contracting as agent, exceeds both his actual and his ostensible authority, no binding relationship arises between the principal and the third party unless the principal chooses to ratify the agent's unauthorised actings. **1–166**

The third party is not entitled to sue the authorised agent *on the contract* which the agent purported to make between the principal and the third party, but has the right to sue the agent on the basis of a collateral contract incorporating an implied undertaking on the agent's part that he had the necessary authority to form a binding relationship between the third party and the principal. **1–167**

If the agent's misrepresentation of his authority was fraudulent, the agent is liable to the third party in damages for fraud. If the agent's misrepresentation was innocent (*i.e.* if he himself really believed that he did have the necessary authority), he is liable to **1–168** the third party in damages for breach of warranty of authority, since the law regards him as having impliedly "warranted" (*i.e.* guaranteed) to the third party that he did have the necessary authority. The measure of damages for breach of warranty of authority is the loss sustained by the third party as a result of his not having a binding relationship with the principal.

1–169 The best-known Scottish case on this topic is *Anderson v. Croall & Sons Ltd* (1903) 6 F. 153:

At the Musselburgh Race Meeting held in October 1902, a mare which had come second in a race was, by an innocent mistake, auctioned by C. Ltd. The successful bidder was A., and the price £36.15s.

A. paid the price and received a delivery-order, but the owner refused to give delivery of the mare, on the ground that the sale had been wholly unauthorised by him.

In May 1903, the mare was sold by auction at York for 70 guineas.

Held that, since an auctioneer, in common with other agents, warrants his authority, A. was entitled to damages from C. Ltd, the sum awarded (£26.5s.) being based on the difference between the two auction prices with a deduction for cost of keep and transit. In addition, A. was entitled to the return of the purchase-price which he had paid to C. Ltd.

1–170 In that case A. had been deprived, through the auctioneer's breach of warranty of authority, of a bargain with the principal which would have given A. possession of a mare worth more than he was paying for her. If, however, it is shown that the third party claiming damages for breach of warranty of authority would have been in no better position even if the contract had been enforceable against the principal, then no damages are awarded other than possibly nominal damages such as can be claimed for the infringement of any legal right. An illustration is *Irving v. Burns*, 1915 S.C. 260:

B., the secretary of the Langside Picture House Ltd, falsely professing that he had the authority of the directors, accepted an offer made by I. for the execution of certain plumber-work in connection with a hall or theatre which the company was about to erect.

After the work had been executed and I. had ascertained that the contract was in fact not binding on the company, I. brought an action against B. for damages for breach of warranty of authority. In this action I. averred that the company had no assets.

Held that since it appeared from this averment that I. would have been in no better position if the contract had bound the company, he had suffered no loss from (and so could recover no damages for) B.'s breach of warranty.

"The defender, no doubt, warranted his authority to contract on behalf of the company. If he had in fact had authority the company would have been bound; but as it has no assets the damage arising from a breach of warranty is nil" (*per* Lord Salvesen at p. 269).

VII TERMINATION OF THE RELATIONSHIP

Agency may be terminated in the following ways: **1–171**

(a) by completion of the transaction or expiry of time;
(b) by mutual agreement;
(c) by revocation by the principal;
(d) by renunciation by the agent; and
(e) by frustration.

(a) Completion of Transaction or Expiry of Time

Agency is brought to an end by completion of the transaction or expiry of the time for which it was created. **1–172**

There is an instance of termination by expiry of time in *Brenan v. Campbell's Trustees* (1898) 25 R. 423: **1–173**

B., a civil engineer and architect with a practice in Oban, was engaged by C. to be factor on C.'s estate for four years from Martinmas 1890 on the express condition that B. should take C.'s stepson as an apprentice for four years from that date.

In October 1894, B. was informed that his services as factor would not be required on C.'s estate after Martinmas 1894.

B., claiming that he was entitled to six months' notice of termination of his factory, raised an action against C. for six months' pay in lieu of notice.

Held that, as B. was not a servant but a professional man employed by a number of clients, he was not entitled to notice of termination of his employment, and further that the special contract limited the period of his factory to four years.

For an implied agency terminated by lapse of time and material change in circumstances see *Ferguson and Lillie v. Stephen* (1864) 2 M. 804 (1–18, above). **1–174**

(b) Mutual Agreement

1–175 Principal and agent may agree that the agency is to be at an end.

1–176 In some situations, however, this does not take effect until third parties are properly notified, because, though the agent's actual authority is at an end, he may have ostensible authority: *e.g.* in partnership a retiring partner's authority is not terminated effectively unless notice of the retirement is given in the *Edinburgh Gazette* and to individual customers of the firm (Partnership Act 1890, s. 36(1) and (2)).

(c) Revocation by Principal

1–177 Some agencies are irrevocable by the principal without the agent's consent. This is so where the authority has been given to enable the agent to do something in his own interest. The agent is then said to have "a procuratory *in rem suam* ('for his own benefit')" (corresponding to "an authority coupled with an interest" in English law).

1–178 An illustration of a procuratory *in rem suam* is *Premier Briquette Co. Ltd v. Gray*, 1922 S.C. 329, a case concerned with an underwriting contract and a sub-underwriting contract relating to shares in a new company, P. Ltd. The purpose of the sub-underwriting contract was to lessen the burden of the shares which might require to be taken up by the underwriter.

G., the sub-underwriter, sent his application for shares, which was addressed to P. Ltd, to the underwriter, M. Ltd, along with a letter stating that the contract and application were irrevocable. M. Ltd passed on G.'s application to P. Ltd and shares were allotted by P. Ltd to G. as a result.

Held that the allotment to G. was valid, since neither the sub-underwriting contract nor the application could have been revoked by G.

The effect of the transaction was that G. as principal had conferred on M. Ltd as agent an irrevocable authority, which was for the benefit of M. Ltd, to apply to P. Ltd for the shares allotted.

1–179 Formerly, under the common law and under section 53(2) of the Bills of Exchange Act 1882 (a subsection which gave effect to the common law and applied only to Scotland) a procuratory *in rem suam* arose where a cheque was presented by its holder to the bank on which it was drawn and the bank had insufficient funds to meet the cheque.

An illustration is *British Linen Co. Bank v. Carruthers and Ferguson* (1883) 10 R. 923, a case decided under the common law:

The holder of a cheque for £161, which had been granted to him in payment of the price of sheep, was refused payment by the drawer's bank because the drawer had no more than £136 in his current account. However, the presentation of the cheque to the bank was held to have operated as an assignation in favour of the holder of the cheque of the funds actually in the account, with the result that the holder of the cheque was entitled to about £136 in the drawer's sequestration.

The holder of the cheque was regarded as having a procuratory *in rem suam* in this case, as was explained by Lord President Inglis (at p. 926):

"A cheque is nothing more than a mandate to the mandatary to go to the bank and get the money. The mandate may be granted for various causes, and the mandatary may be merely the hand of the mandant, to do for him what he might have done for himself. But when a cheque is granted for value then the case is very different. It is a bare procuratory (to use the language of the older law), when it is granted gratuitously, but when it is granted for value it is a procuratory *in rem suam*, which is just one of the definitions of an assignation. Therefore I cannot doubt that this cheque, being granted for onerous causes, was an assignation, and if that is so undoubtedly the demand for payment was a good intimation of it."

Section 11 of the Law Reform (Miscellaneous Provisions) (Scotland) Act 1985 altered the law. The effect of the alteration is that in such circumstances as arose in *British Linen Co. Bank v. Carruthers and Ferguson* the bank would be treated as having no funds at all available for payment of the cheque, and so there would be no assignation of the £136 to the holder of the cheque and no procuratory *in rem suam*.

The alteration affects only cheques and not other bills of exchange. The principle applicable to the latter is that presentment of the bill operates as an assignation of funds in favour of the payee *provided* the drawee has funds available to make payment.

Where it is open to a principal to revoke an agent's authority, **1–180**
the principal must give proper notice to third parties if he wishes to avoid the possibility that they may hold him liable on the ground of the agent's ostensible authority.

1–181 Moreover, the principal may be liable in damages to the agent if the revocation amounts to a breach of a term, express or implied, of the contract of agency between principal and agent. An instance is *Galbraith & Moorhead v. Arethusa Ship Co. Ltd* (1896) 23 R. 1011:

G. & Co., shipbrokers, offered to take £500 in shares in the "A." Ship Co. Ltd, provided that they were appointed sole chartering brokers for the "A." The offer was accepted.

G. & Co. took the shares, and the agreement was acted on for several years. There was then a change in the management, and G. & Co., averring that the "A." Ship Co. Ltd was no longer employing them as sole chartering brokers, raised an action against the company for £500 damages.

Held that the agreement was not terminable at the pleasure of the company.

The underlying reason for the decision, as expressed by Lord Adam (at p. 1015) was as follows: "This case depends solely upon the construction of the agreement . . . by which the pursuers were appointed sole chartering brokers for the 'Arethusa,' and the question is, whether that agreement could be determined by the defenders on reasonable notice, or on reasonable cause only. Now, it will be observed that the pursuers paid for the appointment of sole charterer's brokers, and the consideration was their taking £500 in shares of the company, which it is not disputed they did. I have great difficulty in holding that an agreement for which consideration had been thus given could be terminated at will by the other contracting party.

1–182 By way of contrast, there were in *Walker v. Somerville* (1837) 16 S. 217 circumstances in which authority was held to be revocable at pleasure provided the principal indemnified the agent for his trouble and expenses:

W. by letter promised to S. 15 per cent of any sums which S. might recover by means of an action against W.'s father.

A summons was raised against W.'s father, but within two months of the date of the letter, W. and his father made an agreement by which an annuity was settled on W., and his claims against his father were discharged.

S. claimed that W. had had no power to settle the action to the prejudice of the stipulations in S.'s favour in the letter.

Held that the nature of the agreement between W. and S. was such that W. had been entitled to recall it at pleasure, subject to any claims for disbursement and remuneration for trouble which S. could prove.

(d) Renunciation by Agent

The agent may renounce his agency. **1–183**

The renunciation will in some situations be a breach of the **1–184** contract of agency between principal and agent, making the agent liable in damages to the principal.

(e) Frustration

Frustration operates in agency as in the general law of contract: *e.g.* **1–185** if property which the agent is employed to sell is accidentally destroyed, that amounts to *rei interitus* ("destruction of the subject-matter"), which brings the contract of agency to an end.

Special mention may be made of: **1–186**

(i) death of principal or agent;
(ii) bankruptcy of principal or agent;
(iii) insanity of principal or agent; and
(iv) discontinuance of the principal's business.

(i) *Death of Principal or Agent*

The death of the principal normally terminates the agency. **1–187**

Even the death of one of several principals was held to have **1–188** terminated the agent's authority in *Life Association of Scotland v. Douglas* (1886) 13 R. 910:

A bond and disposition in security had been granted to the Life Association of Scotland by the Athole Hydropathic Co. Ltd and the directors of that company. The deed had been signed by the several granters of it on different dates, between May 11 and July 23. One of the directors, D., who had signed on May 11, died on July 4. The secretary of the company continued to hold the deed until, after it had been signed by all the granters, it was delivered to the Life Association on July 24 in exchange for the sum advanced.

There was failure to pay the full sum in the bond, and the Life Association raised an action against certain of the co-obligants, including D.'s executor.

Held that the executor was not liable, because the implied authority given by D. for delivery of the deed once all the signatures had been obtained had fallen by D.'s death.

1–189 On the other hand, *Campbell v. Anderson* (1829) 3 W. & S. 384 is a departure from the normal rule: a factor on a landed estate who had contracted in the *bona fide* belief that his principal, who had died abroad, was still alive was held to have bound his principal and not to be personally liable on a bill of exchange which he had drawn expressly as agent. The authority of this House of Lords decision may, however, have diminished somewhat owing to the passage of time and the improvement in communications; in addition, the case appears to be contrary to the generally accepted rule that death is a public fact of which no notice need be given.

1–190 The death of the agent likewise normally brings the agency to an end. The general rule that an agent must act in person and not delegate prevents the agent's representatives from taking the deceased's place in the agency.

(ii) *Bankruptcy of Principal or Agent*

1–191 Agency is terminated by the bankruptcy of the principal. An instance is *McKenzie v. Campbell* (1894) 21 R. 904:

Fraser, a corn-factor, had been arrested on various charges of forgery. From prison he wrote to C., a law-agent, asking him to act in his defence. He also delivered to C. about £285, authorising him to use the money for the defence proceedings and for paying out sums as directed by Fraser himself.

A few days later, on October 25, Fraser's estates were sequestrated, and McK., the trustee, called on C. to account for his transactions with Fraser's money.

On December 27, Fraser pleaded guilty and was sentenced.

According to C.'s account, the sum which he had received from Fraser had been more than exhausted by the cost of the defence proceedings coupled with payments made on Fraser's directions.

Held that C.'s agency had fallen by Fraser's sequestration, and that C. was therefore bound to account to McK. for all sums belonging to Fraser in his hands as at October 25.

1–192 Similarly, in *Dickson v. Nicholson* (1855) 17 D. 1011, the authority of a commercial traveller was held to have terminated when his firm stopped payment, and so the traveller was not entitled, in the knowledge of the firm's insolvency, to collect the firm's money from customers and retain it in payment of the remuneration due to himself by the firm.

The bankruptcy of the agent also terminates the agency. Because of the *delectus personae* ("choice of person") involved in the contract of agency between principal and agent, the trustee in bankruptcy is not entitled to adopt the agency. A new agreement to which the principal, the agent and the trustee would be parties could enable the bankrupt agent to continue his work as agent. **1–193**

Bankruptcy, like death, is regarded as a public fact of which no notice need be given. **1–194**

(iii) *Insanity of Principal or Agent*

The effect of a principal's prolonged insanity was fully considered in the early case of *Pollok v. Paterson*, 10 Dec. 1811, F.C., though the question actually before the court for decision was whether or not a sequestration of an insane person should be recalled. **1–195**

David Paterson had carried on business in Edinburgh for many years as a banker and insurance broker. In 1805, on going to London, he granted a procuration in favour of his son, John Paterson, empowering John to manage his affairs in his absence.

When in London, David became insane, and returned to reside at home in Scotland. Visitors of the family knew of his insanity, but no public notice was taken of it until 1811.

Meantime John carried on business on his father's account, making use of the procuration.

In 1809 John enlarged the sphere of his operations and entered into several speculations with a merchant Kerr, but in 1810 the concern with Kerr became bankrupt.

Pollok, the holder of a bill of exchange which had been accepted by John per procuration of David, claimed payment from David.

A petition was presented and granted for David's sequestration, and it was with the recall of this sequestration that the case was directly concerned.

The argument put forward for David's family was that the agency of John had been terminated at the commencement of David's insanity. The argument on the other side was that insanity did not of itself terminate an agency: publication of the insanity was required for that, and here there had been no publication.

The views expressed by the judges were to the general effect that the principal's insanity did not of itself terminate an agency, and that a third party who was bona fide ("in good faith", *i.e.* unaware of the principal's insanity) was entitled to regard the agent as still having authority until notification of the insanity had been given.

In the slightly later case of *Wink v. Mortimer* (1849) 11 D. 995 the court held that a principal's temporary insanity had not terminated the agency. The agent had continued to act as agent during a period when the principal was confined to a lunatic asylum, and later, after the principal had regained his sanity and had had his estates sequestrated, the agent was held to be entitled to claim in the sequestration for the amount of his business account, part of which related to the few weeks of the principal's temporary insanity.

1–196 The unsatisfactory doubt about the effect of a principal's supervening insanity led to the enactment of section 71 of the Law Reform (Miscellaneous Provisions) (Scotland) Act 1990. This provides that any rule of law by which a factory and commission or power of attorney ceases to have effect in the event of the mental incapacity of the granter is not to apply to a factory and commission or power of attorney granted on or after the date when section 71 came into force, which, by section 75(3)(b) of the Act, was January 1, 1991.

The provision is limited to formal appointments of an agent (by a factory and commission or power of attorney), and does not apply retrospectively to appointments made before the section came into force.

"Mental incapacity" means that a person is incapable of managing his property and affairs by reason of mental disorder within the meaning of section 1 of the Mental Health (Scotland) Act 1984.

Parallel, but more elaborate, provisions apply in England under the Enduring Powers of Attorney Act 1985.

1–197 Insanity of the agent terminates the agency.

(iv) *Discontinuance of Principal's Business*

1–198 If the principal discontinues the business in which the agent is engaged, the agency is terminated and the agent is not entitled to damages for breach of contract unless he can show that it was an express or implied term of the agency that the principal should continue the business for a specified period. Illustrative cases include the three following:

1–199 (1) *Patmore & Co. v. B. Cannon & Co. Ltd* (1892) 19 R. 1004: P. & Co., warehousemen, agents and merchants of Glasgow and

Leith, agreed with C. Ltd, of Lincoln, to act as C. Ltd's agents in Scotland for the sale of goods manufactured by C. Ltd, consisting of leather goods, dip and glue, for a period of five years from October 1891.

In January 1892 C. Ltd intimated to P. & Co. its intention to give up its fancy leather trade.

Held that P. & Co. were not entitled to damages for breach of contract, because C. Ltd had not in the agreement bound itself to carry on its business, or any part of it, for five years, or for any other period, simply for the benefit of P. & Co.

Reference was made in the opinions in this case to the decision **1–200**
of the House of Lords in the English case *Rhodes v. Forwood* (1876) 1 App. Cas. 256, in which a colliery owner, who had appointed an agent on a commission basis for seven years for the sale of coal from the colliery, was entitled, when four years later he sold the colliery, to refuse to pay further commission to the agent, the reason being that no term could be implied into the contract that the owner would not sell the colliery and so disable himself from supplying the agent with the coal for sale.

(2) *London, Leith, Edinburgh and Glasgow Shipping Co. v.* **1–201**
Ferguson (1850) 13 D. 51: In 1827 F. had been appointed agent at Greenock for the L. Shipping Co., and was paid by a commission on his transactions. He continued to hold the appointment until April 1847, when the L. Shipping Co. resolved to discontinue its trade at Greenock.

F. claimed commission up to April 1848 on the ground that it had been understood between the parties that his engagement was a yearly one and that there was a custom of trade to that effect.

Held that F., being an agent, had not been engaged from year to year as a servant would have been, and that the L. Shipping Co. was entitled to discontinue its trade whenever it saw fit, without giving prior notice or paying compensation to F.

(3) *S.S. "State of California" Co. Ltd v. Moore* (1895) 22 R. 562: **1–202**
The State Steamship Co. Ltd had for many years carried on a regular series of sailings between Glasgow and New York.

In 1889 certain of the shareholders agreed to form a new company, C. Ltd, for the purpose of acquiring a new steamer of modern type, and the two companies entered into an agreement by which the State Steamship Co. Ltd would for 10 years from the launching of the new steamer give that steamer her regular turn in the transatlantic service along with other steamers.

About a month after the launching of the new steamer in 1891, the State Steamship Co. Ltd passed a resolution for winding up.

C. Ltd claimed damages from the liquidator.

Held that the agreement between the two companies had to be interpreted as being subject to an implied condition that it was to last only so long as the State Steamship Co. Ltd carried on its business, and that C. Ltd was therefore not entitled to damages for breach of contract.

Further Reading

Gloag and Henderson, *The Law of Scotland*, Chapter 22

David M. Walker, *Principles of Scottish Private Law*, Volume II, Chapters 4.7 (part) and 4.14

David M. Walker, *The law of Contracts and related obligations in Scotland*, (3rd ed., 1995, T. & T. Clark) Chapters 6 and 29

The Laws of Scotland: Stair Memorial Encyclopaedia, Volume 1, Title *Agency and Mandate* by Robin G. McEwan

E. B. S. Markesinis and R. J. C. Munday, *An Outline of the Law of Agency* (3rd ed., 1992, Butterworths)

E. G. H. L. Fridman, *The Law of Agency* (7th ed., 1996, Butterworths)

E. *Bowstead on Agency*, 16th ed. by F. M. B. Reynolds (1996, Sweet & Maxwell)

Enid A. Marshall, *Scottish Cases on Agency* (1980, W. Green)

A. F. Phillips, "Agency: Elections and Reflections", 1993 J.R. 133

Ronald A. J. Herd, "The Commercial Agents (Council Directive) Regulations 1993", 1994 S.L.T. (News) 357

John M. Schmidt, "The Commercial Agents Regulations—Some Unfinished Business", 1996 S.L.T. (News) 13

Gordon Junor, "The Estate Agent's Commission: When is an Introduction not an Introduction?" [1996] 64 S.L.G. 60

Chapter 2

PARTNERSHIP

	Para.
Introduction	2–01
I Definition of Partnership	2–12
Joint Adventure	2–16
II Constitution of Partnership	2–18
Rules for Determining Existence of Partnership	2–20
(a) Joint or Common Property or Tenancy, or Part Ownership	2–21
(b) Gross Returns	2–23
(c) Profits	2–25
III Separate *Persona* of the Firm	2–30
(a) Firm as Debtor or Creditor to Partners	2–34
(b) Contracts	2–35
(c) Delicts	2–38
(d) Property	2–41
(e) Compensation	2–44
(f) Bankruptcy	2–46
IV Relations of Partners to Persons Dealing With Them	2–48
(a) Liability for a Firm's Debts	2–50
Authority of Partners and Others to Bind the Firm	2–54
Implied mandate of partners	2–54
Acts on firm's behalf	2–61
Agreed restriction on partner's authority	2–63
Liability of the Firm for Wrongs	2–65
Misapplication by partner of third party's money or property	2–71
Improper employment of trust-property for partnership purposes	2–72
Liability of Incoming Partner	2–73
Liability of Retired Partner	2–80
(i) Debts incurred before retirement	2–81
(ii) Debts incurred after retirement	2–83
Liability by "Holding Out"	2–89
(b) Effect of Change in a Firm on Contracts	2–92
V Relations of Partners to One Another	2–95
Partnership Property	2–98
Rights of Partners	2–104
Partnership at Will	2–106
Fiduciary Character of Partnership	2–113
(a) Duty to Render Accounts and Information (s. 28)	2–114
(b) Accountability for Private Profits (s. 29)	2–116
(c) Duty not to Compete with Firm (s. 30)	2–118
Assignation of Share in Partnership	2–123
VI Termination of Partnership	2–126
(a) Rescission	2–130
(b) Dissolution	2–133
Grounds of Dissolution	2–134
(i) Expiration or notice (s. 32)	2–135
(ii) Death or bankruptcy (s. 33)	2–136
(iii) Illegality (s. 34)	2–139
(iv) Order of the court (s. 35)	2–141
Winding Up	2–142
(i) Right of partners to notify dissolution (s. 37)	2–150
(ii) Continuing authority of partners for purposes of winding up (s. 38)	2–151
(iii) Rights of partners as to application of partnership property (s. 39)	2–155
(iv) Apportionment of premium where partnership prematurely dissolved (s. 40)	2–156
(v) Right of outgoing partner in certain cases to share profits made after dissolution (s. 42)	2–157
(vi) Distribution of assets on final settlement of accounts (s. 44)	2–161
VII Limited Partnerships Act 1907	2–162
(a) Management	2–169
(b) Dissolution	2–171
(c) Winding Up	2–172
(d) Rules Applicable between the Partners	2–175
VIII Business Names Act 1985	2–177
(a) Control of Business Names	2–179
(b) Disclosure of Names of Persons Using Business Names	2–185
IX Goodwill	2–189

INTRODUCTION

2–01 THE main principles of the law of partnership are to be found in the Partnership Act 1890, an Act which, for the most part, applies equally to England and Scotland. Though sometimes described as a codifying Act, it is not a complete code of partnership law (*e.g.* it does not deal with goodwill or bankruptcy). Of the aspects of partnership law which are to be found in other statutes, specially noteworthy are the Limited Partnerships Act 1907 and the Business Names Act 1985. In addition, the Partnerships and Unlimited Companies (Accounts) Regulations 1993 (S.I. 1993 No. 1820), made to implement an E.C. Council Directive (Dir. 90/605), had the effect of removing from "qualifying partnerships" the confidentiality of accounts which had hitherto been one of the main attractions of partnerships in comparison with limited companies. The "qualifying partnerships" include those in which each member is a limited company or an unlimited company or a Scottish firm, each of whose members is a limited company.

2–02 In this chapter references to "the Act" are to the Partnership Act 1890 except where the context indicates otherwise.

2–03 The Act did not substantially alter the common law. Therefore, cases decided before 1890 may be used to illustrate the principles embodied in the Act.

2–04 Further, the Act is itself a comparatively short and simple one, and, to cover situations for which no express provision has been made, it provides that the rules of the common law applicable to partnership continue in force except so far as they are inconsistent with the express provisions of the Act (s. 46).

2–05 A partnership (or "firm") governed by the Partnership Act 1890 must be distinguished from that other important form of business organisation—the limited company registered under the Companies Acts. For legal purposes, the latter is not a "firm"—a term which, despite its colloquial use, should be reserved for a partnership. Company law is dealt with in Chapter 3, below.

2–06 The most striking practical difference between a partnership and a limited company is that the members of a partnership (with the partial exception of a limited partnership) are liable personally without any limitation of liability for the firm's debts, whereas the members of a limited company are liable only for the amount, if any, which is unpaid on their shares.

Further, the liability of the individual partners is "joint and several", so that a creditor of the firm whose debt has not been satisfied by the firm may exact full payment of the debt from any one partner, who will then be left to reimburse himself, as best he may, by claiming a pro rata ("proportionate") amount from his copartners. Creditors of a limited company, on the other hand, have no right to claim payment from individual shareholders. **2–07**

The law of partnership draws major principles from the law of agency (the partners being agents for their firm) and from the law of cautionry (the partners guaranteeing, *i.e.* being in the position of cautioners for, the firm's debts). **2–08**

Other prominent features are the fiduciary nature of the relationship between the partners (evident in the rules against secret competition with the firm's business) and the element of *delectus personae* ("choice of person"), which prevents a person from being introduced as a partner without the consent of all existing partners and enables the firm to be dissolved by notice in certain circumstances under section 32 or by the court as provided for by section 35. **2–09**

Following the arrangements of the Act, the subject-matter of this chapter comes under these headings: **2–10**

I. Definition of partnership;
II. Constitution of partnership;
III. Separate *persona* ("personality") of the firm;
IV. Relations of partners to persons dealing with them;
V. Relations of partners to one another; and
VI. Termination of partnership.

There then follow three additional sections: **2–11**

VII. Limited Partnerships Act 1907;
VIII. Business Names Act 1985; and
IX. Goodwill.

I DEFINITION OF PARTNERSHIP

"Partnership" is defined in section 1(1) of the Act as "the relation which subsists between persons carrying on a business in common with a view of profit". By section 45 of the Act the expression "business" includes every trade, occupation or profession. **2–12**

If left unqualified, this definition in section 1(1) would be too wide: in particular, it would be wide enough to cover the many **2–13** limited companies in which persons carry on business in common with a view of profit. Section 1(2) therefore restricts the definition quoted above by providing that the relation between members of any company or association which is:

(a) registered as a company under one of the Companies Acts; or

(b) formed or incorporated by or under any other Act of Parliament or letters patent or royal charter; or

(c) a company engaged in working mines in the Stannaries (a reference to a special jurisdiction formerly applicable to tin mines in Devon and Cornwall):

is not a partnership for the purposes of the Act.

2–14 From the definition it is apparent that there must be at least two persons before there can be a partnership. A sole trader, therefore, even though he may be trading under a name which suggests that he has business associates (*e.g.* "Andrew Brown & Sons"), is not a partnership.

2–15 An upper limit on the number of partners in a partnership is imposed by the Companies Act 1985 (s. 716): the maximum number of partners is 20, but partnerships of solicitors, of accountants and of members of a recognised stock exchange are exempt from this restriction, and the Department of Trade and Industry has power by statutory instrument to extend the exemption to partnerships formed for other specified purposes. This power has been widely exercised by the making of several Partnerships (Unrestricted Size) Regulations from time to time (*e.g.* the Partnerships (Unrestricted Size) No. 11 Regulations 1996 (S.I. 1996 No. 262) which extend the exemption to partnerships formed for the purpose of carrying on practice as actuaries provided that not less than three-quarters of the partners are either Fellows of the Institute of Actuaries or Fellows of the Faculty of Actuaries). Where the number of persons carrying on the business exceeds 20 and no exemption applies, a company must be formed, the usual procedure being registration under the Companies Acts.

Joint Adventure

2–16 The term "joint adventure" is not defined in the Act. A joint adventure may be described as a partnership of a transient nature. It is entered into for a single "adventure" or undertaking, and is dissolved by the termination of that adventure or undertaking (s. 32).

An instance of a joint adventure occurs in *Mair v. Wood*, 1948 S.C. 83 (see 2–40, below): of the five partners in that joint adventure one contributed the fishing boat and its gear, while the other four contributed their services as crew. **2–17**

Lord President Cooper said (at p. 86): "A joint adventure is simply a species of the genus partnership, differentiated by its limited purpose and duration (which necessarily affect the extent of the rights and liabilities flowing from the relationship), but in all other essential respects indistinguishable from any other partnership."

II CONSTITUTION OF PARTNERSHIP

The contract out of which partnership arises is a "consensual" contract, *i.e.* a contract which may be formed by mere agreement, without writing. Partnership may, therefore, be constituted by a written document ("a contract of copartnery"), or by an oral agreement, or by facts and circumstances (*e.g.* from the fact that X, Y and Z are found to be carrying on a business together and sharing its profits and losses). **2–18**

The question as to whether or not a partnership exists may arise either between the alleged partners or between the alleged partners and a "third party" (an outsider). In the first of these situations, the question is decided by discovering what the intention of the alleged partners was. Where, on the other hand, there is a third party involved, he will usually be attempting to establish that there was a partnership so that he can obtain payment of a debt; in that event the question is decided by considering whether the alleged partners held themselves out to be in partnership, and the court may decide that, even where the alleged partners expressly agreed with one another that they were not to be held to be partners, a partnership was nevertheless constituted. Such a situation came before the court in *Stewart v. Buchanan* (1903) 6 F. 15: **2–19**

Buchanan let business premises to Saunders, and supplied fittings for the premises and capital for the carrying on of the business. An agreement between Buchanan and Saunders provided that Buchanan was not to "be or be held to be a partner in the said business, or liable for its debts and obligations".

Stewart, a wine merchant, brought an action against the alleged partnership and against Saunders and Buchanan for payment of a sum for goods supplied to the business.

Held that Buchanan was liable, the agreement being regarded as merely a device to enable him to carry on the business without incurring liability for its debts.

Rules for Determining Existence of Partnership

2–20 By section 2 of the Act, in determining whether a partnership does or does not exist regard must be had to certain rules. These rules substantially re-enact an Act of 1865 on the law of partnership, known as "Bovill's Act", and are as follows:

(a) *Joint or Common Property or Tenancy, or Part Ownership*

2–21 Joint tenancy, tenancy in common, joint property, common property, or part ownership does not of itself create a partnership, whether the tenants or owners do or do not share any profits made by the use of the property.

2–22 *Sharpe v. Carswell*, 1910 S.C. 391: S. owned 10 sixty-fourth shares of the schooner "Dolphin", and was employed as its master at a fixed remuneration.

S. died as a result of injuries sustained on board while he was in the course of his employment, and his widow claimed compensation under the Workmen's Compensation Act 1906 on the ground that he had been a "workman" in the sense of that Act.

Held that S. had been a "workman", and that the fact that he had been a part owner of the schooner had not made him a partner in its trading.

(b) *Gross Returns*

2–23 The sharing of gross returns does not of itself create a partnership, whether the persons sharing the returns have or have not a joint or common right or interest in any property from which the returns are derived.

2–24 *Clark v. G.R. & W. Jamieson*, 1909 S.C. 132: C. was one of two men engaged to work a small cargo boat in Shetland. His remuneration was a share of the gross earnings of the boat.

C. was drowned by an accident arising out of and in the course of his employment, and when his mother and sister claimed compensation under the Workmen's Compensation Act 1906, the question which the court had to decide was: "Had C. been a 'workman' within the meaning of the Act?"

Held that C. had been a "workman", and not a partner in a joint adventure.

(c) *Profits*

In this rule the word "profits" means net profits, *i.e.* the amount remaining after the expenses of the business have been deducted from the gross returns. **2–25**

The rule is that the receipt by a person of a share of the profits of a business is prima facie evidence that he is a partner in the business, *i.e.* the sharing of net profits is not conclusive evidence of the existence of a partnership but is evidence of its existence unless and until the contrary is proved. **2–26**

Formerly at common law the sharing of profits was regarded as conclusive evidence of partnership, but the decision of the House of Lords in the English case of *Cox v. Hickman* (1860) 8 H.L.C. 268; 11 E.R. 431, established the rule of the common law as being that parties may share profits without necessarily being partners. In that case creditors who were carrying on their bankrupt debtors' business and dividing the net profits amongst themselves in payment of the debts due to them were held not to be partners. **2–27**

In accordance with the decision in *Cox v. Hickman*, the Act provides that the receipt of a share of the profits, or of a payment contingent on (*i.e.* dependent on) or varying with the profits of a business, does not of itself make the recipient a partner in the business. Five situations are then specified illustrating this point: **2–28**

(i) Receipt by a person of a debt by instalments out of the accruing profits of a business does not of itself make him a partner in the business or liable as such.

(ii) A contract for the remuneration of a servant or agent of a person engaged in a business by a share of the profits of the business does not of itself make the servant or agent a partner in the business or liable as such.

(iii) A deceased partner's widow or child who receives as an annuity a portion of the profits made in the business in which the deceased person was a partner is not, merely because of the annuity, a partner in the business or liable as such.

(iv) Where money is lent to a person engaged in a business on a contract that the lender is to receive a rate of interest varying with the profits or is to receive a share of the profits, the lender is not, merely on that account, a partner in the business or liable as such, but so close is the relationship to partnership in this instance that the contract must be in writing and signed by or on behalf of all the parties to it; otherwise the lender would be held to be a partner.

(v) A person who has sold the goodwill of a business and receives as payment a portion of the profits is not, merely on that account, a partner in the business or liable as such.

2–29 With reference to situations (iv) and (v), if the person engaged in the business or the person who has purchased the goodwill becomes bankrupt, the lender or the seller of the goodwill respectively is treated as a postponed creditor, *i.e.* he will not receive any of his loan or any part of the price for the goodwill until the ordinary creditors of the bankrupt have been paid in full (which is unlikely to be the case) (s. 3).

III SEPARATE *PERSONA* OF THE FIRM

2–30 Section 4(1) of the Act provides that persons who have entered into partnership with one another are called collectively a firm, and the name under which their business is carried on is called the firm-name.

2–31 Section 4(2), which applies to Scotland only, preserves a fundamental principle of the common law of partnership in Scotland dating from the seventeenth century: "In Scotland a firm is a legal person distinct from the partners of whom it is composed." It is this provision which is the source of most of the distinctive rules in the Scots law of partnership.

2–32 A firm is not, however, a full corporation, as a limited company is. A firm has no royal charter, nor has it been incorporated by special Act of Parliament or registered under the Companies Acts. It may be formed and dissolved by mere agreement of its members, and, unless there is agreement to the contrary, is dissolved by the death or bankruptcy of any partner (s. 33). "It is a quasi corporation, possessing many, but not all the privileges which law confers upon a duly constituted corporation" (*per* Lord Medwyn in *Forsyth v. Hare and Co.* (1834) 13 S. 42, at p. 47).

Some consequences of the doctrine of the separate *persona* ("personality") of the firm, as well as some of the limitations on that personality are indicated in the following paragraphs. For a fuller description reference may be made to the opinion of Lord Medwyn in *Forsyth v. Hare and Co.* (1834) 13 S. 42, at p. 46, and to that of Lord President Cooper in *Mair v. Wood*, 1948 S.C. 83, at p. 86. For a critical review of the doctrine see Peter C. Hemphill, "The Personality of the Partnership in Scotland", 1984 J.R. 208. **2–33**

(a) Firm as Debtor or Creditor to Partners

A firm may stand in the relation of debtor or creditor to any of its partners, and may sue a partner or be sued by a partner. **2–34**

(b) Contracts

A firm may enter into contracts with third parties, the individual partners acting as agents and the firm being in the position of principal. **2–35**

In accordance with the usual principle of agency, the firm as principal is entitled to sue the third party and is liable to be sued by the third party, while the individual partner who acted as the firm's agent is neither entitled to sue nor liable to be sued. **2–36**

However, since the individual partners are in the last resort liable jointly and severally for the firm's debts (s. 9), any one partner may be held liable by the third party after, but only after, the debt has been constituted against the firm and has not been paid by the firm. The individual partners are liable only *subsidiarie* ("subsidiarily"), and not primarily. They stand in the position of cautioners for the firm, liable to pay only where the firm as principal debtor has itself failed to do so. The Act provides that an individual partner may be charged on a decree or diligence directed against the firm, and on payment of the debts is entitled to relief *pro rata* ("proportionately") from the firm and its other members (s. 4(2)). **2–37**

(c) Delicts

A firm may be the victim of a delict (civil wrong) or may itself commit a delict. A claim for damages may then be made in an action by or against the firm. **2–38**

2–39 In *Gordon v. British and Foreign Metaline Co.* (1886) 14 R. 75, an action for damages for judicial slander, the court held that a firm, despite the fact that its personality is artificial, could be guilty of malice.

2–40 A firm is, however, not liable to one of its partners who has suffered an injury as a result of a delict committed by another partner:

Mair v. Wood, 1948 S.C. 83: M. was one of five partners in a share-fishing joint adventure.

When the boat was at sea, the propeller was fouled, and, to clear the obstruction, the skipper, who was one of the five partners, removed the engine-room floor boards. Before the boards were replaced, M., on descending to the engine-room, put his foot through the opening and was seriously injured.

Held that the firm was not liable to M. for the skipper's negligence.

(d) **Property**

2–41 A firm may own heritable and moveable property. Partnership property must be held and applied exclusively for partnership purposes (s. 20(1)), and not treated by the partners as their own personal property.

2–42 Partners do not own even a share of partnership property: their interest in the property is an indirect one—to a share of the surplus of assets over liabilities when the affairs of the partnership are wound up. This share is moveable property, even although the firm's property is partly or wholly heritable (s. 22)—a point of practical importance in the law of succession on death and in the law of diligence: a deceased partner's share of the firm property will be subject to the legal rights of *jus relictae*, *jus relicti* and legitim which can be claimed by widow, widower and children respectively out of the deceased's moveable (but not heritable) estate, and the appropriate diligence for a creditor who wishes to attach a partner's share of the partnership property for debt is arrestment in the hands of the firm, *i.e.* the diligence used where moveable property is not in the debtor's own possession but in that of a third party.

2–43 Exceptionally, the formal legal title to heritable property held on feudal tenure cannot be taken in the firm-name: it is taken by the partners, or some of them, as trustees for the firm. The formal title to all other property, including leases, may be either in the firm-name or in the name of partners as trustees for the firm. See George L. Gretton, "Who Owns Partnership Property?" 1987 J.R. 163 and George L. Gretton, "Problems in Partnership Conveyancing" (1991) 36 J.L.S. 232.

(e) **Compensation**

Where a question arises as to whether one debt may be wholly or partly set off against another so that the first debt is wholly or partly extinguished, effect is given to the separate personality of a firm by the rule that a partner is not a creditor in a debt due to the firm. Therefore, for instance, if X owes the firm A, B & Co. £5,000, and A, one of the partners in A, B & Co., owes X £1,000, and X brings an action against A for £1,000, A cannot plead compensation of the debt which X owes to the firm. Similarly, if in the same circumstances an action were to be brought by the firm against X for £5,000, X could not plead compensation of the debt of £1,000 due to him by A. **2–44**

On the other hand, because of the ultimate liability of an individual partner for the debts of the firm, a partner is, for the purposes of compensation, treated as a debtor in a debt due by his firm. If, therefore, the firm A, B & Co. owes X £5,000 and X owes the individual partner A £1,000, and A brings an action against X for £1,000, X can plead compensation of the debt which the firm owes to him. **2–45**

(f) **Bankruptcy**

A firm may become bankrupt without any of the partners becoming bankrupt, and conversely individual partners may become bankrupt while the firm remains solvent. **2–46**

However, because individual partners are ultimately liable without any limitation of liability for the debts of the firm, concurrent bankruptcies of firm and individual partners are common. In such a situation, a creditor of the firm who obtains a dividend of so much in the £ from the firm's bankrupt estate can obtain a dividend on the balance from the individual partner's bankrupt estate. The rule against double ranking prevents the creditor from obtaining a dividend on the full amount from both estates. **2–47**

IV RELATIONS OF PARTNERS TO PERSONS DEALING WITH THEM

2–48 The relations of partners to persons dealing with them are described below under two headings:

(a) liability for a firm's debts; and

(b) effect of change in a firm on contracts.

2–49 Partners may, in their contract of copartnery, make provision for the conduct of the firm's external relations. Any such provisions will be binding as amongst the partners themselves, but are not allowed to override the provisions of the Act which are designed to protect third parties (the outsiders).

(a) Liability for a Firm's Debts

2–50 Principles of the law of agency and of the law of cautionry operate here.

2–51 The first question which presents itself is whether the firm itself is liable for a debt incurred or obligation undertaken by a partner. In answering this question the principles of the law of agency are applied, the partner being the agent of the firm and the firm being the principal. The partner is said to be *praepositus negotiis societatis* ("placed in charge of the affairs of the partnership"). Further consideration is given to this question under the heading "Authority of Partners and Others to Bind the Firm", below.

2–52 The second question arising is whether the person dealing with the firm is entitled to hold individual partners or other persons liable for the firm's debts. In answering this question principles of the law of cautionry are applied, individual partners being in the position of cautioners for the firm's debts, liable to pay if the firm itself fails to do so. The leading provision is in section 9: all partners are liable jointly and severally for all the firm's debts and obligations incurred during the partnership. This enables a third party to hold any individual partner liable for the firm's debts and obligations once there has been failure on the firm's part. That partner will then have a right of relief against the other partners, but, if they are bankrupt, that right may be of little value.

2–53 The liability of incoming and outgoing partners requires special consideration, and in certain circumstances a person who is not a partner may be liable on the principle of "holding out".

Authority of Partners and Others to Bind the Firm

Implied mandate of partners

Section 5 of the Act provides that every partner is an agent of the firm and of his other partners for the purposes of the business of the partnership, and then sets out the rule to be applied where the partners have agreed among themselves to limit a partner's authority to some extent: the acts of every partner who does any act for carrying on in the usual way business of the kind carried on by the firm bind the firm and his partners, *unless*: **2–54**

(i) the partner so acting has in fact no authority to act for the firm in the particular matter; *and*

(ii) the person with whom he is dealing *either* knows that he has no authority, *or* does not know or believe him to be a partner.

This gives the third party protection against any secret limitations on a partner's authority.

The implied mandate or authority conferred on each partner by section 5 is restricted to acts "for carrying on in the usual way business of the kind carried on by the firm". For acts beyond that scope the firm will not be bound unless the partner had express authority. **2–55**

In applying section 5 one must take into account not only the nature of the firm's business but also the way in which the partner has been acting. **2–56**

For instance, if the firm is a mercantile or trading firm, each of the partners has an implied mandate to borrow money on behalf of the firm, with the result that the firm will be liable to repay the loan to the lender. Thus, in *Bryan v. Butters Brothers & Co.* (1892) 19 R. 490, where a firm of contractors, engineers and machinery merchants in Glasgow was sued by the wife of one of its partners for repayment of a loan which she had made through her husband to the firm, the firm was held liable. **2–57**

Again, in *Ciceri v. Hunter & Co.* (1904) 12 S.L.T. 293 (O.H.), the circumstances were that S. and H. had entered into a copartnery to carry on a business of hotelkeepers in Edinburgh under the name of "H. & Co.", H. having the sole control of the business and S. not being bound to give personal attention, though he had the right to be consulted on all matters of importance. **2–58**

H. instructed C. to make a revaluation of the furnishings for the purposes of the firm's balance sheet. Before C.'s fee had been paid, H. and H. & Co. became bankrupt.

Held that C. was entitled to recover his fee from S., the solvent partner, because in instructing the revaluation H. had acted within the scope of his mandate as managing partner and so the firm, and not merely H., was bound.

2–59 The Act has further provisions relating to a partner's implied mandate in sections 15 and 16: an admission or representation made by any partner concerning the partnership affairs, and in the ordinary course of its business, is evidence against the firm (s. 15); and notice to any partner who habitually acts in the partnership business of any matter relating to partnership affairs operates as notice to the firm, except in the case of a fraud on the firm committed by or with the consent of that partner (s. 16).

2–60 A question as to the interpretation of section 16 arose in *Campbell v. McCreath*, 1975 S.C. 81; 1975 S.L.T.(Notes) 5 (O.H.): M., the owner of a farm in Ayrshire, after some preliminary negotiations with C., a prospective purchaser, advised his solicitor, a partner in a Whithorn firm, to expect an offer of £70,000 from a Stranraer firm. M. further advised his solicitor that he wished to consider the terms of the offer before instructing his solicitor to accept it.

Three weeks elapsed and M.'s solicitor then, contrary to the instructions given him, sent an offer on M.'s behalf to the Stranraer firm.

The two firms of solicitors consisted of the same two individuals.

The purchaser brought an action against the seller for implement of the missives. M. averred that the fact that M. had not instructed his solicitor in Whithorn to send out the offer was known to C.'s solicitor in Stranraer since the partners of the Whithorn firm were the whole partners of the Stranraer firm. There was, therefore, M. averred, no contract.

Held that the knowledge of M.'s solicitor could not be imputed to C.'s solicitor, and C. was therefore entitled to take advantage of the offer ostensibly made on M.'s behalf.

Lord Stott said (at 1975 S.C. p. 85): "Section 16 of the Act and the relevant commentary in Lindley seem to me to be directed towards a more limited relationship, namely the relationship between a partner and his firm. A partner being the agent of his firm, it follows that notice to him on matters connected with the partnership affairs must be notice to the firm, his principal. But it does not follow that the same applies in matters connected not with the partnership affairs but with the affairs of a client of the partnership."

Acts on firm's behalf

Persons other than partners may also have authority to deal with third parties on behalf of the firm, but such persons have no implied mandate: the third party must be on his guard to see that they have in fact authority. Section 6 provides that an act or document relating to the business of the firm done or signed in the firm-name, or in any other way which shows an intention to bind the firm, by any person authorised to do so, whether a partner or not, is binding on the firm and all the partners. By the Requirements of Writing (Scotland) Act 1995 (s. 7(7) and Sched. 2) the general rule is that a document granted by a partnership is signed by the partnership either by being signed on its behalf by a partner or by being signed by a person authorised to sign the document on its behalf. A person signing on behalf of a partnership may use his own name or the firm-name. **2–61**

A partner may have been given special authority by the other partners to act on the firm's behalf in some way which would not be covered by the implied authority with which section 5 is concerned. It is for the third party to satisfy himself that the partner does in fact have that special authority: otherwise the third party will have to rely on the personal liability of the partner. Section 7 provides that where one partner pledges the credit of the firm for a purpose apparently not connected with the firm's ordinary course of business, the firm is not bound, unless he is in fact specially authorised by the other partners. Special authority is normally required for the undertaking of a cautionary obligation: see *Fortune v. Young*, 1918 S.C. 1 (8–48, below). **2–62**

Agreed restriction on partner's authority

Where partners agree that some restriction be placed on the power of any one or more of them to bind the firm, the agreement is binding on the partners *inter se* ("amongst themselves"), and also on third parties who have notice of (*i.e.* know of) it (s. 8), but it does not affect other third parties. **2–63**

Where the circumstances are such that the third party ought to suspect that the partner is contravening some restriction on his authority, the firm is not bound: **2–64**

Paterson Brothers v. Gladstone (1891) 18 R. 403: The firm of P. Brothers, builders and joiners in Edinburgh, had three partners, Robert, William and John. The contract of copartnery provided that William should have full charge of the financial affairs of the firm and be the only partner to sign the firm's name on financial documents.

Robert signed the firm's name on certain promissory notes in favour of G., a moneylender, discounted them with G. at the rate of 40 per cent and fraudulently applied the proceeds to his own use.

Held that the firm was not liable to pay the promissory notes: G. ought to have suspected that a partner in such a firm would not have authority to raise money in this way for the firm.

Liability of the Firm for Wrongs

2–65 The main rule relating to liability of a firm for wrongs is in section 10: where, by any wrongful act or omission of any partner acting in the ordinary course of the business of the firm, or with the authority of his copartners, loss or injury is caused to any person who is not a partner, or any penalty is incurred, the firm is liable to the same extent as the partner who has been guilty of the act or omission.

2–66 All the partners are jointly and severally liable to third parties for the firm's wrongs (s. 12), though as between the partners themselves an innocent partner is entitled to be relieved by the guilty partner.

2–67 *Kirkintilloch Equitable Co-operative Society Ltd v. Livingstone*, 1972 S.C. 111, gives an illustration of the application of sections 10 and 12 in a case of alleged professional negligence:

A partner in a firm of chartered accountants had acted as auditor of an industrial and provident society from 1952 to 1967, his audit fee being paid to the firm.

After the dissolution of the firm in 1967, the society brought an action of damages for professional negligence based on alleged errors in the audited accounts.

Held that the society was entitled to sue not only the auditor but also his copartners.

2–68 Where the wrong for which a firm is being sued is fraud, the names of the partners who are alleged to have committed the fraud must be specified, because fraud is regarded as always personal (*Thomson & Co. v. Pattison, Elder & Co.* (1895) 22 R. 432).

It is, however, no objection to an action against a firm for a wrong that malice must be proved (*Gordon v. British and Foreign Metaline Co.* (1886) 14 R. 75 (2–39, above)). **2–69**

A firm cannot be made liable to one partner for the fault of another partner (*Mair v. Wood*, 1948 S.C. 83 (2–40, above)): section 10 is concerned only with wrongs done to a person who is not a partner. **2–70**

Misapplication by partner of third party's money or property

Section 11 makes specific provision for two cases where a partner has misapplied money or property belonging to a third party: the firm is liable to make good the loss to the third party where either: **2–71**

(i) a partner acting within the scope of his apparent authority receives the third party's money or property and misapplies it; or

(ii) the firm in the course of its business receives the third party's money or property and it is misapplied by one or more of the partners while it is in the custody of the firm.

Improper employment of trust property for partnership purposes

Section 13 provides that if a partner who is a trustee in a trust improperly employs trust property in the business or on the account of the partnership, no other partner is liable for the trust property to the beneficiaries in the trust. This provision does not, however, affect any liability incurred by another partner who has notice (*i.e.* knows of) the breach of trust, and it does not prevent trust money from being followed and recovered from the firm if it is still in the firm's possession or under the firm's control. **2–72**

Liability of Incoming Partner

A person who is admitted as a partner into an existing firm does not thereby become liable to the creditors of the firm for anything done before he became a partner (s. 17(1)). **2–73**

An incoming partner may, however, incur liability for pre-existing debts, either through an agreement made between the new firm and the creditor (amounting to delegation—the substitution, **2–74** with the creditor's consent, of a new debtor for the original debtor) or because the circumstances show that the new firm has taken over the liabilities of the former firm (involving *jus quaesitum tertio* ("right conferred on a third party"), arising from the express or implied agreement between the partners of the new firm).

2–75 Circumstances which made an incoming partner liable for pre-existing debts are exemplified in the three following cases:

2–76 (i) *Miller v. Thorburn* (1861) 23 D. 359: D., a jeweller in Dumfries, obtained a cash credit from a bank to pay for stock-in-trade and to carry on his business.

Some years later he took his son, John, into partnership. John brought no capital to the business.

The following year D. died, and the firm's estate was sequestrated.

T., a cautioner under the cash credit bond, paid to the bank the balance of £225 due on the cash account, and then claimed to be ranked as a creditor for that amount in the firm's sequestration.

Held that he was entitled to be so ranked.

Lord Cowan said (at p. 362): "In the general case where the whole estate of a company is given over to and taken possession of by a new concern or partnership, the business being continued on the same footing, the estate goes to the new company *suo onere* [literally, 'with its own burden']—that is, the liabilities go along with the effects. . . . This is the general presumption, although there may be special circumstances in particular cases not admitting of its application."

2–77 (ii) *Heddle's Executrix v. Marwick & Hourston's Trustee* (1888) 15 R. 698: M., the owner of a long-established general merchant's business in Kirkwall, took H., the manager of it, into partnership. There was no written contract of copartnery, H. contributed no capital, and the business was carried on as before.

Held that the firm was liable for a pre-existing trade debt which had been contracted by M.

Lord Shand said (at p. 709): "It must always be a question of circumstances whether a new firm becomes responsible for the obligations of the old. On the one hand, if an old-established firm, consisting of one or two partners, arranges to take in a clerk and give him a future share of the profits, or if one of the partners has a son who has just come of age and is taken into the business, and they arrange to give him a share of the profits of the new firm thereby constituted, it appears to me that, if the new firm takes over the stock in trade and the book debts and whole business of the old firm and the goodwill of that business, equity requires that they shall take over its obligations. . . . On the other hand, if a partner comes into a business, paying in a large sum of capital, and the other partners merely put in their shares of a going business as their shares of the capital, a different question might arise. In such a case as that, probably some special circumstances would require to be proved in order to impose liability on the new partner for transactions entered into prior to the date when he became a partner. Then, again, intermediate cases will occur between these two classes. In all of them I think it must be a question of circumstances, to be determined by the Court upon the facts, whether there has been liability undertaken, or adoption of the debt of the old firm."

(iii) *Miller v. MacLeod*, 1973 S.C. 172: In 1955 MacL., a solicitor **2–78**
practising on his own account, undertook the winding up of a large and involved executry estate. Owing to ill health he was unable to attend to his business regularly and his books and accounts got into a state of disorder.

In April 1958 MacL. entered into partnership with Parker, who knew that the financial state of the business was precarious. No agreement was made as to how much, if any, capital Parker would contribute, and the partnership took over and continued MacL.'s business without fresh instructions from clients.

In June 1958 MacL. died, and in 1959 Parker entered into partnership with Piacentini, and the new partnership continued to carry on the business including the winding up of the executry.

In 1962 the executrix, claiming that £10,000 was due to her, raised an action against (1) the firm, (2) Parker, (3) Piacentini and (4) MacL.'s executrix. She sued for (first) an accounting against all four defenders jointly and severally for the period from 1955 to MacL.'s death in June 1958 and (second) an accounting against the first, second and third defenders jointly and severally for the period from MacL.'s death to 1962.

The firm and the partners denied that they were liable to make an accounting for any period before April 1958.

Held that the proper inference from the circumstances was that the firm and its members had accepted the liabilities attaching to the business including liability to account for the period before April 1958.

2–79 A contrasting case is *Thomson & Balfour v. Boag & Son*, 1936 S.C. 2:

B., a joiner, assumed his foreman as a partner. The foreman contributed £340 as capital, and there was an agreement between the partners that B. should realise debts due to him and pay debts due by him in connection with his own business.

Held that neither the partnership nor the foreman was liable for debts incurred when B. had been in business on his own account.

Lord President Normand, referring to the earlier cases, said (at p. 10): "It is a settled principle of law that, when the whole assets of a going concern are handed over to a new partnership and the business is continued on the same footing as before, the presumption is that the liabilities are taken over with the stock. . . . The principle is that it would be inequitable to allow a trader to injure his trade creditors by assuming a partner and handing over his whole trading assets to the new partnership without liability to pay the trade debts. But this presumption must not be extended beyond the circumstances to which it properly applies."

Liability of Retired Partner

2–80 A distinction must be made between:

(i) debts incurred before retirement; and
(ii) debts incurred after retirement.

(i) **Debts incurred before retirement**

2–81 A partner who retires from a firm does not thereby cease to be liable for partnership debts or obligations incurred before his retirement (s. 17(2)).

A retiring partner may be discharged from any existing liability by an agreement to that effect between himself and the members of the firm as newly constituted and the creditors; this agreement may be either express or inferred from the course of dealing between the creditors and the firm as newly constituted (s. 17(3)).

2–82 An agreement amongst the partners themselves does not affect the right of creditors to hold the retiring partner liable. This is in accordance with the general rule of the law of contract that delegation (the substitution of a new debtor) requires the consent of the creditor.

(ii) **Debts incurred after retirement**

The liability of a retired partner for debts of the firm incurred after his retirement rests on the principle of "holding out", a form of personal bar. So far as the rights of creditors are concerned, the question is not what the partners themselves have agreed on, but whether the creditors have been properly notified of the retirement. **2–83**

Section 36(1) provides that where a person deals with a firm after a change in its constitution he is entitled to treat all apparent members of the old firm as still being members of the firm until he has notice of the change. The effect of this is that customers of the business must be individually notified of the retirement of a partner; otherwise they may hold the retired partner liable for future transactions with the new firm; an advertisement will not be sufficient unless the customer can be proved to have read it. **2–84**

As regards persons who have not had dealings with the firm, an advertisement in the Gazette (*i.e.* the *Edinburgh Gazette* if the principal place of business is in Scotland, or the *London Gazette* if the principal place of business is in England or Wales) is sufficient (s. 36(2)). **2–85**

As these rules are based on the principle of holding out, a retired partner who has not been known to the person dealing with the firm to be a partner, is not liable for debts contracted after his retirement whether proper notice has been given or not (s. 36(3)). **2–86**

The estate of a partner who dies, or who becomes bankrupt, is also not liable for partnership debts contracted after the death or bankrupty, these being regarded as public or notorious events (s. 36(3)). **2–87**

A well-known English case involving section 36(3) as well as other provisions of the Act is *Tower Cabinet Co. Ltd v. Ingram* [1949] 2 K.B. 397: **2–88**

In 1946 Ingram and Christmas began to carry on business in partnership as household furnishers under the name of Merry's. By agreement the partnership was dissolved in April 1947. Ingram gave notice of the dissolution to the firm's bankers and arranged with Christmas to notify those dealing with Merry's that Ingram had ceased to be connected with it. No advertisement was put in the *London Gazette*.

In January 1948 T. Ltd, which had not had previous dealings with Merry's, received an order for furniture from it. Without Ingram's knowledge that order was confirmed by Christmas on old headed notepaper bearing Ingram's name.

T. Ltd sought to hold Ingram liable.

Held that (1) Ingram had not knowingly suffered himself to be represented as a partner in Merry's, and so was not liable on the ground of "holding out" (s. 14(1)) (see 2–89, below); (2) he was not liable as an "apparent" member under section 36(1) because the phrase "apparent members" in that provision meant members who were apparently members to the person who was dealing with the firm; and (3) he was protected from liability by section 36(3) because he had not been known to T. Ltd as a partner before the dissolution of the firm.

Liability by "Holding Out"

2–89 A person who is not in fact a partner may be liable for the firm's debts on the principle of "holding out", which is one of the forms of personal bar. The person holding himself out as a partner, or allowing others to do so, may be, for instance, an employee in the business, or a retired partner of whose retirement proper notification has not been given. Section 14(1) provides that every one who by words, spoken or written, or by conduct, represents himself or knowingly suffers himself to be represented as a partner in a particular firm is liable as a partner to anyone who has on the faith of that representation given credit to the firm.

2–90 An illustration of holding out occurs in *Hosie v. Waddell* (1866) 3 S.L.R. 16:

H., when suing W. for a debt, was met by the defence that W. had paid the debt to C., whom he believed to be H.'s partner.

H. maintained that C. had never been his partner, but only manager of the business.

Held that, in the circumstances of the case, C. had been held out as a partner, that W. had made payment of the debt to C. in the bona fide belief that C. was a partner, and that therefore payment to C. was good payment.

2–91 Where after a partner's death the partnership business is continued in the old firm-name, the continued use of that name or of the deceased partner's name as part of it does not of itself make the deceased's estate liable for partnership debts contracted after the death (s. 14(2)).

(b) **Effect of Change in a Firm on Contracts**

The Act does not contain any general provision as to the effect which a change in the membership of a firm has on existing and continuing contracts of the firm. The rule of the common law, therefore, remains applicable, that only contracts involving *delectus personae* ("choice of person") will be terminated. **2–92**

Where, however, there is not merely a change in the membership of the firm, but the conversion of the firm into a registered company, the company is not a party to the contracts of the firm whose business it has taken over (*Grierson, Oldham & Co. Ltd v. Forbes, Maxwell & Co. Ltd* (1895) 22 R. 812, in which the company G., O. & Co. Ltd, which was continuing the wine business of the firm G., O. & Co., was held to have no title to sue for implement of a contract by which F. Ltd had undertaken to pay a rent to the firm for a space in the firm's advertising wine-list for a period of three years). **2–93**

The Act makes express provision for only one type of contract— cautionary obligations (guarantees). Section 18 provides that a continuing cautionary obligation is, in the absence of agreement to the contrary, revoked as to future transactions by a change in a firm where either: **2–94**

(i) the cautionary obligation has been given to the firm, *i.e.* the firm is the creditor; or

(ii) the cautionary obligation has been given in respect of the firm's transactions, *i.e.* the firm is the principal debtor.

V RELATIONS OF PARTNERS TO ONE ANOTHER

Two general principles operate in the relations of partners *inter se* ("amongst themselves"). The first of these is that the contract out of which partnership arises is a contract involving *delectus personae* ("choice of person"): the personal qualities of a partner are important to his copartners. The second general principle is the fiduciary character of the relationship: the partners must act in good faith towards each other, making full disclosure of all matters affecting the partnership to their copartners and not seeking to **2–95** obtain a personal gain in contravention of the partnership agreement.

2–96 These two general principles can be seen to underlie the specific provisions of the Act regulating the relations of partners to one another.

2–97 Another general point is that partners are free to make such agreement as they choose concerning their relations to one another. The agreement may be a written contract of copartnery, or an oral agreement, or an agreement implied by conduct. The partners are also free to agree on variation of their relations from time to time. The provisions of the Act governing relations between the partners themselves apply only where no different provisions have been made by the partners' own agreement. This is in contrast to the provisions of the Act governing relations of partners to persons dealing with them, considered above. Section 19 provides that the mutual rights and duties of partners, whether ascertained by agreement or defined by the Act, may be varied by the consent of all the partners, and such consent may be either express or inferred from a course of dealing.

Partnership Property

2–98 The term "partnership property" is defined in section 20(1) as meaning "all property and rights and interests in property originally brought into the partnership stock or acquired, whether by purchase or otherwise, on account of the firm, or for the purposes and in the course of the partnership business".

2–99 Partnership property belongs to the firm as a separate legal person from the partners, but, since the personality of the firm is artificial, partnership property is in the actual hands of and is managed by the partners, who must not, however, treat it, or even a share of it, as their own personal property. Section 20(1) provides that partnership property must be held and applied by the partners exclusively for the purposes of the partnership, and in accordance with the partnership agreement.

2–100 The formal legal title to partnership property may be either in the name of the firm or in the name of individual partners, with the one exception of the formal legal title to heritable property held on feudal tenure: this cannot be taken in the firm-name; usually it will be in the name of two or more of the partners as trustees for the firm (see also 2–43, above).

One of the rules for determining the existence of partnership is, as was mentioned above (2–21), that joint property, common property, or part ownership does not of itself create a partnership, whether the owners do or do not share any profits made by the use of the property (s. 2). It is also possible, however, that persons may be co-owners of heritable property and be partners as to the profits made by the use of that property without the property being partnership property. For such a situation section 20(3) provides that if the co-owners purchase other heritable property out of the profits for the purpose of using that other property in the same way, then, in the absence of agreement to the contrary, that other property belongs to them, not as partners, but as co-owners. **2–101**

Disputes may arise as to whether property in the possession or in the name of an individual partner is partnership property or his own personal property. There is an instance of such a dispute in *Munro v. Stein*, 1961 S.C. 362 (O.H.), in which Lord Wheatley (Ordinary) held that (i) it was competent to prove by parole evidence that a dance hall was partnership property, and (ii) on the evidence the dance hall had been proved to be such. Section 21 provides that, unless the contrary intention appears, property bought with money belonging to the firm is deemed to have been bought on account of the firm. **2–102**

It follows from the firm's separate personality that where heritable property has become partnership property, it must, unless the contrary intention appears, be treated as between the partners (including the representatives of a deceased partner) as moveable and not as heritable property (s. 22). **2–103**

Rights of Partners

Section 24 sets out nine rules as to the interests of partners in the partnership property and as to their rights and duties in relation to the partnership. These rules are all "subject to any agreement express or implied between the partners". **2–104**

(1) All the partners are entitled to share equally in the capital and profits of the business, and must contribute equally towards the losses, whether of capital or otherwise, sustained by the firm.

(2) The firm must indemnify every partner for payments made and personal liabilities incurred by him:

(a) in the ordinary and proper business of the firm; or

(b) in or about anything necessarily done for the preservation of the business or property of the firm.

(3) A partner making, for the purpose of the partnership, any actual payment or advance beyond the amount of capital which he has agreed to subscribe, is entitled to interest at five per cent from the date of the payment or advance.

(4) A partner is not entitled, before the ascertainment of profits, to interest on the capital subscribed by him.

(5) Every partner may take part in the management of the partnership business.

(6) No partner is entitled to remuneration for acting in the partnership business.

(7) No person may be introduced as a partner without the consent of all existing partners.

(8) Any difference arising as to ordinary matters connected with the partnership business may be decided by a majority of the partners, but no change may be made in the nature of the partnership business without the consent of all existing partners.

(9) The partnership books must be kept at the principal place of business of the partnership, and every partner may, when he thinks fit, have access to and inspect and copy any of them.

2–105 Partners may have a right to expel one of their number, but such a right requires an express provision in the contract of copartnery. Section 25 provides: "No majority of the partners can expel any partner unless a power to do so has been conferred by express agreement between the partners."

Partnership at Will

2–106 A partnership at will exists in either of two situations: (a) where there never has been any time fixed for the duration of the partnership, and (b) where the partnership was originally for a fixed period and has been continued after the expiry of that period without any express new agreement. In the second situation there is said to be "tacit relocation" ("silent renewal").

2–107 It is of the essence of a partnership at will that it may be brought to an end by notice given by any partner. This follows from the *delectus personae* inherent in partnership.

2–108 With reference to situation (a), the Act provides that where no fixed term has been agreed upon for the duration of a partnership, any partner may terminate the partnership at any time on giving notice of his intention to do so to all the other partners (s. 26(1)). If the partnership has originally been constituted by deed (a formal legal document such as a contract of copartnery signed by the partners in the presence of witnesses), a notice in writing, signed by the partner giving it, is sufficient to terminate the partnership (s. 26(2)). The firm will be dissolved as from the date mentioned in the notice as the date of dissolution, or, if no date is mentioned, as from the date of the communication of the notice (s. 32).

With reference to situation (b), the Act provides that where a **2–109** partnership entered into for a fixed term is continued after the term has expired, and without any express new agreement, the rights and duties of the partners remain the same as they were at the expiration of the term, so far as is consistent with the incidents of a partnership at will (s. 27(1)). A continuance of the business by the partners, or by those partners who have been habitually acting in the business during the original term, without any settlement or liquidation of the partnership affairs, is presumed to be a continuance of the partnership (s. 27(2)).

Difficulties can arise as to whether or not a particular clause in **2–110** the original agreement is "consistent with the incidents of a partnership at will", so that it is carried over into the partnership at will under section 27(1). Two contrasting cases may be referred to by way of illustration:

Neilson v. Mossend Iron Co. (1886) 13 R. (H.L.) 50: A contract **2–111** of copartnery for a period of seven years contained a clause stipulating that any partner was to have the option of being bought out by his copartners on condition that he gave notice of his desire to exercise that option "three months before the termination of this contract".

Held that this clause had not been carried forward into the partnership at will which had commenced at the end of the seven-year period.

Lord Watson said (at p. 56): "The condition and the rights and obligations arising out of it are totally inapplicable to a contract-at-will. They have plain reference to a fixed *punctum temporis* ['point of time'], the termination of the original contract; but how are they to be applied to a contract which has no definite currency? Time is of the essence of the condition, but a contract-at-will affords no terminus from which it can be measured or computed."

2–112 *McGown v. Henderson*, 1914 S.C. 839: H., M. and C. entered into a contract of copartnery to carry on a business as wine and spirit merchants for a period of five years. The contract contained a pre-emption clause giving to H., as holder of the licence, the option, at the expiry of the five years, to pay out to M. and C. the amount due to them.

After the expiry of the five years, the partnership continued for several years as a partnership at will. H. then terminated the partnership by notice and claimed the right to exercise the option conferred by the pre-emption clause.

Held that H. was entitled to do so, there being nothing to prevent the pre-emption clause from being carried forward into the partnership at will.

Fiduciary Character of Partnership

2–113 The fiduciary character of partnership underlies the duties of partners to one another set out in sections 28, 29 and 30 of the Act:

(a) *Duty to Render Accounts and Information (s. 28)*

2–114 Partners are bound to render true accounts and full information of all things affecting the partnership to any partner or his legal representatives.

2–115 This provision is illustrated in *Ferguson v. Mackay*, 1985 S.L.T. 94 (O.H.); F. was retiring from a partnership of solicitors. The original terms of the deed of copartnery were departed from and by agreement amongst the partners new provisions were substituted. Under the new terms F. was to receive a salary at a certain level for the year preceding his retiral and a salary as a consultant at a different rate. No payment was made for work in progress, which at the time was extensive and was to bring in substantial fees.

F., claiming that he would not have agreed to the financial terms fixed for his retirement if he had been given full information (in particular as to work in progress), brought an action of damages against his former copartners on the ground that they had been in breach of their fiduciary duty to him.

Held that F. had made out a claim which was open to him and proof before answer was allowed.

(b) *Accountability for Private Profits (s. 29)*

Every partner must account to the firm for any benefit derived by him without the consent of the other partners from any transaction concerning the partnership, or from any use by him of the partnership property, name, or business connection. **2–116**

This section applies also to transactions undertaken after a partnership has been dissolved by the death of a partner, and before its affairs have been completely wound up, either by any surviving partner or by the representatives of the deceased partner. **2–117**

(c) *Duty not to Compete with Firm (s. 30)*

If a partner, without the consent of the other partners, carries on any business of the same nature as and competing with that of the firm, he must account for and pay over to the firm all profits made by him in that business. **2–118**

The following three cases illustrate these fiduciary duties: **2–119**

(i) *McNiven v. Peffers* (1868) 7 M. 181: M. and P. were partners in a wine and spirit business which was carried on in leased premises. P. was sole manager of the business, and the lease was in his name. **2–120**

Shortly before the lease was due to expire, P. entered into negotiations with the landlord which resulted in P.'s obtaining a renewal of the lease for himself. M. was not informed of these proceedings.

Held that P. was bound to share with M. the profits of the business carried on under the new lease.

Lord Justice-Clerk Patton said (at p. 186): "It appears to me perfectly plain that a partner, and especially a managing partner, who goes to the landlord, and, behind the back of his partner, obtains from the landlord a new lease of the partnership premises, is not entitled to retain the profits of that lease for himself. . . .

". . . It follows, as the natural result of the plainest principles of equity applied to such a case, that a partner so acting must communicate the benefit of the lease so obtained to the copartnery, the interests of which he was bound to have attended to. The effect of refusing the remedy would be that a valuable interest in the copartnery, that of goodwill, would be destroyed, and a private benefit secured by an act grossly wrong in itself."

2–121 (ii) *Stewart v. North* (1893) 20 R. 260: In 1876 North obtained from a municipal council in Peru a concession of the exclusive right to supply the town with piped drinking water, and in 1877 he entered into a contract of joint adventure with Speedie and Cockburn for the purpose of carrying out the work.

In 1878, after the work had begun, North, partly by means of the concession, obtained for himself a lease of property belonging to the T. Water Company, which was then supplying stored fresh water to the town. North then stopped the work of the joint adventure, and, in partnership with Speedie, continued the business of the T. Water Company. Cockburn knew of these proceedings, but took no action.

In 1885 Cockburn became bankrupt, and in 1887 his interest in the joint adventure was assigned by his trustee to Stewart.

Stewart brought an action of accounting against North, claiming that the profits derived from the lease of the T. Water Company's property belonged to the joint adventure.

Held that (1) Cockburn would have been entitled to a share of these profits because (a) the business being carried on covered the same ground as that of the joint adventure and (b) North had used the joint adventure's property (the concession) to obtain the lease, but (2) the claim was barred by lapse of time.

Lord Adam said (at p. 270): "I think that where a partner is not bound by a contract entered into by a copartner, but is entitled and desires to have the benefit of it, he must make his claim without delay. He is not entitled to lie by in order to see whether the contract turns out a profitable one or not. If he is to have the benefit he must be prepared to run the risk of loss."

2–122 (iii) *Pillans Brothers v. Pillans* (1908) 16 S.L.T. 611 (O.H.): In 1905 three brothers, Alexander, John and Richard, arranged to become partners in carrying on business as rivet, bolt and nut manufacturers in Motherwell and elsewhere.

The following year, Richard purchased a rivet, bolt and nut manufacturing business at Greenfield, about four miles from Motherwell.

Held that (1) there was a subsisting partnership when the Greenfield works were acquired; (2) that business had to be regarded as having been acquired for the firm; and (3) Richard was therefore bound to account to the firm and his brothers for the profits made at Greenfield.

Assignation of Share in Partnership

Because of the *delectus personae* inherent in partnership, no partner may, without the consent of his copartners, assign his interest in the partnership with the effect of making the assignee a partner in the firm. **2–123**

A partner may assign his share in the partnership, either absolutely or by way of security, but this does not of itself change the constitution of the partnership: the assigning partner (the cedent) remains a partner, and the assignee does not become a partner. **2–124**

During the continuance of the partnership, the assignee is not entitled, as against the other partners, to interfere in the management of the business, or to require any accounts of the partnership transactions, or to inspect the partnership books; he is entitled only to receive the share of profits to which the cedent would otherwise be entitled, and the assignee must accept the account of profits agreed to by the partners (including the cedent) (s. 31(1)). On the dissolution of the partnership, the assignee is entitled to receive the share of the partnership assets to which the cedent is entitled as between himself and the other partners, and, for the purpose of ascertaining that share, the assignee is entitled to an account as from the date of the dissolution (s. 31(2)). **2–125**

VI TERMINATION OF PARTNERSHIP

The relationship of partnership may be brought to an end by: **2–126**

(a) rescission; or

(b) dissolution.

Rescission involves the reduction (setting aside) of the contract out of which the partnership has arisen, and *restitutio in integrum* ("restoration to the original position"). It is governed mainly by the rules of the common law relating to the invalidity of contracts. **2–127**

Dissolution is the ending of a relationship which is regarded as having validly subsisted for some time. It results in a winding up of the partnership affairs, including apportionment of the final balance amongst the individual partners according to their rights and obligations in the contract of copartnery. The main rules relating to dissolution and its consequences are set out in the Act. **2–128**

A point of contrast between the law of partnership and company law is that, whereas in the former dissolution (the termination of **2–129** the relationship) is followed by winding up, in the latter winding up precedes dissolution (*i.e.* the company continues in existence as a legal person until the winding-up (or liquidation) procedure has been completed).

(a) **Rescission**

2–130 As in the general law of contract, the rescission may be on the ground of fraudulent misrepresentation (or fraud) or on the ground of innocent misrepresentation; in the former case, the partner rescinding has also a claim for damages. By section 10 of the Law Reform (Miscellaneous Provisions) (Scotland) Act 1985 a claim for damages may arise where an innocent misrepresentation has been made negligently. It may also be that partnership is one of the contracts *uberrimae fidei* ("of the utmost good faith"), and if so, mere failure to disclose material facts will confer on the other party or parties the right of rescission.

2–131 The case of *Ferguson v. Wilson* (1904) 6 F. 779 is an instance of rescission on the ground of innocent misrepresentation:

W., an engineer in Aberdeen, advertised for a partner. F. replied to the advertisement, and negotiations took place in the course of which W., without fraudulent intent, misrepresented the trading results of his business.

W. and F. agreed to enter into partnership.

Held that F. was entitled to rescind the agreement on the ground that he had entered into it under an essential error induced by W.'s innocent misrepresentation.

2–132 The Act confers certain additional rights on a partner who is entitled to rescind on the ground of fraud or misrepresentation: by section 41 he is entitled:

(i) to a lien on, or right of retention of, the surplus of the partnership assets, after satisfying the partnership liabilities, for any sum of money paid by him for the purchase of a share in the partnership and for any capital contributed by him;

(ii) to stand in the place of the creditors of the firm for any payments made by him in respect of partnership liabilities; and

(iii) to be indemnified by the person guilty of the fraud or making the representation against all the debts and liabilities of the firm.

(b) **Dissolution**

The grounds of dissolution are considered first, and then, under the heading "Winding Up", the consequences of dissolution. 2–133

Grounds of Dissolution

The circumstances which bring about a dissolution of the relationship of partnership are set out in sections 32 to 35 of the Act: 2–134

(i) expiration or notice (s. 32);
(ii) death or bankruptcy (s. 33);
(iii) illegality (s. 34); and
(iv) order of the court (s. 35).

(i) **Expiration or notice (s. 32)**

Subject to any agreement between the partners, a partnership is dissolved: 2–135

(a) if entered into for a fixed term, by the expiration of that term;

(b) if entered into for a single adventure or undertaking, by the termination of that adventure or undertaking;

(c) if entered into for an undefined time, by any partner giving notice to the other or others of his intention to dissolve the partnership.

On (b), see "Joint Adventure", 2–16, above.

In situation (c) the partnership is dissolved as from the date mentioned in the notice as the date of dissolution, or, if no date is mentioned, as from the date of the communication of the notice.

(ii) **Death or bankruptcy (s. 33)**

Subject to any agreement between the partners, every partnership is dissolved as regards all the partners by the death or bankruptcy of any partner. 2–136

An instance of agreement to the contrary may be seen in *William S. Gordon & Co. Ltd v. Mrs Mary Thomson Partnership*, 1985 S.L.T. 122: 2–137

G. Ltd, owners of two fields at Bardowie, Stirlingshire, had leased them to a firm named "Mrs Mary Thomson", the partners of which were Mrs Mary Thomson and two other persons. On the death of Mrs Mary Thomson in 1981, G. Ltd sought to recover possession on the ground that the partnership had been dissolved by her death.

The contract of copartnery provided: "In the event of the death or legal incapacity of any of the Parties . . . the remaining Parties shall decide within two months of the death or declared incapacity, either to wind up the Partnership business or to take over the estate and assets of the Partnership business and to carry on the business to the exclusion of the representatives of the deceased or incapacitated partner and with exclusive right to the goodwill and use of the firm name."

The interpretation given to these words by the Inner House (in agreement with the sheriff, from whose decision an appeal had been allowed by the sheriff principal) was that they constituted an agreement amongst the partners that the death of one of the three was not to result in the dissolution of the partnership.

2–138 However, the mere bequest of estate which includes the deceased's share in a partnership does not make the legatee a partner:

Thomson v. Thomson, 1962 S.C. (H.L.) 28; 1961 S.C. 255: Two brothers, Hector and Andrew, carried on a bakery business in partnership. The deed of copartnery provided that "either partner may by will nominate his widow to his share in the partnership".

Hector died leaving a will in which he bequeathed all his estate to his widow, but did not expressly nominate her as a partner.

Held that the widow was entitled to Hector's share in the partnership assets, but was not nominated as a partner in the business.

(iii) **Illegality (s. 34)**

2–139 A partnership is in every case dissolved by the happening of any event which makes it unlawful for the business of the firm to be carried on or for the members of the firm to carry it on in partnership.

2–140 An instance of dissolution by illegality occurs in *Hugh Stevenson and Sons Ltd v. Aktiengesellschaft für Cartonnagen-Industrie* [1918] A.C. 239 (see 2–160, below): the admitted effect of the outbreak of war between Britain and Germany was to dissolve the partnership between the English company and the German company.

(iv) **Order of the court (s. 35)**

Section 35 sets out six cases in which a partner may apply to the court for the court to decree a dissolution of the partnership. The applicant will not necessarily succeed: the court has a discretion in the matter. The six cases are: **2–141**

(a) when a partner is found lunatic by cognition, or is shown to the satisfaction of the court to be of permanently unsound mind; (In this case the application may be made either by the insane partner's *curator bonis* (his guardian) or by another partner.)

(b) when a partner, other than the partner suing, becomes in any other way permanently incapable of performing his part of the partnership contract;
(In this case much depends on what the partner who has become incapable had necessarily to do himself in the partnership business; an illustration is provided by *Eadie v. MacBean's Curator Bonis* (1885) 12 R. 660:

M., the owner of a long-established manufacturing business in Glasgow, assumed three younger men as partners in the business. The contract of copartnery provided that M. alone was to be entitled to sign cheques and indorse bills of exchange and promissory notes, but that in the event of his indisposition or of his being unable to attend to business from other causes, any of the other partners should be entitled to do so. The three junior partners were to devote their whole time and attention to the business.

M., by a stroke of paralysis, became permanently incapable of taking any further active part in the business, and the other partners petitioned the court to appoint a judicial factor to wind up the partnership affairs.

Petition *refused*, on the ground that it was not an essential part of the contract of copartnery that M. should give his personal services, and that therefore the other partners were not entitled to dissolve the partnership.)

(c) when a partner, other than the partner suing, has been guilty of such conduct as, in the opinion of the court, is calculated to prejudicially affect the carrying on of the business;
(Regard must be had to the nature of the business.)

(d) when a partner, other than the partner suing, wilfully or persistently commits a breach of the partnership agreement, or

otherwise so conducts himself in matters relating to the partnership business that it is not reasonably practicable for the other partner or partners to carry on the business in partnership with him;
(This provision was applied in *Thomson, Petr.* (1893) 1 S.L.T. 59:

A partner, after drawing a cheque in the firm's name, disappeared, taking the money with him.

On the ground that this was a breach of the express terms of the contract of copartnery the other partner petitioned the court to dissolve the partnership.

The court *granted* the order for dissolution.)

(e) when the business of the partnership can only be carried on at a loss;

(f) whenever in any case circumstances have arisen which, in the opinion of the court, render it just and equitable that the partnership be dissolved.
(The court's jurisdiction is not ousted by a general arbitration clause in the partnership contract providing for all disputes to be settled by arbitration (*Roxburgh v. Dinardo*, 1981 S.L.T. 291 (O.H.)).)

Winding Up

2–142 In relation to winding up, the Act includes provision for the following matters:

(i) right of partners to notify dissolution (s. 37);

(ii) continuing authority of partners for purposes of winding up (s. 38);

(iii) rights of partners as to application of partnership property (s. 39);

(iv) apportionment of premium where partnership prematurely dissolved (s. 40);

(v) right of outgoing partner in certain cases to share profits made after dissolution (s. 42); and

(vi) distribution of assets on final settlement of accounts (s. 44).

2–143 Primarily the right and duty to wind up the affairs of a partnership rest on the partners themselves, but, in cases of difficulty, the court has power to appoint a judicial factor whose function it is to wind up the firm's affairs under the eyes of the court. This power existed at common law, and is preserved by the provision in section 39 of the Act that any partner or his representatives may, on the termination of the partnership, apply to the court to wind up the business and affairs of the firm. By the Law Reform (Miscellaneous Provisions) (Scotland) Act 1980 (s. 14) the sheriff court has the same jurisdiction to appoint a judicial factor as does the Court of Session.

The following two cases illustrate circumstances which have been held to justify appointment of a judicial factor: **2–144**

(1) *Allan v. Gronmeyer* (1891) 18 R. 784: A, B and C were partners in a wine and spirit business. The capital of about £22,000 had been contributed entirely by A and B. An article in the contract of copartnery provided that at the termination of the partnership the duty of winding up its affairs was to lie with C. **2–145**

In 1888 the partners agreed that the partnership should be dissolved and that C should wind up its affairs in accordance with that article.

C took no steps towards winding up but carried on the business as a going concern, with its capital undiminished.

In 1890 A and B presented a petition for the appointment of a judicial factor, and the court *appointed* an accountant to that office.

Lord Adam said (at p. 787): "The petitioners . . . have a very clear interest to see that that capital is safe."

(2) *Carabine v. Carabine*, 1949 S.C. 521: A husband and wife were partners in a hotel business, to which both had contributed capital. There was no written contract of copartnery. **2–146**

The partnership terminated when the wife left her husband. All efforts on the wife's part to have the business realised failed, the husband carrying it on against her wishes. There was an imminent risk that a building society to which interest was due would force a sale of the premises in circumstances disadvantageous to both partners.

The court *appointed* a judicial factor in order that the wife might obtain her rights under section 39 of the Act.

Lord Justice-Clerk Thomson said (at p. 527): "Here there is no harmony, and the impression I take from what I have been told is that the respondent has just been staying on running the hotel and that he has not the slightest intention of settling up the partnership affairs unless he is subjected to pressure, and this puts the petitioner in a very awkward position and prevents her from enjoying her rights under the Act. That is just the sort of situation which seems to me to make it necessary or expedient that we should intervene. This is not just a dispute between the winding-up partner and the late partner on some matter of detail or accounting arising out of the winding up; it is something much more fundamental which attacks the propriety of the course adopted altogether."

2–147 On the other hand in *Thomson, Petr.* (1893) 1 S.L.T. 59 (2–141, above) the court, while granting the order for dissolution, refused to authorise winding up by the petitioner or to appoint a judicial factor, on the ground that at common law a partner had on dissolution full power to wind up.

2–148 In *Dickie v. Mitchell* (1874) 1 R. 1030 (a case in which a judicial factor was appointed where the two partners in a joint farming adventure were both incapable of managing the farm), Lord President Inglis (at p. 1033) formulated three general principles:

(1) When all the partners are dead, the court will appoint a judicial factor.

(2) If there are surviving partners without fault or incapacity, the court will not interfere but will leave them to extricate their affairs in their own way.

(3) Where there is a surviving partner who is unfitted for winding up the affairs, the court can, and, if satisfied of the necessity, will appoint a factor. All such cases are, in their nature, cases of circumstances.

2–149 The specific provisions of the Act may now be looked at:

(i) **Right of partners to notify dissolution (s. 37)**

2–150 On the dissolution of a partnership or retirement of a partner any partner may publicly notify the fact, and may require the other partner or partners to concur for that purpose in all necessary or proper acts which cannot be done without his or their concurrence.

The importance of this section in practice is linked to the provisions in section 36, already noticed (2–83–86, above) in connection with the possible liability of retired partners for the future debts of the firm.

(ii) **Continuing authority of partners for purposes of winding up (s. 38)**

2–151 After the dissolution the authority of each partner to bind the firm, and the other rights and obligations of the partners, continue so far as is necessary to wind up the affairs of the partnership, and to complete transactions begun but unfinished at the time of the dissolution, but not otherwise.

However, it is specially provided that the firm is in no case bound by the acts of a partner who has become bankrupt, though this will not affect the liability of any person who has after the bankruptcy represented himself or knowingly allowed himself to be represented as a partner of the bankrupt. **2–152**

Section 38 was applied in *Dickson v. National Bank of Scotland Ltd*, 1917 S.C. (H.L.) 50; 1916 S.C. 589: **2–153**

A sum of money forming part of a trust estate was deposited with a bank. The deposit-receipt stated that the sum was to be repayable on the signature of a legal firm, A, B & C, the law-agents to the trust.

The firm A, B & C was subsequently dissolved, and eight years after the dissolution B, one of the former partners, by signing the firm-name on the deposit receipt, uplifted the money and embezzled it.

The beneficiaries in the trust brought an action against the bank for payment of the sum deposited.

Held that as the uplifting of the deposit was necessary for one or other of the purposes mentioned in section 38, B had authority to sign the firm-name, and the bank was justified in paying over the money to him; and action *dismissed* as irrelevant.

Section 38 was also applied in *Lujo Properties Ltd v. Green*, 1997 S.L.T. 225 (O.H.): **2–154**

L. Ltd let to a firm of solicitors certain heritable property. The tenants were described as being the partnership and the partners as trustees for the firm. Assignees were excluded except with the prior consent of L. Ltd.

The partnership was later dissolved and a judicial factor was appointed.

L. Ltd raised a commercial action against the partners, including those who had been assumed but had resigned before the dissolution, and the judicial factor, seeking declarator that the defenders were liable for the pecuniary obligations of the tenants for the duration of the lease.

Held that, because of section 38, the tenants' pecuniary obligations under the lease prior to dissolution subsisted and imposed upon the former partners in particular an obligation to pay a sum equivalent to the rent otherwise due for the duration of the unexpired term of the lease.

(iii) **Rights of partners as to application of partnership property (s. 39)**

2–155 On the dissolution of a partnership every partner is entitled to have the partnership property applied in payment of the debts and liabilities of the firm, and to have the surplus assets applied in payment of what may be due to the partners respectively after deducting what may be due from them as partners to the firm.

(iv) **Apportionment of premium where partnership prematurely dissolved (s. 40)**

2–156 Section 40 relates to the situation where one partner has paid a premium to another on entering into a partnership for a fixed term, and the partnership is dissolved before that term has expired. The court may then order the repayment of the premium, or of such part of it as the court thinks just, considering the terms of the partnership contract and the length of time during which the partnership has continued, unless:

(1) the dissolution has been caused by the death of a partner; or

(2) the dissolution is, in the court's judgment, wholly or chiefly due to the misconduct of the partner who paid the premium; or

(3) the partnership has been dissolved by an agreement containing no provision for a return of any part of the premium.

(v) **Right of outgoing partner in certain cases to share profits made after dissolution (s. 42)**

2–157 It may be that where a member of a firm has died or otherwise ceased to be a partner, the surviving or continuing partners carry on the business of the firm with its capital or assets without any final settlement of accounts as between the firm and the outgoing partner or his estate. For that situation the Act provides that, in the absence of any agreement to the contrary, the outgoing partner or his estate is entitled to an option, *viz.* either:

(1) such share of the profits made since the dissolution as the court may find to be attributable to the use of his share of the partnership assets; or

(2) interest at five per cent on the amount of his share of the partnership assets (s. 42(1)).

2–158 Difficulty can arise in the application of section 42(1) where the contract of copartnery has not made it abundantly clear how the outgoing or deceased partner's share of the partnership assets is to be valued. The following two contrasting cases may be given in illustration:

(a) *Clark v. Watson*, 1982 S.L.T. 450 (O.H.): Two dentists practised in partnership until the death of one of them in 1977. The contract of copartnery did not make it clear how the share of capital due to the deceased partner's estate was to be determined.

Held that in the absence of an agreement that the share of capital due to the estate was that shown in a specified annual balance sheet, the share had to be ascertained by drawing up a balance sheet as at the date of death in which all the assets of the partnership were inserted at their fair value at that date.

(b) *Thom's Executrix v. Russel & Aitken*, 1983 S.L.T. 335 (O.H.): The partnership agreement for a firm of solicitors provided that on the death of a partner no accounts up to the date of death were to be made up but that his representatives were to be entitled to receive (i) the share standing at his credit in the capital of the firm as determined by the auditors and (ii) profits in proportion to that share up to the date of death.

The executrix of a deceased partner argued that there should be a revaluation of assets; the firm's heritable property had been last revalued in 1968, and she contended that a fair value for that property was its value on the open market, not its book value which had been entered in the annual accounts.

The remaining partners argued that the share of capital was restricted to the book value.

Held, on a construction of the contract of copartnery and in the light of the annual accounts, the deceased's share was to be calculated by reference to the book value of the heritage at the date of death.

Where by the partnership contract an option is given to surviving **2–159** or continuing partners to purchase the interest of a deceased or outgoing partner, and that option is duly exercised, then the estate of the deceased partner, or the outgoing partner or his estate, as the case may be, is not entitled to any further or other share of profits (s. 42(2)).

Section 42 applies even where the dissolution is caused by **2–160** illegality:

Hugh Stevenson and Sons Ltd v. Aktiengesellschaft für Cartonnagen-Industrie [1918] A.C. 239: An English company and a

German company had carried on business as a clamp factory in England until the partnership was dissolved by the outbreak of war between Britain and Germany.

During the war the English company continued to carry on the business and to use the partnership plant.

Held that, at the end of the war, the German company was entitled to a share of the profits made by the carrying on of the business during the war.

(vi) **Distribution of assets on final settlement of accounts (s. 44)**

2–161 In settling accounts between the partners after a dissolution, the following rules must, subject to any agreement, be observed:

(a) Losses, including losses and deficiencies of capital, must be paid first out of profits, next out of capital, and lastly, if necessary, by the partners individually in the proportion in which they were entitled to share profits.

(b) The assets of the firm, including any sums contributed by the partners to make up losses or deficiencies of capital, must be applied as follows:

(1) in paying the debts and liabilities of the firm to persons who are not partners;

(2) in paying to each partner rateably what is due to him for advances as distinct from capital;

(3) in paying to each partner rateably what is due from the firm to him in respect of capital.

The ultimate residue, if any, must then:

(4) be divided among the partners in the proportion in which profits are divisible.

VII LIMITED PARTNERSHIPS ACT 1907

2–162 The Limited Partnerships Act 1907 was passed to enable partnerships to be formed in which one or more (but not all) of the partners are not liable beyond a fixed limit for the firm's debts. Section references here are to sections of the Act of 1907.

2–163 The Act provides that a limited partnership must consist of one or more persons, called "general partners", who are liable in the usual way for all the firm's debts and obligations, and of one or more persons, called "limited partners", who at the time of entering into the partnership contribute a sum as capital, or contribute property valued at a stated amount, and who are not liable for the firm's debts or obligations beyond the amount contributed. A limited partner must not, during the continuance of the partnership, draw out any part of his contribution: if he does so, he remains liable for the firm's debts and obligations up to the amount drawn out (s. 4(2) and (3)).

Limited partnerships, unlike ordinary partnerships, must be **2–164** registered with the registrar of companies (s. 5). For a limited partnership whose principal place of business is situated or proposed to be situated in Scotland the appropriate registration office is that in Edinburgh (ss. 8 and 15).

The particulars which must be registered are: **2–165**

(a) the firm-name;
(b) the general nature of the business;
(c) the principal place of business;
(d) the full names of each of the partners;
(e) the term, if any, for which the partnership is entered into, and the date of its commencement;
(f) a statement that the partnership is limited, and of who are the limited partners; and
(g) the sum contributed by each limited partner, and whether paid in cash or how otherwise (s. 8).

Changes in these particulars must also be registered (s. 9(1)). **2–166**

These provisions for registration are intended to give protection **2–167** to members of the public who deal with a limited partnership. Any person is entitled, on paying the appropriate fee, to inspect, or require copies of or extracts from, the documents filed with the registrar (s. 16(1)). Hence, on account of this publicity, members of the public are deemed to have notice of the fact that at least one of the partners has only a limited liability for the firm's debts. A further provision of the Act designed to secure publicity is the provision that any arrangement by which a general partner becomes a limited partner or by which a limited partner's share is assigned must be immediately advertised in the *Gazette* (*i.e.* the *Edinburgh Gazette* in the case of a limited partnership registered in Scotland): until that is done, the arrangement is deemed to be of no effect (s. 10).

Limited partnerships are governed by the Partnership Act 1890 **2–168** and by the common law to the same extent as ordinary partnerships except in so far as the Limited Partnerships Act 1907 expressly provides otherwise (s. 7). The following are the main modifications made by the Act of 1907:

(a) **Management**

2–169 A limited partner must not take part in the management of the partnership business, and has no power to bind the firm. He may, however, either personally or through an agent, at any time inspect the books of the firm and examine into the state and prospects of the partnership business, and may advise with his copartners on these matters.

2–170 If a limited partner takes part in the management of the partnership business, he becomes liable as if he were a general partner for all the debts and obligations of the firm incurred while he takes part in the management (s. 6(1)).

(b) **Dissolution**

2–171 A limited partnership is not dissolved by the death or bankruptcy of a limited partner, and the lunacy of a limited partner is not a ground for dissolution of the partnership by the court unless the lunatic's share cannot be otherwise ascertained and realised (s. 6(2)).

(c) **Winding Up**

2–172 On the dissolution of a limited partnership its affairs are wound up by the general partners unless the court orders otherwise (s. 6(3)).

2–173 A limited partnership registered in Scotland may be wound up by sequestration (Bankruptcy (Scotland) Act 1985, s. 6(1)). Alternatively, a judicial factor may be appointed.

2–174 Formerly, a limited partnership registered in Scotland could be wound up as an unregistered company under the Companies Acts. This ceased to be permissible on the repeal in part of section 665 of the Companies Act 1985 by section 75(2) of and Schedule 8 to the Bankruptcy (Scotland) Act 1985.

(d) **Rules Applicable between the Partners**

2–175 Subject to any agreement, expressed or implied, between the partners:

(i) any difference arising as to ordinary matters connected with the partnership business may be decided by a majority of the general partners;

(ii) a limited partner may, with the consent of the general partners, assign his share in the partnership, and the assignee then becomes a limited partner with all the rights of the cedent;

(iv) a person may be introduced as a partner without the consent of the existing limited partners;

(v) a limited partner is not entitled to dissolve the partnership by notice (s. 6(5)).

The limited partnership has not been a popular form of business **2–176** organisation, principally because the private limited company, with a minimum membership at that time of two, was introduced in the same year, and enabled two persons, with only a little more formality, to carry on business as a limited company, each securing for himself a limit on his personal liability for the company's debts and at the same time, if appointed as a director, being entitled to take part in the management of the company's business.[1]

VIII BUSINESS NAMES ACT 1985

Provisions on business names, formerly comprising Part II of the **2–177** Companies Act 1981 (headed "Company Names and Business Names"), were consolidated into the Business Names Act 1985, itself part of the major consolidation of company law which took place in 1985. The Act covers all business names, whether the name is that of a partnership, an individual or a company. Section references here are to sections of the Business Names Act 1985.

The provisions fall under two main headings: **2–178**

(a) control of business names; and

(b) disclosure of names of persons using business names.

(a) **Control of Business Names**

The Business Names Act 1985 applies to any person who has a **2–179** place of business in Great Britain and who carries on business in Great Britain under a name which—

[1] On the popularity of limited partnerships as a means of bypassing the agricultural holdings legislation, see Catherine Montgomery Blight, "Land Tenure Forty Years On" (1989) 34 J.L.S. S. 463.

(a) in the case of a partnership, does not consist of the surnames of all partners who are individuals and the corporate names of all partners who are bodies corporate (*e.g.* companies) without any addition other than a permitted addition;

(b) in the case of an individual, does not consist of his surname without any addition other than a permitted addition;

(c) in the case of a company capable of being wound up under the Companies Act 1985, does not consist of its corporate name without any addition other than a permitted addition (s. 1(1)).

2–180 The following are permitted additions—

(a) in the case of a partnership, the forenames of individual partners or the initials of their forenames, or, where two or more individual partners have the same surname, the addition of "s" at the end of that surname;

(b) in the case of an individual, his forename or the initials of his forename;

(c) in any case, any addition merely indicating that the business is carried on in succession to a former owner of the business (s. 1(2)).

2–181 A person to whom the Act applies must not, without the written approval of the Secretary of State, carry on business in Great Britain under a name which—

(a) would be likely to give the impression that the business is connected with the Government or with any local authority; or

(b) includes any word or expression specified in regulations made under the Act (s. 2(1)).

2–182 A person contravening this provision is guilty of an offence and liable to be fined (ss. 2(4) and 7).

2–183 The principal Regulations are the Company and Business Names Regulations 1981 (S.I. 1981 No. 1685), which were made under the Companies Act 1981 and continued in force by section 31(2) of the Companies Consolidation (Consequential Provisions) Act 1985. As amended by the Company and Business Names (Amendment) Regulations 1982 (S.I. 1982 No. 1653), 1992 (S.I. 1992 No. 1196) and 1995 (S.I. 1995 No. 3022), they list about 90 words or expressions for the use of which in a business name the Secretary of State's approval is required (*e.g.* "Chamber of Commerce", "Institute", "Scottish" and "Trade Union"). In the case of many of the words and expressions listed there is a "relevant body" which must first be approached, with a written request that it should indicate whether (and if so why) it has any objections to the proposed use, and a copy of any response received must then be submitted to the Secretary of State (*e.g.* for the expression "Contact Lens" the relevant body is the General Optical Council, for the words "Dental" and "Dentistry" the relevant body is the General Dental Council and for the word "University" the relevant body is the Privy Council).

By the Contracting Out (Functions in relation to the Registration of Companies) Order 1995 (S.I. 1995 No. 1013) the Secretary of State may authorise the exercise by another person, or that person's employees, of the functions conferred on him by section 2. **2–184**

(b) Disclosure of Names of Persons Using Business Names

Section 4(1) provides that any person to whom the Act applies must state in legible characters on all business letters, written orders for goods or services, invoices and receipts and written demands for payment of debts— **2–185**

(i) in the case of a partnership, the name of each partner;
(ii) in the case of an individual, his name;
(iii) in the case of a company, its corporate name; and
(iv) in relation to each person so named, an address in Great Britain at which service of any document will be effective.

These requirements are modified in the case of a partnership of more than 20 persons provided the document states the address of the principal place of business and that a list of the partners' names is open to inspection at that place (s. 4(3)).

A second requirement of section 4(1) is that any person to whom the Act applies must display a notice containing all names and addresses, in a prominent position so that it may be easily read, in any premises where the business is carried on and to which the customers of the business or suppliers of goods or services have access. **2–186**

Section 4(2) provides that any person to whom the Act applies must, on request, give a written notice of all names and addresses in (i) to (iv), above, to any person with whom anything is done or discussed in the course of the business. There is no modification in this provision for partnerships of more than 20 persons. **2–187**

A person who without reasonable excuse contravenes section 4(1) or 4(2) is guilty of an offence and liable to be fined (ss. 4(6) **2–188** and 7). In addition there is, in section 5(1), the following civil remedy: where legal proceedings are brought to enforce any right arising out of a contract entered into at a time when the pursuer was in breach of section 4(1) or 4(2), they will be dismissed if the defender shows that, because of the breach, he has been unable to pursue a claim against the pursuer or has suffered some financial loss; however, to this there is the exception that the court may permit the proceedings to continue if it is satisfied that it is just and equitable to do so.

IX GOODWILL

2–189 One of the assets of a business, whether the business is carried on by a partnership, or by an individual or by a company, is likely to be goodwill, a matter governed by the common law.

2–190 It has been said that "goodwill is an elastic term of which it is not easy, if it is possible, to give an exhaustive definition" (*per* Lord Wellwood in *Hughes v. Assessor for Stirling* (1892) 19 R. 840, at p. 842).

2–191 The best-known attempted definition is that of Lord Chancellor Eldon in the English case *Cruttwell v. Lye* (1810) 17 Ves. Jun. 335; 34 E.R. 129:

L., who had a long-established trade as a common carrier, became bankrupt and his business was sold by auction in lots. Lot 1 was L.'s carrying trade from Bristol and Bath to London with premises and goodwill, and it was purchased by C. Lot 2 was L.'s carrying trade from Bristol and Bath to Warminster and Salisbury with stock on the premises, and it was purchased in trust for L., who commenced trade again to London by that different route.

C. sought but was refused an injunction to prevent L.'s trade: L. had set up a similar trade, but not the same trade as that which had been sold to C.

Lord Eldon said (at 17 Ves. Jun. p. 346; 34 E.R. p. 134) that the goodwill which had been sold to C. was "nothing more than the probability, that the old customers will resort to the old place".

2–192 That definition was criticised by Lord Herschell in *Trego v. Hunt* [1896] A.C. 7, at p. 17, as being "far too narrow" if it had been intended as an exhaustive definition.

The facts in *Trego v. Hunt* were that T., a varnish and japan manufacturer, had taken H. into partnership under an agreement which provided that the goodwill of the business should remain the sole property of T.

H. acquired a list of the firm's customers with a view to obtaining their custom for himself at the termination of the partnership.

The House of Lords held that T. was entitled to an injunction restraining H. from asking any customer of the firm to deal with him after the firm's dissolution.

Lord Herschell said (at p. 17): "It is the connection . . . formed [*with customers*], together with the circumstances, whether of habit or otherwise, which tend to make it permanent, that constitutes the goodwill of a business. It is this which constitutes the difference between a business just started, which has no goodwill attached to it, and one which has acquired a goodwill. The former trader has to seek out his customers from among the community as best he can. The latter has a custom ready made."

Goodwill is an incorporeal asset. It may be heritable or move- **2–193** able or partly heritable and partly moveable. If and in so far as it is associated with premises in which the business has been carried on, it is heritable, and if and in so far as it is associated with the reputation of the trader, it is moveable. Decided cases relating to the valuation of premises, especially licensed premises, and to the law of succession illustrate the importance of the distinction, *e.g.*:

(a) *Hughes v. Assessor for Stirling* (1892) 19 R. 840 was a case in **2–194** which for valuation purposes the goodwill of a publican's business at the Commercial Inn, Denny, was held to be partly heritable and partly moveable.

(b) In *Assessor for Edinburgh v. Caira and Crolla*, 1928 S.C. 398, **2–195** the same decision was reached in relation to a fish restaurant business.

(c) *Graham v. Graham's Trustees* (1904) 6 F. 1015 concerned a **2–196** point in the law of succession. G. had been the occupier of public-houses in Glasgow. On his death the question arose of whether the goodwill formed part of his moveable estate, out of which his son was entitled to claim legitim. The circumstances in the case were such that the court held that the goodwill was heritable (and so was not estate out of which legitim could be claimed).

A person selling the goodwill of his business is barred from **2–197** representing that he is continuing the business himself. He therefore cannot solicit the customers of his former business to transfer their custom to him, nor can he use the firm name to which the goodwill attaches. These two consequences are illustrated in the following cases:

2–198 (a) *Dumbarton Steamboat Co. Ltd v. MacFarlane* (1899) 1 F. 993: The firm of MacFarlane, Lang & Co., whose partners were MacF. and L., had conducted business as carriers at Dumbarton. The firm sold its business and its assets including goodwill to the promoters of D. Ltd, a company which was afterwards formed. MacF. and L. became employees of D. Ltd, but after about three years MacF. was dismissed. He began business on his own account, soliciting orders from the customers of the former firm, and D. Ltd raised a process of interdict against him.

Held that it was against the good faith of the contract of sale for MacF. to solicit the custom of his former firm, the goodwill of which had been transferred to D. Ltd, and interdict *granted.*

2–199 (b) *Smith v. McBride & Smith* (1888) 16 R. 36: James Smith and Joseph McBride had carried on business in partnership as aerated water manufacturers in Greenock under the name "Smith & McBride". In 1884 their partnership terminated, and they agreed that Smith should pay £300 to McBride for the latter's share in the business and that Smith should acquire the business with goodwill, machinery and stock-in-trade and carry it on in his own name.

McBride entered into partnership with William Smith, a brother of James Smith, and traded under the name "Smith & McBride".

Held that James Smith was entitled to an interdict restraining McBride and William Smith from trading under that name.

Further Reading

Scots Mercantile Law Statutes (reprinted every second year from *The Parliament House Book*) for Partnership Act 1890, Business Names Act 1985 and Companies Act 1985

Gloag and Henderson, *The Law of Scotland*, Chapters 38 (part) and 50

David M. Walker, *Principles of Scottish Private Law*, Volume I, Chapter 3.10 and Volume III, Chapters 5.19 (part) and 5.39 (part)

David Bennett, *An Introduction to the Law of Partnership in Scotland* (1995, W. Green/Sweet & Maxwell with The Institute of Chartered Accountants of Scotland)

James Bennett Miller, *The Law of Partnership in Scotland*, 2nd ed. by Gordon H. Brough (1994, W. Green)

The Laws of Scotland: Stair Memorial Encyclopaedia, Volume 16, Title *Partnership* (part) by Judith J. H. Pearson

E. *Lindley and Banks on Partnership*, 17th ed. by R. C. I'Anson Banks (1995, Sweet & Maxwell)

Enid A. Marshall, *Scottish Cases on Partnerships and Companies*, Part I (1980, W. Green)

CHAPTER 3

COMPANIES

	Para.
Introduction	3–01
(a) Registration	3–12
(b) Promoters	3–14
(c) Members, Shareholders and Stockholders	3–17
(d) Directors	3–21
(e) Share Capital	3–26
(f) Debenture and Debenture Stock	3–34
(g) Meetings and Resolutions	3–38
I Classification of Registered Companies	3–43
(a) Companies Limited by Shares, Companies Limited by Guarantee and Unlimited Companies	3–44
(i) Company Limited by Shares	3–45
(ii) Company Limited by Guarantee	3–52
(iii) Unlimited Company	3–61
(iv) Conversion from Limited to Unlimited and *Vice Versa*	3–67
(b) Public Companies and Private Companies	3–71
(i) Definitions of "Public Company" and "Private Company"	3–72
(ii) Differences between Public Companies and Private Companies	3–77
(1) Form of memorandum	3–80
(2) The company's name	3–82
(3) Commencing business	3–86
(4) Directors and secretary	3–86
(5) Capital	3–91
(a) The raising of share capital	3–93
(b) Allotment of share capital	3–94
(c) Payment for share capital	3–97
(d) Maintenance of capital	3–103
(6) Restriction on distribution of assets	3–108
(7) Proxies	3–109
(8) Resolutions	3–110
(9) Conversion from limited to unlimited	3–113
(iii) Conversion from Private to Public and *Vice Versa*	3–114
(1) Conversion from private to public	3–115
(2) Conversion from public to private	3–119
(c) Holding Companies and Subsidiaries	3–123
II The Separate Personality of a Registered Company	3–128
(a) The Registration Provisions	3–129
(b) *Salomon's* Case	3–138
(c) Application of the Principle in *Salomon's* Case	3–142
(d) Lifting the Veil	3–146
(i) Statutory Instances	3–147
(1) Trading with the enemy	3–148
(2) Membership below minimum	3–151
(3) Holding company and subsidiaries	3–152
(4) Department of Trade and Industry investigations	3–154
(5) Sole director not to be secretary	3–156
(6) Disclosure of directors' interests	3–157
(ii) Common Law Instances	3–158
(1) Company formed to enable valid contract in restraint of trade to be broken	3–159
(2) Transfer of land in breach of contract of sale	3–160
(3) Subsidiary company as agent of holding company	3–161
(4) Court's discretion in relation to "take-over bid"	3–162

	Para.
(5) Decision of all the members taking effect as decision of the company	3–164
III Comparison of Registered Companies with Partnerships	3–165
(a) Advantages of Registered Company	3–171
(i) Limited Liability	3–173
(ii) Transferability of Shares	3–174
(iii) Management by Directors	3–176
(iv) No Limit in Number of Members	3–178
(v) Changes in Membership	3–180
(vi) Borrowing and Granting Security	3–181
(b) Advantages of Partnership	3–183
(i) No Formalities in Formation	3–184
(ii) No Formalities in Carrying on Business	3–186
(iii) No Disclosure of Financial Affairs	3–188
(iv) No Restriction on Share Capital	3–190
(v) Arrangements with Creditors	3–192
IV Memorandum of Association	3–193
(a) Relationship between Memorandum and Articles	3–194
(b) Contents of Memorandum	3–198
(i) Name	3–199
(1) Choice of name	3–201
(2) Change of name	3–203
(3) Publication of name (ss. 348–351)	3–205
(4) Business names	3–208
(ii) Statement that Company is to be Public Company	3–209
(iii) Registered Office	3–210
(iv) Objects	3–216
(1) *Ultra vires* doctrine in operation	3–220
(a) Purpose of the doctrine	3–221
(b) Illustrative cases	3–222
(2) Abolition of *ultra vires* doctrine	3–228
(a) Company's capacity not limited by its memorandum (s. 35)	3–229
(b) Powers of directors to bind the company (s. 35A)	3–233
(c) No duty to inquire (s. 35B)	3–237
(3) Alteration of objects	3–238
(v) Statement that Liability is Limited	3–242
(vi) Share Capital	3–244
(vii) Additional Clauses	3–256
(viii) Association Clause	3–258
V Articles of Association	3–262
(a) Form and Contents of Articles	3–263
(b) Alteration of Articles	3–267
(c) Effect of Memorandum and Articles	3–276

INTRODUCTION

THE aim of this chapter is to give an elementary account of the most prominent aspects of company law, a branch of mercantile law of ever-increasing complexity. More than any other topic included in this book, company law is justifiably regarded as a subject in its own right, the principles and practical details of which must be sought in more specialist works. **3–01**

The companies with which this chapter is concerned are *registered* companies, *i.e.* companies incorporated by registration under the Companies Acts. Most, but not all, registered companies are *limited* companies, *i.e.* companies in which the members are liable only up to a fixed amount for the company's debts. **3–02**

The registration system was introduced to Scotland by the Joint Stock Companies Act 1856. This branch of the law is therefore, by legal standards, a modern one, largely consisting of statute law, **3–03** enacted, amended and re-enacted with amendment in a long succession of Companies Acts since that year.

3–04 The most recent comprehensive consolidation took place in 1985. It consisted not of a single Act, as consolidation had formerly done, but of four Acts:

the Companies Act 1985;
the Business Names Act 1985;
the Company Securities (Insider Dealing) Act 1985; and
the Companies Consolidation (Consequential Provisions) Act 1985.

3–05 The principal of these four Acts is the Companies Act 1985, and in this chapter references to sections of a statute are, except where the context requires otherwise, references to sections of that Act. Of the subordinate legislation made under the authority of the Acts the regulations most often referred to below are the Companies (Tables A to F) Regulations 1985 (S.I. 1985 No. 805), the Schedule to which consists of model forms of memoranda and articles for the various types of companies, and in what follows references to Tables are to Tables in that Schedule. Also important for even an elementary study of company law are the Companies (Single Member Private Limited Companies) Regulations 1992 (S.I. 1992 No. 1699) which made it legally possible to have a one-person private limited company, and the Partnerships and Unlimited Companies (Accounts) Regulations 1993 (S.I. 1993 No. 1820) which removed from unlimited companies the advantage of balance-sheet secrecy.

3–06 Since 1985 there have been several amending Acts. In particular, the Insolvency Act 1985 substantially amended the law relating to insolvency and also the law relating to disqualification of company directors. The alterations made by that Act to the consolidation of 1985 were so extensive that two further consolidating Acts were passed in the following year:

the Insolvency Act 1986; and
the Company Directors Disqualification Act 1986.

These Acts were a new consolidation of *parts* of the consolidating Acts of 1985. Further major amendments were made by:

the Financial Services Act 1986; and
the Companies Act 1989.

In addition the Company Securities (Insider Dealing) Act 1985 has been repealed and its provisions restated as Part V of the Criminal Justice Act 1993.

The law relating to companies is now, therefore, to be found mainly in the four consolidating Acts of 1985–86 (the Companies Act 1985, the Business Names Act 1985, the Insolvency Act 1986 and the Company Directors Disqualification Act 1986) as amended by the Financial Services Act 1986 and the Companies Act 1989. **3–07**

The following are prominent features of company law: **3–08**

(i) *Increasing statutory control*—The legislation relating to companies has vastly increased in volume and complexity since its introduction in the middle of the nineteenth century. At no time has the increase been more rapid and extensive than in recent years, and there is no sign of abatement in the near future.

(ii) *Case law*—Despite the great volume of legislation company law has never been codified. The numerous statutes have been superimposed on a basis of common law, as revealed in decided cases. In addition there have been very many cases in which the courts have been called on to interpret and apply the statutory provisions. Where statutory provisions have been carried forward unaltered into new consolidating Acts, cases decided on the earlier enactment retain their authority. On the other hand, there have been several cases which have prompted the legislature to make statutory changes; *e.g.* the case of *Derry v. Peek* (1889) 14 App. Cas. 337 showed the inadequacy of the law relating to mis-statements in a prospectus and led to the passing of the Directors' Liability Act 1890.

(iii) *E.C. influence*—An important feature in the development of company law at the present day is the need to comply with E.C. directives on harmonisation of company law in the Member States. For example, the Companies Act 1989 implemented the Seventh and Eighth Company Law Directives on consolidated accounts and on the regulation of auditors, respectively.

(iv) *A company's wider responsibilities*—A trend which emerged in company legislation in the 1980s was the recognition of a company as an institution with social and economic responsibilities to groups other than its shareholders; *e.g.* the Companies Act 1980 made a start on the recognition of a company's responsibilities to its employees.

3–09 Scots company law is for the most part the same as English company law, but for the following two reasons there are some distinctions:

(i) There are some statutory provisions which make a distinction between Scotland and England. Obvious instances occur in Part XVIII of the Act of 1985 in which the provisions relating to floating charges derived from the Companies (Floating Charges and Receivers) (Scotland) Act 1972 apply only to Scotland and in Part III of the Insolvency Act 1986 which consists of two Chapters, the first entitled "Receivers and Managers (England and Wales)" and the second "Receivers (Scotland)".

(ii) Since company legislation is consolidating, and not codifying, it is superimposed on the common law of the two different legal systems, and that common law is not necessarily the same in Scotland as in England; this point is important because most of the statutory provisions are confined to matters of detail, leaving many of the broad principles to rest still on the common law.

3–10 The selected aspects of company law considered in this chapter are all of an introductory nature. It is appropriate to look first at:

I. The classification of registered companies.

The topic dealt with next is the most important principle of all in company law:

II. The separate personality of a registered company.

The stage has then been reached for appreciating:

III. A comparison of registered companies with partnerships.

The remainder of the chapter is devoted to the two documents which comprise the constitution of a registered company:

IV. The memorandum of association; and

V. The articles of association.

3–11 At this preliminary stage it may be useful for the reader to have a brief explanation of some of the terms commonly met with in any study of company law:

(a) registration;
(b) promoters;
(c) members, shareholders and stockholders;
(d) directors;
(e) share capital;
(f) debentures and debenture stock; and
(g) meetings and resolutions.

(a) **Registration**

Frequent mention is made throughout company law of the need to register documents. Registration means delivery of the documents in question to the appropriate registrar of companies. If the company's registered office is in Scotland, the appropriate registrar is the Registrar of Companies for Scotland, Companies House, 37 Castle Terrace, Edinburgh EH1 2EB. **3–12**

The purpose of the registration requirements is to secure publicity: any member of the public has the right to inspect a company's file kept by the registrar of companies. An inspection will yield information about the company's constitution (contained in the company's memorandum of association and articles of association), and about important matters arising during the company's operation (including special resolutions and its annual accounts). **3–13**

(b) **Promoters**

Promoters are the persons who take the necessary steps to set the company going. They give instructions to solicitors or other professional persons for the preparation and registration of documents such as the memorandum and articles and they may procure capital for the new company. Professional persons employed by the promoters are not, merely because of their employment, promoters themselves. **3–14**

Promoters are not agents for the company which they bring into existence, because until incorporated the company is not a legal person and so can have no agents. Contracts which promoters purport to make on behalf of a company before its formation are binding on the promoters personally (*Kelner v. Baxter* (1866) L.R. 2 C.P. 174 and s. 36C(i) inserted in the 1985 Act by Companies Act 1989, s. 130(4)). Similarly, a new company once formed cannot sue for damages for breach of a pre-incorporation contract entered into on its behalf by its promoters (*Tinnevelly Sugar Refining Co. Ltd v. Mirrlees, Watson & Yaryan Co. Ltd* (1894) 21 R. 1009). **3–15**

Promoters stand in a fiduciary relationship to the company which they are forming, and must disclose any profit which they make out of the promotion either to an independent board of directors or to the existing and intended shareholders. In a small private company **3–16** it is quite usual for the promoters to be themselves the first shareholders and directors, and in that case there is unlikely to be any difficulty over the duty of disclosure.

(c) **Members, Shareholders and Stockholders**

3–17 The members of a company are the persons who together own the company. They are often called "shareholders" because, in the commonest type of company (the company limited by shares), each member holds a number of shares in the capital of the company.

3–18 "Members" is, however, a wider term than "shareholders". This is because companies limited by guarantee and unlimited companies need not have a share capital: some companies, therefore, have no shareholders, but they do have members.

3–19 A member is not necessarily a natural person (*i.e.* an individual): artificial legal persons (such as partnerships and companies) may be members of a company.

3–20 A company may convert its shares, provided they are fully paid up, into *stock* (s. 121(2)). If it has done so, it will have "stockholders" instead of "shareholders". Shares are at the present day usually fully paid up in any case, and so the distinction between shareholders and stockholders is seldom of any practical importance.

(d) **Directors**

3–21 Directors are the persons who manage the company. They may or may not be members. Their powers depend on the provisions of the company's articles of association, and are often wide; *e.g.*:

"Subject to the provisions of the Act, the memorandum and the articles and to any directions given by special resolution, the business of the company shall be managed by the directors who may exercise all the powers of the company . . . " (Table A, reg. 70).

3–22 An important topic in company law is the extent to which members may exercise control over directors.

3–23 Directors, as such, are not employees of the company: they are its officers or agents. It is however possible for a director to be also an employee; *e.g.* a managing director is both a director and an employee of the company.

Directors occupy a fiduciary position (*i.e.* a position of trust) towards the company as a legal person distinct from the individual members. **3–24**

In performing their functions directors must have regard to the interests of the company's employees in general as well as the interests of its members (s. 309(1)). This statutory duty is owed by the directors to the company (and to the company alone) and is enforceable in the same way as any other fiduciary duty owed to the company by its directors (s. 309(2)). **3–25**

(e) **Share Capital**

Most companies have a share capital, and this will be divided into a number of shares of a certain amount each; *e.g.* a company may have a share capital of £100,000, divided into 400,000 shares of 25p each. **3–26**

A distinction is made between *nominal* (also referred to as *authorised*) capital, *allotted* capital, *called-up* capital, and *paid-up* capital. The meaning of the term "*the authorised minimum*" should also be noted. **3–27**

The *nominal* (or *authorised*) capital is the amount stated in the company's memorandum of association as being the capital of the company. The allotted, called-up, or paid-up capital can never exceed the amount of the nominal capital. **3–28**

The *allotted* capital is the amount of capital held by the shareholders; *e.g.* if a company has a nominal capital of £100,000, divided into 400,000 shares of 25p each, it may be that only £75,000 has been allotted; there will then be 300,000 shares of 25p each held by shareholders. **3–29**

Called-up capital is the amount of capital which the company has actually called up from its shareholders. It is usual now for companies to call up all the allotted capital in full very soon after it has been allotted. Usually, therefore, if a company has allotted 300,000 shares of 25p each, its called-up capital will be £75,000 because each shareholder will have been asked to pay the full 25p on each share held. Where a company's allotted capital has not been fully called up, each shareholder remains liable to pay to the company, when a call is made, the amount unpaid on his shares. **3–30**

Paid-up capital is the amount which has actually been paid by the shareholders to the company. Normally it will be the same as **3–31** the called-up capital, but there is the possibility that some shareholders will have fallen into arrears in the payment of calls.

3–32 The term "*the authorised minimum*" means £50,000, or such other sum as the Department of Trade and Industry may, by statutory instrument, specify instead (s. 118(1)). The Act provides that the nominal capital of a *public* company must be not less than the authorised minimum (s. 11), and that before such a company can do business the registrar of companies must be satisfied that the company's allotted share capital is not less than the authorised minimum (s. 117(2)). The capital of a private company may be of any amount.

3–33 The shares forming the share capital are often of two or more different classes, *e.g.* preference shares, entitling their holders to a preference dividend of, say, 7 per cent, and ordinary shares, whose holders will not be entitled to any dividend unless there is a surplus of profits after the preference dividend has been paid. Prima facie ("Unless the contrary is proved") a preference dividend is cumulative, *i.e.* if the profits of one year are insufficient to pay it, the arrears will require to be paid in a subsequent year before any ordinary dividend is paid in that year.

(f) Debentures and Debenture Stock

3–34 In investment circles debentures and debenture stock are bought and sold in much the same way as shares and stock. In law, however, debentures and debenture stock are quite different in nature from shares and stock.

3–35 A debenture is a document in which the company acknowledges that it is liable to pay a specified amount, say, £100. The person holding the debenture (the "debenture holder") is, in law, a *creditor* of the company, entitled to be paid his £100 out of the company's assets before any distribution is made to shareholders. Like other creditors, the debenture holder may or may not have a right in security over property belonging to the company, *i.e.* his debenture may be a secured debenture or an unsecured debenture. The security may be a fixed security (*e.g.* a standard security over the company's heritable property) or a floating charge over all or any of the company's property and undertaking for the time being.

3–36 Debentures differ from debenture stock in that debentures are each for a fixed amount such as £100, whereas debenture stock consists of a mass of indebtedness which may be divided into parcels of any amount desired, so that one debenture stockholder may hold £25 of the debenture stock, another £100 and so on.

The interest which falls due on debentures and debenture stock at fixed intervals is, like the debentures and debenture stock themselves, a *debt* due by the company: there can be no question of paying dividends to shareholders unless and until the interest due to debenture holders and debenture stockholders has been fully paid. **3–37**

(g) Meetings and Resolutions

There are three kinds of meeting of the *members* of a company: **3–38**

(i) annual general meetings, which must be held each calendar year;

(ii) extraordinary general meetings (*i.e.* all general meetings other than the annual general meetings); and

(iii) if the share capital of the company is divided into different classes, class meetings (*e.g.* a meeting of preference shareholders).

Normally these meetings are convened by the directors, but section 368 (as amended by Companies Act 1989, s. 145 and Sched. 19), one of several minority rights' sections in the Acts, enables a general meeting to be requisitioned (*i.e.* demanded) by the holders of not less than one-tenth of the paid-up capital carrying the right to vote at general meetings (or if the company does not have a share capital, members representing not less than one-tenth of the total voting rights of all the members with a right to vote at general meetings). If the directors do not within 21 days from the date of the deposit of the requisition at the company's registered office proceed duly to convene a meeting for a date not more than 28 days after the notice convening the meeting, the requisitionists or the majority of them may themselves convene a meeting.

Business is transacted at company meetings by the passing of resolutions, which may be *ordinary* resolutions (requiring only a simple majority of votes), *special* resolutions (requiring a three-fourths majority and 21 days' prior notice) or *extraordinary* resolutions (also requiring a three-fourths majority but only 14 days' prior notice). **3–39**

The type of resolution required depends on the nature of the business, *e.g.*: **3–40** ordinary resolution—appointment or removal of a director (Table A, reg. 78 and s. 303(1), respectively);

special resolution—alteration of the company's articles of association (s. 9(1));

extraordinary resolution—voluntary winding up on the ground of inability to pay debts (Insolvency Act 1986, s. 84(1)).

Where neither the Acts nor the company's articles of association require a special or an extraordinary resolution, then an ordinary resolution is sufficient.

3–41 Special resolutions are distinct from *those ordinary resolutions which require special notice*: *e.g.* an ordinary resolution for the removal of a director under section 303 requires special notice (s. 303(2)). The procedure for special notice is laid down in section 379; it involves giving notice *to* the company *28 days* before the meeting at which the resolution is to be passed.

3–42 Meetings of the *directors* of a company are referred to as "*board meetings*". Proceedings at these meetings are regulated by provisions in the company's articles of association (see, *e.g.*, Table A, regs. 88 to 98).

I CLASSIFICATION OF REGISTERED COMPANIES

3–43 The classifications of registered companies to be considered here are:

(a) companies limited by shares, companies limited by guarantee and unlimited companies;
(b) public companies and private companies; and
(c) holding companies and subsidiaries.

(a) **Companies Limited by Shares, Companies Limited by Guarantee and Unlimited Companies**

3–44 All registered companies are embraced within this classification, *i.e.* every registered company must take one of the three forms:

(i) company limited by shares;
(ii) company limited by guarantee; and
(iii) unlimited company.

Brief mention will also be made of:

(iv) conversion from limited to unlimited and vice versa.

(i) *Company Limited by Shares*

This is by far the commonest type of registered company. It may be public or private. Its name will always include the word "limited". **3–45**

A company limited by shares is defined as "a company having the liability of its members limited by the memorandum to the amount, if any, unpaid on the shares respectively held by them" (s. 1(2)(a)). The amount unpaid may be called up by the company at any time. It is, however, now usual for all the shares which a company has issued to be fully paid up from a date early in the company's life, and so a member usually has no liability to pay anything at all to the company. **3–46**

When the company is wound up, the member will be entitled to receive back from the company the amount which he (or a former member from whom he has obtained a transfer) has paid to the company on each share, but this repayment of capital to the member is made only where all the company's creditors have been paid in full. **3–47**

The *nominal* value (also referred to as "the par value") of a share (*e.g.* £1 if the company's capital is divided into shares of £1 each) is in law the measure of the member's stake in the company: he may lose his £1 per share, but he cannot be held liable for more, however great the company's own liabilities to its creditors may be. **3–48**

In reality, of course, the member will regard his stake in the company as being the amount which he has paid to the company (if he is one of the original shareholders) or to the former member from whom he has himself obtained the shares by transfer. This purchase price is seldom the same as the nominal or par value of the shares. A company may, for instance, allot its £1 shares at a "premium" of 25p; this means that the applicant will be required to pay £1.25p to the company for each share, that the company will hold the £1 as paid-up capital and transfer the 25p to a special capital account called the "share premium account", and that the shares will be fully paid shares with £1 operating as the measure of the member's entitlement to dividends and, if the company is wound up and all creditors are fully paid, to first the return of nominal capital (*i.e.* £1 per share) and secondly the division of surplus assets. **3–49**

The memorandum of association of a company limited by shares must be in the form (as nearly as circumstances admit) set out in: **3–50**

(1) Table B, if the company is a private company; or

(2) Table F, if the company is a public company (s. 3(1)).

3–51 A company limited by shares need not register articles of association. If it chooses to register articles, these may adopt all or any of the regulations contained in Table A (s. 8(1)). If it does not register articles, the regulations contained in Table A are treated as the company's articles. Further, if the company registers articles, Table A is still treated as containing the company's articles except in so far as the registered articles exclude or modify the regulations contained in Table A (s. 8(2)).

(ii) *Company Limited by Guarantee*

3–52 A company limited by guarantee is defined as "a company having the liability of its members limited by the memorandum to such amount as the members may respectively thereby undertake to contribute to the assets of the company in the event of its being wound up" (s. 1(2)(b)).

3–53 The distinctive clause in the memorandum of a guarantee company is the clause by which "every member of the company undertakes to contribute such amount as may be required (not exceeding £100 (or £200, *etc.*)) to the company's assets if it should be wound up while he is a member or within one year after he ceases to be a member, for payment of the company's debts and liabilities contracted before he ceases to be a member, and of the costs, charges and expenses of winding up, and for the adjustment of the rights of the contributories among themselves". This liability can arise only when the company is being wound up: it is available as a protection for creditors who would otherwise be left not fully paid at the end of the company's life.

3–54 Just as the company cannot during its active existence call up the guarantee fund, so it cannot give any particular creditor security over the fund. An attempt to do this was held to be of no effect in *Robertson v. British Linen Co.* (1890) 18 R. 1225 (O.H.), a case to be contrasted with *Lloyds Bank Ltd v. Morrison & Son*, 1927 S.C. 571, in which a guarantee company was held entitled to assign to its bank a guarantee obtained from M. (who was not a member), quite distinct from the company's statutory guarantee fund.

3–55 There are two forms of guarantee company—commonly described as the "pure" form and the "hybrid" form. The pure form has no share capital: the creditors can look only to the statutory guarantee fund for protection and that will not exist until the company is being wound up. The hybrid form has a share capital (available for the protection of creditors during the company's active existence) as well as a guarantee fund. This hybrid form had been rarely used and since December 22, 1980, the creation of any *further* companies of this kind has been prohibited (s. 1(4) re-enacting Companies Act 1980, s. 1(2)).

By definition a public company must be either a company limited by shares or a company limited by guarantee and having a share capital (s. 1(4)). If follows that all pure forms of guarantee company are private companies. **3–56**

The memorandum of association of a company limited by guarantee must be in the form (as nearly as circumstances admit) set out in: **3–57**

(1) Table C, if the company has no share capital (the pure form of guarantee company and necessarily private); or

(2) Part I of Table D, if the company has a share capital and is a public company (the hybrid form, which will in time die out); or

(3) Part II of Table D, if the company has a share capital and is a private company (again the hybrid form, which will in time die out) (s. 3(1)).

A company limited by guarantee must always register articles of association (s. 7(1)). **3–58**

The model form of articles for the pure form of guarantee company is set out in Table C and the model form of articles for the hybrid form of guarantee company (whether public or private) is stated in Part III of Table D to be the same as the regulations of Table A (s. 8(4)). **3–59**

A private guarantee company is on certain conditions exempt from the requirement that the word "limited" should be part of its name (s. 30(2)). The conditions which must be fulfilled are: **3–60**

(1) the company's objects are the promotion of commerce, art, science, education, religion, charity or any profession and anything incidental or conducive to any of those objects; and

(2) the company's memorandum or articles:

(i) require its profits or other income to be applied in promoting its objects;

(ii) prohibit the payment of dividends to its members; and

(iii) require all the assets which would otherwise be available to its members generally to be transferred on its winding up either to another body with objects similar to its own or to another body whose objects are the promotion of charity and anything incidental or conducive to charity (s. 30(3)).

(iii) *Unlimited Company*

3–61 An unlimited company is defined as "a company not having any limit on the liability of its members" (s. 1(2)(c)).

3–62 This type of registered company was becoming virtually obsolete by 1967, when the Companies Act of that year somewhat revived it, because it was by that Act made the only type of registered company which could keep its balance sheet secret. By the Partnerships and Unlimited Companies (Accounts) Regulations 1993 (S.I. 1993 No. 1820) an unlimited company no longer has that advantage if it is a "qualifying company" as defined in those regulations. An unlimited company is a "qualifying company" if each of its members is (a) a limited company or (b) another unlimited company or a Scottish firm, each of whose members is a limited company (reg. 9(1)). A "qualifying company" must deliver its accounts to the registrar of companies (reg. 10).

3–63 Since by definition a public company must be either a company limited by shares or a company limited by guarantee (and having a share capital) (s. 1(3)), it follows that all unlimited companies are private companies.

3–64 An unlimited company may, but need not, have a share capital. The model form of memorandum and articles for an unlimited company with a share capital is set out in Table E (ss. 3(1) and 8(4)).

3–65 An unlimited company must always register articles (s. 7(1)).

3–66 Much of the common law of Scotland relating to companies came to light as a result of cases involving unlimited companies, especially the Western Bank of Scotland and the City of Glasgow Bank, in the nineteenth century.

(iv) *Conversion from Limited to Unlimited and Vice Versa*

3–67 Procedures for conversion of a limited company into an unlimited company and vice versa are contained in sections 49 and 50 and sections 51 and 52, respectively. Each involves re-registration and the issue by the registrar of companies of a new certificate of incorporation.

The first-mentioned type of conversion might be desired to enable the company to obtain the privilege of keeping its financial affairs secret—a privilege available only to unlimited companies other than unlimited companies which are "qualifying" companies within the meaning of the Partnerships and Unlimited Companies (Accounts) Regulations 1993 (see 3–62, above). The whole procedure hinges on a prescribed form of assent to the company's being re-registered as unlimited; the form must be subscribed by or on behalf of *all* the members: nothing short of unanimity will do. This is in accordance with the dominant principle of company law that no member of a limited company can ever be required, without his written agreement, to undertake a liability which exceeds the fixed limit of his liability (see s. 16). **3–68**

Conversion from an unlimited company to a limited company can be achieved by a special resolution, but in this case it is vital that creditors be given adequate protection since they will no longer be able to rely on the members being liable without limit for the company's debts: if the company goes into liquidation within three years after the conversion, those who were members at the time of the conversion are still liable without limit for debts and liabilities contracted before the conversion (Insolvency Act 1986, s. 77(2)). **3–69**

Each of the procedures is available only once: re-conversion is not permitted. **3–70**

(b) Public Companies and Private Companies

The matters considered here are: **3–71**

(i) the definitions of "public company" and "private company";
(ii) the differences between public companies and private companies; and
(iii) conversion from private to public and vice versa.

(i) *Definitions of "Public Company" and "Private Company"*

The Act gives a definition of "public company", and then provides: "a 'private company' is a company that is not a public company" (s. 1(3)). **3–72**

"Public company" is defined as meaning "a company limited by shares or limited by guarantee and having a share capital, being a company— **3–73** (*a*) the memorandum of which states that it is to be a public company; and

(*b*) in relation to which the provisions of the Act of 1985 or the former Companies Acts as to the registration or re-registration of a company as a public company have been complied with".

3–74 The main provisions as to *registration* are as follows:

The memorandum delivered to the registrar of companies (under section 10(1) of the Act) must state: "The company is to be a public company" (s. 1(3)). The amount of the share capital stated in the memorandum as that with which the company proposes to be registered must not be less than "the authorised minimum" (s. 11). "The authorised minimum" means £50,000 or such other sum as is specified in a statutory instrument made under section 118.

3–75 The certificate of incorporation given by the registrar (under section 13(1)) must contain a statement that the company is a public company; that statement is conclusive (s. 13(6), (7)).

3–76 The provisions as to *re-registration* apply where the company is a private company with a share capital and wishes to convert itself into a public company (s. 43). These provisions will be indicated under heading (iii), below.

(ii) *Differences between Public Companies and Private Companies*

3–77 The prominent difference between a public company and a private company originally was that the minimum number of members in a public company was seven whereas in a private company it was two. The Act of 1980 (s. 2(1)) removed that difference: the minimum membership for either type of company then became two, and by the Companies (Single Member Private Limited Companies) Regulations 1992 (S.I. 1992 No. 1699) is now one for a *private limited* company. In other respects, however, the Acts of 1980 and 1989 greatly accentuated the differences between public and private companies, and the advantages enjoyed by the latter over the former.

3–78 The pre-1980 definition of a private company required the company's articles to include restrictions on the transfer of the company's shares and a limitation on the company's membership to 50 (excluding employees and former employees who had continued to hold shares). Though these distinctive requirements are no longer of statutory force, private companies commonly in practice have restrictions on the transfer of their shares and have a comparatively small membership.

The following are now the main statutory differences between public and private companies: **3–79**

(1) Form of memorandum

The memorandum of a public company must be either in the form of Part I of Table D or in the form of Table F, or as near to one of these forms as circumstances admit (s. 3(1)). Part I of Table D consists of a form of memorandum for a public company limited by guarantee and having a share capital, and Table F consists of a form of memorandum for a public company limited by shares. The former type of company is rare and will eventually disappear completely because of the provision in the Act that in future no company may be formed as, or become, a company limited by guarantee with a share capital (s. 1(4)). **3–80**

The memorandum of a private company takes one of the forms set out in Table B (private company limited by shares), Table C (company limited by guarantee and not having a share capital), Part II of Table D (private company limited by guarantee and having a share capital) and Table E (unlimited company having a share capital) or comes as near to one of these forms as circumstances admit (s.3(1)). **3–81**

(2) The company's name

The name of a public company must end with the words "public limited company". Permitted alternatives are the abbreviation "p.l.c." and the Welsh equivalent "cwmni cyfyngedig cyhoeddus", which may be abbreviated as "c.c.c.". The alternatives in Welsh are permissible only if the memorandum states that the company's registered office is to be situated in Wales (ss. 25(1), 27(1), (4)). **3–82**

A private company may be either limited or unlimited. If it is a limited company, the last word of its name will be "limited" (or the abbreviation "ltd") or (but only if the company is a Welsh company) "cyfyngedig" (or its abbreviation "cyf") (ss. 25(2), 27(1), (4)). An unlimited company must not use "limited" or "cyfyngedig" or any contraction or imitation of either of these words as the last word of its name; penalties are imposed for the **3–83** improper use of these terms (s. 34). A private guarantee company is on certain conditions exempt from the requirement that the word "limited" (or any of its alternatives) should be part of the company's name (s. 30—see 3–60, above).

(3) **Commencing business**

3–84 A private company may commence business on the issue of its certificate of incorporation.

3–85 A public company is prohibited from doing business or exercising any borrowing powers until the registrar of companies has issued to it a certificate entitling it to do so. Before issuing such a certificate the registrar must be satisfied that the nominal value of the company's allotted share capital is not less than "the authorised minimum", and there must be delivered to the registrar a statutory declaration (in a prescribed form and signed by a director or secretary of the company) stating the amount paid up on the allotted share capital, preliminary expenses and the benefits paid to promoters (s. 117(1)–(3)).

(4) **Directors and secretary**

3–86 A private company need have only one director, whereas a public company must have at least two (s. 282).

3–87 In a public company two or more directors cannot be appointed by a single resolution, unless a resolution has first been passed approving of that procedure without any vote being given against it (s. 292(1)). In a private company there is no rule requiring the appointment of directors to be voted on individually.

3–88 The directors of a private company, unlike the directors of a public company, are not required to retire at the age of 70 years, unless the company is a subsidiary of a public company (s. 293(1)–(3)).

3–89 As regards loans by a company to its directors and similar transactions, a private company, unless it is in a group of companies which includes a public company, is in a favourable position. The main provisions are in sections 330 to 342. The provisions start with the basic rule that a company must not make a loan to any of its directors or to any of the directors of its holding company and must not enter into any guarantee or provide any security in connection with a loan made by any person to such a director

(s. 330(2)). Additional prohibitions are then made applicable to "relevant companies" (*i.e.* companies which either are public companies themselves or are private companies within a group which includes a public company); these wider prohibitions extend to "quasi-loans", to persons "connected with" directors, and to "credit transactions"; each of these special terms has a detailed statutory definition (ss. 330(3), (4), 331(6), (7), 346). There are important exceptions both to the basic rule and to the wider prohibitions (ss. 332–338).

A person appointed to the office of secretary of a public company must hold certain qualifications (*e.g.* membership of specified professional bodies) (s. 286). There is no such requirement in the case of a private company. **3–90**

(5) **Capital**

Two differences arise out of the definition of "public company" (3–73 *et seq.*, above): **3–91**

(a) A public company must have a share capital, whereas a private company need not.

(b) The share capital of a public company must not be less than "the authorised minimum" (at present £50,000), whereas the share capital of a private company may be of any amount, however small.

Other differences relating to share capital include the following: **3–92**

(a) *The raising of share capital*

Public companies will normally wish to raise their capital from the investing public, and in doing so must comply with the strict controls in Part IV of the Financial Services Act 1986 or in the Public Offers of Securities Regulations 1995 (S.I. 1995 No. 1537) (relating to official listing on the stock exchange and to offers of unlisted securities, respectively). Private companies are not subject to these provisions. **3–93**

(b) *Allotment of share capital*

The directors of any company must not allot shares unless authorised to do so by the company in general meeting or by the company's articles (s. 80(1)). The authority lasts, in the case of a **3–94** public company, for only five years from the date of the resolution or from the incorporation of the company (s. 80(4)), but in the case of a private company it may last for a fixed longer period or indefinitely, if the company has passed an "elective" resolution (see 3–112, below) to that effect (s. 80A(1), (2), inserted by s. 115(1) of the Companies Act 1989).

3–95 Provision is made for pre-emption offers to existing shareholders: a company proposing to issue "equity" shares (*i.e.* broadly, ordinary, as opposed to preference, shares) for cash must first offer them to existing equity shareholders in proportion to their existing holdings (s. 89(1), (4)), but in the case of a private company this rule may be excluded by a provision in the company's memorandum or articles (s. 91(1)).

3–96 Section 84(1) provides that no allotment can be made of any share capital offered for subscription unless either that capital is subscribed for in full or the other conditions specified in the offer are satisfied. This provision applies only to a public company.

(c) *Payment for share capital*

3–97 In a public company payment for shares or for any premium on shares must not take the form of an undertaking given by any person to do work or perform services, whereas in a private company it may do so (s. 99(1), (2)).

3–98 On an allotment of a share by a public company at least one-quarter of the nominal value of the share and the whole of any premium must be paid; this is not required in the case of a private company (s. 101(1)).

3–99 Where a share is allotted as fully or partly paid up otherwise than in cash, the non-cash consideration must not in the case of a public company include an undertaking which is to be performed more than five years after the allotment (s. 102(1)); there is no such restriction in the case of a private company.

3–100 A public company must not as a general rule allot shares for a non-cash consideration unless that consideration has been valued by an "independent person", *i.e.* a person qualified to be the auditor of the company (ss. 103(1), 108(1)); no such valuation is required in the case of a private company.

3–101 Where a public company is being formed and enters into an agreement with a subscriber to the memorandum for the transfer by him during the company's first two years of one or more non-cash assets, and the consideration to be given by the company is one-tenth or more of the nominal value of the company's issued share capital, the non-cash assets must be valued by an "independent person", and the terms of the agreement must be approved by an ordinary resolution of the company (s. 104(1), (2), (4)); these provisions do not apply to a private company.

In a public company the shares for which a subscriber to the memorandum has undertaken, in the memorandum, to subscribe must be paid up in cash (s. 106); in a private company such shares may be paid for in some other way (*e.g.* by the transfer of property to the company). (The normal practice, however, is for the minimum number of subscribers (now one in a private limited company) to subscribe the memorandum for only one share each; the provision mentioned has therefore only a limited effect.) **3–102**

(d) *Maintenance of capital*

Where the net assets of a public company fall to half or less of the amount of the company's called-up share capital, the directors must call an extraordinary general meeting to consider what steps should be taken to deal with the situation (s. 142(1)); in a private company directors are under no such obligation. **3–103**

There are strict rules as to the treatment of shares in a public company which come to be held by the company itself as a result of various circumstances including forfeiture and surrender (s. 146); these rules do not apply to private companies. **3–104**

As a general rule a public company cannot have a lien or other charge on its own shares (s. 150(1)); there is no similar prohibition applying to a private company. **3–105**

As a general rule it is not lawful for any company to give financial assistance to enable a person to acquire its own shares, but with certain safeguards relaxation of that rule is allowed in the case of private companies (ss. 151(1), 155(1)). **3–106**

Any company, if authorised by its articles, may purchase its own shares (including any redeemable shares) out of distributable profits or out of the proceeds of a fresh issue, but only private companies are permitted to redeem or purchase their own shares out of capital (ss. 162(1), (2), 171(1)). **3–107**

(6) **Restriction on distribution of assets**

3–108 A public company must not make any distribution of its assets, in cash or otherwise, to its members if the company's net assets are less, or by the distribution would become less, than the total of the company's called-up share capital and "undistributable reserves" (*e.g.* the share premium account and the capital redemption reserve (s. 264(1), (3)); there is no such restriction on a private company.

(7) **Proxies**

3–109 In any company with a share capital a member who is entitled to attend and vote at a meeting of the company is entitled to appoint another person (whether a member or not) as his proxy to attend and vote instead of him. In a private company the proxy appointed to attend and vote has the same right to speak at the meeting as the member would have had; in a public company a proxy does not have this statutory right (s. 372(1), (2)).

(8) **Resolutions**

3–110 The Companies Act 1989 introduced several provisions with a view to the de-regulation of private companies.

3–111 Meetings and notice of meetings may, with some exceptions, be dispensed with by private companies, business being transacted instead by written resolutions signed by all the members entitled to attend and vote at the meeting in question (s. 381A inserted by Companies Act 1989, s. 113(1), (2)).

3–112 Further, a private company is permitted to "elect" (*i.e.* choose) not to comply with certain statutory provisions, provided it has first passed an "elective resolution". To be effective such a resolution must have been agreed to at a meeting by all the members entitled to attend and vote at the meeting. The following are the provisions for which an elective resolution may be passed (s. 379A(1), (2), inserted by Companies Act 1989, s. 113(1), (2)):

(a) to decide on the duration of the directors' authority to allot shares under section 80A (see 3–94, above);

(b) to dispense with the laying of accounts and reports before a general meeting under section 252;

(c) to dispense with the holding of an annual general meeting under section 366A;

(d) to fix a lesser majority than 95 per cent (but not less than 90 per cent) as the majority required to authorise short notice of meetings and special resolutions under sections 369(4) and 378(3), respectively; and

(e) to dispense with the appointment of auditors annually under section 386.

(9) **Conversion from limited to unlimited**

A private limited company may convert itself into a private unlimited company under section 49. Such conversion is not available to a public company, since by definition a public company is always a limited company (s. 1(3)). **3–113**

(iii) *Conversion from Private to Public and Vice Versa*

The rules relating to conversion of a private company into a public company and vice versa are in sections 43 to 48 and sections 53 to 55, respectively. **3–114**

(1) **Conversion from private to public**

The procedure is open only to a company which has a share capital (s. 43(1)). Moreover, before the procedure can start, the company must satisfy certain requirements as to its share capital. These correspond to the statutory requirements as to a public company's share capital (see 3–91 *et seq.*, above): the nominal value of the allotted share capital must be not less than "the authorised minimum", each allotted share must be paid up at least as to one-quarter of its nominal value and the whole of any premium, *etc.* (s. 45). **3–115**

The company must pass a special resolution altering its memorandum so that it states that the company is to be a public company and making any other necessary alterations in its memorandum and articles (s. 43(1), (2)). **3–116**

An application for re-registration, in a prescribed form and signed by a director or secretary of the company, is then delivered to the registrar of companies, along with various documents including a printed copy of the memorandum and articles as altered and a copy of a written statement by the company's auditors that in their opinion the balance sheet shows that the **3–117** amount of the company's net assets was not less than the total of its called-up share capital and undistributable reserves (s. 43(3)).

3–118 The registrar retains the application and the other documents and issues a certificate of incorporation stating that the company is a public company. The certificate is conclusive evidence that the statutory requirements for re-registration have been complied with and that the company is a public company (s. 47(1), (5)).

(2) **Conversion from public to private**

3–119 The first step here is for the company to pass a special resolution altering its memorandum so that it no longer states that the company is to be a public company and making any other necessary alterations in its memorandum and articles (s. 53(1), (2)).

3–120 An application for re-registration, in a prescribed form and signed by a director or secretary of the company, is then delivered to the registrar, along with a printed copy of the memorandum and articles as altered (s. 53(1)).

3–121 During the 28 days after the passing of the special resolution dissenting members may apply to the court for cancellation of the special resolution. The minimum number of members for such an application is—

(a) holders of at least five per cent in nominal value of the company's issued share capital or of any class of the company's issued share capital; or
(b) if the company is not limited by shares, at least five per cent of the company's members; or
(c) at least 50 of the company's members.

The court must then make an order either cancelling or confirming the special resolution. The order may be a conditional one; *e.g.* it may provide for the purchase by the company of the shares of certain members or restrict the company's power to alter its memorandum or articles (s. 54(1), (2), (5), (6)).

3–122 Where no application is made to the court or when an application is withdrawn or where the court confirms the special resolution, the registrar issues a certificate of incorporation which is conclusive evidence that the requirements for re-registration have been complied with and that the company is a private company (ss. 53(1), 55(1), (3)).

(c) **Holding Companies and Subsidiaries**

Groups of companies are a common feature of modern business organisation. The Companies Acts give recognition to this feature by defining, and making special provisions for, "holding companies" and "subsidiaries". **3–123**

A company ("S Ltd") is a subsidiary of another company, its holding company ("H Ltd") if H Ltd— **3–124**

(i) holds a majority of the voting rights in S Ltd; or

(ii) is a member of S Ltd and has the right to appoint or remove a majority of S Ltd's board of directors; or

(iii) is a member of S Ltd and controls alone, under an agreement with other shareholders or members, a majority of the voting rights in S Ltd; or

(iv) S Ltd is a subsidiary of any company which is itself a subsidiary of H Ltd (s. 736(1) as substituted by Companies Act 1989, s. 144(1)).

The relationship of holding company and subsidiary may be— **3–125**

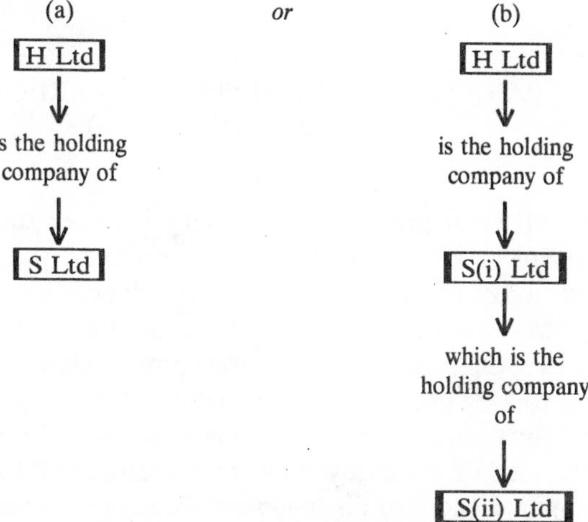

In (b), S(ii) Ltd, as well as being the subsidiary of S(i) Ltd, is the subsidiary of H Ltd, and H Ltd is the holding company of both S(i) Ltd and S(ii) Ltd. The chain of subsidiaries may extend much further—to S(iii) Ltd, S(iv) Ltd, and so on; in theory it is of infinite length.

The definition of the relationship of holding company and subsidiary in section 736, above, is especially important in the application of two sets of provisions: **3–126**

(i) section 23 (as substituted by Companies Act 1989, s. 129(1)), the leading provision of which is that as a general rule a body corporate cannot be a member of a company which is its holding company and any allotment or transfer of shares in a company to its subsidiary is void; there are some exceptions, *e.g.* where the subsidiary holds the shares in a representative capacity as executor or trustee;

(ii) sections 151 to 158, which consist of the prohibitions on the giving by a company of financial assistance to a person for the purpose of acquiring shares in the company or its holding company; there are many exceptions to the general prohibition.

3–127 The definition of the relationship between holding and subsidiary companies in section 736 does *not* apply for the purpose of deciding whether group accounts are required. For that purpose reference must be made to section 258 (as substituted by Companies Act 1989, s. 21(1)) and the supplementary provisions in Schedule 10A (as inserted by Companies Act 1989, s. 21(2)).

II THE SEPARATE PERSONALITY OF A REGISTERED COMPANY

3–128 This most important principle of company law, like several other major principles, is not to be found expressly stated in the Companies Acts; rather it has been developed by the courts professing to interpret the statutory provisions. The relevant provisions are those relating to registration and it is therefore appropriate to look briefly at those provisions before passing to the doctrine of separate personality as illustrated by the cases. By far the most famous of the cases is *Salomon's* case [1897] A.C. 22; it has been applied and also distinguished in many subsequent cases, and the picturesque phrase "lifting the veil" has commonly been used to describe those cases where it has been distinguished. The doctrine of a registered company's separate personality may therefore be considered under these headings:

(a) the registration provisions;
(b) *Salomon's* case;
(c) application of the principle in *Salomon's* case; and
(d) lifting the veil.

(a) The Registration Provisions

For the formation of a registered company certain documents must be delivered to the appropriate registrar of companies and certain fees and stamp duties must be paid. If the registered office of the company is to be in Scotland the appropriate registrar is the Registrar of Companies for Scotland, Companies House, 37 Castle Terrace, Edinburgh EH1 2EB (s. 10). **3–129**

The documents which must be delivered to the registrar are listed below. The first two—the memorandum of association and the articles of association—are the most important: together they comprise the constitution of the company, the memorandum being the dominant document and intended to govern relations between the company and outsiders, and the articles being the regulations for the internal management of the company. These two documents must be "subscribed" (*i.e.* signed) by at least two persons in the presence of at least one witness (ss. 1(1), 2(6), 7(1)), except that if the company is to be a private limited company one person may form the company by subscribing the memorandum and articles in the presence of a witness (ss. 1(3A), 2(6), 7(1), as altered by the Companies (Single Member Private Limited Companies) Regulations 1992 (S.I. 1992 No. 1699)). **3–130**

The documents to be delivered to the registrar are: **3–131**

(i) the memorandum of association, which states amongst other things the objects of the company and the nominal capital with which it is to be registered (s. 3(1));

(ii) the articles of association, providing for such matters as the holding of meetings of the members, the transfer of shares, and the directors' powers of management (s. 8(1), (4)); it is not compulsory for the commonest type of company—the company limited by shares—to register articles: if it does not do so, the regulations contained in Table A will be the regulations of the company just as if they had been contained in duly registered articles (s. 8(2));

(iii) a statement signed by or on behalf of the subscribers of the memorandum:

(1) containing the names and particulars of the first directors and first secretary and a consent signed by each of them to act in the respective capacity (s. 10(2), (3)); and

(2) specifying the intended situation of the company's registered office (s. 10(6)); and

(iv) a statutory declaration by a solicitor engaged in the formation of the company, or by a person named as director or secretary in the statement mentioned in (iii), above, that the requirements of the Act have been complied with (s. 12(3)).

3–132 On receiving these documents, the registrar must be satisfied that all the requirements of the Companies Act have been complied with; he may accept the declaration mentioned in (iv), above, as sufficient evidence of compliance (s. 12(1), (3)).

3–133 If the company is being formed for an unlawful object, the registrar will be justified in declining to register it (*R. v. Registrar of Joint Stock Companies, ex parte More* [1931] 2 K.B. 197 (CA), concerning the formation in England of a company for the sale there of tickets and chances in the Irish lottery authorised by the Parliament of the Irish Free State).

3–134 On registering the company the registrar issues a certificate of incorporation (the company's birth certificate), and from the date of incorporation mentioned in that certificate the subscribers of the memorandum, together with all the other persons who may from time to time become members of the company, are "a body corporate by the name contained in the memorandum. That body corporate is capable forthwith of exercising all the functions of an incorporated company" (s. 13(3), (4)).

3–135 The registrar must publish in the *Edinburgh Gazette* a notice of the issue of any certificate of incorporation to a company registered in Scotland (s. 711(1)).

3–136 A certificate of incorporation is conclusive evidence that the requirements of the Act have been complied with and that the association is a company authorised to be registered and is duly registered (s. 13(7)).

3–137 The certificate is not conclusive as to the legality of the company: if a company were registered for an illegal object, proceedings could be brought to have the registration cancelled (*per* Lord Parker of Waddington in *Bowman v. Secular Society Ltd* [1917] A.C. 406, at p. 439).

(b) *Salomon's* Case

3–138 The doctrine of a registered company's separate personality is always associated with the English case of *Salomon v. Salomon & Co. Ltd* [1897] A.C. 22, in which the House of Lords reversed the judgment of the Court of Appeal.

Aron Salomon had for many years carried on business on his own account as a leather merchant and wholesale boot manufacturer. He transferred his business to a company consisting of himself and members of his own family. The minimum membership was at that time (under the Companies Act 1862) seven, and so Salomon, his wife, a daughter and four sons each subscribed the memorandum for one share each.

Since Salomon was selling his own business to the new company he received 20,000 shares and £10,000 debentures from the company as payment of the purchase-price. Salomon then held 20,001 shares and no other shares were ever issued. The debentures were secured by a floating charge over the company's property.

Before the transfer the business had been prosperous, but the company soon fell upon bad days owing to a depression in the boot trade and strikes of workmen. As a result the company was wound up. The position then was that if the debentures (representing a debt due by the company to Salomon) were paid, there would be nothing left for payment of the unsecured creditors.

It was argued that the six shareholders other than Salomon were mere dummies, his nominees, and held their shares in trust for Salomon, and that the company was really still a one-man business, it making no difference that all the requirements of the Act of 1862 had been duly observed.

Held that the company had been duly formed and was not the mere "alias" or agent of or trustee for Salomon; that he was not liable to indemnify the company against its creditors' claims; that there was no fraud upon creditors or shareholders; and that the company (or its liquidator) was not entitled to rescission of the contract of purchase.

Lord Macnaghten said (at p. 51): "When the memorandum is duly signed and registered, though there be only seven shares taken, the subscribers are a body corporate 'capable forthwith', to use the words of the enactment, 'of exercising all the functions of an incorporated company'. Those are strong words. The company attains maturity on its birth. There is no period of minority—no interval of incapacity. I cannot understand how a body corporate thus made 'capable' by statute can lose its individuality by issuing the bulk of its capital to one person, whether he be a subscriber to the memorandum or not. **The company is at law a different person altogether from the subscribers to the memorandum; and, though**

it may be that after incorporation the business is precisely the same as it was before, and the same persons are managers, and the same hands receive the profits, the company is not in law the agent of the subscribers or trustee for them. Nor are the subscribers as members liable, in any shape or form, except to the extent and in the manner provided by the Act."

The words in bold type are the most famous passage in company law.

3–139 By the time when *Salomon's* case was decided the Scottish courts had already worked out the same doctrine independently; two instances are:

3–140 (i) *Grierson, Oldham & Co. Ltd v. Forbes, Maxwell & Co. Ltd* (1895) 22 R. 812: F. Ltd entered into an agreement with G. & Co., a firm of wine-merchants, for a space in G. & Co.'s advertising wine-list for a period of three years at a rent of £200 per annum. Shortly after the agreement was entered into, G. & Co.'s business was transferred to a newly-formed registered company, G. & Co. Ltd.

Held that G. & Co. Ltd had no title to sue F. Ltd for non-payment of the rent.

Lord Justice-Clerk J.H.A. Macdonald said (at p. 817): "I am of opinion that the new limited company cannot be held to be the same contracting party as the old firm, and that Messrs Forbes, Maxwell, & Company are not under their contract with Messrs Grierson, Oldham, & Company bound to pay for an advertisement in the wine-list of the limited company, with which company they have no contract."

3–141 (ii) *John Wilson & Son Ltd v. Inland Revenue* (1895) 23 R. 18: A partnership, W. & Son, was converted into a registered company, W. & Son Ltd, each partner receiving shares in the new company equal to the value of his holding in the former partnership.

The question arose of whether the conveyance of the assets of the partnership to the new company was a conveyance on sale within the meaning of the Stamp Act 1891.

Held that it was such a conveyance.

Lord McLaren said (at p. 24): "When a number of persons are constituted a company under the Companies Act, the new company is by statute a corporation, having an identity distinct from that of its constituent members or those to whom shares may be allotted."

(c) Application of the Principle in *Salomon's* Case

As a general rule the court will not go behind the separate personality of a registered company to find out who the members of the company are. *Salomon's* case is authority for not "lifting the veil of incorporation". The application of this general rule has the following consequences: 3–142

(i) The property of the company belongs to the company itself and not to the individual members, however many shares they may hold. Therefore neither shareholders nor creditors have any insurable interest in the company's assets, as may be illustrated by *Macaura v. Northern Assurance Co. Ltd* [1925] A.C. 619, which reached the House of Lords from Northern Ireland: 3–143

M., the owner of Killymoon timber estate in county Tyrone, sold the whole of the timber to the Irish Canadian Saw Mills Ltd for £27,000 to be paid in fully-paid shares. M. insured the timber against fire by policies in his own name. M. was also a creditor of the company for £19,000.

The greater part of the timber was destroyed by fire, and M. sued the insurance companies.

M.'s action was unsuccessful because he had no insurable interest, though he was virtually the sole shareholder and sole creditor; the fact that the timber was the company's only asset made no difference.

(ii) A company may be the occupier of, and carry on business in, heritable property. If the property is compulsorily acquired, the individual who is the major shareholder and sole director and who devotes his whole time to the business is not entitled to compensation as occupier. This point arose, in connection with a group of companies, in *Woolfson v. Strathclyde Regional Council*, 1978 S.C. (H.L.) 90; 1977 S.C. 84: 3–144

M. & L. Campbell (Glasgow) Ltd ("C. Ltd") was the occupier of a retail shop and carried on business there. The issued share capital of C. Ltd was 1,000 shares, of which 999 were held by W. and one by W.'s wife. W. was the sole director of C. Ltd, managed the business and was paid a salary which was taxed under Schedule E.

The premises were owned partly by W. and partly by Solfred Holdings Ltd ("S. Ltd"), the shares in which were held as to two-thirds by W. and as to the remaining one-third by W.'s wife.

Glasgow Corporation as highway authority made a compulsory purchase order in respect of the shop.

W. claimed compensation on the basis that he, C. Ltd and S. Ltd should all be treated as a single entity embodied in W. himself.

Held, applying the principle of *Salomon's* case, that W., C. Ltd and S. Ltd were each a separate legal *persona* ("person").

A comparable English case, *DHN Food Distributors Ltd v. Tower Hamlets London Borough Council* [1976] 1 W.L.R. 852 had been differently decided by the Court of Appeal, but was explained both in the Court of Session and in the House of Lords as being clearly distinguishable on its facts from *Woolfson's* case. (The question may be raised of whether the real difference was not as to the facts but as to the approach taken.)

3–145 (iii) Where there are two or more companies, each has a separate legal *persona*, though the companies may in reality be related or form part of the same group; thus in *Taylor, Petitioner*, 1976 S.L.T. (Sh. Ct.) 82, two related companies were held to be separate entities; see also *Woolfson v. Strathclyde Regional Council* (3–144, above).

(d) Lifting the Veil

3–146 The exceptional cases in which the veil of incorporation is lifted (or, as is sometimes said, "pierced") fall into two groups:

(i) statutory instances; and
(ii) common law instances.

(i) *Statutory Instances*

3–147 Statutory instances of lifting the veil are to be found not only in the Companies Act but also in other legislation. Of the instances given below, the first is from such other legislation:

(1) **Trading with the enemy**

3–148 The common law recognised that in time of war a company registered in the United Kingdom was an alien enemy if its agents or the persons *de facto* ("in fact") in control of its affairs were alien enemies, and that the enemy character of individual shareholders and their conduct might be material on the question of control.

3–149 During the two World Wars the common law was strengthened by the Trading with the Enemy Act 1914 and the Trading with the Enemy Act 1939.

A well-known case on this area of the law is *Daimler Co. Ltd v. Continental Tyre and Rubber Co. (Great Britain) Ltd* [1916] 2 A.C. 307: 3–150

C. Ltd was an English company most of whose shares were held by a German company. The holders of the remaining shares (except one) and all the directors were Germans resident in Germany. The one exceptional share was registered in the name of the secretary who had been born in Germany, but who had become a naturalised British subject and resided in England.

An action was commenced in the name of C. Ltd for a sum of money alleged to be due to it by D. Ltd. The summons was opposed on the grounds that the plaintiff and its officers were alien enemies (with the consequence that it could not bring proceedings) and that D. Ltd in paying the amount claimed would be contravening the Trading with the Enemy Act 1914.

The House of Lords held that C. Ltd was an enemy company for the purposes of the Act of 1914 because the effective control was in enemy hands.

(2) **Membership below minimum**

If a company, *other than a private company limited by shares or by guarantee*, carries on business without having at least two members for more than six months, then a person who, after these six months, is a member of the company *and* knows that it is carrying on business with only one member is liable (jointly and severally with the company) for payment of the company's debts contracted after the expiry of the six months. This is an exception to the general rule that the company's debts cannot be enforced against its members (s. 24 with words in italics inserted by the Companies (Single Member Private Limited Companies) Regulations 1992 (S.I. 1992 No. 1699)). 3–151

(3) **Holding company and subsidiaries**

In order to find out whether the relationship of holding company and subsidiary exists, the veil of incorporation is lifted because the membership of the subsidiary company must be looked at (s. 736(1)—see 3–124, above). 3–152

The requirement to have group accounts where the relationship of parent company and subsidiary exists is a further illustration of lifting the veil (ss. 227(1), 258). 3–153

(4) **Department of Trade and Industry investigations**

3–154 An inspector appointed to investigate a company's *affairs* may, if he thinks it necessary, investigate also the affairs of related companies (*e.g.* the holding company and subsidiary companies) (s. 433(1)).

3–155 Department of Trade and Industry investigations into a company's *membership* are a still more obvious instance of lifting the veil (s. 442).

(5) **Sole director not to be secretary**

3–156 Every company must have a secretary, and a sole director must not also be the secretary (s. 283(2)). It is possible for a director or secretary to be not an individual but a corporation (*e.g.* another company), and so, to prevent the provision mentioned being avoided by the device of incorporation, there is the additional provision that it is not permissible for a company—

(a) to have as secretary a corporation whose sole director is also the sole director of the company in question; or

(b) to have as sole director a corporation whose sole director is also the secretary of the company in question (s. 283(4)).

This additional provision amounts to a lifting of the veil for the purpose of ensuring that the two offices of secretary and sole director are in reality, and not merely in theory, held by two different persons.

(6) **Disclosure of directors' interests**

3–157 A director is under an obligation to notify the company of his interests in shares in and debentures of the company (s. 324(1)), and one of the rules designed to give effect to that obligation is the provision that a person ("X") is to be taken to be interested in shares or debentures if a body corporate is interested in them *and*—

(a) that body corporate is accustomed to act in accordance with X's directions or instructions; or

(b) X is entitled to exercise, or control the exercise of, one-third or more of the voting power at general meetings of that body corporate (Sched. 13, para. 4).

The veil is here being lifted to see how the body corporate is controlled.

(ii) *Common Law Instances*

The following are some of the instances in which the courts, in the exercise of their discretion and in the interests of justice and equity as seen by them, have lifted the veil of incorporation: **3–158**

(1) **Company formed to enable valid contract in restraint of trade to be broken**

Gilford Motor Co. Ltd v. Horne [1933] Ch. 935 (CA): H. was managing director of G. Ltd. His contract of employment included a valid covenant in restraint of trade, by which he undertook that after the termination of his employment he would not solicit G. Ltd's customers. **3–159**

Shortly after the termination of his employment H. formed a company, J.M.H. & Co. Ltd, for the sale of spare parts of G. Ltd's vehicles, and sent out circulars to G. Ltd's customers. The business of J.M.H. & Co. Ltd was carried on wholly by H.

Held that J.M.H. & Co. Ltd was a mere channel, a mere cloak or sham for the purpose of enabling H. to commit a breach of his covenant, and an injunction[1] was granted against both H. and J.M.H. & Co. Ltd to restrain further breach of the covenant.

(2) **Transfer of land in breach of contract of sale**

Jones v. Lipman [1962] 1 W.L.R. 832: L. agreed to sell freehold land to J. Before the land was transferred, L., for a lesser price, sold and transferred the land to Alamed Ltd, in which L. and his clerk were the only shareholders and directors. **3–160**

J. brought an action for specific performance[2] against L. and Alamed Ltd.

Held that J. was entitled to the decree of specific performance sought because Alamed Ltd was the creature of, and a mask for, L., who was in a position, through his control of Alamed Ltd, to cause the contract with J. to be completed.

(3) **Subsidiary company as agent of holding company**

Smith, Stone & Knight Ltd v. Birmingham Corporation [1939] 4 All E.R. 116: The case arose out of the compulsory purchase of S. Ltd's factory by Birmingham Corporation for the purpose of **3–161**

[1] The Scots law equivalent is "interdict".
[2] The Scots law equivalent is "specific implement".

building a technical college. The premises had been let by S. Ltd to its subsidiary, Birmingham Waste Co. Ltd, and the question was whether S. Ltd could claim compensation for disturbance of the business carried on by its subsidiary.

Atkinson J. asked six questions and gave an affirmative answer to each:

(a) Were the profits treated as the profits of S. Ltd?

(b) Were the persons conducting the business appointed by S. Ltd?

(c) Was S. Ltd the head and the brain of the trading venture?

(d) Did S. Ltd govern the adventure, decide what should be done and what capital should be embarked on the venture?

(e) Did S. Ltd make the profits by its skill and direction?

(f) Was S. Ltd in effectual and constant control?

The judge concluded that he had no doubt that the business was S. Ltd's business and was being carried on under S. Ltd's direction. S. Ltd was therefore entitled to claim compensation for disturbance of the business.

The judge emphasised that the question is one of fact in each case, depending on the arrangements made between the holding company and the subsidiaries.

The question raised may be the converse one—whether the holding company is the agent of its subsidiary.

Compare the two contrasting cases *Woolfson v. Strathclyde Regional Council* and *DHN Food Distributors Ltd v. Tower Hamlets London Borough Council* (3–144, above).

(4) **Court's discretion in relation to "take-over bid"**

3–162 Sections 428 to 430F (as substituted by Financial Services Act 1986, s. 172 and Sched. 12) enable an "offeror" (usually a company) which has made an offer for the shares of a company and which has had the offer accepted by the holders of nine-tenths of the company's shares to acquire compulsorily the remaining one-tenth held by the shareholders who have not accepted the offer. However, a shareholder who has not accepted the offer has the right to apply to court, and the court may order that the terms on which the offeror is entitled to acquire the applicant's shares shall be "such as the court thinks fit".

3–163 An instance of the exercise of this discretion by the court occurred in *Re Bugle Press Ltd* [1961] Ch. 270 (CA):

B. Ltd, a publishing company, had three shareholders and an issued capital of 10,000 £1 shares, of which Shaw held 4,500, Jackson 4,500 and Treby 1,000.

A new company, Jackson & Shaw (Holdings) Ltd ("J. & S. Ltd"), was formed with only Jackson and Shaw as shareholders and directors. J. & S. Ltd made a "take-over bid" for all the shares of B. Ltd. Treby did not accept the offer, and J. & S. Ltd, as offeror, gave notice of its intention to exercise its right of compulsory acquisition.

Treby applied to court for a declaration that J. & S. Ltd was not entitled to acquire his shares compulsorily.

Held that Treby was entitled to the declaration sought because the statutory provision was being abused for the purpose of enabling the majority shareholders to expropriate or evict the minority.

The court was here lifting the veil for the purpose of revealing that the offeror was in reality the same in identity as the majority shareholders of B. Ltd. Treby won his case by showing that "the [*offeror*] was nothing but a little hut built round his two co-shareholders, and that the so-called scheme was made by themselves as directors of that company with themselves as shareholders and the whole thing, therefore, is seen to be a hollow sham" (*per* Harman L.J. at p. 288).

(5) Decision of all the members taking effect as decision of the company

Where all the members of a company agree to dispense with formalities such as the holding of meetings and the passing of resolutions, their own actings are regarded as the actings of the company, *e.g. Re Express Engineering Works Ltd* [1920] 1 Ch. 466 (CA): **3–164**

Five persons formed a private company in which they were the only shareholders. Having bought a property for £7,000, they sold it to the company for £15,000, the price to be paid by debentures issued by the company. The transaction was carried out at a "board meeting" for the purpose of which the five persons appointed themselves directors. A provision in the articles prohibiting a director from voting on a contract in which he was interested was disregarded.

Held that no fraud was involved, that the company was bound by the unanimous agreement of its members and that consequently the debentures were valid.

III COMPARISON OF REGISTERED COMPANIES WITH PARTNERSHIPS

3–165 In Scots law both registered companies and partnerships are artificial legal persons, distinct from the members of whom they are composed.

3–166 The personality of the two types of body, however, arises from different sources: the personality of a registered company comes from the incorporation effected by the issue of the certificate of incorporation (s. 13(3), (4)), whereas the personality of a partnership depends on the provision in the Partnership Act 1890 (s. 4(2)), reproducing the common law of Scotland, that a firm is a legal person distinct from the partners of whom it is composed; a partnership is an unincorporated body.

3–167 There are some principles of law which credit a partnership with a personality which is less full than the personality of a registered company. In particular[3]:

3–168 (i) In the case of a firm, it is permissible, if the firm itself does not meet its debts and obligations, for a creditor to go behind the firm and hold the individual partners liable jointly and severally for these debts and obligations; this does not happen in the case of a registered company: even when the company is being wound up, and even though it may be hopelessly insolvent, a creditor has no direct access to any individual member; any liability attaching to a member (*e.g.* if the shares which he holds are not fully paid shares) is a liability to pay *to the company* (or its liquidator as representing it in a winding up) and not to the company's creditors.

3–169 (ii) A firm, like a registered company, has rights of ownership in property, both heritable and moveable, but the formal legal title to heritable property held on feudal tenure must be taken in the names of the individual partners or of other individuals in trust for the firm. In the case of a registered company, on the other hand, there is no such obstacle.

---

[3] See also 2–30 *et seq.*, above.

Separate personality is the most striking feature which is common to registered companies and partnerships in Scotland. In considering the differences between the two types of body it is convenient to make a division between: **3–170**

(a) those respects in which a registered company has advantages over a partnership; and
(b) those respects in which a partnership has advantages over a registered company.

(a) **Advantages of Registered Company**

Because the personality of a partnership is less full than that of a registered company, there are some respects in which the registered company is at an advantage (see, *e.g.*, 3–168 and 3–169, above). **3–171**

The following advantages, however, are of greater practical importance: **3–172**

(i) *Limited Liability*

In a registered company (unless the company is an unlimited company) all members enjoy limited liability for the company's debts, whereas in a partnership the general rule is that all the partners are jointly and severally liable for the firm's debts if the firm itself fails to pay. If the partnership is a limited partnership, as is allowed by the Limited Partnerships Act 1907, one or more of the partners may enjoy limited liability, but there must always be one or more general partners who incur the usual joint and several liability; further, in a limited partnership a limited partner must not take part in the management: if he does so, he becomes liable as a general partner; in a registered company, on the other hand, all the members may, by having themselves appointed directors, take part in the management without losing their limited liability. **3–173**

(ii) *Transferability of Shares*

The basic rule in company law is that shares are freely transferable, though it is usual in private companies for the articles to contain some restriction on the transfer of shares (*e.g.* there may be the restriction that a shareholder wishing to transfer his shares must **3–174** first offer them to other shareholders—a "pre-emption" clause). In public companies shares are always freely transferable.

3–175 In a partnership, on the other hand, owing to the element of *delectus personae* ("choice of person"), a new partner cannot be introduced without the consent of all existing partners unless the existing partners have made some agreement to the contrary (Partnership Act 1890, s. 24(7)).

(iii) *Management by Directors*

3–176 In a registered company management is in the hands of directors: they are the agents of the company, and members, as members, have no powers of management. This opens up a great range of possibilities for the business organisation: at one end of the scale there is opportunity for an investor on the stock exchange to purchase shares in a large public company purely as a financial venture, without even contemplating that he would be expected to attend to the day-to-day management of the concern, while at the other end of the scale there is the small private company where all the members of a particular family may so arrange matters that they are all directors as well as shareholders, and so manage the family business in much the same way to outward appearances as if they were in fact partners.

3–177 In partnership, on the other hand, the principle is that every partner is an agent of the firm and his other partners for the purpose of the business of the partnership (Partnership Act 1890, s. 5). As regards the relations between the partners themselves, every partner may take part in the management of the partnership business unless there is agreement to the contrary (Partnership Act 1890, s. 24(5)). The special disability of the limited partner in a limited partnership is mentioned above (3–173). Partnership as a form of business organisation is designed rather for a small concern where all the members are envisaged as taking part in the running of the business; it does not offer anything like the range of possibilities available in registered companies.

(iv) *No Limit in Number of Members*

3–178 The minimum membership for both registered companies and partnerships is two, with the exception that for the formation of a private limited company only one person is required. In a registered company there is no maximum, whereas in a partnership there is a general limit of 20 (Companies Act 1985, s. 716), exceptions being allowed for partnerships of solicitors, accountants, members of a recognised stock exchange and other categories specified in regulations.

A consequence of the limit in the number of partners is that it is **3–179** generally impossible for a partnership to raise such a large capital as may be raised by a registered company.

(v) *Changes in Membership*

Changes in the membership of a registered company do not disturb **3–180** the continuing existence and operation of the company, whereas changes in the membership of a partnership may result in the discontinuance of the partnership; *e.g.* finding a replacement for a retiring partner requires, unless there is agreement to the contrary, consent of all the continuing partners (Partnership Act 1890, s. 24(7)), questions of liability of retiring and new partners to creditors of the firm may arise, and a partnership is, unless there is agreement to the contrary between the partners, dissolved as regards all the partners by the death or bankruptcy of any partner (Partnership Act 1890, s. 33(1)).

(vi) *Borrowing and Granting Security*

A registered company may borrow by issuing debentures and **3–181** debenture stock, and it may grant security to lenders by creating floating charges over the whole or part of its undertaking (Companies Act 1985, ss. 462–466); it may, for instance, grant a floating charge over its moveable stock-in-trade. However, in the case of a small private company, it can often happen that a creditor such as a bank will require a personal guarantee from the person who is in actual control of the company, the effect being that that person will not have the protection of limited liability in respect of the debt due to that creditor.

Partnerships do not issue debentures or debenture stock, and **3–182** they are subject to the ordinary principles relating to rights in security, *i.e.* delivery is essential for the creation of a valid right in security and any attempt to create a floating charge is of no legal effect.

(b) **Advantages of Partnership**

3–183 The advantages of a partnership—normally outweighed by the advantages of a registered company—include the following:

(i) *No Formalities in Formation*

3–184 A partnership may be formed by simple agreement: there is no need for formal writing (though a contract of copartnery is advisable), and the relationship may even be inferred from conduct without any words being spoken. No publicity is necessary. There need be no legal costs.

3–185 A registered company can be formed only by compliance with a registration procedure. A memorandum of association and articles of association together with other documents in proper legal form, delivered to the registrar of companies, involve publicity and expense.

(ii) *No Formalities in Carrying on Business*

3–186 A partnership is not required to deliver to any public office information relating to the carrying on of its business. This again means less publicity and less expense.

3–187 A registered company is required to file an annual return, copies of various resolutions and other documents. These must all be prepared in an acceptable form and are kept open to public inspection at the office of the registrar of companies.

(iii) *No Disclosure of Financial Affairs*

3–188 As a general rule a partnership is not required to file at a public office any copy of the business accounts: its financial affairs are therefore not made public. This can be a highly prized advantage. If, however, the partnership is a "qualifying partnership" within the meaning of the Partnerships and Unlimited Companies Regulations 1993 (S.I. 1993 No. 1820) it will be required to deliver accounts to the registrar of companies (reg. 5), and so will not have the advantage mentioned (see 2–01, above).

3–189 A registered company, on the other hand, (unless it is an unlimited company other than a "qualifying company" (see 3–62, above)) must file with the registrar of companies, and so give publicity to, its annual accounts. Small and medium-sized companies, however, enjoy certain exemptions.

(iv) *No Restrictions on Share Capital*

A partnership is free to alter its capital in any way agreed on by the partners. **3–190**

A registered company, on the other hand, is subject to various restrictions in relation to its share capital; *e.g.* limited companies are subject to the principle of maintenance of capital as modified by the Act and there are statutory procedures for variation of capital and statutory restrictions on the allotment of and payment for share capital. **3–191**

(v) *Arrangements with Creditors*

A partnership is free to make any arrangement with its creditors that is agreed on, whereas a registered company can make only such arrangements as are authorised by the Companies Act (s. 425) or the Insolvency Act 1986 (ss. 1, 8, 110, 165–167). **3–192**

IV MEMORANDUM OF ASSOCIATION

The two documents which contain the constitution of any company (its "constitutional" documents) are the memorandum of association and the articles of association. This part of the chapter will deal first with (a) the relationship between the two documents and then with (b) the contents of the memorandum. **3–193**

(a) **Relationship between Memorandum and Articles**

The memorandum governs the external transactions of the company: it is the public document from which persons dealing with the company may ascertain the company's name, whether the company is public or private, the country of its registration, its objects, whether it is limited or unlimited, and, in the case of a limited company with a share capital, the amount of that share capital; it ends with an association clause which shows, and is signed by, the persons who will be the company's first members. **3–194**

3–195 The articles, on the other hand, govern the company's internal affairs: they deal with such matters as the transfer of shares from one person to another, company meetings, directors and dividends.

3–196 Originally the memorandum was unalterable, whereas the articles were alterable by the members. Although there are now many statutory provisions which permit the several contents of the memorandum to be altered, the original rule is still reflected in the statutory wording:

"A company may not alter the conditions contained in its memorandum except in the cases, in the mode and to the extent for which express provision is made by this Act" (s. 2(7)); and

"Subject to the provisions of this Act and to the conditions contained in its memorandum, a company may by special resolution alter its articles" (s. 9(1)).

3–197 The memorandum is the dominant of the two documents. If, however, there is an ambiguity in its provisions, the articles, being a "contemporaneous" document, may be looked at for assistance in interpretation. Such difficulties can arise where matters which might have been set out in the articles have been included in the memorandum instead, *e.g.*:

Marshall, Fleming & Co. Ltd, Petitioners, 1938 S.C. 873 (O.H.): The memorandum of M. Ltd divided the shares into preference shares and ordinary shares, with certain rights attached to each class. The articles contained a clause enabling special rights to be altered.

Held that M. Ltd could, by following the procedure prescribed in the articles, alter the rights of the different classes of shareholders as set out in the memorandum.

(b) **Contents of Memorandum**

3–198 The Companies (Tables A to F) Regulations 1985 (S.I. 1985 No. 805), made under section 3 of the Act of 1985, provide model forms of memoranda for the different types of registered companies. These have been indicated under "Classification of Registered Companies" (3–43 *et seq.*, above). The contents of a memorandum, together with some of the law associated with them, are considered here under the headings:

(i) name;
(ii) statement that company is to be a public company;

(iii) registered office;
(iv) objects;
(v) statement that liability is limited;
(vi) share capital;
(vii) additional clauses; and
(viii) association clause.

(i) *Name*

The main rules are that the name of a private company limited by shares or by guarantee must have "limited" as the last word of its name (s. 25(2)) and that the name of a public company must end with the words "public limited company" (s. 25(1)). For the permitted abbreviations and the Welsh equivalents, see 3–82 *et seq.*, above, and for the exemption from the use of the word "limited", which on certain conditions is open to private companies limited by guarantee, see 3–60, above. **3–199**

Examples of name clauses in the model memoranda are: **3–200**

"The company's name is 'The South Wales Motor Transport Company cyfyngedig' " (Table B);

"The company's name is 'Western Electronic Public Limited Company' " (Table F); and

"The company's name is 'The Woodford Engineering Company' " (Table E).

(1) **Choice of name**

A company must not be registered by a name which is the same as a name appearing in the index of names (which includes the names of limited partnerships) kept by the registrar of companies or by a name the use of which would in the opinion of the Department of Trade and Industry constitute a criminal offence or by a name which in the opinion of the Department of Trade and Industry is offensive (s. 26(1)). **3–201**

In addition certain names require prior approval of the Department of Trade and Industry; these are:

(a) names likely to give the impression that the company is connected in any way with the Government or with any local authority; and

(b) names including a word or expression specified in regulations (s. 26(2)).

As regards (b), the regulations at present in force are the Company and Business Names Regulations 1981 (S.I. 1981 No. 1685) as amended. Examples of words and expressions specified are "Chamber of Commerce", "Giro", "Stock Exchange" and "Trust". In respect of some words and expressions the regulations also specify a Government department or other body as the "relevant body", *i.e.* as the body which must first be asked whether (and if so why) it has any objections to the proposed name; *e.g.* for the word "University" the relevant body is the Privy Council (s. 29(2)).

3–202 In addition to these statutory provisions there is a principle of the common law which enables a person to obtain an interdict from the court prohibiting the adoption of a name likely to cause confusion between his own existing business and the new concern. An English illustration is *Ewing v. Buttercup Margarine Co. Ltd* [1917] 2 Ch. 1 (CA), in which E., who had a chain of shops trading under the name "Buttercup Dairy Company", was held entitled to an injunction restraining a new company from carrying on business under the name "Buttercup Margarine Co. Ltd". Two Scottish cases in which interdicts were refused because the new name was not calculated to deceive the public are:

Dunlop Pneumatic Tyre Co. Ltd v. Dunlop Motor Co. Ltd, 1907 S.C. (H.L.) 15; (1906) 8 F. 1146: The name "Dunlop Motor Co. Ltd" adopted by a small new motor repairing company in Kilmarnock was held not calculated to deceive the public into purchasing that company's goods in the belief that they were goods of a large English company, Dunlop Pneumatic Tyre Co. Ltd, manufacturers of motoring accessories.

Scottish Union and National Insurance Co. v. Scottish National Insurance Co. Ltd, 1909 S.C. 318: The similarity of names in this case was held not likely to deceive the public because the first-mentioned company carried on general insurance business excluding marine insurance, whereas the newly registered company was to confine its business to marine insurance.

(2) **Change of name**

3–203 A company may change its name by special resolution (s. 28(1)).

3–204 There are statutory provisions under which a company may be required to change its name in certain circumstances: where a company has been registered by a name which is the same as or, in the opinion of the Department of Trade and Industry, too like a name already in the index of names kept by the registrar, the Department of Trade and Industry may within 12 months of the registration direct the company to change its name within a specified period (s. 28(2)); if, in the opinion of the Department of Trade and Industry, the name by which a company is registered gives so misleading an indication of the nature of its activities as to be likely to cause harm to the public, the Department may direct it to change its name, but the company receiving such a direction has a right to apply to the court to set the direction aside (s. 32(1), (3)).

(3) **Publication of name (sections 348–351)**

Every company must: **3–205**

(a) paint or affix its name on the outside of every office or place in which its business is carried on, in a conspicuous position, in letters easily legible;

(b) have its name engraved in legible characters on its seal if it has a seal[4]; and

(c) have the following particulars mentioned in legible characters in all business letters and order forms of the company—the company's place of registration, its registered number, the address of its registered office and, if it is a limited company exempt from using "limited" as part of its name, the fact that it is a limited company.

There are penalties imposed on a company and officers of a company for failure to observe these provisions. **3–206**

In addition, an officer or other person acting on behalf of the company may become personally liable to the holder of a bill of exchange, promissory note, cheque or order for money or goods if the company's name is not mentioned in the document in question and the company itself fails to make due payment. This provision was applied in *Scottish and Newcastle Breweries Ltd v. Blair*, 1967 S.L.T. 72 (O.H.): **3–207**

S. Ltd drew a bill of exchange for £7,500 on Anderson & Blair (Property Development) Ltd, but misnamed the drawee as "Messrs. Anderson & Blair". The bill was accepted on behalf of the company by two directors and the company secretaries.

---

[4] A company need not now have a seal (Companies Act 1989, s. 130(7) and Sched. 17).

On presentation for payment, the bill was dishonoured, and later the company went into liquidation.

Held that the signatories were liable to S. Ltd for the amount of the bill.

(4) **Business names**

3–208 Where a registered company carries on business under a name other than its corporate name, it is subject to the provisions of the Business Names Act 1985 (see 2–177 *et seq.*, above).

(ii) *Statement that Company is to be a Public Company*

3–209 The second clause in the memorandum of a public company is "The company is to be a public company" (Tables D and F). It is part of the definition of "public company" that the memorandum contains this statement (s. 1(3); see 3–73, above).

(iii) *Registered Office*

3–210 The second clause in the memorandum of a private company and the third clause in the memorandum of a public company must state whether the registered office of the company is to be situated in England and Wales or in Scotland (s. 2(1)). Alternatively it may contain a statement that the company's registered office is to be situated in Wales (s. 2(2)). The actual address of the registered office need not be, and in practice never is, stated in this clause, which is an unalterable part of the memorandum. The clause fixes the company's nationality and domicile.

3–211 Every company must at all times have a registered office to which all communications and notices may be addressed. On incorporation the situation of the company's registered office is that specified in the statement delivered to the registrar under section 10 along with the memorandum and articles. The company may change the situation of its registered office from time to time by giving notice in the prescribed form to the registrar; the new address must not be outside the country of the company's domicile. The change takes effect upon the notice being registered by the registrar (s. 287 as substituted by Companies Act 1989, s. 136).

3–212 The registrar must have any notice of a change in the situation of a company's registered office published in the *Edinburgh*

Gazette. This step is referred to in the Act as "official notification" (s. 711).

The Acts do not require any resolution of the company to be passed for a change in the address of the registered office. The change may be decided on by the board of directors. **3–213**

The address of the company's registered office as well as the place of registration and the registered number must be mentioned in legible characters in all business letters and order forms of the company (s. 351(1)). **3–214**

Several books and documents are required to be kept at the registered office, *e.g.* the register of members (unless it is made up at another office) (s. 353(1)), the minutes of proceedings at general meetings (s. 383(1)) and the register of directors and secretaries (s. 288(1)). **3–215**

The time, duration and manner of inspection of these books and documents are governed by regulations made under section 723A (inserted by Companies Act 1989, s. 143).

(iv) *Objects*

The memorandum of every company must state the objects of the company (s. 2(1)). In the case of a private company the objects clause will be the third clause of the memorandum and in the case of a public company it will be the fourth. The statutory example given for a public company limited by shares is: **3–216**

"The company's objects are the manufacture and development of such descriptions of electronic equipment, instruments and appliances as the company may from time to time determine, and the doing of all such other things as are incidental or conducive to the attainment of that object" (Table F).

The model for a private company limited by shares is:

"The company's objects are the carriage of passengers and goods in motor vehicles between such places as the company may from time to time determine and the doing of all such other things as are incidental or conducive to the attainment of that object" (Table B).

In practice the objects clause has been the longest clause in a company's memorandum; it commonly extended to several pages. It would include not only the proposed object, but every possible object, even although the promoters had not the remotest intention **3–217** of pursuing it. It would provide that all the listed objects were to be "independent objects" in no way restricted by reference to the name of the company or to the objects contained in the first or any other paragraph of the clause. It would include as objects a long list of what were truly powers and which did not need to be specified because the company had by implication the powers necessary to attain its stated objects. The aim of all these practices was the avoidance of the *ultra vires* ("beyond the powers") doctrine.

3–218 The operation of the *ultra vires* doctrine was limited to some extent by section 9(1) of the European Communities Act 1972 and was virtually abolished by the Companies Act 1989 (ss. 108–110).

3–219 For the better understanding of the statutory provisions which now apply, a short explanation of the doctrine is included below. A brief account is also given of the statutory provisions for alteration of objects.

(1) Ultra vires doctrine in operation

3–220 The *ultra vires* doctrine is to the effect that an artificial legal person, such as a company, incorporated by or under an Act of Parliament has capacity to pursue only those objects which Parliament has authorised it to pursue. The doctrine was applied to statutory companies such as railway companies in the nineteenth century: the special Act of Parliament incorporating each company was the measure of its capacity. When the doctrine came to be applied to registered companies, the measure of a company's capacity was to be found in the objects as expressed in the company's memorandum—a document open to public inspection: any transaction which the company purported to enter into beyond the scope of its expressed objects was void and could not be ratified even by all its members.

(a) *Purpose of the doctrine*

3–221 The doctrine was intended to have a two-fold purpose: first, it would protect investors in the company: they would know the objects to which their money was to be devoted; secondly, it would protect creditors of the company: they would know that the company's funds were not to be dissipated in unauthorised activities. In fact company law and practice developed in such a way that the doctrine served neither of these purposes: investors came to have no protection because company promoters framed the objects clauses in memoranda in the widest possible terms, while creditors, being unlikely in practice to consult a company's memorandum before transacting with the company, could find themselves without any valid claim against the company if the transaction was in fact beyond the scope of the memorandum.

(b) *Illustrative cases*

The leading case was *Ashbury Railway Carriage and Iron Co. Ltd v. Riche* (1875) L.R. 7 H.L. 653: A. Ltd's objects were: (1) to make, and sell, or lend on hire, railway carriages and wagons; (2) to carry on the business of mechanical engineers and general contractors; (3) to purchase, lease, work and sell mines, minerals, land and buildings, *etc.* **3–222**

The directors entered into a contract to purchase a concession for making a railway in Belgium.

Held that the contract was *ultra vires* of the company and void and that therefore even the whole body of shareholders could not subsequently ratify it.

The words "general contractors" were to be taken along with the immediately preceding words and so indicated the making generally of contracts connected with the business of mechanical engineers.

Lord Chancellor Cairns' speech in this case includes one of the most famous passages in company law: he said (at p. 672):

"Now, I am clearly of opinion that this contract was entirely, as I have said, beyond the objects of the memorandum of association. If so, it was thereby placed beyond the powers of the company to make the contract. If so, my Lords, it is not a question whether the contract ever was ratified or was not ratified. If it was a contract void at its beginning, it was void because the company could not make the contract. If every shareholder of the company had been in the room, and every shareholder of the company had said, 'That is a contract which we desire to make, which we authorise the directors to make, to which we sanction the placing of the seal of the company', the case would not have stood in any different position from that in which it stands now. The shareholders would thereby, by unanimous consent, have been attempting to do the very thing which, by the Act of Parliament, they were prohibited from doing."

3–223 A Scottish illustration of the operation of the doctrine is *Life Association of Scotland v. Caledonian Heritable Security Co. Ltd in Liquidation* (1886) 13 R. 750: C. Ltd had power to lend money on heritable security and to do all things incidental or conducive to the attainment of that object. It lent £10,500 on a postponed heritable bond over property which was already subject to a prior bond of £14,000.

Held that the agreement was *ultra vires* of C. Ltd on the ground that the memorandum did not confer express power to enter into such an agreement and that the agreement could not be regarded as "incidental or conducive to the attainment" of C. Ltd's objects.

3–224 Of the many other decided cases illustrating the doctrine the three following are amongst the best-known twentieth century cases:

3–225 (1) *Re John Beauforte (London) Ltd* [1953] Ch. 131: A company, authorised by its memorandum to carry on business as costumiers and gown-makers, started the business of making veneered panels, which was *ultra vires*.

Builders engaged to erect a factory, persons who had supplied veneers and coke merchants who had sold coke for the factory were all held to have no claims as creditors in the company's liquidation.

3–226 (2) *Parke v. Daily News Ltd* [1962] Ch. 927: D. Ltd had agreed to sell the major part of its business to Associated Newspapers Ltd, but was to continue trading. The board of directors, with the approval of the general meeting, proposed to distribute the proceeds of the sale among former employees.

P., a minority shareholder, was held entitled to veto the proposed distribution, on the ground that it was *ultra vires* of D. Ltd to make a distribution which could not be shown to be for the purpose of promoting its prospects.

3–227 (3) *Introductions Ltd v. National Provincial Bank Ltd* [1970] Ch. 199 (CA): The main object of I. Ltd was to provide entertainments and services for overseas visitors. The objects clause included a power to borrow money and provided that each of the stated objects was to be an independent object.

I. Ltd undertook pig-breeding, which was *ultra vires*, and a bank which had been supplied with a copy of the company's memorandum, made a loan for the purpose of that business and received debentures as security.

Held that as borrowing money was not an end in itself but had to be for some purpose, and as the loan made by the bank had been for an *ultra vires* purpose, the debentures were void.

(2) **Abolition of ultra vires doctrine**

The modifications of the *ultra vires* doctrine made by section 9(1) of the European Communities Act 1972 became section 35 of the Act of 1985 on the consolidation of that year. The abolition of the doctrine by the Companies Act 1989 took the form of a substitution for that section 35 of three new sections (ss. 35, 35A and 35B). **3–228**

(a) *Company's capacity not limited by its memorandum (section 35)*

The leading provision in section 35 is that the validity of an act done by a company is no longer to be called into question on the ground of lack of capacity by reason of anything in the company's memorandum (s. 35(1)). This provision protects outsiders transacting with a company, which would normally be represented by its directors. **3–229**

It was recognised that in such a situation members should not be left without protection, if the directors in transacting with outsiders were going beyond the company's capacity. Hence it is provided that a member may bring proceedings to restrain the doing of an act which would be beyond the company's capacity. This personal right of an individual member is, however, limited by a further provision—he cannot bring proceedings if the act in question is to be done in fulfilment of a legal obligation arising from a previous act of the company (s. 35(2)). **3–230**

Section 35 goes on to provide that it remains the duty of the directors to observe any limitations on their powers flowing from the memorandum, and, if they are in breach of this duty, the directors' action may only be ratified by the company by special resolution. **3–231**

It is further provided that a special resolution ratifying the directors' action does not affect any liability incurred by the directors; relief from such liability must be agreed to separately by special resolution. This has the effect of preserving the company's right to obtain damages from directors for breach of duty in failing to observe limitations on their powers flowing from the memorandum (s. 35(3)). **3–232**

(b) *Power of directors to bind the company (section 35A)*

3–233 Whereas section 35 relates to directors acting beyond the company's capacity (as defined by the memorandum), section 35A relates to the situation where directors are acting within the company's capacity but beyond the authority conferred on them by the company.

3–234 Section 35A provides that, in favour of a person dealing with a company in good faith, the power of the directors to bind the company is to be deemed to be free of any limitation under the "company's constitution" (s. 35A(1)).

For the purposes of this provision—

(i) a person "deals with" a company if he is a party to any transaction or other act to which the company is a party;

(ii) a person is not to be regarded as acting in bad faith merely because he knows that an act is beyond the powers of the directors under the "company's constitution"; and

(iii) a person is presumed to have acted in good faith unless the contrary is proved (s. 35A(2)).

The term "company's constitution" would normally be considered as referring to the company's memorandum and articles. It is given a wider meaning here, because the limitations on the directors' powers may have been imposed, not by the memorandum or articles, but by a resolution at a general or class meeting, or by an agreement between the members of the company or of any class of shareholders (s. 35A(3)).

3–235 The right of a member to bring proceedings to restrain the doing of an act which is beyond the powers of the directors is expressly preserved, but no proceedings can be brought if the act in question is to be done in fulfilment of a legal obligation arising from a previous act of the company (s. 35A(4)).

3–236 Any liability incurred by the directors on account of their exceeding their powers is also preserved (s. 35A(5)).

(c) *No duty to inquire (section 35B)*

3–237 Section 35B provides that a party to a transaction with a company is not bound to inquire as to the company's capacity or as to the authority of the directors.

(3) **Alteration of objects**

Successive Companies Acts progressively increased the extent to which a company might alter its objects. As a result there was unlikely to be a situation where the risk of having an intended activity held *ultra vires* could not be avoided by the company's passing a special resolution for alteration of its objects. **3–238**

The Companies Act 1989 (s. 110(2)) removed the seven specified purposes for which a company might alter its objects by special resolution under section 4 of the Act of 1985, and substituted a new section 4 enabling a company to alter its objects by special resolution for any purpose. **3–239**

The holders of not less than 15 per cent in nominal value of the company's issued share capital or any class of the issued share capital (or, if the company is not limited by shares, not less than 15 per cent of the company's members) may apply to court within 21 days from the passing of the resolution, and the court may make such order as it thinks fit. **3–240**

In *Incorporated Glasgow Dental Hospital v. Lord Advocate*, 1927 S.C. 400, and *Scottish Housing Association Ltd, Petitioners*, 1947 S.C. 17, the statutory provisions for alteration of objects were held not to be restricted to alteration of the objects *clause* but to extend to alteration of objects which happened to be stated in other clauses of the memorandum. **3–241**

(v) *Statement that Liability is Limited*

The memorandum of every limited company must state that the liability of its members is limited (s. 2(3)). The statement always in practice is simply "The liability of the members is limited", and does not reveal whether the company is a company limited by shares or a company limited by guarantee; that information is derived from the clause which immediately follows the limited liability clause. If the company is a company limited by guarantee that succeeding clause will contain the member's guarantee, *e.g.*: **3–242**

"Every member of the company undertakes to contribute such amount as may be required (not exceeding £100) to the company's assets if it should be wound up while he is a member or within one year after he ceases to be a member, for payment of the company's debts and liabilities contracted before he ceases to be a member, and of the costs, charges and expenses of winding up, and for the adjustment of the rights of the contributories among themselves" (Table D, Parts I and II).

3–243 No alteration in a company's memorandum or articles can bind a member, without his written agreement, to take more shares or in any way increase his liability to the company (s. 16).

(vi) *Share Capital*

3–244 In the case of a company having a share capital, the memorandum must state, unless the company is an unlimited company, the amount of the share capital with which the company proposes to be registered and the division of the capital into shares of a fixed amount (s. 2(5)). If the company is an unlimited company with a share capital the *articles* must state the amount of the share capital (s. 7(2)).

3–245 The statutory model share capital clause for a private company limited by shares is: "The company's share capital is £50,000 divided into 50,000 shares of £1 each" (Table B).

3–246 The statutory model clause for a public company limited by shares is: "The company's share capital is £5,000,000 divided into 5,000,000 shares of £1 each" (Table F). The share capital with which a public company proposes to be registered must not be less than the "authorised minimum" (s. 11), a figure which at present is £50,000 but may be altered by statutory instrument (s. 118).

3–247 The share capital stated in the memorandum is the nominal (also referred to as the authorised) capital. For the distinction between this and the allotted, called-up and paid-up capital, see 3–27 *et seq.*, above.

3–248 A company with a share capital may, by section 121, alter the nominal capital stated in its memorandum in any of the following ways:

(a) by increasing the share capital by new shares of such amount as it thinks expedient;

(b) by consolidating and dividing all or any of its share capital into shares of larger amount than its existing shares;

(c) by converting all or any of its paid-up shares into stock, and reconverting that stock into paid-up shares of any denomination;

(d) by subdividing its shares, or any of them, into shares of smaller amount than is fixed by the memorandum (retaining, however, the same proportion between what is paid up and what is unpaid (if any) on each share);

(e) by cancelling shares which have not been taken or agreed to be taken by any person, and diminishing the share capital by the amount cancelled.

The conditions which must be fulfilled for an alteration under section 121 are: 3–249

(1) Authority to alter must be contained in the articles; otherwise the articles would require first to be altered by special resolution.

(2) The power to alter must be exercised by the company in general meeting; the type of resolution required will be that specified in the articles—usually an ordinary resolution.

As regards (a) (increase of capital), a company which is expanding and allotting further shares will usually wish about the same time to increase its nominal share capital, so as to maintain a suitable margin between its nominal capital and its allotted capital.

Mode (b) (consolidation into shares of larger amount) is seldom resorted to. 3–250

Likewise, mode (c) (conversion of paid-up shares into stock and reconversion) has now little practical significance. Shares are distinguishable from stock in that: 3–251

(1) Shares cannot be bought or sold or transferred in fractions, whereas stock is a mass of capital which can be divided into fractions of any amount. However, this point of distinction is lessened by the fact that the articles usually provide for stock to be divided into stock units (*e.g.* stock units of 25p each) which cannot be sub-divided.

(2) Only shares may be allotted in the first instance by the company; if the company wishes to have stock it must exercise the power of conversion under section 121.

(3) Shares may be partly paid (though in practice now they are usually fully paid); stock must always be fully paid.

(4) Formerly each share in a company had to be distinguished by its appropriate number and the main advantage of converting shares into stock was the avoidance of the work involved in the numbering of shares. However, it is now permissible to dispense with distinguishing numbers on shares provided all the allotted shares, or all the allotted shares of a particular class, are fully paid up and rank *pari passu* ("rateably", "equally") for all purposes—which will usually be the case.

Mode (e) (diminution) is distinct from reduction of capital. Diminution relates only to the nominal capital and to shares in that 3–252 capital which have not yet been allotted. Reduction, on the other hand, relates to the allotted capital and involves, for example, extinction of liability on shares which are not fully paid up or cancellation of paid-up share capital which is lost or unrepresented by available assets or which is in excess of the wants of the company. Reduction is permitted under section 135 but only on the conditions that:

(1) authority for reduction is contained in the articles;

(2) the company passes a special resolution for the reduction; and

(3) the court confirms the reduction.

3–253 The shares which comprise the share capital may be divided into different classes (preference, ordinary, deferred, *etc.*). Such division need not be mentioned in the memorandum. Usually the articles will confer power to divide shares into different classes. For example, the statutory model articles for a company limited by shares provide: "Subject to the provisions of the Act and without prejudice to any rights attached to any existing shares, any share may be issued with such rights or restrictions as the company may by ordinary resolution determine" (Table A, reg. 2).

3–254 Articles may, but Table A does not, provide for variation of class rights. Section 125 provides that where rights are attached to a class of shares otherwise than by the memorandum, and the articles do not contain provision for variation of the rights, then the rights may be varied if, but only if—

(a) the holders of three-quarters in nominal value of the issued shares of that class consent in writing to the variation; or

(b) an extraordinary resolution passed at a class meeting sanctions the variation.

3–255 If a company's share capital is divided into different classes of shares and a provision in the memorandum or articles authorises variation of the special rights subject to the consent of a specified proportion of the holders of the shares of the class or subject to the sanction of a resolution passed at a separate class meeting, then, by section 127, after the variation procedure has been followed, holders of not less than 15 per cent of the issued shares of the class, provided they are persons who did not consent to the resolution for variation, have the right to apply to the court to have the variation cancelled. The application must be made within 21 days after the giving of the consent or the passing of the resolution.

If the court is satisfied, having regard to all the circumstances of the case, that the variation would unfairly prejudice the applicants, it will disallow the variation; otherwise it will confirm it.

(vii) *Additional Clauses*

The memorandum may include other clauses which are not required by the Act to be included in it. The commonest instance is an additional clause dealing with the special rights attached to a particular class of shares. **3–256**

Section 17 enables any condition which is contained in a company's memorandum but which could lawfully have been contained in its articles instead to be altered by special resolution in much the same way as the objects of the company may be altered under section 4 of the Act. Section 17, however, does not apply where the memorandum itself provides for or prohibits alteration of the condition, nor does the section authorise any variation or abrogation of the special rights of any class of members. This latter exception makes section 17 of little importance in practice because it is unlikely that an additional clause will relate to anything other than special rights. **3–257**

(viii) *Association Clause*

The association clause is the clause by which the subscribers to the memorandum declare that they desire to form a company and by which they agree to take shares. The clause is followed by a list of the names and addresses of the subscribers, each subscriber stating opposite his name the number of shares which he is taking (s. 2(5)). The memorandum must then be signed by each subscriber in the presence of at least one witness who must also sign (s. 2(6)). **3–258**

However large a company may be contemplated and however many shares in it the subscribers to the memorandum may be intending to take, the memorandum will in practice be subscribed by two persons only, of whom each will take only one share. By the Companies (Single Member Private Limited Companies) Regulations 1992 (S.I. 1992 No. 1699) only one person need subscribe if the company is to be a private limited company. **3–259**

Thus the final part of the model memorandum for a public company limited by shares is in the following form (Table F): **3–260**

"We, the subscribers to this memorandum of association, wish to be formed into a company pursuant to this memorandum; and we agree to take the number of shares shown opposite our respective names:

Names and Addresses of Subscribers	Number of shares taken by each Subscriber
1 James White, 12 Broadmead, Birmingham.	1
2 Patrick Smith, 145A Huntley House, London Wall, London EC2.	1
Total shares taken	2

Dated 19

Witness to the above signatures,
Anne Brown, 13 Hute Street, London WC2."

3–261 The subscribers of the memorandum are deemed to have agreed to become members of the company, and on its registration must be entered as members in the company's register of members (s. 22(1)). Subscribers of the memorandum therefore become members even before their names are entered in the register of members. Persons other than subscribers do not become members until (1) they have agreed to become members and (2) their names have been entered in the register of members (s. 22(2)).

V ARTICLES OF ASSOCIATION

3–262 This part of the chapter is devoted to:

(a) the form and contents of articles;
(b) alteration of articles; and
(c) the effect of the memorandum and articles.

(a) Form and Contents of Articles

3–263 The Act provides that articles must:

(i) be printed;
(ii) be divided into paragraphs numbered consecutively; and
(iii) be signed by each subscriber of the memorandum in the presence of at least one witness, who must also sign (s. 7(3)).

3–264 Table A consists of a model set of articles (or, as they are called in the Act, "regulations") for a company limited by shares. Table A is particularly important because of the provisions of sections 7 and 8 of the Act. The effect of these sections is that a company limited by shares need not register articles along with its memorandum and that if it does not do so, the regulations in Table A will be the articles of the company just as if they had been contained in duly registered articles. A further provision is that if articles are registered a company limited by shares is governed by the regulations in Table A in so far as its own articles do not exclude or modify the contents of Table A. A company limited by guarantee and an unlimited company must always register articles of their own. The promoters of such companies may adopt in whole or in part the model articles in Tables C and E respectively, but there is no statutory provision for the automatic application of these Tables to any company.

The regulations which comprise Table A are grouped under these headings: **3–265**

"Interpretation" (a short list of definitions);

"Share Capital";

"Share Certificates";

"Lien" (the company has a "first and paramount" lien on non-fully-paid shares for money called up or payable at a fixed time in respect of such shares; it may also sell such shares by following a stated procedure);

"Calls on Shares and Forfeiture" (seven regulations specify the conditions on which any amount unpaid on shares may be called up by the directors from the shareholders and four regulations lay down a procedure which enables the directors to forfeit shares of a member who has failed to pay a call);

"Transfer of Shares" (six regulations specify the procedure for transferring shares and deal with the directors' possible right to refuse to register a transfer);

"Transmission of Shares" (transmission occurs when a member dies or becomes bankrupt; regulations specify the rights of other persons who become entitled to the shares on the occurrence of these events);

"Alteration of Capital" (the company is given power to alter its capital under section 121 of the Act by an ordinary resolution and to reduce its capital under section 135; see 3–248 *et seq.*, above);

"Purchase of Own Shares";

"General Meetings" (provisions for the convening of annual and extraordinary meetings of the company); there then follow separate groups of regulations as to notice of and proceedings at general meetings (including the demand for a poll) and as to votes (including proxies); a corporation (such as another company) may appoint a representative to act at company meetings;

"Directors" (here again there are many regulations, covering such matters as appointment, remuneration, directors' expenses, interests and pensions, disqualification, rotation (by which, say, one-third retire each year), proceedings (including meetings and delegation to committees), and appointment of a managing director);

"Secretary" (his appointment and remuneration are decided on by the directors);

"The Seal" (provisions as to the custody and use of the company's seal);

"Dividends" (the company in general meeting may declare dividends but not of a greater amount than is recommended by the directors; interim dividends may be paid by the directors);

"Accounts";

"Capitalisation of Profits" (the company in general meeting upon the recommendation of the directors has power to capitalise profits and reserves, with the result that the shareholders receive what are popularly referred to as "bonus" shares);

"Notices" (provisions as to the giving of notices where there are joint holders of shares, where the shareholder has died or become bankrupt or has no registered address in the United Kingdom, *etc.*);

"Winding Up" (the liquidator, with the sanction of an extraordinary resolution of the company, would have power to divide the company's assets in kind amongst the members); and

"Indemnity" (any director or other officer may be indemnified by the company against liability incurred in civil or criminal proceedings if judgment is given in his favour or if he is acquitted or if the court considers that he ought fairly to be excused for some negligence, default, breach of duty or breach of trust for which he may be liable).

3–266 Because articles are habitually based closely on the statutory model in Table A, questions as to the validity of an article seldom reach the courts. An exception is the case of *St Johnstone Football Club Ltd v. Scottish Football Association*, 1965 S.L.T. 171 (O.H.):

A football club brought an action against an association of football clubs, of which it was itself a member. The association sought to rely on one of its articles which, it maintained, prohibited any member from taking legal proceedings except with the prior consent of the Council of the association.

Held by Lord Kilbrandon (Ordinary) that the article in question was not wide enough to debar the club's action, and that, if it were, it was contrary to public policy and therefore not binding.

(b) **Alteration of Articles**

By section 9, a company may, subject to the provisions of the Act and to the conditions contained in its memorandum, alter its articles by special resolution, and any alterations are, subject to the Act, as valid as if originally contained in the articles and are subject in like manner to alteration by special resolution. **3–267**

A company's power to alter its articles under section 9 is wide: the only limitations on it are: **3–268**

(i) It is subject to the provisions of the Companies Act; *e.g.* no alteration in the articles could require a member, without his written consent, to take more shares or in any way increase his liability to the company (s. 16); nor could any alteration deprive minorities of their various statutory rights (such as the right of a 15 per cent minority to apply to court where special rights have been varied under section 127 of the Act (see 3–255, above)). **3–269**

(ii) The power to alter is also subject to the conditions contained in the company's memorandum. Since the memorandum is the ruling document, any alteration of the articles which would conflict with conditions in the memorandum would be of no effect. **3–270**

(iii) The power to alter must be exercised bona fide for the benefit of the company as a whole. There have been many cases illustrating this common law restriction on the power of alteration, *e.g.*: **3–271**

(1) *Allen v. Gold Reefs of West Africa Ltd* [1900] 1 Ch. 656 (CA): Articles gave the company a lien on partly-paid shares for all debts due by the member to the company. Zuccani had sold property to the company, and was the only holder of fully-paid shares; he also held partly-paid shares. **3–272**

At his death Zuccani was in debt to the company for arrears of calls on his partly-paid shares, and the articles were altered so as to give the company a lien on fully-paid shares.

Held that the alteration was valid because it had been made in good faith for the benefit of the company as a whole.

The alteration was there aimed at only one person and it was in a sense retrospective in that it enabled the company to exercise a lien on Zuccani's fully-paid shares for debts contracted before the date of the alteration.

Lord Lindley M.R. said (at p. 671) that the power conferred on companies to alter articles "must, like all other powers, be exercised subject to those general principles of law and equity which are applicable to all powers conferred on majorities and enabling them to bind minorities. It must be exercised, not only in the manner required by law, but also bona fide for the benefit of the company as a whole, and it must not be exceeded. These conditions are always implied, and are seldom, if ever, expressed."

3–273 In a somewhat similar Scottish case, however, the court refused to allow the alteration to have retrospective effect:

Liquidator of W. & A. McArthur Ltd v. Gulf Line Ltd, 1909 S.C. 732: G. Ltd's articles gave the company a lien on all shares which were not fully paid.

M. (South Africa) Ltd, which held both fully-paid shares and partly-paid shares in G. Ltd, transferred the fully-paid shares to M. Ltd at a time when a call was due on the partly-paid shares.

G. Ltd then altered its articles so as to give it a lien on all shares registered in the name of a member for all calls due on any shares registered in the member's name.

Held that M. Ltd was not affected by that alteration but was entitled to have its name placed on the register of members in accordance with the articles in force at the time when it had presented the transfer for registration.

The alteration came into force only at its own date; further, it had been made not so much because the directors considered it to be required in the general interests of the company as simply to meet the case of one particular transfer.

3–274 (2) An alteration may still be bona fide for the benefit of the company as a whole although it has the effect of prejudicing a particular shareholder or class of shareholders:

Crookston v. Lindsay, Crookston & Co. Ltd, 1922 S.L.T. 62 (O.H.): L. Ltd was a private company in which C. and three other directors held amongst them the whole of the issued shares.

L. Ltd altered its articles so as to include a provision that any member desiring to sell his shares had first to offer them to the directors at par (*i.e.* at their nominal value).

C., alleging that the alteration had been devised to enable the other three directors ultimately to acquire C.'s shares at a price far below their fair value, sought to interdict the alteration.

Held that the alteration was valid, even although it might have the effect of prejudicing C.'s rights under the original articles.

(3) An alteration of the articles which amounts to a breach of a contract entered into by the company is nevertheless valid, but the other party is entitled to damages from the company: **3–275**

Southern Foundries (1926) Ltd v. Shirlaw [1940] A.C. 701: S., a director of S. Ltd, had been appointed managing director for 10 years by a contract outside the articles.

The articles provided that the managing director, *subject to his contract with the company*, could be removed in the same way as the other directors and that if he ceased to be a director he would automatically cease to be managing director.

Later, Federated Foundries Ltd ("F. Ltd") acquired the shares of S. Ltd, and the articles were altered so as to empower F. Ltd to remove any director of S. Ltd.

Before the expiry of the 10 years of S.'s contract, F. Ltd removed S. from his office of director, and treated S. as having ceased to be managing director.

Held that S. was entitled to damages from S. Ltd for breach of the implied term in S.'s contract of employment that S. Ltd would not remove S. from his position as director during the 10 years for which he had been appointed managing director.

(c) Effect of Memorandum and Articles

Section 14(1) of the Act provides that, subject to the provisions of the Act, the memorandum and articles, when registered, bind the company and its members to the same extent as if they had been signed and sealed by each member and contained covenants on the part of each member to observe all the provisions of the memorandum and articles. **3–276**

The effect of section 14(1) is open to some doubt. The following are amongst the points raised by the provision: **3–277**

3–278 (i) Members in their capacity as members are bound to the company as if each member had himself signed and sealed the memorandum and articles. An illustration is *Hickman v. Kent or Romney Marsh Sheep-Breeders' Association* [1915] 1 Ch. 881:

Articles provided that differences between the company and any of its members should be referred to arbitration.

H., a member, brought an action against the company in connection with a dispute as to his expulsion from the company.

Held that the company was entitled to have the action stayed, since the articles constituted a contract between the company and its members in respect of their ordinary rights as members.

3–279 (ii) The provision does not expressly state that the company is bound to its members as if the company had signed and sealed the memorandum and articles, but this has been held to be so:

Wood v. Odessa Waterworks Co. (1889) 42 Ch.D. 636: Articles empowered the company to declare a dividend "to be paid" to the shareholders.

The company, instead of paying a dividend, passed a resolution to issue to the shareholders debenture bonds bearing interest and redeemable over 30 years.

Held that the words "to be paid" meant paid in cash and that a shareholder could therefore restrain the company from acting on the resolution, on the ground that it contravened the articles.

3–280 (iii) The memorandum and articles do not constitute a contract between the company and its members in some capacity other than as members (*e.g.* as promoters, solicitors or directors):

Eley v. Positive Government Security Life Assurance Co. Ltd (1876) 1 Ex. D. 88 (CA): Articles provided that E. should be the solicitor to the company for the usual fees and charges and should not be removed from office except for misconduct.

E. was employed for a time, but later the company ceased to employ him and employed other solicitors.

Held that E. was not entitled to damages for breach of contract, because the articles did not create a contract between the company and E. in his capacity as solicitor to the company.

3–281 (iv) It is, however, possible for the articles to be used as the basis for a contract outside the articles between the company and a member in some capacity other than that of member:

Re New British Iron Co., ex parte Beckwith [1898] 1 Ch. 324: An article provided that remuneration of the directors should be the annual sum of £1,000. The directors, who were also members, accepted office on the footing of that article.

For some time prior to the liquidation of the company the directors acted as such but were not paid.

Held that they were entitled to rank as ordinary creditors for the arrears of remuneration, since the provision in the articles had been embodied in the contract between them (as directors) and the company; the remuneration was not due to the directors in their character of members.

(v) The memorandum and articles constitute a contract between **3–282**
individual members, and if a member thus obtains a personal right, he may enforce the contract directly against another member without the aid of the company:

Rayfield v. Hands [1960] Ch. 1: Articles of a private company required a member who was intending to transfer his shares to inform the directors and provided that the directors should take the shares equally between them at a fair value.

Held that the directors (who were also members) were bound by the articles to take the plaintiff's shares because of the contractual relationship between the plaintiff as a member and the directors as members, and that it was not necessary for the company to be a party to the action.

Further Reading

Scots Mercantile Law Statutes (reprinted from *The Parliament House Book* (W. Green) for Companies Act 1985, Business Names Act 1985, Companies Consolidation (Consequential Provisions) Act 1985, Insolvency Act 1986, Company Directors Disqualification Act 1986, Financial Services Act 1986 and Companies Act 1989

Gloag and Henderson, *The Law of Scotland*, Chapter 51

David M. Walker, *Principles of Scottish Private Law*, Volume I, Chapter 3.13

Charlesworth and Morse Company Law, 15th ed. by Geoffrey Morse (Scottish Editor: Enid A. Marshall) (1995, Sweet & Maxwell)

Palmer's Company Law, 25th ed., Principal Editor: Geoffrey Morse, with Specialist Editors (seven volumes, loose-leaf) (Sweet & Maxwell)

Nicholas Bourne and Brian Pillans, *Scottish Company Law* (1996, Cavendish Publishing Ltd)

Smith & Keenan's Company Law for Students, 10th ed. by Denis Keenan (Scottish Supplement by Josephine R. Bisacre) (1996, Pitman Publishing)

M. C. Oliver and Enid A. Marshall, *Company Law*, 12th ed. by Enid A. Marshall (Scots Law incorporated) (1994, Pitman Publishing)

The Laws of Scotland: Stair Memorial Encyclopaedia, Volume 4, Title *Companies,* Co-ordinator: David A. Bennett

Enid A. Marshall, *Scottish Cases on Partnerships and Companies,* Part II (1980, W. Green)

Chapter 4

SALE OF GOODS

	Para.
Introduction	4–01
I Contracts to which the Act applies	4–14
II Formation of the Contract	4–17
(a) Definition and Nature of the Contract	4–18
"Sale" and "Agreement to Sell"	4–18
Sale and Barter	4–23
Sale and Security	4–27
Capacity to Buy and Sell	4–31
(b) Formalities of the Contract	4–35
(c) Subject-Matter of the Contract	4–36
Existing or Future Goods	4–38
Specific or Generic Goods	4–39
(d) The Price	4–44
(e) Terms of the Contract	4–50
Stipulations as to Time	4–59
Implied Terms about Title, *etc.*	4–64
Sale by Description	4–72
Implied Terms about Quality or Fitness	4–84
(i) Satisfactory quality	4–92
(ii) Fitness for particular purpose	4–97
(iii) Usage	4–110
Sale by Sample	4–111
Remedies for Breach of Contract as respects Scotland	4–116
III Effects of the Contract	4–117
(a) Transfer of Property as between Seller and Buyer	4–118
Unascertained Goods	4–123
Specific or Ascertained Goods	4–131
Rules for ascertaining intention	4–136
(b) Transfer of Title	4–155
(i) Personal Bar	4–158
(ii) Sale under Voidable Title	4–159
(iii) Seller or Buyer in Possession after Sale	4–162
IV Performance of the Contract	4–173
(a) Seller's Duty to Deliver	4–175
General Rules about Delivery	4–177
Delivery of Wrong Quantity	4–183
Instalment Deliveries	4–190
Delivery to Carrier	4–192
Delivery at Distant Place	4–201
(b) Buyer's Duty to Accept	4–202
Buyer's Right of Examination	4–204
Buyer's Right of Rejection	4–205
Buyer's Right of Partial Rejection	4–225
Buyer's Liability for not Taking Delivery	4–229
V Rights of Unpaid Seller against the Goods	4–231
(a) Lien	4–241
(b) Stoppage in Transit	4–251
(i) Duration of Transit	4–254
(ii) How Stoppage in Transit is Effected	4–265
(c) Resale	4–268
[(d) Attachment by Arrestment or Poinding]	4–275
VI Actions for Breach of the Contract	4–278
(a) Seller's Remedies	4–286
(i) Action for Price	4–287
(ii) Damages for Non-Acceptance	4–290
(b) Buyer's Remedies	4–294
(i) Damages for Non-Delivery	4–296
(ii) Specific Performance	4–299
(iii) Damages and Rejection	4–301
VII Auction Sales	4–311
VIII Other Statutory Provisions on Sale of Goods	4–326
Auctions (Bidding Agreements) Acts 1927 and 1969	4–327
Mock Auctions Act 1961	4–330
Trading Stamps Act 1964	4–334
Trade Descriptions Acts 1968 and 1972	4–336
Unsolicited Goods and Services Acts 1971 and 1975	4–344
Fair Trading Act 1973	4–349
Unfair Contract Terms Act 1977	4–356
Consumer Protection Act 1987	4–360
(a) Product Liability	4–361
(b) Consumer Safety	4–373
(c) Misleading Price Indications	4–385

INTRODUCTION

4–01 THE law on the sale of goods was first codified by the Sale of Goods Act 1893. That Act was subsequently amended, notably by the Supply of Goods (Implied Terms) Act 1973, and the Sale of Goods Act 1979 was passed to consolidate the law on the subject. The Act of 1979, which came into force on January 1, 1980, repealed the Act of 1893 and its amendments, but, being a consolidating Act, did not alter the substance of the law.

4–02 Meantime in 1979, before the passing of the Act of 1979, the Law Commission and the Scottish Law Commission had been asked to consider certain aspects of the law relating to the sale and supply of goods. This reference resulted in a joint Report being published in 1987—*Sale and Supply of Goods* (Law Com. No. 160; Scot. Law Com. No. 104; Cm. 137). The Commissions examined the statutory implied terms in contracts for the sale of goods, remedies for breach of those terms and the loss of the right to reject non-conforming goods. Recommendations included:

(a) a reformulation of the implied term as to "merchantable quality" so as to make it clear that it applied to minor defects and covered the durability of the goods;

(b) the introduction of a right of partial rejection;

(c) clarification of the circumstances in which the right to reject is lost;

(d) as regards Scots law, removal of the English terminology of "conditions" and "warranties" and the substitution of the word "terms" in their place; and

(e) extension to Scotland of provisions equivalent to those of Part I of the Supply of Goods and Services Act 1982 (which does not apply to Scotland).

4–03 The recommendations of the Commissions were substantially accepted and became the Sale and Supply of Goods Act 1994, which came into force on January 3, 1995.

4–04 A further joint report of the Law Commission and the Scottish Law Commission—*Sale of Goods Forming Part of a Bulk* (Law Com. No. 215; Scot. Law Com. No. 145)—concerned the rights of purchasers of goods forming part of a larger bulk carried by sea. The Commissions' recommendations became the Sale of Goods (Amendment) Act 1995, which came into force on September 19, 1995.

These two last-mentioned Acts are amending Acts. The code of law on the sale of goods is therefore now to be found in the Sale of Goods Act 1979, as amended, and in this chapter references to sections are, unless the context indicates otherwise, references to sections of the Act of 1979. The amendments have been made by putting "patches" on the Act of 1979, *e.g.* section 1(1) of the Act of 1994 provides that in section 14 of the Sale of Goods Act 1979 (implied terms about quality or fitness) for subsection (2) there are substituted new subsections (2), (2A), (2B) and (2C). The effect is to leave undisturbed the arrangement of the Act of 1979 as a whole. It is also a remarkable, but convenient, feature of the Act of 1979 itself that it adopted for the most part the numbering of sections which had become familiar under the Act of 1893. **4–05**

Most of the statutory provisions dealt with in this chapter apply equally throughout the United Kingdom. **4–06**

The codification which took place in 1893 was based mainly on the common law of England, and was a continuation of the process of assimilation of Scots and English law which had begun with the Mercantile Law Amendment Act Scotland 1856. The effect was to alter substantially the Scots law on sale of goods, since the common law of Scotland had closely followed the Roman law of sale. **4–07**

Especially important was the statutory change made by the introduction of the English theory and principles affecting the time at which the ownership of the goods passed from seller to buyer. By the common law of Scotland, delivery had been essential: a contract for the sale of goods was no more than a contract giving rise to personal rights between seller and buyer: up to the time of delivery the buyer had a *jus ad rem* ("right with regard to the thing") and not a *jus in re* ("right in the thing"), *i.e.* he had not a right of ownership (a "real" as opposed to a "personal" right). By the common law of England, on the other hand, ownership passed to the buyer independently of delivery: the sale was not only a contract but also a conveyance (*i.e.* a transfer of ownership). Founded on this basic difference in theory between Scots and English law there were the different principles applicable, at common law, in the two legal systems: in Scots law the ownership of the goods did not pass to the buyer until the goods were delivered, whereas in English law the ownership passed at the time when the contract was entered into, or if the goods were not then in existence or were for some other reason not then ready for **4–08** delivery, it passed as soon as the goods were ready for delivery. The principles of English law, now applicable to Scotland also, are set out in sections 16 to 20B of the Act of 1979, as amended by the Sale of Goods (Amendment) Act 1995, under the heading "Transfer of property as between seller and buyer".

4–09 The Act of 1979, like its predecessor of 1893, is a comparatively short Act, and does not cover all aspects of the law as to sale of goods: the rules of the common law are expressly preserved in so far as they are consistent with the express provisions of the Act. In particular, the rules relating to agency, and to fraud, misrepresentation and other grounds of invalidity, continue to apply to contracts for the sale of goods (s. 62(2)). The common law of Scotland, therefore, still governs many aspects of the law as to sale of goods.

4–10 In recent years there has been a considerable growth in "consumer-protection" legislation. For the purposes of this chapter such legislation may be regarded as falling into two categories:

4–11 First, there have been the statutes amending the Act of 1893 where the specific provisions of that Act were thought to operate unfairly. The most important provisions within this category were contained in the Supply of Goods (Implied Terms) Act 1973, the Consumer Credit Act 1974, and the Unfair Contract Terms Act 1977. These provisions are now all consolidated in the Act of 1979, which has in its turn been amended by part of the Sale and Supply of Goods Act 1994 and by the Sale of Goods (Amendment) Act 1995.

4–12 Secondly, a number of statutes have been passed to regulate matters which were not dealt with at all by the Act of 1893. Statutes in this second category are the Trading Stamps Act 1964, the Trade Descriptions Act 1968, and the Consumer Protection Act 1987, and, on auction sales, the Auctions (Bidding Agreements) Acts 1927 and 1969 and the Mock Auctions Act 1961. Part of the Sale and Supply of Goods Act 1994 is of this character in that it inserts Part IA ("Supply of Goods as Respects Scotland") into the Supply of Goods and Services Act 1982; the inserted provisions relate to contracts for the transfer of goods, such as barter, not within the sale of goods legislation. These statutes have introduced civil and criminal provisions designed to restrict practices considered to be undesirable. They form distinct bodies of legislation, supplementary to, but outwith, the Sale of Goods Act

1979. Though important in practice, they will receive only incidental mention in this chapter, which is confined to an account of "the law relating to the sale of goods" in the narrower, traditional sense of that phrase.

Following the arrangement of the first six Parts of the Act of 1979, the subject-matter of this chapter comes under these headings: 4–13

I. Contracts to which the Act applies;
II. Formation of the contract;
III. Effects of the contract;
IV. Performance of the contract;
V. Rights of unpaid seller against the goods; and
VI. Actions for breach of the contract.

Part VII of the Act ("Supplementary") includes, as well as miscellaneous provisions, a section on:

VII. Auction sales.

At the end of the chapter a brief indication is given of:

VIII. Other statutory provisions on sale of goods.

I CONTRACTS TO WHICH THE ACT APPLIES

Part I of the 1979 Act consists of only one section. 4–14

The section declares that the Act applies to contracts of sale of goods made on or after (but not to those made before) January 1, 1894 (the date when the Act of 1893 came into force) (s. 1(1)). 4–15

The section then goes on to state what is in effect a transitional provision: in relation to contracts made on certain dates, the Act applies *subject to the modification of certain of its sections*, as mentioned in Schedule 1 to the Act (s. 1(2)). The contracts which are within the transitional provisions are mainly those which were made on or after May 18, 1973 (when the amendments to the 1893 Act made by the Supply of Goods (Implied Terms) Act 1973 came into force) and before January 1, 1980 (the date on which the 1979 Act came into force). 4–16

II FORMATION OF THE CONTRACT

The provisions in Part II of the Act are dealt with below under the following headings: 4–17

(a) definition and nature of the contract;
(b) formalities of the contract;
(c) subject-matter of the contract;
(d) the price; and
(e) terms of the contract.

(a) **Definition and Nature of the Contract**

"Sale" and "Agreement to Sell"

4–18 The statutory definition of "a contract of sale of goods" is such that it covers both (i) a "sale" and (ii) an "agreement to sell".

4–19 "A contract of sale of goods is a contract by which the seller transfers or agrees to transfer the property in goods to the buyer for a money consideration, called the price" (s. 2(1)). Where under a contract of sale the property in (*i.e.* the ownership of) the goods is transferred from the seller to the buyer, the contract is called a "sale", but where the transfer of the property in the goods is to take place at a future time or subject to some condition which has still not been fulfilled, the contract is called an "agreement to sell" (s. 2(4), (5)). An agreement to sell becomes a sale when the time elapses or the conditions are fulfilled (s. 2(6)).

4–20 A contract of sale may be absolute or conditional (s. 2(3)). There are two types of condition to which a contract may be subject—suspensive and resolutive.

4–21 If the condition is a suspensive one, the contract will be held in suspense until the condition is fulfilled. The property in the goods will therefore not be transferred to the buyer, and the contract will necessarily be in the meantime only an "agreement to sell", and not a "sale". There are several instances of suspensive conditions in section 18 of the Act; *e.g.* when goods are delivered to the buyer on approval, the property in the goods passes to the buyer when he indicates his approval to the seller.

4–22 A resolutive condition, on the other hand, does not suspend the completion of the contract, but makes the contract liable to be "resolved" (dissolved) if the condition is fulfilled. Such a condition therefore allows the property in the goods to pass to the buyer, though, if the condition is fulfilled, the property may later require to be restored to the seller. Because the passing of the property to the buyer is not delayed by the presence of a resolutive condition, the contract will be a "sale", and not merely an "agreement to sell", for the purposes of the Act. An instance of a resolutive condition can be seen in *Gavin's Trustee v. Fraser*, 1920 S.C. 674 (see also 4–30, below): a haulage contractor who had sold his plant to a timber merchant was, by the terms of the agreement between them, entitled to buy back the plant within a year for £1,200 with interest at 6 per cent.

Sale and Barter

The words "for a money consideration, called the price" included in the definition serve to differentiate a contract of sale from a contract of barter by which moveable property is exchanged for other moveable property without any money being paid. **4–23**

Straightforward barter is now seldom of commercial importance in purely home transactions, though it can be of considerable utility in some international commerce (*e.g.* to avoid problems of establishing exchange rates). An illustration is *Widenmeyer v. Burn, Stewart & Co. Ltd*, 1967 S.C. 85 (an exchange of a specified quantity of 1962 whisky for a specified quantity of 1964 whisky). **4–24**

Very common, however, especially in the motor trade, are transactions where the price consists partly of money and partly of other moveable property (*e.g.* a vehicle being traded-in). At common law it was important that it should be made clear whether such a transaction was to be categorised as a sale or as barter, since sale was governed by the Act of 1979, whereas in Scotland barter was governed by the common law. In England barter was covered by the Supply of Goods and Services Act 1982, which did not apply to Scotland. **4–25**

Two sheriff court cases, taken together, support the view that where the consideration is partly in goods and partly in money the contract is a sale whereas if the consideration is wholly in goods the contract is barter:

Sneddon v. Durant, 1982 S.L.T. (Sh. Ct.) 39: S. purchased a van for £995. He was allowed a trade-in allowance of £845 for his Ford Cortina estate car and he entered into a consumer credit agreement with D. for the balance of £150.

S. sought to reject the van under section 14(2) of the Sale of Goods Act 1979 on the ground that it was not of "merchantable quality", whereas D. contended that the transaction was barter to which that Act did not apply.

Held that the transaction was a sale.

The sheriff (A. M. Bell) was of the opinion that where money was involved, ordinary people as well as the legal profession would normally regard the transaction as a sale.

Ballantyne v. Durant, 1983 S.L.T. (Sh. Ct.) 38: This case concerned a straight exchange of vehicles: B. exchanged his Lada for a Simca. No money changed hands. The parties were in agreement that the contract was barter.

B. alleged that the Simca was "a lump of scrap", not fit to be driven on the public road, and the main question in that case was whether B. was entitled to exercise a right of rejection three weeks after delivery.

Held that (i) the principle applicable to barter was that where goods had a material latent defect discoverable only by inspection, the barterer was entitled to carry out an inspection after the exchange, provided he did so within a reasonable time; and (ii) in the circumstances three weeks was not an unreasonable time.

For comments on these cases see A.D.M. Forte, "Permutations on the Contract of Sale: The background to *Sneddon v. Durant*, 1982 S.L.T. (Sh. Ct.) 39" (1983) 28 J.L.S.S. 108 and "The Scope of the Right of Rejection in Contracts of Exchange: *Ballantyne v. Durant*, 1983 S.L.T. (Sh. Ct.) 38" (1983) 28 J.L.S.S. 314.

4–26 It is no longer important to categorise a transaction as sale or barter on account of the changes made to the common law by the Sale and Supply of Goods Act 1994, which added a new Part IA (sections 11A to 11L) to the Supply of Goods and Services Act 1982. Sections 11A to 11F relate to contracts for the transfer of property in goods and are relevant to barter, though it is not specifically mentioned. (Sections 11G to 11L relate to contracts for the hire of goods.)

A "contract for the transfer of goods" means a contract under which one person transfers or agrees to transfer to another the property in goods, other than an excepted contract" (s. 11A(1)). Amongst the "excepted" contracts is a contract of sale of goods (s. 11A(2)). A contract is a contract for the transfer of goods whatever is the nature of the consideration for the transfer or agreement to transfer (s. 11A(3)). For instance, the consideration might be a traded-in vehicle alone or in addition to money.

With little modification the implied terms and the remedies for breach of contract which would apply to a contract for a sale of goods under the Act of 1979, as amended by the Act of 1994, are made applicable to contracts for the transfer of goods as defined above (Supply of Goods and Services Act 1982, ss. 11B–11F).

Sale and Security

It is important in certain circumstances to distinguish between a contract of sale and a contract which is in the form of a sale but is really intended to create security over moveables (which remain in the apparent seller's possession) in favour of a creditor who is the apparent buyer. The Act of 1979 does not apply to such fictitious sales: by section 62(4) "the provisions of this Act about contracts of sale do not apply to a transaction in the form of a contract of sale which is intended to operate by way of mortgage, pledge, charge, or other security". **4–27**

The importance and the operation of section 62(4) are most easily understood by an example selected from the many decided cases in which the court has been called upon to apply the corresponding provision (s. 61(4)) of the Act of 1893: **4–28**

Robertson v. Hall's Trustee (1896) 24 R. 120: H. purchased a crane-making business with its machinery, plant and stock of materials. He had, however, no capital, and borrowed £400 from R., a moneylender, to pay the first instalment of the price.

H. and R. agreed that H. "sold" the machinery *etc.* to R., that H. was to remain in possession of it, using it for the purposes of the business, and to pay a "hire" of 20 per cent on the "purchase" price of £400, and that, after the £400 had been repaid (which was to be by half-yearly instalments), R. would "resell" the articles to H.

About a year after this agreement had been entered into, H. became bankrupt, and there was competition for the machinery *etc.* between the trustee in H.'s sequestration and R.

Held that the circumstances showed that the parties had intended a security and not a sale; R.'s claim was therefore repelled because H. had in reality remained the owner.

Section 61(4) of the Act of 1893 was there said to be "in effect a statutory declaration that a pledge of or security over moveables cannot be created merely by completion of what professes to be a contract of sale. If the transaction is truly a sale, the property will pass without delivery. But the form of the contract is not conclusive. The reality of the transaction must be inquired into; and if, contrary to the form of the contract, and even the declaration of the parties, it appears from the whole circumstances that a true sale was not intended, it will be held that the property has not passed and that no effectual security has been acquired" (*per* Lord Moncreiff at p. 134).

4–29 Other cases in which the court came to the same conclusion include *Jones & Co.'s Trustee v. Allan* (1901) 4 F. 374 (J., a bicycle dealer, obtaining a loan from A. and giving A. a receipted invoice stating fictitiously that A. had paid £72 for certain specified bicycles which remained in J.'s possession), *Rennet v. Mathieson* (1903) 5 F. 591 (a landlord "purchasing" his tenant's wood-turning plant and then "hiring" it to the tenant), *Hepburn v. Law*, 1914 S.C. 918 (a creditor obtaining from his debtor a "receipt" for £130 stated to be the price of specified articles of furniture which remained in the debtor's house), and *Scottish Transit Trust Ltd v. Scottish Land Cultivators Ltd*, 1955 S.C. 254 (public works contractors "selling" their tractors and other vehicles to dealers in such vehicles who then advanced a lump sum to the contractors and entered into an apparently ordinary hire-purchase agreement with them).

4–30 The narrowness of the distinction can be seen by contrasting with these cases the case of *Gavin's Trustee v. Fraser*, 1920 S.C. 674, in which the court held that there had truly been a contract of sale where a haulage contractor had sold his plant to a timber merchant for £1,200, had continued to use the plant for the performance of a contract previously entered into with the timber merchant, and was to be entitled to buy back the plant within a year for £1,200 with interest at 6 per cent.

Capacity to Buy and Sell

4–31 Capacity to buy and sell is regulated by the general law concerning capacity to contract, except for the special rule that where necessaries are sold and delivered to a person who by reason of mental incapacity or drunkenness is incompetent to contract, he must pay a reasonable price for the goods. The word "necessaries" means goods suitable to the condition in life of the person, and to his actual requirements at the time of the sale and delivery (s. 3, as amended by Age of Legal Capacity (Scotland) Act 1991, s. 10 and Sched. 2).

4–32 Since the rule requires only a "reasonable" price, and not the contract price, to be paid, it is part of the law of unjust enrichment rather than of contract.

Food and clothing would often be held to be "necessaries", but this would not always be so, as may be illustrated by the well-known English case *Nash v. Inman* [1908] 2 K.B. 1 (CA), a case decided when minors also were covered by the special rule: 4–33

A Savile Row tailor brought an action for £145 10s. 3d., the price of clothing "of an extravagant and ridiculous style" (including 11 fancy waistcoats) supplied to an undergraduate at Cambridge University. He met with the defence of "infancy", the defendant having been under the age of majority (21 years at that time).

Held that the onus was on the plaintiff to prove not only that the goods were suitable to the condition in life of the infant but that he was not sufficiently supplied with goods of that class at the time of the sale and delivery.

The general law now governing the capacity of young persons to contract is in the Age of Legal Capacity (Scotland) Act 1991. The general rule is that persons under 16 have no capacity to enter into any transaction, whereas persons over 16 have legal capacity to enter into any transaction (s. 1(1)). 4–34

An exception to the general rule is that a person under 16 has legal capacity to enter into a transaction of a kind commonly entered into by persons of his age and circumstances provided the terms are not unreasonable (s. 2(1)).

Further, there is some protection given by the Act to 16- and 17-year old persons: the Court of Session or a sheriff court may, if applied to, set aside a transaction entered into while the person was of or over 16 but under 18 provided the transaction was a "prejudicial transaction". The application to court must be made before the person reaches 21. By "prejudicial transaction" is meant a transaction which an adult, exercising reasonable prudence, would not have entered into in the circumstances *and* which has caused or is likely to cause substantial prejudice to the applicant (s. 3(1), (2), (5)).

This protection does not extend to the following transactions:

(a) transaction in the course of the applicant's trade, business or profession;

(b) a transaction induced by fraudulent misrepresentation by the applicant as to his age or other material fact;

(c) a transaction ratified by the applicant after he attains 18 and in the knowledge that he could have applied to the court to set it aside;

(d) a proposed transaction ratified by the court (s. 3(3)).

If it were not for (d), above, persons between 16 and 18 might be unduly hampered from entering into a transaction because the other party would not wish to risk the possibility that the transaction would be set aside. The Act, therefore, provides that the person between 16 and 18 and the other party may make a joint application to the sheriff court to have their *proposed* transaction ratified. The court must not give ratification if it considers that an adult, exercising reasonable prudence and in the circumstances of the parties, would not enter into the transaction. The decision of the sheriff is final (s. 4).

(b) Formalities of the Contract

4–35 Except where there is some provision to the contrary in any statute (as there is, for instance, in the case of the sale of a ship), there are no special formalities, either for constitution of the contract or for proof of it. The contract may be made in writing, or by word of mouth, or partly in writing and partly by word of mouth, or may be implied from the conduct of the parties (s. 4(1)). It may be proved *prout de jure* ("by any competent evidence, including parole evidence"):

Allan v. Millar, 1932 S.C. 620: A tenant was selling to his successor in the tenancy his "whole stock, crop, buildings, implements *etc*". Some items of heritable property—growing raspberry bushes and a shed—were included in the tenant's stock.

Held that since the contract was for the sale of an *universitas* (a "totality") which was preponderatingly moveable it could competently be proved *prout de jure*.

(c) Subject-Matter of the Contract

4–36 The subject-matter of the contract is "goods", defined, in section 61(1), as including "all corporeal moveables except money". Incorporeal moveables, such as stocks and shares, are not "goods". Money is a corporeal moveable, but is necessarily excluded in the definition because in a sale of goods the goods and the price (which must be in money) are contrasted.

4–37 The term "goods" includes industrial growing crops (*e.g.* a growing crop of potatoes at a specified price per acre, as in *Paton's*

Trustee v. Finlayson, 1923 S.C. 872 (4–247, below)), and things attached to or forming part of the land which are agreed to be severed before sale or under the contract of sale (*e.g.* a quantity of growing timber, as in *Munro v. Liquidator of Balnagown Estates Co. Ltd*, 1949 S.C. 49 (4–140, below)) (s. 61(1)). By the Sale of Goods (Amendment) Act 1995 (s. 2), the term also includes an undivided share in goods. It has been decided in an English High Court case that "goods" include instructions on the packaging of goods (*Wormell v. R.H.M. Agriculture (East) Ltd* [1986] 1 W.L.R. 336, concerning misleading instructions on cans of herbicide).

Existing or Future Goods

The goods may be either (i) existing goods, owned or possessed by the seller, or (ii) "future goods", defined as goods to be manufactured or acquired by the seller after the making of the contract of sale. It is possible to have a contract for the sale of goods, the acquisition of which by the seller depends upon a contingency which may or may not happen. There cannot be a present sale of future goods: the contract must, in the case of future goods, operate as an agreement to sell (with the result that the ownership of the goods does not pass to the buyer at the time of the making of the contract) (s. 5): **4–38**

Stark's Trustees v. Stark, 1948 S.C. 41: S., by will dated July 10, 1946, bequeathed to his nephew "any motor car which I may possess at the date of my death". At that date, S. had a car on order.

S. died on August 23, 1946, before the car had been supplied.

Held that since at the date of S.'s death the car was still "future goods", it did not form part of S.'s estate, and that therefore the legacy failed.

Specific or Generic Goods

"Specific goods" are goods identified and agreed on at the time a contract of sale is made and include an undivided share, specified as a fraction or percentage, of goods identified and agreed on at the time a contract of sale is made (s. 61(1) as amended by the Sale of Goods (Amendment) Act 1995, s. 2). **4–39**

The Act has two provisions concerned with the possibility of the destruction of specific goods: **4–40**

4–41 (i) Where there is a contract for the sale of specific goods, and the goods without the knowledge of the seller have perished at the time when the contract is made, the contract is void (s. 6).

4–42 (ii) Where there is an agreement to sell specific goods, and subsequently the goods, without any fault on the part of the seller or buyer, perish before the risk passes to the buyer, the agreement is avoided (s. 7). The passing of the risk is regulated by section 20 (see 4–120, below): the general rule is that prima facie ("unless the contrary is proved") the risk passes from seller to buyer at the same time as the ownership of the goods passes from seller to buyer.

4–43 In contrast to specific goods are generic goods (*e.g.* a specified quantity of a commodity such as flour). There are no provisions in the Act to make a contract for the sale of generic goods void should the goods be destroyed: the theory is *genus nunquam perit* ("the class never perishes"). The effect is that the loss will fall on the seller.

(d) **The Price**

4–44 The price must always be in money (s. 2(1)). Where there is no money the contract would be one of barter (see 4–23 *et seq.*, above).

4–45 The price may be fixed by the contract, or may be left to be fixed in a manner agreed by the contract, or may be determined by the course of dealing between the parties. Where the price is not determined in any of these ways, the buyer must pay a reasonable price, and what is a reasonable price is a question of fact dependent on the circumstances of each particular case (s. 8). A reasonable price is not necessarily, though it often will be, the market price.

4–46 An illustration of the application of the corresponding provisions in section 8 of the Act of 1893 is *Glynwed Distribution Ltd v. S. Koronka & Co.*, 1977 S.C. 1:

G. Ltd delivered to K. & Co., manufacturers of agricultural implements, a quantity of hot rolled steel. K. & Co. accepted the steel, thinking that they had bought "British steel" at a price of £103.50 per tonne; G. Ltd thought that they had sold "foreign steel" at a price of £149 per tonne.

G. Ltd raised an action in the sheriff court at Cupar for the unpaid balance of the price, representing the difference between the two prices.

The sheriff fixed £135 as a reasonable price.

On appeal to the sheriff principal, the decision of the sheriff was reversed on the ground that G. Ltd had not proved that there was a contract to sell at £149 per tonne, and that in any event there was no *consensus in idem* ("mutual agreement").

Held, on an appeal to the Court of Session, that (i) there was an agreement as to the subject-matter, namely, hot rolled steel, and therefore there was *consensus in idem*; and (ii) "reasonable price" meant something different from the market price, and there was a basis in fact upon which the sheriff could reach a decision as to what was a reasonable price in this case.

One of the ways in which the price may be left to be fixed "in a **4–47** manner agreed by the contract" is where a valuation is to be made by a third party. The question may then arise of whether the valuator has adopted the correct basis for his valuation:

Macdonald v. Clark, 1927 S.N. 6 (O.H.): M., the owner of a hotel at Dalmellington, was selling the hotel property and business to C. The parties agreed that the price for the furniture and plant was to be fixed by valuators.

Held that the valuators were justified in valuing the articles, not at their market value, but as parts of a going concern, *i.e.* at a value greater than the sum of the values of the separate articles.

The Act provides that where there is an agreement to sell goods **4–48** at a price to be fixed by the valuation of a third party, and the third party cannot or does not make the valuation, the agreement is avoided (*i.e.* cancelled), but if the goods or any part of them have been delivered to and appropriated by the buyer he must pay a reasonable price for them. Where the third party is prevented from making the valuation by the fault of the seller or buyer, the party not at fault may bring an action for damages against the party at fault (s. 9).

The parties may agree that part of the price is to be paid as a **4–49** "deposit" at the time when the contract is entered into, the stipulation being that the deposit will be forfeited if the buyer does not duly pay the full price at the later date when it becomes due. The deposit is regarded as a guarantee for the due performance of the contract:

Roberts & Cooper Ltd v. Christian Salvesen & Co. Ltd, 1918 S.C. 794: An agreement was entered into for the sale of the vessel "Giralda" by S. Ltd to R. Ltd for £30,000, payable as to £3,000 on the signing of the agreement and as to the balance within five days after the vessel was ready for delivery. The agreement stipulated that failing due payment by the buyers, the sellers were to be at liberty to resell the vessel, the deposit would be forfeited, and any deficiency between the amount realised and the amount due would be borne by the buyers.

R. Ltd failed to obtain the necessary Government permit for their intended trade with the "Giralda", and they repudiated the contract. S. Ltd resold the vessel.

R. Ltd brought an action to recover the deposit on the ground that it was a penalty and that in fact S. Ltd had suffered no loss through R. Ltd's failure to implement the contract.

Held that the £3,000 had been deposited as a guarantee for the performance of the contract, and that R. Ltd were not entitled to recover it.

Lord President Strathclyde said (at p. 806): "It is well-settled law that where, in a contract of sale, the intending buyer deposits part of the price, he cannot, if he repudiates the contract without justification, claim repayment of the deposit. That is upon the ground either that a man who repudiates a contract is not entitled to rescind that contract, or that a man who is in default cannot take advantage of his own default, or that a man who has paid down money as a security for performance of a contract cannot have that money back if he deliberately elects to throw up the contract."

Dicta in this case were followed in *Zemhunt (Holdings) Ltd v. Control Securities plc*, 1991 S.L.T. 653 (O.H.): Z. Ltd were successful bidders for property auctioned by C. plc and in terms of the articles of roup paid a deposit of 10 per cent. When the balance was not paid, C. plc resiled from the contract.

Z. Ltd sued for the return of their deposit, averring that the articles of roup did not provide for forfeiture and that the deposit could only be retained by C. plc to offset any loss which they had suffered and none had been claimed.

C. plc argued that the word "deposit" necessarily implied forfeiture, and that since Z. Ltd were relying on the equitable remedy of restitution, it was not equitable that they should recover the deposit when they themselves were in breach of contract.

Held, action dismissed. "Deposit" in Scots law did not by itself mean more than advance part-payment, and Z. Ltd were not entitled to restitution of their deposit when they were responsible for the termination of the contract. The forfeiture of a deposit was not akin to a penalty or liquidate damages, nor had the court any inherent equitable power to grant relief.

(e) Terms of the Contract

Sections 10 to 15 of the Act relate to the terms of the contract. Some important changes have been made in these sections since their original enactment in 1893: in particular, the Supply of Goods (Implied Terms) Act 1973 and the Consumer Credit Act 1974 substituted new provisions for some of the original provisions, and the Unfair Contract Terms Act 1977 further affected some of the provisions. Substantial amendments have also been made by the Sale and Supply of Goods Act 1994. 4–50

The terms of the contract depend primarily on the agreement made between the parties. There are also terms implied by law. The general effect of twentieth century legislation is to restrict the freedom of contract allowed by the original provisions: parties are no longer as free as they were to choose their own terms and reject the terms implied by statute. The general position is stated in section 55(1) (a provision substituted for the original provision of the 1893 Act by the Supply of Goods (Implied Terms) Act 1973 and itself amended by the Unfair Contract Terms Act 1977): where a right, duty or liability would arise under a contract of sale by implication of law, it may be negatived or varied by express agreement, or by the course of dealing between the parties, or by usage if the usage be such as to bind both of the parties, but this provision is subject to the provisions of the Unfair Contract Terms Act 1977. The Act of 1979 (s. 55(2)), as amended by the Sale and Supply of Goods Act 1994 (Sched. 2, para. 5(8)), further provides that an express term does not negative one implied by the Act unless they are inconsistent. 4–51

The terms of the contract must be distinguished from collateral representations, such as statements contained in advertisements and expressions of opinion. Such representations may have induced the buyer to make the purchase, but they are not themselves terms of the contract. 4–52

Flynn v. Scott, 1949 S.C. 442 (O.H.): S. and F. entered into an oral contract for the purchase by F. of S.'s motor van. In the course of the negotiations F. had informed S. that he wanted the van for 4–53 the general purposes of a haulage contractor and S. had said that the van was in good running order.

Seven days after the sale, the van, loaded with bedding from an aerodrome, broke down at the beginning of a journey, and 21 days after that breakdown F. intimated to S. his rejection of the van, and claimed repayment of the purchase price.

Held that S.'s statement that the van was in good running order was a mere expression of opinion and not a misrepresentation entitling F. to reject the van. (The Lord Ordinary also held that in any event the rejection had not been timeous.)

4–54 As well as using the phrase "terms of the contract" the Act uses the words "stipulations" (*e.g.* "stipulations as to time" in section 10), "conditions" (*e.g.* in sections 12 to 15), and "warranties" (*e.g.* in section 12). The word "stipulation" has no technical meaning: it simply denotes any term of the contract. The words "condition" and "warranty", however, do have technical meanings, and, in addition, these meanings differ as between Scots and English law.

4–55 In English law a "condition" is a fundamental term of the contract. Breach of a condition gives rise to a right to treat the contract as repudiated (s. 11(3)). A "warranty" means an agreement relating to the goods but collateral to the main purpose of the contract, and breach of a warranty gives rise to a claim for damages, but not to a right to reject the goods and treat the contract as repudiated (s. 61(1)). The question whether a term in a particular contract is a condition or a warranty is decided by the interpretation of the contract, and the word chosen by the parties is not conclusive (s. 11(3)). The Act provides that where a seller is in breach of a condition, the buyer may choose to treat that breach as a breach of warranty instead of as a ground for treating the contract as repudiated (s. 11(2)).

4–56 The common law of Scotland draws a distinction between material and non-material parts of a contract, and this distinction corresponds generally to the English distinction between conditions and warranties. Hence section 11(5) provided:

> "In Scotland, failure by the seller to perform any material part of a contract of sale is a breach of contract, which entitles the buyer either within a reasonable time after delivery to reject the goods and treat the contract as repudiated, or to retain the goods and treat the failure to perform such material part as a breach which may give rise to a claim for compensation or damages."

The meaning of the word "warranty" in Scots law approached to the meaning of "condition" in English law, and this accounted for the provision in section 61(2) that as regards Scotland a breach of warranty should be deemed to be a failure to perform a material part of the contract.

This divergence in terminology between Scots and English law **4–57** led to uncertainty in the application to Scotland of sections 12 to 15 of the Act when read along with sections 11(5) and 61(2). The original Act of 1893 was first drafted (by Sir Mackenzie Chalmers) with the intention that it should codify the then existing law of England, and it was only after the Bill had been before Parliament for some four years (1889 to 1892) that the question of extending its provisions to Scotland was settled. Sections 12 to 15 retained the language of the common law of England in so far as they reflected the clear dividing line in that system between a "condition" and a "warranty". As regards Scotland, the Scots common law distinction between material and non-material parts of a contract was introduced by section 11(5), but it was not made clear that in the application of sections 12 to 15 to Scotland the word "condition" was to be read as a material part and the word "warranty" as a non-material part; further, the provision in section 61(2) whereby a breach of warranty was to be deemed to be a failure to perform a material part of the contract suggested that sections 12 to 15 in so far as they dealt with warranties had a different application in the two legal systems.

The Sale and Supply of Goods Act 1994 (referred to in the **4–58** remainder of this chapter as "the Act of 1994"), in accordance with the recommendations of the Law Commissions in their report *Sale and Supply of Goods* (see 4–02, above), substituted the word "terms" for both "conditions" and "warranties" in provisions applicable to Scotland. This involved the repeal of section 11(5), leaving the whole of section 11 not applicable to Scotland, restriction of the definition of "warranty" in section 61(1), so that it would not apply to Scotland, and the repeal of section 61(2).

Stipulations as to Time

Unless a different intention appears from the terms of the contract, **4–59** stipulations as to time of payment are not of the essence of the contract (s. 10(1)). Whether any other stipulation as to time (*e.g.* as to the time of delivery) is or is not of the essence of the contract depends on the terms of the contract (s. 10 (2)).

4–60 The word "stipulation" having no technical meaning, no change was made in the wording of section 10 by the Act of 1994.

4–61 Where one party is in breach of a stipulation as to time which is of the essence of the contract, the other is entitled to rescind the contract. Two contrasting cases may serve as illustrations:

4–62 (i) *Shaw, Macfarlane & Co. v. Waddell & Son* (1900) 2 F. 1070: A contract for the sale of a cargo of coal at a fixed price per ton included a stipulation that the coal should be delivered at Grangemouth for shipment by the "L'Avenir" between April 12 and 16. At the time when the contract was made a strike of miners in Wales was imminent and the price of Scotch coal was rising rapidly.

The "L'Avenir" did not sail from Antwerp for Grangemouth until April 19, and would not have been ready to load until April 23. Meantime the sellers' railway sidings had become completely blocked by the waggons containing the coal intended for the "L'Avenir", and the sellers rescinded the contract.

Held that as in the circumstances the time of taking delivery was of the essence of the contract the sellers were justified in rescinding the contract, and so the buyers were not entitled to damages for the sellers' failure to implement the contract.

4–63 (ii) *Paton & Sons v. David Payne & Co. Ltd* (1897) 35 S.L.R. 112 (HL): In March engineers undertook to supply a new printing machine to be delivered in six weeks. The machine was not supplied until July.

Held, on an interpretation of the correspondence between the parties, that time was not an essential element and that therefore the buyers, though entitled to damages, were not entitled to reject the machine. (The ground on which the House of Lords decided the case was that in any event the rejection of the machine by the buyers had not been timeous.)

Implied Terms about Title, etc.

4–64 Section 12 of the Act of 1893 was altered by the Supply of Goods (Implied Terms) Act 1973, and section 12 of the Act of 1979 consisted of substantially the same provisions as those of the Act of 1973, although a new arrangement was adopted.

Section 12, as amended by the Act of 1994, now has seven subsections. The last of these contains the transitional provisions (see 4–16, above) that in relation to a contract made before May 18, 1973, the provisions in paragraph 3 of Schedule 1 to the Act are to apply instead (*i.e.* the provisions of section 12 of the Act of 1893 are preserved to that extent). **4–65**

The Act of 1994 inserted subsection (5A) to provide that in non-Scottish terminology the term implied by subsection (1) would be a condition and the terms implied by subsections (2), (4) and (5) would be warranties. **4–66**

Subsections (1) to (5) fall into two groups: the first two subsections are those which are of general application, while the remaining three subsections apply to the exceptional situation where there is a limitation on the title which is to be transferred by seller to buyer. **4–67**

(i) Subsections (1) and (2) provide that in a contract of sale, other than one to which subsection (3) applies, there is: **4–68**

(1) an implied term on the part of the seller that in the case of a sale he has a right to sell the goods, and in the case of an agreement to sell he will have such a right at the time when the property is to pass; and

(2) an implied term that—

(a) the goods are free, and will remain free until the time when the property is to pass, from any charge or encumbrance not disclosed or known to the buyer before the contract is made; and

(b) the buyer will enjoy quiet possession of the goods except so far as it may be disturbed by the owner or other person entitled to the benefit of any charge or encumbrance which was disclosed or known.

In *McDonald v. Provan (of Scotland Street) Ltd*, 1960 S.L.T. 231 (O.H.), there were circumstances where (if the facts were proved to be as the pursuer alleged) there had been a breach of the implied terms both in subsection (1) and in (a) and (b) in subsection (2): **4–69**

The front part of a stolen Ford car had been welded to the rear portion of another Ford, and the composite vehicle had then been sold to P. Ltd who acquired it in good faith.

P. Ltd resold the vehicle to M. Three months later, the police took possession of it from M., and M. brought an action for damages against P. Ltd for breach of the three undertakings as to title etc. (as provided for in section 12(1) to (3) of the Act of 1893).

P. Ltd attempted to escape liability by the doctrine of *specificatio* ("manufacture of a new object"), arguing that the composite vehicle was a new entity belonging to the person who had constructed it.

Held that *specificatio* required good faith on the part of the manufacturer, and that therefore there might have been a breach of section 12. (There was, however, wide disagreement as to the facts, and proof before answer was allowed.)

4–70 (ii) Subsections (3) to (5) apply to the situation where the contract or the circumstances show that the seller intends to transfer only such title as he or a third person may have. In that situation there is:

(1) an implied term that all charges or encumbrances known to the seller and not known to the buyer have been disclosed to the buyer before the contract is made; and

(2) an implied term that none of the following will disturb the buyer's quiet possession of the goods, namely—

(a) the seller;

(b) the third person (in a case where the parties intend that the seller should transfer only such title as a third person may have);

(c) anyone claiming through or under the seller or the third person otherwise than under a charge or encumbrance disclosed or known to the buyer before the contract is made.

4–71 The obligations arising from section 12 cannot be excluded or restricted by agreement (Unfair Contract Terms Act 1977, s. 20(1)(a), as amended by 1979 Act, s. 63(1) and Sched. 2, para. 21).

Sale by Description

4–72 Section 13 as originally enacted in the Act of 1893 was amended by the Supply of Goods (Implied Terms) Act 1973 so as to clarify the meaning of sale by description. Before the Act of 1973 it was clear that there would be a sale by description if the buyer did not see the goods, and it was equally clear that a sale of a specific article as such, without any reference (express or implied) to a description, would not be a sale by description. The point which the Act of 1973 put beyond doubt was that a sale might still be a sale by description where the goods were exposed for sale and were selected by the buyer (*e.g.* in a self-service shop) (s. 13(3)).

However, not all difficulties about the meaning of sale by description have yet been eliminated. In particular there is the question whether the word "description" extends to the qualitative character of the goods or is restricted to the identification of the goods. **4–73**

Earlier cases tend to support the former, wider meaning of "description". For example, in *Varley v. Whipp* [1900] 1 Q.B. 513 a seller agreed to sell for £21 a second-hand self-binder reaping machine which the buyer had never seen and which the seller stated had been new the previous year and had been used to cut only 50 or 60 acres. The buyer was held entitled to return the machine on the ground that since it did not correspond with the seller's statements there had been a breach of section 13. **4–74**

Some later English cases included criticisms of this approach, *e.g.*: **4–75**

Ashington Piggeries Ltd v. Christopher Hill Ltd [1972] A.C. 441: H. Ltd, well-known animal feeding stuff compounders, contracted to sell to A. Ltd a mink food to be manufactured according to a formula prepared by A. Ltd and including as one of its ingredients herring meal. **4–76**

Unknown to either parties, some quantities of the food supplied contained in the herring meal a substance called dimethylnitrosamine (DMNA), which was highly toxic to mink.

A. Ltd claimed damages for losses sustained by death of and injury to the mink, alleging breaches of the conditions implied by sections 13 (description), 14(1) (fitness for purpose) and 14(2) (merchantable quality) of the Act of 1893.

Held that there had been breaches of section 14(1) and (2), but not of section 13.

The "key" to section 13 was held to be identification (*per* Lord Diplock at p. 504).

"A term ought not to be regarded as part of the description unless it identifies the goods sold" (*per* Lord Hodson at p. 470).

"Herring meal is still herring meal notwithstanding that it may have been contaminated by DMNA" (*per* Lord Guest at p. 472).

"The proposition is . . . that the herring meal ingredient did not correspond with the description because it contained DMNA. . . .

" . . . I do not believe that the Sale of Goods Act was designed to provoke metaphysical discussions as to the nature of what is delivered, in comparison to what is sold. The test of description, at least where commodities are concerned, is intended to be a broader, more common sense, test of a mercantile character. The question whether that is what the buyer bargained for has to be answered according to such tests as men in the market would apply, leaving more delicate questions of condition, or quality, to be determined under other clauses of the contract or sections of the Act. . . . The defect in the meal was a matter of quality or condition rather than of description. I think that buyers and sellers and arbitrators in the market, asked what this was, could only have said that the relevant ingredient was herring meal, and, therefore, that there was no failure to correspond with description. In my opinion, the appellants do not succeed under section 13" (*per* Lord Wilberforce at p. 489).

4–77 Another House of Lords case, *Reardon Smith Line Ltd v. Hansen-Tangen* [1976] 1 W.L.R. 989, included an interesting *obiter dictum* from the same Law Lord. The case concerned the identification of a vessel which had been given two different yard numbers—one by the builders and the other by the subcontract builders. The authorities as to description in sale of goods cases were held not to extend to the contract in question, but Lord Wilberforce expressed the view (at p. 998) that he found some of the cases on sale of goods by description to be "excessively technical and due for fresh examination in this House".

4–78 A later Scottish case involving the distinction between quality and identification in an alleged sale by description was *Border Harvesters Ltd v. Edwards Engineering (Perth) Ltd*, 1985 S.L.T. 128 (O.H.):

A written contract for the sale of a machine for drying grain included express terms as to its capacity and limited the liability of the sellers for injury, damages or loss to £500,000.

There was a dispute as to the performance of the dryer, and the sellers sought payment of the price in one action while the purchasers sought damages including loss of profits in a counter-action.

Held that the sale was not one by description, which related to the identification of the goods sold; the contract was for a specific type of dryer; such a dryer had been delivered and its capacity was irrelevant.

Lord Kincraig, allowing proof before answer, said (at p. 131): "No doubt in some cases quality could be used as part of the description but it has not in my judgment been so used here." He then referred to *Ashington Piggeries Ltd v. Christopher Hill Ltd* and quoted from Lord Diplock including his observation that "the key to section 13 is identification".

Section 13(1), as amended by the Act of 1994, provides that in a sale by description there is an implied term that the goods will correspond with the description. In non-Scottish terminology the term implied would be a condition (s. 13(1A), inserted by the Act of 1994). If the sale is by sample as well as by description, the bulk of the goods must correspond both with the sample and with the description (s. 13(2)). **4–79**

A typical example of a sale by description would be a sale of a quantity of fertiliser described as having added to it a certain proportion of magnesium sulphate intended to correct a deficiency of magnesium in the soil. If the fertiliser supplied had had added to it the weedkiller sodium chlorate instead of magnesium sulphate, the seller would be in breach of section 13 (see *McCallum v. Mason*, 1956 S.C. 50 (4–104, below)). **4–80**

An instance of a specific article sold by description occurred in *Roberts & Co. v. Yule* (1896) 23 R. 855: **4–81**

Machinery merchants sold a second-hand four-horse power nominal gas-engine, described as in "excellent order", to Y. for £47.10s. Y. found that the engine required an expenditure of £8.10s. on it to put it right.

Held that Y. was entitled to reject the engine as disconform to description.

Contracting out of section 13 is allowed only to a strictly limited extent. No exclusion or restriction at all is allowed as against the consumer in a consumer contract (*i.e.* a contract in which one party is dealing in the course of a business and the other party ("the consumer") is not dealing in the course of a business and the goods are of a type ordinarily supplied for private use or consumption). In any other type of contract any exclusion or restriction is of no effect unless it was fair and reasonable as at the time when the contract was made. The onus of proving that a contract is not a consumer contract lies on the party who claims that it is not, and the onus of proving that an exclusion or restriction was fair and reasonable lies on the party who so contends (Unfair Contract Terms Act 1977, ss. 20(2), 24 and 25, as amended by the 1979 Act, s. 63(1) and Sched. 2, paras. 21 and 22). Guidelines for the application of the reasonableness test are set out in Schedule 2 to **4–82** the Act of 1977: for example, regard should be had to the relative strength of the bargaining positions of the parties, including alternative means by which the customer's requirements could have been met.

4–83 The provisions of section 13 as to sale by description are concerned only with civil law, and are not affected by the Trade Descriptions Act 1968 which makes the use of false "trade descriptions" a criminal offence (see 4–336 *et seq.*, below).

Implied Terms about Quality or Fitness

4–84 Section 14 of the Act of 1979 is derived from section 14 of the Act of 1893 as substituted by the Supply of Goods (Implied Terms) Act 1973 (and also in part by the Consumer Credit Act 1974). It has been extensively amended by the Act of 1994. The section has as its basis the general rule of *caveat emptor* ("let the buyer beware"), but provides for exceptions to that general rule—the situations in which there are implied undertakings as to quality or fitness.

4–85 The rule of *caveat emptor* is derived from the English common law. Under the common law of Scotland sale was a contract *bonae fidei* ("of good faith"), with the result that the seller was bound to supply price-worthy goods.

4–86 The general rule now applicable in both legal systems is that, with the exceptions provided for in sections 14 and 15 of the Act and subject to the provisions of any other Act, there is no implied term about the quality or fitness for any particular purpose of goods supplied under a contract of sale (s. 14(1), as amended by the Act of 1994). As a general rule, therefore, it is for the buyer to satisfy himself that the goods which he is buying are of the quality which he desires and are fit for the purpose for which he requires them.

4–87 The exceptions provided for in section 14 as amended by the Act of 1994 are considered below under the headings:

(i) satisfactory quality;
(ii) fitness for particular purpose; and
(iii) usage.

4–88 Contracting out of these implied undertakings is strictly limited in the same way as contracting out of section 13 is limited (see 4–82, above).

4–89 As regards (i) and (ii) the undertakings apply where the seller is selling the goods "in the course of a business". Non-business sales are therefore excluded, but in other respects the phrase has a wide meaning. The goods are not necessarily goods in which the seller ordinarily deals; for example, if a trader were to sell the delivery vans which he had been using to transport his merchandise, that would seem to be a sale "in the course of a business", and in *Buchanan-Jardine v. Hamilink*, 1983 S.L.T. 149, the seller of the whole stock of a farm business which was itself being sold or wound up was held to be selling "in the course of a business". The statutory definition of "business" also has the effect of making these provisions wide-ranging. "Business" includes a profession and the activities of any government department, or local or public authority (s. 61(1)).

Another point affecting both (i) and (ii) and also (iii) is the **4–90** provision added by the Supply of Goods (Implied Terms) Act 1973 and now constituting section 14(5) of the Act of 1979. This deals with the situation where the person who is selling in the course of a business is acting as agent for another person (his principal). The agent may, for instance, be an auctioneer. He will be selling "in the course of a business", but his principal may or may not be selling "in the course of a business". The statutory provision is designed to protect the buyer: the principal, even though he is a private seller, will be liable in respect of the implied undertakings unless he is in fact not selling in the course of a business *and* either the buyer knows that fact or reasonable steps are taken to bring it to the notice of the buyer before the contract is made.

The section was applied in *Boyter v. Thomson*, 1995 S.C. (H.L.) **4–91** 15:

T. instructed a firm, Harbour Marine and Leisure, Kirkcaldy, to sell a cabin cruiser on his behalf under a brokerage and agency agreement. The firm sold the boat in the course of its business to B., who did not know that the owner was a private individual and thought that the boat belonged to the firm.

The boat proved unseaworthy and unfit for the purpose for which it was bought.

B. raised an action for breach of contract against T., and argued that the firm had sold the boat in the course of a business as agent for T., and although T. was a private individual, section 14(5) had the effect of incorporating into the contract the implied term as to fitness for purpose.

The sheriff assoilzied T., and B. successfully appealed to the sheriff-principal. T. then appealed to the Court of Session and an

Extra Division held that the term had been incorporated. T. then appealed to the House of Lords.

Held (affirming the decision of the Extra Division) that (1) section 14(5) applied to any sale by an agent, whether the principal was disclosed or undisclosed and (2) no attempt having been made to bring to the notice of B. that T. was not selling in the course of a business, it followed that B. was entitled to claim damages from T.

(i) **Satisfactory quality**

4–92 Where the seller sells goods in the course of a business, there is an implied term that the goods supplied under the contract are of satisfactory quality (s. 14(2), as amended by the Act of 1994). In non-Scottish terminology, the term implied would be a condition (s. 14(6), as substituted by the Act of 1994).

4–93 The term "merchantable quality" had been used in the Act of 1893, but had not been defined in that Act, and its interpretation featured in many decided cases. The Supply of Goods (Implied Terms) Act 1973 added a definition, which became section 14(6) of the Act of 1979. The definition appears to have been an attempt to codify the definitions supplied by the decided cases: goods were of "merchantable quality" if they were as fit for the purpose or purposes for which goods of that kind are commonly bought as it was reasonable to expect having regard to any description applied to them, the price (if relevant) and all other relevant circumstances.

4–94 The Law Commissions in their report *Sale and Supply of Goods* (see 4–02, above) identified the following criticisms of the term "merchantable" quality:

(1) The term "merchantable" was itself out-of-date and inappropriate in this context.

(2) The term concentrated too exclusively on fitness for purpose and did not make sufficiently clear that other aspects of quality, such as appearance and finish, and freedom from minor defects, may also be important.

(3) There was no express reference in the Act to the concept of durability or to safety of the goods, though it was often an important aspect of quality that the goods should be reasonably durable or reasonably safe.

4–95 The definition of "merchantable quality" added by the Supply of Goods (Implied Terms) Act 1973 was a source of some uncertainty as can be seen in the case of *Millars of Falkirk Ltd v. Turpie*, 1976 S.L.T. (Notes) 66:

In July 1973, T., a solicitor, took delivery of a new Ford Granada. His Zodiac was taken in part payment and the balance of the price was to be paid by cheque.

The new car had a leak of oil from its steering box and a loose bonnet catch. The dealers made adjustments to correct these faults, but, on finding that there was still a leak of oil, T. intimated his rejection of the car on the ground that it was not of "merchantable quality".

The dealers refused to accept T.'s rejection, and brought an action for the balance of the price. T. counterclaimed for return of the Zodiac or its agreed value of £542.42 and for damages.

Held that as the fault was a comparatively minor matter which could readily have been cured at a cost of no more than £25, the new car was of "merchantable quality", and that T. was therefore not entitled to reject it.

The provisions of section 14, as amended by the Act of 1994, in **4–96**
addition to substituting the word "satisfactory" for "merchantable" (s. 14(2)), enact the following in respect of satisfactory quality. In line with the recommendations of the Law Commissions there is first the statement of a basic principle sufficiently general to apply to all kinds of goods and transactions and secondly a list of aspects of quality any of which could be important in a particular case:

Goods are of satisfactory quality if they meet the standard which a reasonable person would regard as satisfactory, taking account of any description of the goods, the price (if relevant) and all the other relevant circumstances (s. 14(2A)).

The quality of goods includes their state and condition and the following (among others) are in appropriate cases aspects of the quality of goods—

(a) fitness for all the purposes for which goods of the kind in question are commonly supplied,

(b) appearance and finish,

(c) freedom from minor defects,

(d) safety, and

(e) durability (s. 14(2B)).

The term that goods are to be of satisfactory quality (s. 14(2)) does not extend to any matter making the quality of goods unsatisfactory—

(a) if the matter is specifically drawn to the buyer's attention before the contract is made,

(b) if the buyer examines the goods before the contract is made and the matter is one which that examination ought to reveal, or

(c) if, in the case of a contract for sale by sample, the matter would have been apparent on a reasonable examination of the sample (s. 14(2C)).

(ii) **Fitness for particular purpose**

4–97 Apart from the substitution of the Scottish terminology ("term" in place of "condition" (Act of 1994, s. 14(6)), no change was made by the Act of 1994 in section 14(3).

4–98 The provision in section 14(3) as to fitnees for a particular purpose differs according to whether the sale is an ordinary sale or a sale on credit terms.

4–99 In the case of an ordinary sale, where the seller sells goods in the course of a business and the buyer, expressly or by implication, makes known to the seller any particular purpose for which the goods are being bought, there is an implied term that the goods supplied under the contract are reasonably fit for that purpose, whether or not that is a purpose for which such goods are commonly supplied, except where the circumstances show that the buyer does not rely, or that it is unreasonable for him to rely, on the skill or judgment of the seller.

4–100 The provision relating to a sale on credit terms covers the situation where a "credit-broker" (*e.g.* the retailer) sells goods to a finance house which then sells them to the retailer's customer (the buyer) on credit. The buyer has the benefit of the same implied undertaking as to fitness for a particular purpose, provided he makes that purpose known to the credit-broker, except where the circumstances show that the buyer does not rely, or that it is unreasonable for him to rely, on the skill or judgment of the credit-broker. The term "credit-broker" means "a person acting in the course of a business of credit brokerage carried on by him, that is a business of effecting introductions of individuals desiring to obtain credit—

(a) to persons carrying on any business so far as it relates to the provision of credit, or

(b) to other persons engaged in credit brokerage" (s. 61(1)).

4–101 The following three cases illustrate the implied undertaking as to fitness for a particular purpose:

(1) *Jacobs v. Scott & Co.* (1899) 2 F. (H.L.) 70: J., a horse-dealer in Canada, entered into a contract with the Glasgow Tramway and Omnibus Co. Ltd to supply the company with 2,100 tons of "best Canadian Timothy hay". **4–102**

To carry out this contract J. contracted with S. & Co., hay-dealers in Canada, for the supply of 100 tons of "No. 1 export hay". It was proved that S. & Co. knew that the hay to be supplied by them was to be used by J. to implement in part his contract with the Glasgow company, and it was also proved that "No. 1 export hay" was a hay composed partly of Timothy and partly of other grasses and was not of a sufficiently high quality to satisfy the Glasgow market.

The Glasgow company rejected the hay supplied as disconform to the contract between them and J., and J. brought an action against S. & Co. for damages for breach of their contract with him.

Held that in the contract between J. and S. & Co. there had been an implied term that the "No. 1 export hay" supplied should be of the standard required for the Glasgow market.

(2) *Buchanan & Carswell v. Eugene Ltd*, 1936 S.C. 160: B. & Co., hairdressers, bought an electric hair-drying machine from E. Ltd, manufacturers and suppliers of hairdressing appliances. **4–103**

Mrs Pollock, a customer of B. & Co., was injured by the machine when it was in use in B. & Co.'s premises and in an action against B. & Co. received an award of damages for her injuries.

B. & Co. sued E. Ltd to recover these damages on the ground that E. Ltd had supplied a machine which was not reasonably fit for the purpose for which it was required.

Held that this action based on what was then section 14(1) of the Act of 1893 was relevant and that B. & Co. would therefore, if they succeeded in proving that there had been a breach of the implied term, be entitled to an award of damages.

(3) *McCallum v. Mason*, 1956 S.C. 50: In 1953 McC., a nurseryman, whose tomato plants were showing a slightly yellowish tinge, was advised by M., a dealer in fertilisers, to apply to them M.'s "N.P." fertiliser to which M. was to add a quantity of magnesium sulphate to correct a deficiency of magnesium in the soil. McC. purchased two bags supposed to contain these ingredients from M., and applied the contents of one bag to his tomato plants. The plants, however, deteriorated and died, and McC.'s whole tomato crop was lost as a result. **4–104**

The following year McC. applied the contents of the second bag to healthy new tomato plants and to chrysanthemum plants. All the plants deteriorated and died.

Analysis of the mixture showed that it contained no magnesium sulphate but 10 per cent of the weedkiller sodium chlorate.

McC. brought an action of damages against M. for breach of what was then section 14(1) of the Act of 1893 averring that M. had failed to supply goods which were reasonably fit for the purpose for which they were required.

Held that McC.'s case was relevant as far as the first tomato crop was concerned but not as far as the second tomato crop or the chrysanthemums were concerned, since the particular purpose of the purchase as disclosed to M. was limited to the first tomato crop.

4–105 Where goods are commonly used for only one purpose, the purpose is sufficiently made known to the seller by the buyer's merely asking for the goods. For example, actions have been successfully brought against the seller where the plaintiff's wife was scalded by the bursting of a hot water bottle bought from a chemist (*Preist v. Last* [1903] 2 K.B. 148 (CA)), where the plaintiff's wife died from consuming milk containing germs of typhoid fever (*Frost v. Aylesbury Dairy Co. Ltd* [1905] 1 K.B. 608 (CA)), and where the pursuer, having purchased boots for himself, suffered periostitis of a foot as a result of the insole having crumpled up and become knotted and nodular (*Thomson v. J. Sears & Co. (Trueform Boot Co.) Ltd*, 1926 S.L.T. 221 (O.H.)).

4–106 On the other hand, there have been cases where the buyer has not sufficiently made known to the seller the particular purpose for which the goods are required. The following are instances:

4–107 (1) *B. S. Brown & Son Ltd v. Craiks Ltd*, 1970 S.C. (H.L.) 51: B. Ltd, cloth merchants in Manchester, purchased a quantity of rayon cloth from C. Ltd, manufacturers in Forfar, intending to resell it for dress material. The cloth supplied was not suitable for dress material, and B. Ltd sued C. Ltd for breach of what was then section 14(1) of the Act of 1893.

The claim failed because B. Ltd could not prove that they had told C. Ltd of the particular purpose for which they required the cloth.

(B. Ltd also claimed under what was then section 14(2) (merchantable quality) of the Act of 1893. This claim also failed because the cloth was held to be reasonably capable of being used and was saleable for a number of industrial purposes (*e.g.* making bags).)

(2) *Slater v. Finning Ltd*, 1996 S.L.T. 912 (HL): This case was decided under section 14(3), as in the Act of 1979. **4–108**

Three camshafts were successively supplied by marine engineers, F. Ltd for a fishing vessel, *Aquarius II*, owned by S. There was failure on every occasion.

After the third failure S. sold the engine, and it eventually found its way to South Africa, where it was installed in another fishing vessel. The camshaft was not replaced. That vessel then went on extensive fishing trips lasting on average 54 days and logged many thousands of miles without encountering any trouble with the camshaft. There was also evidence that the same design of camshaft had been installed in hundreds of other engines.

S. brought an action for damages against F. Ltd and F. Ltd counterclaimed for payment of an amount alleged to be due to them by S. for goods and services supplied.

It was proved that the cause of the failure of the camshafts was that the *Aquarius II* suffered, unknown to F. Ltd from a defect of having an unusual tendency to produce excessive torsional resonance in the camshafts, with the result that the camshafts became badly worn and unserviceable much sooner than would otherwise have been the case.

Held that S.'s action failed.

Lord Keith of Kinkel, who gave the leading speech, said (at p. 916): "There is no breach of the condition of fitness where the failure of the goods to meet the intended purpose arises from an abnormal feature or idiosyncrasy, not made known to the seller, in the buyer or in the circumstances of the use of the goods by the buyer. That is the case whether or not the buyer is himself aware of the abnormal feature or idiosyncrasy."

He referred by way of illustration to "a new front wheel tyre being purchased for a car which, unknown to the buyer or the seller, had a defect in the steering mechanism as a result of which the tyre wore out after a few hundred miles of use, instead of the many thousands which would normally be expected".

The (English) Court of Appeal case *Griffiths v. Peter Conway Ltd* (see 4–109, below) was approved.

4–109 (3) *Griffiths v. Peter Conway Ltd* [1939] 1 All E.R. 685: G. purchased from C. Ltd a Harris tweed coat which had been specially made for her.

Shortly after G. had begun to wear the coat, she contracted dermatitis, and she sought damages from C. Ltd.

It was proved that G. had an abnormally sensitive skin, a fact not made known to C. Ltd and that there was nothing in the coat which would have affected the skin of a normal person.

Held that G.'s claim failed.

(iii) **Usage**

4–110 An implied term about quality or fitness for a particular purpose may be annexed to a contract of sale by usage (s. 14(4), as amended by the Act of 1994).

Sale by Sample

4–111 A sale is a sale by sample where there is an express or implied term to that effect in the contract (s. 15(1)). A sale is not a sale by sample merely because a sample has been exhibited and has induced the sale.

4–112 In a sale by sample there are two implied terms:

(i) that the bulk will correspond with the sample in quality; and

(ii) that the goods will be free from any defect, making them unsatisfactory, which would not be apparent on reasonable examination of the sample (s. 15(2), as amended by the Act of 1994).

4–113 These implied terms would in non-Scottish terminology be conditions (s. 15(3), substituted by the Act of 1994).

4–114 Contracting out is limited to the same extent as contracting out of sections 13 and 14 is limited (see 4–82, above).

4–115 A well-known case involving sales by sample is *Godley v. Perry* [1960] 1 W.L.R. 9, decided by Edmund Davies J. under the Act of 1893:

G., a boy of six, was injured when firing a stone from a toy plastic catapult which he had bought from P.'s shop: one of G.'s eyes was ruptured and had to be removed.

The catapult had been manufactured in Hong Kong and was one of a quantity bought by P.'s wife from a wholesaler, who had bought from the importer. Both P.'s wife and the wholesaler had tested one of the catapults at the time when they made their respective purchases.

G. brought an action against P. for breach of the implied conditions in section 14(1) and (2) of the Act of 1893 (fitness for purpose and merchantable quality). P. brought in the wholesaler, who in turn brought in the importer, the claims against the wholesaler and the importer being based on breach of the implied condition in section 15 that the goods would be free from any defect, rendering them unmerchantable, which had not been apparent on reasonable examination of the sample.

All the claims succeeded.

Remedies for Breach of Contract as respects Scotland

The Act of 1994 inserted a new section, section 15B, applicable to **4–116**
Scotland only, to state the remedies of the buyer for breach by the seller of the express or implied terms, in accordance with and using the terminology of the common law of Scotland.

The section provides that where in a contract of sale the seller is in breach of any terms of the contract (express or implied), the buyer is entitled:

(a) to claim damages, and

(b) if the breach is material, to reject any goods delivered under the contract and treat it as repudiated (s. 15B(1)).

Where a contract of sale is a consumer contract, then, for the purposes of subsection (1)(b) above, breach by the seller of any term (express or implied):

(a) as to quality of the goods or their fitness for a purpose,

(b) in a sale by description, that the goods will correspond with the description,

(c) in a sale by sample, that the bulk will correspond with the sample in quality,

will be deemed to be a material breach (s. 15B(2)).

III EFFECTS OF THE CONTRACT

Two questions are dealt with in this third Part of the Act: **4–117**

(a) When does the ownership of the goods (referred to in the Act as "the property in the goods") pass from seller to buyer? The provisions of the Act on this question come under the heading "Transfer of Property as between Seller and Buyer".

(b) Where the seller is not the true owner of the goods, what is the buyer's right in (or "title to") the goods? The provisions of the Act on this question come under the heading "Transfer of Title".

(a) Transfer of Property as between Seller and Buyer

4–118 By the common law of Scotland, the property did not pass until the goods were delivered to the buyer. Under the Act, the property may pass independently of delivery: in many cases it will pass when the contract is made, though the goods are still in the possession of the seller.

The rules which govern the passing of the property from seller to buyer are especially important in connection with:

4–119 (i) *bankruptcy*: where one of the parties to the contract becomes bankrupt, his property (in the sense of the items which he owns), whether or not it is in his possession, passes to the trustee in his sequestration; many of the decided cases have involved competing claims asserted on bankruptcy;

4–120 (ii) *passing of risk*: the general rule is expressed in the maxim *res perit domino* (literally, "a thing perishes to the disadvantage of its owner", *i.e.* it is on the owner that a loss falls); the Act provides that unless otherwise agreed, the goods remain at the seller's risk until the property in them passes to the buyer and that thereafter they are at the buyer's risk whether delivery has been made or not (s. 20(1)); there are two exceptions to this general rule:

(1) Where delivery has been delayed through the fault of either buyer or seller, the goods are at the risk of the party at fault as regards any loss which might not have occurred but for such fault (s. 20(2)). (For instance, the seller may have failed to meet a delivery date and the goods may have been destroyed by a subsequent fire in the seller's warehouse.)

(2) The duties or liabilities of either seller or buyer as custodier of the goods are not affected by the statutory provision (s. 20(3)). (For instance, the seller may be storing the goods until the buyer gets entry to a new house.)

4–121 Some of the provisions relating to the transfer of property as between seller and buyer have been amended by the Sale of Goods (Amendment) Act 1995 (referred to in the remainder of this chapter as "the Act of 1995"). In addition to amendments in sections 16 and 18, two new sections, 20A and 20B, were inserted. The reforms were recommended by the Law Commission and the

Scottish Law Commission in their report *Sale of Goods Forming Part of a Bulk* (Law Com. No. 215; Scot. Law Com. No. 145).

The difficulty centred on the provision in section 16, as **4–122** unamended, which provided that where there was a contract for the sale of unascertained goods no property in the goods was transferred to the buyer unless and until the goods were ascertained. The buyer might have paid for the goods and received a document purporting to be a document of title; yet, if the seller became insolvent before the goods were ascertained, both the price and the goods would pass to the insolvent seller's estate to be shared amongst all his creditors.

This unsatisfactory position was highlighted by *The Gosforth*, S. en S. 1985 Nr. 91, a case decided by the Commercial Court in Rotterdam in 1985. Purchasers of goods forming part of a bulk had paid for the goods, but found that the goods still belonged to the seller and so could be arrested by an unpaid creditor who was suing the seller. The contracts were governed by English law which, by section 16 of the Act of 1979, prevented property from passing to the buyer before the goods were ascertained. The case caused concern to commodity traders and led to an approach being made to the Law Commission by one of the leading international commodity trade associations for examination of the law relating to the rights of purchasers of goods forming part of a larger bulk carried by sea.

Unascertained Goods

The first provision of the Act as to the transfer of property from **4–123** seller to buyer is that the goods must be ascertained: where there is a contract for the sale of unascertained goods, no property in the goods passes to the buyer unless and until the goods are ascertained (s. 16).

An illustration of section 16 occurs in *Hayman & Son v. McLintock*, 1907 S.C. 936: **4–124**

McNairn & Co., flour-merchants, had a large number of sacks of flour in H.'s store. They sold 250 sacks to X and 100 sacks to Y, and in implement of these sales handed to X and Y delivery-orders addressed to H. The delivery-orders were intimated to H., who acknowledged to X and Y that he held the 250 sacks and 100 sacks respectively subject to their instructions. However, the individual sacks were not marked or separated from the other sacks in the store.

McNairn & Co.'s estates were sequestrated.

Held that the trustee in the sequestration was entitled to all the sacks of flour in H.'s store, because the goods sold to X and Y were unascertained and so no property in the goods had passed to X and Y.

4–125 Section 16 was by the Act of 1995 made subject to a new rule for sales of goods out of a bulk by the insertion of section 20A into the Act of 1979. The effect is to enable property in unascertained goods in certain circumstances to pass to the buyer. The parties are free to contract out of the provision (s. 20A(2)): section 16, unamended, would then apply to the contract.

4–126 Section 20A applies to a contract for the sale of a specified quantity of unascertained goods if the following conditions are met:

(a) the goods or some of them form part of a bulk which is identified either in the contract or by subsequent agreement between the parties; and

(b) the buyer has paid the price for some or all of the goods which are the subject of the contract and which form part of the bulk (s. 20A(1)).

"Bulk" is defined as "a mass or collection of goods of the same kind which—

(a) is contained in a defined space or area; and

(b) is such that any goods in the bulk are interchangeable with any other goods therein of the same number or quantity" (added to s. 61(1) by the Act of 1995).

An example would be a sale of 100 tonnes of wheat forming an undifferentiated part of the cargo of wheat on a named ship where the buyer has paid for the wheat. The goods must always form part of an *identified* bulk: it still remains the rule that property cannot pass in wholly unascertained goods.

4–127 As soon as the conditions (a) and (b) of section 20A(1) (4–126, above) are met, then unless the parties agree otherwise:

(a) property in an undivided share in the bulk is transferred to the buyer, and

(b) the buyer becomes an owner in common of the bulk (s. 20A(2)).

The buyer's undivided share at any time is the share which the goods paid for and due to him bear to the quantity of goods in the bulk at that time (s. 20A(3)); *e.g.* where there is an identified bulk of 1,000 gallons in an identified storage tank and the buyer has bought 500 gallons, but paid for only 100 gallons, he acquires an undivided one-tenth share in the bulk.

Where a buyer has paid the price for only some of the goods due **4–128**
to him out of a bulk, any delivery to him out of the bulk is ascribed in the first place to the goods for which he has paid (s. 20A(5)); *e.g.* where the buyer had bought 500 gallons out of an identified bulk of 1,000 gallons, but paid for only 100 gallons and had later taken delivery of 100 gallons, he would be held to have taken delivery of the 100 gallons already paid for and not for 100 gallons out of the 400 gallons not yet paid for.

Payment of part of the price for any goods is treated as payment **4–129**
for a corresponding part of the goods (s. 20A(6)). This is contrary to the usual practice: part payments would not normally be related to any proportion of the goods bought.

The purpose of section 20B also inserted by the Act of 1995 is to **4–130**
facilitate normal trading where a person becomes an owner in common of a bulk under section 20A(2), above. The general principle of Scots law is that the consent of all co-owners is necessary before any inroads can be made into the co-owned goods, though any owner in common can raise an action for division or sale. These principles would not be appropriate for the type of ownership in common introduced by section 20A(2). Section 20B therefore provides for "deemed consents". It provides that a person who has become an owner in common of a bulk is to be deemed to have consented to:

(a) any delivery of goods out of the bulk to any other owner in common of the bulk; and

(b) any dealing with or removal, delivery or disposal of goods in the bulk by any other person who is an owner in common of the bulk in so far as the goods fall within that co-owner's undivided share in the bulk at the time of the dealing, removal, delivery or disposal (s. 20B(1)).

Specific or Ascertained Goods

Where the goods are specific or ascertained, the property in them **4–131**
passes to the buyer at such time as the parties intend it to pass, and for the purpose of ascertaining the intention of the parties regard

must be had to the terms of the contract, the conduct of the parties and the circumstances of the case (s. 17).

4–132 The Act sets out in section 18 five rules for ascertaining the intention of the parties as to the time at which the property is to pass, but these rules apply only where no different intention appears. The following three cases give instances of situations where the rules of section 18 were held not applicable because the intention of the parties was to a different effect:

4–133 (i) *Peebles & Co. v. John L. Kerr Ltd* (1902) 9 S.L.T. 372 (O.H.): A contract for the sale of a motor by P. & Co. to K. Ltd provided that the price was to be paid by a bill of exchange payable in three months' time. The contract was silent as to the passing of the property.

When delivered, the machine had riveted upon it a brass plate bearing the words: "the property of P. & Co".

Before the price had become payable, K. Ltd went into liquidation and P. & Co. brought an action for redelivery of the machine on the ground that the property had not passed to K. Ltd.

Held that the sale had been made under a suspensive condition to that effect, and decree of delivery *granted.*

4–134 (ii) *Sir James Laing & Sons Ltd v. Barclay, Curle & Co. Ltd*, 1908 S.C. (H.L.) 1; 1908 S.C. 82: B. Ltd, shipbuilders, contracted to build a ship for an Italian company. The price was to be paid by instalments at certain stages of construction. The contract provided that the ship should not be considered as delivered until it had passed a certain trial trip.

After the ship had been built and the greater part of the price had been paid but before the trial trip, L. Ltd arrested the ship for a debt alleged to be due by the Italian company to L. Ltd.

Held that B. Ltd were entitled to have the arrestment recalled because the contract showed that the parties had not intended the property to pass to the Italian company until the trial trip had taken place.

Lord Robertson said (at p. 2): "The statute supplies certain rules; but these may or may not come into operation, according as the contract requires it. In the present case I find the contract to require no aid or supplement from the statutory rules, for it seems to me to provide from the beginning to completion of this ship for the building of it by the shipbuilders with their materials, and transfers it to the purchasers only as a finished ship and at a stage not in fact yet reached."

(iii) *Woodburn v. Andrew Motherwell Ltd*, 1917 S.C. 533: W., a farmer, sold to M. Ltd six ricks of hay at an agreed price per ton. The contract provided that the hay was to be placed at the disposal of M. Ltd in W.'s stackyard so that M. could pack it in bales, that W. should then cart it to the railway, and that the weight ascertained there for carriage purposes would also be taken as the weight for fixing the total purchase price. **4–135**

Some bales of hay were destroyed by fire before they had been removed from W.'s stackyard.

Held that the terms of the contract clearly indicated that the parties intended the property in the hay to pass when the hay was placed at M. Ltd's disposal, that the risk of loss by fire therefore lay with M. Ltd, and that W. was entitled to recover from M. Ltd the price of the bales which had been destroyed.

Lord President Strathclyde said (at p. 538): "The rules in section 18 are merely intended to be a guide in ascertaining the intention of the parties. But, if the intention of the parties is quite plain—as I think it is in this case—that the property should pass at the time when the goods were placed at the disposal of the buyer that he might convert them into bales, then the rules of section 18 do not come into play at all."

Rules for ascertaining intention

Where no different intention appears, the rules which, by section 18, as amended by the Act of 1995, are to be applied for ascertaining the intention of the parties as to the time at which the property in the goods is to pass to the buyer are as follows: **4–136**

Rule 1

"Where there is an unconditional contract for the sale of specific goods in a deliverable state the property in the goods passes to the buyer when the contract is made, and it is immaterial whether the time of payment or the time of delivery, or both, be postponed." **4–137**

For the purposes of the Act goods are in a "deliverable state" when they are in such a state that the buyer would under the contract be bound to take delivery of them (s. 61(5)). **4–138**

Thus, in *Gowans (Cockburn's Trustee) v. Bowe & Sons*, 1910 2 S.L.T. 17 (O.H.), where B. & Sons, potato merchants, had in August bought farmer C.'s whole growing potato crop (specific or **4–139** ascertained goods), the property in the potatoes passed to B. & Sons once C. had lifted and pitted the potatoes on his farm, with the result that, in C.'s subsequent sequestration, the potatoes did not form part of his estate, and B. & Sons were entitled to remove them.

4–140 Similarly, where there is a contract for the sale of growing trees, the goods are put into a deliverable state when the trees are felled. The property, therefore, passes under rule 1 to the buyer although the timber may not actually have been removed from the estate on which it was grown (*Munro v. Balnagown Estates Co. Ltd*, 1949 S.C. 49).

Rule 2

4–141 "Where there is a contract for the sale of specific goods and the seller is bound to do something to the goods for the purpose of putting them into a deliverable state, the property does not pass until the thing is done and the buyer has notice that it has been done."

4–142 *Brown Brothers v. Carron Co.* (1898) 6 S.L.T. 231 (O.H.): Under a contract for the sale of a steam crane by B. to C. it was arranged that B. should keep the crane in his yard until it was required for erection on C.'s vessel and that B. should make some slight alterations on the crane in the course of erecting it.

C., no longer requiring the crane, refused to take delivery.

Held that the property in the crane had not passed to C., and that therefore B. was not entitled to succeed in an action for the price (see s. 49(1)); his only remedy was damages.

Rule 3

4–143 "Where there is a contract for the sale of specific goods in a deliverable state but the seller is bound to weigh, measure, test, or do some other act or thing with reference to the goods for the purpose of ascertaining the price, the property does not pass until the act or thing is done and the buyer has notice that it has been done."

4–144 In *Woodburn v. Andrew Motherwell Ltd*, 1917 S.C. 533 (4–135, above), M. Ltd made an unsuccessful attempt to have this third rule applied.

Rule 4

"When goods are delivered to the buyer on approval or on sale or return or other similar terms the property in the goods passes to the buyer:— **4–145**

(a) when he signifies his approval or acceptance to the seller or does any other act adopting the transaction; [*or*]

(b) if he does not signify his approval or acceptance to the seller but retains the goods without giving notice of rejection, then, if a time has been fixed for the return of the goods, on the expiration of that time, and, if no time has been fixed, on the expiration of a reasonable time."

A contract of "sale or return" can be seen in *Ross & Co. v. Plano Manufacturing Co.* (1903) 11 S.L.T. 7 (O.H.): Robertson was a commission agent who had obtained 20 binders from the company which manufactured them. At the time of Robertson's bankruptcy the binders were stored with Ross & Co., and competing claims to them were made by the manufacturing company and by Robertson's trustee. **4–146**

Held that as there had been no absolute sale of the binders to Robertson but only a "sale or return" the property in the binders had remained with the manufacturing company.

A transaction of a similar nature was considered by the court in *Bryce v. Ehrmann* (1904) 7 F. 5: E., a wholesale jeweller, sent goods to A., a retail jeweller, on terms that A. was to have power to sell the goods and should then become liable to pay the wholesale price to E. An "approbation note" issued by E. stated that the goods were to remain the property of E. until invoiced by him to A. **4–147**

A., without E.'s knowledge, pledged a diamond necklace, part of the goods, to B., a pawnbroker.

A. subsequently became bankrupt.

Held that, as A.'s trustee did not insist in his claim to the necklace, E. was entitled to delivery of it, but only after satisfying B.'s claim.

Rule 5

"(1) Where there is a contract for the sale of unascertained or future goods by description, and goods of that description and in a deliverable state are unconditionally appropriated to the contract, **4–148** either by the seller with the assent of the buyer or by the buyer with the assent of the seller, the property in the goods then passes to the buyer; and the assent may be express or implied, and may be given either before or after the appropriation is made.

4–149 (2) Where, in pursuance of the contract, the seller delivers the goods to the buyer or to a carrier or other . . . custodier (whether named by the buyer or not) for the purpose of transmission to the buyer, and does not reserve the right of disposal, he is to be taken to have unconditionally appropriated the goods to the contract."

4–150 Paragraphs (3) and (4), below, were added by the Act of 1995. They give statutory expression to the rules on "ascertainment by exhaustion", which was already recognised by the courts. For example, a buyer may purchase and pay for 100 tonnes forming part of an identified bulk, which at the time of payment, contains 2000 tonnes. On payment the buyer owns one-twentieth of the bulk. Later, before delivery to the buyer, 1000 tonnes are withdrawn from the bulk. The buyer's share then becomes one-tenth, and this may be followed by further fluctuations, making the buyer's share larger on each occasion. If and when the bulk comes to be reduced to, or to less than, 100 tonnes, the buyer will own the whole bulk. Paragraph (3) applies to such a situation, *i.e.* to where there is only one contract and one buyer. Paragraph (4) is an extension of paragraph (3): it applies where there are two or more contracts in which the buyer is the same person and where the bulk is reduced to, or to less than, the total of the goods covered by the two or more contracts. The rules are:

4–151 "(3) Where there is a contract for the sale of a specified quantity of unascertained goods in a deliverable state forming part of a bulk which is identified either in the contract or by subsequent agreement between the parties and the bulk is reduced to (or to less than) that quantity, then, if the buyer under that contract is the only buyer to whom goods are then due out of the bulk—

(a) the remaining goods are to be taken as appropriated to that contract at the time when the bulk is so reduced; and

(b) the property in those goods then passes to that buyer.

4–152 (4) Paragraph (3) above applies also (with the necessary modifications) where a bulk is reduced to (or to less than) the aggregate of the quantities due to a single buyer under separate contracts relating to that bulk and he is the only buyer to whom goods are then due out of that bulk."

Section 19 explains how the seller may "reserve the right of disposal." He may do so by stipulating that the property in the goods is not to pass to the buyer until certain conditions are fulfilled (s. 19(1)) (*e.g.* until the price is paid). Where goods are shipped, and by the bill of lading are deliverable to the order of the seller or his agent, the seller is prima facie ("until the contrary is proved") to be taken to reserve the right of disposal (s. 19(2)). Where the seller draws a bill of exchange on the buyer for the price, and sends the bill of exchange and the bill of lading to the buyer together in order that the buyer may accept or pay the bill of exchange, the buyer is bound to return the bill of lading if he does not honour the bill of exchange, and if he wrongfully retains the bill of lading the property in the goods does not pass to him. **4–153**

A contract of sale may include a "Romalpa" clause—so-called after the decision of the Court of Appeal in *Aluminium Industrie Vaassen B.V. v. Romalpa Aluminium Ltd* [1976] 1 W.L.R. 676: **4–154**

A Dutch company sold to an English company aluminium foil, some of which was then sold by the English company to sub-purchasers. The Dutch company's standard conditions of sale included a clause providing that the ownership of the foil was to be transferred to the English company only when they had met all that was owing to the Dutch company, that until the date of payment the English company were, if the Dutch company so desired, to store the foil in such a way that it was clearly the property of the Dutch company, that articles manufactured from the foil were to be kept for the Dutch company as a guarantee for full payment of the sums owed by the English company to the Dutch company, and that if the English company sold the articles to third parties, the English company were, if the Dutch company so required, to hand over to the Dutch company the claims which they might have against the third parties.

The English company got into financial difficulty, and a receiver was appointed under powers contained in a debenture.

Held that because of the "Romalpa" clause, the English company had to be regarded, so far as the Dutch company were concerned, as having sold the foil to the third parties as agents and bailees (custodiers), and so the Dutch company were entitled not only to recover the foil still in the possession of the English company but also to trace and claim the proceeds of sub-sales (held by the receiver in a separate account) in priority to the general body of the English company's other creditors including the debenture holders who had appointed the receiver.

The *Romalpa* case has attracted much academic interest in recent years. The trend of the decided Scottish cases has been that "Romalpa" clauses have been held to be ineffectual (*Clark Taylor & Co. Ltd v. Quality Site Development (Edinburgh) Ltd*, 1981 S.C. 111, *Emerald Stainless Steel Ltd v. South Side Distribution Ltd*, 1983 S.L.T. 162 (O.H.) and *Deutz Engines Ltd v. Terex Ltd*, 1984 S.L.T. 273 (O.H.)), but in 1990 the decision of the House of Lords (reversing the decision of the Lord Ordinary which had been upheld by the Inner House) in *Armour v. Thyssen Edelstahlwerke A.G.*, 1990 S.L.T. 891 (HL), seems likely to have reversed that trend:

A German company, T., had been selling steel strip to Carron Co. Ltd ("C. Ltd"), which carried on a manufacturing business at Falkirk. The contracts of sale were expressed as being subject to T.'s "General Conditions of Delivery and Payment", one provision of which (clause 1.3.(1)) was that all goods delivered by T. remained in T.'s ownership until all debts owed to T. had been paid.

On account of C. Ltd's indebtedness to two banks, receivers were appointed on its assets in 1982, at which time steel supplied by T. with an invoice price of £71,769 (none of which had been paid) was lying at C. Ltd's works.

A dispute arose between the receivers and T. as to whether the steel remained the property of T. because of clause 1.3.(1) or formed part of the assets of C. Ltd available to C. Ltd's preferred or other creditors. The receivers raised an action against T. seeking declarator that the steel was the property of C. Ltd. T. lodged a counterclaim for payment of the invoice price.

The Lord Ordinary and, on appeal, the Second Division decided the case on substantially the same grounds, namely that clause 1.3.(1) constituted an attempt, ineffective under Scots law, to create a right in security over corporeal moveables without transfer of possession, and that the property in the steel had passed to C. Ltd on delivery.

Held by the House of Lords that a provision reserving title to the seller until payment of all debts due to him by the buyer did not amount to the creation by the buyer of a right in security in favour of the seller, and that the provisions of sections 17 and 19(1) of the

Sale of Goods Act 1979 made clause 1.3.(1) effective to prevent property in the steel passing to C. Ltd until all debts due by C. Ltd to T. had been paid.

(b) **Transfer of Title**

The basic rule is expressed in the maxim *nemo dat quod non habet* **4–155**
("no one gives what he does not have"). Therefore, as a general rule, where goods are sold by a person who is not their owner, and who does not have the owner's authority or consent to sell them, the buyer acquires no better title to the goods than the seller had (s. 21(1)). The general rule applies to sales by a person who has merely found goods or has stolen them or has obtained them under a void contract, such as a contract void on account of error in the substantials (*e.g. Morrisson v. Robertson*, 1908 S.C. 332 (4–161, below)). The goods are regarded as having a *vitium reale* ("inherent fault"), which prevents even a bona fide purchaser who has given value for them from obtaining a good title to them: the true owner is entitled to recover them.

There are some exceptions to the general rule, both at common **4–156**
law (*e.g.* in *negotiorum gestio* ("management of affairs", a branch of unjust enrichment)) and by statutory provisions outside the Sale of Goods Act 1979 (*e.g.* the Factors Act 1889, extended to Scotland by the Factors (Scotland) Act 1890, and the Innkeepers Act 1878). Such exceptions are expressly preserved by the Act of 1979 (s. 21(2)).

The Act itself provides for exceptions which are explained below **4–157**
under these headings:

(i) personal bar;
(ii) sale under voidable title; and
(iii) seller or buyer in possession after sale.

In England[1] there was formerly the additional exception of "market overt": where goods were sold in "market overt" (*i.e.* shops within the City of London and public, legally constituted, markets outside it), according to the usage of the market, the buyer acquired a good title to the goods, provided he bought them in good faith and without notice of any defect or want of title on the

[1] but not in Wales—apparently the last surviving distinction between the private law applicable to Wales and that applicable to England (W. A. Wilson: *Introductory Essays on Scots Law*, 2nd ed., p. 37).

part of the seller (s. 22). This provision was repealed by the Sale of Goods (Amendment) Act 1994 (s. 1).

(i) *Personal Bar*

4–158 By the operation of the principle of personal bar, the owner of the goods may be precluded from denying the seller's authority to sell (s. 21(1)). This could occur, for instance, where the seller is an agent or employee of the owner and has been placed in such a position by the owner that the buyer is justified in believing that he has the necessary authority to sell.

(ii) *Sale under Voidable Title*

4–159 When the seller has a voidable title in the goods, but his title has not been "avoided" (*i.e.* set aside) at the time of the sale, the buyer acquires a good title to the goods, provided he buys them in good faith and without notice of the seller's defect of title (s. 23).

4–160 The seller's title may, for instance, be voidable on account of fraud, as in *MacLeod v. Kerr*, 1965 S.C. 253:

A rogue, Galloway, giving his name as "L. Craig", persuaded Kerr to sell a car to him, in return for a cheque from a stolen cheque book.

Galloway then, giving his name as "Kerr", sold the car to Gibson, who in good faith paid £200 for it.

Held that, as the first sale had conferred on Galloway a voidable title which had not been avoided by the time of the second sale, Gibson had obtained a good title of the car.

4–161 The legal position is different where the first sale is not merely voidable, but void, *e.g.* where there has been error in the substantials, as in *Morrisson v. Robertson*, 1908 S.C. 332:

A rogue, Telford, falsely representing that he was the son of Wilson, obtained two cows on credit from Morrisson, who knew Wilson, and relied on Telford's representation.

Telford then sold the cows to Robertson, who purchased them in good faith.

Held that Morrisson was entitled to recover the cows from Robertson, since Telford had, by the first transaction, obtained no title at all to them.

(iii) *Seller or Buyer in Possession after Sale*

Two possible situations are provided for by sections 24 and 25. In both situations a sale by the owner has taken place, and following on that sale the person (who may be the seller or may be the buyer) who is then in possession treats the goods as if he were the owner of them in a second transaction, possibly another sale. Such a person is sometimes referred to as the "reputed owner", and the general effect of sections 24 and 25 is to protect the person who deals with a reputed owner from claims by the true owner. **4–162**

The terms "mercantile agent" and "document of title" are used in both sections. **4–163**

"Mercantile agent" means "a mercantile agent having in the customary course of his business as such agent authority either— **4–164**

(a) to sell goods, or
(b) to consign goods for the purpose of sale, or
(c) to buy goods, or
(d) to raise money on the security of goods" (s. 26).

By section 61(1) of the Act of 1979 "document of title to goods" has the same meaning as it has in the Factors Acts. The effect is that the term "document of title" includes "any bill of lading, dock warrant, warehouse-keeper's certificate, and warrant or order for the delivery of goods, and any other document used in the ordinary course of business as proof of the possession or control of goods, or authorising or purporting to authorise, either by indorsement or by delivery, the possessor of the document to transfer or receive goods thereby represented" (Factors Act 1889, s. 1(4), extended to Scotland by the Factors (Scotland) Act 1890, s. 1). **4–165**

The provisions of sections 24 and 25 are as follows: **4–166**

Section 24: Where a person has sold goods and continues or is in possession of the goods, or of the documents of title to the goods, the delivery or transfer by that person, or by a mercantile agent acting for him, of the goods or documents of title under any sale, pledge, or other disposition of them, to any person receiving them in good faith and without notice of the previous sale, has the same effect as if the person making the delivery or transfer were expressly authorised by the owner of the goods. **4–167**

Section 25: Where a person who has bought or agreed to buy goods obtains, with the seller's consent, possession of the goods or the documents of title to the goods, the delivery or transfer by that **4–168** person, or by a mercantile agent acting for him, of the goods or documents of title, under any sale, pledge, or other disposition of them, to any person receiving them in good faith and without notice of any lien or other right of the original seller over the goods, has the same effect as if the person making the delivery or transfer were a mercantile agent in possession of the goods or documents of title with the consent of the owner (s. 25(1)).

4–169 For the purposes of the provision in section 25(1) the buyer under a conditional sale agreement is to be taken not to be a person who has "bought or agreed to buy goods", and "conditional sale agreement" means "an agreement for the sale of goods which is a consumer credit agreement within the meaning of the Consumer Credit Act 1974 under which the purchase price or part of it is payable by instalments, and the property in the goods is to remain in the seller (notwithstanding that the buyer is to be in possession of the goods) until such conditions as to the payment of instalments or otherwise as may be specified in the agreement are fulfilled" (s. 25(2)).

4–170 The significance of the concluding words of section 25(1) ("as if the person making the delivery or transfer were a mercantile agent in possession of the goods or documents of title with the consent of the owner") is to be found in the Factors Act 1889 (ss. 2 and 5) as applied to Scotland by the Factors (Scotland) Act 1890 (s. 1): under these statutory provisions, where a mercantile agent is, with the consent of the owner, in possession of goods or of the documents of title to them, any sale, pledge, or other disposition made in the ordinary course of his business is as valid as if he were expressly authorised by the owner of the goods, provided the person who receives the goods acts in good faith without notice of the mercantile agent's lack of authority and provided the sale, pledge, or other disposition is made for valuable consideration.

4–171 The provision in the Act of 1893 (s. 25(2)) corresponding to section 25(1) of the Act of 1979 was considered in *Thomas Graham & Sons Ltd v. Glenrothes Development Corporation*, 1967 S.C. 284:

G. Ltd supplied building materials to builders who were engaged on building a housing scheme for the development corporation of the new town of Glenrothes. The builders went into liquidation, and a question arose as to the ownership of the materials which were on the site.

G. Ltd's claim was based on the term in their contract with the builders that the property in the materials was not to pass to the builders until the full price had been paid, and G. Ltd alleged the full price had not been paid.

The development corporation founded on section 25(2) of the Sale of Goods Act 1893, averring that the builders had been in possession with the consent of the owners, and that the corporation had acted in good faith without notice of the terms of the builders' contract with G. Ltd and had paid to the builders 80 per cent of the value of all materials placed on the site, having retained the balance until the amount of a counterclaim which the corporation had against the builders should be ascertained.

Held that the corporation's averments were sufficient to entitle them to an inquiry, and a proof before answer was allowed.

Lord President Clyde said (at p. 293): "Section 25 is a statutory recognition of an exception to the general rule that only an owner of goods can transfer the property in them. The section enables an apparent owner to transfer someone else's goods to a third party in certain specific circumstances."

Lord Clyde's observation was applied by Lord Mayfield in **4–172**
Archivent Sales & Development Ltd v. Strathclyde Regional Council, 1985 S.L.T. 154 (O.H.):

Ventilators had been ordered from A. by R. D. Robertson (Builders) Ltd ("R."), the main contractors on a site owned by S. on which a primary school was being built.

The contract between A. and R. incorporated a suspensive condition that until A. had received full payment of the price, A. should remain the owner of the materials. S. did not know of this condition. The building contract between R. and S. provided that the materials should become the property of S. when they were included in any interim certificate under which R. had received payment.

The ventilators were delivered by A. to R. at the site, and were duly included in an interim certificate. S. made payment to R. in respect of that interim certificate.

R. went into liquidation, and A. raised an action against S. for delivery of the materials and failing delivery for payment of a sum of money.

Held that property in the materials passed to S. in terms of section 25(1), and S. were assoilzied.

IV PERFORMANCE OF THE CONTRACT

4–173 Section 27, which is the first section in Part IV of the Act, sets out the central principle that it is the duty of the seller to deliver the goods, and of the buyer to accept and pay for them, in accordance with the terms of the contract. By section 28, unless otherwise agreed, delivery of the goods and payment of the price are concurrent conditions, *i.e.* the seller must be ready and willing to give possession of the goods to the buyer in exchange for the price, and the buyer must be ready and willing to pay the price in exchange for possession of the goods.

4–174 The more detailed provisions of Part IV may therefore be conveniently dealt with under two headings:

(a) seller's duty to deliver; and
(b) buyer's duty to accept.

(a) Seller's Duty to Deliver

4–175 "Delivery" means the voluntary transfer of possession of the goods from one person to another except that in relation to sections 20A and 20B (see 4–126 *et seq.*, above) it includes such appropriation of goods to the contract as results in property in the goods being transferred to the buyer (s. 61(1) as amended by the Act of 1995). Delivery does not refer to the transfer of ownership of the goods, the rules for which come within Part III of the Act.

4–176 Section 29 consists of some rules about delivery which are of general application. Later sections cover special matters—delivery of the wrong quantity, instalment deliveries, delivery to a carrier, and delivery at a distant place.

General Rules about Delivery

4–177 Whether it is for the buyer to take possession of the goods or for the seller to send them to the buyer is a question depending in each case on the contract, express or implied, between the parties (s. 29(1)).

4–178 Apart from any such contract, express or implied, the place of delivery is the seller's place of business if he has one, and if he has not, then his residence, except that if the contract is for the sale of specific goods, which to the knowledge of the parties when the contract is made are in some other place, then that place is the place of delivery (s. 29(2)).

Where, under the contract of sale, the seller is bound to send the goods to the buyer, but no time for sending them is fixed, the seller is bound to send them within a reasonable time (s. 29(3)). **4–179**

Where the goods at the time of sale are in the possession of a third person, there is no delivery by seller to buyer unless and until the third person acknowledges to the buyer that he holds the documents on his behalf; but this does not affect the issue or transfer of any document of title to the goods (s. 29(4)). **4–180**

Demand or tender of delivery may be treated as of no effect unless made at a reasonable hour. What is a reasonable hour is a question of fact (s. 29(5)). **4–181**

Unless otherwise agreed, the expenses of and incidental to putting the goods into a deliverable state must be borne by the seller (s. 29(6)). **4–182**

Delivery of Wrong Quantity

Section 30, which sets out the rules as to delivery of the wrong quantity, was amended by the Act of 1994, the amendments differing according to whether the contract is governed by Scots law or not. **4–183**

All the rules are subject to any usage of trade, special agreement, or course of dealing between the parties (s. 30(5)). **4–184**

The provisions of section 30, as amended for Scotland, are as follows: **4–185**

(i) Where the seller delivers to the buyer a quantity of goods less than he contracted to sell, the buyer may reject them, but if the buyer accepts them he must pay for them at the contract rate (s. 30(1)). This subsection has been amended by the provision that the buyer will not be entitled to reject the goods unless the shortfall is material (s. 30(2D) inserted by the Act of 1994). **4–186**

An instance of a rejection under section 30(1) before its amendment occurred in *Robertson v. Stewart*, 1928 S.N. 31 (O.H.): **4–187**

Shipbreakers sold to S. the wreck S.S. "Sheila" and all the property which had been salved from her by them.

S. claimed that he was entitled to rescind the contract on the ground that the shipbreakers had not tendered all the subjects sold but had disposed of some property salved by sale or donation to others.

The shipbreakers offered to return the salved property which had been removed, or to credit S. with its value. They brought an action against S. for the price.

Held that S. had been entitled to rescind and was not bound to accept the shipbreakers' offer of a deduction from the price.

4–188 Where the buyer chooses to accept the lesser quantity at the contract rate, he may still have a claim for damages.

4–189 (ii) Where the seller delivers to the buyer a quantity of goods larger than he contracted to sell, the buyer may accept the goods included in the contract and reject the rest, or he may reject the whole (s. 30(2)). This subsection has been amended by the provision that the buyer will not be entitled to reject the whole unless the excess is material (s. 30(2D) inserted by the Act of 1994). If the buyer accepts the whole of the goods delivered he must pay for them at the contract rate (s. 30(3)).

Instalment Deliveries

4–190 Unless otherwise agreed, the buyer is not bound to accept delivery by instalments (s. 31(1)).

4–191 Where, however, there is a contract for the sale of goods to be delivered by stated instalments, which are to be separately paid for, and the seller makes defective deliveries in respect of one or more instalments, or the buyer neglects or refuses to take delivery of or pay for one or more instalments, it is a question in each case depending on the terms of the contract and the circumstances of the case whether the breach of contract is a repudiation of the whole contract or whether it is a severable breach giving rise to a claim for compensation but not to a right to treat the whole contract as repudiated (s. 31(2)).

Delivery to Carrier

4–192 Where, "in pursuance of" (*i.e.* following on) a contract of sale, the seller is authorised or required to send the goods to the buyer, delivery of the goods to a carrier, whether named by the buyer or not, is prima facie ("until the contrary is proved") deemed to be a delivery to the buyer (s. 32(1)), *i.e.* the carrier is treated as the buyer's agent for the purposes of delivery (but not for the purposes of acceptance of the goods as being in conformity with the contract).

Unless otherwise authorised by the buyer, the seller must make such a contract with the carrier on the buyer's behalf as is reasonable considering the nature of the goods and the other circumstances of the case. If the seller omits to do so, and the goods are lost or damaged in transit, the buyer may decline to treat the delivery to the carrier as delivery to himself, or may hold the seller responsible in damages (s. 32(2)). **4–193**

Unless otherwise agreed, where goods are sent by the seller to the buyer by a route involving sea transit, under circumstances in which it is usual to insure, the seller must give sufficient notice to the buyer to enable him to insure the goods during their sea transit, and, if the seller fails to do so, the goods are at the seller's risk during the sea transit (s. 32(3)). **4–194**

Contracts involving sea transit take different forms, including c.i.f., f.o.b., f.a.s. and ex-ship contracts. **4–195**

In a c.i.f. ("cost, insurance, freight") contract, the seller's obligation is to ship the goods, insure them and pay the freight. Section 32(3) does not apply to such a situation. "In the usual course a contract of sale c.i.f. contemplates delivery of the cargo at the port of discharge, not the port of shipment" (*per* Lord Trayner in *McDowall & Neilson's Trustee v. J. B. Snowball Co. Ltd* (1904) 7 F. 35, at p. 45). This does not mean, however, that delivery is postponed until the ship actually arrives at its port of destination, for the bill of lading is treated as a symbol of the goods while they are at sea, and so the goods can be delivered to the buyer if the seller (or his agent in the foreign port) transfers the bill of lading with the other shipping documents (the insurance policy and the invoice) to the buyer in exchange for the price. The fact that the buyer has taken up the shipping documents does not prevent him from exercising his right to reject the goods if, when they are actually landed, they are found to be not in conformity with the contract. **4–196**

In an f.o.b. ("free on board") contract it is the duty of the buyer to arrange the shipping, insure the goods and pay the freight. The seller's duty is to deliver the goods on board ship at the agreed port of shipment. Section 32(3) does apply to this situation. An instance of an f.o.b. contract can be seen in *Glengarnock Iron and Steel Co. Ltd v. Cooper & Co.* (1895) 22 R. 672. The seller must pay all the charges incurred up to the delivery of the goods over the ship's rail, but he is not liable for the costs subsequently incurred, such as the **4–197** cost of stowage on board: these fall on the buyer as owner or charterer of the ship.

4–198 An f.a.s. ("free alongside ship") contract is similar to an f.o.b. one: the seller's duty is to deliver the goods alongside the ship, ready for loading. An instance occurs in *Pini & Co. v. Smith & Co.* (1895) 22 R. 699. The actual loading of the goods over the ship's rail is the buyer's responsibility.

4–199 The distinction between an f.o.b. contract and an f.a.s. contract was commented on by Lord Trayner in *Glengarnock Iron and Steel Co. Ltd v. Cooper & Co.*, at p. 676: "The point of delivery under the two contracts is different, and the consequent risks and the necessary insurance to cover these risks may be very different—the duty of insurance or the risk in the one case lying upon one party, and in the other upon the other party; but as regards the question which is to be at the expense of putting the cargo on board, there is not any difference which I have ever heard between the one contract and the other. In either contract . . . the universal practice is that the ship undertakes the duty and the expense of putting the cargo from the quay or alongside into the hold of the vessel."

4–200 In an ex-ship contract, delivery is made by the seller to the buyer from a ship at the port of destination. In this case the shipping, insurance and freight are all the responsibility of the seller. The price becomes payable when the goods are delivered over the ship's rail at the port of destination. An ex-ship contract was considered by the Privy Council in *Yangtsze Insurance Association Ltd v. Lukmanjee* [1918] A.C. 585, an appeal from the Supreme Court of Ceylon:

A quantity of teak logs had been shipped from Bangkok to Colombo on an ex-ship contract. While the buyer, having paid the price, was taking delivery at Colombo, many of the logs, afloat in the form of rafts, were driven out to sea by a gale and lost.

The buyer sued the insurance company under the insurance policy.

Held that, as the insurance had not been effected on his behalf or to cover his interest, he was not entitled to maintain the suit.

Delivery at Distant Place

4–201 Where the seller agrees to deliver the goods at his own risk at a place other than that where they are when sold, the buyer must, nevertheless, unless otherwise agreed, take any risk of deterioration in the goods necessarily incident to the course of transit (s. 33).

(b) **Buyer's Duty to Accept**

The Act of 1979 included provisions relating to the buyer's right of examining the goods, the buyer's right to reject the goods, and the buyer's liability for not taking delivery of the goods. **4–202**

The Act of 1994 amended the provisions on the first two of these subjects and introduced a new right of partial rejection. **4–203**

Buyer's Right of Examination

Unless otherwise agreed, when the seller tenders delivery of goods to the buyer, he is bound on request to afford the buyer a reasonable opportunity of examining the goods for the purpose of ascertaining whether they are in conformity with the contract and, in the case of a contract for sale by sample, of comparing the bulk with the sample (s. 34, as amended by the Act of 1994). **4–204**

The application of these rules can have the effect of postponing the buyer's acceptance of the goods, thus keeping open his right to reject them. **4–205**

Buyer's Right of Rejection

Section 35 regulates the time at which the buyer is deemed to have accepted the goods, and so given up his right to reject them. The buyer's right of rejection has been strengthened and clarified by amendments made to section 35 by the Act of 1994. The contents of the section have also been rearranged. **4–206**

The buyer is deemed to have accepted the goods: **4–207**

(i) when he intimates to the seller that he has accepted them, or

(ii) when the goods have been delivered to him, and he does any act in relation to them which is inconsistent with the ownership of the seller (s. 35(1), as amended by the Act of 1994).

This provision in section 35(1) does not, however, apply where the goods are delivered to the buyer and he has not previously examined them. In that situation the buyer is not deemed to have accepted the goods under section 35(1) until he has had a reasonable opportunity of examining them for the purpose— **4–208**

(a) of ascertaining whether they are in conformity with the contract, and

(b) in a sale by sample, of comparing the bulk with the sample (s. 35(2), as inserted by the Act of 1994).

4–209 In a consumer contract the buyer cannot lose his right to rely on subsection (2) by agreement, waiver or otherwise. This means that a consumer cannot contract out of the requirement that he should be given a reasonable opportunity of examination of the goods before accepting them (s. 35(3), as inserted by the Act of 1994).

4–210 The buyer is also deemed to have accepted the goods when after the lapse of a reasonable time he retains the goods without intimating to the seller that he has rejected them (s. 35(4), as inserted by the Act of 1994), and for the purposes of this provision the questions which are material in deciding whether a reasonable time has elapsed include whether the buyer has had a reasonable opportunity of examining the goods for the purposes (a) and (b) above.

4–211 Unless otherwise agreed, where the goods delivered to the buyer are goods which he is entitled to refuse to accept, he is not bound to return them to the seller: it is sufficient if he intimates to the seller that he refuses to accept them (s. 36).

4–212 Some comments may be made on these provisions:

4–213 1. It is no longer the case, since the Act of 1994, that the buyer will be deemed to have accepted the goods when he has merely intimated to the seller that he has accepted them: he must now have been given a reasonable opportunity of examining the goods (see 4–208, above). Previously the rule was that where there had been an express acceptance on the buyer's part he was no longer entitled to reject the goods. An illustration occurred in *Mechans Ltd v. Highland Marine Charters Ltd*, 1964 S.C. 48:

H. Ltd contracted to buy two steel water buses, the "Lomond Lass" and the "Lomond Princess", from M. Ltd. The buses were delivered and, after inspection by Ministry of Transport inspectors as provided for in the contract, acceptance certificates were signed by H. Ltd.

After the buses had been used for a few weeks, H. Ltd sought to reject them on the ground of major defects.

Held that, on account of the express acceptance, H. Ltd was no longer entitled to reject the buses.

4–214 2. A buyer on taking delivery may be asked to sign an "acceptance note". The signature might be that of a quite junior employee at the buyer's place of business, and it might not be realised that the signature was not only evidence of the receipt of the goods, but also an agreement that the goods received were in good condition. Receipt is not the same as acceptance. The unsatisfactory result could previously have been that the buyer, on the signing of an "acceptance note" (or some other form of receipt), would be deemed to have accepted the goods (and so lost any right to reject them once he had examined them).

The mere signature of an "acceptance note" is no longer deemed as an acceptance of the goods: a reasonable opportunity for examination must be given (see 4–208 and 4–209, above). **4–215**

3. There was formerly doubt about the interpretation of the words "an act . . . inconsistent with the ownership of the seller". It was not entirely clear whether a subsale, gift or other disposition of the goods by the buyer would be such an act. The doubt has been removed by the provision that the buyer is not deemed to have accepted the goods merely because the goods are delivered to another under a subsale or other disposition (s. 35(6), as inserted by the Act of 1994). **4–216**

4. Similarly there was formerly doubt about whether a buyer who asked for, or agreed to, repair of goods by the seller or under an arrangement with the seller would be deemed to have accepted the goods. It is now an express provision of the Act that a buyer who makes such a request or agreement is not, merely because of that, to be deemed to have accepted the goods (s. 35(6), as inserted by the Act of 1994). **4–217**

This provision would provide a solution to some of the difficulties which could arise with the fitting up of machinery: *e.g.* in *Mechan & Sons Ltd v. Bow, McLachlan & Co. Ltd*, 1910 S.C. 758, where two steel feed-tanks supplied by engineers to shipbuilders were fitted by the shipbuilders into a tug which they were building for the Admiralty, this was held to be an act "inconsistent with the ownership of the seller". **4–218**

The provision would also cover some of the cases involving continued use of machinery or other goods: *e.g.* in *Aird & Coghill v. Pullan & Adams* (1904) 7 F. 258, buyers were held entitled to reject a printing machine which had been fitted in their works and had been used for about a year and a half before rejection, and in *Munro & Co. v. Bennet & Son*, 1911 S.C. 337, the buyer of a deep-well pump from artesian well engineers was held entitled to reject **4–219** the pump after a similar period. In both cases complaints had been made in the time intervening between fitting up and rejection and in response to these complaints the sellers had been attempting to remedy the defects without success.

On the other hand in *Electric Construction Co. Ltd v. Hurry & Young* (1897) 24 R. 312, H. & Y., electrical engineers and contractors who had purchased a dynamo from E. Ltd, sought to reject it as disconform to contract. They continued, however, to use the dynamo for three months.

Held that they were not allowed to found on their alleged rejection.

This case was followed in *Hunter v. Albancode Group plc*, 1989 G.W.D. 39–1843 (Sh. Ct.):

H. purchased a suite of furniture from A. It proved defective, and a replacement also proved defective.

H. then purported to reject the second suite and requested A. plc to remove it and return the price. She admitted that she had still been using the suite because she could not afford to return it to A. plc.

Held H.'s subsequent action against A. plc had to be dismissed because the continued use of the suite was an act inconsistent with the ownership of the seller.

4–220 5. What is a "reasonable" opportunity depends on the circumstances.

4–221 The buyer loses his right of rejection if he does not exercise his right to examine the goods at the proper place and time for that examination. For example, in *Pini & Co. v. Smith & Co.* (1895) 22 R. 699, buyers of soil-pipes did not avail themselves of the opportunity to examine the pipes at Glasgow or Liverpool before having them shipped to Buenos Aires, and were held no longer to be entitled to reject the pipes when the customer in Buenos Aires intimated that the pipes were disconform to contract. Similar failure to examine occurred in *W.M. Strachan & Co. Ltd v. John Marshall & Co.*, 1910 2 S.L.T. 108 (O.H.) (boiler delivered at Glasgow, shipped to Japan and there found to require repairs costing more than the full purchase price), and in *Dick v. Cochrane & Fleming*, 1935 S.L.T. 432 (O.H.) (earthenware shipped from Glasgow to sub-purchasers in South America). Likewise, in *Charles Henshaw & Sons Ltd v. Antlerport Ltd*, 1995 G.W.D. 24–1315 (O.H) cast aluminium panels supplied by H. Ltd to A. Ltd and painted and assembled for two weeks by A. Ltd's subcontractors before being incorporated in a building could no longer be rejected by A. Ltd as defective after the scaffolding had been removed. Lord Penrose observed that while the complexity of the intended function of goods was clearly a prime consideration in assessing a reasonable time in which to reject goods, the period between delivery and rejection in this case had clearly not been reasonable as the panels had no mechanical properties and required examination only for their surface characteristics.

The nature of the goods is an important factor in the decision of **4–222**
what is a reasonable time. For instance, in *Flynn v. Scott*, 1949 S.C. 442 (O.H.) (4–53, above), Lord Mackintosh (Ordinary), holding that the rejection of a motor-van three weeks after it had broken down was not timeous, said (at p. 446) that intimation of rejection ought to have been made "within a very few days". Similarly, in the English case *Bernstein v. Pamson Motors (Golders Green) Ltd* [1987] 2 All E.R. 220 B. was held to have lost his right of rejection of a new car which he had bought for just under £8,000 and which had broken down on a motorway after having been driven only 140 miles; three weeks had elapsed since B.'s purchase of the car. A longer time could be reasonable in the case of goods such as works of art, but in *Hyslop v. Shirlaw* (1905) 7 F. 875, a buyer was held not entitled to reject four paintings as not being genuine a year and a half after their delivery to him. "Prima facie a delay of eighteen months is unreasonable. . . . The *onus* is on the pursuer to shew that he could not, by any examination reasonably possible, have discovered earlier the disconformity on which his rejection proceeded" (*per* Lord Kyllachy at p. 882). Mere length of time, however, is not *per se* ("of itself") conclusive, as was recognised in *Burrell v. Harding's Executrix*, 1931 S.L.T. 76 (O.H.), in which Lord Moncrieff (Ordinary) allowed a proof before answer in the case of a sale by an art dealer of a supposedly fifteenth-century English reredos, which the buyer sought to reject after a lapse of more than two years on the ground that an expert examination had shown that it was partly modern. Amongst the circumstances to be considered were that in *Hyslop's* case the pictures had been hanging in the buyer's house for a year and a half, whereas in *Burrell's* case the reredos had been in store.

6. The Act of 1994 introduced a new concept of the "commer- **4–223**
cial unit" and provided that where the contract is for the sale of

goods making one or more commercial units, a buyer accepting any goods included in a unit is deemed to have accepted all the goods making the unit. "Commercial unit" is defined as "a unit division of which would materially impair the value of the goods or the character of the unit" (s. 35(7) as inserted by the Act of 1994).

4–224 The effect of the provision is, for instance, that a buyer who accepted part only of a set, such as a single volume of an encyclopaedia which is sold as a set, would be deemed to have accepted the whole set, and that a buyer who accepted one shoe of a pair would be deemed to have accepted the pair.

Buyer's Right of Partial Rejection

4–225 A buyer's right of partial rejection was an innovation made by the Act of 1994. Formerly a right of partial rejection existed where the seller delivered to the buyer the goods which he contracted to sell mixed with goods of a different description not included in the contract; the buyer had then the right to accept the goods which were in accordance with the contract and reject the rest, or to reject the whole (s. 30(4)). That provision applied only to goods of a different description, not to goods of defective quality. The Law Commissions considered that in commercial terms it was reasonable for a buyer to be able to retain satisfactory goods and reject defective goods.

4–226 Section 35A, inserted in the Act of 1979 by the Act of 1994, provides that if the buyer—

(a) has the right to reject the goods by reason of a breach on the part of the seller which affects some or all of them, but

(b) accepts some of the goods, including, where there are any goods unaffected by the breach, all these goods,

he does not by accepting them lose his right to reject the rest (s. 35A(1)).

This provision also applies to instalment deliveries: in the case where a buyer has the right to reject an instalment, the references to "the goods" in subsection (1) will be read as "the goods comprised in the instalment" (s. 35A(2)), *i.e.* the right to reject a non-conforming instalment is not lost by the acceptance of another instalment.

4–227 Goods are "affected" by a breach if on account of the breach they are not in conformity with the contract (s. 35A(3)).

4–228 The right of partial rejection exists only where there is no contrary intention apparent in, or to be implied from, the contract (s. 35A(4)).

Buyer's Liability for not Taking Delivery

When the seller is ready and willing to deliver, and requests the buyer to take delivery, and the buyer does not within a reasonable time after that request take delivery, he is liable to the seller for any loss caused by his neglect or refusal to take delivery, and also for a reasonable charge for the care and custody of the goods (s. 37(1)). This provision does not affect the rights of the seller where the neglect or refusal of the buyer to take delivery amounts to a repudiation of the contract (s. 37(2)). **4–229**

In *Shaw, Macfarlane & Co. v. Waddell & Son* (1900) 2 F. 1070 (4–62, above), there were circumstances in which the buyers' failure to take delivery of coal timeously amounted to a repudiation of the contract which justified the sellers in rescinding the contract. **4–230**

V RIGHTS OF UNPAID SELLER AGAINST THE GOODS

Under Part V of the Act a seller has certain rights against the goods themselves, as distinct from his remedies against the buyer (which come into Part VI of the Act). **4–231**

The three main rights in Part V belong only to an "unpaid seller", and a seller is an "unpaid seller" for the purposes of the Act— **4–232**

(a) when the whole of the price has not been paid or tendered; or

(b) when a bill of exchange or other negotiable instrument has been received as conditional payment, and the condition on which it was received has not been fulfilled by reason of the dishonour of the instrument or otherwise (s. 38(1)).

The term "seller" in Part V includes any person who is in the position of a seller, *e.g.* an agent of the seller to whom the bill of lading has been indorsed, or a consignor or agent who has himself paid (or is directly responsible for) the price (s. 38(2)). **4–233**

The unpaid seller's rights against the goods are: **4–234**

(a) a lien on the goods or right to retain them for the price while he is in possession of them;

(b) in the case of the insolvency of the buyer, a right of stopping the goods in transit[2] after he has parted with them; and

---

[2] The Latin phrase "*in transitu*" used in the Act of 1893 was replaced by its English translation in the Act of 1979.

(c) a right of resale as limited by the Act (s. 39(1)).

Also included in Part V of the Act there formerly was:

[(d) in Scotland a seller's right of attachment by arrestment or poinding (s. 40).]

4–235 The rights of lien and stoppage in transit are appropriate only if the goods are no longer owned by the seller, *i.e.* only if the property has passed to the buyer. The Act, however, in effect extends these rights to the situation where the seller is still the owner, by providing that where the property in goods has not passed to the buyer, the unpaid seller has, in addition to his other remedies, a "right of withholding delivery similar to and co-extensive with his rights of lien or retention and stoppage in transit where the property has passed to the buyer" (s. 39(2)).

4–236 Further provisions of the Act which relate to both lien and stoppage in transit may be appropriately noted here before these rights are separately considered:

4–237 (1) These rights are not as a general rule affected by any sale or other disposition of the goods which the buyer may have made, unless the seller has assented to it (s. 47(1)).

4–238 However, where a document of title to goods has been lawfully transferred to any person as buyer or owner of the goods, and that person transfers the document to a person who takes it in good faith and for valuable consideration, then—

(a) if that transfer was by way of sale, the unpaid seller's right of lien or retention or stoppage in transit is defeated; and

(b) if the transfer was by way of pledge or other disposition for value, the unpaid seller's right of lien or retention or stoppage in transit can only be exercised subject to the rights of the transferee (s. 47(2)).

4–239 Further, since the general rule stated in section 47(1) is made "subject to this Act", the provisions in sections 21 to 26 as to transfer of title (see 4–155 *et seq.*, above) must be kept in mind.

4–240 (2) The contract of sale is not as a general rule rescinded by the mere exercise by an unpaid seller of his right of lien or retention or stoppage in transit (s. 48(1)), but where an unpaid seller who has exercised his right of lien or retention or stoppage in transit resells the goods, the buyer acquires a good title to them as against the original buyer (s. 48(2)).

(a) Lien

The unpaid seller who is in possession of the goods is entitled to retain possession of them until payment or tender of the price in the following cases: **4–241**

(i) where the goods have been sold without any stipulation as to credit; or

(ii) where the goods have been sold on credit but the term of credit has expired; or

(iii) where the buyer becomes insolvent (s. 41(1)).

A person is deemed to be insolvent for the purposes of the Act if he either has ceased to pay his debts in the ordinary course of business or cannot pay his debts as they become due (s. 61(4)). He need not have had his estates sequestrated, nor need he be "apparently insolvent" within the meaning of the Bankruptcy (Scotland) Act 1985: practical, as distinct from absolute, insolvency is all that is required. **4–242**

The fact that the seller is in possession of the goods as agent or custodier for the buyer does not prevent him from exercising his lien or right of retention (s. 41(2)). **4–243**

Where the seller has made part delivery, he may exercise his lien or right of retention on the remainder, unless the part delivery has been made under such circumstances as to show an agreement to waive the lien or right of retention (s. 42). **4–244**

The seller's lien or right of retention is terminated: **4–245**

(i) when the seller delivers the goods to a carrier or other custodier for transmission to the buyer without reserving the right of disposal of the goods (which he could do by the terms of the contract or by making the goods deliverable to his own agent in a foreign port); or

(ii) when the buyer or his agent lawfully obtains possession of the goods; or

(iii) by waiver of the lien or right of retention (s. 43(1)).

The seller does not lose his lien or right of retention merely because he has obtained a decree from the court against the buyer for the price (s. 43(2)). **4–246**

A case which illustrates this right of the unpaid seller is *Paton's Trustee v. Finlayson*, 1923 S.C. 872: **4–247**

P., a potato merchant, had bought a farmer's growing crop of potatoes at a specified price per acre. P. supplied the labour to lift the potatoes and pit them on the farm, but by the terms of the contract the farmer undertook to cart the potatoes to the pits and later to the railway. While the potatoes were in the pits and before the full price had been paid, P.'s estates were sequestrated.

Held that the farmer was still in possession of the potatoes, and was therefore entitled to exercise a lien over them. (It was not disputed that the property in the potatoes, as distinct from possession of them, had passed to P. at the time when they were removed from the soil: see *Gowans (Cockburn's Trustee) v. Bowe & Sons*, 1910 2 S.L.T. 17 (O.H.) (4–139, above)).

4–248 The Act does not expressly provide for the revival of the unpaid seller's lien in the situation where the unpaid seller, having once parted with possession of the goods, regains possession of them. There is a sheriff court case which is authority for the proposition that the lien does not revive:

4–249 *London Scottish Transport Ltd v. Tyres (Scotland) Ltd*, 1957 S.L.T. (Sh. Ct.) 48: T. Ltd had sold and delivered to L. Ltd tyres and allied accessories which were not paid for.

T. Ltd, suspecting that L. Ltd was on the verge of insolvency, instructed one of its agents to retake possession of as much of the goods supplied as could be found at L. Ltd's depot at Alva. Goods to the value of £548 9s. thus came again into the possession of T. Ltd.

L. Ltd went into liquidation, and an action was brought by that company and its liquidator against T. Ltd for redelivery of the goods or alternatively for payment of their value.

T. Ltd claimed that its lien had revived.

Held that in the circumstances of the case T. Ltd's lien, having been lost on delivery of the goods, had not been revived.

Sheriff-Substitute (W. J. Bryden) said (at p. 49): "Before it could be argued that a lost lien had revived it would be necessary, in my opinion, to show that the goods had been handed back to the sellers by the purchasers with the particular intention that the sellers' lien should revive."

4–250 It is possible that the legal position would be different if the goods were repossessed by the seller in circumstances from which it could be inferred that the buyer had accepted that all the original conditions attaching to the contract continued to exist; the argument for revival would then be based on the broad principle of mutuality of obligations. This possibility was left open in *Hostess*

Mobile Catering v. Archibald Scott Ltd, 1981 S.L.T. (Notes) 125 (O.H.):

S. Ltd had sold and delivered to H. a piece of equipment called a Paragon refreshment trailer unit. A few months later the unit had, by agreement, been taken back to S. Ltd's premises so that S. Ltd might repair it under a guarantee contained in the original contract. When the repairs had been completed, S. Ltd refused to redeliver the unit to H. until a balance of the original purchase price, which S. Ltd claimed was still due, was paid.

The Lord Ordinary (McDonald) rejected the argument that the right of lien "ran" with the goods (with the effect that it could be exercised by the unpaid seller, whatever the means by which he had regained possession), but as regards the argument based on the principle of mutuality of obligations the Lord Ordinary was not prepared to decide the case without further knowledge of the circumstances under which repossession had been obtained and he allowed the parties a proof before answer.

(b) Stoppage in Transit

The unpaid seller who has parted with possession of the goods has **4–251** the right to stop them in transit in one case only, *viz.* when the buyer becomes "insolvent" in the sense explained above. This right enables the seller to resume possession of the goods as long as they are in course of transit to the buyer, and then retain them until payment or tender of the price (s. 44).

The right appears to have been first recognised as being part of **4–252** Scots law in the case of *Jaffrey and Others, Partners of the Stirling Banking Company (Stein's Creditors) v. Allan, Stewart & Co.* (1790) 3 Pat. 191:

S. had been carrying on an extensive distilling trade under great financial difficulties until he finally stopped payment in February 1788. Between October 1787 and February 1788, while S. was "verging towards and on the eve of bankruptcy", A. & Co. had supplied him with 20 or 30 cargoes of grain. At the time of S.'s bankruptcy in February 1788 four of the cargoes were not landed but were lying in the ships at the port of delivery.

Held that A. & Co. were entitled to take possession of these four cargoes.

Lord Chancellor Thurlow said (at p. 196): "Within the last hundred years, a rule has been introduced, from the customs of foreign nations, that in the case of the vendee's bankruptcy, the vendor might stop and take back the goods *in transitu*[3], or before they came into the hands of the vendee; and this is certainly now a part of the law of England, and I understand it to be the law likewise of Scotland."

4–253 The common law on the subject as worked out in cases decided before the Act of 1893 is now represented by the rules set out in sections 45 and 46 of the Act of 1979 as to:

(i) duration of transit; and
(ii) how stoppage in transit is effected.

(i) *Duration of Transit*

4–254 The rules in section 45 as to duration of transit are:

4–255 (1) Goods are deemed to be in course of transit from the time when they are delivered to the carrier or other custodier for the purpose of transmission to the buyer, until the buyer or his agent takes delivery of them from the carrier or other custodier.

4–256 (2) If the buyer or his agent obtains delivery of the goods before their arrival at the appointed destination, the transit is at an end.

4–257 (3) If, after the arrival of the goods at the appointed destination, the carrier or other custodier acknowledges to the buyer or to the buyer's agent that he holds the goods on his behalf and continues in possession of them as custodier for the buyer or the buyer's agent, the transit is at an end, and it does not matter that a further destination for the goods may have been indicated by the buyer.

4–258 This third rule was considered in *Muir v. Rankin* (1905) 13 S.L.T. 60 (O.H.):

M., a farmer, had sold oats to R. and had consigned them in 100 sacks to Buchanan Street goods station, Glasgow. No part of the price was ever paid, and M. on being informed of R.'s insolvency intimated to the company that delivery to R. was stopped.

In the meantime, however, R. had obtained possession of three of the sacks, and had received an "advice note" and had also signed the "advice note delivery book"—formalities which, according to the railway company's practice, signified that it was holding the grain on behalf of the consignee.

(The ground of the decision was that M. was entitled to rescind the contract because of R.'s fraudulent representation as to his financial standing.)

[3] "in transit".

(4) If the goods are rejected by the buyer, and the carrier or other custodier continues in possession of them, the transit is not deemed to be at an end, even if the seller has refused to receive them back. **4–259**

(5) When goods are delivered to a ship chartered by the buyer it is a question depending on the circumstances of the particular case whether they are in the possession of the master as a carrier or as agent of the buyer. **4–260**

Illustrations are to be found in *McDowall & Neilson's Trustee v. J. B. Snowball Co. Ltd* (1904) 7 F. 35, in which the New Brunswick seller of timber which by the bill of lading was to be delivered at Glasgow to the seller's order was held entitled to stop the timber on the ship's arrival at Glasgow, and in *Cowdenbeath Coal Co. Ltd v. Clydesdale Bank Ltd* (1895) 22 R. 682, in which opinions were expressed that the coal company had no right of stoppage in transit over a cargo of coal shipped for export to a sub-purchaser in a vessel chartered by the buyer, the bill of lading being in the buyer's name. **4–261**

(6) Where the carrier or other custodier wrongfully refuses to deliver the goods to the buyer or to the buyer's agent, the transit is deemed to be at an end. **4–262**

(7) Where part delivery of the goods has been made to the buyer or his agent, the remainder of the goods may be stopped in transit, unless the part delivery has been made under such circumstances as to show an agreement to give up possession of the whole of the goods. **4–263**

In *Mechan & Sons Ltd v. North-Eastern Railway Co.*, 1911 S.C. 1348, where there had been a contract for the sale of two lifeboats, which were dispatched to the purchaser by rail, the railway company, after it had given up possession of one of the boats to a carter, received notification of stoppage in transit from the sellers. It nevertheless delivered the second boat to the liquidator on the buyer's estate. **4–264**

Held that the railway company was liable in damages to the sellers. The court found no evidence that the delivery of the first boat had been made under such circumstances as to show an agreement to give up possession of the other boat.

(ii) *How Stoppage in Transit is Effected*

4–265 The unpaid seller may exercise his right of stoppage in transit either by taking actual possession of the goods, or by giving notice of his claim to the carrier or other custodier in whose possession the goods are (s. 46(1)). The notice may be given either to the person in actual possession of the goods or to his principal (s. 46(2)), but in the latter case the notice must be given at such a time and under such circumstances that the principal, by the exercise of reasonable diligence, will be able to communicate it to his servant or agent in time to prevent delivery to the buyer (s. 46(3)).

4–266 The carrier or other custodier who receives notice of stoppage in transit must re-deliver the goods to, or according to the directions of, the seller, and the expenses of the re-delivery must be borne by the seller (s. 46(4)).

4–267 As the case of *Mechan & Sons Ltd v. North-Eastern Railway Co.* (4–264, above) shows, a carrier who disregards a notice of stoppage in transit (with the result that the goods pass into the hands of the trustee or liquidator who is administering the bankrupt buyer's estate instead of being returned to the seller) is liable to the seller in damages for the loss caused to the seller by disregard of the notice.

(c) **Resale**

4–268 An unpaid seller has no general right to resell the goods: he has only a right of resale "as limited by" the Act (s. 39(1)).

4–269 In some circumstances the seller who is unpaid will be justified in treating the buyer's failure to pay as a repudiation of the contract and be entitled to rescind the contract, thus placing himself in a position to enter into another contract of sale. However, as was noticed above (4–240), the Act provides that a contract of sale is not rescinded by the mere exercise by an unpaid seller of his right of lien or retention or stoppage in transit (s. 48(1)). If, therefore, the contract has not been rescinded, the seller may retain the goods and at some later date, when he is confident that he will be paid, deliver them or send them for delivery to the buyer.

4–270 It has also been already noticed (4–240, above) that if a seller who has exercised his right of lien or retention or stoppage in transit resells the goods, the buyer acquires a good title to the goods as against the original buyer (s. 48(2)). This is not to say, however, that in all cases the seller who has exercised one of these rights has necessarily then a right to resell to a second buyer: the provision is intended to protect the second buyer, and does not affect the legal relationship between the seller and the original buyer. Therefore, if the first sale has not been rescinded, the seller, by thus putting it out of his power to implement that contract, will be liable to the buyer in damages for breach of contract.

The limited right of resale which is provided for by the Act is as follows: **4–271**

(i) Where the goods are of a perishable nature, or where the unpaid seller gives notice to the buyer of his intention to resell, and the buyer does not within a reasonable time pay or tender the price, the unpaid seller may resell the goods and recover from the original buyer damages for any loss caused by his breach of contract (s. 48(3)). **4–272**

(ii) Where the seller expressly reserves a right of resale in case the buyer should make default, he may then, on the buyer's default, resell the goods. The original contract is rescinded, but without prejudice to any claim which the seller may have for damages (s. 48(4)). **4–273**

The fact that rescission of the original contract is specifically provided for in section 48(4) and not in section 48(3) caused some controversy, the question being whether, in the situation covered by section 48(3), the original contract must be treated as still in existence at the time of the resale. The point has a practical importance where the seller makes a profit out of the resale: if the contract has not been rescinded, the seller will be selling as holder of the goods in security and will be bound to account to the original buyer for the profit, whereas if the contract has been rescinded, he will be selling as owner and be entitled to retain the profit. The former view was supported by *Gallagher v. Shilcock* [1949] 2 K.B. 765, in which a seller who had resold a motor-boat for a higher price than the original contract price was held to be bound to account to the original buyer for part of the deposit which that buyer had already paid. That decision, however, was overruled by the Court of Appeal in *R. V. Ward Ltd v. Bignall* [1967] 1 Q.B. 534: **4–274**

B. contracted to buy a Ford Zodiac and a Vanguard estate car from W. Ltd for £850 and paid a deposit of £25, leaving the cars in W. Ltd's possession pending payment of the balance.

Later, alleging misrepresentation as to the age of the Vanguard, B. suggested that either the price should be reduced to £800 or he should purchase only the Zodiac for £500. W. Ltd, rejecting both suggestions, gave notice that, if the full price was not paid, they would sell both cars elsewhere and claim damages from B.

W. Ltd resold the Vanguard for £350, and sued B. for damages of £497 10s., being the balance of the purchase price (£825), less £350, plus £22 10s. advertising costs.

The Court of Appeal found W. Ltd entitled to only £47 10s. damages, *i.e.* £497 10s less the agreed value of the Zodiac (£450), holding that the resale had not left the original contract intact as *Gallagher v. Shilcock* suggested but had necessarily rescinded the original contract and caused the property in the cars, if it had passed to B., to revert to W. Ltd.

(d) **Attachment by Arrestment or Poinding**

4–275 Section 40 provided that in Scotland a seller might attach the goods while they were in his own hands or possession by arrestment or poinding[4], and that such arrestment or poinding was to have the same operation and effect in a competition or otherwise as an arrestment or poinding by a third party.

4–276 The right differed from the other rights in Part V of the Act in that it belonged to "a seller", not merely to "the unpaid seller". Another peculiarity was that the terms "arrestment" and "poinding" normally referred to moveables which were in the hands of a third party or the debtor, respectively, whereas in the context of section 40 they referred to goods which were in the creditor's hands.

4–277 Section 40 was repealed by the Debtors (Scotland) Act 1987 (Sched. 8).

VI ACTIONS FOR BREACH OF THE CONTRACT

4–278 Part VI of the Act is divided into two Parts:

---

[4] pronounced "pinding."

(a) seller's remedies; and
(b) buyer's remedies.

The provisions of the Act do not, however, amount to a comprehensive codification of the remedies available to the parties, and much is left to rest on the general principles of the common law of contract. **4–279**

Partly this is achieved by express saving of particular rights—*e.g.* the seller's right to interest on the price (s. 49(3)), the buyer's right of specific implement (s. 52(4)) and the right of the buyer or the seller at common law to recover interest or special damages or to recover money paid where the consideration for the payment of it has failed (s. 54). **4–280**

Special damages become payable at common law where, because of special circumstances known to both parties at the time of the formation of the contract, a breach of contract results in losses greater than those which would normally be foreseeable. The distinction between ordinary damages and special damages is always associated with the English case of *Hadley v. Baxendale* (1854) 9 Ex. 341. The Act gives guidance as to the measure of ordinary damages, but has no provisions as to special damages beyond the saving in section 54 of the common law right to such damages in appropriate circumstances. **4–281**

The right to recover money paid where the consideration for the payment of it has failed arises out of unjust enrichment in accordance with the principle *condictio causa data causa non secuta* ("the action applicable where consideration has been given and where consideration for it has not followed"). An illustration is *Cantiere San Rocco S.A. v. Clyde Shipbuilding and Engineering Co. Ltd*, 1923 S.C. (H.L.) 105, in which a buyer of marine engines was held entitled to recover an instalment of the price when fulfilment of the contract became impossible owing to an outbreak of war. **4–282**

In addition to the express saving of particular rights, there is the general saving of the common law in section 62(2): the rules of the common law, except in so far as they are inconsistent with the provisions of the Act (and in particular the rules relating to principal and agent and to the effect of fraud, misrepresentation, duress or coercion, or other invalidating cause) are made to continue to apply to contracts for the sale of goods. **4–283**

This general saving would apply to the common law right which a buyer has to damages for wrongful detention of the goods by the **4–284** seller (and in certain situations by a third party) where the property in the goods has passed to the buyer and he does not obtain delivery of them; the damages are measured by the value of the goods.

4–285 What follows here is restricted to a consideration of the statutory remedies.

(a) **Seller's Remedies**

4–286 The seller has two remedies against the buyer personally (as distinct from the rights which he has against the goods themselves under Part V):

(i) He may bring an action against the buyer for the price.
(ii) He may claim damages for non-acceptance.

(i) *Action for the Price*

4–287 The seller may bring an action against the buyer for the price in the following cases:

(1) where, under the contract, the property in the goods has passed to the buyer, and the buyer wrongfully neglects or refuses to pay for the goods according to the terms of the contract (s. 49(1)); or

(2) where, under the contract, the price is payable on a certain day irrespective of delivery, and the buyer wrongfully neglects or refuses to pay on that day.

In case (2), the action for the price may be brought even although the property in the goods has not passed and even although the goods have not been appropriated to the contract (s. 49(2)).

4–288 When sued for the price, the buyer may put forward the defence that he has a claim for damages against the seller in respect of a breach of the contract by the seller. This is not expressly provided for in the Act, but is in accordance with the general principle that in mutual contracts even an illiquid claim may be used as a defence so as to extinguish or diminish a liquid claim of the other party. The point was established with reference to a contract for the sale of goods by *British Motor Body Co. Ltd v. Thomas Shaw (Dundee) Ltd*, 1914 S.C. 922:

B. Ltd sued S. Ltd for £135 10s., the agreed price of a car-body which B. Ltd had built and supplied to S. Ltd. The order had been given in February, 1912, and the body was delivered in October, 1912. No specific time for delivery was specified in the contract.

S. Ltd put forward the defence that the body had not been delivered within a reasonable time, and that they were entitled to set off £75 as damages against the price.

Held that this was a competent defence.

The seller's common law right to recover interest on the price **4–289** from the date of tender of the goods, or from the date on which the price was payable, as the case may be, is expressly preserved by the Act (s. 49(3)).

(ii) *Damages for Non-Acceptance*

Where the buyer wrongfully neglects or refuses to accept and pay **4–290** for the goods, the seller may sue him for damages for non-acceptance (s. 50(1)).

The measure of damages is the estimated loss directly and **4–291** naturally resulting, in the ordinary course of events, from the buyer's breach of contract (s. 50(2)).

Where there is an available market for the goods in question, the **4–292** measure of damages is prima facie ("unless the contrary is proved") to be ascertained by the difference between the contract price and the market or current price at the time when the goods ought to have been accepted, or, if no time was fixed for acceptance, then at the time of the refusal to accept (s. 50(3)).

An instance of an action for damages for non-acceptance is **4–293** *Govan Rope and Sail Co. Ltd v. Weir & Co.* (1897) 24 R. 368:

A rope-manufacturing company contracted to supply 20 tons of a specified quality of rope to W. & Co., shipowners, in quantities to be ordered by W. & Co., the whole of the rope to be taken by the end of 1894.

By that date, however, W. & Co. had ordered and obtained delivery of only about five and a half tons of rope, and the manufacturers sued for damages for non-acceptance in respect of the balance.

W. & Co. put forward the defence that the rope supplied had been of inferior quality to that specified in the contract, but failed to prove this.

Held that, as there was no "market or current" price for the kind of rope contracted for, the measure of damages to which the manufacturers were entitled was the "loss directly and naturally resulting in the ordinary course of events" from W. & Co.'s breach of contract, *i.e.* in this case the difference between the contract price of the 14½ or so tons and the cost of the raw material required for its manufacture plus the cost of manufacture.

(b) Buyer's Remedies

4–294 Part VI as amended by the Act of 1994 sets out provisions relating to the following two remedies of the buyer:

(i) damages for non-delivery; and

(ii) specific performance.

In addition, under section 15B in Part II of the Act, there are the remedies for breach by the seller of any of the terms of the contract, *viz.*

(iii) (a) damages, and

(b) if the breach is material, rejection of the goods.

4–295 The remedy for breach of "warranty" no longer applies to Scotland (s. 53 as amended by the Act of 1994).

(i) *Damages for Non-Delivery*

4–296 Where the seller wrongfully neglects or refuses to deliver the goods to the buyer, the buyer may sue the seller for damages for non-delivery (s. 51(1)).

4–297 The measure of damages is the estimated loss directly and naturally resulting, in the ordinary course of events, from the seller's breach of contract (s. 51(2)).

4–298 Where there is an available market for the goods in question, the measure of damages is prima facie ("unless the contrary is proved") to be ascertained by the difference between the contract price and the market or current price of the goods at the time when they ought to have been delivered, or, if no time was fixed, then at the time of the refusal to deliver (s. 51(3)).

(ii) *Specific Performance*

4–299 If the goods are specific or ascertained, the court may, if it thinks fit (on an application being made to it by the buyer), direct that the contract be performed specifically, *i.e.* the court will not give the seller the option of retaining the goods and merely paying damages (s. 52(1)). The decree of the court may be unconditional, or on such terms and conditions as to damages, payment of the price, and otherwise, as seem just to the court (s. 52(3)). This remedy of specific performance is supplementary to, and does not derogate from, the common law right of specific implement in Scotland (s. 52(4)).

The term "specific performance" is derived from English law, and section 52(1) enacted the English principle that specific performance would be granted only at the court's discretion. In contrast, the remedy of specific implement in Scots law is regarded as the primary remedy where a seller has failed to deliver a specific article, the court being bound to grant specific implement except in a limited number of situations (such as where implement would be impossible or inequitable). **4–300**

(iii) Damages and Rejection

Whereas sections 51 and 52 relate to situations where the seller fails to deliver goods, other forms of breach of contract are covered by the common law or, where applicable, by section 15B ("Remedies for breach of contract as respects Scotland") and section 53A ("Measure of damages as respects Scotland"). Both section 15B and section 53A were inserted in the Act of 1979 by the Act of 1994, and to a substantial extent restore to Scotland the rules which had applied at common law. **4–301**

The rule of the common law is that if the seller's breach of contract is in some minor respect, he is not entitled to reject the goods, but he may claim damages; for the right to reject the goods the breach must be a material one. **4–302**

The question of whether a breach is material or not depends on the circumstances of each case. **4–303**

In accordance with the common law, section 15B of the Act provides that where the seller is in breach of any term of the contract, express or implied, the buyer is entitled— **4–304**

(a) to claim damages, and

(b) if the breach is material, to reject any goods delivered under the contract and treat it as repudiated (s. 15B(1)).

The buyer in a consumer contract is then assisted by the provision that, for the purposes of (1)(b), the following breaches **4–305** are to be deemed to be material: breach by the seller of any term, express or implied—

(a) as to the quality of the goods or their fitness for a purpose,

(b) if the goods are sold by description, that the goods will correspond with the description,

(c) if the goods are sold by sample, that the bulk will correspond with the sample in quality (s. 15B(2)).

4–306 Apart from this provision in section 15B(2), the Act gives little guidance as to what will be material. It will be noted that no mention is made in section 15B(2) of terms about title; whether or not breach of a term about title is material in a consumer contract is left to rest on the common law: it will depend on the circumstances of the case. Section 10 deals expressly with stipulations about time: unless a different intention appears from the terms of the contract, stipulations as to time of payment are not of the essence of the contract (s. 10(1)), and whether any other stipulation as to time is or is not of the essence of the contract depends on the terms of the contract (s. 10(2)). A seller's failure, therefore, to deliver goods by a stipulated date would not, unless the time of delivery was of the essence of the contract, entitle the buyer to reject the goods, but would give him a claim for damages. In *Paton & Sons v. David Payne & Co. Ltd* (1897) 35 S.L.R. 112 (HL) (4–63, above), for instance, the time of the delivery of the printing machine was held not to have been of the essence of the contract and so, on the seller's failure to deliver by the agreed date the buyers, while not entitled to reject the machine, were entitled to damages.

4–307 The measure of damages is the estimated loss directly and naturally resulting, in the ordinary course of events, from the breach (s. 53A(1)). Where the breach consists of the delivery of goods which are not of the quality required by the contract, and the buyer retains the goods, that loss is prima facie ("unless the contrary is proved") the difference between the value of the goods at the time of delivery to the buyer and the value which they would have had if they had fulfilled the contract (s. 53A(2)).

4–308 The right of rejection must be exercised timeously. In particular, it is no longer open if the buyer has accepted the goods. On this, see "*Buyer's Right of Rejection*" (4–206 *et seq.*, above), where some illustrative cases have been included.

4–309 The right of rejection may still be open although the property in the goods has passed to the buyer:

Nelson v. William Chalmers & Co. Ltd, 1913 S.C. 441: C. Ltd entered into a contract to build a motor yacht for N. A clause in the contract provided that the property in the yacht was to pass to N. on payment of the first of the four instalments of the price.

The first instalment was paid. When completed the yacht was disconform to contract, and N. rejected it and brought an action against C. Ltd for repayment of the instalment paid and for damages. C. Ltd maintained that N. was barred from rejecting the yacht because, under the terms of the contract, it had become his own property.

Held that as N. had never accepted the yacht as conform to contract, he was not barred from rejecting it.

By a provision in Part VII ("Supplementary") of the Act, where **4–310**
a buyer has elected to accept goods which he might have rejected, and to treat a breach of contract as only giving rise to a claim for damages, he may, if sued by the seller for the price, be required, in the court's discretion, to consign or pay into court the price of the goods or part of the price or to give other reasonable security for its due payment (s. 58). This discretion, as it existed under the common law, was exercised by the court in *George Cohen Sons & Co. Ltd v. Jamieson & Paterson*, 1963 S.C. 289 (O.H.):

C. Ltd had supplied to J. & P., scrap merchants, a hydraulic scrap metal press. J. & P. refused to pay the contract price, though they continued to use the machine.

C. Ltd brought an action against J. & P. for the price.

C. Ltd asked the court to require J. & P. to consign the sum sued for.

Held that at common law the court had a discretion to order consignation in such circumstances; and J. & P. *ordained* to consign half of the sum sued for.

VII AUCTION SALES

The Act in some respects altered the common law of Scotland as to **4–311**
sales by auction. As a result, the rules applicable to auction sales of goods differ to some extent from the rules applicable to auction sales of heritable property and incorporeal moveables.

Section 57 sets out the following rules as to auction sales: **4–312**

(a) Where goods are put up for sale by auction in lots, each lot is **4–313**
prima facie ("unless the contrary is proved") deemed to be the subject of a separate contract of sale (s. 57(1)).

4–314 The rule of the common law was to the same effect, as is clear from *Couston, Thomson & Co. v. Chapman* (1872) 10 M. (H.L.) 74; (1871) 9 M. 675, in which the buyer of several lots of wine by sample at an auction was held not to have timeously rejected three of the lots which were disconform to sample, and so was liable to pay the price of all the lots.

"There can be no question whatever that the purchase of each lot was a separate and distinct contract, and that it was perfectly competent to the defenders to object to the completion of the purchase with respect to the three lots they object to, if they had good grounds for so doing, irrespective wholly of the view which they might take of the other purchases which they made, and with which they are content" (*per* Lord Chancellor Hatherley at p. 76).

4–315 (b) A sale by auction is complete when the auctioneer announces its completion by the fall of the hammer, or in other customary manner; until that announcement is made any bidder may retract his bid (s. 57(2)).

4–316 From this provision the court deduced in *Fenwick v. Macdonald, Fraser & Co. Ltd* (1904) 6 F. 850 that until the fall of the hammer the exposer is free to withdraw the goods from sale. "There is no sale until the fall of the hammer, and . . . until then any competitor is entitled to withdraw his bid. Of course, it follows that any proprietor is entitled to withdraw the article he is selling. One party is not bound while the other is free" (*per* Lord Young at p. 853).

4–317 As was explained by Lord Trayner in that case (at pp. 853–854), the common law rule was different: a bidder could not withdraw his bid, and the seller, even if only one bid had been made, could not withdraw the article from sale.

4–318 (c) A sale by auction may be notified to be subject to a reserve or upset price, and a right to bid may also be reserved expressly by or on behalf of the seller (s. 57(3)).

4–319 Where a right to bid is expressly reserved (but not otherwise) the seller or any one person on his behalf may bid (s. 57(6)).

4–320 The distinction in practice between a reserve and an upset price is that the former is in writing, sealed up and only made known after the fall of the hammer, whereas an upset price is made known to prospective bidders before the sale has begun. Reserve prices have been commoner in England, and upset prices in Scotland.

4–321 (d) Where a sale by auction is not notified to be subject to a right to bid by or on behalf of the seller, it is not lawful for the seller to bid himself or to employ any person to bid at the sale, or for the auctioneer knowingly to take any bid from the seller or from that other person (s. 57(4)).

A sale which contravenes that rule may be treated as fraudulent by the buyer (s. 57(5)). **4–322**

A person employed by the seller to bid with a view to raising the price is commonly referred to as a "white-bonnet". **4–323**

These statutory rules operate within a framework provided by the common law of agency: the auctioneer is a mercantile or commercial agent, selling on behalf of a disclosed or undisclosed principal; he has a lien on the price for the charges and commission due to him by the seller (*Mackenzie v. Cormack*, 1950 S.C. 183), he is freed from liability to the buyer if the buyer, having discovered the identity of the previously undisclosed seller, elects to return the goods to the seller (*Ferrier v. Dods* (1865) 3 M. 561), and if the auctioneer sells without having the seller's authority to sell, with the result that the buyer loses a bargain, he is liable to the buyer in damages for "breach of warranty of authority" (*Anderson v. Croall & Sons Ltd* (1903) 6 F. 153) (see also 1–42 *et seq.*, above). **4–324**

Auction sales are also governed by other statutes (see 4–327 *et seq.*, below). **4–325**

VIII OTHER STATUTORY PROVISIONS ON SALE OF GOODS

There are numerous other statutory provisions besides the Act of 1979 which affect particular aspects of contracts for the sale of goods. The legislation since the 1960s, with its accompanying subordinate legislation, is voluminous, and must be looked for in more specialised works. What follows here is no more than an indication of the existence of the main statutes and their subject-matter. **4–326**

Auctions (Bidding Agreements) Acts 1927 and 1969

The Act of 1927 made it an offence for any dealer to give any gift or consideration to any other person to induce that other person to abstain from bidding at an auction sale, and also for any person to accept or attempt to obtain from a dealer any gift or consideration for such purpose (s. 1(1)). A "dealer" for the purposes of the Act **4–327** is "a person who in the normal course of his business attends sales by auction for the purpose of purchasing goods with a view to reselling them" (s. 1(2)).

4–328 The amending Act of 1969 introduced increased penalties for offences under the Act of 1927 (s. 1(1)), empowered the court to prohibit convicted persons from attending auctions for up to three years (s. 2(1)), and provided the civil remedy by which the seller may avoid the contract (s. 3(1)) and if the goods are not restored to him may recover any loss sustained by him not only from the buyer but from any of the parties to the prohibited bidding agreement (s. 3(2)).

4–329 Copies of both Acts must be exhibited at the auction (1927 Act, s. 3; 1969 Act, s. 4).

Mock Auctions Act 1961

4–330 This Act made it an offence to promote a "mock auction" at which lots of, or including, "prescribed" articles are offered for sale (s. 1(1)).

4–331 A "mock auction" is a sale of goods by competitive bidding at which:

(a) a lot is sold to a person for less than the amount of his highest bid, or part of the price is repaid or credited to him; or

(b) the right to bid is restricted or stated to be restricted to persons who have bought or agreed to buy one or more articles; or

(c) any articles are given away or offered as gifts (s. 1(3)).

4–332 The "prescribed" articles are any plate, plated articles, linen, china, glass, books, pictures, prints, furniture, jewellery, articles of household or personal use or ornament or any musical or scientific instrument or apparatus (s. 3(2)).

4–333 An example of a "mock auction" within the meaning of the Act is given in *Aitchison v. Cooper*, 1982 S.L.T. (Sh. Ct.) 41:

At a public sale C. had required those wishing to bid to purchase first an undisclosed item for 10p. These undisclosed items were orange boxes, and the right to bid was restricted to orange box holders.

C. had also secured offers of £50 and £100 from two persons for undisclosed items, had returned £20 to one and £50 to the other and had then revealed that these persons had purchased a cassette recorder and a television set respectively.

Unknown to C. there were present at the sale two officers of the Consumer Protection Department, who took notes.

C. was found guilty: both (a) and (b), above, in the definition of a "mock auction" were satisfied.

Trading Stamps Act 1964

This Act was passed to regulate the issue and redeeming of trading stamps. **4–334**

It requires the promoter of the trading stamp scheme to redeem the stamps for their cash value if the holder so chooses and the stamps have an aggregate cash value of at least 25p (s. 3(1)). Each stamp must bear on its face a value expressed in the current coin of the realm (*e.g.* ".033p") and the promoter's name (s. 2(1) and (2)). **4–335**

Trade Descriptions Acts 1968 and 1972

The 1968 Act replaces, but is of much wider scope than, the Merchandise Marks Acts 1887 to 1953. It is aimed against false or misleading trade descriptions, and is part of the criminal law: contravention of the Act does not of itself affect the validity or enforceability of a contract (s. 35). **4–336**

The leading provision of the Act is that any person who, in the course of a trade or business,— **4–337**

(a) applies a "false trade description" to any goods, or

(b) supplies or offers to supply any goods to which a "false trade description" is applied,

is guilty of an offence (s. 1(1)).

"Trade description" is any indication, direct or indirect, and by whatever means given, of a wide variety of matters relating to goods, *e.g.* quantity, size, method of manufacture, fitness for purpose, approval by any person, history (s. 2(1)) (*e.g.* a false mileometer reading on a second-hand car as in *MacNab v. Alexanders of Greenock Ltd*, 1971 S.L.T. 121). **4–338**

"False trade description" means a trade description which is false "to a material degree" (s. 3(1)), but the Act also provides that if a trade description is misleading, though not false, it is deemed to be a false trade description (s. 3(2)) (*e.g.* "where whisky which is not made in Scotland is placed in a bottle bearing a label pictorially suggestive of Scottish origin but also disclosing in small print the **4–339** actual place of manufacture" (G. H. Treitel in his annotation to this provision in *Current Law Statutes Annotated*)).

4–340 A person charged with an offence will be acquitted if he proves that:

(a) the commission of the offence was due to a mistake or to reliance on information supplied to him, or to the act or default of "another person", an accident or some other cause beyond his control; *and*

(b) he took all reasonable precautions and exercised all due diligence to avoid the commission of the offence by himself or any person under his control (s. 24(1)).

4–341 The best-known case on the Act was concerned with the interpretation of this statutory defence:

Tesco Supermarkets Ltd v. Nattrass [1972] A.C. 153: T. Ltd, at one of its branch supermarkets, was advertising a "special offer" of "Radiant washing powder at 2s. 11d. instead of the normal price of 3s. 11d. Some packets marked at 3s. 11d. were in fact on the shelves, and a customer who selected one of these was charged 3s. 11d.[5]

T. Ltd was successful in its defence to a charge under the Act, since the commission of the offence had been due to the default of "another person", namely, the store manager whose duty it was to see that the correct goods were on the shelves, and since T. Ltd also satisfied part (b) of the defence by having devised a proper system for the store and having done all it could do to see that the system was implemented.

The decision has led to some criticism of the defence as making it too easy for parties in the position of T. Ltd to obtain immunity.

4–342 A short amending Act of 1972 required certain names and marks applied to imported goods to be accompanied by an indication of the country of origin of the goods. That Act was repealed by the Consumer Protection Act 1987 (s. 48(2)) and replaced by the Trade Descriptions (Place of Production) (Marking) Order 1988 (S.I. 1988 No. 1771) which provides that where goods are presented in such a way as to indicate that they were manufactured or produced elsewhere than is the case, they must be marked with a

[5] Provisions on false or misleading indications as to price comprised s. 11 of the Trade Descriptions Act 1968. That section was repealed by the Consumer Protection Act 1987, Pt. III of which consists of revised provisions on misleading price indications (see 4–385 *et seq.*, below).

clear statement as to the place where they were manufactured or produced.

The most commonly reported cases on trade descriptions have been appeals against convictions arising from the sale of motor vehicles with false odometer readings, and the point at issue has usually been whether the appellant had taken all reasonable precautions and exercised all due diligence to avoid the commission of the offence. Examples are *Ford v. Guild*, 1990 S.L.T. 502 (motor dealer had made no attempt to confirm that an owner previous to the immediate seller existed), *Amag Ltd v. Jessop*, 1989 S.C.C.R 186; [1989] C.L.Y. 4935 (appellants had not taken any steps to check the accuracy of the odometer such as making inquiries of the dealers from whom the car was purchased) and *Costello v. Lowe*, 1990 S.C.C.R 90; [1990] C.L.Y. 5786 (appellant had failed to check police records which would have provided the true mileage of a former taxi). **4–343**

Unsolicited Goods and Services Acts 1971 and 1975

These Acts are aimed at protecting persons who receive "unsolicited" goods, *i.e.* goods sent to them without any prior request having been made for the goods by or on behalf of the recipients (1971 Act, s. 6). **4–344**

The Acts enable the recipient of unsolicited goods, provided certain conditions are satisfied, to use, deal with or dispose of them as if they were an unconditional gift to him, all the rights of the sender to the goods being extinguished (1971 Act, s. 1(1)). The recipient must have no reasonable cause to believe that the goods were sent with a view to their being acquired for the purposes of a trade or business. He must not have agreed to acquire them, nor must he have agreed to return them. He must not have unreasonably refused to permit the sender to take possession of them, and he must either have held the goods for six months or have given the sender 30 days' notice (1971 Act, s. 1(2)). **4–345**

A person who makes demands for payment for unsolicited goods is guilty of an offence (1971 Act, s. 2(1)). **4–346**

The amending Act of 1975 added to the Act of 1971 a new section enabling regulations to be made as to the contents and form of notes of agreement, invoices and similar documents (1971 Act, s. 3A). **4–347**

4–348 An illustration is *The Readers Digest Association v. Pirie*, 1973 S.L.T. 170 (High Court of Justiciary): Subscribers to the *Readers Digest* had cancelled their subscriptions as from the end of 1971 and later confirmed their cancellation. Employees of the Association failed to alter the computer, and magazines and bills continued to be sent out.

The Association was convicted in the sheriff court under section 2(1) of the Act of 1971, and appealed by stated case.

Held that the Association's system was to rely on the instructions of the computer to which all relevant information ought to have been fed; that it was reasonable for the Association to so rely and the system broke down owing to mistakes on the part of the junior staff whose knowledge could not be imputed to the Association; and appeal allowed.

Fair Trading Act 1973

4–349 This long Act, consisting of 140 sections and 13 Schedules, established the office of Director General of Fair Trading (s. 1(1)), whose duty it is to keep under review commercial activities relating to goods or services supplied to consumers in order to make himself aware of practices which might adversely affect the economic interests of consumers (s. 2(1)). The Director has further functions both under this Act and under the Consumer Credit Act 1974.

4–350 The Act empowers the Secretary of State for Trade and Industry to make orders, in the form of statutory instruments, to control certain "consumer trade practices" (s. 22). Failure to comply with an order is an offence (s. 23).

4–351 A "consumer trade practice" is any practice which is carried on in connection with the supply of goods (whether by sale or otherwise) to consumers or in connection with the supply of services for consumers and which relates to a variety of matters (*e.g.* the terms or conditions on which goods or services are supplied, methods of salesmanship employed in dealing with consumers, the way in which goods are packed, or methods of demanding payment) (s. 13).

4–352 A recommendation for the exercise of the Secretary of State's powers to make orders may be made by the Director where it appears to the Director that a consumer trade practice has the effect, or is likely to have the effect—

(a) of misleading consumers as to, or withholding from them adequate information as to, or an adequate record of, their rights and obligations under consumer transactions, or

(b) of otherwise misleading or confusing consumers with respect to any matter in connection with consumer transactions, or

(c) of subjecting consumers to undue pressure to enter into consumer transactions, or

(d) of causing the terms or conditions on which consumers enter into consumer transactions to be so adverse to them as to be inequitable (s. 17(1) and (2)).

The Act includes provisions enabling the Director to take action against persons who in carrying on business persist in a course of conduct which is unfair to consumers by involving the commission of offences (*e.g.* under the Trade Descriptions Act) or breach of contract or breach of duty. The Director must "use his best endeavours" to obtain from the person concerned a satisfactory written assurance that he will refrain from continuing his course of conduct (s. 34). If the Director fails to obtain such an assurance or if the assurance is given but not observed, the Director may bring proceedings against the person concerned before the Restrictive Practices Court (s. 35). **4–353**

Another notable provision of the Act is the duty imposed on the Director to encourage associations to prepare and distribute to their members codes of practice for guidance in safeguarding and promoting the interests of consumers (s. 124(3)). The existence of such codes of practice in many trades has the effect of reducing consumers' complaints. **4–354**

The Director must make an annual report to the Secretary of State (s. 125(1)). He may also publish information and advice for consumers (s. 124(1)), and there are now numerous booklets and leaflets available free of charge in accordance with this provision. **4–355**

Unfair Contract Terms Act 1977

The main provisions of this Act are directed against exclusion-of-liability clauses which one party to a contract may seek, by the exercise of superior bargaining strength, to impose on the other party. Amongst the contracts to which these provisions apply are contracts relating to the transfer of the ownership of goods. **4–356**

4–357 In general, any clause excluding or restricting liability for death or personal injury is void, and of clauses excluding or restricting liability for other matters, some are void (*e.g.* in consumer contracts) while the others are of no effect unless they satisfy a "reasonableness" test.

4–358 The provisions of the Act which affected sections 12 to 15 of the Sale of Goods Act 1893 were incorporated in the Sale of Goods Act 1979 and have been considered earlier in this chapter (see 4–64 *et seq.*, above).

4–359 Overlapping the Act of 1977 to some extent are the Unfair Terms in Consumer Contracts Regulations 1994 (S.I. 1994 No. 3159) which implemented the E.C. Council Directive on Unfair Contract Terms (Dir. 93/13). A person wishing to ascertain whether a term is valid must check it both against the Act and against the regulations. The latter are of wider scope than the Act. The central provision in the regulations is that an unfair term in a contract concluded with a consumer by a seller or supplier is not binding on the consumer.

Consumer Protection Act 1987

4–360 The three major Parts of this Act consist of provisions on:

(a) product liability (Part I);
(b) consumer safety (Part II); and
(c) misleading price indications (Part III).

Whereas Part I is concerned with civil law, Parts II and III are mainly concerned with criminal law.

(a) *Product Liability*

4–361 Part I of the Act has the effect of implementing the E.C. Council Directive on Product Liability (Dir. 85/374) (s. 1(1)).

4–362 The central provision of this Part is that strict liability is imposed for damage caused by a defect in a product, *i.e.* the pursuer need not prove any fault or negligence (s. 1(1)).

4–363 "Product" has a wider definition than that of "goods" in the Sale of Goods Act 1979: "product" means any goods or electricity and includes a product which is comprised in another product, whether as a component part or raw material or otherwise (s. 1(2)); further, in the interpretation section of the Act of 1987 "goods" is defined as including "substances, growing crops and things comprised in land by virtue of being attached to it and any ship, aircraft or vehicle", and "substance" is stated to mean "any natural or artificial substance, whether in solid, liquid or gaseous form or in the form of a vapour", and to include substances which are comprised in or mixed with other goods (s. 45(1)); a reference in the Act to "things comprised in land by virtue of being attached to it" is in Scotland a reference to moveables which have become heritable by accession to heritable property (s. 45(5)).

Primary liability is imposed on: **4–364**

(i) the producer of the product;

(ii) any person who, by putting his name on the product or using a trade mark or other distinguishing mark in relation to the product, has held himself out to be the producer of the product (commonly referred to as an "own-brander");

(iii) any person who has imported the product from outside the European Community in order, in the course of any business of his, to supply it to another (s. 2(1)); and

(iv) if the person primarily liable cannot be identified, the supplier (s. 2(3)).

Where two or more persons are liable, their liability is joint and several (s. 2(5)).

For the purposes of (i), above, the "producer" of a product **4–365**
means:

(1) the person who manufactured it;

(2) in the case of a substance which has not been manufactured but has been won or abstracted, the person who won or abstracted it (as in mining or quarrying);

(3) in the case of a product which has not been manufactured, won or abstracted but essential characteristics of which are attributable to an industrial or other process having been carried out (*e.g.* in relation to agricultural produce), the person who carried out that process (s. 1(2)).

Liability does not attach to any person for any defect in any **4–366**
game or agricultural produce provided it has not undergone an industrial process (s. 2(4)).

The Act does not prejudice any liability arising otherwise, *e.g.* **4–367**
from negligence or breach of contract (s. 2(6)).

The term "defect" is related to safety: there is not a "defect" in a **4–368**
product merely because it wears out quickly or does not function.

This follows from the definition of "defect" in section 3, which provides that there is a defect in a product for the purposes of Part I of the Act if the *safety* of the product is not such as persons generally are entitled to expect and that for those purposes "safety", in relation to a product, includes safety with respect to products comprised in that product and safety in the context of risks of loss of or damage to property (including land), as well as in the context of risks of death or personal injury (ss. 3(1) and 5(1)). In deciding what "persons generally are entitled to expect" all the circumstances must be taken into account, including:

(i) the manner in which, and purposes for which, the product has been marketed, its get-up, the use of any mark in relation to the product and any instructions for, or warnings with respect to, doing or refraining from doing anything with or in relation to the product;

(ii) what might reasonably be expected to be done with or in relation to the product; and

(iii) the time when the product was supplied by its producer to another (s. 3(2)).

4–369 There is no liability under the provisions of the Act for the loss of or any damage to the product itself (s. 5(2)).

4–370 Where the claim is for loss of or damage to property, there is no liability under the Act unless the property is:

(i) of a description of property ordinarily intended for private use, occupation or consumption; *and*

(ii) intended by the person suffering the loss or damage mainly for his own private use, occupation or consumption (s. 5(3)).

4–371 To avoid trivial claims, it is provided that no loss of or damage to property falls within the provisions of the Act if it does not exceed £275 (s. 5(4)).

4–372 An obligation arising from liability under section 2 of the Act is extinguished on the expiry of 10 years (Prescription and Limitation (Scotland) Act 1973, as amended by s. 6(6) of and Sched. 1 to the 1987 Act).

(b) *Consumer Safety*

4–373 Legislation on the safety of goods was formerly covered by the Consumer Safety Act 1978 (itself repealing the Consumer Protection Acts 1961–71). The Act of 1978 was amended by the

Consumer Safety (Amendment) Act 1986, and Part II of the Consumer Protection Act 1987 is a consolidation of the Acts of 1978 and 1986 with some further amendment.

Section 10 relates to what is called "the general safety requirement". A person is guilty of an offence if he supplies any consumer goods which fail to comply with the general safety requirement or if he offers or agrees to supply any such goods or if he exposes or possesses any such goods for supply (s. 10(1)). The references to a person's supplying goods are confined to references to that person's supplying goods in the course of a business of his (s. 46(5)). **4–374**

The term "consumer goods" means any goods which are ordinarily intended for private use or consumption, other than certain listed items which are covered by other legislation, *e.g.* growing crops, water, food, feeding stuff or fertiliser, gas, aircraft or motor vehicles, controlled drugs or licensed medicinal products (s. 10(7)). **4–375**

Consumer goods fail to comply with "the general safety requirement" if they are not reasonably safe in the light of all the circumstances, including: **4–376**

(i) the manner in which, and purposes for which, the goods are being or would be marketed, the get-up of the goods, the use of any mark in relation to the goods and any instructions or warnings which are given or would be given with respect to the keeping, use or consumption of the goods;

(ii) any standards of safety published by any person (*e.g.* the British Standards Institute) either for goods of a description which applies to the goods in question or for matters relating to goods of that description; and

(iii) the existence of any means by which it would have been reasonable (taking into account the cost, likelihood and extent of any improvement) for the goods to have been made safer (s. 10(2)).

"Safe", in relation to any goods, means such that there is no risk, or no risk apart from one reduced to a minimum, that the goods will cause the death of, or any personal injury to, any person (s. 19(1)). The provisions of Part II, therefore, are not concerned with whether the goods supplied will cause damage to other property. **4–377**

Under section 11 the Secretary of State for Trade and Industry has a wide power to make regulations ("safety regulations") for the purpose of securing: **4–378**

(i) that goods are safe;

(ii) that goods which would be unsafe in the hands of particular descriptions of persons are not made available generally; and

(iii) that appropriate information is, and inappropriate information is not, provided in relation to goods (s. 11(1)).

4–379 Safety regulations may relate to composition or contents, design, construction, finish or packing of goods, to standards for goods and to many other matters listed in section 11(2). Failure to comply with certain safety regulations is an offence (s. 12), and may also give rise to civil proceedings (s. 41).

4–380 The Secretary of State has also power to serve on a person "a prohibition notice" (*i.e.* a notice prohibiting the person, except with the Secretary of State's consent, from supplying the goods which the Secretary of State considers are unsafe and which are described in the notice) and "a notice to warn" (*i.e.* a notice requiring the person at his own expense to publish a warning about goods which the Secretary of State considers are unsafe, which that person supplies or has supplied and which are described in the notice) (s. 13(1)). A person who contravenes a prohibition notice or a notice to warn is guilty of an offence (s. 13(4)).

4–381 Where an enforcement authority (*i.e.* a government department or a local weights and measures authority) has reasonable grounds for suspecting that any safety provision has been contravened, the enforcement authority may serve "a suspension notice" (*i.e.* a notice prohibiting the person on whom it is served for a period of up to six months from supplying the goods described in the notice) (s. 14(1) and (2)). A person who contravenes a suspension notice is guilty of an offence (s. 14(6)). There is a right of appeal to the sheriff court for a suspension notice to be set aside (s. 15(1) and (2)).

4–382 A sheriff may make an order for forfeiture of any goods in relation to which there has been a contravention of a safety provision (s. 17(1)).

4–383 Wide powers are conferred on the Secretary of State to obtain information for the purpose of deciding whether to make, vary or revoke any safety regulations, or to serve, vary or revoke a prohibition notice or to serve or revoke a notice to warn (s. 18(1)).

4–384 Overlapping Part II of the Act are the General Product Safety Regulations 1994 (S.I. 1994 No. 2328) which implemented the E.C. Council Directive on General Product Safety (Dir. 92/59). The "general safety requirement" in the Act is restricted by the regulations since the regulations also contain a general safety requirement and provide that, where it applies, the requirement of the Act does not apply. The range of products covered by the regulations is wider than that of the Act. The central provision in the regulations is that no producer shall place a product on the market unless the product is a safe one.

(c) *Misleading Price Indications*

Part III of the Act replaces provisions in section 11 of the Trade Descriptions Act 1968, which had been found to contain loopholes. Further, section 11 did not apply to services or accommodation. Part III of the Act of 1987 applies to misleading price indications relating to goods, services, accommodation or facilities, and it includes a lengthy definition of "misleading". It also provides for an approved code of practice, and confers on the Secretary of State power to make regulations. **4–385**

Section 20(1) provides that a person is guilty of an offence if, in the course of any business of his, he gives (by any means whatever) to any consumers an indication which is misleading as to the price at which any goods, services, accommodation or facilities are available. The word "consumer" means: **4–386**

(i) in relation to goods, any person who might wish to be supplied with the goods for his own private use or consumption;

(ii) in relation to services or facilities, any person who might wish to be provided with the services or facilities otherwise than for the purposes of any business of his; and

(iii) in relation to accommodation, any person who might wish to occupy the accommodation otherwise than for the purposes of any business of his (s. 20(6)).

The definition of the word "misleading" is to the general effect that the price indication is to be looked at from the consumer's point of view: it is what the consumer might reasonably be expected to infer from the indication that is in question—not what the trader intended to convey by the indication (s. 21). **4–387**

Before approving any code of practice on price indications the Secretary of State must consult the Director General of Fair Trading. The purpose of a code is to give practical guidance on the provisions of the Act on price indications, and to promote what **4–388** appear to the Secretary of State to be desirable practices (s. 25(1)). Contravention of a code does not of itself give rise to any criminal or civil liability, but compliance or non-compliance with it is taken into account by the court in deciding whether an offence has been committed (s. 25(2)).

4–389 The Secretary of State's power to make regulations is likewise to be exercised only after consultation with the Director General of Fair Trading (s. 26(1)).

Further Reading

Scots Mercantile Law Statutes (reprinted every second year from *The Parliament House Book*) for Sale of Goods Act 1979, as amended

Gloag and Henderson, *The Law of Scotland*, Chapters 16 and 17

David M. Walker, *Principles of Scottish Private Law*, Volume III, Chapter 5.33

W. Cowan H. Ervine, *Consumer Law in Scotland*, Chapters 1 to 8 and 10 to 12

Encyclopedia of Consumer Law, General Editor: W. H. Thomas; Scottish Editor: W. Cowan H. Ervine (loose-leaf, 1980— Sweet & Maxwell, W. Green & Son)

The Laws of Scotland: Stair Memorial Encyclopaedia, Volume 20, Title *Sale and Exchange* by William J. Stewart, and Volume 6, Title *Consumer Protection* by W. C. H. Ervine.

W. Cowan H. Ervine, "The Sale and Supply of Goods Act 1994", 1995 S.L.T. (News) 1

H. L. MacQueen, "The Sale and Supply of Goods Act 1994" (1995) 63 S.L.G. 5

Keith R. Wotherspoon, "The Sale and Supply of Goods Act 1994" (1995) 40 J.L.S.S. 88

CHAPTER 5

CONSUMER CREDIT

	Para.
Introduction	5–01
(a) General Meaning of Term "Consumer Credit"	5–06
(b) General Aim of the Act	5–09
(c) The Crowther Report	5–14
(d) Structure of the Act	5–19
I Administration	5–29
II Definitions	5–39
(a) "Regulated Agreement"	5–44
(i) "Consumer Credit Agreement"	5–46
(ii) "Consumer Hire Agreement"	5–51
(iii) "Exempt Agreement"	5–58
(b) The Subdivisions of Regulated Consumer Credit Agreements	5–62
(i) "Running-Account Credit" and "Fixed-Sum Credit"	5–64
(ii) "Restricted-Use Credit" and "Unrestricted-Use Credit"	5–79
(iii) "Debtor-Creditor-Supplier Agreements" and "Debtor-Creditor Agreements"	5–88
(c) "Credit-Token Agreement"	5–99
(d) "Small Agreement"	5–104
(e) "Multiple Agreement"	5–108
(f) "Linked Transaction"	5–116
III Trading Control	5–121
(a) Licensing of Credit and Hire Businesses	5–122
Licensing Principles	5–123
Issue of Licences	5–132
Renewal, Variation, Suspension and Revocation of Licences	5–134
Miscellaneous	5–140
Representations to Director	5–140
The register	5–141
Duty to notify changes	5–143
Death, bankruptcy, *etc.*, of licensee	5–144
Criminal and civil consequences of contravention of licensing provisions	5–147
Appeals	5–149
(b) Seeking Business	5–152
(i) Advertising	5–154
Advertisements to which Part IV applies	5–154
Form and content of advertisements	5–160
Offences	5–165
(ii) Canvassing, etc.	5–167
Canvassing off trade premises	5–167
Circulars to minors	5–171
Prohibition of unsolicited credit-tokens	5–173
(iii) Quotations, etc.	5–174
Quotations	5–174
Display of information	5–177
Conduct of business regulations	5–178
IV Agreement Control	5–179
(a) Entry into Credit or Hire Agreements	5–180
(i) Preliminary Matters	5–181
Disclosure of information	5–181
Antecedent negotiations	5–182
(ii) Making the Agreement	5–186
Form and content of agreements	5–186
Proper and improper execution	5–189
(iii) Cancellation of Certain Agreements within Cooling-off Period	5–196
(iv) Exclusion of Certain Agreements from Part V	5–203
(b) Matters Arising During Currency of Credit or Hire Agreements	5–206
Liability of Creditor for Breaches by Supplier	5–207
Duty to Give Notice before Taking Certain Action	5–211
Duty to Give Information	5–214
Appropriation of Payments	5–220
Variation of Agreements	5–222
Misuse of Credit-Tokens and Other Credit Facilities	5–224
Duty on Issue of New Credit Tokens	5–226

	Para.
Death of Debtor or Hirer . . .	5–227
(c) Default and Termination	5–230
(i) Default Notices	5–231
(ii) Further Restriction of Remedies for Default . . .	5–237
Retaking of protected goods	5–237
Recovery of possession of goods or land	5–241
Interest not to be increased on default	5–242
Summary diligence not competent	5–243
(iii) Early Payment by Debtor .	5–244
(iv) Termination of Agreements	5–248
Notice of termination in non-default cases	5–249
Termination of hire-purchase and conditional sale agreements	5–250
Termination of hire agreement	5–252
Termination statements . .	5–254
Landlord's hypothec . . .	5–255
(d) Security	5–256
(i) General	5–259
Form and content of securities	5–259
Duty to give information to surety	5–260
Duty to give information to debtor or hirer	5–262
Realisation of securities . .	5–263
Act not to be evaded by use of security	5–264
(ii) Pledges	5–265
Pawn-receipts	5–267
Redemption period	5–269
Redemption of pawn . . .	5–272
Realisation of pawn	5–276
Order to deliver pawn . . .	5–278
(iii) Negotiable Instruments . .	5–279
(iv) Heritable Securities	5–284
(e) Judicial Control	5–285
(i) Enforcement and Other Orders	5–290
Enforcement orders in cases of infringement . . .	5–292
Enforcement orders on death of debtor or hirer . .	5–295
Time orders	5–297
Protection orders	5–301
Financial relief in hire agreements	5–302
Special powers of court in hire-purchase and conditional sale agreements . .	5–303
(ii) Extortionate Credit Bargains	5–307
When bargains are extortionate	5–311
Reopening of extortionate agreements	5–314
V Ancillary Credit Businesses	5–317
(a) Definitions	5–320
(i) Credit Brokerage	5–324
(ii) Debt-Adjusting	5–329
(iii) Debt-Counselling	5–332
(iv) Debt-Collecting	5–335
(v) Credit Reference Agency .	5–337
(b) Licensing	5–341
(c) Seeking Business	5–344
(d) Entry into Agreements	5–347
(e) Credit Reference Agencies . . .	5–349
(i) Name, *etc.*, of Agency . . .	5–351
(ii) Copy of File	5–353
(iii) Correction of Wrong Information	5–359
VI Enforcement of the Act	5–362
Enforcement Authorities	5–363
Entry and Inspection	5–365
Power to Make Test Purchases, *etc.*	5–370
Obstruction of Authorised Officers	5–371
Notification of Convictions and Judgments to Director	5–374
Penalties, Defences and Onus of Proof	5–376
Statements by Creditor or Owner to be Binding	5–381
Contracting-out Forbidden	5–383
VII Motor Vehicles on Hire-Purchase or Conditional Sale	5–384

INTRODUCTION

5–01 THE most important Act on the subject of "consumer credit" is the Consumer Credit Act 1974, and references in this chapter are, unless the context otherwise requires, references to provisions of that Act.

5–02 The Act applies to the whole of the United Kingdom. Many of its provisions, phrased initially in the terminology of English law, are followed by adaptations for Scotland and Northern Ireland; two examples are:

(a) in section 1 and elsewhere in the Act there is the expression "bailment or (in Scotland) hiring of goods";

(b) section 37 refers to the possibility that the holder of a licence may be "adjudged bankrupt", and section 38 provides that in the application of section 37 to Scotland the phrase "has his estate sequestrated" is to be substituted.

The Act is a long one, consisting of 193 sections and five **5–03** Schedules, but it is by no means complete in itself. It is in wide terms and is intended as a framework of legal principles. Practical and specific details are to be looked for in regulations and orders made by the Secretary of State for Trade and Industry and amended by him from time to time (s. 182).

Only a few of the provisions of the Act came into operation on **5–04** the date of its passing (July 31, 1974). For the remainder there were "appointed days", fixed by commencement orders in the form of statutory instruments made over the next 11 years, the final one being the Consumer Credit Act 1974 (Commencement No. 9) Order 1984 (S.I. 1984 No. 436), which, along with the Consumer Credit Act 1974 (Commencement No. 8) Order 1983 (S.I. 1983 No. 1551), had the effect of bringing into operation on May 15, 1985, most of the provisions of the Act which had not been brought into force at any earlier date. The Consumer Credit Act 1974 (Commencement No. 10) Order 1989 (S.I. 1989 No. 1128) had an amending effect: it related to licensing requirements for consumer credit business carried on by individuals and which only did business resulting in the making of agreements for credit not exceeding £30 which had previously been exempt by the Consumer Credit (Commencement No. 2) Order (S.I. 1977 No. 325). Exceptionally there are certain provisions in the Act which the Government has proposed not to bring into force because there is thought to be no need for them to be implemented, *e.g.* in section 53 ("Duty to display information") the power to make regulations is proposed not to be exercised.

As a preliminary to the outline of the Act, it is appropriate to **5–05** look briefly at:

(a) the general meaning of the term "consumer credit";

(b) the general aim of the Act;

(c) the Crowther Report; and
(d) the structure of the Act.

(a) **General Meaning of Term "Consumer Credit"**

5–06 The phrase "consumer credit" is a comparatively recent addition to the language of the law. Its exact meaning depends on several definitions (especially the definition of "regulated agreement") in Part II of the Act (see 5–44, below). For the present it is sufficient to appreciate that the word "consumer" denotes the ordinary citizen, the "man in the street", who immediately requires something of material value for his own use, while the word "credit" indicates that that same party, being typically without sufficient capital resources of his own, obtains the necessary finance, by way of loan or some similar transaction, from another party who is in business for that very purpose.

5–07 The Act is therefore not concerned with finance for industry, but with the various forms of borrowing to which the "small man" resorts when it is impossible or inconvenient for him to pay the full cash price immediately.

5–08 Two points of practical importance are:

(i) The consumer may be an individual or may be a partnership, but the Act does not treat a registered company (however small) as a consumer.

(ii) Most of the provisions of the Act do not apply if the amount of the credit exceeds £15,000, and some of the provisions do not apply where only £50 or less is involved. However, these and other monetary limits may be increased or reduced by statutory instrument.[1]

(b) **General Aim of the Act**

5–09 In a consumer credit transaction the consumer is likely to be the weaker party, and is therefore in danger of being required to pay an excessive amount to the other party. The general aim of the Act of 1974 is to embrace within a single Act all the major principles to be applied in the protection of a consumer who enters into a consumer credit transaction.

[1] The figures £15,000 and £50 just mentioned were substituted for £5,000 and £30 respectively (which were the original amounts in the Act) by the Consumer Credit (Increase of Monetary Limits) Order 1983 (S.I. 1983 No. 1878).

The Act is part of a wider movement which has gained momentum in recent years: Parliament has increasingly considered it desirable to protect the consumer by legislation which restricts the freedom which the stronger party would otherwise have at common law to impose his own terms on the consumer. This legislation has not been confined to consumer *credit* transactions; the Act of 1974 is only one of several "consumer-protection" measures; other examples are the Trade Descriptions Act 1968, the Unfair Contract Terms Act 1977 and the Consumer Protection Act 1987. **5–10**

The principles of the Act of 1974 are, however, not solely of recent origin. Even in the nineteenth century Parliament had regarded the consumer *who was obtaining credit* as being in a particularly vulnerable position. Several statutes had been passed long before 1974 to curb the various abuses as they became apparent, but these statutes were restricted in their scope to particular types of consumer credit transactions; examples are the Pawnbrokers Acts 1872 and 1960, the Moneylenders Acts 1900 to 1927, and hire-purchase legislation consolidated by the Hire-Purchase (Scotland) Act 1965. The general terms "consumer" and "credit" were not in common use, and the legislation was piecemeal and not capable of being extended to new forms of providing credit as these came to be devised. **5–11**

Since about 1950 there had been a rapid growth in the demand for consumer credit. As is stated in the opening paragraph of the White Paper *Reform of the Law on Consumer Credit* of 1973 (Cmnd. 5427) (see 5–17, below): **5–12**

> "Without the use of credit, the standard of living of many, particularly those in the process of setting up home and starting a family, would be lower."

Legislation was seen as not having kept pace with the changed needs of society.

What the circumstances of modern life required was wide-ranging legislation which would catch all existing forms of consumer credit arrangements and also new arrangements as they came to be devised, and this is what the Act of 1974 was intended to be. It applies comprehensively to the whole field of consumer credit: whether the transaction takes the form of an agreement with a pawnbroker, or a loan by a moneylender, or a hire-purchase agreement, or any other form, it will be subject to the Act provided it falls within the general description of being a consumer credit transaction covered by the Act. **5–13**

(c) The Crowther Report

5–14 The historical background to the passing of the Act of 1974 centres on the Crowther Report *Consumer Credit*, published in 1971 (Cmnd. 4596).

The Committee on Consumer Credit had been appointed by the Government in 1968 under the chairmanship of Lord Crowther to review the then existing law and practice governing the provision of consumer credit and to make recommendations.

5–15 The Committee found it impracticable to examine the law of *consumer* credit in isolation, particularly because existing legislation, such as the Moneylenders Acts, was not confined to *consumer* transactions. The Committee therefore extended its study to cover the general legal framework within which the granting of credit and the taking of security were required to operate.

5–16 The Committee recommended the repeal of all the then existing legislation affecting credit and security (the Moneylenders Acts, the Hire-Purchase Acts, the English Bills of Sale Acts, etc.), and its replacement by two new Acts which would clearly distinguish between rules of general application and rules for *consumer* credit transactions; the two Acts would be:

(i) a Lending and Security Act, which would be of general application and which would establish a security register; and

(ii) a Consumer Sale and Loan Act, which would apply a uniform code to consumer sale and consumer loan credit agreements, strengthen the protection of the consumer and provide for proper enforcement through a licensing system operated by a Consumer Credit Commissioner.

5–17 In September 1973, the Government in its White Paper *Reform of the Law on Consumer Credit* (Cmnd. 5427) intimated its intention to give effect to almost all of the recommendations of the Crowther Committee on *consumer* credit, but to postpone any attempt at the fundamental restructuring of the general law of credit and security until consultations with those closely concerned could take place in the light of the situation which would exist after the passing of the Consumer Credit Bill.

5–18 The Bill, introduced to Parliament in November 1973, was lost on the dissolution of Parliament in February 1974. A new Bill, in substantially the same terms, was introduced by the new Government and was passed on July 31, 1974.

(d) **Structure of the Act**

The Act is intended to give effect to three main principles laid down by the Crowther Committee for the protection of consumers: 5–19

(i) the redress of bargaining inequality;
(ii) the control of trading malpractices; and
(iii) the regulation of remedies for default.

The Act is divided into 12 Parts: 5–20

I. Director General of Fair Trading;
II. Credit Agreements, Hire Agreements and Linked Transactions;
III. Licensing of Credit and Hire Businesses;
IV. Seeking Business;
V. Entry into Credit or Hire Agreements;
VI. Matters Arising During Currency of Credit or Hire Agreements;
VII. Default and Termination;
VIII. Security;
IX. Judicial Control;
X. Ancillary Credit Businesses;
XI. Enforcement of Act; and
XII. Supplemental.

Part I is preliminary, dealing with the system of administering the Act. The system is under the control of the Director General of Fair Trading. 5–21

Part II is also preliminary. It defines the basic concepts: a new terminology was required for the new system of control being introduced. 5–22

Parts III and IV are concerned with the methods by which the business activities of those who provide credit are to be regulated. The methods are a licensing system (Part III of the Act) and control of advertisements and other ways in which those providing credit seek customers (Part IV of the Act). These two Parts together may be regarded as dealing with "trading control", because they control the conduct of the trader's business. 5–23

Then come five Parts which deal with what may be called "agreement control", because they regulate individual credit or hire agreements. Part V is concerned with the making of the agreement, Part VI with matters arising during the currency of the agreement, Part VII with default by the consumer and with the 5–24 termination of the agreement generally, Part VIII with security granted by the consumer or by someone else on his behalf, and Part IX with control exercised by the courts over the agreement.

5–25 The remaining three Parts of the Act extend or supplement the earlier Parts. Part X extends Parts III and IV to "ancillary credit businesses" (*e.g.* "credit brokerage" and "debt-collecting"). Part XI deals with enforcement of the Act, and Part XII consists of supplementary provisions (including the comprehensive definition section—section 189—which sets out or refers to the 117 definitions occurring in the Act).

5–26 The Act also has five Schedules. Of these Schedule 2 is particularly interesting: it sets out examples of the use of the new terminology, and so is of considerable assistance in bridging the gap between the theoretical language used in the Act and the types of agreement which are commonly met with in practice. For instance, if one is still puzzled by the terms "credit-broker" and "credit brokerage" after reading the definitions of these terms in sections 189 and 145 respectively, a reference to Schedule 2 can be illuminating: Example 2 in that Schedule explains that a shopkeeper who introduces one of his customers to a finance company with whom the shopkeeper has a business relationship is a credit-broker.

5–27 In the light of the structure of the Act as outlined above, this chapter may be conveniently divided into:

I. Administration (Part I of the Act);
II. Definitions (Part II of the Act);
III. Trading control (Parts III and IV of the Act);
IV. Agreement control (Parts V to IX of the Act);
V. Ancillary credit businesses (Part X of the Act); and
VI. Enforcement of the Act (Part XI of the Act).

The main provisions of Part XII of the Act ("Supplemental") are incorporated into one or more of these divisions.

5–28 In addition, since the Hire-Purchase Act 1964 is not wholly repealed by the Act of 1974, a brief account is given of its provisions on:

VII. Motor vehicles on hire-purchase or conditional sale.

I ADMINISTRATION

5–29 Administration of the Act is dealt with mainly by Part I of the Act, which is headed "Director General of Fair Trading".

All the provisions of Part I of the Act came into force on the date when the Act was passed (July 31, 1974). 5–30

The office of Director General of Fair Trading was already in existence when the Act was passed. It had been established by the Fair Trading Act 1973 to exercise functions in three main fields—monopolies and mergers, restrictive trade practices and consumer protection. The holder of the office is appointed by the Secretary of State for Trade and Industry for a period of not more than five years at a time. 5–31

The general functions of the Director General of Fair Trading under the Act of 1974 fall into three groups: 5–32

(a) to administer the licensing system set up by the Act, including the issue, renewal, variation, suspension and revocation of licences;

(b) to superintend the working and enforcement of the Act and the regulations made under it; and

(c) to keep under review and from time to time advise the Secretary of State about social and commercial developments in the United Kingdom and elsewhere relating to the provision of credit or hiring of goods to individuals (s. 1).

Additional functions may be conferred on the Director by the Secretary of State (s. 2). 5–33

The Director's functions are partly executive, partly administrative and partly judicial. In the exercise of his judicial functions the Director is regarded as a "Schedule 1 tribunal" for the purposes of the Tribunals and Inquiries Act 1992 (replacing the Tribunals and Inquiries Act 1971) (s. 3); he therefore comes under the supervision of the Council on Tribunals, and he must give reasons for his decisions. 5–34

The Director must arrange for the dissemination of information and advice to the public about the operation of the Act (s. 4). In accordance with this provision the Office of Fair Trading has published many booklets and leaflets for guidance of laymen and professional bodies on different aspects of the Act. 5–35

The Director makes an annual report to the Secretary of State on all his activities, including directions given to him by the Secretary of State under the Act of 1974. The report is laid before Parliament and published in such manner as the Secretary of State may consider appropriate (Fair Trading Act 1973, s. 125 and 1974 Act, s. 5). 5–36

5–37 Applications to the Director (*e.g.* for the issue of a licence) must be in writing, and in such form, and accompanied by such particulars, as the Director may specify by general notice, and must be accompanied by the specified fee. The Director may require the applicant to publish details of his application (s. 6).

5–38 It is an offence for persons knowingly or recklessly to give to the Director information which, in a material particular, is false or misleading (s. 7). Further details on this aspect of the Act are set out in Schedule 1.

II DEFINITIONS

5–39 The terms for which definitions have been included in the Act fall into two categories: first there are terms which would be virtually meaningless unless they were defined, *e.g.* the term "debtor-creditor-supplier agreement"; they are part of the new language adopted, if not actually invented, for the purposes of the Act; secondly, there are terms which are part of normal English, but for which the Act supplies a precise definition not always coinciding with ordinary usage, *e.g.* the terms "business", "credit", and "individual".

5–40 The scheme followed in the Act in relation to definitions is that (a) *all* terms defined in the Act are listed in the definition section—section 189 in Part XII ("Supplemental")—from which one may either immediately obtain the definition or be referred to another section of the Act where the definition is to be found, and (b) terms in the first category—the special language of the Act—are also defined at the point in the Act where they are first used; *e.g.* the term "ancillary credit business" is defined in section 145, the first section in Part X ("Ancillary Credit Businesses").

5–41 Before the Act was passed, there was no terminology in ordinary English which suitably described all the various forms of credit which the Act seeks to cover: a completely new set of terms had to be found and given precise definitions before any statutory provisions could be proceeded with. Therefore most of the new terminology is set out as a preliminary to the operative parts of the Act and depends on definitions in sections 8 to 20 which comprise Part II of the Act. These are the definitions which fix the scope of the Act.

5–42 Statutory definitions are not always easily understood, and this is especially so where the statutory provision is defining a term which has itself no recognisable meaning in ordinary usage. Schedule 2 to the Act, however, gives some assistance by setting out 24 "Examples" illustrating the use of the Act's terminology. The Examples are not exhaustive, and in the case of conflict between the Schedule and any other provision of the Act, the other provision prevails. The Secretary of State may by subordinate legislation amend the Schedule by adding further Examples or in any other way (s. 188).

A further complication is that the definitions about to be **5–43** considered are not self-explanatory but include terms which themselves require to be defined and the meaning of which will be found set out in another provision of the Act. To overcome this difficulty, one must proceed step by step through each definition, exploring each term used in it, before passing on to the next definition in the list.

(a) "Regulated Agreement"

The definition which is, as it were, the peg on which the provisions **5–44** of the Act are made to hang is that of "regulated agreement". The answer to the question "What is the scope of the Act?" is: "The Act applies to regulated agreements". The next question is obvious: "What is a regulated agreement?"

A "regulated agreement" means "a consumer credit agreement, **5–45** or consumer hire agreement, other than an exempt agreement" (s. 189(1)). There are three terms in this definition which themselves require to be defined:

(i) "consumer credit agreement";
(ii) "consumer hire agreement"; and
(iii) "exempt agreement."

A more detailed account of these terms than is attempted here would reveal some circularity: in section 16 the term "exempt agreement" is explained as including certain "debtor-creditor-supplier" agreements and certain "debtor-creditor" agreements, and these two latter terms are defined in sections 12 and 13 respectively as being "*regulated* consumer credit agreements" with certain characteristics.

(i) *"Consumer Credit Agreement"*

5–46 A "consumer credit agreement" is "a personal credit agreement by which the creditor provides the debtor with credit not exceeding £15,000"[2] (s. 8(2)). In common with other monetary limits in the Act the figure of £15,000 may be increased or reduced by statutory instrument (s. 181). One must now explore the terms "personal credit agreement" and "credit".

5–47 A "personal credit agreement" is "an agreement between an individual ('the debtor') and any other person ('the creditor') by which the creditor provides the debtor with credit of any amount" (s. 8(1)). "Individual" is defined as including "a partnership or other unincorporated body of persons not consisting entirely of bodies corporate" (s. 189(1)).

5–48 "Credit" includes "a cash loan, and any other form of financial accommodation" (s. 9(1)), but an item entering into the "total charge for credit" is not treated as credit even though time is allowed for its payment (s. 9(4)).

5–49 "Total charge for credit" means "a sum calculated in accordance with regulations under section 20(1)" (s. 189(1)). The principal regulations in force are the Consumer Credit (Total Charge for Credit) Regulations 1980 (S.I. 1980 No. 51). The Regulations prescribe what items (interest charges and other charges affecting the cost of borrowing) are to be treated as entering into the total charge for credit, and the method of calculating the rate of the total charge for credit, *i.e.* the true annual percentage rate ("APR"), which enables consumers to compare the cost of borrowing from one lender with the cost of borrowing from another. The simplest way of finding the APR is to use the "Consumer Credit Tables", specially prepared mathematical tables sold in 15 parts by HMSO.

5–50 A simple example may now be taken from Schedule 2:

"*Facts*. E agrees to sell to F (an individual) an item of furniture in return for 24 monthly instalments of £10 payable in arrears. The property in the goods [*i.e.* the ownership of them] passes to F immediately.

Analysis. This is a credit-sale agreement. . . . The credit provided amounts to £240 less the amount which, according to regulations

[2] £15,000 substituted for £5,000 by Consumer Credit (Increase of Monetary Limits) Order 1983 (S.I. 1983 No. 1878).

made under section 20(1), constitutes the total charge for credit. . . . Accordingly the agreement falls within section 8(2) and is a consumer credit agreement" (Example 5).

(ii) *"Consumer Hire Agreement"*

A "consumer hire agreement" is "an agreement made by a person with an individual (the 'hirer') for the hiring of goods to the hirer, being an agreement which— **5–51**

(*a*) is not a hire-purchase agreement, and

(*b*) is capable of subsisting for more than three months, and

(*c*) does not require the hirer to make payments exceeding £15,000"[3] (s. 15(1)).

The provision of the Act relating to the monetary limit and the definition of the term "individual" for the purposes of the Act have already been noted. What requires to be explored is the distinction between a "consumer hire agreement" and a "hire-purchase agreement" implied in condition (*a*). What, then, is the Act's definition of "hire-purchase agreement"? **5–52**

A "hire-purchase agreement" means "an agreement, other than a conditional sale agreement, under which— **5–53**

(*a*) goods are hired in return for periodical payments by the person to whom they are hired, and

(*b*) the property in the goods will pass to that person if the terms of the agreement are complied with and one or more of the following occurs—

(i) the exercise of an option to purchase by that person,

(ii) the doing of any other specified act by any party to the agreement,

(iii) the happening of any other specified event" (s. 189(1)).

Put shortly (and with some sacrifice of accuracy) a hire-purchase agreement is an agreement for the hire of goods with an option (but no obligation) to purchase them.

A "conditional sale agreement", on the other hand, commits the buyer to buying as well as the seller to selling: there is to be a sale but the ownership of the goods is to remain with the seller until some condition is fulfilled. The Act's definition of a "conditional **5–54**

---

[3] £15,000 substituted for £5,000 by Consumer Credit (Increase of Monetary Limits) Order 1983 (S.I. 1983 No. 1878).

sale agreement" is "an agreement for the sale of goods or land under which the purchase price or part of it is payable by instalments, and the property in the goods or land is to remain in the seller (notwithstanding that the buyer is to be in possession of the goods or land) until such conditions as to the payment of instalments or otherwise as may be specified in the agreement are fulfilled" (s. 189(1)).

5–55 Both hire-purchase agreements and conditional sale agreements are, of course, within the scope of the Act, but they form part of the first leg of the definition of "regulated agreement" (*i.e.* they are consumer *credit* agreements, not consumer *hire* agreements). Typical of the consumer hire agreements forming the second leg of the definition of "regulated agreement" are machinery or equipment leases.

5–56 An illustration based on Example 20 in Schedule 2 is:

Facts. K agrees with L (an individual) to let out goods on hire to L for three years at £6,000 a year, payable quarterly. The agreement contains no provision for the passing of the property in the goods to L.

Analysis. This is not a hire-purchase agreement, because it does not satisfy paragraph (*b*) in the definition of "hire-purchase agreement", and it is capable of lasting for more than three months. Paragraphs (*a*) and (*b*) in the definition of "consumer hire agreement" are therefore satisfied. Paragraph (*c*), however, is not satisfied, because the payments will exceed £15,000. So the agreement is not a consumer hire agreement, though it would have been such if the hire charge had been, say, £4,000.

5–57 Where by a hire agreement the hirer agrees to pay VAT and the result is that payments to be made under the agreement exceed the upper limit of (at present) £15,000, the hire agreement does not fall within the definition of "consumer hire agreement":

Apollo Leasing Ltd v. Scott, 1984 S.L.T. (Sh.Ct.) 90: A "leasing agreement" for the hiring of video equipment by A. Ltd to S. provided for rental payments of a total sum of £4,395 "plus VAT". At the time of the agreement the upper limit under section 15(1) of the Act was £5,000 and the rate of VAT was 15 per cent. The result would have been that the total payments to be made by S. would have been £5,055.

A. Ltd brought an action of payment for the recovery of unpaid rental charges. S. contended that the agreement was a consumer hire agreement and unenforceable under section 40 of the Act (which relates to enforcement of agreements made by unlicensed traders—see 5–148, below). A. Ltd submitted that the agreement was not a consumer hire agreement since VAT fell to be taken into account in calculating the total payments payable for the purposes of the limit in section 15(1).

Held by Sheriff Principal P. I. Caplan, affirming the decision of Sheriff D. B. Smith, that the agreement was not a consumer hire agreement since at the time of executing the agreement the minimum total sum to be paid by S. exceeded £5,000, VAT being very much part of the contractual consideration payable by him. The agreement was therefore enforceable.

(iii) *"Exempt Agreement"*

"Exempt agreement" means "an agreement specified in or under section 16" (s. 189(1)). The terms "regulated agreement" and "exempt agreement" are opposites of one another. Exempt agreements are not within the scope of the Act at all except that sections 137 to 140 ("extortionate credit bargains") are applicable to them as well as to regulated agreements (s. 140). **5–58**

The statutory instrument now in force under section 16 is the Consumer Credit (Exempt Agreements) Order 1989 (S.I. 1989 No. 869), which revoked and consolidated several earlier orders and which has in its turn been amended many times. **5–59**

There are six categories of exemption provided for by section 16 when taken along with these Orders, *e.g.*: **5–60**

1. certain consumer credit agreements where the creditor is a local authority, a building society or a bank *and* the agreement is secured by a heritable security;
2. certain consumer credit agreements where the creditor is a *specified* insurance company, friendly society, organisation of employers or organisation of workers, charity, land improvement company, body corporate named in a public general Act or in an order made under provisions of the Housing (Scotland) Act 1987, *and* the agreement is secured by a heritable security; the list of specified bodies is to be found in a schedule to the principal Order, as amended;
3. certain consumer credit agreements where the number of payments to be made by the debtor does not exceed the number specified in an order (at present four);

4. certain consumer agreements where the rate of the total charge for credit does not exceed the specified rate (at present the higher of 13 per cent and 1 per cent above the highest of the banks' base rates 28 days before the making of the agreement);

5. certain consumer credit agreements where the agreement has a connection with a country outside the United Kingdom; and

6. consumer hire agreements of a description specified in an order where the owner is a gas, electricity or water authority and the subject of the agreement is a meter or metering equipment to be used in connection with the supply of gas, electricity or water, as the case may be.

5–61 It may be useful to list the essentials of a "regulated agreement" which have been gathered from the definitions so far considered. The agreement will be:

(i) a consumer credit agreement or a consumer hire agreement;

(ii) between two parties, of whom one (the creditor in a consumer credit agreement or the owner in a consumer hire agreement) may be a person of any status (individual, partnership or company) and the other (the debtor in a consumer credit agreement or the hirer in a consumer hire agreement) must be an "individual" (a term so defined as to include a partnership, but not a company, however small);

(iii) for credit or for hire charges not exceeding £15,000 and

(iv) not an exempt agreement.

(b) **The Subdivisions of Regulated Consumer Credit Agreements**

5–62 The first leg of the definition of "regulated agreement" requires further consideration, because the Act makes three subdivisions of consumer credit agreements. There is only one form of consumer *hire* agreement but a consumer *credit* agreement may take one of a great variety of forms. The classification is based on the Crowther Report.

5–63 The three subdivisions referred to hinge on the distinction between each of the following pairs:

(i) "running-account credit" and "fixed-sum credit";

(ii) "restricted-use credit" and "unrestricted-use credit"; and

(iii) "debtor-creditor-supplier agreements" and "debtor-creditor agreements",

(i) *"Running-Account Credit" and "Fixed-Sum Credit"*

It is easiest to approach the statutory definitions of these two terms with a few simple instances in mind. Examples of running-account credit are bank overdrafts and shop budget accounts. Examples of fixed-sum credit are personal and bank loans, pawnbrokers' loans, and hire-purchase, credit sale and conditional sale agreements. **5–64**

The distinction between the two types of credit is made by defining running-account credit; the definition of fixed-sum credit is then relatively easy, because fixed-sum credit is in effect any credit other than running-account credit. **5–65**

"Running-account credit" is defined as "a facility under a personal credit agreement whereby the debtor is enabled to receive from time to time (whether in his own person, or by another person) from the creditor or a third party cash, goods and services (or any of them) to an amount or value such that, taking into account payments made by or to the credit of the debtor, the credit limit (if any) is not at any time exceeded" (s. 10(1)(a)). **5–66**

"Fixed-sum credit" is defined as "any other facility under a personal credit agreement whereby the debtor is enabled to receive credit (whether in one amount or by instalments)" (s. 10(1)(b)). **5–67**

Some further points require to be noted concerning the definition of "running-account credit". **5–68**

The term "credit-limit" used in that definition means the maximum debit balance which, under the agreement, is allowed to stand on the account; any term of the agreement allowing the maximum to be exceeded merely temporarily is disregarded for this purpose (s. 10(2)). From the definition of "regulated agreement" it follows that if the credit limit in a running-account credit is fixed above £15,000, the agreement will not be within the scope of the Act. A credit limit fixed at £15,000 or any lower figure brings the agreement within the scope of the Act. **5–69**

There is an obvious need for some anti-avoidance provisions; otherwise a creditor could place himself beyond the reach of the Act by simply having no fixed credit limit expressed in the credit agreement or by fixing an artificially high credit limit of, say, £30,000 in the knowledge that the credit would not be likely to extend beyond, say, £10,000. Therefore the Act provides that a **5–70** credit facility which is without limit or which has a limit in excess of £15,000[4] will nevertheless be governed by the Act—

(i) if the debtor is not enabled to draw more than £15,000 credit at any one time; or

(ii) if the rate of the total charge for credit increases, or any other condition favouring the creditor comes into operation, on a rise of the debit balance above a given amount of £15,000 or less; or

(iii) at the time of the making of the agreement it is probable, having regard to the terms of the agreement and any other relevant considerations, that the debit balance will not at any time rise above £15,000 (s. 10(3)(b)).

5–71 In connection with the distinction between running-account credit and fixed-sum credit a specific provision of the Act concerning a hire-purchase agreement should be noted: the person by whom the goods are hired out to an individual under a hire-purchase agreement is to be taken as providing the individual with fixed-sum credit to finance the transaction of an amount equal to the full price of the goods less the total of the deposit (if any) and the total charge for credit (s. 9(3)). An item entering into the total charge for credit is not treated as credit even though time is allowed for its payment (s. 9(4)).

5–72 Some examples may now be looked at as illustrations of the distinction; all are based on the examples in Schedule 2:

5–73 1. *Facts:* A agrees to make a cash loan to B of £4,500 in nine monthly instalments of £500.

Analysis: This falls within section 10(1)(b) and is fixed-sum credit amounting to £4,500 (Example 9).

5–74 2. *Facts:* A issues to B a credit-card for use in obtaining cash on credit from A. The credit limit is £300. On one occasion B uses the credit-card in a way which increases his debit balance with A to £400. A writes to B agreeing to allow the excess on that occasion only, but stating that it must be paid off within one month.

Analysis: In exceeding his credit limit B, by implication, requests A to allow him a temporary excess, and A grants this implied request. The agreement to allow the excess varies the original agreement by adding a new term, but under section 10(2) the new term is disregarded in arriving at the credit limit (Example 22).

---

[4] £15,000 substituted for £5,000 by Consumer Credit (Increase of Monetary Limits) Order 1983 (S.I. 1983 No. 1878).

3. *Facts:* The G Bank grants H an unlimited overdraft, with an increased rate of interest on so much of any debit balance as exceeds £2,000. **5–75**

Analysis: Although the overdraft purports to be unlimited, the stipulation for increased interest above £2,000 brings the agreement within section 10(3)(b)(ii) and it is a consumer credit agreement (Example 6).

4. *Facts:* J is an individual who owns a small shop which usually carries a stock worth about £1,000. K makes a stocking agreement under which he undertakes to provide on short-term credit the stock needed from time to time by J without any specified limit. **5–76**

Analysis: Although the agreement appears to provide unlimited credit, it is probable, having regard to the stock usually carried by J, that his indebtedness to K will not at any time rise above £15,000. Accordingly the agreement falls within section 10(3)(b)(iii) and is a consumer credit agreement (Example 7).

5. *Facts:* C agrees to hire goods to D in return for periodical payments. The agreement provides for the property in the goods to pass to D on payment of a total of £7,500 and the exercise by D of an option to purchase. The sum of £7,500 includes a down-payment of £1,000. It also includes an amount which, according to the Consumer Credit (Total Charge for Credit) Regulations 1980, constitutes a total charge for credit of £1,500. **5–77**

Analysis: This is a hire-purchase agreement with a deposit of £1,000 and a total price of £7,500. By section 9(3), it is taken to provide credit amounting to £7,500–(£1,500 + £1,000), which equals £5,000. Under section 8(2), the agreement is therefore a consumer credit agreement, and under section 9(3) it is a credit agreement for fixed-sum credit (Example 10).

6. *Facts:* H agrees with J to open a loan account in J's name on which the debit balance is not to exceed £17,000. Interest is to be payable in advance on this sum, with provision for yearly adjustments. H is entitled to debit the account with interest, a "setting-up" charge, and other charges. Before J has an opportunity to draw on the account it is initially debited with £2,250 for advance interest and other charges. **5–78**

Analysis: This is a running-account credit agreement with a credit limit of £17,000. By section 9(4), however, the initial debit of £2,250 is not to be treated as credit even though time is allowed for its payment. Although the credit limit of £17,000 exceeds the amount (£15,000) specified in section 8(2) as the maximum for a consumer credit agreement, the agreement is caught by section 10(3)(b)(i), because at the beginning J. can effectively draw as credit no more than £14,750. The agreement is therefore a consumer credit agreement (Example 19).

(ii) *"Restricted-Use Credit" and "Unrestricted-Use Credit"*

5–79 Easily recognisable instances to have in mind here are—for restricted-use credit, hire-purchase, credit sale and conditional sale agreements and shop budget accounts, and for unrestricted-use credit, overdraft facilities, cheque cards and loans of money the use of which is at the free disposal of the borrower.

5–80 With this pair of terms again only the first is specifically defined, and the second—"unrestricted-use credit"—is then in effect declared to be the opposite of "restricted-use credit".

5–81 A "restricted-use credit agreement" is defined as "a regulated consumer credit agreement—

(*a*) to finance a transaction between the debtor and the creditor, whether forming part of that agreement or not, or

(*b*) to finance a transaction between the debtor and a person (the 'supplier') other than the creditor, or

(*c*) to refinance any existing indebtedness of the debtor's, whether to the creditor or another person" (s. 11(1)).

5–82 An "unrestricted-use credit agreement" is defined as "a regulated consumer credit agreement not falling within section 11(1)" (s. 11(2)).

5–83 An agreement is not considered as a "restricted-use credit agreement" if the credit is in fact provided in such a way as to leave the debtor free to use it as he chooses (even though certain uses would be contrary to agreement) (s.11(3)).

5–84 The following are illustrative examples based on the examples in Schedule 2:

5–85 1. *Facts:* The N Bank agrees to lend O £7,000 to buy a car from P. To make sure the loan is used as intended, the N Bank stipulates that the money must be paid by it direct to P.

Analysis: The agreement is a consumer credit agreement because of section 8(2). Since it falls within section 11(1)(b), it is a restricted-use credit agreement, P being the supplier. If the N Bank had not stipulated for direct payment to the supplier, section 11(3) would have operated and made the agreement into one for unrestricted-use credit (Example 12).

2. *Facts:* Q, a debt-adjuster, agrees to pay off debts owed by R to various moneylenders. For this purpose the agreement provides for the making of a loan by Q to R in return for R's agreeing to repay the loan by instalments with interest. The loan money is not paid over to R but retained by Q and used to pay off the moneylenders. **5–86**

Analysis: This is an agreement to refinance existing indebtedness of the debtor's, and if the loan by Q does not exceed £15,000 is a restricted-use credit agreement falling within section 11(1)(c) (Example 13).

3. *Facts:* The P bank decides to issue cheque cards to its customers under a scheme whereby the bank undertakes to honour cheques of up to £100 in every case where the payee has taken the cheque in reliance on the cheque card, whether the customer has funds in his account or not. The bank issues a cheque card to Q, who uses it to pay by cheque for goods costing £70 bought by Q from R, a major retailer. At the time, Q has £500 in his account at the P Bank. **5–87**

Analysis: The agreement under which the cheque card is issued to Q is a consumer credit agreement because Q is free to draw out his whole balance and then use the cheque card, in which case the bank has bound itself to honour the cheque. In other words the cheque card agreement provides Q with credit, whether he avails himself of it or not. It is an unrestricted-use credit agreement (Example 21).

(iii) *"Debtor-Creditor-Supplier Agreements" and "Debtor-Creditor Agreements"*

The distinction between the two members of this third pair of terms may be more easily grasped if the terms used by the Crowther Committee are substituted, namely "connected loans" and "unconnected loans", a connected loan being one made by the supplier himself or by some other person with whom he has some arrangement, and an unconnected loan being one made by an independent lender who is not himself involved in the transaction for which the debtor needs the money. Where there is a connected loan, the lender and the seller are the same person or are engaged in a joint venture to their mutual advantage, and the two transactions of loan and sale cannot be treated in isolation as they may be in the case of an unconnected loan. **5–88**

5–89 The term used in the Act for a connected loan—"debtor-creditor-supplier agreement"—suggests at first sight that three parties are involved. It is clear from the last paragraph that this is not necessarily so: the creditor and the supplier may very well be the same person; they will at least have some arrangements with one another.

5–90 A "debtor-creditor-supplier agreement" is defined as "a regulated consumer credit agreement being—

(*a*) a restricted-use credit agreement which falls within section 11(1)(a), or

(*b*) a restricted-use credit agreement which falls within section 11(1)(b) and is made by the creditor under pre-existing arrangements, or in contemplation of future arrangements, between himself and the supplier, or

(*c*) an unrestricted-use credit agreement which is made by the creditor under pre-existing arrangements between himself and a person (the 'supplier') other than the debtor in the knowledge that the credit is to be used to finance a transaction between the debtor and the supplier" (s. 12).

5–91 Section 13 has a definition of similar length for a "debtor-creditor agreement", the effect of which simply is that a debtor-creditor agreement is any regulated consumer credit agreement other than a debtor-creditor-supplier agreement. (Typical instances of debtor-creditor agreements are normal bank loans and overdrafts, loans by moneylenders, and personal loans where there is no actual or contemplated arrangement between lender and supplier.)

5–92 It is appropriate, therefore, to concentrate on the definition of "debtor-creditor-supplier agreement" set out in section 12.

5–93 The use of the word "supplier" is liable to cause confusion, because it is defined in two different ways: " 'supplier' has the meaning given by section 11(1)(b) or 12(c) . . . or, in relation to an agreement falling within section 11(1)(a), means the creditor . . . " (s. 189(1)). Looking back to section 11(1)(b) and 12(c), one finds the word "supplier" appearing in brackets: in section 11(1)(b) "supplier" denotes a person other than the creditor; in section 12(c) "supplier" denotes a person other than the debtor. The result is that in relation to both these provisions three parties are involved—the creditor, the debtor and the supplier; the situation is truly a tripartite one. Looking now to section 11(1)(a), one finds that that provision relates to a restricted-use credit agreement financing a transaction between the debtor and the creditor (whether forming part of that agreement or not); here there are only two parties—the debtor and the creditor—and by definition in this situation the "supplier" is the creditor. This emphasises the point already mentioned that in a "debtor-creditor-supplier agreement" there are not necessarily three parties: there may be only two—the debtor and the creditor (also called the "supplier").

It is now possible to proceed to a clearer understanding of the definition of "debtor-creditor-supplier agreement" in section 12. The definition has three limbs. **5–94**

Limb (a) is "a restricted-use credit agreement which falls within section 11(1)(a)". This covers those agreements in which creditor and supplier are the same person: simple examples are the sale of goods or the supply of services by creditor to debtor on credit. Limb (a) also covers the common form of hire-purchase, in which the finance house buys the goods from a dealer and then lets them on hire-purchase to the customer, because the finance house (not the dealer) is the "supplier" in this situation, and so creditor and supplier are the same person. **5–95**

Limb (b) is "a restricted-use credit agreement which falls within section 11(1)(b) and is made by the creditor under pre-existing arrangements, or in contemplation of future arrangements, between himself and the supplier". A three-party agreement is involved here, the "supplier" being, as specially defined in section 11(1)(b), a person other than the creditor. The credit will necessarily take the form of a loan, *e.g.* a loan paid by a finance house (the creditor) to a motor-dealer (the supplier) at the request of the person buying a car (the debtor). The agreement must have been made "under pre-existing arrangements" *or* "in contemplation of future arrangements" between the creditor and the supplier. Guidance on the interpretation of these two phrases is given in section 187 of the Act; *e.g.* an agreement is to be treated as entered into under pre-existing arrangements if it is entered into "in accordance with, or in furtherance of, arrangements previously made" between creditor and supplier or their associates (s. 187(1)), and where the creditor is an associate of the supplier's, the agreement is treated, unless the contrary is proved, as entered into under pre-existing arrangements between creditor and supplier (s. 187(5)). The term "associate" is defined in section 184: it **5–96** covers, in the case of individuals, husband or wife and specified relatives while in the case of bodies corporate it depends on the element of control.

5–97 Limb (c) is "an unrestricted-use credit agreement which is made by the creditor under pre-existing arrangements between himself and a person (the 'supplier') other than the debtor in the knowledge that the credit is to be used to finance a transaction between the debtor and the supplier". As in limb (b), there are three parties. An instance would be where, as the result of an arrangement previously made between a finance house and a dealer, a customer of the dealer's is directed to the finance house by the dealer and obtains a loan which theoretically is at his free disposal but which, to the knowledge of the finance house, is to be used by him to purchase goods from the dealer. The arrangement must be a pre-existing one: mere "contemplation of future arrangements" is not sufficient to bring an *unrestricted-use* credit agreement within the definition of debtor-creditor-supplier agreement: this is the point of distinction between limb (b) and limb (c).

5–98 Finally, Example 8 in Schedule 2 may be referred to as illustrating the key position held by the phrase "pre-existing arrangements" in the distinction between "debtor-creditor-supplier agreements" and "debtor-creditor agreements":

Facts: U, a moneylender, lends £500 to V knowing that V intends to use it to buy office equipment from W. W introduced V to U, it being his practice to introduce customers needing finance to him. Sometimes U gives W a commission for this and sometimes not. U pays £500 direct to V.

Analysis: At first sight this falls under section 11(1)(b) (a restricted-use credit agreement to finance a transaction between the debtor (V) and a supplier (W, a person other than the creditor)). However, section 11(3) prevents this from being so by providing that if the credit is in fact provided in such a way as to leave the debtor free to use it as he chooses, the agreement will not be a restricted-use agreement. Here U pays the £500 direct to V, and so V would be free to use the credit as he chose. The agreement is therefore an unrestricted-use credit agreement and so, if it is to be a debtor-creditor-supplier agreement, it must satisfy section 12(c), *i.e.* it must have been made by the creditor (U) under pre-existing arrangements between himself and the supplier (W) in the knowledge that the credit was to be used to finance the transaction between V and W. The question then arises under section 187(1) of whether the agreement can be taken to have been entered into "in accordance with, or in furtherance of arrangements previously made" between U and W. If it cannot be so treated it will be a debtor-creditor agreement.

(c) "Credit-Token Agreement"

A "credit-token agreement" is "a regulated agreement for the provision of credit in connection with the use of a credit-token" (s. 14(2)). The term "credit-token" was invented for the purposes of the Act, and is defined in section 14(1). Some examples help to make the definition more readily understood. Examples of credit-tokens are: a credit card issued by a shop authorising the holder to purchase goods from the shop and have his account debited with the price on credit terms; a bank credit card enabling the holder to draw cash from a bank or to buy goods from a third party such as a shop having an arrangement with the bank to accept the card; and a card enabling the holder to draw cash from a machine. **5–99**

Section 14(1) provides that a credit-token is "a card, check, voucher, coupon, stamp, form, booklet or other document or thing given to an individual by a person carrying on a consumer credit business, who undertakes— **5–100**

(*a*) that on the production of it (whether or not some other action is also required) he will supply cash, goods and services (or any of them) on credit, or

(*b*) that where, on the production of it to a third party (whether or not any other action is also required), the third party supplies cash, goods and services (or any of them), he will pay the third party for them (whether or not deducting any discount or commission), in return for payment to him by the individual".

For the purposes of that definition, use of an object to operate a machine provided by the person giving the object or a third party is to be treated as the production of the object to him (s. 14(4)). Thus a bank card issued by a bank to enable a customer to obtain cash from an automatic teller is a credit-token if (but only if) the bank has agreed to grant overdraft facilities to the customer. **5–101**

The definition of "credit-token" was considered by the court in *Elliott v. Director General of Fair Trading* [1980] 1 W.L.R. 977 (DC): **5–102**

E. had been convicted of contravening section 51 of the Act which provides that it is an offence to give a person a credit-token if he has not asked for it.

The document which E. had sent to selected members of the public had the appearance of a plastic card like a bank credit card. On its face it had the words "The E. Account" and a series of computer figures, and on the reverse there was a box marked "Signature", along with the statements: "1. This credit card is valid for immediate use. 2. The sole requirement is your signature and means of identification. 3. Credit is immediately available if you have a bank account". In fact these statements were untrue since the production of the card did not entitle the customer to a supply of goods on credit but only to apply for a credit card when he had signed an agreement.

The argument for E. was that the word "undertakes" in the definition was not satisfied in this case because other matters had to be carried out before credit could be obtained.

The court, however, held that the word "undertakes" did not mean that a contractual agreement had to exist; by the wording on the card, E. did "undertake" that, on the production of the card, cash or goods would be supplied; the fact that none of the statements was true did not prevent the card from being what it purported to be—a credit-token. In any event the words "whether or not some other action is also required" in section 14(1) brought the card within the definition.

E.'s appeal against conviction therefore failed.

This case has attracted considerable academic criticism.

5–103 It should be noted that a cheque card is *not* a credit-token. A cheque card is an undertaking by a bank to suppliers generally to whom the card is produced that it will honour cheques drawn by its customer up to the limit stated on the card; the bank, in paying the supplier, is not paying for the goods, but is honouring its guarantee of payment of the cheque.

(d) "Small Agreement"

5–104 It is not a principle of the Act that small agreements should be exempt. The principle is that the provisions of the Act apply to *all* regulated agreements, however small. There are, however, certain provisions of the Act which do not apply to small agreements; in particular, it was felt that it would be burdensome for a creditor to be required to comply with the documentation and cancellation provisions where only a small transaction was involved; so certain categories of small agreement are made exempt from the provisions of Part V of the Act ("Entry into Credit or Hire Agreements") other than the disclosure provisions (s. 74(2)).

Obviously the Act had to include a precise definition of "small agreement". By section 17(1) a "small agreement" is: **5–105**

"(*a*) a regulated consumer credit agreement for credit not exceeding £50,[5] other than a hire-purchase or conditional sale agreement; or

(*b*) a regulated consumer hire agreement which does not require the hirer to make payments exceeding £50,[5]

being an agreement which is either unsecured or secured by a guarantee or indemnity only (whether or not the guarantee or indemnity is itself secured)".

This definition is supported by anti-avoidance provisions to prevent some of the provisions of the Act from being avoided by the splitting up of what is really not a small agreement into two or more small agreements, whether made between the same parties or between associates of these parties (s. 17(3) and (4)). **5–106**

The figure £50 may be altered by statutory instrument (s. 181). **5–107**

(e) "Multiple Agreement"

There are various types of agreement which fall into more than one category; the cause of this may be *either* that the agreement is made up of different parts which belong to different categories *or* that the agreement, though indivisible, includes terms which place it in two or more categories. **5–108**

"Multiple agreement" is defined as an agreement whose "terms are such as:

(*a*) to place a part of it within one category of agreement mentioned in this Act, and another part of it within a different category of agreement so mentioned, or within a category of agreement not so mentioned, or

(*b*) to place it, or a part of it, within two or more categories of agreement so mentioned" (s. 18(1)).

---

[5] £50 substituted for £30 by the Consumer Credit (Increase of Monetary Limits) Order 1983 (S.I. 1983 No. 1878).

5–109 As an instance of an agreement falling within (*a*) one may think of an agreement part of which is for fixed-sum credit and another part of which is for running-account credit, or an agreement part of which is a consumer credit agreement and part of which is concerned with the provision of credit to a company (a category of agreement not mentioned in, and so not within the scope of, the Act).

5–110 As an instance of an agreement falling within (*b*) one may think of a credit-card agreement in which the credit card may be used to obtain cash (a debtor-creditor agreement for unrestricted-use credit) or to obtain goods (a debtor-creditor-supplier agreement for restricted-use credit).

5–111 The Act has two separate provisions for the two different types of multiple agreement.

5–112 For multiple agreements within (*a*) the provision is that each part must be treated as a separate agreement (s. 18(2)). As a result of this provision it may happen that a multiple agreement providing credit of more than £15,000 will be brought within the scope of the Act because it will require to be treated as two or more separate agreements, each below the £15,000 ceiling.

5–113 For multiple agreements within (*b*) the provision is that the agreement must be treated as an agreement in each of the categories in question (s. 18(3)).

5–114 The following is an example of the (*a*) type of multiple agreement:

Facts: F has a current account with the G Bank. Though usually in credit, the account has recently been allowed by the G Bank to become overdrawn.

Analysis: Part of the agreement, *i.e.* the part not dealing with the overdraft, falls within a category of agreement not mentioned in the Act. It is to be treated as a separate agreement from the part of the agreement relating to the overdraft—which is a debtor-creditor agreement for unrestricted-use running-account credit (Sched. 2, Example 18).

5–115 The following is an example of the (*b*) type of multiple agreement:

Facts: Under an unsecured agreement, A (Credit), an associate of the A Bank, issues to B (an individual) a credit card for use in obtaining cash on credit from A (Credit), to be paid by branches of the A Bank, or goods from suppliers who have agreed to honour credit cards issued by A (Credit). The credit limit is £50.

Analysis: This is a credit-token agreement. It is a regulated consumer credit agreement for running-account credit. Since the credit limit does not exceed £50, the agreement is a small agreement. So far as the agreement relates to goods it is a debtor-creditor-supplier agreement providing restricted-use credit, and in so far as it relates to cash it is a debtor-creditor agreement providing unrestricted-use credit. Since the whole agreement falls within several of the categories of agreement mentioned in the Act, it is to be treated as an agreement in each of those categories (Sched. 2, Example 16).

(f) "Linked Transaction"

The Act recognises that where a debtor has entered into a regulated agreement there are quite likely to be other transactions linked to that regulated agreement, and that such linked transactions also should be to some extent governed by statutory provisions for the better protection of the weaker party. The definition of "linked transaction" is such as to enable the Act to cast its net far and wide. However, the definition is long and complex, and what follows here is no more than an introduction to the definition. **5–116**

Preliminary points about the definition, which is in section 19, are: **5–117**

(i) The transaction need not be one entered into by the debtor or hirer himself: it may be entered into by a "relative" of his, and "relative" has a wide definition: it means an "associate" (s. 189(1)).

(ii) The other party to the transaction need not be the creditor: all that is necessary is that the other party should be a person other than the first party.

(iii) A transaction for the provision of security is *not* a "linked transaction".

(iv) The regulated agreement to which the "linked transaction" is connected is referred to as the "principal agreement".

The definition embraces three main categories: a transaction is a "linked transaction" if: **5–118**

(a) the transaction is entered into in compliance with a term of the principal agreement; or

(b) the principal agreement is a debtor-creditor-supplier agreement and the transaction is financed by the principal agreement; or

(c) the creditor or owner (or some other person associated with or representing him) initiated the transaction by suggesting it to the debtor or hirer or his relative, and the latter party enters into the transaction for a purpose connected with the principal agreement (*e.g.* to induce the creditor or owner to enter into the principal agreement).

5–119 Instances of each of (a), (b) and (c) will help to clarify this skeleton of the definition.

(a): The regulated agreement may include a term requiring the debtor or hirer to maintain or insure the goods; the contract for maintenance or of insurance will then be a "linked transaction" because it is entered into "in compliance with" a term in the principal agreement.

(b): The regulated agreement may be a loan to purchase goods made by a finance house under pre-existing arrangements with the supplier; the contract for the purchase of the goods will be a "linked transaction".

(c): The finance house may have suggested to the debtor that he should take out a life insurance policy. If the debtor then does so (either to induce the finance house to enter into the regulated agreement or because he wishes to cover his repayments in the event of his death), the contract of life insurance will be a "linked transaction".

5–120 Finally, Example 11 in Schedule 2 may be referred to:

Facts: X (an individual) borrows £500 from Y (Finance). As a condition of the granting of the loan, X is required—

(a) to grant a standard security on his house in favour of Y (Finance), and

(b) to take out a policy of insurance on his life with Y (Insurances), an associate of Y (Finance).

It is a term of the loan agreement that the policy should be assigned in security to Y (Finance).

Analysis: The standard security on X's house does not count as a "linked transaction" because it is a transaction for the provision of security. The taking out of the insurance policy is a linked transaction because it is taken out in compliance with a term in the principal agreement. The assignation of the policy in security is again a security transaction expressly excluded by the definition.

The only "linked transaction" is therefore the taking out of the insurance policy. If X had not been *required* by the loan agreement to take out the policy, but it had been done at the suggestion of Y (Finance) to induce them to enter into the loan agreement, it would have been a "linked transaction".

III TRADING CONTROL

The provisions on trading control are divided into two parts: **5–121**

(a) licensing of credit and hire businesses (corresponding to Part III of the Act); and

(b) seeking business (corresponding to Part IV of the Act).

(a) **Licensing of Credit and Hire Businesses**

The enforcement machinery of the Act centres on the licensing **5–122** system operated by the Director. The following is an outline of the statutory provisions on licensing:

Licensing Principles

The general principle is that a licence is required to carry on a **5–123** consumer credit business or consumer hire business, but the following do not require a licence to do so—a local authority and a body corporate empowered by a public general Act naming it to carry on the business (*e.g.* electricity boards) (s. 21). It should be noted that what is being referred to here is an exemption from the *licensing* provisions: these bodies are required to comply with the other provisions of the Act; the only *general* exemption from the provisions of the Act is that arising from "exempt agreements" as defined in section 16 (see 5–58, above).

A licence may be either a "standard" licence, or a "group" **5–124** licence (s. 22).

For a standard licence the person seeking the licence applies to **5–125** the Director; the licence names the applicant and covers the activities described in the licence; the licence lasts for the "prescribed" period, which was at first three years (Consumer Credit (Period of Standard Licence) Regulations 1975 (S.I. 1975 No. 2124)), then 10 years (Consumer Credit (Period of Standard Licence) (Amendment) Regulations 1979 (S.I. 1979 No. 796)), then 15 years (Consumer Credit (Period of Standard Licence) (Amendment) Regulations 1986 (S.I. 1986 No. 1016)) and is now five years (Consumer Credit (Period of Standard Licence) (Amendment) Regulations 1991 (S.I. 1991 No. 817)).

5–126 A group licence may be issued by the Director on an application being made to him or it may be issued by him of his own motion; it covers the persons and activities described in the licence; it lasts for such period as the Director thinks fit, which may be indefinitely. The Director may issue a group licence only if it appears to him that the public interest is better served by doing so than by requiring each person in the group concerned to apply separately for a standard licence. A group licence may exclude named persons if the Director thinks fit. Group licences so far issued include one to the Law Society of Scotland in relation to solicitors holding current practising certificates.

5–127 A licence may cover all lawful activities done in the course of the business, or it may be limited to certain types of agreement only or in any other way. A licence covers the canvassing off trade premises of debtor-creditor-supplier agreements or regulated consumer hire agreements only if the licence specifically so provides, and such a provision must not be included in a group licence (s. 23).

5–128 A standard licence authorises the licensee to carry on the business under the name or names specified in the licence, but not under any other name (s. 24), and a licence is not assignable (s. 22(2)).

5–129 To obtain a standard licence the applicant must satisfy the Director that—

(a) he is a fit person to engage in activities covered by the licence, and

(b) the name under which he applies to be licensed is not misleading or otherwise undesirable.

In deciding point (a) the Director must have regard to any circumstances appearing to him to be relevant, and in particular any evidence tending to show that the applicant (or any of his employees, agents or associates, past or present) (or, if the applicant is a body corporate, any controller of it) has—

(i) committed any offence involving fraud or other dishonesty, or violence,

(ii) contravened any statutory provision regulating the provision of credit to individuals or other transactions with individuals,

(iii) practised discrimination on grounds of sex, colour, race or ethnic or national origins in carrying on any business, or

(iv) engaged in business practices appearing to the Director to be deceitful or oppressive, or otherwise unfair or improper (s. 25). These provisions give the Director a wide discretion: he is not bound by strict rules of evidence: he is entitled to base his decision on "evidence tending to show".

An English case illustrative of section 25 is *North Wales Motor Auctions Ltd v. Secretary of State for Trade* [1981] C.C.L.R. 1, a decision of Sheen J. in the High Court: **5–130**

In 1977 Thomas applied for a consumer credit licence on behalf of N. Ltd and two other limited companies, of which he appeared to the Director to be the "controller".

In 1974 Thomas had been convicted of six offences of fraud on the Inland Revenue committed between 1965 and 1970. These had resulted in his being sentenced to two and a half years' imprisonment and a fine of £9,000 and ordered to pay costs of £3,000.

The Director refused the licence applied for, and N. Ltd appealed from the Director's decision to the Secretary of State for Trade, who upheld the Director's decision.

N. Ltd then appealed to the court on the ground that the Secretary of State was wrong in law in holding that the frauds were sufficient to justify the refusal of the licence; N. Ltd contended that it was wrong in law and a denial of natural justice and disproportionate for further punishment to be inflicted by the refusal of the licence in the absence of evidence of improper practices in relation to consumers and customers.

Held that there was evidence on which the Director could reach the conclusion, having regard to all the circumstances which appeared to him to be relevant, that N. Ltd was not a fit person to be granted a licence.

Sheen J. said (at p. 2): "I do not regard the refusal of a licence as being a punishment. The granting of a licence is a privilege and it is a privilege which is to be granted only to those who are thought by the Director General of Fair Trading, on proper evidence, to be fit persons."

Section 26 enables regulations to be made as to the conduct of a licensee's business, specifying in particular— **5–131**

(a) the books and other records to be kept by the licensee, and

(b) the information to be furnished by him to persons with whom he does business or seeks to do business, and the way it is to be furnished.

Regulations which have been made under this section are the Consumer Credit (Conduct of Business) (Credit References) Regulations 1977 (S.I. 1977 No. 330) and the Consumer Credit (Conduct of Business) (Pawn Records) Regulations 1983 (S.I. 1983 No. 1565).

Issue of Licences

5–132 Unless the Director decides to issue a licence which has been applied for, he must, before deciding the application—

(a) notify the applicant, giving his reasons, that he is minded to refuse the application, or to grant it in terms different from those applied for, and

(b) invite the applicant to submit to him representations in support of the application (s. 27).

5–133 Where the Director is minded to issue a group licence (whether on the application of any person or of his own motion), and in doing so to exclude any person from the group by name, he must, before deciding the matter—

(a) give notice of that fact to the person proposed to be excluded, giving his reasons, and

(b) invite the person to submit representations against his exclusion (s. 28).

Renewal, Variation, Suspension and Revocation of Licences

5–134 If the licensee under a standard licence, or the original applicant for, or any licensee under, a group licence of limited duration, wishes the Director to renew the licence, he must apply to the Director for its renewal. The Director may of his own motion renew any group licence (s 29).

5–135 Variation of a licence may be by request (s. 30) or compulsory (s. 31).

5–136 Variation by request takes place where the Director varies a standard or group licence in response to an application made to him by the licensee who originally applied for the licence. Variation by request may also take place where a person originally excluded from a group licence applies to the Director to vary the terms of the licence so as to remove the exclusion. Unless the Director decides to vary a licence in accordance with the request being made, he must, before deciding the application—

(a) notify the applicant, giving his reasons, that he is minded to refuse the application, and

(b) invite the applicant to submit to him representations in support of the application.

During the currency of a licence the Director may come to be of the opinion that, if the licence had expired at that time, he would have been minded to renew it on different terms. If so, he may compulsorily vary the licence during its currency, but in the case of a standard licence he must first inform the licensee and invite him to submit representations and in the case of a group licence he must first give a general notice of the proposed variations and in that general notice invite any licensee to submit representations; in the case of a group licence originally issued on application the Director must also give individual notice to the applicant and invite him to submit representations; where the variation of a group licence is for the purpose of excluding a named person, individual notice and an invitation to submit representations must likewise be given to that named person. **5–137**

The procedure for suspension and revocation of a licence by the Director is similar to that for compulsory variation. Suspension may be for a specified period or may be indefinite; in the latter case the suspension may be ended by a notice given by the Director to the licensee or, if the licence is a group one, by general notice. On revoking or suspending a licence the Director may give directions authorising a licensee to carry into effect agreements made by him before the revocation or suspension (s. 32). **5–138**

A licensee may apply to the Director to end a suspension (whether the suspension was for a fixed or for an indefinite period) (s. 33). **5–139**

Miscellaneous

Representations to Director

A person who has been invited to submit representations to the Director in connection with the issue, etc., of a licence has 21 days (or longer if the Director so allows) in which to submit written **5–140** representations or to give notice that he wishes to make oral representations. Both types of representations must be taken into account by the Director in reaching his decision (s. 34). Further details are contained in the Consumer Credit Licensing (Representations) Order 1976 (S.I. 1976 No. 191).

The register

5–141 The Director is required to maintain a register containing particulars relating to licences and applications for licences and such other matters as he thinks fit. Members of the public are entitled on payment of specified fees to inspect the register, take copies of any entry and obtain certified copies of any entry from the Director (s. 35).

5–142 The register, which is kept in London, is arranged alphabetically under the names of the applicants for licences and existing licences. The particulars take the form of photocopies of documents (or parts of documents) which are required to be registered under the Act.

Duty to notify changes

5–143 The holder of a standard licence has a duty to notify the Director of certain changes within 21 working days after their occurrence. The changes include changes in the officers of a company or of its controller and changes in the members of a partnership. Where a change in a partnership has the result that the business ceases to be carried on under the name specified in the standard licence, the licence ceases to have effect (s. 36).

Death, bankruptcy, *etc.*, of licensee

5–144 A licence held by one individual terminates if he dies or has his estate sequestrated or becomes incapable of managing his own affairs (ss. 37 and 38).

5–145 However, the provisions of the Act on these subjects are supplemented by the Consumer Credit (Termination of Licences) Regulations 1976 (S.I. 1976 No. 1002). These Regulations list other events which terminate licences, whether held by an individual, an unincorporated body such as a partnership or a body corporate such as a company. It is to be noted that the events listed do not include the liquidation of a company; this is because the separate *persona* ("personality") of a company continues during the winding-up process and if the liquidator continues the business he does so in the company's name and not in his own; if the statutory provision were that the licence automatically terminated at the commencement of the liquidation, the liquidator would be unable to continue the business without incurring personal liability. The Regulations also provide a period of deferment (limited to 12 months, with no mention of further extension) during which a licence continues in force despite the occurrence of a terminating event; *e.g.* on a licensee's death the licence continues in force for 12 months thereafter, to the obvious convenience of his personal representatives. The effect of this provision as to deferment can be to prolong (but by not more than 12 months) the life of a licence which was about to expire.

A licence can also be voluntarily relinquished by the giving by **5–146** the licensee of written notice to the Director. The period of deferment is in this case one month after receipt of the notice (Consumer Credit (Termination of Licences) (Amendment) Regulations 1981 (S.I. 1981 No. 614)).

Criminal and civil consequences of contravention of licensing provisions

The Act makes it an offence to engage in activities covered by **5–147** the Act without having a licence. It is also an offence for the holder of a standard licence to carry on business under a name not specified in the licence and for a person to fail to notify changes as required by section 36 (s. 39).

In addition to these criminal consequences, there is the import- **5–148** ant civil consequence that a regulated agreement, other than a non-commercial agreement, if made when the creditor or owner was unlicensed, is enforceable against the debtor or hirer only where the Director has made an order under section 40. The effect of obtaining such an order is that the regulated agreements made by the "trader" (*i.e.* the unlicensed person) are treated as if he had been licensed. Application for such an order is made by the trader to the Director. There are the usual safeguards to ensure that the Director will act judicially: before deciding the application adversely to the applicant he must—

(a) notify the applicant, giving his reasons, that he is minded to refuse the application, or to grant it in terms different from those applied for, and

(b) invite the applicant to submit representations in support of the application.

In deciding whether or not to make an order under section 40 the Director must consider, in addition to any other relevant factors—

(a) how far debtors or hirers were prejudiced by the trader's conduct,

(b) whether or not the Director would have been likely to grant a licence to the trader for that period if it had been applied for, and

(c) the degree of culpability for the failure to obtain a licence.

The Director may limit the order to specified agreements or make the order conditional on the doing of specified acts by the applicant.

Appeals

5–149 A person aggrieved by a determination of the Director (*e.g.* a refusal to issue or renew a licence, an exclusion from a group licence or a refusal to make an order under section 40) may appeal to the Secretary of State (s. 41).

5–150 Details of how appeals are conducted are in the Consumer Credit Licensing (Appeals) Regulations 1976 (S.I. 1976 No. 837). Appeals may be dealt with in certain cases by the Secretary of State without a hearing. In other cases there will be a hearing before an "appointed person" or "appointed persons" drawn from a panel maintained by the Secretary of State. The recommendation made by the appointed person or persons is not binding on the Secretary of State, but is usually accepted by him.

5–151 A further appeal is available on a point of law: the aggrieved person may require the Secretary of State to state a case for the opinion of the Court of Session on any question of law (s. 42).

(b) **Seeking Business**

5–152 The main purpose of Part IV of the Act ("Seeking Business") is to give effect to the "truth-in-lending" principle which is at the heart of the Act: the aim is that information given to the public should fairly and in sufficient detail indicate the nature and true cost of the credit terms being offered.

5–153 The controls on seeking business are imposed on three main activities:

(i) advertising (ss. 43 to 47);
(ii) canvassing, etc. (ss. 48 to 51); and
(iii) quotations, etc. (ss. 52 to 54).

(i) *Advertising*

Advertisements to which Part IV applies

The advertisements to which Part IV of the Act applies are defined in wide terms in section 43: Part IV applies to "any advertisement, published for the purposes of a business carried on by the advertiser, indicating that he is willing— **5–154**

(a) to provide credit, or

(b) to enter into an agreement for the hiring of goods by him" (s. 43(1)).

A case on the interpretation of section 43(1) is *Jenkins v. Lombard North Central PLC* [1984] 1 W.L.R. 307 (DC): **5–155**

L. Ltd, which provided financial services to the public including the granting of credit facilities, supplied price stickers to a motor dealer to place on vehicles which he was offering for sale. The stickers stated the cash price of the vehicle concerned and also bore the name "L. Ltd" and its insignia (consisting of a capital letter "L", stylised to resemble a £ sign, mounted on a black diamond).

L. Ltd was accused of being in breach of the Consumer Credit (Advertisements) Regulations 1980 and the case turned on whether the stickers were advertisements within the meaning of section 43(1) of the Act.

Held that because the stickers did not contain or constitute a statement of L. Ltd's *willingness* to provide credit, there was no advertisement within the meaning of section 43(1) and so there was no requirement to comply with the Consumer Credit (Advertisements) Regulations 1980 and no offence had been committed.

By section 189(1) "advertisement" includes "every form of advertising, whether in a publication, by television or radio, by display of notices, signs, labels, showcards or goods, by distribution of samples, circulars, catalogues, price lists or other material, by exhibition of pictures, models or films, or in any other way". **5–156**

From the provision quoted from section 43(1) it is clear that Part IV applies to a wider range of transactions than "regulated agreements". There are, however, certain limitations on the provision in section 43(1): Part IV does not apply unless the advertiser **5–157** carries on a consumer credit business or consumer hire business or a business in the course of which he provides credit to individuals secured on land; nor does Part IV apply to an advertisement which indicates that—

(1) (in relation to the provision of credit) the credit must exceed £15,000, and that no security is required, or the security is to consist of property other than land; or

(2) (in relation to the provision of credit) the credit is available only to a body corporate; or

(3) (in relation to hiring of goods) the advertiser is not willing to enter into a consumer hire agreement (s. 43(2)–(4)).

Although the general effect of these limitations is to restrict Part IV to the consumer field, nevertheless Part IV applies more widely than other provisions of the Act.

5–158 Further, an advertiser who carries on business consisting of *unregulated* agreements governed by the law of a foreign country is subject to Part IV of the Act in relation to advertisements published in this country if the agreements would have been regulated agreements under United Kingdom law (s. 43(2)(c)).

5–159 The Secretary of State may by order provide that Part IV is not to apply to advertisements of a description specified in the order (s. 43(5)). The order at present in operation under this provision is the Consumer Credit (Exempt Advertisements) Order 1985 (S.I. 1985 No. 621). Amongst the exclusions are:

(1) advertisements relating to certain consumer credit agreements where the number of payments does not exceed a certain number or the rate of the total charge for credit does not exceed a specified rate;

(2) advertisements relating to certain consumer credit agreements connected with foreign trade; and

(3) advertisements relating to certain consumer hire agreements for the hire of metering equipment used in connection with the authorised supply of electricity or water.

Form and content of advertisements

5–160 By section 44 the Secretary of State must make regulations as to the form and content of advertisements, and the regulations must contain provisions appropriate for ensuring that an advertisement conveys a fair and reasonably comprehensive indication of the nature of the credit or hire facilities offered by the advertiser and of their true cost to persons using them.

The regulations which are at present in operation are the Consumer Credit (Advertisements) Regulations 1989 (S.I. 1989 No. 1125). These divide advertisements into three categories—simple, intermediate and full. **5–161**

Simple advertisements are those whose purpose is to keep the name of the advertiser in the public eye, *e.g.* brief messages appearing at a sponsored sporting event or printed on business cards. The Regulations *limit* the information which may be included in a simple advertisement to the advertiser's name, logo, address, telephone number, occupation and any information *other than* information that a person is willing to provide credit or the price of any goods, etc. An example is: **5–162**

"A. CREDITOR LTD
MONEYLENDER".

Intermediate advertisements also allow the advertiser some choice as to what is to be included. Facts which *must* always be given are the creditor's name, his address or telephone number, and an indication that his terms of business may be obtained on application to that address or number. An example is: **5–163**

"A. CREDITOR LTD
PHONE **123–4567**
FOR WRITTEN DETAILS OF
CREDIT TERMS".

There are other facts which *must* be given if they apply to the credit being offered; these include any need for security or to take out a life insurance policy, and where the credit is for a fixed sum (*e.g.* hire-purchase) and is advertised as being available for the purchase of particular goods, the cash price and also the APR.[6] Further information *may* be given, *e.g.* a statement that the credit is limited to, say, £500, or is available only to persons over a specified age.

Full advertisements must contain the full range of relevant information specified in the Regulations. There are different levels of disclosure for different types of agreements. Full advertisements must always include, in addition to the information compulsorily included in intermediate advertisements, an indication that the **5–164**

[6] the total cost of the credit, expressed as an annual percentage rate of charge.

credit is restricted to a particular class of persons (if such is the case), the extent to which credit purchasers are treated differently from persons paying cash (if such is the case), and the APR.

Offences

5–165 It is an offence—

(1) to contravene the regulations made under section 44 (s. 167(2));

(2) to advertise restricted-use credit facilities relating to goods or services unless the goods or services are available for cash (s. 45); and

(3) to publish an advertisement which conveys information which in a material respect is false or misleading (even though the advertisement may comply with the regulations) (s. 46(1)).

This criminal liability extends to the publisher of the advertisement, to any person who, in the course of a business carried on by him, devised the advertisement and to any person who procured the publication of the advertisement (s. 47(1)). A defence open to the publisher is that he had no reason to suspect that the publication would be an offence (s. 47(2)).

5–166 The following are three instances of successful prosecutions:

1. *Metsoja v. H. Norman Pitt & Co. Ltd* [1990] C.C.L.R. 12; [1990] C.L.Y. 620: A dealer advertised new cars under a finance scheme which stated that the interest payable was to be "nought per cent APR".

A trading standards officer visited the dealer's premises and ascertained that under the finance scheme he would be given a part-exchange allowance of £3,258.75 against his old car, but that if he arranged his own finance the allowance would be £3,500 to £3,600.

The dealer was prosecuted for (1) procuring the publication of an advertisement which was false in a material particular and (2) procuring the publication of an advertisement proclaiming nought per cent APR when a purchaser seeking to use the finance scheme would have to pay more than a cash purchaser.

Held that the advertisement was false because it clearly indicated that a purchaser using the finance scheme would pay the same as a cash purchaser; the difference between the part-exchange allowances represented a hidden charge or interest payment.

2. *Ford Credit plc v. Normand*, 1994 S.L.T. 318: F. plc devised for Arnold Clark Automobiles Ltd an advertisement which used

the expression "0% finance or 10% discount". Both parties were prosecuted by N., procurator fiscal at Glasgow, for breach of regulation 7(c) of the Consumer Credit (Advertisements) Regulations 1989, which provides that a credit advertisement must not include the expression "interest free" or any expression to the like effect indicating that a customer is liable to pay no greater amount in respect of a transaction financed by credit than he would be liable to pay as a cash purchaser, except where the total amount payable by the debtor does not exceed the cash price.

The accused objected on the ground that the expression was neither false nor misleading since it explicitly stated that a cash sale would cost 10 per cent less than a credit sale.

The sheriff repelled that objection and the accused appealed to the High Court of Justiciary.

Held that the fact that the alternative of "10% discount" was added did not alter the fact that the advertisement included the words "0% finance", which were equivalent to "interest free". The sheriff had therefore been well founded in concluding that the advertisement was in breach of regulation 7(c).

The court observed that the regulations may well be designed to cover cases which are not caught by the provisions of the Act dealing with false or misleading advertisements.

3. *Rover Group Ltd v. Sumner* [1995] C.C.L.R. 1; [1996] C.L.Y. 104: An advertisement stated the price of a new Rover Metro to be "just £5,995". An asterisk was attached to the first mention of this price indicating that a further £400 required to be paid before the agreement for the sale of the car could be completed. No similar qualification was made at other points in the advertisement where the price of "just £5,995" was stated.

Held in a prosecution under section 46(1) that the statements as to the price of the car were in a material respect misleading; the reason for stating the price as "just £5,995" had obviously been to suggest a price of less than £6,000, which was not the true price.

(ii) *Canvassing, etc.*

Canvassing off trade premises

A definition is given in section 48 of "canvassing off trade premises". The definition is based on a contrast between business premises (whether of the creditor or of the debtor) and other premises (*e.g.* the doorstep of the debtor's home). **5–167**

5–168 To canvass a regulated agreement off trade premises means to solicit the consumer to enter into the agreement by making oral representations during a visit carried out by the canvasser for the purpose of making these oral representations and not carried out in response to a request made on a previous occasion, provided the place of the visit is not a place where a business is carried on (whether on a permanent or temporary basis) by—

(a) the creditor or owner, or

(b) a supplier, or

(c) the canvasser, or the person whose employee or agent the canvasser is, or

(d) the consumer (s. 48).

The representations need not be made to the consumer himself: they may be made to any person who is at the place where the unsolicited visit is carried out (*e.g.* representations made to a wife for the purpose of inducing her to persuade her husband to enter into the agreement).

5–169 It is an offence to canvass debtor-creditor agreements off trade premises. Criminal liability can be avoided only where the visit has been carried out in response to a *written* request made on a previous occasion (s. 49(1) and (2)). Current accounts of a banking character have been excluded from these provisions by a determination made by the Director General of Fair Trading in the exercise of a power conferred on him (s. 49(3)).

5–170 It is not an offence to canvass debtor-creditor-supplier agreements off trade premises. The provisions are aimed against what the Crowther Committee called "unconnected loans" (*e.g.* personal loans), not against transactions such as hire-purchase, conditional sale, credit sale and rental facilities ("connected loans").

Circulars to minors

5–171 A person commits an offence if, with a view to financial gain, he sends to a minor any document inviting him to—

(1) borrow money, or

(2) obtain goods on credit or hire, or

(3) obtain services on credit, or

(4) apply for information or advice on borrowing money or otherwise obtaining credit, or hiring goods.

A "minor" is a person under the age of 18 years (Age of Majority (Scotland) Act 1969 (s. 1(1) and (2)) and Age of Legal Capacity

(Scotland) Act 1991 (s. 1(3)(d))). It is a defence for the person charged with the offence to prove that he did not know, and had no reasonable cause to suspect, that he was a minor. Where a document is received by a minor at any school or other educational establishment for minors, the person sending it to him at that establishment knowing or suspecting it to be such an establishment is deemed to have "reasonable cause to suspect" that he is a minor (s. 50).

It is *sending* which is made an offence by this section: handing over a document to the minor in person is not covered by the provision, and an offence would be committed even where the document which had been sent never arrived. **5–172**

Prohibition of unsolicited credit-tokens

It is an offence to give a person a credit-token if he has not asked for it. To avoid this criminal liability the request must have been a written request except that in the case of a small debtor-creditor-supplier agreement it may have been oral. The prohibition does not apply to the giving of a credit-token for use under a credit-token agreement already made or in renewal or replacement of a credit-token under an existing credit-token agreement (s. 51). **5–173**

"Give" means "deliver or send by post to" (s. 189(1)).

(iii) *Quotations,* etc.

Quotations

Section 52 authorises the making of regulations— **5–174**

(1) as to the form and content of any document (a "quotation") by which a person who carries on a consumer credit business or consumer hire business, or a business in the course of which he provides credit to individuals secured on land, gives prospective customers information about the terms on which he is prepared to do business;

(2) requiring a person carrying on such a business to provide quotations to such persons and in such circumstances as are prescribed.

The section extends to *persons who carry on the types of business mentioned*: the particular agreement which is the subject-matter of the quotation need not be a regulated agreement. **5–175**

5–176 The regulations which are now in operation are the Consumer Credit (Quotations) (Revocation) Regulations 1997 (S.I. 1997 No. 211). The aim is to ensure that the consumer is provided with all the relevant details of a prospective transaction.

Display of information

5–177 Section 53 enables regulations to be made requiring a person who carries on a consumer credit business or consumer hire business, or a business in the course of which he provides credit to individuals secured on land, to display prescribed information at any premises where the business is carried on and to which the public have access.

Conduct of business regulations

5–178 The regulations made under section 26 as to the conduct by a licensee of his business may include provisions regulating the seeking of business by the licensee (s. 54) (5–131, above).

IV AGREEMENT CONTROL

5–179 The five Parts of the Act which are concerned with the control of individual credit or hire agreements are:

(a) Part V ("Entry into Credit or Hire Agreements");

(b) Part VI ("Matters Arising During Currency of Credit or Hire Agreements");

(c) Part VII ("Default and Termination");

(d) Part VIII ("Security"); and

(e) Part IX ("Judicial Control").

(a) Entry into Credit or Hire Agreements

5–180 The provisions of Part V of the Act fall under four headings:

(i) preliminary matters;

(ii) making the agreement;

(iii) cancellation of certain agreements within cooling-off period; and

(iv) exclusion of certain agreements from Part V.

(i) *Preliminary Matters*

Disclosure of information

5–181 Regulations may require specified information to be disclosed in the prescribed manner to the debtor or hirer before a regulated agreement is made (s. 55).

Antecedent negotiations

The phrase "antecedent negotiations" has an elaborate definition. It means any "negotiations with the debtor or hirer— 5–182

(*a*) conducted by the creditor or owner in relation to the making of any regulated agreement, or

(*b*) conducted by a credit-broker in relation to goods sold or proposed to be sold by the credit-broker before forming the subject-matter of a debtor-creditor-supplier agreement within section 12(a), or

(*c*) conducted by the supplier in relation to a transaction financed or proposed to be financed by a debtor-creditor-supplier agreement within section 12(b) or (c)" (s. 56(1)).

Typical examples of creditors in each of the three categories may assist— 5–183

(a) a finance company supplying goods under a hire-purchase agreement;

(b) a dealer selling goods to a finance house to be let out on hire-purchase to a person introduced by the dealer to the finance house;

(c) a supplier selling goods against a credit card, and a motor dealer selling a car for cash advanced to the buyer by a finance house to whom the buyer was introduced by the dealer.

In (b) and (c) the negotiations are deemed to be conducted by the negotiator in the capacity of agent of the creditor as well as in his actual capacity (s. 56(2)). The effect is that the creditor will be liable to the debtor for any misrepresentations made by the negotiator since these will be deemed to have been made by the negotiator as his agent. 5–184

The agency in section 56(1)(b) is restricted to "goods sold or proposed to be sold" and does not extend to other goods which may form the subject-matter of another debtor-creditor-supplier agreement: *Powell v. Lloyds Bowmaker Ltd*, 1996 S.L.T. (Sh.Ct.) 117:

P. entered into a hire-purchase agreement with a finance company ("AIB") for a Vauxhall Cavalier car.

While the agreement was still current, P. decided to trade in the Vauxhall for another car. He went to a garage and spoke to a salesman there (Robb). He was interested in buying a Nissan Sunny car and ascertained that to discharge his indebtedness to AIB he had to pay them £1,300.

It was agreed between P. and Robb that the price of the Nissan car would be £4,995, that the trade-in allowance on the Vauxhall would be £1,500, leaving a balance due of £3,495. It was also agreed that there would be a further hire-purchase agreement between P. and another finance company, L. Ltd.

Robb insisted that P. should make out a cheque payable to the garage for the full cash element which he was putting into the transaction, with a view to £1,300 being applied to paying off AIB and the balance being attributed to the down payment on the Nissan. Robb undertook that the garage would repay AIB £1,300, but it failed to do so.

P. brought an action of damages against L. Ltd for the loss which he suffered as a result of the garage's failure to make payment to AIB, averring that by virtue of section 56(2) of the Act of 1974 L. Ltd were liable for the breach of the undertaking given by their deemed agents, the garage.

Held that Robb's undertaking to pay AIB was not a representation made by him "in relation to the goods sold or proposed to be sold"; any deemed agency was restricted to antecedent negotiations in relation to the Nissan car.

P.'s action was therefore dismissed.

5–185 Antecedent negotiations are taken to begin when the negotiator and the debtor or hirer first enter into communication (including communication by advertisement) (s. 56(4)). They may therefore begin before the creditor is aware of the existence of his debtor.

(ii) *Making the Agreement*

Form and content of agreements

5–186 Section 60 requires the Secretary of State to make regulations as to the form and content of documents embodying regulated agreements. The purpose of the regulations is to ensure that the debtor or hirer is made aware of—

(a) the rights and duties conferred or imposed on him by the agreement,

(b) the amount and rate of the total charge for credit (in the case of a consumer credit agreement),

(c) the protection and remedies available to him under the Act, and

(d) any other matters which, in the opinion of the Secretary of State, it is desirable for him to know about in connection with the agreement.

The Director General of Fair Trading has power to direct that an applicant need not comply with some particular requirement of the regulations if compliance would be impracticable, but the Director must be satisfied that the exemption will not prejudice the interests of debtors or hirers. **5–187**

The regulations which have been made under section 60 are the Consumer Credit (Agreements) Regulations 1983 (S.I. 1983 No. 1553, as amended by S.I. 1984 No. 1600, 1985 No. 666 and 1988 No. 2047). **5–188**

Proper and improper execution

By section 65 a regulated agreement which is improperly executed cannot be enforced against the debtor or hirer except on an order of the court. **5–189**

A regulated agreement is not properly executed unless— **5–190**

(a) a document in the prescribed form itself containing all the prescribed terms and conforming to the regulations made under section 60 is signed in the prescribed manner both by the debtor or hirer and by or on behalf of the creditor or owner, and

(b) the document embodies all the terms of the agreement, other than implied terms, and

(c) the document is, when presented or sent to the debtor or hirer for signature, in such a state that all its terms are readily legible (s. 61(1)).

Sections 62 and 63 provide for copies to be supplied to the debtor or hirer. The provisions vary according to the circumstances in which the document is executed (*i.e.* signed by the parties): **5–191**

(1) If the document is *presented personally* to the debtor or hirer for his signature, and, *on the occasion* when he signs it, the document becomes an executed agreement, a copy of the executed agreement must be there and then delivered to him (s. 63(1)); no further copy is required.

(2) If the document is *presented personally* to the debtor or hirer for his signature, but the creditor or owner does not immediately execute the agreement, then—

(a) a copy of the unexecuted agreement must there and then be delivered to the debtor or hirer (s. 62(1)), and

(b) a further copy of the agreement must be given to him within seven days of its execution (s. 63(2)).

(3) If the document is *sent* to the debtor or hirer for his signature, a copy of it must be sent to him at the same time

(s. 62(2)). A further copy of the agreement must be given to him within seven days of its execution, except where the unexecuted agreement became an executed agreement upon the debtor or hirer signing it (which would be so where the document was already signed by the creditor or owner before being sent to the debtor or hirer) (s. 63(2)).

5–192 The copies supplied under these provisions must be accompanied by any other document referred to in them.

5–193 An exception applies to a credit-token agreement: the seven-days' time limit need not be complied with provided the copy is given before or at the time when the credit-token is given to the debtor (s. 63(4)).

5–194 A regulated agreement is not properly executed if the requirements of sections 62 and 63 are not observed (ss. 62(3) and 63(5)).

5–195 By section 64, in the case of a cancellable agreement (see (iii), below) notice must be given to the debtor or hirer of his right to cancel, how and when that right is exercisable, and the name and address of a person to whom notice of cancellation may be given. The form of notice is prescribed in regulations (Consumer Credit (Cancellation Notices and Copies of Documents) Regulations 1983 (S.I. 1983 No. 1557, as amended by S.I. 1984 No. 1108, 1985 No. 666, 1988 No. 2047 and 1989 No. 591)). A cancellable agreement is not properly executed if the statutory requirements as to notice of the cancellation right are not observed.

(iii) *Cancellation of Certain Agreements within Cooling-off Period*

5–196 The provisions under this heading had their origin in the hire-purchase legislation aimed at discouraging certain forms of door-step selling: a "cooling-off" period was introduced in respect of hire-purchase agreements not signed at "appropriate trade premises". The provisions of the Act of 1974 are more sophisticated.

5–197 By section 67 a regulated agreement may be cancelled by the debtor or hirer if the antecedent negotiations included oral representations made when in the presence of the debtor or hirer by an individual acting as, or on behalf of, the negotiator, *unless*—

(a) the agreement is secured on land, or is a restricted-use credit agreement to finance the purchase of land or is an agreement for a bridging loan in connection with the purchase of land, or

(b) the unexecuted agreement is signed by the debtor or hirer at premises at which any of the following is carrying on any business (whether on a permanent or temporary basis)—

(i) the creditor or owner;

(ii) any party to a linked transaction (other than the debtor or hirer or a relative of his);

(iii) the negotiator in any antecedent negotiations.

The word "representation" is widely defined in section 189(1) as including "any condition or warranty, and any other statement or undertaking, whether oral or in writing". It was commented on in *Moorgate Services v. Kabir, The Times*, April 25, 1995; [1995] C.L.Y. 722:

K. appealed against a decision that he was liable to make payment to M. in respect of a credit agreement which had been held not to be cancellable under section 67. The negotiations had included oral representations made in K.'s presence.

Held that the wide definition of "representation" in section 189(1) should be interpreted to mean a statement or undertaking which was capable of inducing the borrower to enter into the agreement; it was not necessary to show that the representation did in fact induce, or had been intended to induce, the agreement entered into; the representations made to K. were capable of such inducement and therefore the agreement could be cancelled.

Further, as M. had not given K. notice of his right to cancel, the court had no power to enforce the agreement.

The length of the cooling-off period is dealt with in section 68: **5–198**
the debtor or hirer may serve notice of cancellation between his signing of the unexecuted agreement and the end of the fifth day following the day on which he received his second copy (if such is required) or (in other cases) the notice required to be given to him of the cancellation right under section 64.

By section 69 the notice of cancellation may be served on— **5–199**

(a) the creditor or owner, or

(b) the person specified in the notice given under section 64, or

(c) the agent of the creditor or owner.

As regards (c), the section provides that the following are to be deemed to be the agent of the creditor or owner for the purpose of receiving a notice of cancellation—

(i) a credit-broker or supplier who is the negotiator in antecedent negotiations, and

(ii) any person who, in the course of a business carried on by him, acts on behalf of *the debtor or hirer* in any negotiations for the agreement.

5–200 The notice need not be expressed in any particular words: provided it indicates the intention of the debtor or hirer to withdraw from the agreement, the notice has the effect of cancelling the agreement and any linked transaction and of withdrawing any offer by the debtor or hirer, or his relative, to enter into a linked transaction.

5–201 A notice of cancellation sent by post is deemed to be served at the time of posting, even though it is not actually received.

5–202 The remaining sections under this heading are concerned with the rights and duties which arise on the cancellation of an agreement. Section 70 deals with the recovery of money paid by the debtor or hirer, section 71 with repayment of the credit (if the debtor has already received it), section 72 with return of goods already in the possession of the debtor or hirer, and section 73 with goods delivered by the debtor or hirer in part-exchange during antecedent negotiations.

(iv) *Exclusion of Certain Agreements from Part V*

5–203 Section 74 provides that Part V (except section 56 ("antecedent negotiations")) does not apply to—

(a) a non-commercial agreement (defined in section 189(1) as a consumer credit agreement or a consumer hire agreement not made by the creditor or owner in the course of a business carried on by him), or

(b) a debtor-creditor agreement enabling the debtor to overdraw on a current account (*e.g.* an ordinary bank overdraft), or

(c) a debtor-creditor agreement to finance the making of certain prescribed payments connected with a person's death.

The exclusions in (b) and (c) apply only where the Director so decides and he must be of the opinion that the exclusion is not against the interests of debtors. An addition was made here in relation to (b) by the Banking Act 1979 (s. 38(1)): if the creditor is a bank the Director *must* now decide that the exclusion applies unless he considers that it would be against the public interest to do so; the underlying aim of the amendment is to allow flexibility in bank overdraft systems.

5–204 Further, none of Part V except sections 55 (disclosure of information prior to the agreement being made) and 56 ("antecedent negotiations") applies to a small debtor-creditor-supplier agreement for restricted-use credit (*e.g.* a credit-sale agreement where the amount of the credit does not exceed £50).

The effect is that the agreements mentioned in section 74 are exempt from the statutory provisions relating to the form, content and execution of agreements and the cancellation of agreements. 5–205

(b) Matters Arising During Currency of Credit or Hire Agreements

Part VI has provisions relating to the following matters which may arise during the currency of a credit or hire agreement: 5–206

Liability of Creditor for Breaches by Supplier

Section 75 makes the creditor in a debtor-creditor-supplier agreement jointly and severally liable with the supplier for misrepresentation and breach of contract. A creditor who is held liable to the debtor under this provision is entitled to be indemnified by the supplier. 5–207

The section applies even though the debtor, in entering into the transaction, may have exceeded the credit limit in his agreement or may have otherwise contravened a term in the agreement.

The section does not apply to a claim— 5–208

(a) under a non-commercial agreement, or

(b) relating to a single item to which the supplier has attached a cash price not exceeding £100[7] or more than £30,000.[7]

Section 75 was applied in *United Dominions Trust v. Taylor*, 1980 S.L.T. (Sh.Ct.) 28: 5–209

UDT, a finance company, made a loan to T. for the purchase of a used car from Parkway Cars (the "supplier").

T., alleging that the supplier had misrepresented the condition of the car and had refused to remedy its faults, returned it to the supplier and refused to pay the monthly instalments of the loan repayment as they fell due.

UDT sued T. for the balance of the loan and interest.

T. put forward the defence that as the contract of sale had been rescinded on the ground of the supplier's misrepresentation and

[7] figures substituted for £30 and £10,000, respectively, by Consumer Credit (Increase of Monetary Limits) Order 1983 (S.I. 1983 No. 1878).

breach of contract, the rescission, by section 75 of the Act, affected also the contract of loan.

UDT's reply was that there were two contracts and that the grounds of rescission of the contract with the supplier (namely, misrepresentation and breach of contract) could only apply to that contract.

The sheriff principal, reversing the decision of the sheriff, held that the effect of the Act was that where two contracts were economically part of one credit transaction, the fate of each contract depended on the other, even where the parties to the contracts were different; the rescission of the contract of sale therefore operated as rescission of the credit agreement linked to it, since both contracts formed part of a debtor-creditor-supplier agreement.

5–210 In 1995 the Director General of Fair Trading made recommendations that the provisions of section 75 should be changed so as to lessen the liability on the credit card industry. The Department of Trade and Industry then issued a consultation document, but after consideration of the responses received, the Government decided that the provisions gave useful and desirable protection to consumers buying goods and services on credit and did not impose an unwarranted burden on business. The provisions of section 75 have therefore been retained (DTI Press Notice, P96/803, October 28, 1996).

Duty to Give Notice before Taking Certain Action

5–211 Section 76 deals with the situation where a regulated agreement is for a specified period and before that period has ended, the creditor or owner wishes to enforce a term of the agreement by—

(a) demanding earlier payment of any sum, or

(b) recovering possession of any goods or land, or

(c) treating any right conferred on the debtor or hirer by the agreement as terminated, restricted or deferred.

5–212 The creditor or owner must give the debtor or hirer no less than seven days' notice of his intention to take any of these steps. The form of notice is prescribed in regulations (Consumer Credit (Enforcement, Default and Termination Notices) Regulations 1983 (S.I. 1983 No. 1561, as amended by S.I. 1984 No. 1109)).

5–213 This section does not apply to a right of enforcement arising from a breach by the debtor or hirer—a situation governed by the default notice provisions in Part VII of the Act.

Duty to Give Information

Sections 77 to 80 are concerned with circumstances in which one of the parties to a regulated agreement has a duty to give information to the other. None of these provisions apply to a non-commercial agreement (*i.e.* a consumer credit agreement or a consumer hire agreement not made by the creditor or owner in the course of a business carried on by him—s. 189(1)). **5–214**

(i) The creditor under a regulated agreement for *fixed-sum credit* must, on a written request from the debtor, give the debtor a copy of the executed agreement and of any other document referred to in it, together with a signed statement showing— **5–215**

(1) the total sum paid under the agreement by the debtor;

(2) the amounts which have become payable under the agreement by the debtor but remain unpaid, with dates; and

(3) the amounts which are to become payable under the agreement by the debtor, with dates.

The creditor need not comply with a request made less than one month after complying with a previous request (s. 77).

(ii) The creditor under a regulated agreement for *running-account credit* is under a similar duty, but the information to be shown is necessarily different— **5–216**

(1) the state of the account;

(2) the amount currently payable under the agreement by the debtor to the creditor; and

(3) the amounts (with dates) of any payments which, if the debtor does not draw further on the account, will later become payable under the agreement by the debtor to the creditor.

In addition, the creditor in a running-account credit agreement is under a duty to give the debtor, without any request being made, statements at regular intervals of not more than 12 months showing the state of the account. This latter provision does not apply to a small agreement (s. 78). **5–217**

(iii) The owner under a regulated consumer *hire* agreement must, on a written request from the hirer, give the hirer a copy of the executed agreement and of any other document referred to in it, together with a signed statement showing the amounts (with dates) which have become payable under the agreement by the hirer but remain unpaid (s. 79). **5–218**

(iv) Where a regulated agreement requires the debtor or hirer to keep goods to which the agreement relates in his possession or **5–219** control, he must, within seven working days after receiving a written request from the creditor or owner, tell the creditor or owner where the goods are (s. 80).

Appropriation of Payments

5–220 The normal rule in contract is that where several separate debts are due, the debtor may, when making payment, appropriate the money to a particular debt, but that if he makes no appropriation, the creditor may appropriate the money as he chooses. This normal rule is modified in relation to regulated agreements by section 81.

5–221 The debtor or hirer is entitled to appropriate the payment in any way he sees fit, but if he does not do so and one or more of the agreements is a hire-purchase or conditional sale agreement, or a consumer hire agreement, or an agreement for which any security is provided, then the payment must be appropriated towards the satisfaction of the sums due under the several agreements in the proportions which those sums bear to one another.

Variation of Agreements

5–222 There may be a power in a regulated agreement enabling the creditor or owner to vary the agreement (*e.g.* to alter the rate of interest payable). In exercising such a power the creditor or owner must first give notice in the prescribed manner. This provision does not apply to a non-commercial agreement (s. 82).

5–223 The regulations which prescribe the manner of giving notice are the Consumer Credit (Notice of Variation of Agreements) Regulations 1977 (S.I. 1977 No. 328, as amended by S.I. 1979 Nos. 661 and 667).

Misuse of Credit-Tokens and other Credit Facilities

5–224 There is a general provision in section 83 that a debtor under a regulated consumer credit agreement is not to be liable to the creditor for any loss arising from use of the credit facility by another person (who is not the debtor's agent). This provision does not apply to a non-commercial agreement or to any loss arising from the misuse of cheques and other documents grouped with cheques by the Cheques Act 1957.

Section 84 modifies that general provision, but deals only with credit-tokens (*e.g.* a credit card). The section provides that a debtor can be made liable in certain situations and within certain limits for loss to the creditor arising from misuse of a credit-token: **5–225**

(i) The debtor may be made liable to any extent for the creditor's loss if the person misusing the credit-token acquired possession of it with the debtor's consent.

(ii) The debtor may be made liable to the extent of £50[8] (or the credit limit if less) if the person misusing the credit-token does so when the credit-token is not in the possession of an "authorised person" (defined as the debtor, the creditor or any person authorised by the debtor to use the credit-token).

(iii) Once oral or written notice has been received by the creditor that the credit-token has been lost or stolen or is for any other reason liable to misuse, the debtor ceases to incur any further liability.

(iv) The credit-token agreement must contain in the prescribed manner particulars of the name, address and telephone number for the giving of notice of loss, etc.; if it does not do so, the debtor is free from liability for the creditor's loss. The relevant regulations are the Consumer Credit (Credit-Token Agreements) Regulations 1983 (S.I. 1983 No. 1555).

Duty on Issue of New Credit-Tokens

When a credit-token (other than the first) is given by the creditor to the debtor, the creditor must give the debtor a copy of the executed agreement and of any other document referred to in it. This provision does not apply to small agreements (s. 85). **5–226**

Death of Debtor or Hirer

Section 86 deals with the situation where the debtor or hirer dies before the expiry of the period for which a regulated agreement is specified to last. The section is intended to discourage the creditor or owner from taking such steps as terminating the agreement, demanding earlier payment of any sum, recovering possession or enforcing any security. **5–227**

---

[8] substituted for £30 by Consumer Credit (Increase of Monetary Amounts) Order 1983 (S.I. 1983 No. 1571).

5–228 The main provisions are:

(i) If at the death the agreement is fully secured, the creditor or owner is not entitled to take any such step.

(ii) If at the death the agreement is only partly secured or is unsecured, the creditor or owner is entitled to take such a step but only on an order of the court.

5–229 The section does not prevent termination, etc., of the agreement on death if no period for its duration was specified in the agreement, nor does it prevent the creditor from treating the right to draw on any credit as restricted or deferred (*e.g.* he may refuse to allow further withdrawals).

(c) **Default and Termination**

5–230 The provisions of Part VII of the Act fall under four headings:

(i) default notices;
(ii) further restriction of remedies for default;
(iii) early payment by debtor; and
(iv) termination of agreements.

(i) *Default Notices*

5–231 Where there is a breach by the debtor or hirer of a regulated agreement, service of a "default notice" is necessary before the creditor or owner can become entitled, by reason of the breach,—

(a) to terminate the agreement, or

(b) to demand earlier payment of any sum, or

(c) to recover possession of any goods or land, or

(d) to treat any right conferred on the debtor or hirer by the agreement as terminated, restricted or deferred, or

(e) to enforce any security.

This provision does not prevent the creditor from treating the right to draw upon any credit as restricted or deferred; for instance, he may refuse to allow further withdrawals, even without serving a default notice.

5–232 Regulations may provide that default notices are not to be necessary in the case of certain agreements (s. 87), *e.g.* non-commercial agreements for which no security has been provided.

5–233 A default notice must be in a form prescribed by regulations and must specify—

(a) the nature of the alleged breach;

(b) if the breach is capable of remedy, what action is required to remedy it and the date before which that action is to be taken;

(c) if the breach is not capable of remedy, the sum (if any) required to be paid as compensation for the breach, and the date before which it is to be paid.

The date specified in (b) or (c) must not be less than seven days after the date of service of the default notice.

The notice must contain information in the prescribed terms about the consequences of failure to comply with the notice (s. 88). **5–234**

The relevant regulations for sections 87 and 88 are the Consumer Credit (Enforcement, Default and Termination Notices) Regulations 1983 (S.I. 1983 No. 1561, as amended by S.I. 1984 No. 1109). **5–235**

If before the specified date the debtor or hirer takes the required action (in the case of (b)) or pays the required compensation (in the case of (c)), the breach must be treated as not having occurred (s. 89). **5–236**

(ii) *Further Restriction of Remedies for Default*

Retaking of protected goods

Sections 90 and 91 enact a restriction which is additional to the need for a default notice. The sections are derived from similar provisions in the hire-purchase legislation, and relate to "protected goods" in hire-purchase and conditional sale agreements. **5–237**

The restriction is that at any time when— **5–238**

(a) the debtor is in breach of a regulated hire-purchase or a regulated conditional sale agreement relating to goods, and

(b) the debtor has paid to the creditor one-third or more of the total price of the goods, and

(c) the property in (*i.e.* ownership of) the goods remains in the creditor,

the creditor is not entitled to recover possession of the goods from the debtor except on an order of the court.

The provision does not apply where the debtor voluntarily terminates the agreement (s. 90). **5–239**

If goods are recovered by the creditor in contravention of section 90, then— **5–240**

(a) the regulated agreement terminates, and

(b) the debtor is released from all liability under the agreement and is entitled to recover from the creditor all sums paid by the debtor under the agreement (s. 91).

Recovery of possession of goods or land

5–241 Section 92 prohibits the creditor or owner in a regulated hire-purchase, conditional sale or consumer hire agreement relating to goods from entering, without an order of the court, any premises to take possession of the goods, and similarly prohibits the creditor in a regulated conditional sale agreement relating to land from recovering possession of the land without an order of the court when the debtor is in breach of the agreement.

Interest not to be increased on default

5–242 By section 93, where the debtor under a regulated consumer credit agreement is in breach of the agreement he cannot be required to pay interest on the outstanding sums at a rate which exceeds the rate of interest provided for in the agreement.

Summary diligence not competent

5–243 By section 93A, inserted by the Debtors (Scotland) Act 1987 (s. 108(1) and Sched. 6), summary diligence is not competent in Scotland to enforce payment of a debt due under a regulated agreement or under any related security.

(iii) *Early Payment by Debtor*

5–244 The debtor under a regulated consumer credit agreement is entitled at any time, by notice to the creditor and the payment to the creditor of all amounts payable by the debtor to him under the agreement (less any rebate), to discharge the debtor's indebtedness under the agreement (s. 94).

5–245 One of the important recommendations of the Crowther Committee was that the debtor should be entitled to a rebate of charges where there was an early settlement, and so section 95 enables regulations to be made providing for such a rebate. The regulations may extend to other cases of early settlement besides the case where the debtor exercises his right under section 94, above: for instance, they may cover the case where the debtor's indebtedness becomes payable before the time fixed by the agreement because the debtor is in breach of the agreement. Calculation of rebates is as prescribed by the regulations. The relevant regulations are the Consumer Credit (Rebate on Early Settlement) Regulations 1983 (S.I. 1983 No. 1562).

The early settlement of a regulated consumer credit agreement automatically discharges the liability of the debtor, and any "relative" (associate) of his, under a linked transaction, except as regards a debt which has already become payable. This provision does not apply to a linked transaction which is itself an agreement providing the debtor or his relative with credit, and regulations may make further exceptions for linked transactions of a prescribed description (s. 96). **5–246**

By section 97 the creditor under a regulated consumer credit agreement must, on the written request of the debtor, give the debtor a statement, in a form prescribed by regulations, indicating the amount required to discharge the debtor's indebtedness under the agreement. The relevant regulations are the Consumer Credit (Settlement Information) Regulations 1983 (S.I. 1983 No. 1564). **5–247**

(iv) *Termination of Agreements*

Termination on the debtor's or hirer's default was dealt with in (i), above. The provisions under the present heading relate to other modes of termination. **5–248**

Notice of termination in non-default cases

Where there is no breach of the agreement by the debtor or hirer, the creditor or owner is not entitled to terminate a regulated agreement without giving the debtor or hirer not less than seven days' notice of the termination, but this applies only where a period for the duration of the agreement is specified in the agreement, and it does not prevent a creditor from treating the right to obtain *further* credit as restricted or deferred. Regulations (Consumer Credit (Enforcement, Default and Termination Notices) Regulations 1983 (S.I. 1983 No. 1561, as amended by S.I. 1984 No. 1109)) prescribe the form of the notice and also exempt certain agreements from this requirement for notice (s. 98), *e.g.* non-commercial agreements for which no security has been provided. **5–249**

Termination of hire-purchase and conditional sale agreements

5–250 By section 99, at any time before the final payment by the debtor under a regulated hire-purchase or regulated conditional sale agreement falls due, the debtor is entitled to terminate the agreement by giving notice to any person entitled or authorised to receive the sums payable under the agreement. This does not affect any liability which has already accrued, and it does not apply to a conditional sale agreement relating to land after the title to the land has passed to the debtor or to a conditional sale agreement relating to goods which have become vested in the debtor and which the debtor has then transferred to a third party.

5–251 On termination under section 99, the debtor is liable (unless the agreement provides for a smaller payment, or does not provide for any payment) to pay to the creditor the amount (if any) by which one-half of the total price exceeds the total of sums already paid and sums due immediately before the termination. If the court is satisfied that the loss sustained by the creditor as a result of the termination is in fact less than that amount, then the court may order that only the amount of the loss is to be paid. If the debtor has failed to take reasonable care of the goods or land, the amount payable is increased so as to recompense the creditor for the debtor's failure (s. 100).

Termination of hire agreement

5–252 By section 101 the hirer under a regulated consumer hire agreement is entitled to terminate the agreement by giving notice to any person entitled or authorised to receive the sums payable under the agreement. This does not affect any liability which has already accrued.

5–253 There are two provisions as to the length of notice:

(1) The notice must not expire earlier than 18 months after the making of the agreement.

(2) The minimum period of notice is three months except where the agreement itself specifies a shorter period or the agreement provides for the making of payments by the hirer to the owner at intervals which are shorter than three months (in which cases the shorter period is treated as the minimum period of notice).

This right to terminate a hire agreement after only 18 months was likely to cause undue difficulty in equipment leases where the period of hire was usually envisaged by the equipment leasing company as being for a four or five year term. There are therefore several exceptions in section 101 (*e.g.* the section does not apply to agreements in which the payments exceed £900[9] in any year), and in addition the Director General of Fair Trading may grant an exemption to a particular applicant if he thinks that would be in the interest of hirers.

Termination statements

Section 103 gives the debtor or hirer under a regulated agreement the right to obtain, on request, from the creditor or owner a termination statement to the effect that the indebtedness is discharged and that the agreement is at an end. If it were not for this statutory provision a debtor or hirer might have difficulty in obtaining from the creditor or owner written evidence of termination. The provision does not apply to non-commercial agreements. **5–254**

Landlord's hypothec

In a hire-purchase or conditional sale agreement goods which have not become vested in (*i.e.* have not yet come into the ownership of) the debtor are not to be treated as subject to the landlord's hypothec (see 7–44, below) during the following periods: **5–255**

(1) during the period between the service of a default notice and the date on which the notice is complied with (or, if the notice is not complied with, the date on which it expires); and

(2) (in the case of an agreement which can be enforced only on an order of the court) during the period between the commencement and termination of an action by the creditor to enforce the agreement (s. 104).

(d) **Security**

The provisions on security comprise Part VIII of the Act. **5–256**

The term "security" is widely defined: it means "a mortgage, charge, pledge, bond, debenture, indemnity, guarantee, bill, note or other right provided by the debtor or hirer, or at his request

[9] substituted for £300 by Consumer Credit (Increase of Monetary Amounts) Order 1983 (S.I. 1983 No. 1571).

(express or implied), to secure the carrying out of the obligations of the debtor or hirer under the agreement" (s. 189(1)).

5–257 The person by whom any security is provided is referred to in the Act as the "surety" (s. 189(1)).

5–258 The provisions in Part VIII are grouped under four headings:

(i) general;
(ii) pledges;
(iii) negotiable instruments; and
(iv) heritable securities.

(i) *General*

Form and content of securities

5–259 The security provided must be expressed in writing. The document is referred to as a "security instrument", and must comply in form and content with regulations (Consumer Credit (Guarantees and Indemnities) Regulations 1983 (S.I. 1983 No. 1556)). A copy of the security instrument and a copy of the regulated agreement, and also of any other document referred to in the latter, must be given to the surety. If these provisions are not complied with, the security can be enforced against the surety on an order of the court only (s. 105). If the court dismissed an application, the security would be an "ineffective security", to be treated as never having had effect, and any property lodged with the creditor or owner solely for the purposes of the security would require to be returned immediately, the creditor or owner would require to have entries in any register removed or cancelled, and any amount received by the creditor or owner on a sale of the security would require to be repaid to the surety (s. 106).

Duty to give information to surety

5–260 Sections 107, 108 and 109 impose on the creditor or owner a duty to give certain information to the surety under a fixed-sum credit agreement, a running-account credit agreement and a consumer hire agreement, respectively. For instance, in the case of fixed-sum credit agreement the information to be supplied on the surety's written request is:

(1) a copy of the executed agreement and of any other document referred to in it;

(2) a copy of the security instrument; and

(3) a signed statement showing the total sum paid by the debtor, the amounts payable by him and remaining unpaid (with dates), and the amounts to become payable (with dates).

A request for information need not be complied with if made less than a month after compliance with a previous request. None of the provisions apply to non-commercial agreements.

By section 111, when a default notice or a notice of termination is served on a debtor or hirer, a copy of the notice must be served by the creditor or owner on the surety; otherwise the security can be enforced against the surety on an order of the court only. 5–261

Duty to give information to debtor or hirer

Section 110 places the creditor or owner under the duty, on the written request of the debtor or hirer, to give the debtor or hirer a copy of a security instrument. A request made less than one month after compliance with a previous request need not be complied with, and the section does not apply to non-commercial agreements. 5–262

Realisation of securities

Regulations may provide for any matters relating to the sale or other realisation, by the creditor or owner, of property provided by way of security. The regulations[10] will not extend to non-commercial agreements, and the provision is subject to section 121 which has specific provisions as to the realisation of a pawn (s. 112). 5–263

Act not to be evaded by use of security

Section 113 contains a number of provisions designed to ensure that the protection given by the Act is not evaded by the use of security. The general provision of the section is that where a security is provided in relation to an actual or prospective regulated agreement, the security is not to be enforced so as to benefit the creditor or owner, directly or indirectly, to a greater extent than would be the case if the security were not provided. Therefore, for example, where a regulated agreement can be enforced only on an 5–264

[10] No regulations have yet been made under this provision.

order of the court or of the Director, any security can be enforced where such an order has been made, but not otherwise.

(ii) *Pledges*

5–265 Sections 114 to 122 replace the Pawnbrokers Acts 1872 and 1960. They do not apply to non-commercial agreements (s. 114(3)).

5–266 "Pawn" is defined as "any article subject to a pledge" (s. 189(1)). The person who pledges the article is referred to as the "pawnor" and the person who receives it is referred to as the "pawnee".

Pawn-receipts

5–267 The pawnee must at the time when he takes the article in pawn under a regulated agreement give the pawnor a "pawn-receipt" in a form prescribed by the Consumer Credit (Pawn-Receipts) Regulations 1983 (S.I. 1983 No. 1566).

5–268 A person who takes any article in pawn from an individual whom he knows to be, or who appears to be and is, a minor, commits an offence (s. 114).

Redemption period

5–269 A pawn is redeemable at any time within six months after it was taken, but, subject to that limitation, the redemption period is the period fixed by the parties for the duration of the credit secured by the pledge or such longer period as the parties may agree.

5–270 If the pawn is not redeemed by the end of the redemption period, it still remains redeemable until it is realised by a sale or (in the case of credit not exceeding £25[11]) until the ownership passes automatically to the pawnee.

5–271 No special charge can be made for redemption of a pawn after the end of the redemption period, and charges for the safe keeping of the pawn must not be at a higher rate after the end of the redemption period than before (s. 116).

Redemption of pawn

5–272 On surrender of the pawn-receipt, and payment of the amount owing, the pawnee must (so long as the pawn is redeemable) deliver the pawn to the bearer of the pawn-receipt unless the

---

[11] substituted for £15 by Consumer Credit (Increase of Monetary Amounts) Order 1983 (S.I. 1983 No. 1571).

pawnee knows or has reasonable cause to suspect that the bearer of the pawn-receipt is neither the owner of the pawn nor authorised by the owner to redeem it. A pawnee who acts in accordance with that provision is not liable in delict to any person for delivering the pawn or refusing to deliver it (s. 117).

On the loss of a pawn-receipt the person entitled to redeem the pawn may do so by tendering to the pawnee a prescribed form of statutory declaration or (in the case of credit not exceeding £25[12]) a prescribed form of written statement (s. 118). The regulations which prescribe the forms are the Consumer Credit (Loss of Pawn-Receipt) Regulations 1983 (S.I. 1983 No. 1567). **5–273**

If the pawnee without reasonable cause refuses to allow the pawn to be redeemed, he commits an offence (s. 119). **5–274**

If at the end of the redemption period the pawn has not been redeemed, then— **5–275**

(1) if the redemption period is six months and the credit does not exceed £25[12], the property in (*i.e.* ownership of) the pawn passes to the pawnee; or

(2) in any other case, the pawn becomes realisable by the pawnee (s. 120).

Realisation of pawn

Details of the procedure for realisation of a pawn are prescribed by the Consumer Credit (Realisation of Pawn) Regulations 1983 (S.I. 1983 No. 1568). The pawnee must give the pawnor notice prior to selling and information as to proceeds and expenses after the sale has taken place. The result of the sale may be to discharge the debt (in which case any surplus must be paid by the pawnee to the pawnor) or merely to diminish its amount. **5–276**

If the pawnor alleges that the true market value has not been obtained for the pawn, it is for the pawnee to prove that he and any agents employed by him in the sale used reasonable care to ensure that the true market value was obtained, and similarly if the pawnor alleges that the expenses of the sale were unreasonably high, it is for the pawnee to prove that they were reasonable (s. 121). **5–277**

[12] substituted for £15 by Consumer Credit (Increase of Monetary Amounts) Order 1983 (S.I. 1983 No. 1571).

Order to deliver pawn

5–278 Where a pawn is either an article which has been stolen or an article which has been obtained by fraud, and a person is convicted of the theft or fraud, the court by which the person is convicted may order delivery of the pawn to the owner or other person entitled to it, and may make such an order subject to such conditions as to payment of the debt secured by the pawn as it thinks fit (s. 122).

(iii) *Negotiable Instruments*

5–279 Restrictions are placed by the Act on the taking and negotiation of negotiable instruments in connection with consumer credit and consumer hire transactions. The restrictions do not apply to non-commercial agreements. The provisions are aimed at situations where a consumer wishing, for instance, to have central heating installed in his home would give the supplier a bill of exchange or a promissory note which the consumer would be required to pay at a future date to a holder in due course (often a finance house to which the supplier negotiated the instrument), even though the installation was defective.

5–280 Section 123 has three leading provisions designed to protect the consumer from such practices:

(1) A creditor or owner must not take a negotiable instrument, other than a bank note or cheque, in discharge of any sum payable—

(a) by the debtor or hirer under a regulated agreement, or

(b) by any person as surety in relation to the agreement.

(2) The creditor or owner who has taken a cheque as payment must not negotiate the cheque except to a bank; this prevents any person other than a bank from becoming a holder in due course.

(3) The creditor or owner must not take any negotiable instrument as security.

5–281 The Secretary of State may by order provide that section 123 is not to apply where the regulated agreement has a connection with a country outside the United Kingdom. The Consumer Credit (Negotiable Instruments) (Exemption) Order 1984 (S.I. 1984 No. 435) excludes from the application of section 123 consumer hire agreements which have a connection with a country outside the United Kingdom but only if the goods are hired in the course of the hirer's business.

Failure to comply with section 123 makes the agreement or the security, as the case may be, unenforceable except on an order of the court (s. 124). **5–282**

A creditor or owner who takes a negotiable instrument in contravention of section 123 is not a holder in due course, and is not entitled to enforce the instrument, and where a creditor or owner negotiates a cheque in contravention of section 123, his doing so constitutes a defect in his title for the purposes of the Bills of Exchange Act 1882. These provisions do not, however, affect the rights of a holder in due course of any negotiable instrument or prevent a negotiable instrument which has been taken or negotiated in contravention of section 123 from coming into the hands of a holder in due course: the instrument may have been negotiated by the creditor or owner to a person who took it in good faith and without notice of the contravention of section 123. The debtor, hirer or surety ("the protected person") may, therefore, find himself liable to a holder in due course; the Act provides that in such a situation the creditor or owner must indemnify the protected person (s. 125). **5–283**

(iv) *Heritable Securities*

A heritable security securing a regulated agreement can be enforced only on an order of the court (s. 126). **5–284**

(e) **Judicial Control**

Part IX of the Act is concerned with the powers which the court may exercise in connection with regulated and other agreements. **5–285**

The powers fall into two broad groups: **5–286**

(i) the power to make enforcement orders in actions by creditors or owners; and

(ii) the power to reopen "extortionate credit bargains".

The term "court" in relation to Scotland in (i) means the sheriff court (s. 189(1)), and in (ii) means either the sheriff court or the Court of Session (ss. 139 and 189(1)). **5–287**

The particular sheriff court which has jurisdiction to enforce regulated agreements, securities relating to them and linked transactions is in general the court for the place where the debtor or hirer is domiciled or carries on business or for the place where any **5–288** moveable property in question is situated (s. 141, as substituted by Civil Jurisdiction and Judgments Act 1982, Sched. 12).

5–289 An application to have a credit bargain reopened on the ground that it is extortionate may be made to the Court of Session or to the sheriff court for the district in which the debtor or surety resides or carries on business (s. 139).

(i) *Enforcement and Other Orders*

5–290 The provisions under this heading apply only to regulated agreements.

In making an order the court has a general power to—

(1) make the order conditional on the doing of specified acts by any party to the proceedings; and

(2) suspend the operation of the order for a time or until the occurrence of a specified act or omission (s. 135).

5–291 The court has also power to include in an order such provision as it considers just for amending any agreement or security so as to give proper effect to an order which it is making (s. 136). The provision does not enable the court to fix a different rate of interest: *Murie McDougall Ltd v. Sinclair*, 1994 S.L.T. (Sh.Ct.) 74 (see 5–297, below).

Enforcement orders in cases of infringement

5–292 As has been mentioned above, there are cases where the creditor or owner must obtain an enforcement order from the court before he can enforce the agreement. This is so where—

(1) the agreement has been improperly executed (s. 65);

(2) a security is not in writing or is improperly executed (s. 105);

(3) a surety has not had a default notice or a notice of termination served on him (s. 111); or

(4) a negotiable instrument has been taken or negotiated in contravention of section 123 (s. 124).

5–293 In an application for an enforcement order the court must have regard to prejudice caused to any person by the contravention in question, and the degree of culpability for it. If it appears to the court just to do so, the court may in an enforcement order reduce or discharge any sum payable by the debtor or hirer, or any surety, so as to compensate him for prejudice suffered as a result of the contravention in question.

There are some cases of infringement where the court has no power to make an enforcement order. A prominent instance is infringement of section 64 which requires the debtor or hirer in a cancellable agreement to be given a notice of his right to cancel (s. 127). 5–294

Enforcement orders on death of debtor or hirer

It was noted above that by section 86 on the death of a debtor or hirer the creditor or owner is entitled, where the agreement is not fully secured or is unsecured, to take certain steps, such as terminating the agreement, but only if he obtains an order from the court. 5–295

By section 128 the court must make an order under section 86 if, but only if, the creditor or owner proves that he has been unable to satisfy himself that the present and future obligations of the debtor or hirer under the agreement are likely to be discharged. 5–296

Time orders

A "time order" is an order of the court providing for one or both of the following, as the court considers just— 5–297

(a) the payment by the debtor or hirer or any surety of any sum owed under a regulated agreement or a security by such instalments, payable at such times as the court, having regard to the means of the debtor or hirer and any surety, considers reasonable;

(b) the remedying by the debtor or hirer of any breach of a regulated agreement (other than non-payment of money) within such period as the court may specify (s. 129).

However, by an amendment made by the Debtors (Scotland) Act 1987 (s. 108(1) and Sched. 6), it is not competent to make a time order if a time-to-pay direction or a time-to-pay order has already been made in relation to the same debt.

An instance of an unsuccessful application for a time order was *Murie McDougall Ltd v. Sinclair*, 1994 S.L.T. (Sh.Ct.) 74:

M. Ltd, who specialised in high risk lending, entered into a regulated agreement with S. under which S. agreed to repay to M. Ltd a total sum of £12,480 (being an advance of £8,000 plus interest of £4,480) over a period of 208 weeks at the rate of £60 per week; the interest was fixed at 27.1 per cent APR; earlier payment could be demanded by the service on S. of a default notice under the Act of 1974; and failure to comply with the terms of the notice would result in the whole of the remaining balance becoming payable immediately.

After a few months S. fell into arrears and M. Ltd claimed payment of an outstanding balance of nearly £12,000 to be paid within 10 days.

S. had a net disposable income of £163 per month and was willing to pay £160 per month. He applied for a time order under section 129, to substitute £160 per month for the contractual instalments of £60 per week. The proposed instalments would have had the result that the loan would not be paid off for more than 40 years.

S. also sought a further order under section 136 to have the agreement amended by the substitution of an interest rate of 10.95 per cent; the loan would then have taken 13 years to pay off.

Held that (1) an order under section 129 could not be considered "just" in that the loan would not be paid off for an inordinate length of time; (2) section 136 could only come into play when a time order was made and could not be used to make a "just" order where one could not otherwise exist; and (3) neither singly nor in combination did section 129 or section 136 give the court power to vary the contractual interest rate.

The sheriff (J. T. Fitzsimons) did not find the English cases authoritative, and there had been no previous reported Scottish case.

In the case of a hire-purchase or conditional sale agreement only, a time order of type (a), above, may deal with sums which are not yet due but which are to become payable if the agreement continues in force.

5–298 Where, following the making of a time order in relation to a regulated hire-purchase or conditional sale agreement or a regulated consumer hire agreement, the debtor or hirer is in possession of the goods, he must be treated (except in the case of a debtor to whom the creditor's title has passed) as a custodier of the goods under the terms of the agreement, notwithstanding that the agreement has been terminated. The effect of this provision is that, subject to the time order, the obligations of the debtor or hirer under the terminated agreement are notionally revived: payments again become due under the agreement (as controlled by the time order), and other obligations (*e.g.* as to insurance and maintenance) are restored.

While a time order of type (b), above, is in force, the creditor or owner cannot take certain steps, such as terminating the agreement, until the specified period has elapsed. **5–299**

The court has power to vary or revoke a time order on an application being made to the court by any person affected by the order (*i.e.* by *either* creditor or owner *or* debtor or hirer) (s. 130). **5–300**

Protection orders

Section 131 gives the court power, on the application of the creditor or owner under a regulated agreement, to make such orders as it thinks just for protecting any property of the creditor or owner, or property subject to any security, from damage or depreciation pending the determination of legal proceedings under the Act. The orders which may be made include orders restricting or prohibiting use of the property or giving directions as to its custody. **5–301**

Financial relief in hire agreements

The provisions mentioned in (ii), below, on extortionate credit bargains do not apply to hire agreements, but the hirer in a regulated consumer hire agreement is protected from oppression by section 132, which provides that where the owner recovers possession of the goods the court may order that the whole or part of any sum paid by the hirer to the owner be repaid, and that the obligation to pay the whole or part of any sum owed by the hirer to the owner is to cease. In considering whether it is just to make such an order, the court must have regard to the extent of the enjoyment of the goods by the hirer. **5–302**

An illustration is *Automotive Financial Services Ltd v. Henderson*, 1992 S.L.T. (Sh.Ct.) 63: A car was leased by A. Ltd to H. for 36 months. After six months H. returned the car to A. Ltd and stopped the rental payments.

A. Ltd sold the car, terminated the rental agreement and claimed from H. the total of the sums due on termination under the agreement.

H. claimed under section 132 that the court should order that their obligations under the agreement should cease or be restricted.

The sheriff refused to order such relief and granted decree to A. Ltd.

H. appealed to the sheriff principal.

Held (by Sheriff Principal R. D. Ireland) that the sheriff had taken all relevant matters into account and that the exercise of his discretion ought not to be disturbed on appeal.

Special powers of court in hire-purchase and conditional sale agreements

5–303 Section 133 enables the court, if it considers it just, to make "return orders" and "transfer orders" in relation to regulated hire-purchase or conditional sale agreements. A "return order" is an order for the return of the goods to the creditor. A "transfer order" is an order for the transfer to the debtor of the creditor's title to certain goods ("the transferred goods") and the return to the creditor of the remainder of the goods.

5–304 A transfer order can be made only where the paid-up sum exceeds that part of the total price which attaches to the transferred goods by at least one-third of the unpaid balance of the total price. The part of the total price which attaches to any goods may be specified in the agreement, but usually there will be no such express provision and in that case it will be for the court to fix an amount which it considers reasonable.

5–305 Even though a return order or a transfer order has been made, the debtor can still, before the goods actually enter the possession of the creditor, claim the goods by paying off the balance of the total price and fulfilling any other necessary conditions.

5–306 If goods are not returned to the creditor as required by a return order or a transfer order, the court may order the debtor to pay the creditor the unpaid portion of that part of the total price which attaches to the goods in question.

(ii) *Extortionate Credit Bargains*

5–307 The provisions of the Act concerning extortionate credit bargains are similar to, but more extensive than, provisions previously applicable under the Moneylenders Acts of 1900 and 1927. Moreover, the wording of the Act of 1974 is different: "grossly exorbitant" has replaced "excessive"; the test is thus a stricter one.

5–308 The leading provision is in section 137:

"If the court finds a credit bargain extortionate it may reopen the credit agreement so as to do justice between the parties."

The term "credit agreement" as used in this sentence means "any agreement between an individual (the 'debtor') and any other person (the 'creditor') by which the creditor provides the debtor with credit of any amount". "Individual", as elsewhere in the Act, includes a partnership or other unincorporated body of persons not consisting entirely of bodies corporate (s. 189(1)). Sections 137 to 140 are therefore not confined to regulated agreements: they extend to all credit agreements other than those in which the debtor is a body corporate or a partnership of bodies corporate. The credit may be of an amount well beyond the £15,000 ceiling generally applicable under the Act, and there is no exemption for "exempt agreements", "small agreements" or "non-commercial agreements". **5–309**

The scope of the provisions in sections 137 to 140 is further widened by the use of the term "credit bargain", which means the credit agreement together with any other transaction taken into account in computing the total charge for credit: the power of the court is therefore not confined to an examination of the terms of the credit agreement itself unless no other transaction is to be taken into account in computing the total charge for credit. **5–310**

When bargains are extortionate

Section 138 provides that a credit bargain is extortionate if it— **5–311**

(1) requires the debtor or an associate of his to make payments (whether unconditionally, or on certain contingencies only) which are grossly exorbitant, or

(2) otherwise grossly contravenes ordinary principles of fair dealing.

In deciding whether a credit bargain is extortionate the court must look at evidence on— **5–312**

(a) interest rates prevailing at the time when it was made,

(b) factors in relation to the debtor including—

(i) his age, experience, business capacity and state of health, and

(ii) the degree to which, at the time of making the credit bargain, he was under financial pressure, and the nature of that pressure,

(c) factors in relation to the creditor including—

(i) the degree of risk accepted by him, having regard to the value of any security provided,

(ii) his relationship to the debtor, and

(iii) whether or not a colourable cash price was quoted for any goods or services included in the credit bargain (the reason for this inclusion being that if the cash price is inflated, the stated rate of charge for credit will be misleading),

(d) factors in relation to a linked transaction including the question how far the transaction was reasonably required for the protection of debtor or creditor, or was in the interest of the debtor, and

(e) any other relevant considerations.

For the purposes of the Act the meaning of "extortionate" is confined to these statutory provisions, and it is not permissible to attach to it a meaning which it could have outside the Act: *Davies v. Directloans Ltd* [1986] 1 W.L.R. 823.

5–313 There is an illustration of how the court applies these provisions in *A. Ketley Ltd v. Scott* [1981] I.C.R. 241:

To finance the purchase of two flats S. obtained a loan of £20,500 from K. Ltd at 12 per cent for three months, *i.e.* at an annual rate of 48 per cent. S. had a protected tenancy of one of the flats. K. Ltd was given a legal charge on the property.

In an action by K. Ltd against S. for £22,960 (the principal sum plus interest at the agreed rate), S. applied for the agreement to be reopened on the ground that the credit bargain was extortionate.

The court (Foster J.) refused the application, being influenced by the following points:

Under (a): The rate of interest had to be compared with the prevailing rates for the *sort of transaction* in question, namely a loan which was the borrower's last resort.

Under (b): S., in view of his earnings and his experience in business, knew exactly what he was doing. The "financial pressure" alleged was his need to save the deposit of £2,250 and take advantage of the reduction in price arising from his protected tenancy, but he could easily have forfeited the deposit and remained in the property as a protected tenant; there was no question of his finding himself without a roof over his head. In the court's opinion there was no real "financial pressure".

Under (c): The degree of risk accepted by K. Ltd was considerable: there had been no time to check S.'s financial position, and to lend 82 per cent of the value of a property worth about £25,000 was highly speculative.

Under (e): It was clear that S. knew the rate of interest, and to enable the purchase to be completed the money had had to be provided with extraordinary speed—within a matter of hours—with the result that it was impossible to make inquiries as to S.'s financial position.

The judge further referred to the provision in section 139 that an agreement may be reopened "if the court thinks just", and held that it would not have been just to reopen the agreement in this case, since S. had failed to disclose several material facts to K. Ltd including his bank overdraft secured by a legal charge which, if registered, would have had priority over K. Ltd's charge.

Likewise in *Davies v. Directloans Ltd* (5–312, above) after considering the various factors the court (Edward Nugee, Q.C.) held that D.'s claim to have an agreement reopened also failed since neither were the payments required of D. "grossly exorbitant" nor was there gross contravention of "ordinary principles of fair dealing".

Reopening of extortionate agreements

By section 139 a credit agreement may, if the court thinks just, be reopened on the ground that the credit bargain is extortionate. The application to the court for this purpose may be made by the debtor or any surety. **5–314**

In reopening the agreement, the court may, for the purpose of relieving the debtor or a surety from payment of any sum in excess of that fairly due and reasonable, by order— **5–315**

(1) direct an accounting to be made between any persons,

(2) set aside the whole or part of any obligation imposed on the debtor or a surety by the credit bargain or any related agreement,

(3) require the creditor to repay the whole or part of any sum paid under the credit bargain or any related agreement by the debtor or a surety, whether paid to the creditor or any other person,

(4) direct the return to the surety of any property provided for the purposes of the security, or

(5) alter the terms of the credit agreement or of any security instrument.

It is no obstacle to the making of any of these orders that the effect of the order is to place a burden on the creditor in respect of an advantage unfairly enjoyed by another person who is a party to a linked transaction. For instance, if the total charge for credit in a credit agreement relating to goods includes the cost to the creditor **5–316** of having the goods serviced by a third party with whom the creditor has a maintenance contract, the court may, if it considers that the maintenance charge is extortionate, require the creditor to repay the whole or part of the sum paid under the credit agreement, even though the effect may be that the creditor has to bear the burden of paying sums due to the third party under the extortionate maintenance agreement.

V ANCILLARY CREDIT BUSINESSES

5–317 Part X of the Act brings within the scope of the Act various types of businesses which are connected with the provision of credit or hire facilities to consumers. These businesses are given the collective title of "ancillary credit businesses".

5–318 Broadly, the effect of Part X is to make "ancillary credit businesses"—a term requiring a statutory definition—subject to the licensing provisions of Part III of the Act, to impose on certain classes of ancillary credit business controls as to the seeking of business similar to the controls imposed by Part IV on consumer credit and consumer hire businesses, to enable regulations to be made as to the entry into ancillary credit agreements, and to protect consumers against the operation of "credit reference agencies", which maintain files of information as to the financial standing of individual consumers.

5–319 The provisions of Part X, therefore, fall under the following headings:

(a) definitions;
(b) licensing;
(c) seeking business;
(d) entry into agreements; and
(e) credit reference agencies.

(a) **Definitions**

5–320 The definitions set out in section 145, together with the exceptions stated in section 146, fix the scope of Part X.

5–321 An "ancillary credit business" is defined as "any business so far as it comprises or relates to"—

(i) credit brokerage,
(ii) debt-adjusting,

(iii) debt-counselling,
(iv) debt-collecting, or
(v) the operation of a credit reference agency.

Each of the terms in (i) to (v) is then in turn defined.

Note should be taken of the words "any business so far as it comprises or relates to" in the definition of ancillary credit business: the words imply that the person engaged in ancillary credit business may be carrying on that business within the framework of a business set up for some other purpose, *i.e.* it is the *activity* of ancillary credit business which is being brought within the scope of the Act, whether or not the activity itself constitutes a business. **5–322**

An important exception made by section 146 is that solicitors and advocates in preparing for and conducting court or arbitration proceedings are not to be treated as doing so in the course of any ancillary credit business. If it were not for this exception solicitors and advocates acting regularly for creditors might be considered to be carrying on the activity of debt-collecting, while those acting regularly for debtors might be considered to be carrying on the activity of debt-adjusting or debt-counselling. **5–323**

(i) *Credit Brokerage*

The definition of "credit brokerage" in section 145 is wide and complicated. In outline, the term means the effecting of introductions— **5–324**

(1) of individuals desiring to obtain credit to persons carrying on a consumer credit business or (in the case of a house-purchase) to any person carrying on a business in the course of which he provides credit secured on land, or

(2) of individuals desiring to obtain goods on hire to persons carrying on a consumer hire business, or

(3) of individuals desiring to obtain credit, or to obtain goods on hire, to other credit-brokers.

The persons introduced must always be "individuals" as defined in the Act: introducing companies to sources of credit is therefore not "credit brokerage" for the purposes of the Act. **5–325**

On the other hand, credit brokerage is not confined to regulated agreements: the introductions may be to creditors or owners whose agreements would be exempt or unregulated agreements. **5–326**

5–327 The result is that the term "credit brokerage" embraces a wide range of activities which would not normally be described as "brokerage": "credit-brokers" for the purposes of the Act include motor dealers and retail shops introducing retail customers to finance houses for hire-purchase, credit sale, conditional sale or rental facilities or personal loans, solicitors regularly negotiating advances for clients, and estate agents introducing house purchasers to building societies.

5–328 An exception is made by section 146 for introductions effected by an individual by canvassing off trade premises either a restricted-use credit agreement to finance a transaction between debtor and creditor or a regulated consumer hire agreement, *provided* the introductions are not effected by the individual in the capacity of an employee. This exception would exclude from the definition, for example, individuals who as part-time agents for mail-order companies canvass applications from persons wishing to acquire goods on credit sale from the mail-order companies.

(ii) *Debt-Adjusting*

5–329 "Debt-adjusting" is, in relation to debts due under consumer credit agreements or consumer hire agreements,—

(1) negotiating with the creditor or owner, on behalf of the debtor or hirer, terms for the discharge of a debt, or

(2) taking over, in return for payments by the debtor or hirer, his obligation to discharge a debt, or

(3) any similar activity concerned with the liquidation of a debt (s. 145(5)).

5–330 This is a wide definition, going well beyond persons whose main business is that of debt-adjustment; it covers, for example, solicitors who, without resorting to legal proceedings, negotiate on behalf of clients who are debtors, and banks providing overdrafts to customers in place of overdrafts outstanding from the customers to other banks.

5–331 The width of the definition makes it necessary to have some exclusions; for example, it is not "debt-adjusting" where the person negotiating, etc., is himself the "supplier" (s. 146(6)).

(iii) *Debt-Counselling*

5–332 "Debt-counselling" is "the giving of advice to debtors or hirers about the liquidation of debts due under consumer credit agreements or consumer hire agreements" (s. 145(6)).

Examples of debt-counsellors may include accountants, bankers, Citizens' Advice Bureaux, and free legal advice organisations. 5–333

Again, it is necessary to have some exclusions to prevent, for example, the creditor, owner or "supplier" from being himself counted as a debt-counsellor (s. 146(6)). 5–334

(iv) *Debt-Collecting*

"Debt-collecting" is "the taking of steps to procure payment of debts due under consumer credit agreements or consumer hire agreements" (s. 145(7)). 5–335

Again there are exclusions so that, for example, the creditor, owner or "supplier" who takes steps to procure payment is not to be treated as carrying on the business of debt-collecting (s. 146(6)). 5–336

(v) *Credit Reference Agency*

A "credit reference agency" is "a person carrying on a business comprising the furnishing of persons with information relevant to the financial standing of individuals, being information collected by the agency for that purpose" (s. 145(8)). 5–337

The use of the terms "person" and "individuals" should be noted: "person" includes a company (Interpretation Act 1978); "individual" includes partnerships (but not companies) (1974 Act, s. 189(1)). 5–338

The information must have been collected *for the purpose* of furnishing it to persons: the mere furnishing of information about an individual's financial standing does not amount to the operation of a credit reference agency; therefore a bank, for example, furnishing information based on its accounts between itself and one of its customers is not operating a credit reference agency. 5–339

It should be noted that the definition of "credit reference agency" makes no reference to consumer credit or consumer hire agreements, and so is not restricted to information collected and furnished in connection with such agreements. 5–340

(b) **Licensing**

The provisions of Part III of the Act ("Licensing of Credit and Hire Businesses") are extended to ancillary credit business (s. 147). 5–341

5–342 A person who carries on ancillary credit business without having the necessary licence cannot enforce any agreement for his services against the other party unless he obtains an order under section 148 from the Director General of Fair Trading. The provisions concerning applications to the Director in this connection are similar to those applicable under Part III (see 5–122 to 5–151, above); they include the right of an unlicensed person to make representations against the Director's refusal of an order and the right of the unlicensed person to appeal to the Secretary of State and, on a question of law, to the Court of Session (ss. 148 and 150). The effect is that the unlicensed person will be unable to claim his fees or commission from the person who uses his services, unless he applies for and obtains an order under section 148.

5–343 A further consequence of failure to obtain a licence for an ancillary credit business is that, by section 149, a regulated agreement itself, if made by a debtor or hirer who was introduced to the creditor or owner by an unlicensed credit-broker, is unenforceable against the debtor or hirer unless an order is obtained from the Director. An order to avoid this provision as to unenforceability of a regulated agreement may be granted to the credit-broker under section 149. The provisions for representations and appeals apply also to applications under section 149 (ss. 149 and 150). Because of section 149 those who carry on consumer credit and consumer hire businesses must be on their guard to ensure that the credit-brokers with whom they deal are duly licensed; for example, a finance company would be unable to enforce a hire-purchase agreement without an order from the Director if the supplier who introduced the finance company to the consumer was not licensed as a credit-broker.

(c) **Seeking Business**

5–344 Broadly the effect of sections 151 to 154 is to extend the provisions of Part IV on advertising, canvassing, etc., and quotations, display of information and conduct of business—see 5–152 to 5–178 above) to persons engaged in the business of credit brokerage, debt-adjusting and debt-counselling.

5–345 In section 153 there is a definition of "canvassing off trade premises" in similar terms to the definition in section 48 (see 5–167, above), and by section 154 it is an offence to canvass off trade premises the services of a person carrying on a business of credit brokerage, debt-adjusting or debt-counselling.

Section 155 provides that a credit-broker is not entitled to more than £3[13] as a fee or commission for his services if the introduction which he has made does not result in the individual's entering into a relevant agreement within six months after the introduction. Any excess over £3 may be recovered by the individual. The provision is aimed against the abuse of commission being charged by credit-brokers, supposedly trying to procure a loan, while knowing that they were unlikely to succeed. **5–346**

(d) **Entry into Agreements**

By section 156 regulations may make provision, in relation to agreements entered into in the course of a business of credit brokerage, debt-adjusting or debt-counselling, corresponding (with such modifications as the Secretary of State thinks fit) to the provision made under the sections in Part V ("Entry into Credit or Hire Agreements") which deal with regulations applicable to regulated agreements (see 5–180 to 5–205, above). **5–347**

No regulations have yet been made under section 156. **5–348**

(e) **Credit Reference Agencies**

The provisions under this heading are designed to deal with the difficulties faced by a consumer who is refused credit because of erroneous information as to his financial standing supplied to prospective lenders by a "credit reference agency" (defined in section 145 as "a person carrying on a business comprising the furnishing of persons with information relevant to the financial standing of individuals, being information collected by the agency for that purpose"). These difficulties were considered by the Crowther Committee and also by the Younger Committee on Privacy whose report was published in 1972 (Cmnd. 5012). The Younger Committee's recommendations were adopted in a strengthened form in the Act of 1974. **5–349**

The consumer has three basic rights conferred on him: **5–350**

---

[13] substituted for £1 by Consumer Credit (Increase of Monetary Amounts) Order 1983 (S.I. 1983 No. 1571).

(i) the right to obtain from a creditor, owner or negotiator the name and address of any credit reference agency consulted;

(ii) the right to obtain from the credit reference agency a copy of its file on him; and

(iii) the right to require wrong information on the file to be corrected.

(i) *Name, etc., of Agency*

5–351 By section 157 a creditor, owner or "negotiator" (*i.e.* a person who has conducted "antecedent negotiations" as defined in section 56 with the debtor or hirer) must on the written request of the debtor or hirer give him, within the prescribed period, notice of the name and address of any credit reference agency from which the creditor, owner or negotiator has, during the antecedent negotiations, applied for information about his financial standing. This provision does not apply to a request received more than 28 days after the termination of the antecedent negotiations. A creditor, owner or negotiator who fails to comply with section 157 commits an offence.

5–352 The period prescribed for the giving of the notice under section 157 is seven working days (Consumer Credit (Credit Reference Agency) Regulations 1977 (S.I. 1977 No. 329)).

(ii) *Copy of File*

5–353 By section 158 a credit reference agency, within the prescribed period after receiving a written request from the consumer and the particulars reasonably required by the agency to enable it to identify the file, and also a fee of £1,[14] must give the consumer a copy of the file relating to him kept by the agency. At the same time the agency must give the consumer a statement in the prescribed form of his rights under section 159 to have the file corrected. The word "file" means all the information about the consumer kept by the agency, regardless of how the information is stored, and "copy of the file" means, if the information kept is not in plain English (*e.g.* if it is coded), a transcript reduced into plain

[14] substituted for 25p by Consumer Credit (Increase of Monetary Amounts) Order 1983 (S.I. 1983 No. 1571).

English. If the agency does not keep a file relating to the consumer, it must give him notice of that fact. An agency which contravenes section 158 commits an offence.

The regulations applicable are the Consumer Credit (Credit Reference Agency) Regulations 1977; they prescribe a period of seven working days for the giving of the copy of the file. **5–354**

It was recognised that the right conferred by section 158 could seriously affect the ability of a credit reference agency to provide a proper service to its subscribers concerning business consumers (*i.e.* sole traders and partnerships): the copy of the file would almost certainly reveal the agency's sources of information, and these sources, while willing to give the information in confidence, would decline to do so in view of the new right conferred by section 158. An alternative procedure is therefore available under section 160 in relation to business consumers. **5–355**

For the operation of the alternative procedure an application must be made to the Director General of Fair Trading by the credit reference agency, and the Director must be satisfied that— **5–356**

(1) compliance with section 158 in the case of consumers carrying on a business would adversely affect the service provided by the agency to its customers, and

(2) having regard to the methods employed by the agency and to any other relevant factors, it is probable that consumers carrying on a business would not be prejudiced by the substitution of the alternative procedure.

If the application is successful, the agency has then an option when it receives a request for a copy of a file from a consumer who carries on a business: the agency may elect to comply with section 158 or, instead of giving the consumer a copy of the file, it may give the consumer such information included in or based on entries in the file as the Director may direct. If, within 28 days after receiving such information (or any longer period allowed by the Director), the consumer gives notice to the Director that he is dissatisfied with the information and satisfies the Director that he has taken reasonable steps, in relation to the agency, with a view to removing the cause of his dissatisfaction, the Director may direct the agency to give the Director a copy of the file, and the Director may then disclose to the consumer such of the information on the file as the Director thinks fit. **5–357**

5–358 An agency which elects to deal with a request under section 160 and then fails to comply with the requirements of that section commits an offence.

(iii) *Correction of Wrong Information*

5–359 By section 159 a consumer who has been given a copy of his file under section 158 and considers that an entry on it is incorrect and that, if it is not corrected, he is likely to be prejudiced, may give notice to the agency requiring it either to remove the entry from the file or to amend it.

5–360 There are further elaborate provisions designed to reinforce this right: within 28 days after receiving such a notice the agency must inform the consumer that it has removed the entry from the file or amended the entry, or taken no action; the consumer then has a further 28 days in which he may, unless he has been informed by the agency that it has removed the entry, serve a further notice on the agency requiring it to add to the file an accompanying notice of correction (not exceeding 200 words) drawn up by the consumer, and include a copy of it when furnishing information included in or based on that entry; if the consumer does not then receive a notice from the agency confirming that it is to comply with the consumer's second notice, the consumer may apply to the Director; the agency also has the right to apply to the Director if it appears to the agency that the notice of correction is incorrect, defamatory, frivolous, scandalous or for any other reason unsuitable; the Director may make such order as he thinks fit, and a person who fails to comply with the order commits an offence.

5–361 These provisions in section 159 apply also to information given to business consumers under the alternative procedure of section 160 (s. 160(5)).

VI ENFORCEMENT OF THE ACT

5–362 The following are among the provisions in Part XI of the Act ("Enforcement of Act").

Enforcement Authorities

5–363 The enforcement authorities are the Director General of Fair Trading and the local weights and measures authorities (which in Scotland are the local government councils).

Every local weights and measures authority must, whenever the Director requires, report to him in such form and with such particulars as he requires on the exercise of their functions under the Act (s. 161). 5–364

Entry and Inspection

A duly authorised officer of an enforcement authority may exercise the following powers of entry and inspection at all reasonable hours and on production, if required, of his credentials: 5–365

(a) He may, in order to ascertain whether a breach of the Act has been committed, inspect any goods and enter any premises, other than premises used only as a dwelling.

(b) He may, if he has reasonable cause to suspect that a breach has been committed, require the production of business books and documents and legible reproductions of information recorded otherwise than in a legible form.

(c) He may seize and detain any goods, books or documents which he has reason to believe may be required as evidence in criminal proceedings under the Act. In this connection he may, if this is reasonably necessary, require any container to be broken open by any person having authority to do so, and, if that person does not comply, break it open himself.

Where admission to premises is likely to be refused or where an application for admission would defeat the object of the entry, a warrant may be obtained from a sheriff or justice of the peace authorising an officer of an enforcement authority to enter the premises (by force if need be). 5–366

An officer entering premises, either with or without a warrant, may take with him such other persons and such equipment as he thinks necessary. 5–367

Regulations may provide that, in cases described by the regulations, an officer of a local weights and measures authority is not to be taken as a "duly authorised" officer unless he is authorised by the Director (s. 162). The relevant regulations are the Consumer Credit (Entry and Inspection) Regulations 1977 (S.I. 1977 No. 331, as amended by S.I. 1984 No. 1046). 5–368

Where, in exercising the powers mentioned, an officer seizes and detains goods and their owner suffers loss because of the seizure or because of the loss, damage or deterioration of the goods during 5–369 detention, then, unless the owner is convicted of an offence under the Act, the authority must compensate him for the loss suffered. Any dispute as to the right to or amount of any compensation is decided by arbitration (s. 163).

Power to Make Test Purchases, etc.

5–370 An enforcement authority may make, or authorise any of its officers to make, purchases of goods and may authorise any of its officers to procure services or facilities or enter into agreements or other transactions such as may appear to it expedient for determining whether the statutory provisions are being complied with (s. 164).

Obstruction of Authorised Officers

5–371 A person commits an offence if he wilfully obstructs an officer of an enforcement authority, wilfully fails to comply with a requirement properly made for entry and inspection under section 162, above, or without reasonable cause fails to give an officer other assistance or information which the officer reasonably requires in performing his functions under the Act. Refusing to speak to an enforcement officer and failure to hand over certain documents requested by him were held to be offences under these provisions in *Aitchison v. Rizza*, 1985 S.C.C.R. 297.

5–372 It is also an offence for a person, in giving information, to make any statement which he knows to be false.

5–373 A person, however, need not answer any question or give any information if to do so might incriminate himself or (if he is married) his spouse (s. 165).

Notification of Convictions and Judgments to Director

5–374 Where a person is convicted of an offence or has a decree given against him by a court in the United Kingdom and it appears to the court (having regard to the functions of the Director under the Act of 1974) that the conviction or decree should be brought to the Director's attention and that it might not be brought to his attention unless the court made arrangements for that purpose, the court may make such arrangements, even after the proceedings have been finally disposed of (s. 166).

The proceedings referred to in section 166 are not necessarily proceedings (civil or criminal) *under the Act*. The purpose of the provision is to make available to the Director information which it would be relevant for him to have when exercising his licensing powers under Parts III and X of the Act. **5–375**

Penalties, Defences and Onus of Proof

Schedule 1 to the Act tabulates 35 offences created by the Act, setting opposite each the mode of prosecution (summary, or solemn) and the maximum imprisonment or fine (s. 167). **5–376**

In proceedings for an offence under the Act it is a defence for the person charged to prove— **5–377**

(a) that his act or omission was due to a mistake, or to reliance on information supplied to him, or to an act or omission by another person, or to an accident or some other cause beyond his control, and

(b) that he took all reasonable precautions and exercised all due diligence to avoid such act or omission by himself or any person under his control.

Where this defence involves the allegation that the act or omission was due to an act or omission by another person or to reliance on information supplied by another person, the person charged is not entitled, without leave of the court, to rely on the defence unless, at least seven clear days before the hearing, he gives the prosecutor as much information as he has for the purpose of identifying the other person (s. 168). **5–378**

Where at any time a body corporate (*e.g.* a company) commits an offence under the Act with the consent or connivance of, or because of neglect by, any individual, then the individual commits the same offence if at that time— **5–379**

(a) he is a director, manager, secretary or similar officer of the body corporate, or

(b) he is purporting to act as such an officer, or

(c) the body corporate is managed by its members and he is one of them (s. 169).

Section 171 provides for where the onus of proof is to lie in various proceedings, *e.g.* if, under section 139, the debtor or any surety alleges that the credit bargain is extortionate it is for the creditor to prove the contrary. **5–380**

Statements by Creditor or Owner to be Binding

5–381 Section 172 lists a number of provisions under which the creditor or owner is required to supply the debtor, hirer or surety with a statement (*e.g.* section 77(1) which requires the creditor to furnish the debtor with information as to the amounts paid and payable under a regulated agreement for fixed-sum credit), and provides that the statements given by the creditor or owner are to be binding on him.

5–382 The court has a discretion to grant relief to the creditor or owner from the operation of this provision where in court proceedings it is sought to rely on a statement and the statement is shown to be incorrect.

Contracting-out Forbidden

5–383 Section 173 prohibits contracting out of the protection given by the Act. The section provides that a term in a regulated agreement or linked transaction is void if it is inconsistent with a provision in the Act or regulations for the protection of the debtor or hirer or his associate or any surety.

VII MOTOR VEHICLES ON HIRE-PURCHASE OR CONDITIONAL SALE

5–384 The major Act on hire-purchase in Scotland before the Act of 1974 was the consolidating Hire-Purchase (Scotland) Act 1965. That Act, like the corresponding Act applicable to England—the Hire-Purchase Act 1965—was one of the Acts wholly repealed by the Act of 1974 (s. 192(3)(b) and Sched. 5).

5–385 Part III of the Hire-Purchase Act 1964, applicable to both countries, and concerned with the protection of private purchasers of motor vehicles, was not repealed by the Act of 1974, and is reproduced, with some changes in terminology only, in Schedule 4 to the Act of 1974.

5–386 The provisions apply where a motor vehicle has been hired under a hire-purchase agreement, or has been agreed to be sold under a conditional sale agreement, and, before the property in the vehicle (*i.e.* the ownership of the vehicle) has passed to the debtor, he disposes of the vehicle to another person (1964 Act, s.27(1)).

The other person may be a "private purchaser" or a "trade or finance purchaser". The latter term means a purchaser who carries on a business which consists, wholly or partly,— **5–387**

(a) of purchasing motor vehicles for the purpose of offering or exposing them for sale, or

(b) of providing finance by purchasing motor vehicles for the purpose of hiring them under hire-purchase agreements or agreeing to sell them under conditional sale agreements.

"Private purchaser" means a purchaser who does not carry on any such business (1964 Act, s. 29(2)).

Section 27 of the Act of 1964 provides that where the vehicle is disposed of to a private purchaser who purchases it in good faith without notice of the hire-purchase or conditional sale agreement affecting it, the private purchaser obtains as good a title to the vehicle as he would have obtained if the debtor had been the owner. Similar protection is extended to a private purchaser in the situation where the vehicle has first been disposed of to a trade or finance purchaser from whom it has been purchased by the private purchaser. **5–388**

The provisions apply even where the debtor in the hire-purchase or conditional sale agreement is a body corporate and the price exceeds £15,000. **5–389**

Further Reading

Gloag and Henderson, *The Law of Scotland*, Chapter 18

W. A. Wilson, *The Scottish Law of Debt*, Chapters 3 and 4

David M. Walker, *Principles of Scottish Private Law*, Volume II, Chapter 4.12 (part), and Volume III, Chapter 5.34 (part)

W. Cowan H. Ervine, *Consumer Law in Scotland*, Chapter 9

The Laws of Scotland: Stair Memorial Encyclopaedia, Volume 5, Title *Consumer Credit* by Judith J. H. Pearson

E. *Encyclopedia of Consumer Credit Law*, A. G. Guest, Michael G. Lloyd and Eva Lomnicka (Editors) (loose-leaf, Sweet & Maxwell)

E. R. M. Goode, *Consumer Credit Law* (1989, Butterworths)

CHAPTER 6

BILLS OF EXCHANGE, CHEQUES AND PROMISSORY NOTES

	Para.
Introduction	6–01
(a) Negotiable Instruments in General	6–06
(b) Some Functions of a Bill of Exchange	6–08
I Bills of Exchange	6–14
(a) Definitions of Bills	6–16
"Unconditional Order in Writing"	6–20
"Addressed by One Person to Another	6–21
"Signed by the Person Giving it"	6–22
"To Pay on Demand or at a Fixed or Determinable Future Time"	6–28
"A Sum Certain in Money"	6–33
"To or to the Order of a Specified Person or to Bearer"	6–35
(b) Acceptance of a Bill	6–37
(c) Issue of a Bill	6–40
(i) "Delivery"	6–41
(ii) "Complete in Form"	6–42
(iii) "Holder"	6–45
(d) Holder in Due Course	6–47
(i) "Good Faith"	6–50
(ii) "Value"	6–51
(iii) "Defect in Title"	6–57
(e) Negotiation of a Bill	6–62
(f) Presentment for Acceptance and Presentment for Payment	6–69
(i) Presentment for Acceptance	6–70
Rules as to presentment for acceptance	6–72
Excuses for non-presentment for acceptance	6–73
(ii) Presentment for Payment	6–77
Rules as to presentment for payment	6–78
Excuses for delay or non-presentment for payment	6–79
(g) Procedure on Dishonour	6–80
(i) Notice of Dishonour	6–81
Rules as to notice of dishonour	6–82
Excuses for delay or non-notice	6–83
(ii) Protest	6–84
(1) Noting	6–86
(2) Protest	6–89
Excuses for delay or non-protest	6–91
(h) Liabilities of Parties	6–92
(i) Liability of Drawee	6–98
(ii) Liability of Acceptor	6–106
(iii) Liability of Drawer	6–108
(iv) Liability of Indorser	6–111
(v) Liability of Transferor by Delivery	6–115
(vi) Liability of Referee in Case of Need	6–117
(i) Measure of Damages on Dishonour	6–118
(j) Enforcement of Liability by Summary Diligence	6–119
(k) Discharge of Bill	6–125
(i) Payment in Due Course	6–127
(ii) Acceptor Becoming Holder	6–130
(iii) Renunciation or Waiver	6–131
(iv) Cancellation	6–132
(v) Alteration	6–133
(vi) Prescription	6–135
(l) Acceptance and Payment for Honour *supra* Protest	6–136
(i) Acceptance for Honour *supra* Protest	6–138
(ii) Payment for Honour *supra* Protest	6–141
(m) Miscellaneous Statutory Provisions	6–142
(i) Lost Bills	6–143
(ii) Bill in a Set	6–144
(iii) Conflict of Laws	6–145
II Cheques	6–147
(a) Relation of Banker and Customer	6–150
(i) Who is a "Banker"	6–152
(ii) Who is a "Customer"	6–155

	Para.
(iii) Banker's Duties to Customer	6–159
(1) Banker's duty of secrecy	6–161
(2) Banker's duty to honour cheques	6–164
(a) "If the account is in credit"	6–165
(b) "Drawn by a customer"	6–168
(c) "A mandate to the banker to pay"	6–169
(d) "According to the tenor of the cheque"	6–171
(iv) Customer's Duties to Banker	6–175
(1) Reasonable precautions in drawing cheques	6–176
(2) Timeous notification of forgeries	6–177
(b) Presentment of Cheque for Payment	6–178
(c) Crossed Cheques	6–182
(i) General and Special Crossings	6–185
(ii) Who is Entitled to Cross a Cheque	6–188
(iii) Effect of Crossing	6–192
(iv) Effect of Addition of "Not Negotiable"	6–194
(v) Effect of Addition of "Account Payee"	6–195
(d) Protection of Bankers	6–196
(i) Protection of Paying Banker	6–197
(1) Bills of Exchange Act 1882, section 60	6–203
(2) Bills of Exchange Act 1882, section 80, as amended by Cheques Act 1992, section 2	6–204
(3) Cheques Act 1957, section 1	6–205
(ii) Protection of Collecting Banker	6–207
III Promissory Notes	6–225
(a) Delivery	6–235
(b) Joint and Several Notes	6–236
(c) Note Payable on Demand	6–237
(d) Presentment for Payment	6–240
(e) Liability of Maker	6–242

INTRODUCTION

THE law relating to bills of exchange, cheques and promissory notes was codified by the Bills of Exchange Act 1882, which, with a few exceptions, applies equally to Scotland and England. In this chapter references to sections are, except where the context otherwise requires, references to sections of that codifying Act. The only major amendments of the Act are those concerning cheques, and are now to be found in the Cheques Act 1957 as amended by the Cheques Act 1992. **6–01**

Bills of exchange, cheques and promissory notes are the principal (but not the only) instances of "negotiable instruments", *i.e.* they are documents having the quality of "negotiability", which enables them to pass from one person to another with much the same effect as that with which cash passes from one person to another. **6–02**

The 100 sections of the Act of 1882 substantially codified the then existing common law of Scotland and England on the subject. In *McLean v. Clydesdale Bank Ltd* (1883) 11 R. (H.L.) 1; (1883) 10 R. 719, a case decided under the common law shortly after the Act **6–03** of 1882 had received the royal assent, Lord Blackburn said (at 11 R. (H.L.) p. 3):

"The general law merchant for many years has in all countries caused bills of exchange to be negotiable. That is a common ground which belongs to all, or almost all, countries, and it has been adopted as the law in all civilized countries. There are in some cases differences and peculiarities which by the municipal law of each country are grafted upon it, and which do not affect other countries; but the general rules of the law merchant are the same in all countries, and before the recent Act (the Bills of Exchange Act) which received the royal assent in August 1882, the general law of Scotland and the general law of England were the same. Some peculiarities there were in the municipal law of Scotland as to the mode in which it was to be enforced. . . . Upon the general question of negotiability the law has always been the same in both countries, and we have always been in the habit of treating the authorities of each country as authorities in the other."

The Bill was originally an English measure, and it was said to be generally known that it was Professor Dove Wilson who was mainly influential in having it extended to Scotland (*per* Sheriff-Substitute Brown in *McRobert v. Lindsay* (1898) 14 Sh.Ct.Rep. 89; (1898) 5 S.L.T. 317).

The Act provides that the rules of common law including the law merchant, except in so far as they are inconsistent with the express provisions of the Act, continue to apply to bills of exchange, cheques and promissory notes (s. 97(2)).

6–04 This chapter has three divisions:

I. Bills of exchange;
II. Cheques; and
III. Promissory notes.

These divisions correspond to Parts II to IV of the Act.

Parts I and V of the Act consist of preliminary and supplementary provisions respectively, equally applicable to bills of exchange, cheques and promissory notes (*e.g.* the definition of terms such as "bearer", "holder", and "indorsement" (s. 2), and rules concerning good faith (s. 90), signature (s. 91) and the calculation of time (s. 92)).

Part II (on bills of exchange) is by far the longest Part of the Act (ss. 3 to 72). The statutory provisions applicable to cheques (ss. 73 to 82 of the Act of 1882 along with the eight sections of the

Cheques Act 1957) and to promissory notes (ss. 83 to 89 of the Act of 1882) appear at first sight to be much shorter. It must, however, be kept in view that a cheque is by definition a "bill of exchange drawn on a banker payable on demand", with the result that, except where the sections expressly applicable to cheques provide otherwise, the provisions of Part II of the Act apply to cheques (s. 73), and that by section 89 the provisions of Part II are, with some necessary modifications and exceptions, made to extend also to promissory notes.

To assist in the appreciation of the subject-matter of this chapter, a brief explanation is first given of: **6–05**

(a) negotiable instruments in general; and

(b) some functions of a bill of exchange.

(a) Negotiable Instruments in General

Negotiable instruments form one category of incorporeal moveable property and so have some affinity with other incorporeal moveable property such as policies of life assurance, shares in companies, claims of damages, goodwill, and patents. The distinctive feature of negotiable instruments is the quality of "negotiability", by which they are exceptions to two rules which are generally applicable to the transfer of incorporeal moveable property. A policy of life assurance, for instance, may be transferred by the policy-holder to another person by an assignation, the policy-holder being the cedent and the person to whom the policy is assigned being the assignee. The debtor (*i.e.* the party liable to pay the proceeds of the policy on the cedent's death) continues to be the assurance company. According to the general rules: **6–06**

(i) the assignation must be intimated to the assurance company in order to enable the assignee to collect the proceeds of the policy from the company on the cedent's death; and

(ii) the assignee cannot obtain any better right to payment from the assurance company than the cedent had, the maxim applicable being *assignatus utitur jure auctoris* ("the assignee enjoys (only) the right of his cedent"); *e.g.* if the policy was voidable as between the original policy-holder and the company on account of misrepresentation by the former as to his state of health, the policy remains voidable after the assignation.

In contrast, where a negotiable instrument is transferred:

(i) no assignation or intimation is necessary; if the document is payable to "bearer", the mere handing over of the document is sufficient, while if the document is payable to "order" the mere indorsement (signature on the back of the document) followed by handing over is sufficient; and

(ii) the person to whom the transfer is made, provided he takes the document in good faith, for value and without notice of any defect in the transferor's title, obtains a good title to the obligation, although the transferor may have had no title or only a defective title.

6–07 Examples of negotiable instruments are bills of exchange (including cheques), promissory notes (including bank notes), share warrants issued to bearer (which entitle the bearer to the shares specified), debentures payable to bearer, and dividend warrants. The following are not negotiable instruments—postal orders, deposit receipts, share certificates, and bills of lading. The class of negotiable instruments is not closed: other documents may, by statute or by decisions of the courts giving effect to mercantile usage, be added to the class. It is not, however, permissible for contracting parties to create a new form of negotiable instrument by mere agreement unsupported by mercantile usage: any isolated agreement of this kind would be binding only on the parties to it and would not affect the rights of subsequent holders of the document; but if the agreement were of a type in common use in mercantile circles, the courts might hold that the document in question should be added to the class of negotiable instruments.

(b) Some Functions of a Bill of Exchange

6–08 Bills of exchange were developed in medieval Europe to meet the needs of merchants engaged in foreign trade. Such documents enabled the merchants to overcome the difficulty in transmitting coins from one country to another. In Scotland by the end of the seventeenth century bills of exchange were in use for both foreign and inland trading, as is proved by the passing of a Scots Act in 1681 providing for summary diligence on foreign bills, followed by a further Scots Act in 1696 extending summary diligence to inland bills.

6–09 With the expansion of trade, the use of bills of exchange increased, so that by 1882 the law relating to bills had emerged as a sufficiently important and well-defined branch of commercial law as to merit the codification of that year.

Bills of exchange other than cheques are now seldom encountered in inland transactions. Even in foreign trade they are now used in fewer transactions than formerly, though a significant part of foreign trade is still conducted by transactions which *include* the use of bills of exchange (*e.g.* a bill of exchange may be one of the documents specified in a "documentary credit"). The chief importance of the law relating to bills of exchange at the present day, at least in inland transactions, is that it includes the law relating to cheques. Since a cheque is by definition "a bill of exchange drawn on a banker payable on demand", and since the statutory provisions applying to bills of exchange are made to apply (with some modifications) to cheques (s. 73), the law relating to cheques, obviously of supreme importance to the present-day business community, must be approached via the law relating to bills of exchange in general. **6–10**

Bills of exchange have fulfilled various functions, and have often featured in complex transactions as can be seen from reported cases. The question of whether or not a particular document is a bill of exchange depends on whether or not it satisfies the statutory definition (6–16, below). A preliminary glance at some of the functions of a bill of exchange will make the study of the precise terms of that definition more meaningful. Two situations, shorn of all the complexities which often beset actual practice and decided cases, are given here as illustrations: **6–11**

(i) A bill of exchange may be used in conjunction with a bill of lading to ensure that a seller who ships goods to a buyer will obtain, by the time when the goods are delivered to the buyer, either immediate payment or at least an easily enforceable written undertaking by the buyer to pay. **6–12**

For example, B, a seller in Brazil, will receive on shipping a cargo to G, a buyer from Glasgow, a bill of lading from the master of the ship (in practice usually from the master's agent). This is both a receipt for the goods and a document of title to them. The master will deliver the cargo only to the person who, at Glasgow, presents the bill of lading to him.

B sends the bill of lading to his own agent in Glasgow, attaching to it a bill of exchange for the price of the goods. In the bill of exchange B orders G to pay to some specified person, such as B's

Glasgow agent, the sum of money which is the price of the goods. The Glasgow agent will hand over the bill of lading to G (putting G in a position to collect the cargo from the ship) only if G pays, or at least accepts, the bill of exchange.

This is an over-simplification of what happens in practice: the transactions are conducted through banks as agents for the parties themselves. Accordingly, B would not normally send the bill of lading with the bill of exchange attached direct to a Glasgow agent: he would hand over the documents to his bank in Brazil, and that bank would then transmit them to its Glasgow agent (usually a Scottish bank).

6–13 (ii) A bill of exchange, although it may not be payable until some future date, can be used by its holder to provide immediate cash. This is accomplished where the holder "discounts" the bill at his bank.

For example, one merchant, X, who has sold the goods to another merchant, Y, may wish to allow Y three months' credit, and so he will draw on Y a bill of exchange payable three months after its date. When Y accepts this bill, X may obtain immediate cash for it by having it discounted at his bank. X will receive the sum for which the bill was drawn, less a discount.

I BILLS OF EXCHANGE

6–14 A bill of exchange has three principal characteristics:

(i) It contains an obligation to pay money. The person who holds it has therefore a document, of at least potential value, which he may use to obtain cash or credit for himself. If the bill has been accepted by the drawee, it is the acceptor who is primarily liable to pay it, but there are circumstances in which other parties to the bill, provided they have signed the bill, are liable to pay it. Hence the liability of the drawer and of indorsers, as well as that of the acceptor, must be taken into account.

(ii) It is a negotiable instrument. The results are that: (1) it may be transferred by one holder to another holder without the need for intimation to the acceptor or other person liable on the bill; and (2) the second, or subsequent, holder acquires a good title to the bill (provided certain conditions are fulfilled), so that his rights against the acceptor or other person liable are unaffected by any defects in the title of a previous holder.

(iii) It operates as an assignation of funds held by the drawee, when it is intimated to the drawee. This characteristic is of practical importance where the holder presents the bill to the drawee at a time when the drawee has insufficient funds in his hands to pay the full amount of the bill, and because of that does not accept the bill. Such funds as he has are, by the mere fact that the bill has been presented to him, assigned to the holder. The presentment takes effect as an intimated assignation. In this respect there is a distinction between Scots and English law: the common law of Scotland is expressly preserved by section 53(2), except as regards those bills of exchange which are stopped cheques. On this see 6–99 *et seq.*, below. Under English law a bill does not, of itself, operate as an assignment of funds in the hands of the drawer (s. 53(1)).

These three major characteristics underlie the specific statutory **6–15** provisions of Part II of the Act, which are considered below under these headings:

(a) definitions of bills;
(b) acceptance of a bill;
(c) issue of a bill;
(d) holder in due course;
(e) negotiation of a bill;
(f) presentment for acceptance and presentment for payment;
(g) procedure on dishonour;
(h) liabilities of parties;
(i) measure of damages on dishonour;
(j) enforcement of liability by summary diligence;
(k) discharge of bill;
(l) acceptance and payment for honour *supra* protest;
(m) miscellaneous statutory provisions (lost bills, bill in a set and conflict of laws).

(a) **Definitions of Bills**

The Act defines a bill of exchange as follows: "A bill of exchange is **6–16** an unconditional order in writing, addressed by one person to another, signed by the person giving it, requiring the person to whom it is addressed to pay on demand or at a fixed or determinable future time a sum certain in money to or to the order of a specified person, or to bearer" (s. 3(1)). A document which does not comply with these conditions, or which orders any act to be done in addition to the payment of money, is not a bill of exchange (s. 3(2)).

6–17 Before some explanatory comments are made on this definition, it is appropriate to set out the statutory definitions of inland and foreign bills.

"An inland bill is a bill which is or on the face of it purports to be

(*a*) both drawn and payable within the British Islands, or

(*b*) drawn within the British Islands upon some person resident therein.

Any other bill is a foreign bill." "British Islands" mean any part of the United Kingdom, the islands of Man, Guernsey, Jersey, Alderney, and Sark, and the islands adjacent to any of them if they are part of Her Majesty's dominions (s. 4(1)).

6–18 The only important legal distinction between an inland bill and a foreign bill is that, if a foreign bill is dishonoured, it must be "protested" for non-acceptance or for non-payment; this procedure is not necessary if the bill is an inland bill (s. 51(1) and (2)). Unless the contrary appears on the face of the bill, the holder of the bill may treat it as an inland bill (s. 4(2)).

6–19 The wording of the definition of a bill of exchange will now be examined with reference to the following fictitious specimen bill:

Glasgow,
£1,000 November 6, 1991
At sight pay to Peter Piper or order the sum of One thousand pounds. Value received.

Derek Driver

To Arthur Dee,
15 High Street,
Edinburgh.

Alternatives to "At sight" would be "On demand", "Three months after date", "Six months after sight", etc., and instead of "Peter Piper or order" one might have "Peter Piper or bearer", "me" or "bearer".

This specimen includes some items which, though usual, are not essential to the validity of the bill. A bill is not invalid if it is not dated ("November 6, 1991"), or if it does not include the words "Value received", or if it does not specify the place where it is drawn ("Glasgow"). A bill may specify the place where it is payable (*e.g.* "at the Bank of Scotland Head Office" or (more usually) at a particular branch), but this is also not essential (s. 3(4)). Nor is a bill invalid merely because it is ante-dated or post-dated, or bears a date which is a Sunday (s. 13(2)).

"Unconditional Order in Writing"

This is the word "pay", an order given by Derek Driver to Arthur **6–20**
Dee. If conditions could be attached to the order, the document would not serve the needs of the commercial community, because investigation would be necessary to ascertain whether or not the conditions had been fulfilled.

An instance of a conditional order is an order to pay out of a particular fund. It is, however, permissible to have an unqualified order to pay, coupled with either:

(i) an indication of a particular fund out of which Arthur Dee is to reimburse himself or a particular account to be debited with the amount; or

(ii) a statement of the transaction which gave rise to the bill.

Such an order is regarded as "unconditional" (s. 3(3)).

A document expressed as a conditional order may, if transferred to a third party, be used by him as proof of a debt, but it is not a bill of exchange (*Lawson's Executors v. Watson*, 1907 S.C. 1353).

"Writing" includes print (s. 2). A bill may therefore be partly printed.

"Addressed by One Person to Another"

The order is addressed by Derek Driver, who is referred to as the **6–21**
"drawer", to Arthur Dee, who is referred to as the "drawee".

The drawee must be named or otherwise indicated in the bill with reasonable certainty (s. 6(1)). The purpose is to ensure that the holder of the bill will know to whom he is to present the bill for acceptance or payment.

A bill may be addressed to two or more drawees (*e.g.* to partners), but an order addressed to two drawees in the alternative or to two or more drawees in succession is not within the definition of a bill (s. 6(2)).

"Signed by the Person Giving it"

6–22 Derek Driver must sign the bill. If, and as long as, his signature is the only signature on the bill, he is the only party liable to pay the bill. He may, however, insert an express stipulation in the bill negativing or limiting his own liability (s. 16(1)).

The requirement that the drawer must sign the bill is part of the wider principle applicable to bills of exchange (and also to cheques and promissory notes) that signature is essential for liability: no person is liable as drawer, indorser, or acceptor unless he has signed the bill (s. 23). Other statutory provisions as to signature may be conveniently noted here, although they are not restricted to the drawer's signature.

6–23 It is not necessary that the drawer (or the other person concerned) should sign the bill (or cheque or promissory note) with his own hand: it is sufficient if the signature is written by some other person by or under his authority (s. 91(1)). In the case of corporations (including limited and other registered companies) sealing with the corporate seal is sufficient as a signature, but sealing is not essential (s. 91(2)). By the Companies Act 1985 (s. 37), a bill of exchange or promissory note is deemed to have been made, accepted or indorsed on behalf of a company if made, accepted, or indorsed in the name of, or by or on behalf or on account of, the company by any person acting under its authority.

6–24 Where a person signs a bill in a trade or assumed name, he is liable on the bill as if he had signed it in his own name (s. 23, proviso (1)). The signature of the name of a firm is equivalent to the signature of all the partners, provided the person signing the firm's name has the necessary express or implied authority to bind the firm (s. 23, proviso (2)). The circumstances may be such that the person who takes the bill ought to suspect that a partner signing the firm's name has no authority to do so (*cf. Paterson Brothers v. Gladstone* (1891) 18 R. 403 (2–64, above), in which a partner who had signed the firm name on promissory notes was held not to have been acting in the ordinary course of the firm's business, with the result that the firm (and so ultimately the other partners) could not be held liable to pay the notes).

6–25 An unauthorised signature is not the same as a forged signature: the former may be ratified and so become binding on the party on whose behalf it purported to be made, whereas a forged signature cannot be ratified. That distinction apart, however, the statutory rule applicable to forged and to unauthorised signatures on bills is the same: subject to the provisions of the Act, the signature is wholly inoperative, and no right to retain the bill or to give a discharge for it or to enforce payment of it against any party can be acquired through that signature, unless the party against whom the bill is being retained or enforced is barred from saying that the signature was forged or unauthorised (s. 24). An instance of such a bar is given in section 54: the acceptor against whom the bill is being enforced is barred from saying that the drawer's signature was forged. *Greenwood v. Martins Bank Ltd* [1933] A.C. 51 supplies another instance:

G's wife repeatedly forged her husband's signature on cheques, and drew out money which she applied to her own uses. G became aware of the forgeries in October 1929, but his wife begged him not to inform the bank; she said that she had used the money to help her sister in legal proceedings relating to a house. In the hope of a favourable outcome to the sister's legal proceedings and for his wife's sake, G said nothing to the bank.

In June 1930 G discovered that his wife had deceived him, there being no legal proceedings. He said that he would go at once to the bank, and he went out. He did not actually go to the bank, but on his return home his wife shot herself.

G brought an action against the bank to recover the sums paid out on the forged cheques.

Held that G had owed a duty to the bank to disclose the forgeries when he became aware of them so as to enable the bank to recover the sums wrongfully paid, and that since his failure to fulfil this duty had prevented the bank from bringing an action against G and his wife for the tort (wrong) committed by the wife until after her death, G was "estopped" (the English equivalent of "personally barred") from saying that the signatures were forgeries, and so was not entitled to recover the sums from the bank.

(According to the law applicable at the date of the case, a husband was liable for the torts of his wife and the liability ceased on the wife's death. The Law Reform (Married Women and Tortfeasors) Act 1935 (s. 3) abolished a husband's liability for his wife's torts.)

Lord Tomlin said (at p. 58): "The respondents' case is that the duty [*to disclose the forgeries*] ought to have been discharged by the appellant immediately upon his discovery in October 1929, and that if it had been then discharged they could have sued the appellant's wife in tort and the appellant himself would have been responsible for his wife's tort. They claim that his silence until after the wife's death amounted in these circumstances to a representation that the cheques were not forgeries and deprived the respondents of their remedy. . . .

"The appellant's silence . . . was deliberate and intended to produce the effect which it in fact produced—namely, the leaving of the respondents in ignorance of the true facts so that no action might be taken by them against the appellant's wife. The deliberate abstention from speaking in those circumstances seems to me to amount to a representation to the respondents that the forged cheques were in fact in order, and assuming that detriment to the respondents followed there were, it seems to me, present all the elements essential to estoppel."

6–26 A signature may be a signature "by procuration". This occurs where, expressly or by implication, one person makes another person his "procurator" (agent) for the purpose of signing. In practice the words "per pro" are often used to indicate that the signature is of this character. By section 25 of the Act a signature by procuration operates as notice that the agent has only a limited authority to sign, and the principal is only bound by such signature if the agent in signing was acting within the actual limits of his authority.

6–27 It is also possible that a person who signs his own name may add to his signature words which indicate that he is *signing* for or on behalf of a principal, or in a representative character. A drawer, indorser, or acceptor who adds such words to his signature is not personally liable. However, the mere addition of words *describing* the person as an agent, or as filling a representative character, does not exempt him from personal liability (s. 26(1)). For example, in *Brebner v. Henderson*, 1925 S.C. 643, where a promissory note was signed:

> "JAS. R. GORDON, Director
> ALEX HENDERSON, Secretary
> The Fraserburgh Empire Limited",

the words added to the two signatures were held to be no more than descriptive and not to indicate that the signature was "for and on behalf of" the company. In determining whether a signature on a bill is that of the principal or that of the agent by whose hand it is written, the interpretation most favourable to the validity of the document is adopted (s. 26(2)).

"To Pay on Demand or at a Fixed or Determinable Future Time"

The time at which a bill falls due is referred to as the "maturity" of the bill. A bill which is not paid at its maturity becomes "overdue". **6–28**

A bill is payable "on demand" if it is expressed to be payable "on demand", or "at sight", or "on presentation", or if no time for payment is expressed (s. 10(1)).

A "fixed future time" is some specified future date.

A bill is payable at a "determinable future time" if it is expressed to be payable at a fixed period after date or sight (*e.g.* "three months after date" and "six months after sight"), or on or at a fixed period after the occurrence of a specified event which is certain to happen, though the time of happening may be uncertain (*e.g.* on the death of a named individual or six months after the death of a named individual). A document which is expressed to be payable on a "contingency" (an event which may or may not happen, *e.g.* the arrival of a named ship) is not within the definition of a bill of exchange even if the event happens (s. 11).

There may have been an omission to insert a date which is **6–29** necessary for fixing the maturity of the bill: this occurs if a bill expressed to be payable at a fixed period after date is in fact undated, or if the drawee in accepting a bill which is payable at a fixed period after sight does not date his acceptance. Any holder is then entitled to insert the true date of issue or acceptance as the case may be, and the bill is then payable accordingly. If the holder in good faith and by mistake inserts a wrong date, and in every case where a wrongly dated bill comes into the hands of a "holder in due course" (6–47 *et seq.*, below), the bill is payable as if the wrong date were the true date (s. 12).

Where the bill or acceptance or any indorsement is dated, that **6–30** date is, unless the contrary be proved, deemed to be the true date of the drawing, acceptance, or indorsement, as the case may be (s. 13(1)).

Where the drawee chooses to accept a bill which is already **6–31** overdue he becomes liable on the bill as if it were a bill payable on demand (s. 10(2)).

6–32 The rules for calculation of the time of payment are in section 14, as amended by the Banking and Financial Dealings Act 1971:

(1) A bill is due and payable on the last day of the time of payment as fixed by the bill or, if that is a "non-business day", on the succeeding business day. Days of grace, formerly allowed in the payment of bills other than those payable on demand, were abolished by the Act of 1971. By section 92, as amended by the Act of 1971, where the time limited for doing any act or thing is less than three days, "non-business days" are excluded. "Non-business days" are:

(a) Saturday, Sunday, Good Friday and Christmas Day (or December 26 if Christmas Day is a Sunday);

(b) a bank holiday specified in Schedule 1 to the Act of 1971 (New Year's Day (or January 3 if New Year's Day is a Sunday), January 2 (or January 3 if January 2 is a Sunday), the first Monday in May and the first Monday in August);

(c) a day appointed by royal proclamation as a public fast or thanksgiving day;

(d) a day declared by an order under the Act of 1971 to be a non-business day.

Any other day is a business day.

(2) Where a bill is payable at a fixed period after date, or after the happening of a specified event, the time of payment is determined by excluding the day from which the time is to begin to run and by including the day of payment.

(3) Where a bill is payable at a fixed period after sight, the time begins to run from the date of acceptance, or, if the bill is dishonoured by non-acceptance, from the date of "noting" or "protest".

(4) The term "month" in a bill means calendar month.

"A Sum Certain in Money"

6–33 The sum payable still qualifies as a "sum certain" although it is required to be paid:

(a) with interest;

(b) by stated instalments;

(c) by stated instalments, with a provision that upon default in payment of any instalments the whole will become due; or

(d) according to an indicated rate of exchange (s. 9(1)).

Where a bill is expressed to be payable with interest, then, unless there is provision to the contrary, interest runs from the date of the bill, and, if the bill is undated, from the issue of the bill (s. 9(3)).

As the specimen bill indicates, the amount of the bill may be expressed both in words and in figures. If there is a discrepancy between the two, the sum expressed in words is the amount payable (s. 9(2)). In the case of a cheque, the banking practice is to return the cheque unpaid, with the remark "words and figures differ", unless the discrepancy is not large and it is the smaller amount which is being claimed by the collecting bank.

By the Decimal Currency Act 1969, a bill of exchange (or **6–34** promissory note) drawn (or made) after February 15, 1971 ("Decimal Day"), is invalid if the sum payable is an amount wholly or partly in shillings or pence.

"To or to the Order of a Specified Person, or to Bearer"

These words refer to the payee of the bill. If a bill is not payable to **6–35** bearer, the payee must be named or otherwise indicated with reasonable certainty (s. 7(1)).

A bill may be made payable to two or more payees jointly, or it may be made payable in the alternative to one of two, or one or some of several, payees. It may also be made payable to the holder of an office for the time being (s. 7(2)).

Where the payee is a fictitious or non-existing person, the bill may be treated as payable to bearer (s. 7(3)).

A bill may be an "order bill" (*e.g.* payable to "Peter Piper or **6–36** order", or payable to "me or my order"), or a "bearer bill" (*e.g.* payable to "Peter Piper or bearer"). In practice bearer bills are rare. Either type of bill is "negotiable" (*i.e.* may be transferred by the payee to another person as a negotiable instrument) (s. 8(2)). If, however, a bill contains words prohibiting transfer, or indicating an intention that it should not be transferable, it is valid as between the parties to it, but it is not negotiable (s. 8(1)).

The words "or order" need not appear in an order bill. Any negotiable bill which is expressed to be payable to a particular person counts as an order bill (s. 8(4)). It is also of no consequence whether the phrase used is "to the order of Peter Piper" instead of "to Peter Piper or order": in either case Peter Piper has the option of enforcing payment himself or "negotiating" (transferring) the bill to another person (s. 8(5)).

A bill which is not originally a bearer bill may become one in the process of negotiation. This occurs where the indorsement (signature on the back of the specified payee) is a blank indorsement (*i.e.* does not name the new payee) (s. 34(1)). Hence the bill on which the only or the last indorsement is a blank indorsement is considered to be payable to bearer (s. 8(3)).

(b) **Acceptance of a Bill**

6–37 The acceptance of a bill is "the signification by the drawee of his assent to the order of the drawer" (s. 17(1)).

In order to be valid an acceptance must comply with the following conditions:

(i) It must be written on the bill and be signed by the drawee. The mere signature of the drawee without additional words is sufficient.

(ii) It must not express that the drawee will perform his promise by any other means than the payment of money (s. 17(2)).

6–38 A bill need not always be presented to the drawee for acceptance (see 6–71, below). However, the drawer or holder of the bill may wish to obtain the drawee's acceptance because its effect is to make the acceptor primarily liable to pay the bill when it becomes due.

In normal cases the acceptance would be obtained soon after the bill had been signed by the drawer and well before the time when it was due to be paid, but it is permissible for a bill to be accepted:

(i) before it has been signed by the drawer, or while it is otherwise incomplete; or

(ii) when it is overdue, or after it has been dishonoured by a previous refusal to accept, or by non-payment (s. 18).

6–39 An acceptance may be either general or qualified (s. 19(1)).

A general acceptance is one by which the drawee assents, without any qualification, to the order of the drawer. A qualified acceptance varies the effect of the bill as drawn. In particular an acceptance is qualified if it is:

(i) conditional, *i.e.* makes payment by the acceptor dependent on the fulfilment of a condition;

(ii) partial, *i.e.* to pay part only of the amount for which the bill is drawn;

(iii) local, *i.e.* to pay *only* at a particular specified place; an acceptance to pay at a particular place is a general acceptance, unless it expressly states that the bill is to be paid there only and not elsewhere;

(iv) qualified as to time; or

(v) the acceptance of some one or more of the drawees, but not of all (s. 19(2)).

The holder of the bill may refuse to take a qualified acceptance (s. 44(1)).

(c) Issue of a Bill

The "issue" of a bill is defined as "the first delivery of a bill, complete in form, to a person who takes it as a holder" (s. 2). Three terms in this definition should be noted: **6–40**

(i) "delivery";
(ii) "complete in form"; and
(iii) "holder".

The liabilities of the various parties to the bill and the rights and duties of the holder of the bill arise only after the bill has been issued.

(i) *"Delivery"*

"Delivery" means transfer of possession, actual or constructive, from one person to another (s. 2). Every contract on a bill, whether it be the drawer's, or the acceptor's, or an indorser's contract, is incomplete and revocable until there is delivery. Where, however, an acceptance is written on a bill and the drawee gives notice to the person who is entitled to the bill that he has accepted it, the acceptance then becomes complete and irrevocable (s. 21(1)). In most cases the transfer takes the form of the physical delivery of the bill from one person to another. A "constructive" delivery occurs where, for instance, a person who originally held the bill as agent for another party comes to hold the bill for himself. **6–41**

In order to be effectual the delivery must be made either by or under the authority of the party drawing, accepting, or indorsing the bill, as the case may be, and the delivery may be shown to have been conditional or for a special purpose only (and not for the purpose of transferring the ownership of the bill). A "holder in due course" (see 6–47 *et seq.*, below), however, has special protection in this connection: if the bill is in the hands of a "holder in due course" there is a conclusive presumption that the bill was validly delivered by all parties prior to him so as to make them liable to him (s. 21(2)).

Where a bill is no longer in the possession of a party who has signed it as drawer, acceptor, or indorser, the bill is presumed, until the contrary is proved, to have been validly and unconditionally delivered (s. 21(3)). This presumption, which is not a conclusive presumption, gives some assistance to the holder who is not a "holder in due course".

(ii) *"Complete in Form"*

6–42 For an explanation of "complete in form", reference must be made to the definition of a bill (6–16, above). It follows from the definition that the bill will have at least one signature—that of the drawer—and will identify the drawer and the payee. If the bill has already been accepted by the drawee, it will also bear the acceptor's signature, and if it is an order bill and has already been indorsed by the payee, it will also bear the signature of the payee as indorser. As has been noticed, signature is essential for liability (s. 23); hence a "bearer" who has parted with possession of a bill by merely handing it over to another "bearer" is not liable on the bill.

6–43 However, liability on a bill may arise although the bill is not "complete in form" but merely "inchoate". This occurs where a simple signature on a blank paper is delivered by the signer in order that it may be converted into a bill; the person to whom it is delivered has a prima facie[1] authority to fill it up as a complete bill for any amount using the signature for that of the drawer, or the acceptor, or an indorser. Similarly, when a bill is wanting in any material particular, the person in possession of it has a prima facie[1] authority to fill up the omission in any way he thinks fit (s. 20(1)). For the bill to be enforceable against prior parties to it, it must be filled up within a reasonable time and strictly in accordance with the authority given, except that if, after completion, the bill is negotiated to a "holder in due course" it is valid and effectual for all purposes in his hands, and he may enforce it as if it had been filled up within a reasonable time and strictly in accordance with the authority given (s. 20(2)).

---

[1] "until the contrary is proved".

An instance of the application of section 20 is *Kinloch, Campbell & Co. v. Cowan* (1890) 27 S.L.R. 870, in which acceptors of a bill who had delivered it blank in the name of the drawer were held not entitled to have a charge at the instance of the drawer (who claimed that he had given value for the bill) suspended without finding caution. **6–44**

Lord President Inglis said (at p. 871): "It appears to me that when a man sends acceptances blank in the name of the drawer into circulation he must take all the consequences of his rashness, which enables anyone to sign as drawer and become creditor of the acceptor."

(iii) *"Holder"*

"Holder" means either: **6–45**

(1) the payee or indorsee of a bill who is in possession of it; or

(2) the bearer of it.

"Bearer" is defined as the person in possession of a bill which is payable to bearer (s. 2). Possession is therefore essential: an indorsee who is no longer, or not yet, in possession of the bill is not a "holder", nor is a person who has been, but no longer is, in possession of a bearer bill a "holder".

A holder is entitled to sue on the bill in his own name all or any of the parties who are liable to pay it (s. 38(1)), but the party being sued may be able to put forward some defence which would not be available to him if the holder were a "holder in due course" (6–48, below). **6–46**

See also 6–59 and 6–60, below.

(d) **Holder in Due Course**

The definition of "holder in due course" is of central importance, since it is only in the hands of a holder in due course that a bill of exchange is fully a negotiable instrument, *i.e.* the holder in due course holds the bill free from any defect of title of prior parties, as well as free from mere personal defences available to prior parties among themselves, and he may enforce payment of the bill against any party who is liable on it (s. 38(2)). **6–47**

A "holder in due course" is defined as a holder who has taken a bill, complete and regular on the face of it, under the following conditions: **6–48**

(a) that he became the holder of it before it was overdue, and without notice that it had been previously dishonoured, if such was the fact; and

(b) that he took the bill in good faith and for value, and that at the time the bill was negotiated to him he had no notice of any defect in the title of the person who negotiated it (s. 29(1)).

With regard to condition (b), the Act includes further provisions as to the meaning of:

(i) "good faith";
(ii) "value"; and
(iii) "defect in title".

6–49 In addition it should be noted that provisions in the Consumer Credit Act 1974 intended to protect consumers prevent a creditor from becoming a holder in due course of a bill of exchange other than a cheque (1974 Act, s. 125; see 5–283, above).

(i) *"Good Faith"*

6–50 A thing is deemed to be done in good faith provided it is in fact done honestly, whether it is done negligently or not (s. 90).

(ii) *"Value"*

6–51 "Value" means "valuable consideration" (s. 2), and in this connection the Act was framed to match the doctrine of consideration which is part of the common law of contract in England but has no place in that of Scotland.

6–52 The Act provides that "valuable consideration" for a bill may be constituted by:

(a) any consideration sufficient to support a "simple contract" (a term of English law, which distinguishes between simple contracts and contracts under seal); or

(b) an antecedent debt or liability (which, according to English law, would not normally count as consideration because of the rule that "consideration must not be past") (s. 27(1)).

Under the common law of Scotland a bill of exchange could be enforced although it was gratuitous. An acceptor, therefore, could not put forward as a defence to an action against him by the drawer that the drawer had given him no consideration for the bill (*Law v. Humphrey* (1875) 3 R. 1192). The Act gives no separate explanation of how "valuable consideration" may be constituted for Scots law, but from the definition of "holder in due course" it may be inferred that valuable consideration is now essential if a bill is to take full effect as a negotiable instrument.

Where a holder of a bill has a "lien" on it (*i.e.* a right to retain it in security for a debt due to him by the owner of the bill), he is deemed to be a holder for value to the extent of the sum for which he has the lien (s. 27(3)). **6–53**

Although a holder in due course must, to satisfy the definition, have given value for the bill, he is not required to prove that he has done so; the "onus" (burden) of proof lies on the defender (the acceptor or other party being sued as liable on the bill) to prove that he (the holder) did not in fact give value; every party whose signature appears on a bill is prima facie[2] deemed to have become a party to the bill for value (s. 30(1)). This rule is in accordance with the common law of Scotland: "onerosity of a bill is to be assumed" (*per* Lord President Inglis in *Law v. Humphrey* (1875) 3 R. 1192, at p. 1193). However, the Act altered the common law with regard to the method by which this assumption could be proved wrong: by the common law, non-onerosity could be proved only by writ or oath, but by section 100 of the Act "parole evidence" (the oral evidence of witnesses) is now allowed for the proof of any fact relevant to liability on a bill. **6–54**

While the holder in due course must, by definition, have given value for the bill to his immediate predecessor, it does not follow that the person from whom he seeks payment (the acceptor or other party whose signature is on the bill) has received value when he parted with the bill. The bill may have passed through a series of transactions before payment is demanded, and it could be that in one or more of these transactions no value was given for the transfer of the bill. The Act provides that where value has at any time been given for a bill, the holder is deemed to be a holder for value as regards the acceptor and all parties to the bill who became parties to the bill before the stage at which value was given (s. 27(2)). **6–55**

A person who has received no value for a bill may be an "accommodation party", defined as a "person who has signed a bill as drawer, acceptor, or indorser, without receiving value therefor, **6–56**

---

[2] "until the contrary is proved".

and for the purpose of lending his name to some other person" (s. 28(1)). An accommodation party is liable to a holder for value, and it makes no difference whether or not the holder knew, when he took the bill, that it was in fact an accommodation bill (s. 28(2)).

(iii) *"Defect in Title"*

6–57 The title of the person who is transferring the bill is "defective" if he himself obtained the bill (or the acceptance of the bill) by fraud, duress, or force and fear, or other unlawful means, or for an illegal consideration, or when he is acting in breach of faith, or under circumstances amounting to a fraud (s. 29(2)).

6–58 By section 125 of the Consumer Credit Act 1974 if a creditor negotiates a cheque to some person other than a bank his doing so amounts to a "defect in title" (see 5–283, above).

6–59 A holder (whether for value or not), who derives his title to a bill through a holder in due course, and who is not himself a party to any fraud or illegality affecting it, has all the rights of that holder in due course as regards the acceptor and all parties to the bill prior to that holder (s. 29(3)).

6–60 A holder whose title is defective and who is therefore not himself a holder in due course, may negotiate the bill to another holder, who may, if he satisfies the definition, be a holder in due course, with a good and complete title to the bill (s. 38(3)).

6–61 Every holder of a bill is prima facie[3] deemed to be a holder in due course; but if in an action on a bill it is admitted or proved that the acceptance, issue, or subsequent negotiation of the bill is affected with fraud, duress, or force and fear, or illegality, the burden of proof is shifted, unless and until the holder proves that, subsequent to the alleged fraud or illegality, value has in good faith been given for the bill (s. 30(2)).

(e) **Negotiation of a Bill**

6–62 A bill is negotiated when it is transferred from one person to another in such a manner as to make the transferee the holder of the bill (s. 31(1)). A bill payable to bearer is negotiated by delivery

[3] "until the contrary is proved".

(s. 31(2)). A bill payable to order is negotiated by the indorsement of the holder (*i.e.* the holder's signature, usually on the back of the bill) completed by delivery (s. 31(3)). Thus, if the specimen bill (6–19, above) is again referred to, the first indorser would be Peter Piper; if the bill were payable to "me", the first indorser would be Derek Driver. The indorsement would in both cases require to be completed by delivery of the bill to the indorsee (the new holder indicated in the indorsement). If the bill were payable to "Peter Piper or bearer" or simply to "bearer", no indorsement would be required in order to negotiate the bill: mere delivery of the document by Derek Driver to another holder would be sufficient.

Where the holder of a bill payable to his order transfers the bill for value without indorsing it, the transfer gives the transferee the title which the transferor had, and the transferee in addition acquires the right to have the indorsement of the transferor (s. 31(4)). This provision was considered by the court in *Hood v. Stewart* (1890) 17 R. 749, in which the transferee, who had given value for the bill, was held entitled to recover payment from the acceptor, on the ground that section 31(4) conferred on the transferee a title as complete as that of the transferor had been, *i.e.* the transferee had a title equivalent to a duly intimated assignation (although there had in fact been no intimation). Lord Justice-Clerk J.H.A. Macdonald explained the distinction between negotiation and mere transfer as follows (at p. 753): **6–63**

"The title obtained by transference is not necessarily the same as the title obtained by indorsement. It is well known that an indorser may confer on an indorsee a better title than he himself possessed. This cannot happen in the case of mere transference. The transferee acquires the title of the transferor, and nothing more. Hence such exceptions[4] may be stated to the pursuer's title as might have been stated against the title of the transferor. As in an assignation, *utitur jure auctoris*,[5] and if the title of his author is bad, his own is no better."

An indorsement, in order to operate as a negotiation, must comply with the following conditions: **6–64**

(1) It must be written on the bill itself and be signed by the indorser. The simple signature of the indorser, without additional

[4] defences.

[5] "he enjoys the right of his author".

words, is sufficient, and the indorsement may be written on an "allonge" (a piece of paper attached to the bill to allow room for more indorsements) or on a copy of the bill issued or negotiated in a country where copies are recognised.

(2) It must be an indorsement of the entire bill, and not a partial indorsement attempting to transfer part only of the amount to the indorsee or attempting to divide the bill between two separate indorsees.

(3) Where the bill is payable to the order of two or more payees or indorsees who are not partners, all must indorse, unless the one indorsing has authority to indorse for the others (s. 32(1)–(3)).

Where, in a bill payable to order, the payee or indorsee is wrongly designated, or his name is misspelt, he may indorse the bill according to the description in the bill, adding, if he thinks fit, his proper signature (s. 32(4)).

Where there are two or more indorsements on a bill, each indorsement is deemed to have been made in the order in which it appears on the bill, until the contrary is proved (s. 32(5)).

6–65 Where a bill purports to be indorsed conditionally, the condition may be disregarded by the payer, and payment to the indorsee is valid whether the condition has been fulfilled or not (s. 33).

6–66 An indorsement may be "in blank" or it may be "special". An indorsement "in blank" specifies no indorsee (*e.g.* where the indorser simply signs his name on the back of the bill). A bill indorsed in this way becomes payable to bearer. A "special" indorsement specifies the person to whom, or to whose order, the bill is to be payable (*e.g.* where the indorser writes on the back of the bill "pay Ina McNee or order" followed by his signature). The indorsee under a special indorsement ("Ina McNee") is then in the position of payee of the bill. The holder of a bill may convert a blank endorsement into a special indorsement by writing above the indorser's signature a direction to pay the bill to or to order of himself or some other person (s. 34).

6–67 It is also possible to have a "restrictive" indorsement, *i.e.* an indorsement which prohibits the further negotiation of the bill, or which expresses that it is a mere authority to deal with the bill in the way directed and not a transfer of the ownership of the bill (*e.g.* "Pay D only", or "Pay D for the account of X", or "Pay D or order for collection"). A restrictive indorsement gives the indorsee the right to receive payment of the bill and to sue any party whom his indorser could have sued, but gives him no power to transfer his rights as indorsee unless it expressly authorises him to do so. Where a restrictive indorsement authorises further transfer, all subsequent indorsees take the bill with the same rights and subject to the same liabilities as the first indorsee under the restrictive indorsement (s. 35).

A bill which is negotiable in its origin continues to be negotiable until it has been either restrictively indorsed or discharged by payment or otherwise. However, if an overdue bill is negotiated, it can only be negotiated subject to any defect of title affecting it at its maturity: no person who takes the bill thereafter can acquire or give a better title than that which the person from whom he took it had. A bill which is payable on demand is deemed to be "overdue" for this purpose when it appears on the face of it to have been in circulation for an unreasonable length of time, and what is an unreasonable length of time is a question of fact. Except where an indorsement is dated after the maturity of the bill, every negotiation is prima facie deemed to have been effected before the bill was overdue. Where a bill which is not overdue has been dishonoured, any person who takes it with notice of the dishonour takes it subject to any defect of title attaching to it at the time of dishonour (s. 36). These provisions are to be linked to the definition of "holder in due course" (6–48, above): a holder in due course must have become the holder of the bill before it was overdue and without notice that it had been previously dishonoured (if such was the fact) (s. 29(1)). **6–68**

(f) Presentment for Acceptance and Presentment for Payment

In certain circumstances it is the duty of the holder, if he is to exercise his full rights on a bill, to present the bill for acceptance and to present it for payment. **6–69**

(i) *Presentment for Acceptance*

It is *advisable* for the holder to present the bill to the drawee for acceptance. If the drawee accepts the bill, the holder thus obtains the right to enforce payment of the bill against the acceptor and is in a position to pass on to a new holder a document of better currency. If the drawee refuses to accept the bill, the holder will **6–70** acquire an immediate right to hold other parties who have signed the bill (drawer and indorsers) liable to pay it.

6–71 Presentment for acceptance is, however, not *necessary*, except in the three following cases:

(1) where a bill is payable "after sight" (*e.g.* "six months after sight", *i.e.* six months after the drawee sees it): presentment for acceptance is necessary in this case in order to fix the maturity of the bill; a holder to whom a bill payable after sight has been negotiated must either present it for acceptance or himself negotiate it within a reasonable time (regard being had to the nature of the bill, the usage of trade and the facts of the particular case); if he does not do so, the drawer and all prior indorsers are discharged;

(2) where a bill expressly stipulates that it must be presented for payment; and

(3) where a bill is drawn payable elsewhere than at the residence or place of business of the drawee; in this case, if the holder has not time (with the exercise of reasonable diligence) to present the bill for acceptance before presenting it for payment on its due date, the delay caused by presenting the bill for acceptance is excused and does not discharge the drawer and indorsers (ss. 39 and 40).

Rules as to presentment for acceptance

6–72 The Act sets out the following rules as to presentment for acceptance:

(a) The presentment must be made by or on behalf of the holder to the drawee or to some person authorised to accept or refuse acceptance on his behalf at a reasonable hour on a business day and before the bill is overdue.

(b) Where a bill is addressed to two or more drawees who are not partners, presentment must be made to them all, unless one has authority to accept for all, in which case presentment may be made to him only.

(c) Where the drawee is dead, presentment *may* be made to his personal representative.

(d) Where the drawee is bankrupt, presentment *may* be made to him or to his trustee.

(e) Where authorised by agreement or usage, a presentment through the post office is sufficient (s. 41(1)).

Excuses for non-presentment for acceptance

Presentment in accordance with these rules is excused, and a bill may be treated as dishonoured by non-acceptance: **6–73**

(a) where the drawee is dead or bankrupt, or is a fictitious person or person not having capacity to contract by bill;

(b) where, after the exercise of reasonable diligence, presentment in accordance with the rules cannot be effected; or

(c) where, although the presentment has been irregular, acceptance has been refused on some other ground (s. 41(2)).

The fact that the holder has reason to believe that the bill, on presentment, will be dishonoured does not excuse presentment (s. 41(3)). **6–74**

When a bill is duly presented for acceptance and is not accepted within the customary time, the person presenting it must treat it as dishonoured by non-acceptance. If he does not, the holder loses his right of recourse against the drawer and indorsers (s. 42). The common law, which was to the same effect, is to be found expressed in *Martini & Co. v. Steel & Craig* (1878) 6 R. 342. The "customary" time is usually 24 hours. **6–75**

As has been noted (6–39, above), the holder of a bill may refuse to take a qualified acceptance. If he does not obtain an unqualified acceptance, he may treat the bill as dishonoured by non-acceptance. Where the holder takes a qualified acceptance and the drawer or an indorser has not authorised him to do so and does not subsequently assent to his having done so, the drawer or indorser is discharged from his liability on the bill, unless the qualified acceptance is a "partial" acceptance (*i.e.* to pay part only of the amount for which the bill is drawn) and due notice has been given. When the drawer or an indorser receives notice of a qualified acceptance, and does not within a reasonable time express his dissent to the holder, he is deemed to have assented to the taking of the qualified acceptance (s. 44). **6–76**

(ii) *Presentment for Payment*

Subject to the provisions of the Act a bill must be "duly presented" for payment (s. 45). When a bill has been accepted generally, presentment for payment is not necessary in order to make the **6–77** acceptor liable (s. 52(1)). The effect of not duly presenting a bill for payment is that the drawer and indorsers (but not the acceptor) are discharged (s. 45). Another effect, applicable only to Scotland, is that a bill which has not been duly presented for payment cannot be enforced by summary diligence (see 6–119 *et seq.*, below) even against the acceptor; this follows from section 98 of the Act which left the law of Scotland on summary diligence unaltered (*Neill v. Dobson, Molle & Co. Ltd* (1902) 4 F. 625).

Rules as to presentment for payment

6–78 A bill is "duly presented" for payment if it is presented in accordance with rules set out in section 45 of the Act:

(1) Where the bill is not payable on demand, presentment must be made on the day it falls due (not, for example, on September 10 if it had become payable on July 8 as in *Neill v. Dobson, Molle & Co. Ltd*, above).

(2) Where the bill is payable on demand, presentment must be made within a reasonable time after its issue in order to make the drawer liable, and within a reasonable time after its indorsement in order to make the indorser liable. In deciding what is a reasonable time, regard must be had to the nature of the bill, the usage of trade and the facts of the particular case.

(3) Presentment must be made by the holder or by some person authorised to receive payment on his behalf at a reasonable hour on a business day, at the "proper place" (as defined in rule (4)), either to the person specified in the bill as the payer, or to some person authorised to pay or refuse payment on his behalf, if with the exercise of reasonable diligence such person can there be found.

(4) A bill is presented at the "proper place":

(a) where a place of payment is specified in the bill and the bill is there presented;

(b) where no place of payment is specified, but the address of the drawee or acceptor is given in the bill, and the bill is there presented;

(c) where no place of payment is specified and no address given, and the bill is presented at the drawee's or acceptor's place of business if known, and if not, at his ordinary residence if known;

(d) in any other case if presented to the drawee or acceptor wherever he can be found, or if presented at his last known place of business or residence.

In *Neill v. Dobson, Molle & Co. Ltd*, above, the bill, which specified no place of payment, was addressed to "Mr. J. Neill, 1 Morrison Place, Piershill, Edinburgh" (Neill's private address). The bill, which had been accepted by Neill, was presented for payment at his place of business in George Street, Edinburgh, and, by an application of rule (4)(b), this was held not to be presentment at the "proper place". Summary diligence could therefore not be used to enforce the bill against Neill.

(5) Where a bill is presented at the proper place, and after the exercise of reasonable diligence no person authorised to pay or refuse payment can be found there, no further presentment to the drawee or acceptor is required.

(6) Where a bill is drawn upon, or accepted by, two or more persons who are not partners, and no place of payment is specified, presentment must be made to them all.

(7) Where the drawee or acceptor is dead, and no place of payment is specified, presentment *must* be made to a personal representative, if there is one and with the exercise of reasonable diligence he can be found.

(8) Where authorised by agreement or usage, a presentment through the post office is sufficient.

Excuses for delay or non-presentment for payment

Delay in making presentment for payment is excused when the delay is caused by circumstances beyond the control of the holder and not due to his default, misconduct or negligence. When the cause of delay ceases to operate, presentment must be made with reasonable diligence (s. 46(1)). **6–79**

The fact that the holder has reason to believe that the bill will, on presentment, be dishonoured, does not dispense with the necessity for presentment. Presentment for payment is dispensed with:

(a) where after the exercise of reasonable diligence presentment cannot be effected;

(b) where the drawee is a fictitious person;

(c) as regards the drawer, where the drawee or acceptor is not bound, as between himself and the drawer, to accept or pay the bill, and the drawer has no reason to believe that the bill would be paid if presented;

(d) as regards an indorser, where the bill was accepted or made for the accommodation of that indorser (see 6–56, above), and he has no reason to expect that the bill would be paid if presented; or

(e) by waiver of presentment, express or implied (s. 46(2)).

The effect of (c) and (d) is that the drawer (in (c)) and the indorser (in (d)) are, contrary to the general rule, not discharged by the fact that there has been no presentment for payment.

The question of waiver of presentment was considered in *Mactavish's Judicial Factor v. Michael's Trustees*, 1912 S.C. 425: A bill, which had been indorsed, was not presented for payment, and no notice of its dishonour was given to the indorser. The indorser paid part of the bill, but was proved to have done so under the erroneous belief that she was not an indorser, but a joint acceptor.

Held that the part payment gave rise to a presumption that the indorser had waived presentment for payment and notice of dishonour, but that this presumption had been rebutted by proof that the payment had been made in error; and that the indorser was therefore free from liability because the holder had not complied with statutory requirements.

(g) Procedure on Dishonour

6–80 On the dishonour of a bill by non-acceptance or non-payment the holder obtains an immediate "right of recourse" against the drawer and indorsers (ss. 43(2) and 47(2)), but in order to preserve this right of recourse the holder must comply with statutory procedure as to:

(i) notice of dishonour; and

(ii) protest.

(i) *Notice of Dishonour*

6–81 When a bill has been dishonoured by non-acceptance or by non-payment, the general rule is that notice of dishonour must be given to the drawer and each indorser and that any drawer or indorser to whom notice is not given is discharged. Exceptions to the general rule are:

(1) Where a bill is dishonoured by non-acceptance, and notice of dishonour is not given, the rights of a holder in due course subsequent to the omission are not prejudiced by the omission.

(2) Where a bill is dishonoured by non-acceptance and due notice of dishonour is given, it is not necessary to give notice of a subsequent dishonour by non-payment unless the bill has in the meantime been accepted (s. 48).

Rules as to notice of dishonour

Notice of dishonour in order to be valid and effectual must be **6–82**
given in accordance with 15 rules set out in section 49:

(1) The notice must be given by or on behalf of the holder, or by or on behalf of an indorser who, at the time of giving it, is himself liable on the bill.

(2) The notice may be given by an agent either in his own name or in the name of any party entitled to give notice.

(3) Where the notice is given by or on behalf of the holder, it enures for the benefit of all subsequent holders and all prior indorsers who have a right of recourse against the party to whom notice is given.

(4) Similarly, where the notice is given by or on behalf of an indorser, it enures for the benefit of the holder and all indorsers subsequent to the party to whom notice is given.

(5) The notice may be given in writing or by personal communication, and may be given in any terms which sufficiently identify the bill and intimate its dishonour.

(6) The return of a dishonoured bill to the drawer or an indorser is deemed a sufficient notice of dishonour.

(7) A written notice need not be signed, and an insufficient written notice may be supplemented and made valid by verbal communication. A misdescription of the bill does not vitiate the notice unless the party to whom the notice is given is in fact misled by the misdescription.

(8) The notice may be given either to the party himself or to his agent.

(9) Where, to the knowledge of the party giving the notice, the drawer or indorser is dead, the notice must be given to a personal representative, if there is one and with the exercise of reasonable diligence he can be found.

(10) Where the drawer or indorser is bankrupt, notice may be given either to the party himself or to the trustee.

(11) Where there are two or more drawers or indorsers who are not partners, notice must be given to each, unless one has authority to receive notice for the others.

(12) The notice may be given as soon as the bill is dishonoured, and must be given within a reasonable time. In order to satisfy the standard of "reasonable time", the notice must, if the parties giving and receiving the notice reside in the same place, be given in time to reach the recipient on the day after the dishonour, and if the parties reside in different places, be sent off not later than the day after the dishonour (or if there is no convenient post on that day, by the next post).

(13) When the bill is, at the time of its dishonour, in the hands of an agent, he may either give notice to the parties liable on the bill, or he may give notice to his principal. If the agent chooses the latter alternative, the principal will then have the same "reasonable time" for giving notice to the parties liable on the bill.

(14) Where a party receives due notice of dishonour, he has then the same "reasonable time" for giving notice to prior parties.

(15) Where a notice of dishonour is duly addressed and posted, the sender is deemed to have given due notice of dishonour, notwithstanding any miscarriage by the post office.

Excuses for delay or non-notice

6–83 Delay in giving notice of dishonour is excused where the delay is caused by circumstances beyond the control of the party giving the notice, and not due to his default, misconduct, or negligence. When the cause of delay ceases to operate, notice must be given with reasonable diligence (s. 50(1)).

Notice of dishonour is dispensed with:

(a) when, after the exercise of reasonable diligence, it cannot be given to or does not reach the drawer or indorser;

(b) by waiver, express or implied (which may be either before the time of giving notice has arrived, or after the omission to give due notice);

(c) as regards the drawer, in the following cases:

(1) where drawer and drawee are the same person;

(2) where the drawee is a fictitious person or a person lacking capacity to contract;

(3) where the drawer is a person to whom the bill is presented for payment;

(4) where the drawee or acceptor is, as between himself and the drawer, under no obligation to accept or pay the bill; or

(5) where the drawer has countermanded payment (*i.e.* given notice that the bill should not be paid);

(d) as regards the indorser, in the following cases:
(1) where the drawee is a fictitious person or a person lacking capacity to contract;
(2) where the indorser is the person to whom the bill is presented for payment; or
(3) where the bill was accepted or made for his accommodation (see 6–56, above) (s. 50(2)).

(ii) *Protest*

As well as giving notice of dishonour, the holder of a bill which appears on the face of it to be a foreign bill must "protest" the bill when it is dishonoured by non-acceptance or by non-payment, and if it is not duly protested, the drawer and indorsers are discharged (s. 51(2)). The purpose of protest is to provide proof, in a form acceptable to any court at home or abroad, that the bill has been duly presented and has been dishonoured. **6–84**

In the case of an inland bill, the holder may, if he thinks fit, protest it on its dishonour, but, if he chooses not to do so, he does not thereby lose his right of recourse against the drawer or indorsers (s. 51(1)). However, where it is desired to enforce a bill by the process of summary diligence (available only in Scotland and not altered by the Act of 1882 (see s. 98)), protest is essential.

The procedure for protesting a bill has two stages: **6–85**

(1) noting, which is informal; and
(2) protest, which is formal.

Both stages require the services of a notary public, but the Act provides that if the services of a notary cannot be obtained at the place where the bill is dishonoured, any householder or "substantial resident" of the place may, in the presence of two witnesses, give a certificate, signed by them all and narrating the presentment and dishonour of the bill. A form suitable for use in these circumstances is set out in the First Schedule to the Act. Such a certificate operates as if it were a formal protest (s. 94), but it is doubtful whether summary diligence could follow on such a certificate (see 6–120, below).

(1) **Noting**

Noting takes place when a notary presents the bill to the drawee for acceptance or payment, and notes on the bill the date, the fact that the bill is protested for non-acceptance ("P.N.Ac.") or **6–86** non-payment ("P.N.P."), and his own initials followed by the abbreviation "N.P.".

6–87 The place at which this proceeding must normally be carried out is the place where the bill is dishonoured, but when a bill is presented through the post office and is returned by post dishonoured, the noting may be at the place to which the bill is returned (s. 51(6)). In *Sommerville v. Aaronson*, a promissory note, expressed to be payable at Bradford, was duly presented there and was dishonoured. Some months later the note was presented to the maker of it personally at Millport, in Bute, and, there being no notary resident at Millport, a householder's certificate was obtained. *Held* that, as the place of payment and of dishonour was Bradford, the householder's certificate issued at Millport was of no effect.

6–88 By the Act of 1882, as amended by the Bills of Exchange (Time of Noting) Act 1917, the noting must take place either on the day of dishonour or on the next succeeding business day (or, in the case of a bill returned by post, on the day of its return or on the next business day after that). When a bill has been duly noted, the protest (the second and formal stage) may be left until later but will take its date from that of the noting (s. 51(4) and (6)).

(2) **Protest**

6–89 The document referred to as a "protest" is a formal notarial certificate, based on, and bearing the date of, the noting, but in practice drawn up at the notary's office at a convenient later date.

The protest must contain a copy of the bill, must be signed by the notary, and must specify:

(a) the person at whose request the bill is protested; and

(b) the place and date of protest, the cause or reason for protesting the bill, the demand made, and the answer given (if any), or the fact that the drawee or acceptor could not be found (s. 51(7)). These statutory provisions were applied in *Bartsch v. Poole & Co.* (1895) 23 R. 328:

A bill, accepted by B., was expressed to be payable at the office of P. & Co., the drawers. The bill was dishonoured and was protested for non-payment. The protest stated that the notary "presented the said bill at the place where payable to a clerk there, who made answer that no funds had been provided to meet said bill, and payment was refused accordingly".

Held that, since the clerk, being an employee of P. & Co., could not be regarded as agent for B., the protest was invalid because it did not state, as required by section 51(7), that the acceptor could not be found. By accepting the bill payable at P. & Co.'s office, B. had undertaken to be at that office with the money on the date when the bill was due. (It is, however, familiar practice for a bill to be made payable at a named bank, and in that case the bank would be considered to be the agent for the acceptor.)

The protest must exactly conform to the noting: for example, if **6–90** the noting is dated September 24, the date included in the formal certificate must also be September 24, and if the notary substitutes September 25 (even though that may have been the true date of the noting), the protest is invalid (*McPherson v. Wright* (1885) 12 R. 942).

Excuses for delay or non-protest

These are the same as the excuses for delay in giving notice of **6–91** dishonour, and for dispensing with notice of dishonour (see 6–83, above) (s. 51(9)).

(h) Liabilities of Parties

The normal function of a bill is to enable the holder of it to obtain **6–92** payment of the amount of the bill when the bill becomes due. In an ordinary transaction, it is most likely that the holder, on presenting the bill to the drawee (who will be the acceptor, if the bill has been accepted), will be duly paid the amount of the bill. However, the Act necessarily includes provisions to cover the situation where the transaction does not follow the ordinary course. Hence the frequent references in the Act to dishonour of the bill, which in practice is exceptional.

The general principle is that all parties to the bill (*i.e.* all persons **6–93** who have signed the bill) are liable, jointly and severally, to pay the amount of the bill to a holder in due course (see 6–47 *et seq.*, above). The effect is that not only the acceptor but also the drawer and the indorsers may be held liable to pay the bill to a holder in due course, and that, on the other hand, no liability to pay the bill attaches to the drawee who has not yet accepted the bill or to a person who transfers a bearer bill to another bearer by simple delivery without indorsing it.

6–94 This does not mean that the holder is in every case completely free to choose from among the signatories any one particular person whom he is to hold liable to pay the bill. A distinction must be drawn between primary liability and secondary liability. If the bill has been accepted, the person primarily liable to pay it is the acceptor, and the other parties are only secondarily or subsidiarily liable. If the bill has not yet been accepted, the person primarily liable to pay it is the drawer, and the indorsers have only a secondary liability. Once the holder has duly received payment from the person who is primarily liable to pay the bill, the liability of all the other parties is at an end. It is only where the party primarily liable to pay fails to do so that the holder can have recourse to the parties who are secondarily liable. Further, as can be seen from the sections above on presentment for acceptance and presentment for payment (6–69 *et seq.*, above), and on procedure on dishonour (6–80 *et seq.*, above), the holder may lose his right of recourse against such parties if he fails to comply with the statutory requirements.

6–95 On presenting a bill for payment the holder must exhibit the bill to the person from whom he demands payment, and, when it is paid, the holder must immediately hand it over to the person paying it (s. 52(4)).

6–96 Where a bill has been dishonoured by non-acceptance by the drawee or by non-payment by the acceptor, the holder may naturally turn to the person from whom he obtained the bill, hold that party liable to him and, on receiving payment, hand over the bill to him. In this way the dishonoured bill may pass backwards through a chain of parties, each indorsee holding his own indorser liable to reimburse him for what he has had to pay to the later party, until ultimately the bill reaches the party who, as drawer or acceptor, is primarily liable to pay. Such procedure is not essential: the holder is entitled to choose from among the prior parties which party he is to hold liable to himself on the dishonoured bill, or he may himself immediately enforce payment from the party who is primarily liable.

6–97 The main provisions of the Act relating to the liabilities of the various parties are as follows:

(i) *Liability of Drawee*

6–98 The drawee, not having signed the bill, is not liable as a party to the bill.

Where, however, the drawee has in his hands funds available for the payment of the bill, the bill operates as an "assignment" of the sum for which it is drawn in favour of the holder, from the time when the bill is presented to the drawee (s. 53(2)). This provision of the Act applies to Scotland only and is derived from the common law of Scotland. It caused difficulty in connection with those bills of exchange which were countermanded (*i.e.* "stopped") cheques, and amendments were consequently made by section 11 of the Law Reform (Miscellaneous Provisions) (Scotland) Act 1985. The words "Subject to section 75A of this Act" were added at the beginning of subsection 53(2), and the new section 75A, inserted by the Act of 1985, provides that on the countermand of payment of a cheque the banker is to be treated as having no funds available for the payment of the cheque. **6–99**

There is a dearth of cases actually decided on section 53(2), but the following four cases, all relating to cheques, have at least some bearing on it. For a comprehensive study of the provision and its common law background see D. J. Cusine, "The Cheque as an Assignation", 1977 J.R. 98, and on the present law see George L. Gretton, "Stopped Cheques: the new law", 1986 S.L.T. (News) 25. **6–100**

(1) *British Linen Co. Bank v. Carruthers and Fergusson* (1883) 10 R. 923: David F. gave a cheque for £161 drawn on his current account with the B. Bank to John F. The cheque was handed by John F. to his own bank, which presented it to the B. Bank for payment. As the balance at the credit of David F.'s current account was only £135 13s. 10d., the B. Bank refused payment. **6–101**

A few months later David F. became bankrupt, and C. was appointed the trustee in his sequestration. The B. Bank had then in its hands £156 8s. belonging to David F., and competing claims were made, John F. claiming that he was entitled to at least £135 13s. 10d. because the presentation of the cheque had operated as an assignation to him of the funds then at the credit of David F.'s account, and C. on the other hand claiming that the whole fund was to be treated as part of the sequestrated estate to be divided amongst David F.'s creditors.

An action of multiplepoinding was raised—the type of action used to settle disputed claims in such a situation.

Held that John F. was entitled to £135 13s. 10d. out of the funds held by the B. Bank.

"The result of the presentation of the cheque was to give a right to the funds of the drawer which the banker had in his hands at the time" (*per* Lord Shand at p. 928).

Since the transaction had taken place before the passing of the Act of 1882, the case was decided under the common law, but the observation was made that "the statute only carries out what it is understood was intended—a consolidation of the existing Scotch law. There is nothing new in it" (*per* Lord Shand at p. 927).

6–102 (2) *Bank of Scotland v. Reid* (1886) 2 Sh.Ct.Rep. 376: On March 2, 1886, Stewart, a joiner, granted to Knox, a glazier, a cheque for £14 drawn on the Bank of Scotland. Knox passed the cheque to his own bank—the Royal Bank—which paid him cash for it. The cheque was then presented, through the clearing-house, to Stewart's bank on March 4.

Stewart, however, had died on March 3, and his death had been intimated to his bank before the cheque was presented.

Stewart's estate was bankrupt, and Reid, as trustee on that estate, claimed £83 18s., which was the sum lying at Stewart's credit in the Bank of Scotland. The Royal Bank claimed £14 out of that amount, and an action of multiplepoinding was raised to settle the competing claims.

Held (i) that the cheque from its date was an incomplete "assignment" to Knox and through him to the Royal Bank of the £14, (ii) that that assignment did not fall by Stewart's death and so it became operative as an assignment on being presented to Stewart's bank after his death, and (iii) that, although by section 75 of the Act of 1882 the bank's duty and authority to pay the cheque were terminated by notice of Stewart's death, that did not prevent the Royal Bank from proving its right to the fund in a legal action.

Sheriff-Substitute Erskine Murray, referring to section 53(2) of the Act, said (at p. 379): "The words 'operates as an assignment' must be held equivalent to 'become a completed and thus operative assignment'. If so, it just means that the assignment is incomplete without presentation or intimation; but, as an unintimated assignation is good though intimated after death, the intimation subsequent to death completed the Royal Bank's right, though section 75 barred the Bank of Scotland from paying without legal process."

6–103 (3) *Kirkwood & Sons v. Clydesdale Bank Ltd*, 1908 S.C. 20: This case is the highest reported authority on the application of section

53(2), and will be considered more fully in connection with the banker's duty to honour cheques (see 6–167, below).

The court held that a cheque presented after the customer's death did not operate as an assignment under section 53(2) of any part of the credit balance on the customer's current account, because on a combination of all the customer's accounts the bank had no "funds available" for the payment of the cheque within the meaning of the statutory provision.

(4) *Dickson v. Clydesdale Bank Ltd*, 1937 S.L.T. 585 (O.H.): D. **6–104**
was a customer of the C. Bank, and occasionally sent Taylor to the bank to cash her cheques.

On one occasion Taylor obtained from D. a cheque for £166 payable to Mrs Taylor. On July 20, 1933, Taylor attempted to obtain cash for it from the C. Bank, but the bank refused his request.

The following day Taylor returned with the same cheque, but with the letter "s" deleted from "Mrs" and with the date altered from July 20 to July 21. The alterations were initialled "M.L.D.". The C. Bank then paid Taylor £166.

D. claimed that the bank was not entitled to debit her account with the £166.

Held that the cheque was a forgery and therefore not a good mandate to the bank to debit D.'s account.

One of the arguments put forward by counsel for the bank was that on presentation the cheque had operated as an assignment on July 20 in favour of someone—either Mrs Taylor or Mr Taylor—and that D. could therefore not challenge the debiting of her account.

Lord Carmont (Ordinary) rejected that argument, saying (at p. 586) with reference to section 53(2): "It must not be overlooked that the statute says that the assignment is *in favour of the holder*. . . . When John Taylor sought to obtain cash for the cheque payable to 'Mrs Taylor' on 20th July he was not the holder although he was in physical possession of it. . . . It was only the following day that on the footing that Taylor was himself the holder as payee . . . presentation was recognised by the defenders. But as the cheque was then a forged document the defenders cannot put it forward as having operated a valid assignment of the pursuer's funds."

6–105 A point on which the cases give no guidance is whether the words "when the bill is presented to the drawee" in section 53(2) cover presentment for acceptance as well as presentment for payment. There is no express exclusion of presentment for acceptance, but a view which appears to be generally held in banking circles is that the presentment referred to in the provision is restricted to presentment for payment and that presentment for acceptance would not operate as an "assignment", *i.e.* would not attach funds. The question is unlikely to arise in connection with those bills of exchange which are cheques because they are not usually, and perhaps could not competently be, presented for acceptance in any case: Lord Wright, delivering the judgment of the Privy Council, in *Bank of Baroda Ltd v. Punjab National Bank Ltd* [1944] A.C. 176 (a case in which the marking or certification of a cheque as "good for payment" was held not to be an acceptance in the statutory sense) said (at p. 184): "So far as their Lordships know, there is no case in the books of the acceptance of a cheque." Further, there is no doubt that on presentment of any bill of exchange for *payment*, funds would be attached. The only remaining situation then is where a bill of exchange other than a cheque is presented for acceptance. There seems to be no authority available either to support or to challenge the practice which would be followed if such a situation arose, *viz.*, that funds would not be attached.

(ii) *Liability of Acceptor*

6–106 Where a bill is accepted "generally" (see 6–39, above), presentment for payment is not necessary in order to make the acceptor liable (s. 52(1)).

Where, by the terms of a qualified acceptance, presentment for payment is required, the acceptor is not discharged by the mere omission to present the bill for payment on the day on which it matures: an express stipulation would be required for such a discharge (s. 52(2)).

In order to make the acceptor liable, it is not necessary to protest it, or that notice of dishonour should be given to him (s. 52(3)).

6–107 The acceptor, by accepting the bill, engages that he will pay it according to the tenor of his acceptance, and he is barred from denying to a holder in due course:

(a) the existence of the drawer, the genuineness of the drawer's signature, and the drawer's capacity and authority to draw the bill;

(b) in the case of a bill payable to drawer's order, the then capacity of the drawer to indorse (but not the genuineness or validity of his indorsement);

(c) in the case of a bill payable to the order of a third person, the existence of the payee and his then capacity to indorse (but not the genuineness or validity of his indorsement) (s. 54).

On the liability of an "acceptor for honour" see 6–138 *et seq.*, below.

(iii) *Liability of Drawer*

The drawer, by drawing the bill, engages that on due presentment it will be accepted and paid according to its tenor, and that, if it is dishonoured, he will compensate the holder or any indorser who is compelled to pay it, provided that the necessary proceedings on dishonour are duly taken. He is barred from denying to a holder in due course the existence of the payee and the payee's then capacity to indorse (s. 55(1)). **6–108**

However, it is open to the drawer to insert in the bill an express stipulation negativing or limiting his own liability to the holder (*e.g.* the words "without recourse"). Another option open to the drawer is to waive as regards himself some or all of the holder's duties (*e.g.* as to notice of dishonour) (s. 16). **6–109**

On a general view, the drawer may be regarded as cautioner for the drawee or acceptor. **6–110**

(iv) *Liability of Indorser*

The indorser, by indorsing the bill, engages that on due presentment it will be accepted and paid according to its tenor, and that, if it is dishonoured, he will compensate the holder or a subsequent indorser who is compelled to pay it, provided that the necessary proceedings on dishonour are duly taken. He is barred from denying to a holder in due course the genuineness and regularity in all respects of the drawer's signature and all previous indorsements, and he is barred from denying to his immediate or a subsequent indorsee that the bill was at the time of his indorsement a valid and subsisting bill and that he had then a good title to it (s. 55(2)). **6–111**

6–112 An indorser has the same ability as the drawer to negative or restrict his liability by an express stipulation, and to waive, as regards himself, some or all of the holder's duties (s. 16).

6–113 On a general view, the indorser may be regarded as in the position of a cautioner to later parties (including the holder) for those who are already parties to the bill. Ultimate liability does not lie with the indorser: his liability is secondary only, and he is entitled to recover from prior parties the whole of what he has himself paid out to the holder or other later party.

6–114 Where a person signs a bill otherwise than as a drawer or acceptor, he incurs the liabilities of an indorser to a holder in due course (s. 56).

(v) *Liability of Transferor by Delivery*

6–115 A "transferor by delivery" is a holder of a bill payable to bearer, who negotiates it by delivery without indorsing it.

6–116 A transferor by delivery is not liable *on the bill* (signature being essential for such liability), but he "warrants" (*i.e.* guarantees) to his immediate transferee, provided that transferee is a holder for value, that the bill is what it purports to be, that he has a right to transfer it, and that at the time of transfer he is not aware of any fact which makes it valueless (s. 58).

(vi) *Liability of Referee in Case of Need*

6–117 The drawer and any indorser may insert in the bill the name of a person to whom the holder may resort in case of need, *i.e.* in case the bill is dishonoured by non-acceptance or non-payment. Such person is called "the referee in case of need". The holder has an option to resort to the referee in case of need or not, as he thinks fit (s. 15).

(i) Measure of Damages on Dishonour

6–118 Where a bill is dishonoured, the measure of damages, which will be deemed to be liquidate damages, is as follows:

(1) The holder may recover from any party liable on the bill:

(a) the amount of the bill;

(b) interest from the time of presentment for payment if the bill is payable on demand, and from the maturity of the bill in any other case;

(c) the expenses of noting, or, where protest is necessary and the protest has been drawn up, the expenses of protest.

Similarly, the drawer who has been compelled to pay the bill may recover those amounts from the acceptor, and an indorser who has been compelled to pay the bill may recover those amounts from the acceptor or from the drawer, or from a prior indorser.

(2) Where by the Act interest may be recovered as damages, the interest may, if justice require it, be withheld wholly or in part, and where a bill is expressed to be payable with interest at a given rate, interest as damages may or may not be given at the same rate as interest proper (s. 57).

(j) Enforcement of Liability by Summary Diligence

Liability on a bill may be enforced by an ordinary action for **6–119** payment founded on the bill as the document of debt. An alternative method of enforcement is the procedure of summary diligence, which dispenses with the need to bring an action in court. The procedure is peculiar to Scotland, and is governed by two Scots Acts—the Bills of Exchange Act 1681 and the Inland Bills Act 1696—and by the Bills of Exchange (Scotland) Act 1772, along with decided cases. Nothing in the Act of 1882 in any way alters or affects the Scots law and practice in regard to summary diligence (s. 98).

The bill must be duly presented, noted and protested. If, **6–120** therefore, the place at which the bill has been presented for payment is not the proper place, the bill cannot be enforced by summary diligence (*Neill v. Dobson, Molle & Co. Ltd* (1902) 4 F. 625 (6–77 *et seq.*, above)). There is some doubt as to whether a householder's certificate can take the place of the formal notarial certificate for this purpose. That it can do so is supported by Lord Kyllachy (Ordinary) in *Sommerville v. Aaronson* (1898) 25 R. 524 and by Sheriff-Substitute Brown in *McRobert v. Lindsay* (1898) 14 Sh.Ct.Rep. 89; (1898) 5 S.L.T. 317 (in which, where a bill fell due at Aberchirder in Banffshire and the acceptor had moved to Aberdeen, the holder was held not to have been entitled to incur the expense of having a notary sent from Banff, nine miles away, to protest the bill in Aberchirder). However, the rule in the Act of 1882 (s. 45) that where a bill is not payable on demand presentment for payment must be made on the day it falls due need not be complied with where summary diligence is being used against the acceptor; it is enough if the whole procedure has been completed within six months of the date when the bill was dishonoured; this was held to be so in *McNeill & Son v. Innes, Chambers & Co.*, 1917 S.C. 540, on the ground that this had been the established practice before the Act of 1882 and the Act expressly saved the then existing law and practice in regard to summary diligence (s. 98).

6–121 The formal protest once it has been drawn up is registered in the Books of Council and Session in Edinburgh or in the books of the sheriff court of the sheriffdom which has jurisdiction over the person who is to be charged. An "extract" (*i.e.* a certified copy) may then be obtained by the holder of the bill, and this contains a warrant to charge the party liable on a six or 14 days' induciae, *i.e.* the party liable must pay the amount due within six days if he resides in Scotland[6] or within 14 days if he resides "furth of" (outside) Scotland.

6–122 Summary diligence is therefore a speedy and simple procedure enabling the creditor in the bill, without raising a court action, to obtain a warrant which is equivalent to a decree of the court ordering the debtor to pay the amount due. The creditor has also the right at once to arrest in the hands of third parties any money or goods belonging to the debtor. If the debtor fails to pay by the end of the induciae, the creditor may proceed to poind and sell the debtor's goods, or he may petition the court for the debtor's sequestration.

6–123 If the debtor considers that he has grounds for avoiding liability, he may present a "note of suspension" in the Court of Session to have the summary diligence suspended, but in order to succeed in having the note passed he is usually required to find caution (*e.g. Simpson v. Brown* (1888) 15 R. 716).

6–124 There are some restrictions on the use of summary diligence:

(i) Summary diligence may be used only to obtain payment of the amount of the bill and interest: for the recovery of damages and expenses, an ordinary action is required (Erskine, *An Institute of the Law of Scotland*, III, ii, 36).

(ii) It may be used only against a person who is subject to the jurisdiction of the Scottish courts (*Charteris v. Clydesdale Banking*

[6] Orkney and Shetland are no longer exceptional: the Act 1685, c. 43 ("Act in favour of the Inhabitants of Orkney and Zetland"), was wholly repealed by the Statute Law Revision (Scotland) Act 1964 (s. 1 and Sched. 1).

Co. (1882) 19 S.L.R. 602 (O.H.), in which summary diligence was held incompetent against an acceptor who was resident in Manchester, though the bills were payable in Leith).

(iii) It cannot be used if there is an alteration or vitiation in some essential part of the bill (*e.g.* where a bill has been torn into three pieces and pasted together again: *Thomson v. Bell* (1850) 12 D. 1184).

(iv) It cannot be used where the liability of the person charged does not appear *ex facie* ("on the face") of the bill but would require to be proved by extrinsic evidence.

(v) It cannot be used to enforce payment of an unpaid cheque (*Glickman v. Linda*, 1950 S.C. 18 (O.H.)): under the Acts of 1681 and 1696 it applied only to bills of exchange other than cheques, and it was extended to promissory notes by the Act of 1772.

(k) **Discharge of Bill**

The Act provides for five methods of discharge of a bill: **6–125**

(i) payment in due course;
(ii) acceptor becoming holder;
(iii) renunciation or waiver;
(iv) cancellation; and
(v) alteration.

A bill may also be discharged under the Prescription and Limitation (Scotland) Act 1973 by:

(vi) prescription.

It is possible for one or more of the parties to a bill to be **6–126** discharged without the bill itself being discharged: for instance, where a bill has been dishonoured by non-payment and notice of dishonour has not been given to one of the indorsers, that indorser is discharged (s. 48) but the parties to whom notice of dishonour has been duly given (the drawer and other indorsers) remain liable and the bill continues to be enforceable as a bill.

(i) *Payment in Due Course*

A bill is discharged by payment in due course *by or on behalf of the* **6–127** *drawee or acceptor*. "Payment in due course" means payment made at or after the maturity of the bill to the holder of the bill in good faith and without notice that his title to the bill is defective (s. 59(1)).

6–128 When a bill is paid *by the drawer or an indorser*, it is not discharged, but:

(a) Where the bill is payable to, or to the order of, a third party, and is paid by the drawer, the drawer may enforce payment against the acceptor, but is not permitted to re-issue the bill. (In this case the drawer is not an indorser, and the only right which the drawer has is to claim payment from the acceptor.)

(b) Where the bill is paid by an indorser, or where it is a bill payable to, or to the order of, the drawer and is paid by the drawer (who in this case is an indorser), the party paying it is remitted to his former rights as regards the acceptor or antecedent parties to the bill, and he may, if he thinks fit, strike out his own and subsequent indorsements, and again negotiate the bill (s. 59(2)). An accommodation bill (see 6–56, above) is an exception to these provisions of section 59(2): where an accommodation bill is paid in due course *by the party accommodated* the bill is discharged (s. 59(3)).

6–129 For proof of the payment of a bill of exchange writ or oath was required according to the rule of the common law and the provision in section 100 of the Act allowing parole proof of any fact "relevant to any question of liability" on a bill was held not to make parole proof of payment competent (*Nicol's Trustees v. Sutherland*, 1951 S.C. (H.L.) 21). Any requirement for proof by writ or oath was abolished by the Requirements of Writing (Scotland) Act 1995, section 11.

(ii) *Acceptor Becoming Holder*

6–130 When the acceptor is or becomes the holder of the bill at or after its maturity, in his own right, the bill is discharged (s. 61). This is discharge *confusione* ("by merging").

(iii) *Renunciation or Waiver*

6–131 When the holder of a bill *at or after its maturity* absolutely and unconditionally renounces his rights against the acceptor, the bill is discharged. The renunciation must be in writing, unless the bill is delivered up to the acceptor (s. 62(1)).

The liability of any party to a bill may similarly be renounced by the holder, and this may be done before as well as at or after its maturity (s. 62(2)).

However, the rights of a holder in due course are not affected by any renunciation of which he has no notice (s. 62(2)).

(iv) *Cancellation*

Where a bill is *intentionally* cancelled by the holder or his agent and the cancellation is *apparent*, the bill is discharged (s. 63(1)). **6–132**

Similarly, any party liable on a bill may be discharged by the intentional cancellation of his signature by the holder or the holder's agent. In such a case any indorser who would have had a right of recourse against the party whose signature is cancelled, is also discharged (s. 63(2)).

A cancellation made unintentionally, or under a mistake, or without the authority of the holder is inoperative, but where a bill or any signature on it appears to have been cancelled the burden of proof lies on the party who alleges that the cancellation was made unintentionally, or under a mistake, or without authority (s. 63(3)).

(v) *Alteration*

Where a bill or acceptance is *materially* altered without the assent of all parties liable on the bill, the bill is avoided (*i.e.* is of no effect) except as against a party who has himself made, authorised, or assented to the alteration, and as against subsequent indorsers, but there is this exception made to protect a holder in due course: where a bill has been materially altered *and the alteration is not apparent* (compare cancellation, above), a holder in due course may avail himself of the bill as if it had not been altered and may enforce payment of it according to its original tenor (s. 64(1)). **6–133**

The following alterations are material—any alteration of the date, the sum payable, the time of payment, the place of payment, and, where the bill has been accepted generally, the addition of a place of payment without the acceptor's assent (s. 64(2)).

The acceptor of a bill of exchange is not under a duty to take precautions against fraudulent alterations in the bill after acceptance: **6–134**

Scholfield v. Earl of Londesborough [1896] A.C. 514: Sanders drew a bill for £500 on Scholfield, and Scholfield accepted it. The stamp on the bill was of much larger amount than was necessary, and there were spaces in the bill.

Sanders fraudulently inserted the figure "3" between "£" and "5" in the figures section and the words "three at the end of the second line and "thousand" at the beginning of the third line before the words "five hundred" in the body of the bill, thus converting the bill into one which purported to be for £3,500.

Sanders negotiated the bill, and it came into the hands of a holder in due course, who brought an action against Scholfield for £3,500. Scholfield paid £500 into court.

Held that Scholfield was liable for no more than £500, because he owed no duty to the holder to take precautions against fraudulent alterations and so was guilty of no negligence.

Cheques differ from other bills of exchange on this point: bank customers have a duty to take reasonable precautions in drawing cheques (see 6–176, below).

(vi) *Prescription*

6–135 Under the Bills of Exchange (Scotland) Act 1772, a bill of exchange ceased to be an enforceable document of debt on the lapse of six years from the date when it became payable. This sexennial prescription was replaced under the Prescription and Limitation (Scotland) Act 1973, as from 1976, by a five-year prescription, which also wholly extinguishes the bill.

A condition which must be satisfied for the operation of this prescription is that the creditor has for five years made no "relevant claim" (*i.e.* he must not have brought court or arbitration proceedings, or lodged a claim in the debtor's sequestration or liquidation or executed any form of diligence). Bills of exchange (and promissory notes) are exceptions to the general rule that for the operation of the prescription there must also have been no "relevant acknowledgment" of the subsistence of the debt by the debtor during the five-year period. It is therefore possible in the case of bills of exchange and promissory notes for the prescriptive period to continue to run even where the debtor has clearly indicated, by conduct or by an unequivocal written admission, that the obligation still subsists.

(l) Acceptance and Payment for Honour *supra* Protest

6–136 When a bill has been dishonoured by non-acceptance or by non-payment, the holder has the option of resorting to the "referee in case of need" if the drawer or any indorser has inserted the name of such a person on the bill (s. 15) (see 6–117, above). Where a dishonoured bill contains a reference in case of need, it must be protested for non-payment before it is presented for payment to the referee in case of need (s. 67(1)).

It is also possible that the holder may be entitled to avail himself of either: **6–137**

(i) an acceptance for honour *supra* protest (after protest); or
(ii) payment for honour *supra* protest.

(i) *Acceptance for Honour* supra *Protest*

Where a bill has been protested for dishonour by non-acceptance and is not overdue, any person who is not a party already liable on it may, with the consent of the holder, intervene and accept the bill *supra* protest, for the honour of any party liable on it, or for the honour of the person for whose account the bill is drawn (s. 65(1)). **6–138**

An acceptance for honour *supra* protest in order to be valid must be written on the bill, must indicate that it is an acceptance for honour, and must be signed by the acceptor for honour (s. 65(3)).

Where an acceptance for honour does not expressly state for whose honour it is made, it is deemed to be an acceptance for the honour of the drawer (*i.e.* the party primarily liable to pay a bill which has no acceptance on it) (s. 65(4)).

The undertaking of the acceptor for honour is that he will, on due presentment, pay the bill if it is not paid by the drawee, provided it has been duly presented for payment and protested for non-payment, and that he receives notice of these facts (s. 66(1)). The protest for non-payment must precede the presentment for payment to the acceptor for honour (s. 67(1)). The acceptor for honour is liable to the holder and to all parties to the bill subsequent to the party for whose honour he has accepted (s. 66(2)). **6–139**

If a bill is dishonoured by the acceptor for honour, it must be protested for non-payment by him (s. 67(4)). **6–140**

(ii) *Payment for Honour* supra *Protest*

Where a bill has been protested for non-payment, any person may intervene and pay it *supra* protest for the honour of any party liable on it, or for the honour of the person for whose account the bill is drawn (s. 68(1)). **6–141**

Payment for honour *supra* protest may be attested by a "notarial act of honour", which may be appended to the protest or form an extension of it (s. 68(3)). The notarial act of honour must be founded on a declaration made by the payer for honour declaring his intention to pay the bill for honour and for whose honour he pays (s. 68(4)).

Where a bill has been paid for honour, all parties subsequent to the party for whose honour it is paid are discharged, but the payer for honour obtains for himself the rights which the holder has as regards the party for whose honour he pays and as regards all parties liable to that party (s. 68(5)). The payer for honour on paying to the holder the amount of the bill and the notarial expenses connected with its dishonour is entitled to receive both the bill and the protest (s. 68(6)).

(m) **Miscellaneous Statutory Provisions**

6–142 At the end of Part II of the Act there are sections on:

(i) lost bills;
(ii) bill in a set; and
(iii) conflict of laws.

(i) *Lost Bills*

6–143 Where a bill has been lost before it is overdue, the person who was the holder of it may apply to the drawer to give him another bill of the same tenor. The drawer may be compelled to give a replacement, but he may, as a condition of complying, require the holder to indemnify him against all persons whomsoever in case the bill alleged to have been lost should be found again (s. 69). If the drawer does not take this precaution, the possible result is that the acceptor or (if the bill has not been accepted) the drawer may find himself liable to pay the amount of the bill twice over—once to the holder of the original bill and again to the holder of the bill which replaces the "lost" bill.

(ii) *Bill in a Set*

6–144 A bill may be drawn "in a set", *i.e.* there may be more than one copy of it. Each part of the set is numbered (*e.g.* "first of exchange", "second of exchange", etc.) and contains a reference to the other parts. In practice the use of bills in a set is confined to overseas trade, the object being to ensure that at least one of the set will duly and at a conveniently early date reach the desired destination. The whole of the two, three or more parts of a bill in a set constitute only one bill (s. 71(1)).

The acceptance may be written on any part, and it must be written on *one* part only. If the drawee accepts more than one part, and these different parts get into the hands of different holders in due course, the acceptor is liable on every part as if it were a separate bill (s. 71(4)).

The general principle is that where any one part of the bill is discharged by payment or otherwise, the whole bill is discharged (s. 71(6)). Accordingly, where the acceptor pays one part, he ought to require the part bearing his acceptance to be delivered up to him, and if he does not do so and that part at maturity is outstanding in the hands of a holder in due course, the acceptor is liable to that holder (s. 71(5)).

A holder who indorses two or more parts to different persons is liable on each part, and every indorser subsequent to him is liable on the part which he has himself indorsed as if the parts were separate bills (s. 71(2)).

(iii) *Conflict of Laws*

The rules of private international law are of particular importance in relation to bills of exchange, since these documents (apart from cheques) are mostly confined to the foreign trading scene. **6–145**

Section 72 of the Act sets out a number of rules, but these are not exhaustive; rather they form a basis, and they have been augmented by decided cases which have applied general principles of private international law. Full treatment of this subject is beyond the scope of this work: only the provisions of section 72 are noted here: **6–146**

(1) As regards form, the general rule is that the validity of the bill is determined by the law of the place of issue, and the validity of later contracts, such as acceptance and indorsement, is determined by the law of the place where the contract was made (s. 72(1)). The place at which a contract is "made" is the place of delivery, not necessarily the place of signing, because of the rule that every contract on a bill is revocable until delivery (s. 21(1)).

There are two exceptions to this general rule:

(a) Where a bill is issued out of the United Kingdom it is not invalid merely because it is not stamped as required by the law of the place of issue.

(b) Where a bill, issued out of the United Kingdom, conforms to the law of the United Kingdom, it may, for the purpose of enforcing payment, be treated as valid as between all persons who negotiate, hold, or become parties to it in the United Kingdom (s. 72(1)).

(2) As regards essential validity, the interpretation of the drawing, indorsement or acceptance is determined by the law of the place where the contract is made, except that where an inland bill is indorsed in a foreign country the indorsement is, as regards the payer, interpreted according to the law of the United Kingdom (s. 72(2)).

(3) Presentment for acceptance or payment, protest and notice of dishonour are governed by the law of the place where the act is done or the bill is dishonoured (s. 72(3)).

(4) Where a bill is drawn in one country and is payable in another, its due date is determined according to the law of the place where it is payable (s. 72(5)).

II CHEQUES

6–147 A cheque is defined as a "bill of exchange drawn on a banker payable on demand". The provisions of the Act of 1882 applicable to bills of exchange payable on demand apply to cheques except where there is some provision to the contrary, either in the Act of 1882 or in the Cheques Act 1957 as amended by the Cheques Act 1992 (s. 73).

6–148 The definition calls for some examination of the term "banker", and the statutory provisions which are peculiar to cheques relate mainly to presentment for payment, to crossing of cheques and to the protection of bankers. These matters are considered below under the headings:

(a) relation of banker and customer;
(b) presentment of cheque for payment;
(c) crossed cheques; and
(d) protection of bankers.

6–149 As has been seen (6–124, above), summary diligence—a process unaffected by the Act of 1882 (s. 98)—cannot be used to enforce payment of an unpaid cheque (*Glickman v. Linda*, 1950 S.C. 18 (O.H.)).

(a) **Relation of Banker and Customer**

The relation of banker and customer is principally a contractual one, but, because of the variety of services provided by bankers, the contract is not the same category of contract in every situation. Thus, where the customer has placed money in the hands of his banker on deposit or current account, there is a contractual relationship of creditor and debtor as between customer and banker. Where, on the other hand, the banker has advanced money to the customer, the relationship is the reverse one of creditor and debtor as between banker and customer. In paying cheques drawn by the customer and in collecting payment of cheques on behalf of the customer, the banker is in the position of agent for his customer, and the principles of the law of agency govern their relationship. Again, where the banker accepts articles (such as jewellery) and documents (such as share certificates) for his customer for safe keeping, the relationship between the parties is governed by the law of deposit. **6–150**

The law on the relation of banker and customer is mainly to be found in decided cases rather than in specific statutory provisions. Some of the more important aspects of the relation are indicated below under the headings: **6–151**

(i) who is a "banker";
(ii) who is a "customer";
(iii) banker's duties to customer; and
(iv) customer's duties to banker.

(i) *Who is a "Banker"*

The Act of 1882 provides that "banker" includes a body of persons whether incorporated or not who carry on the business of banking (s. 2). The Cheques Act 1957, which must be construed along with the Act of 1882 (Cheques Act 1957, s. 6(1)), makes no advance on that definition. Some other statutes have supplied definitions of "banker", each for its own purposes. **6–152**

In more recent years the most notable statutes on banking—the Banking Act 1979 and the Banking Act 1987 (which latter almost **6–153** wholly repealed the Act of 1979)—were passed mainly to control deposit-taking in the interests of depositors. A central provision of the Act of 1979 was that a "recognised bank" was exempt from the general prohibition placed by the Act on the acceptance of deposits (1979 Act, s. 2). For "recognition" as a bank for the purposes of the Act, the Bank of England had to be satisfied that criteria in Part I of Schedule 2 to the Act were fulfilled (1979 Act, s. 3).

The Banking Act 1987 strengthened the Bank of England's supervisory functions. The term "recognised bank" was dropped, and instead the Act restricted the taking of deposits (with certain exemptions) to "authorised institutions" (1987 Act, s. 3). For "authorisation" under the Act, the Bank of England must be satisfied that the criteria in Schedule 3 to the Act are fulfilled. These come under the headings of:

(1) directors, etc., to be fit and proper persons;
(2) business to be directed by at least two individuals;
(3) composition of board of directors;
(4) business to be conducted in prudent manner;
(5) integrity and skill; and
(6) minimum net assets (£1 million).

The Act also imposes restrictions on the use of banking names: only certain "authorised institutions" may use the name "bank", the principal requirement being an issued share capital or undistributable reserves of at least £5 million (s. 67).

6–154 The case-law relating to the definition of "banker" culminated in the Court of Appeal case *United Dominions Trust Ltd v. Kirkwood* [1966] 2 Q.B. 431, which gave support to the traditional view that an essential characteristic of a banker was that he paid cheques drawn on himself. The question in the case was whether the plaintiff finance company ("U.D.T.") carried on the business of banking (and so would have been exempt from provisions of the Moneylenders Act 1900). All three members of the Court of Appeal described the characteristics of banking as being:

(1) the acceptance of money from, and collection of cheques for, customers, and the placing of them to the customers' credit;

(2) the honouring of cheques or orders drawn on the bank by their customers when presented for payment, and the debiting of the customers accordingly; and

(3) the keeping of some form of current or running accounts for the entries of customers' credits and debits.

(The Court of Appeal held that the evidence in this case did not establish that U.D.T.'s conduct of its business had the usual characteristics of banking, but the Court, by a majority, further held that the evidence of the company's reputation of carrying on the business of banking was sufficient to prove that it carried on the business of banking.)

(ii) *Who is a "Customer"*

The Act of 1882 did not define "customer", although it used the word in section 82 (now replaced by section 4 of the Cheques Act 1957). Nor is there any definition of "customer" in the Cheques Act 1957. **6–155**

The leading English case is *Great Western Railway Co. v. London and County Banking Co. Ltd* [1901] A.C. 414, in which the House of Lords held that to make a person a "customer" of a bank for the purposes of section 82 of the Act of 1882 "there must be some sort of account, either a deposit or a current account or some similar relation" (*per* Lord Davey at p. 420). The decision in the case was therefore that a person who had for 20 years been in the habit of having cheques cashed for him by the bank but who had no account with the bank was not a "customer" (the result being that the bank did not enjoy the protection which it would otherwise have had under section 82 of the Act). **6–156**

The general rule as stated by Lord Davey in that case may require to be qualified in the light of a more recent English case—*Woods v. Martins Bank Ltd* [1959] 1 Q.B. 55: **6–157**

On May 9, 1950, W. was induced to invest £5,000 in shares of Brocks Refrigeration Ltd ("B.R."), following advice given by the manager of a branch of Martins Bank Ltd that B.R., a customer of the bank, was financially sound and that the investment was a wise one to make.

On June 1, 1950, the bank opened a current account for W., and W. made further investments in B.R. after that date.

There were no grounds on which the branch manager could reasonably have advised that B.R. was in a sound or strong financial position, and still less could the investment be reasonably recommended as a wise one.

W. lost all the £14,800 which he had invested in B.R., and brought an action against the bank and the branch manager.

Held that it was within the scope of the bank's business to advise on all financial matters and the bank owed a duty to W. to advise him with reasonable care and skill, that from May 9 the relationship of banker and customer existed, and that W. had made out his case in negligence both against the bank and against the manager.

Salmon J., in considering what was and what was not within the scope of the bank's business, looked at the bank's own publications and concluded (at p. 71): "I find that it was and is within the scope of the defendant bank's business to advise on all financial matters and that, as they did advise him, they owed a duty to the plaintiff to advise him with reasonable care and skill."

In dealing with the point taken by the bank that W. was not a customer of the bank at the date of the first transaction in May 1950, in that no current account had then been opened, Salmon J. held that W. was a customer of the bank on May 9, 1950.

The case suggests two possible alternative qualifications to Lord Davey's statement: *either* a person may be a customer if he is about to open an account *or* a person may be a customer if he avails himself of facilities offered by the bank other than deposit or current account facilities (in this case advice on investments). The second qualification is the more radical of the two.

6–158 A "customer" does not require to have had habitual dealings with the bank: he becomes a customer from the moment he opens an account. This may be illustrated by the Privy Council case *Commissioners of Taxation v. English, Scottish and Australian Bank Ltd* [1920] A.C. 683:

On June 7, a person giving his name as "Thallon" opened a current account with the bank and paid £20 in cash into it.

On the following day, a cheque for some £786, which had been stolen from the Commissioners of Taxation, was handed into the bank with a pay-in slip to be credited to Thallon's account.

Held that Thallon was a customer of the bank.

Lord Dunedin, giving the judgment, said (at p. 687): "The word 'customer' signifies a relationship in which duration is not of the essence. A person whose money has been accepted by a bank on the footing that they undertake to honour cheques up to the amount standing to his credit is . . . a customer of the bank in the sense of the statute, irrespective of whether his connection is of short or long standing."

(iii) *Banker's Duties to Customer*

The banker's duties to his customer depend on the terms of the contract between them: if the customer has a deposit or savings account, the banker will be bound to pay him the agreed interest on the credit balance of that account and to repay the amount deposited when required to do so; if money has been lodged on deposit receipt, the banker will be bound to pay the money deposited with interest to the person named in the deposit receipt (who is not necessarily the person who deposited the money); where the contract is for the safe keeping of the customer's property, either for a charge or gratuitously, the banker will incur the obligations of an onerous or gratuitous depositary as the case may be. **6–159**

Of special importance are: **6–160**

(1) the banker's duty of secrecy; and

(2) the banker's duty to honour cheques.

(1) **Banker's duty of secrecy**

The relation of banker and customer is of a confidential nature, and so, as a general rule, the banker has a duty not to disclose his customer's affairs. **6–161**

This duty was considered and given effect to by the Court of Appeal in *Tournier v. National Provincial and Union Bank of England* [1924] 1 K.B. 461. Bankes L.J. said (at pp. 472–473) that the duty was not absolute but qualified, and he classified the qualifications under four heads: **6–162**

(a) where disclosure is compelled by law (*e.g.* where a court requires a banker to give evidence in legal proceedings or where some statutory provision confers on an official a right of inspection);

(b) where there is a duty to the public to disclose (*e.g.* where, in wartime, the customer is transacting with the enemy);

(c) where the interests of the bank require disclosure (*e.g.* where the bank brings an action in court claiming repayment of the customer's overdraft); and

(d) where the disclosure is made by the express written consent of the customer (*e.g.* where the customer has requested the banker to act as a referee concerning the customer's financial position).

Before 1994 it was an established practice that bankers gave information about their customers to other bankers without asking for permission from the customers. This practice was perhaps justified on the ground that, on opening an account, a customer *impliedly* consented to such disclosure. In 1994 the major banks introduced a new status inquiry system: individuals or businesses wishing to obtain a banker's opinion send their request direct to the bank concerned and that bank responds direct to the inquirer. There is no longer any implied authority to respond to an inquiry: the bank will only respond where the customer has given express consent.

6–163 Other points included in Bankes L.J.'s judgment were that the duty of secrecy did not cease the moment the customer closed his account—the information gained during the currency of the account remained confidential—and that the confidence was not confined to the actual state of the customer's account but extended to information derived from the keeping of the account.

(2) **Banker's duty to honour cheques**

6–164 "The relation between banker and customer is that of debtor and creditor, with a superadded obligation on the part of the banker to honour the customer's cheques if the account is in credit. A cheque drawn by a customer is in point of law a mandate to the banker to pay the amount according to the tenor of the cheque" (*per* Lord Finlay L.C. in *London Joint Stock Bank Ltd v. Macmillan and Arthur* [1918] A.C. 777, at p. 789). This concise quotation involves a number of considerations:

(a) *"If the account is in credit"*

6–165 The banker is under no obligation to allow an overdraft. Where, however, a banker has insufficient funds to meet a cheque which is presented to him for payment, he must set aside such funds as he has, since, by section 53(2), the presentment of the cheque has the effect in Scotland of assigning these funds to the holder of the cheque (see 6–99 *et seq.*, above).

6–166 The question can arise of whether a banker is entitled, without prior notice to his customer, to mass several current accounts kept by the customer, at one or more branches of the bank, in order to ascertain whether there are funds to meet a cheque. The question would usually be covered by an agreement made between banker and customer, as in the English case of *National Westminster Bank Ltd v. Halesowen Presswork & Assemblies Ltd* [1972] A.C. 785:

In February 1968 H. Ltd's current account was overdrawn to the extent of £11,339. An agreement was made between the bank and H. Ltd that in order to support H. Ltd's business so that it could be disposed of as a going concern, the current account, to be called "No. 1 account", would be frozen and that a new account, the "No. 2 account", would be opened and maintained in credit.

In June 1968 H. Ltd went into liquidation, and the liquidator claimed from the bank the sum of about £8,611, then standing at the credit of the No. 2 account. The bank on the other hand claimed to be entitled to set off this amount against H. Ltd's indebtedness on the No. 1 account.

Held, on an interpretation of the agreement, that the parties had not contemplated that the agreement should continue in force after liquidation; the bank was therefore entitled to consolidate the two accounts and exercise the right which existed on a winding-up to set off the balance on the No. 2 account against H. Ltd's debt on the No. 1 account.

Where no event such as the customer's liquidation or death has occurred to stop the current accounts, the generally accepted view, based on the English case of *Garnett v. McKewan* (1872) L.R. 8 Ex. 10, is that, in the absence of any agreement or course of dealing to the contrary, the banker is entitled without prior notice to mass the customer's several current accounts even if kept at different branches of the bank.

If the several accounts are of a different kind (*e.g.* a deposit **6–167**
account and a current account), the banker is not entitled to combine them without prior notice to the customer. This was taken to be an established rule in *Kirkwood & Sons v. Clydesdale Bank Ltd*, 1908 S.C. 20:

Moffatt, a Glasgow stockbroker, had a current account, a loan account and several cash accounts with his bank. A cheque drawn by Moffatt in favour of K. & Sons was presented to the bank at a time when the credit balance on the current account was more than sufficient to meet it, but payment was refused on the ground that Moffatt had died earlier the same day. K. & Sons argued that the cheque had the effect of assigning funds under section 53(2).

Held that (i) the cheque, as a cheque, lapsed at Moffatt's death; and (ii) the cheque did not operate as an "assignment" under section 53(2) because, on a combination of all Moffatt's accounts, he was indebted to the bank and so the bank had no "funds available" for the payment of the cheque, within the meaning of that subsection.

(b) *"Drawn by a customer"*

6–168 The customer's signature must be genuine. If the banker pays a cheque on which the drawer's signature has been forged, he is not entitled to debit the customer's account with the amount because he has no mandate (authority) to do so. The loss therefore falls on the banker.

(c) *"A mandate to the banker to pay"*

6–169 In paying cheques the banker is the agent for the customer whose funds he holds.

6–170 This mandate or agency is terminated in various circumstances either by statute or at common law. These circumstances include:

(i) countermand of payment (*i.e.* where the drawer, before the cheque has been paid, instructs the banker not to pay it) (s. 75); formerly presentment of the cheque for payment operated, under section 53(2) of the Act, as an assignation of funds in the banker's hands available for payment, and the banker had therefore to transfer the amount of the cheque (or the whole credit balance if that was less than the amount of the cheque) to a suspense account; where the holder of the cheque and the drawer of it did not then agree as to the disposal of the funds, the matter had to be settled by a court process known as a "multiplepoinding"; by amendments made by section 11 of the Law Reform (Miscellaneous Provisions) (Scotland) Act 1985, assignation of funds no longer takes place where a cheque has been countermanded, and the banker is treated as having no funds available for the payment of the cheque (s. 53(2) as amended and s. 75A of the 1882 Act); cheques which have been issued along with production of a cheque card cannot, according to the usual terms of the agreement between banker and customer, be countermanded;

(ii) notice of the customer's death (s. 75); presentment of a cheque after notice of the customer's death will operate as an assignation under section 53(2) (*Bank of Scotland v. Reid* (1886) 2 Sh.Ct.Rep. 376 (6–102, above)), but in this situation all the customer's accounts are taken into consideration in the decision of whether the banker has any "funds available" (*Kirkwood & Sons v. Clydesdale Bank Ltd* (6–167, above));

(iii) the drawer's sequestration (Bankruptcy (Scotland) Act 1985, s. 32(8)); any credit balance vests in the permanent trustee as at the date of the sequestration (1985 Act, s. 31(1)); however, if the banker proves that, despite the customer's sequestration, he paid a cheque in the ordinary course of business at a time when he was unaware of the sequestration and had no reason to believe that the customer's estate had been sequestrated or was the subject of sequestration proceedings, payment of the cheque cannot be challenged (1985 Act, s. 32(9)); section 53(2) of the Act of 1882 may operate here also: if, before sequestration, a cheque has been presented and payment of it has been refused on account of there being insufficient funds to meet it, the holder of the cheque and not the trustee is entitled to any funds which, on the occasion of the presentment of the cheque, were at the credit of the account;

(iv) notice given by either party of the closing of the account, but a banker giving notice to his customer is bound to pay cheques drawn prior to, though not presented until after, the date of receipt of the notice (*King v. British Linen Co.* (1899) 1 F. 928); and

(v) appointment of a *curator bonis* ("guardian") on the mental incapacity of the drawer (*Mitchell & Baxter v. Cheyne* (1891) 19 R. 324).

(d) *"According to the tenor of the cheque"*

The banker must follow the instructions of his principal, the **6–171** customer. He must, therefore, observe any crossing which there may be on the cheque (see 6–182 *et seq.*, below), and if the customer has postdated the cheque, the banker must not pay it until that date has arrived.

A banker who wrongfully fails to honour his customer's cheques **6–172** commits a breach of contract, and is liable in damages measured by the actual loss sustained by the customer on the transaction and by the injury to his credit and reputation. If the customer is in business he is entitled to substantial damages under the latter head without proving actual injury (*e.g.* £100 to a hay and grain merchant in *King v. British Linen Co.* (1899) 1 F. 928), but a person who is not in business must prove his actual injury; otherwise he is entitled only to nominal damages (*e.g.* £2 for wrongful dishonour of a cheque payable to a landlord in *Gibbons v. Westminster Bank Ltd* [1939] 2 K.B. 882). In both of the cases mentioned the claim was founded on breach of contract.

6–173 An alternative ground would be delict, since it is defamatory to cast unjustifiable doubts upon a person's financial soundness. An English case which is an example of a successful claim for libel (corresponding to written slander in Scots law) is *Davidson v. Barclays Bank Ltd* [1940] 1 All E.R. 316: A cheque for £2 15s. 8d. drawn by a credit bookmaker had been dishonoured by his bank because the bank had not given effect to a stop order placed by the customer on a previously drawn cheque for £7 15s. 9d. The customer obtained damages of £250. Hilberry J. in that case said that he could not imagine anything much more damaging to a credit bookmaker than a statement which suggested that he could not meet a cheque for such a small amount as £2 15s. 8d. "Substantial damage", he continued (at p. 325), "is done, for the very good reason that nothing about a man travels so fast as that which is to his discredit. . . . What is a proper sum to be given as a reasonable compensation for the injury which has been done to the plaintiff . . . must be sufficient to mark beyond a shadow of doubt the complete lack of justification for making the aspersion which was made by this means on the plaintiff's credit."

6–174 In the cases concerning damages for dishonour of a cheque (whether founded on breach of contract or founded on delict) the emphasis placed on damage to the customer's credit in his business cannot readily be reconciled with the provision in section 57(1) of the Act of 1882 that the measure of damages for the dishonour of any bill of exchange is to be the amount of the bill, plus interest from the time of presentment for payment and the expenses of noting and of protest (where protest is necessary) (David M. Walker, *Civil Remedies*, p. 413).

(iv) *Customer's Duties to Banker*

6–175 In relation to cheques, the customer has a duty towards the banker:

(1) to take reasonable precautions to prevent fraudulent alteration of cheques drawn; and

(2) to notify the banker timeously of any forgeries known to the customer.

There are no further *implied* duties and any additional duties would require to be expressed in clear and unambiguous terms:

Tai Hing Cotton Mill Ltd v. Liu Chong Hing Bank Ltd [1986] A.C. 80 (P.C.): A company which had current accounts with three banks authorised the banks to pay cheques drawn on its behalf by its managing director. Between November 1974 and May 1978 an accounts clerk forged the managing director's signature on about 300 cheques. The banks honoured the cheques and the forgeries were not discovered until May 1978.

The company brought an action against the three banks. It was unsuccessful in the Court of Appeal in Hong Kong, but its appeal to the Judicial Committee of the Privy Council was allowed.

Held that (1) the only duties of a customer to a bank were to exercise due care in the drawing of cheques so as not to facilitate fraud or forgery and to notify the bank immediately of any unauthorised cheques of which he had become aware: there was no wider duty, requiring the customer to take even reasonable precautions in the management of his business so as to prevent forged cheques being presented for payment, or requiring him to check the periodic bank statements; such duties were not implied in the relationship of banker and customer;

(2) the express terms were not sufficiently clear and unambiguous as to impose upon the company an obligation to examine the periodic bank statements;

(3) since the company was not in breach of any implied or express duty to the banks, it was not barred from asserting that the accounts had been incorrectly debited, and the banks were therefore liable to pay the sums of the cheques to the company.

(1) **Reasonable precautions in drawing cheques**

"It is beyond dispute that the customer is bound to exercise reasonable care in drawing the cheque to prevent the banker being misled. If he draws the cheque in a manner which facilitates fraud, he is guilty of a breach of duty as between himself and the banker, and he will be responsible to the banker for any loss sustained by the banker as a natural and direct consequence of this breach of duty" (*per* Lord Finlay L.C. in *London Joint Stock Bank Ltd v. Macmillan and Arthur* [1918] A.C. 777). The facts of the case referred to are a memorable illustration: **6–176**

"On the morning of February 9, 1915, one of the plaintiff partners, Mr. Arthur, was going out to lunch about mid-day. He had his hat on and was leaving the office when the clerk came up to him and said he wanted £2 for petty cash and produced a cheque for signature. The clerk had repeatedly presented cheques for signature to get petty cash, but usually for £3, and Mr. Arthur asked him why it was not £3 on this occasion. The clerk replied that £2 would be sufficient. Mr. Arthur thereupon signed the cheque. . . . On the next day the clerk did not come to business. . . .

". . . Mr. Arthur was in a great hurry when he signed the cheque, and . . . when he signed it there were no words at all in the space left for words; that space was a blank. There were the figures ' 2 .0.0' in the space left for figures. The clerk, having obtained Mr. Arthur's signature to the cheque in this condition properly dated and payable to 'ourselves,' added the words 'one hundred and twenty pounds' in the space left for words, and the figures '1' and '0' on either side of the figure '2'."[7]

The clerk had absconded with the £120, and Macmillan and Arthur brought an action claiming a declaration that the bank was not entitled to debit the plaintiffs' account with the £120.

The House of Lords held that the bank was entitled to do so on the ground of the customer's failure to take reasonable and ordinary precautions against forgery.

(2) **Timeous notification of forgeries**

6–177 The customer has a duty to notify the banker of forged cheques known to the customer: otherwise, the customer may be barred from objecting when further forged cheques are debited to his account. An illustration is *Greenwood v. Martins Bank Ltd* [1933] A.C. 51 (6–25, above).

(b) Presentment of Cheque for Payment

6–178 In all but exceptional cases a cheque is intended to operate as an immediate payment out of the drawer's funds to the payee. While in theory the cheque is an "order" on the banker to pay to the payee, in reality it is an appropriation to the payee by the drawer of what the drawer regards as his own funds. Primary liability, therefore, lies with the drawer, and presentment to the banker for acceptance would be inappropriate.

---

[7] Narrative adopted by Lord Finlay L.C. (at p. 787) from the judgment of Sankey J.

There is, however, the possibility of certification (or "marking") of a cheque. In certifying a cheque the banker undertakes that the customer has sufficient funds to meet it. The banker might write on the face of the cheque words such as "This cheque is good for payment", accompanied by an authorised signature and a date, but the usual Scottish practice is to stamp the back of the cheque with a rubber stamp stating that if the cheque is presented within seven days it will be paid. This procedure can enhance the creditworthiness of the drawer in the eyes of the payee. Though certification does not amount to "acceptance" in the statutory sense (*Bank of Baroda Ltd v. Punjab National Bank Ltd* [1944] A.C. 176), it is an undertaking binding on the banker, and in order to protect himself the banker immediately, at the time of granting the certification, debits the customer's account with the amount of the cheque and places the amount at the credit of another account such as "Sundry Credits": on presentation of the cheque, the amount is then recredited to the customer's account and the cheque is paid out of his account. Certified cheques are in common use in some other Commonwealth countries, but in this country bankers' drafts are preferred. (A banker's draft is a document in the form of a cheque drawn by the banker on himself. It is issued at the customer's request, is payable to a named payee, and the amount of the draft is debited, at that time, to the customer's account. Funds are thus available in the banker's hands to pay the draft to the payee when it is presented.) **6–179**

Presentment for payment is one of the matters on which the Act of 1882 differentiates between cheques and other bills of exchange. The rule applicable to bills of exchange in general is that where a bill is payable on demand (as a cheque always is), presentment for payment must be made within a reasonable time after its issue in order to make the drawer liable, and within a reasonable time after its indorsement, in order to make the indorser liable (s. 45, rule (2)). In the case of a cheque, however, the extent to which the drawer is discharged by the holder's failure to present the cheque for payment within a reasonable time is much more limited: the Act provides that where a cheque is not presented for payment within a reasonable time of its issue and the drawer suffers actual damage through the delay, he is discharged to the extent of that damage, *i.e.* to the extent to which he is a creditor of the banker to a larger amount than he would have been had his cheque been **6–180** paid (s. 74(1)). The effect of this provision is that the drawer will be discharged only if the banker becomes insolvent. As the failure of a bank is an event of very rare occurrence, the practical result is that a drawer remains liable to pay the cheque until the lapse of the prescriptive period of five years. As a matter of Scottish banking practice, however, a cheque which is over six months old when it is presented for payment is returned by the banker to the person presenting it, in order that it may be confirmed by the drawer before it is paid.

The Act further provides that where the unusual circumstances mentioned in section 74(1), above, do occur, the holder of the cheque becomes a creditor of the banker for the amount of which the drawer has been discharged (s. 74(3)).

6–181 By the Deregulation (Bills of Exchange) Order 1996 (S.I. 1996 No. 2993), made under the Deregulation and Contracting Out Act 1994, a new section 74A was inserted in the Act of 1882 to allow cheques to be presented at an address specified by the paying bank in the *London*, *Edinburgh* and *Belfast Gazettes*, and a new section 74B was inserted to enable cheques to be presented for payment by notification of their essential features by electronic means or otherwise, rather than by physical presentment. A new section 74C disapplies section 52(4) (which relates to the duty of the holder when presenting a bill for payment to exhibit the bill, etc.: see 6–95, above) to cheques presented in the way provided for in section 74B.

(c) Crossed Cheques

6–182 The effect of crossing a cheque is to give a direction to the banker on whom it is drawn (the "paying banker") that payment of it should only be made to another banker (the "collecting banker"). The advantage of crossing is that it helps to ensure that the cheque will be paid only to the person for whom it is intended.

6–183 The normal procedure is for the recipient of the cheque to pay the cheque into his own bank account, and his banker will then collect the amount of the cheque by presenting the cheque to the banker on whom it is drawn. If the recipient of the cheque does not himself have a bank account, he will require to enlist the help of another person who does have a bank account and who will obtain payment of the cheque by presenting it, through his bank account, to the banker on whom the cheque is drawn. It would be exceptional for the recipient of a crossed cheque to present it for payment in cash to the banker on whom it is drawn; the banker would be under no obligation to pay it in cash, but if he chose to do so, he would not be acting illegally: he would be without the statutory protection conferred on paying bankers who observe crossings (see 6–204 *et seq.*, below) and he might incur liability under section 79(2) to the true owner of the cheque for any loss sustained by the true owner as a result of the cheque having been paid in disregard of the crossing. A more likely occurrence is where the payee of a crossed cheque hands it to the paying banker along with a giro credit slip, thus transferring the amount of the cheque to his own account at another bank. The use of giro credits is becoming increasingly common, but there is doubt as to how the statutory provisions apply to that system: in particular, is the banker who ultimately receives the proceeds of the crossed cheque a collecting banker enjoying the same protection as that conferred on a banker collecting a crossed cheque? Other questions which are still open are whether the handing in of the giro credit slip and the cheque to the drawee bank is effective as a presentment of the cheque for the purposes of section 53(2) (assignation of funds—see 6–99 *et seq.*, above), and whether the cheque is paid at the moment of the handing in of the giro credit slip, so that countermand of payment would thereafter be impossible.

The statutory provisions are considered under these headings: **6–184**

(i) general and special crossings;
(ii) who is entitled to cross a cheque;
(iii) effect of crossing; and
(iv) effect of addition of "not negotiable".

A note is also included on:

(v) effect of addition of "account payee only".

(i) *General and Special Crossings*

A cheque may be crossed generally or specially. **6–185**

A cheque is crossed generally if it bears across its face an **6–186**
addition of:

(1) the words "and company", or any abbreviation of these words, between two parallel transverse lines, either with or without the words "not negotiable"; or

(2) two parallel transverse lines simply, either with or without the words "not negotiable" (s. 76(1)).

The following are therefore general crossings:

and Company

& Co.

6–187 A cheque is crossed specially if it bears across its face an addition of the name of a banker, either with or without the words "not negotiable" (s. 76(2)). The Act does not require two parallel transverse lines in this case, but such lines are commonly used.

Examples of special crossings are:

Bank of Scotland

Royal Bank of Scotland plc

(ii) *Who is Entitled to Cross a Cheque*

6–188 A cheque may be crossed generally or specially by the drawer. Where a cheque is uncrossed, the holder may cross it generally or specially, and where a cheque is already crossed generally, the holder may cross it specially. Where a cheque is crossed generally or specially, the holder may add the words "not negotiable" (s. 77(1)–(4)).

Where an uncrossed cheque, or a cheque crossed generally, is sent to a banker "for collection", *i.e.* in order that he may obtain payment of it from the banker on whom it is drawn, he may cross it specially to himself (s. 77(6)). **6–189**

There is only one situation in which a cheque may be crossed specially to more than one banker, namely, where the banker to whom the cheque is crossed specially again crosses it specially to another banker for collection (s. 77(5)). If in any other situation a cheque is crossed specially to more than one banker, the banker on whom it is drawn must refuse payment of the cheque (s. 79(1)). **6–190**

Crossing as authorised by the Act is a material part of a cheque, and it is not lawful for any person to obliterate or (with the exceptions mentioned above) to add to or alter the crossing (s. 78). **6–191**

(iii) *Effect of Crossing*

Crossing imposes certain duties on, and gives some protection to, the drawee bank, *i.e.* the bank on which the cheque is drawn. The duties imposed are considered here, and the protection conferred is dealt with later (see 6–197 *et seq.*, below). **6–192**

If a cheque is uncrossed, the holder of it may himself present it to the bank on which it is drawn and obtain cash for it. Alternatively, he may request his own bank to collect payment on his behalf from the bank on which the cheque is drawn.

In the case of a crossed cheque, only the second alternative is open to the holder. If the crossing is a general crossing, the cheque must be presented for payment through a bank, and if the crossing is a special crossing, the cheque must be presented for payment through the bank which is specially named in the crossing.

If the banker on whom the cheque is drawn pays it in contravention of the general or special crossing which it bears, he is liable to the true owner of the cheque for loss sustained. An exception to this liability is made where a cheque, when presented for payment, does not appear to be crossed or to have had a crossing which has been obliterated, or added to or altered in some way not authorised by the Act: to avail himself of this exception the banker must have paid the cheque in good faith and without negligence (s. 79(2)). **6–193**

There is an illustration of the consequences of failure to observe a crossing in *Godfrey Phillips Ltd v. Italian Bank Ltd*, 1934 S.L.T. 78 (O.H.):

P. Ltd of London were wholesale tobacconists. Moyes, one of P. Ltd's travellers, obtained in the course of his duties cheques from customers in favour of P. Ltd. On one occasion Moyes, having obtained three crossed cheques drawn on the Italian Bank Ltd, Glasgow, presented them to the bank for payment, received payment in cash and applied the proceeds to his own purposes.

Held, on an application of section 79(2), that P. Ltd were entitled to recover the amount of the three cheques from the bank.

(iv) *Effect of Addition of "Not Negotiable"*

6–194 When a person takes a crossed cheque which bears on it the words "not negotiable", he does not himself obtain, and is not capable of giving, a better title to the cheque than that which the person from whom he took it had (s. 81). The cheque can still be transferred, but each transferee will take the cheque subject to any defects in the title of previous parties.

(v) *Effect of Addition of "Account Payee"*

6–195 Section 81A, added to the Act of 1882 by the Cheques Act 1992 (s. 1), makes provision for non-transferable cheques: where a cheque is crossed and bears across its face the words "account payee" or "a/c payee" either with or without the word "only" the cheque is not transferable but is only valid as between the parties to it (s. 81A(1)).

(d) **Protection of Bankers**

6–196 Statutory protection is given to both:

(i) the paying banker (*i.e.* the banker on whom the cheque is drawn); and

(ii) the collecting banker (*i.e.* the banker who, as agent for the holder of the cheque, collects payment of it from the paying banker).

(i) *Protection of Paying Banker*

6–197 The statutory provisions under this heading modify, as regards cheques, the rule of section 24 applicable to bills of exchange in general, *viz.*, that where a signature on a bill is forged or unauthorised, the forged or unauthorised signature is wholly inoperative and no right to retain the bill or to give a discharge for it or to enforce payment of it against any party can be acquired through or under that signature, unless the party against whom it is sought to retain or enforce payment of the bill is barred from saying that there has been forgery or want of authority (see 6–25, above).

Where it is the drawer's signature which is forged or unauthorised, the paying banker has no statutory protection. He is not permitted to debit his customer's account with the amount of the cheque, unless the drawer has himself in some way so materially contributed to the forged or unauthorised signature that he is barred from saying to the banker that it ought not to have been paid. **6–198**

The statutory protection is therefore confined to the situation where the cheque has one or more indorsements which have been forged or made without authority. **6–199**

Before the statutory provisions themselves are considered, it is first necessary to distinguish "bearer" cheques (those payable to a named payee "or bearer") from "order" cheques (those payable to a named payee "or order"). **6–200**

Bearer cheques, like any other bills of exchange payable to bearer, may be transferred from one person to another by simple delivery without any indorsement. If in fact a bearer cheque is indorsed, it is not the indorsement which gives the holder of the cheque his title to it: his title is derived from the delivery of the cheque to him. If, therefore, a bearer cheque has a forged or unauthorised indorsement and the banker on whom the cheque is drawn pays it to the holder, the banker will be considered as having paid the cheque in due course, the cheque will be discharged and the amount will be properly debited to the drawer's account. The rule in section 24 does not apply in such a case because the holder has not acquired the right "through or under" the forged or unauthorised signature, but by delivery. **6–201**

As regards order cheques, there are three statutory provisions giving protection to the paying banker: **6–202**

(1) **Bills of Exchange Act 1882, section 60**

This applies to any bill payable to order on demand and drawn on a banker. Provided the banker pays the bill "*in good faith and in the ordinary course of business*", he need not show that the **6–203** indorsement of the payee or any subsequent indorsement was made by or with the authority of the person whose indorsement it purports to be, and he is deemed to have paid the bill in due course, although the indorsement has in fact been forged or made without authority.

Both crossed and uncrossed cheques would come within this provision. If, however, the banker paid a crossed cheque over the counter, that would not be payment "in the ordinary course of business", and he would not be able to rely on section 60; nor would he be protected by this provision if he paid a cheque which bore an irregular indorsement.

(2) **Bills of Exchange Act 1882, section 80 as amended by Cheques Act 1992, section 2**

6–204 This applies only to crossed cheques (including non-transferable cheques). Provided the banker "*in good faith and without negligence*" pays the cheque in accordance with its general or special crossing, the banker is entitled to the same rights and is placed in the same position as if payment of the cheque had been made to the true owner of it.

This provision is differently worded from that in section 60, and there is some overlapping of the two provisions. The explanation appears to be that section 80 is a reproduction of an earlier statutory provision relating to cheques in the Crossed Cheques Act 1876.

By the Cheques Act 1992 (s. 1, inserting s. 81A(2) of the Act of 1882) a banker is not liable for negligence merely because he has failed to concern himself with any purported indorsement of a non-transferable cheque.

(3) **Cheques Act 1957, section 1**

6–205 Neither section 60 nor section 80 gave the paying banker protection if an indorsement on the cheque was missing or was irregular on its face. It was therefore necessary for the banker to check all indorsements to verify that they were apparently regular. This time-taking procedure may be dispensed with under section 1 of the Cheques Act 1957, the effect of which is to extend the paying banker's protection to cheques, whether crossed or uncrossed, which are unindorsed or which are irregularly indorsed.

The provision is that where a banker "*in good faith and in the ordinary course of business*" pays a cheque which is not indorsed or is irregularly indorsed, he does not, in doing so, incur any liability merely because of the absence of, or irregularity in, indorsement, and he is deemed to have paid the cheque in due course.

Questions can arise as to whether the banker has acted "in the ordinary course of business" within the meaning of (1) and (3), above, and as to whether he has acted "without negligence" within the meaning of (2), above. In interpreting these phrases, the courts look to banking practice. It is, for instance, banking practice for a banker to require a cheque to be indorsed if it is presented for payment over the counter and not through a bank. If, therefore, a paying banker were to disregard that practice and pay the cheque over the counter, he would not be protected. **6–206**

(ii) *Protection of Collecting Banker*

The banker who collects the proceeds of a cheque may incur liability if the person from whom he takes the cheque has in fact no title or only a defective title to the cheque. The purpose of the statutory provision under this heading is to protect the collecting banker from such liability on certain conditions. **6–207**

The statutory provision used to be section 82 of the Act of 1882: **6–208**

"Where a banker *in good faith and without negligence receives payment for a customer* of a cheque crossed generally or specially to himself, and the customer has no title or a defective title thereto, the banker shall not incur any liability to the true owner of the cheque by reason only of having received such payment."

That provision was amended by section 1 of the Bills of Exchange (Crossed Cheques) Act 1906 as a result of the decision of the House of Lords in the English case *Capital and Counties Bank Ltd v. Gordon* [1903] A.C. 240. The case established that bankers were protected by section 82 of the Act of 1882 *only where they received payment of a crossed cheque as agents for collection for a customer* and were not protected by the section when they received payment as holders of the cheque on their own account. An outline of the facts is as follows: **6–209**

Gordon was the holder for value of various crossed cheques. His clerk, Jones, forged indorsements on these cheques and took the cheques to the C. Bank, where Jones had an account. Jones also indorsed the cheques in his own name, and the C. Bank credited his account with the amounts. Jones then drew on his account. The bank manager dealt in perfect good faith and without negligence. The vital point was that the bank did not wait until the cheques paid in by Jones had been passed through the clearing-house before their amounts were placed to his credit: they were placed to his credit when he paid the cheques in, and he was allowed to draw upon his account as increased by them. The C. Bank received the amounts in due course from the banks on which the several cheques had been drawn.

Jones' frauds were later discovered and he was prosecuted and convicted.

Gordon, who had been robbed of the cheques and wrongfully deprived of the money represented by them, brought an action against the C. Bank to recover the money which that bank had received.

Gordon was successful since the House of Lords, on an interpretation of section 82 of the Act of 1882, held that it was impossible to say that the bank had received payment of the cheques *for their customer* (Jones). Observations were made on the desirability of amending section 82 so that protection would be extended to collecting bankers acting in the way that the C. Bank had acted in the case.

6–210 Amendment took the form of section 1 of the Bills of Exchange (Crossed Cheques) Act 1906:

"A banker receives payment of a crossed cheque for a customer within the meaning of section 82 of the Bills of Exchange Act 1882 notwithstanding that he credits his customer's account with the amount of the cheque before receiving payment thereof."

6–211 Both section 82 of the Act of 1882 and the amendment of it in the Act of 1906 were repealed in 1957, and replaced by section 4(1) of the Cheques Act 1957. The protection conferred by section 4(1) of the Act of 1957 applies not only to cheques, whether crossed or uncrossed, but to certain other documents for the payment of money, including bankers' drafts and non-transferable cheques (1957 Act, s. 4(2), as amended by Cheques Act 1992, s. 3).

6–212 The statutory protection for the collecting banker now is that where a banker, "*in good faith and without negligence*":

(a) "*receives payment for a customer*" of the cheque or other document; or

(b) "*having credited a customer's account*" with the amount, receives payment for himself;

and the customer has no title, or a defective title, to the document, the banker does not incur any liability to the true owner of the document merely because he has received payment of it (1957 Act, s. 4(1)).

A further provision in section 4 of the Act of 1957 had the effect of enlarging the area of a collecting banker's protection. Before the Act of 1957, if the cheque being collected was not properly indorsed the banker was considered to be acting negligently and so was not protected by section 82 of the Act of 1882. Section 4(3) of the 1957 Act changed the law on this point by providing that a banker is not to be treated as having been negligent merely because he has failed to concern himself with the absence of, or irregularity in, indorsements. The provision has relieved bankers of the need to check the indorsements in the majority of ordinary transactions involving the collection of cheques for customers, namely those in which the customer pays into his own account cheques which have been drawn in favour of the customer himself. As a matter of banking practice, however, a collecting banker still requires indorsement of cheques in certain circumstances, namely: **6–213**

(1) where the payee of the cheque is not the customer into whose account the cheque is being paid (the banker would look for the indorsement of the payee and at any subsequent indorsements up to the stage when his own customer became the holder); if a cheque is specially indorsed to the customer for whose account it is tendered for collection, no further indorsement is necessary (but the banker may write on the customer's name for easy reference);

(2) where the payee's name is misspelt, or the payee is incorrectly described, and the surrounding circumstances are suspicious; or

(3) where the cheque is payable to joint payees and is being paid into an account to which they are not all parties.

Section 4(3) of the Act of 1957 is so worded that a court, looking to banking practice for guidance, could still hold that a banker who failed to observe these usual precautions would be liable to the true owner of the cheque if his customer had no title or a defective title to it.

There is a dearth of Scottish case law on the statutory provisions relating to the protection of the collecting banker, and the assumption may have been too readily made that the statutory provisions **6–214** apply in the same way to Scotland as to England. English case law, however, has this importance, that it has been the basis for standard banking practice in both countries, and it is likely that in any Scottish case relating to the statutory provisions the court would look to standard banking practice. There would therefore appear to be some value in referring to English cases particularly those concerned with the interpretation of the central phrase "without negligence". The following are two instances of how the English courts have relied on banking practice in interpreting the phrase:

6–215 (1) *Lloyds Bank Ltd v. E. B. Savory & Co.* [1933] A.C. 201: In this case the House of Lords held that the practice of the bank in question had been defective in certain respects.

A clerk employed by a firm of stockbrokers had opened a private account with the bank, but had not been asked for the name of his employers.

He stole numerous crossed cheques from his employers and paid them into his private account.

The bank was held to have failed to prove that it had acted "without negligence", and so it was not entitled to the benefit of the statutory protection then in section 82 of the Act of 1882.

Lord Warrington of Clyffe said (at p. 221): "There is here no special duty, contractual or otherwise, towards the true owners of the cheques. The standard by which the absence, or otherwise, of negligence is to be determined must in my opinion be ascertained by reference to the practice of reasonable men carrying on the business of banking, and endeavouring to do so in such a manner as may be calculated to protect themselves and others against fraud."

6–216 (2) *Marfani & Co. Ltd v. Midland Bank Ltd* [1968] 1 W.L.R. 956: In this case, decided by the Court of Appeal under section 4 of the Cheques Act 1957, reference was made to the standard of the "reasonable banker". The bank was in this case held not to have been guilty of negligence.

Diplock L.J. explained (at p. 972): "Where the customer is in possession of the cheque at the time of delivery for collection and appears upon the face of it to be the 'holder', *i.e.* the payee or indorsee or the bearer, the banker is, in my view, entitled to assume that the customer is the owner of the cheque unless there are facts which are, or ought to be, known to him which would cause a reasonable banker to suspect that the customer was not the true owner."

Reasonable care was, he said (at p. 975), to be judged by "the practice of careful bankers".

The ground of liability which a collecting banker would incur if he were not protected by the statutory provision now in section 4(1) of the Cheques Act 1957 is different in Scots law from what it is in English law. For a full account of the distinction reference should be made to the article "The Collecting Banker's Protection in Scots Law" by D.J. Cusine (1978) 23 J.R. 233. **6–217**

As explained in that article, the statutory provisions were enacted to give the collecting banker protection from liability for the tort of conversion, by which the true owner could under English law sue a bona fide intermediary who had obtained stolen property and parted with it again.

Scots law has no equivalent to the tort of conversion: in Scots law if a person who has parted with possession of property is to be made liable to the true owner it will be on the ground of restitution, and liability on that ground will arise only if the intermediary made a profit from the disposal or if he acted in bad faith. The collecting banker in Scotland, therefore, stood in no need of special statutory protection. **6–218**

A case governed by the common law of Scotland was *Clydesdale Banking Co. v. Royal Bank of Scotland* (1876) 3 R. 586: **6–219**

The case concerned a crossed cheque for £4,800 purporting to be drawn upon the Clydesdale Bank by Dixon Brothers, who were customers of that bank, in favour of Paul, who was a customer of the Royal Bank.

Paul's clerk presented the cheque, apparently indorsed by Paul, to the Royal Bank, and that bank, regarding the cheque as in order, paid its contents to the clerk. The cheque was then presented by the Royal Bank through the clearing house to the Clydesdale Bank, and paid by that bank. The Royal Bank retained the cash thus received.

It was then discovered that both the drawer's signature and the indorsement were forged, and the question was, on which of the two innocent banks was the loss to fall.

Held that the loss fell on the Clydesdale Bank.

The position was thus described by Lord Ardmillan (at p. 590): "The cheque was drawn on the Clydesdale Bank and presented to the Royal Bank, and the Royal Bank merely acted as the medium for cashing it. . . . There is no ground for holding that the Royal Bank acted otherwise than in regular course, and in good faith, and they merely were the hands through which the crossed cheque, drawn on the Clydesdale Bank by their customer, found its way to the Clydesdale Bank."

A passage in the opinion of the Lord Ordinary (Rutherfurd Clark) is still more illuminating as to the position of the collecting banker under the common law of Scotland (at p. 589): "The Royal Bank were . . . the mere agents for recovering payment of the cheque. That they paid in anticipation does not . . . affect the position. They took the risk of the cheque being honoured by the pursuers. But when it was honoured, they received the money on account of the person who presented it to them; and having already paid him the money, they are in the same position as if they had first presented the cheque for payment, received the money, and then handed it over to him. *There is no allegation that they were not in good faith, or that they were in any way richer by the transaction.*"

(A sequel to this case gives some further information as to the facts: *Clydesdale Banking Co. v. Paul* (1877) 4 R. 626, in which the Clydesdale Bank successfully sued Paul for the amount of the forged cheque, shows that the clerk had represented his employer in stock exchange transactions, Paul being a member of the stock exchange, that the clerk had engaged in speculative transactions unauthorised by Paul, and that on settling-day the clerk had used the proceeds of the cheque (on which he had himself forged both the drawer's signature and the indorsement) to pay the adverse balance on Paul's stock exchange account which would otherwise have led to Paul's being deprived of his membership of the stock exchange. The ground on which the action succeeded was that Paul was liable to the extent to which he had been benefited by the fraud of his agent (the clerk).)

6–220 The common law as applied in *Clydesdale Banking Co. v. Royal Bank of Scotland* may be regarded as having been re-stated in section 82 of the Act of 1882, the main possible difference being that the common law required the collecting banker to have *acted only as agent*, whereas the statutory provision required that the collecting banker was *receiving payment for a customer*.

Further, in view of the decision in *Clydesdale Banking Co. v. Royal Bank of Scotland*, there was no need in Scotland for the amendment of section 82 of the Act of 1882 made by the Act of 1906. **6–221**

The final paragraph of the article referred to (6–217, above) states: **6–222**

"The author's conclusion is that there is no Scottish equivalent of conversion, and, for that reason, the English cases are of little assistance in an assessment of the collecting banker's protection. It is sufficient to examine the common law as enunciated in *Clydesdale Bank v. Royal Bank*, the ratio of which found expression in section 82 of the 1882 Act, the amendments to which have created confusion in Scotland because they are otiose and in England because there is still considerable doubt about the decision in the *Gordon* case."

It appears that in practice claims are quite frequently made in Scotland against collecting bankers, probably the main reason being that many cheques are now issued by bodies such as Government departments to persons who do not have bank accounts and who therefore negotiate cheques through the local grocer or public house. In the event of such a claim the collecting banker puts forward section 4 of the Cheques Act 1957 as a defence. However, it would be exceptional for a case to come to court, since (1) the amount is usually quite small and (2) it is usually quite obvious where any negligence lies; the result would normally be a fairly amicable settlement out of court. **6–223**

In practice, therefore, it seems that the position in Scotland is much the same as that in England and if a case did come to court in Scotland the leading modern English case *Baker v. Barclays Bank Ltd* [1955] 1 W.L.R. 822 would be highly persuasive: **6–224**

Baker and Bainbridge were trading in partnership under the name "Modern Confections". Bainbridge misappropriated nine cheques amounting to about £1,160 payable to the partnership, by indorsing the cheques and handing them to Jeffcott who paid them into his account at Barclays Bank. Jeffcott also paid into his account cheques payable to, and indorsed by, Bainbridge.

On the occasion when the second of the nine cheques was paid in, the bank manager asked Jeffcott for an explanation, and Jeffcott's reply was that Bainbridge was the sole partner in Modern Confections and that he, Jeffcott, was assisting Bainbridge with the financial side of the business with a view to going into partnership with him later.

Baker eventually brought an action against Barclays Bank for damages for conversion in respect of the nine cheques.

Held that the bank's defence under section 82 of the Act of 1882 failed because the bank could not show that it had acted without negligence.

Devlin J. said (at p. 825): "Of course, cheques are indorsed over to third parties, but usually for small sums and only occasionally. When the bank manager sees it happening for large sums and quite regularly, I think that he is put on inquiry. . . .

"The explanation which Jones, the bank manager, received when he asked for one was not, I think, one which would have satisfied a bank manager. . . . I do not think that he appreciated the significance of a number of indorsed cheques coming in one after the other, or also the significance that the payments out included substantial sums for cash. If he had, I think that he would have found Jeffcott's story less convincing, for within less than a month Bainbridge had received from people who were presumably his customers cheques amounting to £2,000 or £3,000. Surely a man whose business was on that scale and was done in cheques might have been expected to have a bank account of his own?"

III PROMISSORY NOTES

6–225 A promissory note is defined as "an unconditional promise in writing made by one person to another signed by the maker, engaging to pay, on demand or at a fixed or determinable future time, a sum certain in money, to, or to the order of, a specified person or to bearer" (s. 83(1)). A document which, in addition to the promise to pay a sum of money, included a promise to employ and pay the staff of a business was held not to be a promissory note in *Dickie v. Singh*, 1974 S.L.T. 129 (O.H.).

6–226 A simple specimen promissory note might take the form:

"£500

Glasgow,
December 1, 1996.

On demand I promise to pay to Peter Piper or order the sum of Five hundred pounds. Value received.

Mark Anthony"

Alternatives to "On demand" and "Peter Piper or order" would be respectively "Three months after date" and "Peter Piper or bearer". The word "promise" is not essential: in *McTaggart v. MacEachern's Judicial Factor*, 1949 S.C. 503, the words "I the undersigned herewith agree to repay the sum of £200 borrowed today 10th August 1944 . . ." were held to be a promissory note.

An ordinary bank note comes within the definition: it is made by a banker and is payable to bearer on demand. **6–227**

A document in the form of a note payable to maker's order is not within the statutory definition unless and until it is indorsed by the maker (s. 83(2)). **6–228**

A note is not valid merely because it contains also a pledge of collateral security with authority to sell or dispose of the security (s. 83(3)). The maker may therefore confer on his creditor a right in security over property, to which the creditor may wish to have recourse if the maker fails to fulfil his promise to pay. **6–229**

An "inland note" is "a note which is, or on the face of it purports to be, both made and payable within the British Islands", Any other note is a "foreign note" (s. 83(4)). **6–230**

The provisions of the Act of 1882 relating to bills of exchange apply, with some necessary modifications, to promissory notes (s. 89(1)). There are also some provisions in Part IV of the Act which relate only to promissory notes. **6–231**

The modifications referred to are as follows: **6–232**

(a) In applying to promissory notes the provisions of Part II of the Act (*i.e.* the provisions relating to bills of exchange) the maker of a note is deemed to correspond to the acceptor of a bill, and the first indorser of a note is deemed to correspond to the drawer of an accepted bill payable to drawer's order (s. 89(2)).

(b) The following provisions as to bills do not apply to notes, namely, provisions relating to:

(i) presentment for acceptance;
(ii) acceptance;
(iii) acceptance *supra* protest; and
(iv) bills in a set (s. 89(3)).

(c) Where a foreign note is dishonoured, protest of it is unnecessary (s. 89(4)).

The provisions in Part IV of the Act relating only to promissory notes are considered below under these headings: **6–233**

(a) delivery;

(b) joint and several notes;
(c) note payable on demand;
(d) presentment for payment; and
(e) liability of maker.

6–234 The process of summary diligence (6–119 *et seq.*, above), which is left untouched by the Act of 1882 (see s. 98), may be used to enforce payment of a promissory note.

(a) **Delivery**

6–235 A promissory note is "inchoate" (*i.e.* not yet of legal effect) and incomplete until it is delivered to the payee or bearer (s. 84). This differs from the provision as to delivery of a bill of exchange: by section 21 (see 6–41, above) a party to a bill of exchange may *revoke his contract* on the bill until he delivers it, but the bill itself is not inchoate or incomplete.

(b) **Joint and Several Notes**

6–236 A promissory note may be made by two or more makers, and their liability will be "joint" (*i.e.* each will be liable for only his pro rata ("proportionate") share) or "joint and several" (*i.e.* each will be liable for the whole amount), according to the tenor of the note (s. 85(1)).

Where a note runs "I promise to pay", and is signed by two or more persons, it is deemed to be their joint and several note (s. 85(2)). This is an instance of a statutory provision rebutting the presumption which is generally applicable in Scots law to debts undertaken by more than one party, namely that prima facie ("until the contrary is proved") each party is liable only pro rata.

(c) **Note Payable on Demand**

6–237 A bill of exchange which is payable on demand is normally intended to be presented for payment almost immediately, but a promissory note, though it may be expressed to be payable on demand, is often intended to operate as a continuing security. Special provision is therefore made in section 86 with the twofold purpose of:

(i) protecting an indorser from liability to pay a note if an unreasonably long time has elapsed since he indorsed it; and

(ii) enabling the full negotiability of the note to continue even although an unreasonably long time has elapsed since the note was issued.

The first purpose is achieved by the provision that where a note payable on demand has been indorsed, it must be presented for payment within a reasonable time after the indorsement; otherwise the indorser is discharged (s. 86(1)). In deciding what is a reasonable time, one must look to the nature of the document, the usage of trade, and the facts of the particular case (s. 86(2)). **6–238**

For the full negotiability of the note to exist, the note must be in the hands of a "holder in due course" (see 6–48, above), for only such a person will be unaffected by defects of title. However, one of the conditions which, by definition, a holder in due course must satisfy is that he became the holder of the document *before it was overdue*—a condition which the holder of a note would often be unable to satisfy if the same rules applied to promissory notes as to bills of exchange. The Act therefore provides that where a note payable on demand is negotiated, it is not deemed to be overdue, for the purpose of affecting the holder with defects of title of which he had no notice, merely because it appears that a reasonable time for presenting it for payment has already elapsed since its issue (s. 86(3)). The effect is that the holder of the note may still qualify as a holder in due course, although by the time he received the note it appeared to have been an unreasonably long time in circulation. **6–239**

(d) Presentment for Payment

Presentment for payment is not necessary in order to render the *maker* liable to pay the note except in one case, namely, where the note is in the body of it made payable at a particular place; it must then be presented for payment at that place (s. 87(1)). The presentment at that particular place need not be on the day when payment is due (*Gordon v. Kerr* (1898) 25 R. 570). **6–240**

Presentment for payment, however, is necessary in order to make an *indorser* liable (s. 87(2)). Where a note is in the body of it made payable at a particular place, presentment at that place is necessary in order to make an indorser liable, but if the place of payment is indicated only by way of memorandum, an alternative is available—either presentment at that place or presentment to the maker elsewhere (s. 87(3)). **6–241**

(e) **Liability of Maker**

6–242 The maker of a promissory note by making it:

(i) engages that he will pay it according to its tenor; and

(ii) is barred from denying to a holder in due course the existence of the payee and the payee's then capacity to indorse (s. 88).

Further Reading

Scots Mercantile Law Statutes (reprinted every second year from *The Parliament House Book*) for Bills of Exchange Act 1882 and Cheques Act 1957

Gloag and Henderson, *The Law of Scotland*, Chapter 23

David M. Walker, *Principles of Scottish Private Law*, Volume II, Chapters 4.23 and 4.24

Wallace and McNeil's Banking Law, 10th ed. by Donald B. Caskie (1991, W. Green), Chapters 1 to 9

Lorne D. Crerar, *The Law of Banking in Scotland* (1977, Butterworths)

W. A. Wilson, *The Scottish Law of Debt*, Chapters 5 and 6

The Laws of Scotland: Stair Memorial Encyclopaedia, Volume 2, Title *Banking and Financial Institutions* (part) by D. J. Cusine and Volume 4, Title *Commercial Paper: Negotiable Instruments* by Alan R. Barr

The Chartered Institute of Bankers in Scotland, *Law of Banking*, Book 1 (part) and Book 2 (part), 2nd ed. (1996)

E. *Byles on Bills of Exchange*, 26th ed. by Frank R. Ryder and Antonio Bueno (1988, Sweet & Maxwell)

CHAPTER 7

RIGHTS IN SECURITY OVER MOVEABLES

	Para.
Introduction	7–01
I The General Principle—The Need for Possession	7–15
II Exceptions to the General Principle—Hypothecs and Statutory Charges	7–30
(a) Conventional Hypothecs	7–34
(b) Legal Hypothecs	7–43
(i) Landlord's Hypothec for Rent	7–44
What are *invecta et illata?*	7–46
Rents covered	7–52
Enforcing the hypothec	7–54
Warrant to carry back	7–56
(ii) Superior's Hypothec for Feu-Duty	7–59
(iii) Solicitor's Hypothec for Costs of Action	7–62
(iv) Maritime Hypothecs or Maritime "Liens"	7–66
III Securities Founded on Possession and Created by Express Contract	7–73
(a) Securities over Corporeal Moveables	7–75
Pledge	7–78
(i) Actual delivery	7–82
(ii) Symbolical delivery	7–83
(iii) Constructive delivery	7–86
(b) Securities over Incorporeal Moveables	7–93
Stocks and Shares	7–97
(c) The Two General Forms of Constituting Security and their Effects	7–105
(i) Creditor's Power to Sell	7–109
(ii) Scope of Security	7–111
(d) The Obligations of the Security Holder	7–113
IV Securities Founded on Possession and Implied by Law—Lien and Retention	7–120
(a) Liens	7–122
(i) Need for Possession	7–128
(ii) Distinction between Special and General Liens	7–139
Examples of special liens	7–141
Examples of general liens	7–146
Lien of factor or mercantile agent	7–150
Lien of banker	7–155
Lien of solicitor	7–157
(b) Retention on Property Title	7–176
(i) Sale of Goods	7–178
(ii) *Ex Facie* Absolute Transfer	7–184
(c) Retention of Debt	7–189

INTRODUCTION

THE term "right in security", as explained by the leading authority **7–01**
on this branch of Scots law, denotes "any right which a creditor may hold for ensuring the payment or satisfaction of his debt, distinct from, and in addition to, his right of action and execution against the debtor under the latter's personal obligation" (Gloag and Irvine, *Law of Rights in Security, Heritable and Moveable, including Cautionary Obligations*, p. 1).

"Whatever the special form of the right in security may be, its **7–02**
effect is in all cases to put the party entitled to it in a position of

advantage, and to render his power of realising payment of his debt more sure" (*op. cit.*, p. 2). In other words, a creditor holding a right in security is better protected than his debtor's other creditors (referred to as "general" or "ordinary" creditors) because he has at his disposal some means of obtaining payment or performance of the obligation due to him, distinct from, and in addition to, the means—available to the general creditors also—of relying on the debtor's personal credit only.

7–03 From this description of the general nature of rights in security, two immediate consequences follow:

(a) There must be a principal obligation to which the right in security is accessory or subsidiary.

(b) The test of the validity of a right in security is the debtor's bankruptcy: as long as the debtor remains solvent (*i.e.* able to pay his debts), the creditor will have no need to resort to any right in security; he will be content to rely, in common with all the other creditors, on the debtor's personal credit; once, however, it becomes clear that the debtor is insolvent (*i.e.* unable to pay all his creditors in full) the creditor who holds a right in security emerges in an advantageous position; it follows that the general creditors will then, since they will be at a corresponding disadvantage, have an interest to challenge and to have set aside any right in security which has not been validly created.

7–04 There are two major classes of rights in security:

7–05 First, there are the rights in security which create a *nexus* ("bond") over property—usually over the debtor's property. These give the creditor a *jus in re* ("real right") over the property, and in the event of the debtor's bankruptcy the creditor will be entitled to use the property in payment of the debt which the debtor is personally unable to pay; general creditors will have no share in that property (unless there is a surplus left after full payment of the secured creditor's debt).

7–06 Secondly, there are the rights in security which are known in Scots law as "cautionary[1] obligations". These give the creditor a *jus in personam* (literally, "right against a person") or *jus ad rem* (literally, "right with reference to a thing"), *i.e.* a personal right, against some person other than the debtor. In the event of the debtor's bankruptcy the creditor will be entitled to go against that

[1] pronounced "káy-shun-ary".

other person for the payment which the debtor himself is unable to make. The general creditors, in contrast, have no such right: they can look only to the debtor himself and his property, and that will mean that, if the debtor is bankrupt, they will get only part-payment of the debts due to them.

This chapter is concerned with rights in security in the first class. Rights in security in the second class are dealt with in Chapter 8, below. **7–07**

The most important general principle relating to the creation of rights in security over property is that there must be some form of delivery of the property to the creditor—some overt act which will make other parties such as potential general creditors aware of the preference being conferred on the secured creditor: a mere agreement between the debtor and the favoured creditor that the debtor *will* make delivery of the property concerned is not enough to create a valid right in security. **7–08**

The form of delivery varies according to the type of property. In the case of heritable property delivery has taken the form of registration of the document creating the security (now a "standard security" in accordance with the Conveyancing and Feudal Reform (Scotland) Act 1970) in the Register of Sasines. Under the registration of title system, now being extended area by area under the Land Registration (Scotland) Act 1979, delivery takes the form of an entry on the title sheet in the Land Register of Scotland. In the case of corporeal moveable property (*e.g.* furniture, stock-in-trade and personal effects) delivery normally involves an actual physical transfer of the articles, while in the case of incorporeal moveable property (*e.g.* the right to a debt due, or a fund held by a third party) delivery takes the form of an intimation to the third party that the property in question has been assigned to the creditor. **7–09**

There are some exceptions to the general principle as to delivery: in particular, there are, under the common law, hypothecs (see 7–30 *et seq.*, below) which enable a creditor to exercise rights in security over moveable property of which he does not have possession, and various statutes have created exceptions, of which the most important is the floating charge affecting heritable and moveable property of companies, introduced in 1961 and now governed by the Companies Act 1985 as amended by the Insolvency Act 1986 and the Companies Act 1989. **7–10**

7–11 Rights in security which are not exceptional are said to be "founded on possession", because they comply with the general principle mentioned above. It is usual to divide securities founded on possession into two classes—those created by express contract and those implied by law. Into the first class fall the standard security over heritable property, and the pledge of moveable property, while securities implied by law are lien and retention.

7–12 Rights in security over heritable property are outside the scope of this book. They are regulated by the Heritable Securities (Scotland) Act 1894, the Conveyancing and Feudal Reform (Scotland) Act 1970 and the Land Registration (Scotland) Act 1979, and are generally regarded as part of the topic of conveyancing. This chapter is therefore confined to consideration of rights in security over moveables, and is divided as follows:

I. The general principle—the need for possession;
II. Exceptions to the general principle—hypothecs and statutory charges;
III. Securities founded on possession and created by express contract; and
IV. Securities founded on possession and implied by law—lien and retention.

7–13 The subject-matter is largely common law. Its origins are in Roman law as brought to Scotland principally through the Netherlands and France during the formative era of Scots law.

7–14 English authorities are not a reliable guide, the main distinguishing feature being the insistence of Scots law on the need for delivery. There has, however, been some English influence; for example the term "lien" has been imported from English law. Moreover, the provisions of the Consumer Credit Act 1974 on security provided in relation to "regulated agreements" within the meaning of that Act are almost identical in the two legal systems; they comprise Part VIII of the Act (see 5–256 *et seq.*, above).

I THE GENERAL PRINCIPLE—THE NEED FOR POSSESSION

7–15 The general principle is that there must be some form of delivery of the property to the security holder: mere agreement is not enough to give him the "real" right which will put him in an advantageous position on the debtor's bankruptcy. The general principle is expressed in the maxim "*traditionibus, non nudis pactis, dominia rerum transferuntur*" ("by delivery, not by mere agreements, are real rights in property transferred").

A well-known illustration of the general principle is *Clark v. West Calder Oil Co. Ltd* (1882) 9 R. 1017: **7–16**

C. and others were the trustees for debenture-holders who had lent money to W. Ltd. As security for the loans, W. Ltd had assigned to the trustees certain mineral leases in which it was tenant, together with the moveables on the ground.

The assignation was duly intimated to the landlords, but the trustees took no steps to enter into possession of the leases or of the moveables. W. Ltd went into liquidation.

Held that the trustees had no priority over the leases or moveables, since no possession had followed on the assignation.

"There is no principle more deeply rooted in the law than this, that in order to create a good security over subjects delivery must be given. If possession be retained no effectual security can be granted" (*per* Lord Shand at p. 1033).

(At the date of this case floating charges were not valid rights in security in Scotland.)

Various attempts have been made to avoid the application of the general principle, *e.g.*: **7–17**

(a) *The trust theory*: The theory was put forward that if the debtor had *agreed* to transfer some specific thing to a particular creditor by way of security, the debtor then held the thing *in trust for* that creditor, the result being that if the debtor became bankrupt the specific thing would not be counted part of the bankrupt's estate but would be made available to the creditor for whom it was supposed to be held in trust. **7–18**

The theory was finally rejected in *Bank of Scotland v. Liquidators of Hutchison, Main & Co. Ltd*, 1914 S.C. (H.L.) 1; 1913 S.C. 255: **7–19**

H. Ltd arranged with its bank, to which it was indebted, that the bank would surrender golf balls to the value of £2,000 belonging to H. Ltd and held by the bank in security, and would take instead as security a debenture which H. Ltd was to obtain from J. Ltd, a company indebted to H. Ltd.

The golf balls were duly surrendered, and the debenture was issued by J. Ltd to H. Ltd, but, before H. Ltd had assigned the debenture to the bank, H. Ltd went into liquidation.

The bank claimed the debenture on the ground that H. Ltd held it merely as a trustee for the bank.

Held that H. Ltd had, at most, come under a contractual obligation to assign the debenture to the bank, and it was an inaccurate use of language to describe H. Ltd as a "trustee" of the debenture. The bank's claim was therefore rejected.

The debenture was part of H. Ltd's property at the date of the liquidation: the bank had no *jus in re* ("real right"), but only a personal right to compel H. Ltd to assign the debenture to the bank. Since the assignation had not been obtained by the date of the liquidation, the debenture formed part of the estate for equal distribution among all H. Ltd's creditors.

7–20 (b) *Fictitious sale*: The statutory provisions considered under this heading formed part of the codifying Sale of Goods Act 1893 and are now to be found in the consolidating Sale of Goods Act 1979.

7–21 In a contract for the sale of specific or ascertained goods, the property in (*i.e.* the ownership of) the goods passes from seller to buyer at whatever time the parties intend it to pass (Sale of Goods Act 1979, s. 17(1)). In a sale, therefore, the buyer may have a real right (namely, the right of ownership) in goods which still are in the possession of the seller: it is all a matter of the intention of the parties, as gathered from "the terms of the contract, the conduct of the parties and the circumstances of the case" (Sale of Goods Act 1979, s. 17(2)).

7–22 The legislation on sale of goods does not extend to what are here called "fictitious sales", *i.e.* "sales" in which the true position is that the "seller" is obtaining a loan from the "buyer" under a contract which provides that the ownership of the goods is to pass immediately to the "buyer" though the goods are to remain in the "seller's" possession. The express statutory provision which prevents the sale of goods legislation from applying to fictitious sales is:

"The provisions of this Act about contracts of sale do not apply to a transaction in the form of a contract of sale which is intended to operate by way of mortgage, pledge, charge, or other security" (Sale of Goods Act 1979, s. 62(4)).

7–23 The following are two instances of fictitious sales, which were held to be struck at by the corresponding provision in the Sale of Goods Act 1893 (s. 61(4)):

7–24 (i) *Jones & Co.'s Trustee v. Allan* (1901) 4 F. 374: J., a bicycle dealer, applied to A., an agent of the Royal Bank of Scotland Ltd, for a loan of £40. A. stipulated for some security as a condition of making the loan. J. offered six bicycles. A. lent the £40 to J. on receiving from J. a promissory note for that amount, payable in three months' time. J. delivered to A. a receipt as for six bicycles amounting to £72 12s. The six bicycles listed in the receipt were not set apart in any way but remained in J.'s shop along with 20 or 30 other bicycles.

After J. had granted a trust deed for creditors, his salesman sold five of the six bicycles and paid the proceeds to A.

Not many days later J.'s estates were sequestrated, and the trustee in the sequestration successfully claimed repayment of the proceeds from A. on the ground that the transaction was truly an attempt to create a security without giving possession of the goods to the creditor.

(ii) *Hepburn v. Law*, 1914 S.C. 918: L. was pressing his debtor **7–25**
Rev. J. S. Weir for payment of £130. Weir offered security over his furniture. An inventory was made of certain articles of furniture estimated to be of the value of £130 and was incorporated in a document which stated: "Received from L. . . . the sum of £130, in payment of the following specified articles of furniture belonging to me in the Manse of Rayne and sold to him at date hereof." No money passed, nor was possession taken by L. of the furniture.

H., another of Weir's creditors, having obtained a decree against Weir, proceeded to poind Weir's moveables including the furniture specified in the inventory.

Held that L. was not entitled to have the articles in the inventory withdrawn from the poinding.

"The reality of the transaction was . . . nothing but a security, and a bad security, over the furniture. The transaction is exactly struck at by section 61(4) of the statute" (*per* Lord Johnston at p. 921).

(c) *Fictitious hire-purchase transaction*: Section 61(4) of the Sale **7–26**
of Goods Act 1893 was held to have the effect of defeating a fictitious hire-purchase transaction in *Scottish Transit Trust Ltd v. Scottish Land Cultivators Ltd*, 1955 S.C. 254:

The defenders were public works contractors who were short of money to cover their operating costs. They suggested to the pursuers, whose business included the financing of hire-purchase transactions, that the pursuers should purchase some of the defenders' vehicles and then hire these out to the defenders under an ordinary hire-purchase agreement. The effect was that the defenders received a cheque for £4,000 and became liable to pay to the pursuers £4,600 by 24 monthly instalments with an option to purchase the vehicles for 10s. when all instalments had been paid. The vehicles never at any time left the possession of the defenders.

Payments of the instalments became irregular, and the pursuers brought an action for delivery of the vehicles and payment of the instalments in arrear.

Held that as the transaction had been intended to operate by way of security for a loan, the provisions of the 1893 Act did not apply, that the property in the vehicles had not passed to the pursuers, and that their claim for delivery failed. The pursuers were, however, entitled to repayment of the advances which they had made, under deduction of the instalments received.

7–27 (d) *Fictitious lease*: In a genuine lease the landlord has a right in security for the rent over the tenant's *invecta et illata* (literally, "things brought in and things carried in", *i.e.* the tenant's moveables). In *Heritable Securities Investment Association Ltd v. Wingate & Co.'s Trustee* (1880) 7 R. 1094, the lease was a fictitious one: W. & Co. had purported to transfer their shipbuilding yard to H. Ltd, and then to become tenants of H. Ltd at an annual rent of £4,800. The value in the valuation-roll was only £1,800. In reality, the transaction was a loan by H. Ltd to W. & Co. of £55,000, repayable in annual instalments of £4,800.

W. & Co. became bankrupt, and H. Ltd sought to exercise the landlord's right in security over the *invecta et illata*.

Held that the relationship of landlord and tenant never truly existed and that the supposed lease was only an attempt to create a security over moveables which Scots law did not recognise.

7–28 (e) *Sasine and other ineffectual procedures*: The ceremony of sasine was used for the transfer of, and granting of security over, heritable property, but it was ineffectual when applied to moveables. An instance is *Stiven v. Cowan* (1878) 15 S.L.R. 422:

W., of Pitscottie cotton spinning-mills, had obtained an advance of £2,000 from his bank. C. and another were cautioners (*i.e.* were guaranteeing repayment of the advance). In order to give the cautioners a security over the mills and machinery, a ceremony of sasine took place at the mills and deeds were recorded in the Register of Sasines.

In W.'s sequestration the court held that a valid security had been created over the mills themselves and the fixed machinery, but that the transaction as regarded the moveables was an attempt to create a security over moveables *retenta possessione* ("with possession retained")—a form of security not recognised in Scots law.

Other ineffectual procedures have included an inventory of furniture (*Fraser v. Frisbys* (1830) 8 S. 982) and a ceremony of delivery and "instrument of possession" for moveables on a farm (*Roberts v. Wallace* (1842) 5 D. 6). **7–29**

II EXCEPTIONS TO THE GENERAL PRINCIPLE—HYPOTHECS AND STATUTORY CHARGES

A hypothec is "a real right in security, in favour of a creditor, over subjects which are allowed to remain in the possession of the debtor" (Gloag and Irvine, *op. cit.*, p. 406). It is an exception to the general rule that for the creation of a real right in security (as opposed to a personal right against the debtor), the creditor must have possession of the property. **7–30**

In some early authorities the term "hypothec" has a wider meaning, extending to rights in security founded on possession; *e.g.* in Morison's *Dictionary* cases on a solicitor's lien appear under the heading of "hypothec". **7–31**

Hypothecs in the now accepted sense of rights in security without possession are recognised by the common law in a limited number of situations. Several statutes have enlarged the exceptions to the general rule by permitting similar rights in security to be created in other situations as defined in the statutes. Such statutory rights are usually termed "charges"; *e.g.* the solicitor's common law hypothec has been extended by statute so that the solicitor may also have a "charge" in certain other circumstances. The most prominent of these charges created by statute is the floating charge by which a company may now grant security over all or any of its heritable and moveable property for the time being. **7–32**

Hypothecs are either: **7–33**

(a) "conventional", *i.e.* created by contract; or

(b) "legal" or "tacit", *i.e.* implied by law.

(a) **Conventional Hypothecs**

The only conventional hypothecs recognised by Scots law are bonds of bottomry and bonds of respondentia. **7–34**

7–35 A bond of bottomry creates a right in security over a ship, whereas a bond of respondentia creates a right in security over a ship's cargo.

7–36 Such bonds can be granted by the master of a ship when the ship is in a foreign port and is unable to proceed on its voyage without an advance of money (*e.g.* to pay for essential repairs or for supplies). The master's first duty is to obtain the advance on the personal credit of the shipowners, and it is only when this fails that the master is entitled to resort to the far more costly mode of raising money on a bond of bottomry or respondentia (*Miller & Co. v. Potter, Wilson & Co.* (1875) 3 R. 105, *per* Lord Gifford at p. 111).

7–37 Before granting such bonds the master must communicate with the owner of ship or cargo as the case may be, if that is possible. If communication is impossible, the master may act as a *negotiorum gestor* ("manager of affairs") (see 1–28 *et seq.*, above).

7–38 A bond of bottomry entitles the lender to arrest the ship and have it sold so that he may be repaid out of the proceeds of sale. The enforceability of the bond depends on the safe arrival of the ship at its port of destination; if that condition is not fulfilled the lender has no right in security.

7–39 Where two or more bottomry bonds have been granted by the master at different stages of the same voyage, the latest bond has priority over the earlier ones, since it was presumably the last loan which enabled the voyage to be completed.

7–40 A bond of respondentia entitles the lender to have the cargo attached and sold so that he may be repaid out of the proceeds of sale. The bond can be enforced only if the cargo arrives at the port of destination, but it is not necessary that the ship itself should arrive at that port.

7–41 Where a bond of respondentia has been enforced, the shipowner is liable to the cargo-owner for the value of the cargo. An illustration is *Anderston Foundry Co. v. Law* (1869) 7 M. 836:

The "Black Eagle" owned by L. and others sailed from Glasgow for Bombay via Melbourne with a cargo including railway chairs shipped by the A. Co. for delivery to an Indian railway company at Bombay.

Having encountered tempestuous weather the vessel put into Rio de Janeiro in a disabled condition. There the master, being unable otherwise to pay the debt of £5,230 incurred for repairs, granted a bond of bottomry and respondentia, payable 10 days after the arrival of the vessel at Melbourne.

The holders of the bond failed to obtain payment at Melbourne, and as a result ship and cargo were sold.

Held that the shipowners were liable to indemnify the owners of the railway chairs for the loss caused to them by the sale of the railway chairs at Melbourne under the bond.

Bonds of bottomry and respondentia have become virtually obsolete owing to improvement in communications. **7–42**

(b) Legal Hypothecs

The recognised legal or tacit hypothecs are those of the landlord, the superior, and the solicitor, and certain maritime hypothecs (also referred to as maritime "liens"). **7–43**

(i) *Landlord's Hypothec for Rent*

A landlord has a hypothec over certain moveables of his tenant called the "*invecta et illata*" (literally, "things brought in and things carried in"). **7–44**

By the Hypothec Abolition (Scotland) Act 1880 this hypothec was abolished in the case of agricultural property over two acres in extent. **7–45**

What are invecta et illata?

The *invecta et illata* are the ordinary corporeal moveables in the premises—the furniture in the tenant's house and the equipment and stock-in-trade in the case of business premises. Money and incorporeal moveables such as stocks and shares, bonds and bills of exchange are not included in the *invecta et illata*. **7–46**

The general rule is that the hypothec covers only moveables belonging to the tenant and not moveables belonging to other persons. Thus in *Bell v. Andrews* (1885) 12 R. 961 the landlord B. was held not to have a hypothec over a piano belonging to his tenant A.'s minor daughter who had received it as a gift from her grandmother, and in *Pulsometer Engineering Co. Ltd v. Gracie* (1887) 14 R. 316 pumps belonging to P. Ltd and placed in a tenant's premises for exhibition purposes were held not to be subject to a hypothec in favour of the landlord of the premises. Similarly articles which are on the premises for the purposes of repair do not fall under the landlord's hypothec. On the other **7–47** hand, in *Scottish & Newcastle Breweries Ltd v. Edinburgh District Council*, 1979 S.L.T. (Notes) 11 (O.H.), kegs belonging to a brewery company and kept temporarily but regularly at a public house were held to be subject to the hypothec on the ground that they were part of the ordinary equipment and stock-in-trade of the public house.

7–48 Difficulties have arisen over articles hired by the tenant. The authorities were reviewed in *Dundee Corporation v. Marr*, 1971 S.C. 96:

The Corporation of the City of Dundee, owners of the Scrambled Egg Café in High Street, Lochee, let the premises to M. at a rent payable monthly. The rent fell into arrear, and the Corporation wished to avail itself of its hypothec.

The question was whether a record player belonging to the Ditchburn Organisation (Sales) Ltd and hired out by that company for four years to M. and his partner fell under the landlord's hypothec.

Held that the record player did fall under the hypothec.

7–49 The early case of *Penson and Robertson, Petitioners*, June 6, 1820, F.C., relating to a hired musical instrument, was taken as clear authority by the court in *Dundee Corporation v. Marr.*

7–50 On the other hand, in *Edinburgh Albert Buildings Co. Ltd v. General Guarantee Corporation Ltd*, 1917 S.C. 239, the landlord's hypothec was held not to extend to a hired piano in a furnished let where the rent was payable in advance: the fact that the hall was let furnished showed that the landlord did not intend it to be furnished by the tenant with articles which would be subject to the landlord's hypothec, and the fact that the rent was payable in advance indicated that the landlord was relying on the tenant's personal credit without contemplating that he would have a right in security over property brought in by the tenant.

7–51 By the Consumer Credit Act 1974 (s. 104) goods comprised in a hire-purchase or conditional sale agreement are in certain circumstances not to be treated as subject to the landlord's hypothec (see 5–255, above).

Rents covered

7–52 The hypothec covers one year's rent but not prior arrears:

Young v. Welsh (1833) 12 S. 233 (decided before the abolition of the hypothec in agricultural property over two acres in extent): The rent for two farms for the year 1830 was payable at Candlemas and Whitsunday, 1831. In September 1830, when the rent for part of 1828 and the whole of 1829 was still unpaid, the landlord took proceedings to enforce his hypothec in security of the rent for 1830.

The proceeds of the resulting sale of crop and stock considerably exceeded the rent for 1830. W., a creditor of the tenant, arrested purchase money in the hands of Y. and others, who had not yet paid the price of their purchases.

Held that the landlord was not entitled to apply the proceeds of the sale except for the rent for 1830, and that the surplus could be arrested by W.

The usual practice is for the landlord to enforce the hypothec for **7–53** the rent actually due and in security of the rent to become due at the next term.

Enforcing the hypothec

The procedure for enforcing the hypothec is known as "land- **7–54** lord's sequestration for rent". This type of diligence, which takes the form of an "initial writ" in the sheriff court, must be used within three months of the last term at which the rent to be recovered fell due. The landlord applies to the sheriff court for a warrant, the articles are inventoried and valued by a sheriff-officer, and are ultimately sold by auction under another warrant from the sheriff. Once the inventory has been made, the articles are regarded as being *in manibus curiae* ("in the hands of the court"), and must not be removed by the tenant or by anyone else.

The jurisdiction of the sheriff court in landlord's sequestration **7–55** for rent is privative (*i.e.* exclusive): proceedings brought in the Court of Session would be dismissed as incompetent. In *Duncan v. Lodijensky* (1904) 6 F. 408, therefore, a Russian, who was tenant of business premises in Sauchiehall Street, Glasgow, was held not entitled to argue that the sheriff court at Glasgow had no jurisdiction to grant a warrant in a sequestration for rent brought against him by his landlord.

Warrant to carry back

Where *invecta et illata* have been removed from the premises **7–56** before the landlord has commenced his sequestration for rent, he may obtain a warrant to have them brought back. An instance is *Nelmes & Co. v. Ewing* (1883) 11 R. 193:

E. let premises to Neilson to be occupied as a billiard-room. Neilson obtained on hire from N. & Co. a billiard-table and its equipment, but a few years later fell into arrear with the hire charges payable to N. & Co., with the result that N. & Co. removed these furnishings.

E. then came forward, applying for a sequestration for rent and a warrant to carry back to the premises the items which had been removed.

Held that E. was entitled to enforce the hypothec against the items carried back.

7–57 A warrant to carry back is, however, regarded as an extraordinary warrant, only to be granted with great care and after full consideration of the circumstances said to make it necessary. In particular, only in exceptional circumstances would it be granted without notice being given to the opposite party. *Johnston v. Young* (1890) 18 R. (J.) 6 is an instance of a warrant being recalled on an appeal to the High Court of Justiciary from the former small debt court:

Y., a tenant of a house owned by J. at Leith, removed in January 1890 to a house in Greenock, where he had obtained work at better wages, and took his furniture with him. His tenancy of the Leith house did not expire until Whitsunday 1890, and J. raised a summons of sequestration in security of the rent to become due and sought a warrant to carry back the furniture. No notice of these proceedings was given to Y.

The sheriff granted the warrant, and a sheriff-officer proceeded to Y.'s new abode and brought back the furniture to J.'s house at Leith.

Held that no circumstances had been set forth to justify the sheriff in granting the warrant without notice to Y.

7–58 A landlord who wrongly executes a warrant to carry back is liable in damages to the tenant. This can occur where there is a genuine dispute as to the amount of the rent due (as in *Jack v. Black*, 1911 S.C. 691) or where the circumstances do not justify such extreme measures (as in *Gray v. Weir* (1891) 19 R. 25).

(ii) *Superior's Hypothec for Feu-Duty*

7–59 A superior has a hypothec, similar to that of a landlord, over the *invecta et illata* of the owner of the feu. It takes priority over a landlord's hypothec.

As it is not mentioned in the Hypothec Abolition (Scotland) Act 1880, it probably exists over agricultural as well as over urban property. 7–60

In *Yuille v. Lawrie* (1823) 2 S. 155, the court refused to grant an interdict which would have prohibited the execution of a superior's hypothec: 7–61

Herbertsons were the owners of heritable property which included a wood-yard and a house. The feu-duty on the property was £276, payable to L. as superior.

Herbertsons became bankrupt and Y. and others purchased materials which Herbertsons had procured for repairing houses belonging to these parties. By Whitsunday 1820 all the materials had in this way been removed from the yard, and L. applied to the sheriff for warrant to bring back and sell the materials on the ground that they were subject to his right of hypothec for the feu-duty due at Whitsunday. The warrant was granted.

Y. and others sought to interdict the execution of the superior's hypothec on the grounds that the superior had no hypothec in urban property and that they had, at any rate, purchased the materials fairly and in good faith.

Held that the superior in urban property did possess a hypothec, and that that right could not be defeated by a sale of the moveables.

(iii) *Solicitor's Hypothec for Costs of Action*

At common law a solicitor who has incurred costs in connection with court proceedings which he has conducted on his client's behalf has a hypothec over any expenses awarded by the court to the client. Expenses are normally awarded to the successful party in an action. 7–62

The solicitor can make this right effectual by asking the court to grant the decree for expenses in his own name as "agent-disburser" instead of in the name of the client. 7–63

In certain circumstances the solicitor is entitled to be sisted as a party to the action (*i.e.* take his client's place in the action, as pursuer or defender) in order to make his hypothec effectual. The need for this can arise where the parties to the action settle their dispute out of court, with the result that the court proceedings would terminate before reaching the stage at which a decree for 7–64 expenses would finally be made. An instance is *Ammon v. Tod*, 1912 S.C. 306:

A., whose headquarters were in Manchester, was the sole export agent for a U.S. company. A. engaged T. to represent him in Scotland.

T. went to America and there succeeded in filching the agency which A. held from the American company. T. then intimated to A. that he would cease to represent A. in Scotland, and terminated the then current agreement between himself and A., which had still four months to run.

A. raised an action against T. in the sheriff court at Glasgow for interdict, accounting and damages, and obtained a decree for £68 in the accounting and for £100 as damages, with expenses.

T. appealed to the Court of Session, and, while the case was awaiting hearing, A. and T. settled their case without knowledge or consent of A.'s solicitors, A. agreeing to take £70 in full settlement of all claims of principal and expenses. In accordance with this settlement T. lodged a note craving the Court of Session to assoilzie (*i.e.* discharge) him and to find no expenses due to or by either party.

A.'s solicitors, however, lodged a minute craving that they might be sisted as parties to the action as agents-disbursers in order that a decree might be pronounced against T. in their favour as agents-disbursers.

Held that the solicitors were entitled to be sisted in that way.

7–65 At common law a solicitor had no hypothec over property recovered for his client, but a statutory charge, introduced by the Law Agents and Notaries Public (Scotland) Act 1891, improved the solicitor's position in this respect. The statutory provision, now in section 62 of the consolidating Solicitors (Scotland) Act 1980, is that where a solicitor has been employed by a client in an action, the court may declare the solicitor entitled to a charge upon, and a right to payment out of, any property which has been recovered or preserved on behalf of the client in the action. The court has a discretion whether to grant or refuse an application by a solicitor for such a declaration. The Act further provides that where a declaration is made any subsequent acts and deeds of the client, *unless they are in favour of a bona fide purchaser or lender*, are absolutely void as against the charge or right; the effect of this further provision is that the statutory charge is not a full right in security.

(iv) *Maritime Hypothecs or Maritime "Liens"*

These rights in security over a ship, though often referred to as "liens", are properly hypothecs, because the creditor does not have possession of the ship. They are enforced by a "judicial sale" of the ship (*i.e.* a sale authorised by a warrant from the court). Creditors holding a hypothec have priority over mortgagees of the ship. **7–66**

Seamen have a maritime hypothec for their wages, the master of a ship for his wages and disbursements, and a salvor for the amount found due to him for salvage. Where there has been a collision, the owner of the damaged ship has a maritime hypothec over the ship for damages, but there is no such right where one ship has been injured, without any actual collision, through the action of the master and crew of another ship, as was decided in the well-known case *Currie v. McKnight* (1898) 24 R. (H.L.) 1; (1895) 22 R. 607: **7–67**

Three vessels were moored alongside an open quay in the Sound of Islay. The "Dunlossit" was in the centre, and the "Easdale", owned by C., was moored outside the "Dunlossit" by ropes passing over the deck of the "Dunlossit."

One night when, owing to a violent gale, the "Dunlossit" was in danger of being damaged from contact with the other two vessels, her crew cut the mooring ropes of the "Easdale" and stood out to sea. The "Easdale" was driven ashore and damaged.

The "Dunlossit" was sold by McK., who held a mortgage over her, and a competition then arose between McK. and C., the latter claiming a maritime hypothec for the damages due to him as a result of the wrongful action of the crew.

Held that, as there was no hypothec where damage had been done by the crew and not by the vessel itself, C. had no preferable claim on the proceeds of sale.

The case is especially noted for the observations made in the House of Lords to the effect that the maritime law to be applied in Admiralty questions, such as maritime hypothecs, was the same in Scotland as in England. **7–68**

There is no maritime hypothec for repairs executed or necessaries supplied in a home port: *Clydesdale Bank Ltd v. Walker & Bain*, 1926 S.C. 72: **7–69**

The bank had lent money to the Stevens, owners of the "Arbonne", a ship registered at Leith, and in security for the loan the Stevens had granted a mortgage over the ship in favour of the bank.

Ultimately, when the Stevens were bankrupt, the ship was sold, and shipbrokers at Grangemouth claimed that they had a hypothec over the proceeds of sale for disbursements made on behalf of the Stevens as owners when the ship was lying at that port.

Held that as the services had been rendered in a home port (though not the port where the ship was registered), the shipbrokers had no hypothec.

7–70 The earlier Outer House case of *Constant v. Christensen*, 1912 S.C. 1371 (O.H.), is authority for the statement that there is no maritime hypothec for necessaries even when these have been supplied to the ship in a foreign port:

The "Baltic" was owned by Klompus, a Russian, and was registered at a Russian port. The vessel had been mortgaged to Constant, a London shipowner, in security of an advance of £2,400. Klompus failed to pay instalments in accordance with his agreement with Constant, and ultimately the vessel was sold by judicial warrant. The proceeds were £1,255.

Christensen, a coal merchant in Copenhagen, claiming £150 for coal supplied and cash advanced to the master for the purchase of necessaries when the vessel had been in Copenhagen, maintained that he was entitled to be ranked preferably on the proceeds because he had a maritime hypothec.

Held, applying English authorities, that Christensen had no hypothec.

7–71 An extensive review of English authorities is to be found in *Bankers Trust International Ltd v. Todd Shipyards Corporation* (*The Halcyon Isle*) [1981] A.C. 221, which was an appeal to the Privy Council from the judgment of the Court of Appeal in Singapore where English Admiralty law applied:

"The Halcyon Isle", a British ship, had repairs executed on her in New York by T. Later she was arrested in Singapore by B. Ltd, an English bank which held a mortgage on her. She was then sold for a sum insufficient to satisfy all creditors' claims in full, and the question was whether in the distribution of the proceeds T. had a claim preferable to that of B. Ltd.

Held that the question fell to be decided by the *lex fori* (literally, "law of the court") of the country whose court was distributing the proceeds, *i.e.* by the Singapore Admiralty law, which, unlike United

States law, did not recognise a maritime hypothec for repairs, and that B. Ltd had therefore priority over T.

There is no maritime hypothec where the creditor has relied on the personal credit of the shipowner: **7–72**

Clark v. Bowring & Co., 1908 S.C. 1168: The owners of the ship "Abbey Holme" became bankrupt, and the ship was sold at Glasgow. Shipbrokers B. & Co. claimed a hypothec for payments made in New York for repairs, for the supply of necessaries and for wages due to the crew.

Held that (1) the question whether any claimants had a hypothec over the ship had to be decided by the *lex fori* (*i.e.* Scots law) and not by American law, and (2) the payments made in New York had been made on the credit of the owners and not of the ship and were therefore not secured by any hypothec.

III SECURITIES FOUNDED ON POSSESSION AND CREATED BY EXPRESS CONTRACT

Rights in security which adhere to the general principle of being founded on possession take different forms according to whether the moveables over which they exist are corporeal (*i.e.* physical objects which can be seen and touched such as furniture, stock-in-trade and jewellery) or incorporeal (*i.e.* rights which have no physical substance (though they may be *represented by* documents of title) *e.g.* stocks and shares and claims under policies of insurance). It is appropriate, therefore, to consider separately: **7–73**

(a) securities over corporeal moveables; and

(b) securities over incorporeal moveables.

In addition, a brief account is included of certain principles applicable to both corporeal and incorporeal property: **7–74**

(c) the two general forms of constituting security and their effects; and

(d) the obligations of the security holder.

(a) **Securities over Corporeal Moveables**

Securities over ships are subject to special provisions contained in the consolidating Merchant Shipping Act 1995 (s. 16 and Sched. 1, paras. 7–13). A registered ship, or share in a registered ship, may be made a security for the repayment of a loan or the discharge of **7–75** any other obligation. The "instrument" (document) creating such a security is referred to as a "mortgage" and is in the form prescribed by registration regulations. When a mortgage is produced to the Registrar General of Shipping and Seamen it is registered by him in the prescribed manner in the register of British ships. Where several mortgages have been granted over the same ship, priority depends on the order of entry in the register. Provision is also made for the transfer of a registered mortgage by an instrument in a form prescribed by registration regulations.

7–76 Mortgaging of aircraft is also governed by statutory provisions—the Civil Aviation Act 1982 (s. 86) (re-enacting the Civil Aviation Act 1968 (s. 16)), with detailed provisions in the Mortgaging of Aircraft Order 1972 (S.I. 1972 No. 1268), as amended by the Mortgaging of Aircraft (Amendment) Orders of 1981 and 1986 (S.I. 1981 No. 611 and S.I. 1986 No. 2001, respectively). A register of aircraft mortgages is kept by the Civil Aviation Authority, and priority depends on the order of entry in that register. Forms for an aircraft mortgage and for the transfer of an aircraft mortgage are specified in Schedules 1 and 2, respectively, to the Order of 1972.

7–77 As regards corporeal moveables other than ships and aircraft, the usual mode of creating security is pledge. The general law of pledge is common law, but the form of pledge known as "pawn" has been governed by statute—the Pawnbrokers Acts 1872 and 1960 and the Moneylenders Act 1927, all now replaced by provisions of the Consumer Credit Act 1974. The word "pawn" in the Act of 1974 has a wide definition: it means "any article subject to a pledge" (1974 Act, s. 189(1)). It must be kept in mind, however, that these provisions of the 1974 Act apply only where the article is pledged under a "regulated agreement" as defined by the 1974 Act (see 5–44 *et seq.*, above). For an account of the provisions of the 1974 Act (sections 114 to 122) on "pledges", see 5–265 to 5–278, above. In the present chapter only some of the general principles of the common law on pledge will be noted.

Pledge

7–78 Pledge is a contract by which the owner of a corporeal moveable deposits it with a creditor for it to be retained by the creditor until payment or satisfaction of the debt or other obligation due to the creditor. The person who owns the moveable is called the "pledger", and the creditor who obtains the moveable in security is called the "pledgee".

"The creditor has no right of use during his possession; and the security expires with loss of possession" (Bell's *Principles*, § 206). This passage was considered in *Wolifson v. Harrison*, 1977 S.C. 384, to support the view that loss of possession by the pledgee would amount to a material breach of the contract of pledge whereas the pledgee's use of the moveable would not do so: **7–79**

H. lent money to a company of which W. was a director and principal shareholder. W.'s wife gave to H. four items of diamond jewellery as a pledge for the loan to the company.

W., alleging that H. donated items of the jewellery to his wife and daughter, sought delivery of the jewellery on the ground that the donation and permitted use of the jewellery amounted to fundamental breaches of the contract of pledge.

H. denied that he had donated the jewellery and claimed that he had never regarded the jewellery as being out of his possession and control when worn by his wife or daughter.

Held that (i) in view of H.'s denial of donation and of loss of possession and control, an inquiry, by way of "proof before answer", was required in order to ascertain the facts; and (ii) use of the jewellery did not of itself constitute such a material breach of the contract of pledge as to terminate the contract.

In relation to the second point reference was made to a surprisingly apposite passage in Baron Hume's *Lectures* (Stair Society Publication, vol. IV, pp. 2 and 3). Lord Justice-Clerk Wheatley said (at p. 391):

"This passage exempts from breach of contract of pledge use of the pledge which is in the interest of all concerned. Examples of this are said to be milking of cows or shearing of sheep. On the other hand Hume states that in the absence of a permissive condition to do so the pledgee is not entitled for example to wear the watch or give the jewels to his wife or daughters to appear with at public places and the like. 'If he does otherwise, he must pay a hire for the jewels.' This clearly indicates that in Hume's view such a breach of the contract of pledge is not a fundamental one terminating the contract, which . . . continues to exist subject to an accounting. . . . As I read and apply Hume's view the use of the jewellery *per se*[2] does not constitute a fundamental breach warranting the termination of the contract."

7–80 Delivery is essential for the proper constitution of a pledge. A mere "assignation" of furniture, for instance, creates no effective right in security (*Pattison's Trustee v. Liston* (1893) 20 R. 806).

7–81 The delivery required for pledge may be:

(i) actual delivery;
(ii) symbolical delivery; or
(iii) constructive delivery.

(i) **Actual delivery**

7–82 There is actual delivery where the pledger physically transfers the moveables to the pledgee. It can also take place where the moveables are confined in a space which can be locked and the key to which is handed to the pledgee; *e.g.* in *Pattison's Trustee v. Liston*, above, it seems that the handing over by the debtor P. of the house keys to the lender L. would have given L. a good security over the furniture, had it not been that L. was acting as house-agent for the purpose of letting the house and was held to be in possession of the keys merely in his capacity as house-agent for A.

(ii) **Symbolical delivery**

7–83 The main instance of symbolical delivery is the bill of lading, which is regarded as a symbol of the goods shipped: transfer of the bill of lading has the same legal effect as actual delivery of the goods themselves; intimation to the master of the ship is not required. See *Hayman & Son v. McLintock*, 1907 S.C. 936 (7–91, below).

7–84 A wider form of symbolical delivery is provided for by the Factors Act 1889, extended to Scotland by the Factors (Scotland) Act 1890: a "mercantile agent", who is in possession of "documents of title" to goods with the consent of the owner of the goods, may make as valid a pledge of the documents of title as if he were expressly authorised by the owner of the goods, provided:

(1) he is acting in the ordinary course of business of a mercantile agent when making the pledge;

(2) the pledgee is acting in good faith and has given valuable consideration; and

---

[2] "of itself".

(3) the pledge is not for a debt already due by the mercantile agent to the pledgee.

In this statutory context the expression "mercantile agent" means "a mercantile agent having in the customary course of his business as such agent authority either to sell goods, or to consign goods for the purpose of sale, or to buy goods, or to raise money on the security of goods", and the expression "document of title" includes "any bill of lading, dock warrant, warehouse-keeper's certificate, and warrant or order for the delivery of goods, and any other document used in the ordinary course of business as proof of the possession or control of goods, or authorising or purporting to authorise, either by endorsement or by delivery, the possessor of the document to transfer or receive goods thereby represented". It is expressly provided that a pledge of the documents of title is to be deemed to be a pledge of the goods.

Symbolical delivery may be confined to these two instances: **7–85** certainly other attempts to create rights in security over corporeal moveables by the use of symbols have proved unsuccessful (*e.g. Stiven v. Cowan* (1878) 15 S.L.R. 422 (7–28, above)).

(iii) **Constructive delivery**

The term "constructive delivery" is used where goods are in a **7–86** store, and the pledger delivers them by addressing a delivery-order to the storekeeper or by indorsing the storekeeper's warrant.

Constructive delivery is effectual only if the following conditions **7–87** are satisfied:

(1) The transfer must be intimated to the storekeeper; a **7–88** delivery-order or storekeeper's warrant is not, apart from the statutory provision mentioned in 7–84, above, regarded as a symbol of the goods as is a bill of lading. The effect of intimation to the storekeeper is to convert him from a holder for the pledger into a holder for the pledgee. An illustration is *Inglis v. Robertson & Baxter* (1898) 25 R. (H.L.) 70; (1897) 24 R. 758:

Goldsmith, the owner of certain whisky in a bonded warehouse in Glasgow, held a warrant granted by the warehouse-keepers, stating that they held the whisky to order of Goldsmith "or assigns by indorsement hereon". He borrowed £3,000 from I. on the security of the whisky and indorsed and delivered the warrant to I. This assignation was not intimated to the warehouse-keepers.

R. & B., creditors of Goldsmith, arrested the whisky in the hands of the warehouse-keepers, and an action of multiplepoinding was raised to decide between the competing claims of I. and R. & B.

Held that as the assignation had not been intimated to the warehouse-keepers, the real right remained in Goldsmith and so was subject to the diligence of his creditors R. & B.

7–89 (2) Intimation must be to an actual storekeeper, not merely to an excise officer who holds a key to a bonded warehouse:

Rhind's Trustee v. Robertson & Baxter (1891) 18 R. 623: R. was the tenant of a bonded warehouse in Edinburgh. He used the warehouse entirely for his own goods. The warehouse could not be entered without the use of two keys, one of which remained throughout in the possession of R. and the other in the possession of an excise officer.

When R. had a large quantity of wines and spirits in the warehouse, he obtained a loan from R. & B., and as security gave R. & B. delivery-orders addressed to the excise officer. R. & B. intimated these delivery-orders to the excise officer, who then entered R. & B.'s name in his register as transferees of the goods.

R. became bankrupt.

Held that R. & B. had no valid security over the goods since the goods had remained in the possession of R. down to the date of his sequestration.

7–90 (3) The storekeeper must be an independent third party, not an employee of the pledger:

Anderson v. McCall (1866) 4 M. 765: Jackson & Son were grain-merchants and storekeepers whose foreman, Angus, had the management of their store. They obtained from McC. an advance of £1,250 giving to McC. as security a document which they had obtained from Angus stating that a certain quantity of wheat had been transferred to the account of McC.

Jackson & Son became bankrupt, and the trustee on their sequestrated estate claimed the wheat.

Held that as Angus was an employee of Jackson & Son, the transfer in Angus's books did not amount to delivery.

7–91 (4) The goods pledged must be sufficiently identified, *e.g.* by being set apart or separately marked. A case which illustrates this condition and also suggests a possible distinction between symbolical and constructive delivery in this respect is *Hayman & Son v. McLintock*, 1907 S.C. 936:

This was an action of multiplepoinding raised for the purpose of determining the right to 1,174 sacks of "Golden Flower" flour lying in H.'s store. The sacks were the balance of various lots of flour which had been purchased by McNairn & Co. from America and then shipped to Glasgow.

McNairn & Co. became bankrupt, and the trustee in the sequestration claimed that all the sacks belonged to McNairn & Co. and therefore formed part of the sequestrated estate, but his claim was resisted by (a) holders of bills of lading (relating in all to 750 sacks), who had lent money to McNairn & Co. on the security of the bills of lading, and (b) holders of delivery-orders (relating in all to 321 sacks), who had purchased and paid for but not yet taken delivery of these sacks, though they had intimated the delivery-orders to H.

Held that (a) the holders of the bills of lading had obtained a good security and were therefore entitled to delivery out of H.'s store of, in all, 750 sacks in preference to the trustee, but (b) the holders of the delivery-orders were not entitled to any such preference since the 321 sacks, not having been separately marked, were unascertained goods, the ownership of which could not, by section 16 of the Sale of Goods Act 1893, pass to the buyers.

(The holders of the delivery-orders could now be protected by the Sale of Goods (Amendment) Act 1995 (see 4–125 *et seq.*, above).)

A contrasting case is *Price & Pierce Ltd v. Bank of Scotland*, 1912 **7–92**
S.C. (H.L.) 19; 1910 S.C. 1095:

A limited company of timber merchants borrowed money on the security of delivery-orders for quantities of logs lying in a store. The delivery-orders were intimated to and acknowledged by the store-keepers, and the logs were identified by marks being stamped on them by the storekeepers.

The company went into liquidation and was hopelessly insolvent.

Held that the logs transferred by the delivery-orders had been sufficiently identified, and that the holders of the delivery-orders had therefore a claim prior to that of the liquidators.

(b) Securities over Incorporeal Moveables

Incorporeal moveables may be transferred in security by a written **7–93**
assignation followed by intimation to the debtor. The word "debtor" here denotes the person who is liable to pay the debt over

which security is being granted; *e.g.* where the holder of a life policy wishes to borrow money on the security of his policy, the "debtor" to whom intimation must be given is the insurance company, and where shares in a company are transferred in security, the "debtor" is the company. Merely depositing with a lender a document such as a life policy or a share certificate gives him no valid right in security. Two illustrations are:

7–94 (i) *Strachan v. McDougle* (1835) 13 S. 954: In 1825 S. took out a policy of insurance for £1,000 upon his life. In 1830, when he was liable to pay £1,000 to Miss McD., he sent to her a promissory note for £1,000 and the life policy which he intended, as was clear from a covering letter, to be a security for due payment of the promissory note.

In March 1832 S. granted a promissory note for £1,621 10s. in favour of his son, and the following month the son, for the purpose of enforcing payment of this promissory note, arrested the proceeds of the life policy in the hands of the insurance company. Not many days later S. died.

It was not until June 1832 that Miss McD. intimated her right to the insurance company.

Held that the son's arrestment had priority over Miss McD.'s unintimated assignation.

7–95 (ii) *Gourlay v. Mackie* (1887) 14 R. 403: On December 23, 1885, a firm of coalmasters obtained a loan from M., and in exchange granted to M. a promissory note and a letter stating that they were handing over as security 100 shares of £6 paid in the Holmes Oil Company and were binding themselves to transfer the shares at any time desired by M. The share certificate was at that date delivered to M.

On January 14, 1886, a circular was issued intimating that the coalmasters were in financial difficulties. On the following day M. obtained a transfer of the shares from the coalmasters, and this transfer was immediately intimated to the Holmes Oil Company.

The estates of the coalmasters were sequestrated on January 28, 1886, and G., the trustee in the sequestration, raised an action against M. for reduction of the transfer and for delivery of the share certificate.

Held that the transfer, having been granted within 60 days before bankruptcy to secure a pre-existing debt, was reducible under the Bankruptcy Act 1696.

(The Act of 1696 was repealed by the Bankruptcy (Scotland) Act 1985; the corresponding period would now be six months (1985 Act, s. 36).)

Life insurance policies and stocks and shares are commonly used as security. Much less usual was the situation in *Liquidator of the Union Club Ltd v. Edinburgh Life Assurance Co.* (1906) 8 F. 1143, where a club, which was a registered limited company, gave to its landlord as security for the lease of its premises an assignation of its uncalled capital of 5s. per share on each of its issued £1 shares; the same general principle as to intimation applied: as the assignation had not been intimated to the individual shareholders who might be called on to pay up the 5s. on their shares, the landlord had no valid right in security and so no preference over the general body of creditors in the liquidation of the club. **7–96**

Stocks and Shares

There is a marked difference between Scots and English law in relation to the constitution of security over stocks and shares of a company. English law recognises both a legal mortgage (*i.e.* where there is a transfer of the shares to the mortgagee (the lender) and the transfer is registered by the company) and an equitable mortgage (*i.e.* where the share certificate is deposited with the lender, usually accompanied by a "blank" transfer (a transfer signed by the borrower but with the transferee's name left blank so that the transfer may, if necessary, be later completed by the lender and then registered with the company)). The English equitable mortgage does not give the lender absolute security, because the borrower is still registered as the holder in the company's register of members and so might fraudulently sell the shares to a third party who would then, by registering his transfer with the company, become, as far as the company would be concerned, the undisputed owner of the shares. **7–97**

Scots law does not recognise any form of "equitable mortgage": the only effective way of granting security over shares corresponds to the "legal mortgage" of English law, *i.e.* the borrower hands over to the lender the share certificate accompanied by a completed transfer which is registered with the company so as to substitute the lender's name for that of the borrower in the company's register of members. This procedure involves expense **7–98** and publicity (since the company's register of members is open to public inspection), and it is particularly unsuitable in the now rare instances where the shares are only partly paid (since the lender, being himself registered as the holder of the shares, will then be liable to pay to the company any calls made by it on the shares). Alternative procedures are therefore sometimes followed, but none of these is completely satisfactory from the lender's point of view:

7–99 (i) The borrower may merely deposit his share certificate with the lender and give an undertaking to execute a transfer whenever required by the lender to do so. For the time being the lender has no valid right in security at all; the only immediate value of the procedure is that it places an obstacle in the way of the borrower's selling his shares or granting security over them to some other party, but that obstacle is not an insurmountable one, particularly if the borrower is fraudulent.

7–100 The lender has the right to call on the borrower to execute a transfer at any time, and may decide to exercise this right if he sees the borrower getting into financial difficulties. The lender may thereby convert himself from an unsecured creditor into a secured creditor. The chances are, however, that other creditors of the borrower also will become aware of the borrower's financial difficulties about the same time, the borrower will become "apparently insolvent" and a sequestration will follow within the next six months. The transfer of the shares to the lender will then be reducible under section 36 of the Bankruptcy (Scotland) Act 1985 as an "unfair preference" (namely, giving security for a previously unsecured debt), and the lender will revert to being an unsecured creditor (see *Gourlay v. Mackie*, 7–95, above).

7–101 (ii) The borrower may hand over to the lender not only his share certificate but also a duly executed transfer, ready to be registered with the company whenever the lender wishes to send it in. The understanding between borrower and lender then is that the transfer will not be registered unless the borrower fails to implement his obligations to the lender. In the event of such a failure the lender will be in a position to acquire a right in security over the shares by having them registered in his own name; no further act of the borrower will be required at that stage.

7–102 An instance is *Guild v. Young* (1884) 22 S.L.R. 520 (O.H.): Duly executed transfers had been delivered to the creditor, enabling him to register the shares in his own name without further intervention of the debtor. In fact the transfers were not registered until the debtor was on the eve of sequestration.

Held that the transfers were not reducible under the Bankruptcy Act 1696, because the date of the grant of the security was taken to be the date of the delivery of the transfers to the creditor, not the date of their registration with the company.

(iii) The borrower may deposit with the lender, along with his share certificate, a "blank" transfer, in accordance with English practice (see 7–97, above). The intention of the parties is that, so long as the borrower implements his obligations to the lender no further steps will be taken in relation to the shares, but that in the event of the borrower's failure to implement his obligations the lender may then proceed to complete the transfer by inserting his own or another party's name and having it registered with the company. **7–103**

Formerly in Scotland the validity of blank transfers was doubtful because the Blank Bonds and Trusts Act 1696 declared null "bonds, assignations, dispositions or other deeds" subscribed blank in the name of the person or persons to whom they had been granted but that Act was repealed by the Requirements of Writing (Scotland) Act 1995. **7–104**

(c) The Two General Forms of Constituting Security and their Effects

The express contracts by which securities founded on possession are constituted may take one or other of two general forms: **7–105**

(1) The contract may take the form of a transfer to the creditor expressly as a security. Pledge belongs to this category. The creditor obtains possession of the moveables but the right of ownership remains with the person who is granting the security. **7–106**

(2) The contract may take the form of an *ex facie* ("apparently") absolute transfer to the creditor, so that he appears to become the owner, not merely the possessor, of the moveables. The true nature of the transaction will be explained in a separate document—a "back-letter" or other agreement—in which the creditor will undertake to retransfer the moveables to the debtor when the debt has been repaid. **7–107**

7–108 The two forms have different effects in relation to:

(i) the creditor's power to sell; and
(ii) the scope of the security.

(i) *Creditor's Power to Sell*

7–109 A creditor to whom moveables are transferred expressly in security (*e.g.* a pledgee) has no implied power to sell them. In order to sell he must either have an express power to do so conferred on him by the transferor or he must obtain a power of sale from the court.

7–110 If, on the other hand, the creditor has had the moveables transferred to him *ex facie* absolutely, he does have a power of sale, which he may exercise even without giving notice to the debtor. In the "back-letter" or other agreement the creditor may have undertaken not to sell the moveables or to follow a specified procedure in selling them, and if he violates any such undertaking, he will be liable in damages to the debtor for breach of contract, but the title of the purchaser will not be affected.

(ii) *Scope of Security*

7–111 A security which is an express security (*e.g.* pledge) covers only the debt for which it was granted, not debts subsequently incurred. This rule was applied in *National Bank of Scotland v. Forbes* (1858) 21 D. 79:

Laing assigned a policy of insurance for £1,000 on his own life as security for a debt of £500 owed by him to F. Laing later incurred a further debt of £700 to F., but in that second transaction no mention was made of the insurance policy.

Laing died a bankrupt, and the proceeds of the policy were claimed by F. as security for both debts.

Held that F.'s title to the proceeds was limited to security for the £500 debt, because the assignation was an assignation specially in security of that one particular debt.

7–112 Where, on the other hand, the security has taken the *ex facie* absolute form, the creditor has a right of retention which enables him to use the security to cover other debts incurred to him by the debtor. An instance is *Hamilton v. Western Bank of Scotland* (1856) 19 D. 152 (see 7–185, below).

(d) The Obligations of the Security Holder

The obligations of the security holder have been more fully developed, both by statutory provisions and by decided cases, in relation to heritable property than in relation to moveable property. The most general of the obligations apply to both types of property. These are: **7–113**

(i) The security holder must take reasonable care of the property while it is in his possession. A case which illustrates this principle as applied to shares held in security is *Waddell v. Hutton*, 1911 S.C. 575: **7–114**

By an agreement between W. and H., 599 shares of a limited company came to be held by H. as security for certain advances which he had made to W.

While the shares were standing in H.'s name, the company made an issue of new shares at par, offering proportional quantities of the new shares to persons then on its register. The par value of the shares was £10 and their market value was £20. H. declined to take up more than a certain small number of the new shares offered to him, and he did not inform W. of the offer which had been made.

W. averred that he had thus lost the opportunity of taking up at par 101 shares of £10 each, and brought an action against H. for £1,010 as damages for H.'s breach of duty as security holder.

Held that W.'s averments were relevant, and proof *allowed*.

The security holder is not, however, liable for the accidental loss or destruction of the property, and neither of these eventualities prevents him from recovering the debt due to himself. **7–115**

(ii) On payment of the debt for which the security was given, the security holder must restore to the debtor the exact property which was given in security. If, therefore, the property given in security was a holding of shares in a company, the specific shares (and not merely the corresponding quantity of shares) will require, according to the strict rule, to be restored. If, however, the practice is to the contrary and the debtor knows of and acquiesces in that practice, he cannot insist on specific shares being restored to him. Such was the position in *Crerar v. Bank of Scotland*, 1922 S.C. (H.L.) 137; 1921 S.C. 736: **7–116**

C. obtained advances from her bank and in security transferred to the bank and its nominees numbered shares of J. & P. Coats

Ltd. According to its usual practice the bank credited C. with the appropriate quantity of shares without preserving the identifying numbers. This practice was known to and approved by C.'s stockbrokers.

C. brought an action against the bank for an accounting and averred that the bank had sold her shares without her authority, in breach of its obligation to retain the specific shares and to retransfer the identical shares on repayment of the loan.

Held that as C. had to be deemed to have known and acquiesced in the bank's practice, she was barred from insisting in the action.

7–117 If the security holder is, on account of his own fault, unable to restore the property, he cannot demand payment of the debt.

7–118 (iii) Where the security holder has power to sell the property, he must in the exercise of that power proceed exactly according to the authority conferred on him with due regard for the interests of the debtor.

7–119 (iv) Special rules apply where there are catholic and secondary securities. A catholic creditor is one who holds security over two or more subjects while the secondary creditor holds security over only one of these subjects.

The underlying principle is that a catholic creditor is not entitled to act in such a way as to harm the interests of the secondary creditor without obtaining any advantage for himself.

The main rule is therefore that where the catholic creditor, A, holds a prior security over two items of the debtor's property, X and Y, and the secondary creditor, B, holds a postponed security over item X only, A must use item Y before item X in satisfying the debt due to him, or, alternatively, if he chooses to use item X, must assign to B his own security over item Y. The main rule does not apply where the catholic creditor can obtain some advantage for himself by using item X first; *e.g.* if A held item Y as security for two debts and item X as security for only one of these debts, he would be quite entitled to use item X himself, disregarding the interests of B in that item.

An illustration of the main rule is *Littlejohn v. Black* (1855) 18 D. 207:

Robert Black was the owner of heritable property and also of three ships. The Scottish Provident Institution for money advanced to him held security over both the heritable property and the ships.

John Black held a postponed security over the heritable property only.

Robert Black became bankrupt and L. was appointed trustee on his estate.

Held that John Black was entitled to insist that the Institution should make good its debt in the first instance out of the ships and should have a claim against the heritable property, only for the balance, the effect being to make the heritable property, as far as possible, available for the claims of the secondary creditor.

Lord President McNeill said (at p. 212): "In the ordinary case of a catholic creditor—*i.e.*, a creditor holding security over two subjects, which for the sake of simplicity I shall suppose to be heritable subjects—and another creditor holding a postponed security over one of them, there can be no doubt that the catholic creditor is entitled to operate payment out of the two subjects as he best can for his own interest, but he is not entitled arbitrarily or nimiously to proceed in such a manner as to injure the secondary creditor without benefiting himself—as, for instance, capriciously to take his payment entirely out of the subjects over which there is a second security, and thereby to exhaust that subject, to the detriment of the second creditor, leaving the other subject of his own security unaffected or unexhausted. The second creditor will be protected against a proceeding so contrary to equity, and the primary creditor will be compelled either to take his payment in the first instance out of that one of the subjects in which no other creditor holds a special interest, or to assign his right to the second creditor, from whom he has wrested the only subject of his security."

IV SECURITIES FOUNDED ON POSSESSION AND IMPLIED BY LAW—LIEN AND RETENTION

The law on this topic is complicated by the lack of uniformity in the definitions of the terms "lien" and "retention". The term "lien" was adopted from English law, and the original Scottish term was "retention", which denoted a wide variety of rights in security including the liens of English law. **7–120**

The three categories to be considered are: **7–121**

(a) liens;
(b) retention on property title; and
(c) retention of debt.

(a) Liens

7–122 A lien is "the right of a creditor to retain moveable property, belonging to the debtor but entrusted to the creditor's possession for some purpose, until the creditor's claims against the debtor are satisfied" (David M. Walker, *Principles of Scottish Private Law* (4th ed.), Vol. III, p. 399).

7–123 According to this definition a lien may be either created by express contract or implied by law. Where created by express contract, a lien comes very near to being a pledge: the point of distinction is that lien will arise out of another contract collateral to it or associated with it, whereas pledge will be a transaction in its own right. Thus *Gloag and Irvine* (after defining "retention") explains (at p. 303): "It is distinguished . . . from an express pledge or other right in security, because it is not, generally speaking, a part of the express contract between the parties, but is implied by law as a tacit condition or corollary of that contract."

7–124 Support for the contractual basis of lien is also to be found in the opinion of Lord Young in *Miller v. Hutcheson & Dixon* (1881) 8 R. 489, a case in which a firm of auctioneers was held to have a lien over horses for a balance due to the firm on a series of transactions (*i.e.* a general, as opposed to a special, lien). Lord Young said (at p. 492): "Lien is just a contract of pledge collateral to another contract of which it is an incident. . . . People can contract as to liens as they please."

7–125 Normally, however, liens are not created by an express contract, but are implied by law from various contractual relationships established between parties for other purposes; *e.g.* where the owner of goods hands them over to a person who is to repair them, the repairer has by implication of law a special lien over the goods for his charges, and where parties stand in the relationship of solicitor and client, the solicitor has, by implication of law, a general lien over the client's documents for payment of legal fees.

7–126 A lien merely entitles the holder of it to *retain* the moveables; he has no right to sell them unless authorised by the court.

7–127 The other main points arising in connection with liens are:

(i) the need for possession; and

(ii) the distinction between special and general liens.

(i) *Need for Possession*

Lien is described as a "possessory" right because it exists only where the person claiming it has possession of the moveables. 7–128

The following points have been established by decided cases: 7–129

(1) Mere custody, as distinct from possession, is not enough. The distinction between possession and custody is brought out in *Gladstone v. McCallum* (1896) 23 R. 783: 7–130

McC. had been secretary of a limited company until its liquidation, at which time a sum of £17 11s. was due to McC. for his services as secretary. McC. claimed a lien over the company's minute-book. The court, however, ordered him to deliver the minute-book to the liquidator.

Lord McLaren explained (at p. 785): "I think there is no foundation in the facts . . . for any claim either of retention or of lien. Retention, as I understand it, is the right of an owner of property to withhold delivery of it under an unexecuted contract of sale or agreement of a similar nature, until the price due to him has been paid, or the counter obligation fulfilled. Lien, again, is the right of a person who is not the owner of property but is in possession of it on a lawful title, and whose right of lien, if it is not a general one—of which class of liens there are not many examples—is a right to retain the property until he has been compensated for something which he has done to it. In this case there is no right of retention, because the books belong to the company, and there is no right of lien, because they are not in the possession of the respondent but of the company."

It does not matter whether the secretary does his work on the books in the company's premises or in his own private office: the latter situation is covered by *Barnton Hotel Co. Ltd v. Cook* (1899) 1 F. 1190, in which an Edinburgh accountant, who had been secretary of B. Ltd and whose private office had been registered as the company's registered office, was held not entitled to retain the company's books and papers as security for payment of the amount due to himself for his services as secretary. 7–131

(2) The possession must be actual possession, not mere constructive or fictitious possession. In some situations there can be doubts as to whether this requirement is satisfied, *e.g.*: 7–132

(a) *Paton's Trustee v. Finlayson*, 1923 S.C. 872: P., a potato merchant, entered into contracts with farmers, by which P. 7–133 acquired the right to use the farmers' ground for growing potatoes, P. supplying the seed potatoes and artificial manure and lifting the crop, and the farmers doing the horse work, supplying straw for covering pits and carting the potatoes to the railway station. P. was to pay £15 per acre to the farmers for the use of the ground.

P. became bankrupt at a time when potatoes were in pits on the farms and P. had not yet paid the agreed sums to the farmers.

Held that the farmers had under the contracts acquired possession of the potatoes, either at the time of planting or at the time of pitting, and that they had therefore a lien over the potatoes until payment of the sums due by P. for the use of the ground.

(There was no doubt about the *ownership* of the potatoes: both parties accepted that the property in (*i.e.* the ownership of) the potatoes had passed to P. when his servants removed them from the soil; the crucial question was whether the farmers had *possession*, an essential factor if they were to be entitled to exercise a lien. If the property in the potatoes had still remained with the farmers, the right which they would have claimed would have been a right of retention (see the passage quoted from Lord McLaren's opinion in *Gladstone v. McCallum* (7–130, above) and section (b)—"Retention on Property Title" (7–176 *et seq.*, below)).)

7–134 (b) *Ross & Duncan v. Baxter & Co.* (1885) 13 R. 185: Engineers contracted with shipbuilders to put engines into a vessel which was in the course of being built. The engineers claimed a lien over the vessel, and for this purpose they required to establish that they were in possession of the vessel.

Held that the engineers had never obtained possession, because (i) the contract provided that the vessel was to continue in charge of the shipbuilders while the engines were being put in; and (ii) the shipbuilders kept a representative on board during the whole of the time when the work was being done.

Lord Mure said (at p. 197): "This action is laid expressly on an alleged right of lien . . . ; and the question depends upon whether the pursuers had obtained actual and exclusive possession of the ship during the time her engines were being fitted in. If they had, then the lien is good, if they had not, it is bad."

7–135 (3) The possession must be lawful possession: it must not have been acquired by fraud, or under a void contract, or by mere accident or mistake. An illustration of the last is *Louson v. Craik* (1842) 4 D. 1452:

C., junior, purchased for his father, C., senior, a quantity of yarn which was to be sent by the seller in Montrose to C., senior, in Forfar. C., junior, was a cautioner for his father in the transaction.

By mistake the carrier delivered the yarn to the premises of C., junior.

A few days later, C., senior, became bankrupt, and L., the trustee in his sequestration, applied to the court to have C., junior, ordered to hand over the yarn as part of the sequestrated estate of C., senior. C., junior, proposed to retain the yarn as security for his liability as cautioner.

Held that since the possession of C., junior, was not lawful possession but had only been acquired by mistake, he had no lien.

(4) The ground of the possession must not be inconsistent with the creation of a lien. An illustration is *Brown v. Sommerville* (1844) 6 D. 1267: **7–136**

Sutherland, the publisher of a periodical entitled "Wilson's Tales of the Borders", delivered stereotype plates to B., a printer, for the purpose of printing from them.

Sutherland became bankrupt, and the trustee in his sequestration sought to have the plates delivered up to him. B. resisted, however, on the ground that he had a lien over the plates for £800 which he alleged was due to him by the bankrupt.

Held that B. had no lien; the plates had been put into his possession for a special and limited purpose and not in order that he might expend work upon them.

(5) When possession is lost, the lien is at an end unless the loss of possession has been due to error or fraud. **7–137**

The holder of a lien may be compelled by the court to give up possession under reservation of his lien, and the court may authorise the owner to sell the moveables if they are deteriorating in the creditor's hands: **7–138**

Parker v. Brown & Co. (1878) 5 R. 979: Maize belonging to P. in B. & Co.'s stores deteriorated in value through heat and contamination with weevils. P. alleged that the deterioration had been caused by B. & Co.'s negligence. B. & Co. claimed a lien for their charges.

Held that P. was entitled to a warrant from the court authorising him to sell the maize on condition that he consigned the proceeds as the court should direct.

(ii) *Distinction between Special and General Liens*

7–139 A special lien is one which entitles the holder of the moveables to retain them until satisfaction of an obligation arising out of the contract through which he obtained possession of them. A general lien, on the other hand, entitles the holder of the moveables to retain them until a balance due to him on a whole course of dealing is discharged. For instance, a carrier, whose lien is a special lien, is entitled to retain a parcel until he receives payment of his charge for the carriage of that particular parcel (but not any outstanding charges for the carriage of parcels previously carried), whereas a solicitor, whose lien is a general lien, is entitled to retain his client's papers until his business account and ordinary outlays for a whole series of transactions are met.

7–140 Normally only special liens are allowed; general liens are recognised only in a limited number of situations, and the law does not favour their extension to new situations. Hence, in *Laurie v. Denny's Trustee* (1853) 15 D. 404, a storekeeper was held not entitled to retain grain as security for payment of the balance on a whole account but only for payment of the charges applicable to the particular grain then in his store, and there are observations in *Findlay* (*Liquidator of Scottish Workmen's Assurance Co. Ltd*) *v. Waddell*, 1910 S.C. 670, and other cases, to the effect that an auditor or other accountant has no general lien comparable to that of a solicitor but is only entitled to retain papers until he is paid for the particular piece of work for which he obtained possession of the papers.

Examples of special liens

7–141 The ordinary rule in any contract for the performance of services is that, by the doctrine of mutuality, if the party performing the services has obtained possession of moveables belonging to the employer, he is entitled to retain them until he is paid for the work which he has done. The rule does not apply where the relationship between the parties is that of employer and employee (arising out of a contract *of service*), since an employee has merely custody and not possession of his employer's property: the relationship must be that between employer and independent contractor (arising out of a contract *for services*).

7–142 *Meikle & Wilson v. Pollard* (1880) 8 R. 69 is a well-known illustration of special lien: M. & W. were "accountants and business agents" who were employed by Smith, a baker, to recover debts for him. For this purpose books and documents belonging to Smith were handed over to M. & W.

When Smith became bankrupt and P., the trustee in the sequestration, sought delivery of the books and documents, M. & W. were held entitled to refuse to deliver them until their account for the work which they had done was paid.

This case was followed in *Robertson v. Ross* (1887) 15 R. 67—a case in which a bank-agent who had acted as factor for a landed proprietor had in that capacity obtained possession of documents relating to the estate. **7–143**

Meikle & Wilson v. Pollard was also referred to in *Findlay (Liquidator of Scottish Workmen's Assurance Co. Ltd) v. Waddell* (7–140, above), but the decision in that case was that under the Companies (Consolidation) Act 1908 the liquidator was entitled to an order for the delivery to himself of the company's books and papers in the accountant's possession, "without prejudice to any lien" which the accountant might have. **7–144**

For another instance of a special lien, see *Paton's Trustee v. Finlayson* (7–133, above). **7–145**

Examples of general liens

General liens are recognised by usage of trade in a limited number of situations. **7–146**

English cases may be referred to in this connection: if a general lien is in a particular situation clear and well-established in England, comparatively slight proof of the practice in Scotland will be enough to establish its existence also in Scotland: such was the attitude taken by the Court of Session in *Strong v. Philips & Co.* (1878) 5 R. 770: **7–147**

A firm of Turkey red dyers in Glasgow had been in the habit of employing a firm of packers there to pack goods.

When the dyers became bankrupt and S., the trustee in the sequestration, claimed delivery of yarn which was in the packers' hands, the packers were held entitled to a lien on the yarn for the general balance due to them by the dyers, such a general lien being seemingly recognised by usage of trade in Glasgow and being well settled in England.

Although usage of trade is the normal basis for claiming a general lien, it is possible for such a lien to be created by the **7–148** express terms of a contract. An instance is *Anderson's Trustee v. Fleming* (1871) 9 M. 718: bleachers employed by manufacturers to bleach and finish goods were held in that case to have a general lien constituted by a notice sent out on each occasion when the bleachers returned goods; the notice stated: "N.B.—All goods received by us are subject to a lien, not only for the work done thereon, but also for the general balance of our accounts." (According to observations made by the judges, the court would have held (if that had been necessary) that by usage of trade the bleachers had a general lien extending to charges for all goods sent to them within the previous year.)

7–149 The most prominent of the general liens recognised by usage of trade are those of the factor or mercantile agent, the banker, and the solicitor.

Lien of factor or mercantile agent

7–150 A factor or mercantile agent has a general lien over all the property of his principal which has come into his possession in the course of his employment. It covers the amount due by the principal to the agent as a result of the agency (including the agent's salary or commission and any liabilities incurred by the agent on the principal's behalf). An instance of a corn factor having a general lien, so that he was able to retain commission for an earlier transaction out of the proceeds of sale in a later transaction, occurred in *Sibbald v. Gibson* (1852) 15 D. 217 (see 1–139, above).

7–151 The lien of a factor or mercantile agent does not extend to a debt due to him by his principal but arising out of a transaction other than an agency transaction: an illustration is *Miller v. McNair* (1852) 14 D. 955:

Clarke employed Miller, commission merchant in Glasgow, to sell certain goods to Smith. Miller instructed Smith not to pay the price to Clarke but to hold it on behalf of himself, Miller.

Shortly afterwards Clarke became bankrupt, and there was a competition for the price between McNair, the trustee in the sequestration, and Miller who claimed that he had a lien for a debt due to him by Clarke on a distinct transaction.

Held that Miller had no such lien, and the trustee's claim was therefore preferred.

7–152 An auctioneer is classified as a mercantile agent and so has a general lien (*e.g. Miller v. Hutcheson & Dixon* (1881) 8 R. 489

(7–124, above)). It is not necessary that the articles should be brought to the auctioneer's own premises: he is entitled to exercise a lien even if he conducts the sale in his principal's premises (*e.g.* *Mackenzie v. Cormack*, 1950 S.C. 183, where a sale of furniture by auction took place in the seller's castle).

A stockbroker has a similar general lien, entitling him to retain **7–153** his principal's documents in security of a general balance, and not merely in security of the amount due for the particular transaction to which the documents relate (*Glendinning v. Hope & Co.*, 1911 S.C. (H.L.) 73).

A factor managing an estate is not within the category of factor **7–154** or mercantile agent, and he does not have a general lien. Hence, in *Macrae v. Leith*, 1913 S.C. 901, L. who had acted as a factor on an estate was held to have no lien on leases and other estate documents which he held.

Lien of banker

A banker has a general lien over negotiable instruments, such as **7–155** bills of exchange (including cheques) and promissory notes, belonging to his customer, provided they have come into the possession of the banker in his capacity as monetary agent; it does not cover documents which are non-negotiable (*e.g.* share certificates) or negotiable instruments which have been lodged with the banker for some specific purpose inconsistent with the creation of a lien (*e.g.* bills of exchange lodged for safe-keeping only).

The lien may, in circumstances where it would otherwise exist, **7–156** be excluded by agreement, express or implied, *e.g.*:

Robertson's Trustee v. Royal Bank of Scotland (1890) 18 R. 12: R. had from time to time deposited certain bonds, which were negotiable instruments, with his bank, and had received receipts from the bank stating that the bonds were held "for safe-keeping on your account and subject to your order". There was, however, evidence to show that on each occasion when a bond was deposited R. was seeking an overdraft or additional overdraft corresponding to the exact amount of the bond deposited.

Held in R.'s sequestration that the terms of the receipts were not sufficient to exclude the creation of a lien in view of the inference which could be drawn from the other evidence; the bank was therefore entitled to retain the bonds as security for payment of the balance due to it by R.

Lien of solicitor

7–157 A solicitor has a general lien over his client's papers in his possession, for payment of amounts due to him by his client.

7–158 The early case which is regarded as having established the solicitor's lien is *Ranking of Hamilton of Provenhall's Creditors* (1781) Mor. 6253, in which the "hypothec" of Wilson, a writer to the signet, on the papers of a bankrupt was found to be preferable to another creditor's infeftment on the bankrupt's lands, although the infeftment was prior in date to the writer's account. (This particular aspect of the solicitor's lien has since been altered by statute: by the Conveyancing (Scotland) Act 1924 (s. 27), where there is a creditor with an existing heritable security already recorded, a solicitor acting for the owner or for other creditors with postponed securities cannot acquire a lien which will be effective against the first-mentioned creditor.)

7–159 There is a wealth of Scottish cases on the solicitor's lien; some of the points established by them are as follows:

7–160 *Over what papers does the lien exist*? It exists over title deeds (*Ranking of Hamilton of Provenhall's Creditors*, above), and in general over all other deeds and documents, including share certificates. It exists over the client's will, even when both client and solicitor are dead:

Paul v. Meikle (1868) 7 M. 235: Mrs Duncan by her will, which had been prepared by her solicitor, M., conveyed heritable property to her son. She owed M. £35 10s. 2d. for professional services.

On Mrs Duncan's death, her son conveyed the property to P. by a disposition containing the usual assignation of writs clause, but M.'s representatives claimed that they were entitled to retain Mrs Duncan's will until the business account was paid.

Held that they were entitled to do so.

7–161 The lien does not extend to a company's register of members, because it would interfere with the public's right of access to the register (*Liquidator of the Garpel Haematite Co. Ltd v. Andrew* (1866) 4 M. 617).

7–162 *What does the lien give the solicitor security for*? It gives him security for his business account and for outlays made in the ordinary course of business, such as fees to counsel, but not for cash advanced to the client:

Christie v. Ruxton (1862) 24 D. 1182: C. entered into a contract to sell his heritable property for £300, and the title deeds were handed over to R., a solicitor, to enable him to carry the contract into effect on behalf of the purchaser.

Before the price was paid, the purchaser became bankrupt, and C. brought an action against R. for the return of the title deeds.

Held that R. had a lien for the business account incurred to him but not for £35 advanced to the purchaser.

In *Liquidator of Grand Empire Theatres Ltd v. Snodgrass*, 1932 S.C. (H.L.) 73, the House of Lords held that a solicitor's lien did not extend to accounts incurred by the solicitor on his client's behalf to English solicitors and auctioneers, at least where the solicitor had not himself paid the accounts or become personally liable to pay them. **7–163**

Is the solicitor entitled to a lien where he acts for both lender and borrower? Where a solicitor acts for both lender and borrower he is bound to reveal to the lender any lien which he has over the borrower's title deeds; otherwise he is barred from afterwards setting up that claim against the lender: **7–164**

Gray v. Graham (1855) 2 Macq. 435; 18 D. (H.L.) 52 (*sub nom. Gray v. Wardrop's Trustees* (1851) 13 D. 963):

Gray, a solicitor, was in possession of the title deeds of his client Charles Cunningham, who owed him £609 12s. 7d. Part of that amount consisted of Gray's fee for preparing a heritable security over the client's house for £700 borrowed from the client's sister, Janet Cunningham. Gray had acted for both Charles and Janet in the transaction.

Charles Cunningham died bankrupt, and Gray claimed a preference on account of his lien over the title deeds.

Held that, as Gray had never communicated to Janet Cunningham that he held a lien over the title deeds, he was barred from claiming a preference as against her.

It is, however, only in a question with the lender that the solicitor is barred from claiming his lien: **7–165**

Drummond v. Muirhead & Guthrie Smith (1900) 2 F. 585: Waldie purchased heritable property, and the title deeds were delivered to his solicitors, M. & G.S. Waldie then borrowed money from trustees, who were also clients of M. & G.S.

Waldie became bankrupt, with a large business account owing to M. & G.S. D., the trustee in the sequestration, raised an action against M. & G.S. to have it declared that M. & G.S. had no lien against him over the title deeds.

Held that D. was not entitled to challenge M. & G.S.'s lien: only the trustees, as lenders, could have challenged the lien.

7–166 *What is the effect of the lien?* A peculiarity of the solicitor's lien is that it exists over papers which cannot be made available for payment of the debt due to the solicitor: *e.g.* the fact that the solicitor has title deeds in his possession does not entitle the solicitor to sell the client's heritage and obtain payment out of the proceeds. Title deeds and other documents over which the lien exists are said to be *extra commercium* ("outside commerce"), *i.e.* they are not articles which can be traded in.

7–167 The practical value to the solicitor of his lien is that by retaining the documents in his possession he will cause inconvenience to his client (because the client will be unable to produce evidence of his right to heritable or moveable property to other parties) and thus may induce the client to pay what is due to himself.

7–168 In some situations, however, the solicitor is deprived of the right even to retain the documents:

7–169 (1) The solicitor is not entitled to stop the procedure in a litigation by withholding the documents relating to that litigation from his client:

Callman v. Bell (1793) Mor. 6255: C. employed B., a writer to the signet, to raise an action of declarator of marriage and other proceedings. The court decided against C., and B., on her behalf, appealed. While the action was at the appeal stage, C. notified B. that she was to change her solicitor and insisted that B. should deliver to her all the papers relating to the court proceedings. B. refused to comply on the ground that he had a "hypothec" over the papers in his possession until he obtained payment of his account.

Held that B. was not entitled to withhold the papers from C.

7–170 (2) If the client is sequestrated, the solicitor is not entitled to withhold documents from the trustee in the sequestration. However, on surrendering the documents to the trustee, the solicitor becomes entitled to a preference in the division of the estate.

7–171 The position under the common law is seen in *Skinner v. Henderson* (1865) 3 M. 867, in which a solicitor was held bound to deliver up to the trustee in his client's sequestration all the deeds in his possession affecting the bankrupt's estate, but was entitled in doing so to reserve all the rights which he would have had against the estate by retaining the deeds.

The statutory provisions which now apply in a sequestration in relation to title deeds and other documents are in section 38 of the Bankruptcy (Scotland) Act 1985. The permanent trustee takes possession of any document in the debtor's possession or control relating to the debtor's assets or business or financial affairs (s. 38(1)) and is entitled to have access to all such documents sent by the debtor to a third party (s. 38(2)). The permanent trustee may require delivery to him of any title deed or other document even where a right of lien is claimed over the title deed or other document, but delivery does not prejudice any preference of the holder of the lien (s. 38(4)). **7–172**

A solicitor would similarly require to surrender documents to a liquidator if the client were a company which was being wound up (Insolvency Act 1986, s. 144). **7–173**

There is little authority on the precise preference to which the solicitor becomes entitled on surrendering the documents: *Miln's Judicial Factor v. Spence's Trustees*, 1927 S.L.T. 425 (O.H.) (a case concerning surrender of a trust deed for creditors to a judicial factor), suggests that expenses of administration of the sequestration or liquidation would have priority over the solicitor's claim, but it is an open question whether the solicitor would rank before other preferential creditors. Section 51 of the Bankruptcy (Scotland) Act 1985, which sets out the order of priority in the distribution of the debtor's estate, makes no express mention of lien except in section 51(6)(b) which provides that nothing in section 51 is to affect any preference of the holder of a lien over a title deed or other document which has been delivered to the permanent trustee under section 38(4) of the Act. **7–174**

(3) The court has an equitable control on the exercise of a lien, and this control enables the court to intervene to prevent an abuse of the solicitor's lien (*e.g.* where the estate would be likely to suffer great prejudice if the lien were exercised or where the solicitor unreasonably refused to surrender the papers in return for a good substituted security). There are observations to that effect in *Ferguson and Stuart v. Grant* (1856) 18 D. 536, though in the circumstances of that case the court found no sufficient grounds to **7–175**

intervene so as to compel the solicitor to accept the security of caution in place of his lien.

(b) Retention on Property Title

7–176 This right is based on property (*i.e.* on ownership), not on possession; it may be exercised by a creditor who owns the moveables, even though they are in the possession of another party. It may be explained in this way (David M. Walker, *Principles of Scottish Private Law* (4th ed.), Vol. III, p. 405): "Where one party has a title of property to some subject, heritable or moveable, but is under a personal obligation to transfer or convey it to another, he is entitled to retain it in security of the payment of any debt, or the performance of any obligation, due to him by the party to whom he is bound to convey."

7–177 Illustrations of this right in relation to corporeal moveable property fall into two main categories:

(i) contracts for the sale of goods where the property in the goods does *not* pass to the buyer at the time when the contract is made; and

(ii) rights in security created by an express contract which is *ex facie* ("apparently") absolute, though truly in security (see 7–107, above).

(i) *Sale of Goods*

7–178 The rule of the common law was that goods which parties had agreed should be sold remained the property of the seller until they were delivered. In the interval between the agreement and the delivery the seller was therefore in a position which satisfied the requirements of the right of retention as described in the quotation given above: he had a "title of property" to a moveable subject but was "under a personal obligation to transfer or convey it" to the buyer. He was therefore entitled to "retain it in security of the payment of *any* debt, or the performance of *any* obligation due to him" by the buyer.

7–179 The statutory rules now applicable under the Sale of Goods Act 1979 to the passing of property from seller to buyer usually have the effect of denying to the seller this right of retention which the common law allowed him. The Act (re-enacting provisions of the

Sale of Goods Act 1893) provides that where there is a contract for the sale of specific or ascertained goods the property in them is transferred to the buyer at such time as the parties to the contract intend it to be transferred (s. 17(1)), and that, *unless a different intention appears*, the rule to be applied, where there is an unconditional contract for the sale of specific goods in a deliverable state, is that the property passes to the buyer when the contract is made, and that it does not matter that the time of payment or of delivery or both be postponed (s. 18). The "terms of the contract, the conduct of the parties and the circumstances of the case" must always be looked at (s. 17(2)): a "different intention" may then appear: *e.g.* the parties may have agreed that the property is not to pass to the buyer until delivery. A right of retention can therefore still arise, provided the contract is such that it expressly or by implication excludes the ordinary statutory rule. The use of retention of title clauses in contracts of sale became much more common as a result of the Court of Appeal's judgment in the *Romalpa* case (*Aluminium Industrie Vaassen B.V. v. Romalpa Aluminium Ltd* [1976] 1 W.L.R. 676) but the trend seems likely to be reversed in view of the House of Lords decision in *Armour v. Thyssen Edelstahlwerke A.G.*, 1990 S.L.T. 891 (see 4–154, above).

A simple illustration of the common law position is *Mein (Landale and Company's Trustee) v. Bogle and Company* (1828) 6 S. 360: B. sold to L. three lots of sugar. L. received delivery, but did not pay the price. L. then bought a fourth lot of sugar from B. and paid the greater part of the price for that lot but became bankrupt before the lot was delivered to him. **7–180**

Held that B. was entitled to retain the fourth lot of sugar in security for payment of the price of the first three lots. The court emphasised that its judgment did not rest on the special point that the full price for the fourth lot had not been paid but on the general ground that B. had a right of retention over the fourth lot in security of the balance due by L. to B. in respect of all four lots.

Two further cases, also decided under the common law, may be mentioned for the purpose of illustrating how this right of retention operates where third parties have become involved (*e.g.* through subsales): **7–181**

(1) *Melrose v. Hastie* (1851) 13 D. 880: H. sold to Bowie 1,533 bags of sugar which were at that time held by a storekeeper as H.'s property. Bowie then resold 761 of the bags to M., and M. **7–182**

obtained delivery of 170 of them, which left 591 bags still in the warehouse in H.'s name. The price was duly paid both in the sale to Bowie and in the subsale to M., but the delivery-orders used in the transactions were not intimated to the storekeeper.

On two further occasions H. sold quantities of sugar to Bowie, and these had been only partly paid for when Bowie became bankrupt, with a balance due to H. for the second and third purchases of £4,000.

Held that H. was entitled to retain the 591 bags as security for payment of the balance of £4,000. As there had been no actual or constructive delivery, H. had remained the undivested owner of these bags, and his right was a right of retention on a property title, and not a lien.

7–183 (2) *Distillers Co. Ltd v. Russell's Trustee* (1889) 16 R. 479: D. Ltd sold certain lots of whisky which were lying in D. Ltd's warehouse. Several subsales followed over the next few years, and on the occasion of each transaction a delivery-order was intimated to D. Ltd.

R., a wine-merchant, was the last subvendee in the chain. He became bankrupt, and the trustee in his sequestration demanded delivery of the whisky, which had continued to lie in D. Ltd's warehouse. D. Ltd claimed a right to retain the whisky, which was valued at some £200, to set it off against the outstanding balance of some £2,000 which D. Ltd claimed was due to it on its account with R.

Held that D. Ltd had continued to be the undivested owner of the whisky and therefore had a right of retention over it for the balance due by R.

(Intimation of the delivery-orders did not operate as constructive delivery in this case, because the warehouse was D. Ltd's own warehouse, not that of an independent party. The effect of the intimation was merely to notify D. Ltd that the right to demand delivery had passed from the original or earlier purchaser to the next subvendee in the chain.)

(ii) Ex Facie *Absolute Transfer*

7–184 The effect of an *ex facie* absolute transfer is to make the security-holder apparently the owner of the goods, though in a separate document he will declare that the transaction is truly a transfer in security and not an absolute transfer, and so he will undertake to retransfer the goods when they are no longer required as security. The transferee, as apparent owner, has a right to retain the goods for a general balance: his right is not restricted to the particular transaction for which the security was first given.

An illustration of how a right of retention can arise from an *ex facie* absolute transfer of a delivery-order is *Hamilton v. Western Bank of Scotland* (1856) 19 D. 152: **7–185**

In December 1853 Miller applied to the bank to discount a bill of exchange for £650 which was payable in May 1854. Having discounted the bill, the bank required security from Miller for the advance which it was thus making, and Miller gave the bank a delivery-order for 300 cases of brandy to be "collateral security" until the bill matured.

In May 1854, Miller arranged with the bank for a renewal of the bill to the extent of £500 until August and for the continuation of the collateral security until then. In July 1854 Miller obtained a further £400 from the bank.

In September 1854 Miller became bankrupt, and H., the trustee in the sequestration, raised an action against the bank for delivery of the brandy and for damages for wrongful detention of it after payment of the bill for £500 in August. The bank claimed that it was entitled to retain the brandy as security for the advance of £400 which was still outstanding.

Held that as the transaction had not been one of pledge but had been the transfer of a right of ownership, the bank was entitled to retain the brandy until *all* advances were repaid.

The distinction between retention on a property title and lien is explained by Lord Curriehill (at p. 163) thus: "Retention entitles a party who is the owner, or *dominus* of property, to withhold performance of some personal obligation to transfer his right of ownership to another, until the latter perform a counter obligation; whereas lien entitles a party who is in possession of what is another's property, to continue to withhold it from its real owner, until the latter perform a counter obligation. And, on the other hand, the corresponding right to demand possession of the property, on the counter obligation being performed, is, in the former case, merely a personal right, or *jus crediti*; while, in the latter case, it is the real right of property." **7–186**

On the difference in principle applicable to a case of pledge and to the case of an *ex facie* absolute transfer, Lord Deas observed (at **7–187**

p. 166): "In a case of pledge the property remains with the pledger, and, consequently, if the article be pledged for a specific debt, the right to withhold it is limited to that debt. But in a transference like this the property passes to the transferee, subject only to a personal obligation to reconvey, and consequently the right of retention for the general balance, competent by the law of Scotland to a party in whose favour the property has been transferred, comes to be applicable—just as happens in the case of an absolute disposition to heritage, or an intimated assignation to a debt, qualified by a back-bond."

7–188 (Most of the cases on *ex facie* absolute transfers have been concerned with heritable property; by the Conveyancing and Feudal Reform (Scotland) Act 1970, however, the *ex facie* absolute disposition is no longer a permissible form for creating a heritable security.)

(c) Retention of Debt

7–189 This right is based on the doctrine of mutuality in the law of contract: a party who has not performed his part of a contract cannot insist on the other party's paying what is due under the contract. "In the exercise of a right of retention a party to a mutual contract may withhold payment due to the other in security of performance by the other of the obligations due by him" (David M. Walker, *Principles of Scottish Private Law* (4th ed.), Vol. III, p. 407).

7–190 Exercise of this type of retention brings compensation (also called "set off") into operation: the lesser claim will be extinguished and the greater claim will be diminished *pro tanto* ("to the extent of so much", *i.e.* to the extent of the lesser claim).

7–191 The following are two illustrations:

7–192 (i) *Johnston v. Robertson* (1861) 23 D. 646: J. contracted with a parochial board to erect a poor-house for £1,742. By the contract J. undertook to complete the work by March 31, 1856, under a "penalty" of £5 for every week during which the work remained unfinished after that date.

J. brought an action against the board for an alleged balance of the contract price and also for payment for extra work. The board alleged that, since the work had not been completed by March 31, 1856, J. was, under the "penalty" clause, liable to the board for a greater sum than the sum sued for.

Held that (1) the stipulated "penalty" was liquidate damages and not penalty, and was therefore enforceable; and (2) in a mutual contract the principle applicable was that one party was not entitled to enforce performance without showing that he had himself performed his part of the contract.

(ii) *Gibson and Stewart v. Brown and Co.* (1876) 3 R. 328: G. & **7–193**
S., storekeepers, received from B. & Co., grain importers, a quantity of corn to be stored.

After re-delivering the greater part, G. & S. presented a petition to the sheriff for warrant to sell the remainder and apply the proceeds towards payment of their charges, which B. & Co. refused to pay.

B. & Co. stated as a counterclaim damage to a greater amount done to the corn re-delivered, owing to the neglect of G. & S. B. & Co., by minute, restricted their counterclaim to the amount of G. & S.'s claim.

Held that set off was competent, since both claims arose out of the same contract; and objection that this was an attempt to set off an illiquid against a liquid claim *repelled*.

The general rule is that, for the operation of retention, both **7–194**
claims must arise out of the same contract; retention was not allowed, for instance, in *Smart v. Wilkinson*, 1928 S.C. 383:

S. sold his medical practice to W. for £500, payable in three instalments. W. paid the first two instalments, but when sued for the balance of the price, *viz.*, £200, he pleaded that he had been induced to enter into the contract by false and fraudulent misrepresentations made by S. regarding the practice, and he counterclaimed for £500, his estimate of the loss which he had suffered as a result of S.'s representations.

Held that as W.'s claim did not arise out of the contract, but out of an alleged delict which had preceded the making of the contract, it could not be pleaded as a defence and was not a competent counterclaim.

The right of retention is not an absolute right but is subject to **7–195**
equitable control by the court. It may be excluded by the court where it would produce an inequitable result, and on the other hand it may be extended, in the interests of equity, to situations where the claims do not arise out of the same contract; *e.g.* in bankruptcy, if a debtor of the bankrupt has an illiquid claim against him he is entitled to withhold payment of a liquid debt which he

owes to the bankrupt, even though the debts arise out of different contracts: it would be inequitable that the debtor of the bankrupt should be required to pay his own debt in full to the bankrupt and then receive only a dividend on the debt due to himself by the bankrupt.

Further Reading

Gloag and Henderson, *The Law of Scotland*, Chapters 13 (part) and 19

David M. Walker, *Principles of Scottish Private Law*, Volume III, Chapters 5.30 and 5.40

W. A. Wilson, *The Scottish Law of Debt*, Chapters 7, 8 and 13

David M. Walker, *The law of Contracts and related obligations in Scotland*, Chapter 33 (part)

The Laws of Scotland: Stair Memorial Encyclopaedia, Volume 20, Title *Rights in Security over Moveables* by Alexander James Sim.

Gloag and Irvine, *Law of Rights in Security, Heritable and Moveable, including Cautionary Obligations*, Chapters I and VII–XVIII

Enid A. Marshall, *Scottish Cases on Rights in Security over Moveables* (1981, Author)

Chapter 8

CAUTIONARY OBLIGATIONS

	Para.
Introduction	8–01
I General Nature of Cautionary Obligations	8–10
(a) Definitions of Cautionary Obligation	8–13
(b) Similar Obligations	8–17
(i) Independent Obligation	8–18
(ii) Delegation	8–22
(iii) Indemnity	8–24
(iv) Representation as to Credit	8–26
II Kinds of Cautionary Obligations	8–29
(a) Contract of Cautionry to which Creditor is Party	8–30
(b) Contract of Cautionry to which Creditor is not Party	8–33
(c) Implication of Law	8–34
III Constitution and Form	8–36
(a) Constitution	8–37
(b) Form	8–40
(i) The Former Law	8–42
(ii) The New Law	8–43
IV Validity	8–44
(a) Capacity and Authority of Cautioner	8–45
(b) Disclosure by Creditor	8–50
(i) Guarantee of a Debt	8–52
(ii) Fidelity Guarantee	8–54
(c) Obligations by Several Cautioners	8–57
V Extent of Cautioner's Liability	8–61
(a) Interpretation of Cautionary Obligations	8–63
(b) Cautionary Obligations Limited as to Amount	8–67
(c) Cautionary Obligations Limited as to Time	8–75
VI Rights of Cautioners	8–80
(a) *Beneficium Ordinis* ("Benefit of Discussion")	8–83
(b) *Beneficium Divisionis* ("Benefit of Division")	8–89
(c) Right of Relief against Principal Debtor	8–92
(d) Right of Relief against Co-Cautioners	8–96
(e) *Beneficium Cedendarum Actionum* (Right to Assignation)	8–99
(f) Right to Share in Securities held by Co-Cautioners	8–102
VII Termination of Cautionary Obligations	8–105
(a) Termination Resulting from Extinction of Principal Obligation	8–106
(i) Discharge	8–107
(ii) Novation	8–110
(iii) Compensation	8–111
(iv) Rule in *Clayton's Case*	8–113
(v) Prescription	8–116
(b) Other Modes of Termination	8–117
(i) Discharge of Cautioner	8–118
(ii) Revocation by Cautioner	8–119
1. Guarantee for payment of debt	8–122
2. Fidelity guarantee	8–125
(iii) Death	8–128
(iv) Change in a Firm	8–132
(iv) Conduct of Creditor	8–134
1. Giving time to principal debtor	8–135
2. Otherwise altering the principal contract	8–143
3. Releasing co-cautioners	8–148
4. Giving up securities	8–149
(iv) Prescription	8–151

INTRODUCTION

A CAUTIONARY[1] obligation may be shortly described as an obligation of guarantee. Its purpose is to protect a creditor from loss if his principal debtor fails to pay or fails to perform some other **8–01**

[1] pronounced "káy-shun-ary".

obligation: the cautionary obligation gives the creditor the right to recover his loss from a person other than his principal debtor, that other person being referred to as a cautioner.[2]

8–02 As with rights in security over a debtor's property (see Chapter 7, above), the ultimate test of the validity of cautionary obligations comes with the bankruptcy of the principal debtor, but whereas the creditor holding security over some item of his debtor's property has a real right (*i.e.* a *jus in re* ("right in a thing")), the creditor who is protected by a cautionary obligation has a personal right (*i.e.* a *jus in personam* ("right against a person")) against the cautioner. Just as the value to the creditor of his right in security over property depends on the price at which the property may be sold, so the value of a cautionary obligation depends on the solvency of the cautioner.

8–03 The word "cautionry"[3] is used to denote the branch of the law relating to cautionary obligations.

8–04 The law on this subject is mainly common law; a few statutory provisions, notably those of the Mercantile Law Amendment Act Scotland 1856, are mentioned below at the appropriate points.

8–05 Three parties are involved in a cautionary obligation:

A, the creditor, a person to whom a debt must be paid or for whom some service must be performed;

B, the principal debtor, the person who has incurred the debt or who is to perform the service; and

C, the cautioner, the person who guarantees that if B fails to pay or perform, he, C, will be liable to A.

8–06 Other terms which are used are "principal obligant" for B, and "guarantor" or "surety" for C. The last-mentioned is the usual English law equivalent of the Scots law term "cautioner", just as "suretyship" in English law corresponds to "cautionry" in Scots law. However, the terminology in this branch of the law is not kept rigidly distinct in Scottish legal literature; see, *e.g.*, the use of "surety" in the definitions quoted below from Bell's *Principles* (8–15) and from *Gloag and Irvine* (8–16).

8–07 The Scots law of cautionry is founded on the Roman law contract of *fidejussio* ("guarantee").

8–08 As to the value of English decisions Lord Justice-Clerk Cooper in *Aitken's Trustees v. Bank of Scotland*, 1944 S.C. 270 (see 8–108, below) commented (at p. 279):

[2] pronounced "káy-shun-er".
[3] pronounced "káy-shun-ry".

"Now I readiiy agree, as was pointed out by George Joseph Bell in his Commentaries ((7th ed.) vol. I, p. 364), that the general principles of the Scots Law of cautionary obligations are 'nearly the same' as those of the English Law of suretyship, and that this statement is as true to-day as when it was first made. I also agree that, in so far as it is related to these general principles, the *ratio decidendi*[4] of a decision in the one country may have value, and even persuasive authority, in the other; and for this limited purpose many English decisions are cited in our Scottish works on rights in security. But it is only for this limited purpose that English decisions may be used, and through our unfamiliarity with a different legal system we shall incur the risk of being misled if we attempt to follow English decisions not merely when they enunciate general principles common to the two countries but when they apply these principles to the specialties of other branches of English Law and to the special facts of individual cases."

A similar attitude was taken in an observation by Lord Ross in *Lord Advocate v. Maritime Fruit Carriers Co. Ltd*, 1983 S.L.T. 357 (O.H.), on the question of whether a creditor selling a security (in this case a ship) owed a duty to a cautioner. Lord Ross said (at p. 359):

"There is an absence of Scottish authority . . . *Standard Chartered Bank Ltd v. Walker* [1982] 1 W.L.R. 1410 (C.A.) . . . supports the proposition that a creditor does owe a duty to a guarantor to obtain the best possible price when he sells the security subjects, so that the guarantor is made liable for as little as possible under the guarantee. As I indicated, there is no direct authority in Scotland. . . .

" . . . I am not persuaded that the Law of Scotland is necessarily different."

(Proof before answer was allowed.)

Cautionary obligations are part of the law of contract, and are therefore subject to the general principles of the law of contract. Only the specialties affecting cautionary obligations as distinct from other contractual obligations are dealt with in this chapter. They come under the following headings: **8–09**

I. General nature of cautionary obligations;

II. Kinds of cautionary obligations;

III. Constitution and form;

---

[4] basic reasoning.

IV. Validity;
V. Extent of cautioner's liability;
VI. Rights of cautioners; and
VII. Termination of cautionary obligations.

I GENERAL NATURE OF CAUTIONARY OBLIGATIONS

8–10 It is of the essence of a cautionary obligation that it is accessory to another obligation. There must always be a principal obligation either already in existence or contemplated at the time when the cautionary obligation is undertaken, and it is essential for the continuance of the cautionary obligation that the principal obligation should also continue. Accordingly, if the principal obligation is a nullity, there can be no valid cautionary obligation. Similarly, if the principal obligation which was contemplated never in fact comes into existence, there will be no cautionary obligation, and if the principal obligation is brought to an end (*e.g.* by prescription or novation), the cautionary obligation will automatically terminate with it.

8–11 If, however, a cautioner knows, at the time when he undertakes his cautionary obligation, that the principal obligation is invalid, he will be bound by the cautionary obligation:

Stevenson v. Adair (1872) 10 M. 919: Mackenzie, a minor, entered into an indenture of apprenticeship with S. A., as cautioner, bound himself to indemnify S. to the extent of £50 for Mackenzie's omissions or defaults during the apprenticeship. A. knew that Mackenzie's father was alive and had not consented to the indenture.

Mackenzie abandoned his apprenticeship.

Held that S. was entitled to recover damages from A. in accordance with the cautionary obligation.

The case may be explained by the principle of personal bar.

8–12 For the fuller understanding of the general nature of a cautionary obligation, consideration is given below to:

(a) some definitions of cautionary obligation; and

(b) some obligations which are in some respects similar to, and in other respects different from, cautionary obligations.

(a) Definitions of Cautionary Obligation

8–13 There is no statutory definition. The following are amongst the best-known definitions appearing in books of authority:

(i) "By a cautionary obligation one becomes bound that the principal debtor shall pay to the creditor the debt which, by the principal obligation, he engages to pay; or that he shall deliver or perform what, by that principal obligation, he has undertaken"—Bell's *Commentaries*, Vol. I, p. 364. **8–14**

(ii) Cautionry is "an engagement or obligation, as surety for another, that the principal obligant shall pay the debt or perform the undertaking for which he has engaged"—Bell's *Principles*, § 246. **8–15**

(iii) "A cautionary obligation or guarantee is an obligation accessory to a principal obligation, to answer for the payment of some debt or the performance of some duty, in case of the failure of another person, who is himself, in the first instance, liable to such payment or performance. . . . The person who gives the promise is the cautioner, surety, or guarantor; the person to whom the promise is given is the creditor; and the person whose liability is the foundation of the contract is the principal debtor"—Gloag and Irvine in their authoritative *Law of Rights in Security, Heritable and Moveable, including Cautionary Obligations* (published in 1897), p. 642. **8–16**

(b) **Similar Obligations**

It is sometimes difficult but important to distinguish between a cautionary obligation and: **8–17**

(i) an independent obligation;
(ii) delegation;
(iii) indemnity; and
(iv) representation as to credit.

(i) *Independent Obligation*

Cautionary obligations are always accessory, never independent, obligations, but the distinction is sometimes narrow. **8–18**

One party, X, may for the benefit of another party, Y, undertake an obligation to a third party, Z, without necessarily becoming a cautioner for Y. X.'s obligation would be an independent obligation unless the circumstances showed that it was intended that Y was to be primarily liable. **8–19**

The question of whether X's obligation is a cautionary obligation or an independent one becomes important when Z wishes to enforce **8–20**

X's obligation. If X is a cautioner, Z will require to allow to X the rights to which cautioners are entitled. The test to be applied is: "On whose credit did Z rely?" If the answer is that he relied solely on X's credit, the obligation will be held to be an independent one, whereas if he relied on the credit of both X and Y, and primarily on the credit of Y, the obligation will be held to be a cautionary one.

8–21 *Stevenson's Trustee v. Campbell & Sons* (1896) 23 R. 711: A builder who had certain building contracts in hand became unable to complete them without financial assistance. Arrangements were made by which the builder became the servant of S., a property speculator who was to pay for the materials to be ordered by the builder for the completion of the contracts.

C. & Sons, metal merchants, supplied material to the builder on the understanding that S. was to pay for it.

S. died before payment was made, and S.'s estate was sequestrated. The trustee in the sequestration rejected C. & Sons' claim for the price of the material on the ground that S. had been merely a cautioner and that there was no valid evidence of the cautionary obligation.

Held that C. & Sons had a claim in the sequestration on the basis that S. had been the buyer of the material.

Lord President J. P. B. Robertson said (at p. 714): "The present case is in substance and very nearly exactly that stated by the Court in *Birkmyr v. Darnell* (1 Smith's Leading Cases, 10th ed. 287), 'If two come to a shop and one buys and the other . . . says, Let him have the goods, I will be your paymaster . . . this is an undertaking as for himself and he shall be intended to be the very buyer, and the other to act but as his servant.' "

(ii) *Delegation*

8–22 Delegation (the substitution of a new debtor with the creditor's consent) is distinct from cautionry because in delegation the obligation of the original debtor is extinguished, whereas in cautionry the creditor gains the benefit of an additional obligant against whom he may have recourse on the failure of the principal debtor, who remains primarily liable.

8–23 There is a presumption against delegation, *i.e.* until the contrary is proved, the new party is regarded as an additional obligant.

(iii) *Indemnity*

A contract of indemnity is one by which one party undertakes to relieve another of loss incurred by that other in certain circumstances. For instance, X may in a contract of indemnity undertake to relieve Z of any liability which Z may incur in his transactions with Y. The contract of indemnity between X and Z is not accessory to the contract governing the transactions between Y and Z, and is therefore distinct from a cautionary obligation. **8–24**

Guarantee policies issued by insurance companies are contracts of indemnity which come very close to cautionry. The insurance company agrees to pay any loss which may be incurred by the insured through the default of the insured's debtor. The distinction between such a policy and a cautionary obligation is important when the question arises of whether all material facts have been disclosed by the insured to the insurance company. A contract of insurance, being a contract *uberrimae fidei* ("of the utmost good faith"), will be voidable unless full disclosure has been made, whereas there is no such rule generally applicable to cautionary obligations. A further point of distinction is that a guarantee policy is an arrangement made by the *creditor* with the insurance company, whereas in cautionry it is usual for the arrangements for the guarantee to be made by the principal debtor. **8–25**

(iv) *Representation as to Credit*

A representation as to credit may be briefly described as a statement made by one party, X, to another party, Z, as to the trustworthiness of a third party, Y. This brings out the similarity between such a representation and a cautionary obligation. A fuller description of a representation as to credit, based on the now repealed section 6 of the Mercantile Law Amendment Act Scotland 1856, was: **8–26**

> a representation or assurance "as to the character, conduct, credit, ability, trade, or dealings of any person, made or granted to the effect or for the purpose of enabling such person to obtain credit, money, goods, or postponement of payment of debt, or of any other obligation demandable from him."

"Ability" in that context was construed as referring to financial ability (*Irving v. Burns*, 1915 S.C. 260, in which a statement relating to a company commencing business that £3,000 of the capital had been subscribed was held to be a representation as to credit within the statutory definition).

8–27 The Act required such representations, as well as cautionary obligations, to be in writing. This requirement, owing to the repeal of section 6 by the Requirements of Writing (Scotland) Act 1995 (s. 14(2) and Sched. 5) applies only to things done before the commencement of the Act of 1995 on August 1, 1995 (s. 14(3)).

8–28 A representation as to credit, unlike a cautionary obligation, does not give rise to liability on the part of the person making it, merely because the person obtaining credit comes to be in default. The person making the representation will incur no liability for a representation honestly and carefully made, even although it may in fact be false. Where liability is incurred, it will be on the ground of delict, not contract, and will take the form of damages for fraud or for negligence.

II KINDS OF CAUTIONARY OBLIGATIONS

8–29 There are three kinds of cautionary obligations:

(a) those constituted by a contract of cautionry to which the creditor is a party;
(b) those constituted by a contract of cautionry to which the creditor is not a party; and
(c) those arising by implication of law.

(a) **Contract of Cautionry to which Creditor is Party**

8–30 Here a distinction must be made between proper and improper cautionry.

8–31 In proper cautionry the cautioner is bound to the creditor expressly as cautioner for the principal debtor.

8–32 In improper cautionary the cautioner is bound to the creditor as a co-obligant jointly and severally with the principal debtor. This enables the creditor to hold either the cautioner or the principal debtor liable *in solidum* ("for the full amount"). The true relationship of principal debtor and cautioner will rest on some other provision; *e.g.* one of the parties may be described expressly as "cautioner and co-principal", or the contract may contain a clause of relief conferring on one of the apparent co-principals (the cautioner) the right to recover from the other (the principal debtor) the amount which he has had to pay to the creditor, or in the case of a cash credit bond one of the apparent co-principals (the principal debtor) may have the sole right to operate the account though both are made liable for the sum advanced. Wherever it can be established that one of the co-obligants is truly a cautioner for the other, he is entitled to the rights of a cautioner (see 8–80, below).

(b) Contract of Cautionry to which Creditor is not Party

The relation of principal debtor and cautioner may be constituted in an agreement separate from the agreement between these two parties on the one hand and the creditor on the other hand. As long as the creditor does not know the true relationship between his two debtors, he need not treat the one as cautioner for the other: he simply has two debtors. If, however, he comes to know of the true relationship of the two debtors, he must observe all the duties which are imposed on a creditor in a cautionary obligation. **8–33**

(c) Implication of Law

Cautionry arises by implication of law where, without there being any contract of cautionry, two parties are liable for the same debt, the liability of one party being primary and the liability of the other being secondary. **8–34**

Instances of this type of cautionry occur in the law of partnership and in the law relating to bills of exchange: in partnership the individual partners are in the position of cautioners for the debts of the firm, *i.e.* they are liable to pay the firm's debts if the firm itself fails to do so; in the case of a bill of exchange which has been accepted, the acceptor is in the position of principal debtor, and the drawer and indorsers are in the position of cautioners, liable to pay the amount of the bill to the holder if the acceptor fails to pay. **8–35**

III CONSTITUTION AND FORM

The constitution of cautionary obligations is governed by the principles of the common law of contract, but their form depends partly on statute. **8–36**

(a) Constitution

The rules of offer and acceptance apply. **8–37**

8–38 The offer may be an undertaking, addressed by the intending cautioner to a particular creditor, to guarantee the debt or actings of a third party (the principal debtor). The contract will be concluded by either an express acceptance, addressed by the creditor to the cautioner, or an acceptance implied by actings, such as the giving of credit by the creditor to the principal debtor on the faith of the cautioner's undertaking.

An illustration of acceptance implied by actings occurs in *Scottish Metropolitan Property plc v. Christie*, 1987 S.L.T. (Sh.Ct.) 18: The missives for a lease to be granted by Scottish Metropolitan Property plc ("M. plc") to Stuart (Leisure) Ltd ("S. Ltd") included a term that the tenants' part of the lease would be guaranteed by C.

M. plc acted on that undertaking and granted the lease. No formal executed guarantee, however, was ever delivered and S. Ltd failed to pay any rent.

Held (by Sheriff I. D. Macphail) that on the commencement of the lease a binding cautionary obligation had come into being.

8–39 Alternatively, the offer may be contained in a letter or other document, not addressed to anyone in particular, but handed by the intending cautioner to the prospective principal debtor on the understanding that the latter will show it to a prospective creditor, *e.g.*:

"The bearer, Mr Fortune, we have known for a long number of years, and have pleasure in testifying as to his good and straightforward character, and guarantee that his financial standing is all in order . . . to the extent of from £1,600 to £1,800" (*Fortune v. Young*, 1918 S.C. 1 (8–48, below)).

Actings by the creditor on the faith of such document then constitute acceptance.

(b) **Form**

8–40 The law relating to the form of cautionary obligations was altered by the Requirements of Writing (Scotland) Act 1995 which repealed section 6 of the Mercantile Law Amendment Act Scotland 1856 (s. 14(2) of, and Sched. 5 to, the Act of 1995). However, since nothing in the Act of 1995 is to apply to any document executed or anything done before the commencement of that Act on August 1, 1995 (s. 14(3) of the Act of 1995), the pre-existing law will continue to apply to pre-1995 cautionary obligations. Both the former and the new law are therefore summarised below.

Section 14(6) of the Act of 1995 provides that if it cannot be ascertained whether a document was executed before or after August 1, 1995, there will be a presumption that it was executed on or after that date. **8–41**

(i) *The Former Law*

By section 6 of the Mercantile Law Amendment Act Scotland 1856 all cautionary obligations had to be in writing and had to be subscribed by the person undertaking them or by some person duly authorised by him; otherwise they had no effect. **8–42**

The Act did not state that the writing had to be probative. Probably it did not require to be probative, but the point was undecided. It was, however, clear that:

1. If there was an improbative writing and the creditor had acted in reliance on it, a binding cautionary obligation would have been formed:

National Bank of Scotland Ltd v. Campbell (1892) 19 R. 885: A bank agreed to make advances to a firm of builders in Oban on their obtaining a guarantee from C., a shipmaster in Oban.

A formal letter of guarantee was prepared by the bank and handed to the builders so that they would have it executed by C.

The builders obtained C.'s signature and afterwards got two persons to sign as "witnesses" although these persons had neither seen C. sign or nor heard him acknowledge his signature.

The builders then returned the document to the bank, and the bank advanced money to them on the faith of the guarantee.

Later, when the bank sought to enforce the guarantee against C., C. pleaded that he was not bound because the document was not probative.

Held that as C. had signed the document and delivered it to the builders who were acting as agents for the bank in this matter, the guarantee was binding on C. in accordance with the doctrine of *rei interventus* ("actings following on" [an informal document]).

2. If the cautionary obligation was *in re mercatoria* ("on a commercial matter"), the writing did not need to be probative:

B.O.C.M. Silcock Ltd v. Hunter, 1976 S.L.T. 217: A company supplying feedstuffs to grain merchants obtained from H., the individual principally interested in a company of grain merchants, a document by which H. personally guaranteed all such sums as should be due by his company to the suppliers. The document was signed in the presence of one witness only.

Feedstuffs to the value of £45,198.91 were supplied, and the grain merchant company failed to discharge its indebtedness. H. refused to pay under the guarantee on the ground that the document was neither holograph nor tested.

Held that, being a writ *in re mercatoria*, the document was binding on H.

The opinion of the First Division was (at p. 224):

"Before a guarantee will be held to qualify as a writing *in re mercatoria* it must be granted in a course of dealing between merchants. Further . . . it must . . . be seen from all the circumstances which surrounded its origin to be an informal writing of the kind which merits its treatment as a mercantile writing."

(ii) The New Law

8–43 In the Requirements of Writing (Scotland) Act 1995 cautionary obligations are not specifically mentioned in the restricted list of obligations which require writing for their constitution (s. 1(2)). Some will, however, fall into the category of gratuitous unilateral obligations, except those undertaken in the course of business (s. 1(2)(a)(ii)). The only formality required is subscription by the granter or, where there is more than one granter, each granter (s. 2(1)). Cautionary obligations undertaken in the course of business (*e.g.* bonds of caution granted by insurance companies for a premium) do not require writing for their constitution (s. 1(1)).

The Act introduces a new form of *rei interventus*, which will come into operation where there is not a validly executed document (and one is required). The effect is that the cautioner is not entitled to withdraw from the obligation (s. 1(3)), and the cautionary obligation is not treated as invalid, if the following conditions are fulfilled:

1. the creditor has acted or refrained from acting in reliance on the cautionary obligation with the knowledge and acquiescence of the cautioner;

2. as a result of 1, above, the creditor has been affected to a material extent; and

3. the creditor would be affected to a material extent if the cautioner were to be allowed to withdraw (s. 1(3),(4)).

While no witness is required in order to constitute a gratuitous unilateral cautionary obligation (except one undertaken in the course of business) the document will only become "probative" (self-proving, *i.e.* bearing on its face sufficient proof of its authenticity) if it is witnessed by one witness (s. 3(1),(7)) who either sees the cautioner subscribe or hears him acknowledge his subscription and who then signs the document. Where the document containing the cautionary obligation is probative there is a presumption that it was subscribed by the cautioner (s. 3(1)).

The Act of 1995 (s. 11(3)(b)(ii)) abolishes any rule of the common law which confers any privilege on a writ in *re mercatoria.*

IV VALIDITY

Questions as to the validity of cautionary obligations are mostly **8–44** decided according to the general principles of the law of contract. The following matters, however, call for special attention:

(a) capacity and authority of the cautioner;

(b) disclosure by the creditor; and

(c) the situation where there are several cautioners for the same debt.

(a) **Capacity and Authority of Cautioner**

The ordinary rules as to capacity and authority are applied with a **8–45** greater strictness.

Accordingly, while by the Age of Legal Capacity (Scotland) Act **8–46** 1991 (s. 1(1)) a person of or over the age of 16 years has legal capacity to enter into any transaction, it is unlikely that a person between 16 and 18 years of age would be an acceptable cautioner, since up to the age of 21 such a person has the right, under section 3(1) of the Act, to apply to court for a "prejudicial transaction" entered into when he was 16 or 17 years old to be set aside.

Similarly, an agent usually requires express authority if he is to **8–47** undertake a cautionary obligation on behalf of his principal. Authority would be implied only if the granting of guarantees was part of the ordinary business (*e.g.* if the principal were a guarantee association). An ordinary commercial agent has no such authority.

Partners, as agents of their firm, and directors, as agents of their **8–48** company, likewise normally require special authority for the undertaking of a cautionary obligation which will be binding on the firm or company. An instance relating to partnership is *Fortune v. Young*, 1918 S.C. 1:

Y., a partner of the firm James Tait & Co., signed the firm-name, without the authority of the firm, on a letter guaranteeing the financial standing of an applicant for the lease of a farm.

As a result of the letter, the farm was let to the applicant.

On the subsequent bankruptcy of the applicant, an action was brought against Y. as an individual to enforce the guarantee.

Held that Y. was liable.

Lord Justice-Clerk Scott Dickson said (at p. 6): "It is not suggested that this cautionary obligation was within the scope of the business of the firm. . . . If it had been sought to make the firm or the partner other than the one who signed the firm-name liable, there might have been a good defence. . . . A partner who signs an obligatory document outwith the scope of his copartnery does not bind the firm, but he undoubtedly binds himself."

8–49 The Partnership Act 1890 (s. 7) provides that where one partner pledges the credit of the firm for a purpose apparently not connected with the firm's ordinary course of business, the firm is not bound, unless he is in fact specially authorised by the other partners, but that provision does not affect any personal liability incurred by an individual partner.

(b) Disclosure by Creditor

8–50 When a cautionary obligation is being undertaken, the creditor must ensure that he makes such disclosure to the cautioner as the law requires, so that the cautioner will be liable to assess the degree of risk which he is to run as cautioner.

8–51 In this connection a distinction has been made between:

(i) the guarantee of a debt; and
(ii) a fidelity guarantee.

(i) *Guarantee of a Debt*

8–52 The rule has been that where the principal obligation was the payment of a sum of money, the creditor was not required to give the cautioner any information or warning as to the extent of the risk which he was undertaking; *e.g.* a bank was not bound to disclose to a prospective cautioner the state of the principal debtor's bank account which the cautioner was to guarantee:

Young v. Clydesdale Bank Ltd (1889) 17 R. 231: Y., who had been in the habit of granting accommodation bills to his brother for sums between £300 and £400, gave a letter to his brother's banker in which he guaranteed "payment of any advances made and which may hereafter be made" to his brother. Y. had signed the letter without reading it, and the bank-agent had not informed Y. that his brother's account was overdrawn to the amount of about £5,000.

The bank sued Y. for £5,303 0s.9d. under the letter of guarantee, and Y. brought an action of reduction of the letter.

Held that there had been no duty on the bank-agent to inform Y. of the state of his brother's account.

Lord Adam said (at p. 240): "It is well settled that it is not the duty of a bank to give any information to a proposed cautioner as to the state of accounts with the principal. That is quite settled. If the cautioner desires to know the state of accounts with the principal it is his duty to ask and to inform himself, but no duty lies upon a party seeking security to give any information of that kind."

A similar case was *The Royal British Bank v. Greenshields*, 1914 S.C. 259: A bank-agent had represented to an intending cautioner, G., that a customer of the bank, Hutchison, was indebted to the bank for less than £300, without disclosing that Hutchison was also indebted to the bank in respect of certain promissory notes amounting to about £1,100.

Held in an action by the bank against G., that there had been no duty on the bank-agent to disclose the total indebtedness of Hutchison to the bank, and decree for payment was granted.

Lord President (Strathclyde) (at p. 266) said: "The law applicable to the case is well settled. A bank-agent is entitled to assume that an intending guarantor has made himself fully acquainted with the financial position of the customer whose debt he is about to guarantee. And the bank-agent is not bound to make any disclosure whatever regarding the customer's indebtedness to the bank."

This long-established rule has been recently altered by the decision of the House of Lords in *Smith v. Bank of Scotland*, 1997 S.C. (H.L.) 111.

The case started as two cases: *Mumford v. Bank of Scotland*; *Smith v. Bank of Scotland*:

Mrs M. and Mrs S. were the wives of two partners in business who in April 1986 approached the Bank of Scotland seeking an overdraft facility. The husbands were advised that the facility would be granted provided they obtained for the bank a standard security over their respective dwelling-houses.

Mrs M.'s husband was the heritable proprietor of their house and Mrs M. was the "non-entitled" spouse within the meaning of section 1(1) of the Matrimonial Homes (Family Protection) (Scotland) Act 1981. On April 21, 1986, she executed a form of consent for the purposes of that Act and her husband granted a standard security.

Mrs S. and her husband were the heritable proprietors of their house with the title to it in their joint names, and on April 23, 1986, they granted a standard security.

Mrs M. and Mrs S. brought actions for reduction, founding on the House of Lords decision in the English case *Barclays Bank plc v. O'Brien* [1994] 1 A.C. 180. That case was authority for the argument that where the relationship between co-cautioners was close, such as that of husband and wife, and where one party had no direct financial interest in the transaction but was put at a financial disadvantage because of it, the lender was put on inquiry and was under a duty to take reasonable steps to satisfy himself that the disadvantaged party's agreement to give security had been properly obtained.

In the Court of Session, both the Outer House (Lord Johnston) (1994 S.L.T. 1288) and the First Division (1996 S.L.T. 392), declined to follow that English authority and held that in the absence of actual knowledge of undue influence or misrepresentation, the lenders were under no duty either to explain to the wives the nature of the transactions into which they were entering and their consequences or to require them to take independent advice.

Mrs S. appealed to the House of Lords.

Held, appeal allowed and proof before answer allowed.

There were said to be no social or economic considerations which would justify a difference between the two jurisdictions on the point in question; the basis on which *O'Brien's* case should be extended to Scotland was that of constructive notice, the circumstances being such that the intimate relationship of the cautioner with the debtor ought to have made the bank reasonably suspect that the validity of the cautionary obligation was undermined; the bank ought to have warned Mrs S. of the possible consequences of entering into the obligation and to have advised her to take independent advice.

8–53 If, however, the creditor spontaneously or in answer to questions gives information to the cautioner, his statement must be true; otherwise the cautioner will be freed from liability.

(ii) *Fidelity Guarantee*

In a fidelity guarantee the creditor is usually an employer, the principal debtor is usually his employee, and the cautioner is guaranteeing that the employee is honest: the cautioner's liability will then arise if the employee proves dishonest. The cautionary obligation here, therefore, is in substance an insurance against the employee's dishonesty, and the same rule of law applies to fidelity guarantees as to contracts of insurance, namely, that full disclosure of material facts must be made. For instance, an employer who knows that an employee has not been trustworthy in the past must disclose that fact to the prospective cautioner; the result of non-disclosure would be that the cautioner would not be liable: **8–54**

French v. Cameron (1893) 20 R. 966: F. engaged Jamieson as a commercial traveller.

After his first journey Jamieson was about £32 short in his cash account, and his explanation was that his pocket had been picked at a procession in Dublin. F. accepted that excuse, and an arrangement was made for retention off wages to make up the deficiency.

Jamieson then left for a second journey. At first he sent the proper returns, but on the latter part of the journey he failed to do so, and on his return he was found to be about £30 short. He admitted that he had been "drinking and misbehaving himself", and he begged forgiveness. F. consented to give him another chance out of sympathy for his wife, but only on condition that he found security for his deficiency and for his further transactions.

Jamieson approached C. and B., stating that F. had resolved to promote him to a position of greater trust and responsibility on condition that he procured cautioners. C. and B. then signed a cautionary obligation for £50.

Thereafter Jamieson again misconducted himself and was dismissed. F. raised an action against the cautioners.

Held that because of F.'s failure to disclose the circumstances in which the cautionary obligation was demanded the cautioners were not bound.

The duty of full disclosure continues throughout the course of the fidelity guarantee: if, for instance, the employee is guilty of some dishonesty after the guarantee has been given, the employer must inform the cautioner of that fact; otherwise the cautioner would cease to be liable: **8–55**

Snaddon v. London, Edinburgh and Glasgow Assurance Co. Ltd (1902) 5 F. 182: By a bond of guarantee S., a publican, of Devonside Inn, Tillicoultry, became cautioner to an insurance company for Jack, who was appointed the company's superintendent at Alva in December 1896.

The following year these events took place: on August 11 Jack embezzled £25 by putting a forged indorsement on a cheque which had been entrusted to him by the company so that he might hand it over to a policy-holder. He also sent to the company a forged receipt by the policy-holder for the money. On September 25 he confessed the crime to the company, and was suspended. On October 8 he absconded. On October 11 the company intimated to S. that he was liable for £25 under the bond of guarantee.

Held that the company had failed to intimate Jack's criminal conduct timeously to S., and was therefore barred from claiming against S. under the bond of guarantee.

Lord Young said (at p. 186): "On the general rules of law if any company of this kind employs an employee whose honesty is guaranteed by another, and if the employee commits a crime such as forgery, and his employers get to know of it, they are not entitled to retain him a day in their employment under the guarantee, unless they inform the cautioner, and he is prepared to continue the guarantee on the footing that the employee remains in their service."

8–56 These rules as to disclosure by the creditor in a fidelity guarantee are justified on the ground that an employer, both before he engages an employee and during the course of the employment, has a greater opportunity than the cautioner has of discovering any faults in the employee.

(c) Obligations by Several Cautioners

8–57 There may be several cautioners guaranteeing the same principal debt. If so, the creditor must ensure that, after one cautioner has undertaken liability, the co-cautioners also do so, since there is an implied condition that each of the several co-cautioners undertakes liability only if the others do so. The underlying reason is that the co-cautioner who undertook liability would be deprived of his expected right of relief against co-cautioners if they did not sign (see 8–96 *et seq*., below).

8–58 The rule applies even where the co-cautioners are jointly and severally liable to the creditor (provided the creditor knows that they are really cautioners):

Paterson v. Bonar (1844) 6 D. 987 (a majority decision of the whole Court of Session): A bond in favour of a bank stated that M. (who was the principal debtor), C., P. and W. (who were cautioners) were bound "conjunctly and severally" to pay £1,500 to the bank in respect of advances to be made by the bank to M. W. did not sign the bond.

M. became bankrupt, owing the bank upwards of £2,000, and the bank sued P. for £1,500.

Held that since one co-cautioner had not signed the bond, the others were not liable for the advances made under it.

"None are bound until all have subscribed" (*per* Lord Jeffrey at p. 1015).

The result is the same if the signature of a co-cautioner has been forged: **8–59**

Scottish Provincial Assurance Co. v. Pringle (1858) 20 D. 465: The S. Co. agreed to give a loan of £150 to X upon a personal bond to be granted by X and four other persons, P., V., K., and M., as joint and several obligants. The bond was given to X so that he might obtain the signatures of the other obligants.

P., V., and K. signed the bond. M. did not sign it, but X forged M.'s signature and those of two witnesses.

X then returned the bond to the S. Co., and the money was paid to him.

X became bankrupt, and the forgeries were discovered.

The S. Co. sued P., V., and K.

Held that P., V., and K. were not liable.

Judicial cautionry (*i.e.* cautionary obligations required in various court proceedings) is an exception: in that case a cautioner is bound even though the signature of his co-cautioner is forged (*Simpson v. Fleming* (1860) 22 D. 679). **8–60**

V EXTENT OF CAUTIONER'S LIABILITY

A cautioner is never liable for more than the whole loss actually resulting from the principal debtor's failure. The whole loss would include not only the capital sum due by the principal debtor but also unpaid interest and any expenses reasonably incurred by the creditor in trying to enforce the debt against the principal debtor (*Struthers v. Dykes* (1847) 9 D. 1437). **8–61**

Apart from that general principle, the extent of the cautioner's liability depends on the terms of his undertaking. Three matters call for special attention: **8–62**

(a) the interpretation of cautionary obligations;
(b) the situation where the cautionary obligation is limited as to amount; and
(c) the situation where the cautionary obligation is limited as to time.

(a) Interpretation of Cautionary Obligations

8–63 A cautionary obligation is construed in the narrowest sense which the words will reasonably bear.

8–64 An illustration of how a cautionary obligation will not be extended to transactions which, according to a strict interpretation, are outside its scope is:

North of Scotland Banking Co. v. Fleming (1882) 10 R. 217: F. had been appointed a bank-agent by the North of Scotland Banking Co. F.'s brother and another party became cautioners for the faithful discharge by F. of his duties. One of the terms of their bond of caution was that they were to be jointly and severally liable for loss resulting to the bank from overdrafts allowed by F. without the bank's consent.

F. opened a current account in his own name, and, with the bank's knowledge, allowed overdrafts on that account.

Held that the cautioners were not liable to the bank for the overdrafts on F.'s own account, since these were truly advances made by the bank to F. as an individual, whereas the risk intended to be covered by the bond of caution related to overdrafts allowed by F. to customers without the bank's consent.

Similarly, in *Ayr County Council v. Wyllie*, 1935 S.C. 836, W., the cautioner for a sheriff officer, was held not liable for sums embezzled by the sheriff officer when the officer was acting not in his official capacity as sheriff officer but as debt collector for the county council.

8–65 The interpretation of cautionary obligations often is *contra proferentem* ("against the party putting them forward"), the obligation being contained in a formal document issued by the creditor (*e.g.* a guarantee of a bank overdraft contained in a printed form supplied by the bank, as in *Aitken's Trustees v. Bank of Scotland*, 1944 S.C. 270 (8–108, below).

8–66 However, the rules that a cautionary obligation is to be strictly construed and to be construed *contra proferentem* apply only where there is some ambiguity or where the words have no clear meaning at all:

Caldwell v. Keith Bros. (Environmental Services) Ltd, 1990 G.W.D. 10–555 (O.H.): C. leased premises to K. Ltd and obtained guarantees from K. Ltd's directors who bound themselves jointly and severally with K. Ltd, "so long as K. Ltd are the lessees", for payment of the rent.

The lease was terminated in 1985 and C. sued the directors for the rent then outstanding.

The directors argued that the guarantee had to be construed strictly and *contra proferentem* and that as the lease was no longer current they were therefore no longer liable.

Lord Caplan, rejecting these arguments, held that the guarantee was obviously intended to cover rents which had become due during the currency of the lease.

(b) Cautionary Obligations Limited as to Amount

Where there is a limitation on the amount for which the cautioner is **8–67**
to be liable, a distinction must be made between:

(i) a cautionary obligation which guarantees only a part of the principal debtor's debt; and

(ii) a cautionary obligation which guarantees the whole of the principal debtor's debt, though placing a limit on the amount which the cautioner is liable to pay.

Obligations of category (i) are favourable to the cautioner, those of category (ii) are favourable to the creditor.

The distinction is of practical importance when the principal **8–68**
debtor becomes bankrupt, and the cautioner pays the creditor the full amount of his guarantee. The question then is: "Is the cautioner entitled to rank on the bankrupt principal debtor's estate to recover a dividend on the amount which he has paid to the creditor?" If the cautionary obligation falls into category (i), the answer to that question will be in the affirmative, and if the obligation falls into category (ii), the answer will be in the negative.

Because of the stringent interpretation applied to cautionary **8–69**
obligations, precise language is required for the creation of obligations in category (ii).

The following cases will clarify the distinction: **8–70**

(i) *Harmer & Co. v. Gibb*, 1911 S.C. 1341: M. was starting **8–71**
business as a retail clothier. H. & Co., wholesale clothiers, agreed

to supply him with goods provided G. granted a letter of guarantee in their favour.

The letter signed by G. was in these terms: "I, G., hereby undertake to guarantee to you the due payment of all such goods as you may from time to time sell and deliver to M. up to the value of £200."

Several years later, M. sold off his business and disappeared, leaving H. & Co. unpaid to the extent of about £300. In addition to the guarantee, H. & Co. held as security a policy of insurance on M.'s life, the surrender value of the policy being £116.

H. & Co. sued G. under the guarantee for £200.

Held, on an interpretation of the terms of the guarantee, that G. had guaranteed only the first £200 of M.'s debt to H. & Co., and that in paying to H. & Co. under the guarantee, G. was therefore entitled to deduct from £200 that proportion of the value of the policy which £200 bore to the whole debt due by M. to H. & Co. (*i.e.* approximately two-thirds of £116 had to be deducted from H. & Co.'s claim against G.).

8–72 (ii) *Harvie's Trustees v. Bank of Scotland* (1885) 12 R. 1141: This case gives an example of an "ultimate loss clause", which entitles the creditor to regard the cautioner as having guaranteed the whole of the principal debtor's debt, not merely the debt up to the stated limit of the guarantee. The effect of such a clause is to deprive the cautioner of his right of relief against the principal debtor.

H. granted a letter of guarantee to a bank, guaranteeing "due payment of all sums for which M. is or may become liable to you, the amount which I am to be bound to pay under this guarantee not to exceed £15,000, . . . and I further declare that I shall not be entitled to demand from you an assignation of this guarantee, so long as the said M. is indebted to you in any sums such as aforesaid".

The estates of M. were sequestrated. Shortly afterwards, on February 28, H. paid £10,000 into the bank. On March 14 he paid a further £5,000. On March 18 he died.

H.'s trustees claimed a ranking for £15,000 in M.'s sequestration. The bank claimed to be ranked for £44,000, the amount due to it by M. at the date of the sequestration, without deduction of the £15,000 paid by H. (*Both* claims could not be allowed, since this would have amounted to double ranking, to the extent of £15,000.)

The trustee in M.'s sequestration rejected the claim of H.'s trustees, and sustained that of the bank. H.'s trustees appealed against that decision.

Held that, in view of the terms of the letter of guarantee, H.'s trustees were not entitled to interfere with the bank's ranking for the full £44,000.

Lord Shand said (at p. 1146): "It appears to me that the case does not raise any question of general principle, but must be determined on a construction of the particular terms of the letter of guarantee.

"The words which occur towards the close of the document, 'and I further declare that I shall not be entitled to demand from you an assignation of this guarantee so long as the said Andrew Hislop Maclean is indebted to you in any sums such as aforesaid,' are quite conclusive of the present question. . . . The plain meaning of these words is that so long as any sum whatever is due by Maclean to the bank the claims of the cautioner shall not come into conflict with theirs."

A case to be contrasted with *Harvie's Trustees v. Bank of Scotland* is *Veitch v. National Bank of Scotland Ltd*, 1907 S.C. 554: This case indicates the careful choice of language which must be made when the parties intend to create an effective "ultimate loss clause": in particular, the use of a phrase such as "a covering security for the creditor's ultimate loss" is not of itself sufficient. While the case emphasises again that each case turns entirely on the construction of the actual terms of the cautionary obligation, the inclusion of a provision, as in *Harvie's Trustees v. Bank of Scotland*, that the cautioner is not to be entitled to demand an assignation of the guarantee from the creditor as long as any indebtedness is outstanding emerges as being of vital importance: 8–73

R., V. and H. granted a bond of cash-credit in favour of a bank. The current account was in the name of R.; V. and H. were truly cautioners. The bond stated that the bank had agreed to allow credit to the extent of £1,500, and that the parties bound themselves, conjunctly and severally, to repay all sums advanced to R. not exceeding £1,500 in all, "it being the express meaning of these presents that this bond shall to the extent foresaid be a covering security to said bank against any ultimate loss that may arise on the transactions of R. with the said bank."

R. ultimately granted a trust deed for creditors. The sum then due by R. to the bank was £5,855, upon which the bank received a dividend of 13s.4d. in the £ from R.'s estate, leaving £1,951 as the balance still due.

The bank claimed repayment of this balance to the extent of £1,500 from V.

Held that, on a sound construction of the bond, V.'s guarantee was limited to repayment of an advance of £1,500 to be made to R. by the bank, and that as the bank had already recovered (by receiving 13s.4d. in the £) £1,000 of that advance, V. was liable only for repayment of the remaining £500.

(If V. had paid the £1,500 to the bank, he would have been entitled in relief to an assignation of the bank's right to rank on R.'s estate for that sum.)

Lord Stormonth-Darling said (at p. 560): "The judgment in *Harvie's Trustees* proceeded entirely on the ground that by the express words of the guarantee the cautioner had given up the right to demand an assignation so long as the principal debtor was indebted to the bank in any sum whatever."

8–74 An ultimate loss clause such as that in *Harvie's Trustees v. Bank of Scotland* operates only on the bankruptcy of the principal debtor:

Mackinnon's Trustee v. Bank of Scotland, 1915 S.C. 411: In 1907 for the purpose of guaranteeing M.'s bank account Zollner had signed a letter of guarantee in the same terms as that signed by Harvie except that the maximum amount was not to exceed £2,500.

In 1912 Zollner desired to terminate his liability, which he did by paying £2,500 to the bank and then realising property which M. had assigned to him as security for the guarantee.

In 1913 M. became bankrupt, and the bank claimed that it was entitled to rank for the full amount of M.'s indebtedness without deducting the amount paid to it by Zollner.

Held that as the payment by Zollner had been made before M.'s bankruptcy, the bank was entitled to rank on M.'s estate only for the balance due to it after deduction of Zollner's payment.

(c) Cautionary Obligations Limited as to Time

8–75 A cautionary obligation may be either limited as to its duration or continuing and indefinite as to its duration.

8–76 A limitation on duration may arise:

(i) from an express term specifying the limited duration; or

(ii) by inference from other terms in the obligation, from the general nature of the obligation, and from its surrounding circumstances.

Scott v. Mitchell (1866) 4 M. 551: In 1853 M. granted to S. a letter of guarantee in the following terms: "As you have become security to Clydesdale Bank for £150, on account of Mr James Wood, for the purpose of assisting him in his business, I hereby guarantee you against any loss by your so doing." The "security" referred to was a cautionary obligation, to the extent of £150, undertaken by S. to the bank in respect of Wood's cash-credit account with the bank. **8–77**

Wood operated on his account with the bank between 1853 and 1861. In the latter year the balance due to the bank was £151 17s.1d.

The bank obtained a decree against S. for £150, and S. brought an action of relief against M.

Held that M.'s letter of guarantee was to be construed as a guarantee against loss in respect of one advance of £150 and not as a continuing guarantee with reference to all advances on Wood's cash-credit account.

Lord Cowan said (at p. 553): "This letter has no reference to a cash-credit account such as the pursuer undertook. It refers to a single transaction, and by its terms the defender became security for £150. . . . It would be contrary to the principles on which such obligations are to be construed, to enlarge the scope of the obligation undertaken beyond what its terms fairly import."

M.'s obligation had terminated at the time when Wood, in operating on the account, paid into it sufficient to wipe out the original debit of £150.

There was no doubt that S.'s obligation to the bank in respect of Wood's cash-credit account was a continuing guarantee.

It is natural that a cautionary obligation attached to a current account with a bank should be of a continuing nature and not restricted to a single advance only. There was held to be such a continuing obligation in *Caledonian Banking Co. v. Kennedy's Trustees* (1870) 8 M. 862, although the ultimate decision in the case was that the cautioner had been liberated by transactions between the creditor and the principal debtor, such as the giving of time to the principal debtor. Lord Justice-Clerk Moncreiff made the following observations concerning continuing guarantees (at p. 867): **8–78**

"I am of opinion that there is no presumption either way in regard to the construction of the document, but that it must be fairly construed according to its terms, read in the light of the subject-matter of it, and of the surrounding circumstances. . . . The question is, whether, so read, the granter meant to bind himself for one advance, or for the balance of continuous transactions. I do not think much assistance is to be derived from precedent on this matter, as each case must be judged of by the words used, and the circumstances in which they were used."

8–79 A cautioner in a continuing guarantee may withdraw his undertaking as regards future transactions by giving notice to the creditor; in practice the length of notice required would be specified in the guarantee.

VI RIGHTS OF CAUTIONERS

8–80 The rights or privileges of cautioners fall under these headings:

(a) *beneficium ordinis* ("benefit of discussion");
(b) *beneficium divisionis* ("benefit of division");
(c) right of relief against principal debtor;
(d) right of relief against co-cautioners;
(e) *beneficium cedendarum actionum* ("benefit of having rights of action assigned"); and
(f) right to share in securities held by co-cautioners.

8–81 These rights may be varied or waived by agreement of the parties concerned. For instance, as regards (c), there could be an agreement between cautioner and principal debtor that the cautioner would have no right of relief against the principal debtor unless the principal debtor's financial circumstances allowed it (*Williamson v. Foulds*, 1927 S.N. 164 (O.H.)), and, as regards (f), there may be an agreement amongst co-cautioners that one of their number is to have the sole benefit of a security which he has obtained over the principal debtor's estate (*Hamilton & Co. v. Freeth* (1889) 16 R. 1022), while the ultimate loss clause in *Harvie's Trustees v. Bank of Scotland* (8–72, above), by which the cautioner agreed that he was not to be entitled to demand an assignation from the creditor, involved a surrender of right (e).

8–82 Rights (a) and (b) arise only in proper cautionry. The other rights arise in both proper and improper cautionry.

(a) Beneficium Ordinis ("Benefit of Discussion")

"Discuss" in this context means "sue" or "bring a legal action against". **8–83**

The common law relating to this right was altered by section 8 of the Mercantile Law Amendment Act Scotland 1856. **8–84**

At common law the cautioner in proper cautionry was entitled to insist that the creditor should first discuss and do diligence against the principal debtor before calling upon the cautioner. **8–85**

The Act made it competent for the creditor to proceed against both the principal debtor and the cautioner or against either of them for payment of the debt covered by the cautionary obligation, except where the cautioner had stipulated in the document containing the cautionary obligation that the creditor was to be bound, before proceeding against him, to discuss and do diligence against the principal debtor. **8–86**

The Act refers only to cautionary obligations for the payment of a debt. It would appear therefore that where the principal debtor's obligation is *ad factum praestandum* ("for the performance of an act"), the common law would still apply, the result being that the cautioner would be liable only when the creditor had failed to recover from the principal debtor the full amount of damages. **8–87**

The benefit of discussion has never existed in improper cautionry. **8–88**

(b) Beneficium Divisionis ("Benefit of Division")

Where, in proper cautionry, there are two or more cautioners, each cautioner is liable to the creditor only for his *pro rata* ("proportionate") share. **8–89**

If any cautioner is insolvent, then each solvent co-cautioner is liable *pro rata* ("proportionately") for the insolvent's share. **8–90**

In improper cautionry, on the other hand, the creditor is entitled to hold any one co-cautioner liable *in solidum* ("for the whole debt"). **8–91**

(c) Right of Relief against Principal Debtor

A cautioner who has had to pay to the creditor is entitled to recover what he has paid from the principal debtor. **8–92**

8–93 The law protects this right of relief in two ways:

(i) The cautioner is treated as having an implied mandate to pay the principal debt. As soon, therefore, as any sum has become due by the principal debtor to the creditor, the cautioner is entitled to pay the sum, so terminating his own liability, and then sue the principal debtor for the amount paid.

The principal debtor's obligation to repay the cautioner becomes enforceable at the date when payment is made by the cautioner. The right of relief is therefore not lost through prescription, provided the cautioner's payment is made within the five years immediately before the raising of the cautioner's action for relief against the principal debtor:

Smithy's Place Ltd v. Blackadder & McMonagle, 1991 S.L.T. 790 (O.H.): S. Ltd purchased a public house business in Stirling intending to finance the purchase by means of a loan from a brewery company which was to become available once a recorded lease of the premises had been completed. On the advice of solicitors, B. & M., S. Ltd took entry to the premises before the loan was available and, since the sellers required immediate payment of the purchase price, it became necessary for S. Ltd to obtain bridging finance from the Bank of Scotland. This took the form of a loan from the Bank of Scotland to S. Ltd of £40,000 with interest. The two directors of S. Ltd, Mr Kilmartin and Mr Smith, were required to become cautioners for the loan and interest.

By September 1983 the lease had still not been completed and the proposed loan from the brewery company was not forthcoming. The bank withdrew the bridging finance and called on S. Ltd to pay the balance outstanding of over £48,000. S. Ltd had no funds available and in November 1983 the bank raised an action against Mr Smith.

From March 1986 until August 1989 Mr Smith made payments to the bank under the guarantee and in December 1989 he raised an action against S. Ltd claiming by way of relief about £80,000.

S. Ltd then raised an action against B. & M. for damages for their failure to have the lease completed and among the items of loss claimed was S. Ltd's obligation to grant relief to Mr Smith.

B. & M. contended that S. Ltd's obligation had prescribed five years after the bank had raised its action against Mr Smith.

Held (by Lord Cameron of Lochbroom) that a principal debtor's obligation to repay a cautioner became enforceable only when payment was made by the cautioner and that, in this case, as all payments had been made within the period of five years before the raising of the action for relief, the obligation on S. Ltd to relieve Mr Smith had not prescribed.

(ii) If the principal debtor is *vergens ad inopiam* ("tending towards insolvency"), the cautioner may take steps to secure his right of relief, even although the time for payment of the debt has not arrived; *e.g.* he may attach goods belonging to the principal debtor or retain funds belonging to him.

In proper cautionry there may be, in the document which expressly binds the cautioner as cautioner, a clause by which the principal debtor expressly undertakes to relieve the cautioner, but this is not essential, since the right of relief is implied by the express constitution of the cautionary obligation. **8–94**

In improper cautionry the cautioner claiming his right of relief must be able to establish that he is in fact a cautioner, though expressly bound to the creditor as a co-obligant with the principal debtor. Parole evidence is permissible to prove the true relationship. **8–95**

(d) Right of Relief against Co-Cautioners

Where there are several cautioners, each is liable, in a question with his co-cautioners, only for his *pro rata* ("proportionate") share, although his liability in a question with the creditor may be *in solidum* ("for the whole debt"). Any cautioner, therefore, who has paid more than his *pro rata* share is entitled to relief from his co-cautioners to the extent of the excess: **8–96**

Marshall & Co. v. Pennycook, 1908 S.C. 276: McDonald entered into a contract to construct water-works for Selkirk Town Council. M. and P. were bound jointly and severally as cautioners for the due performance of the contract.

McDonald became unable to continue the contract, and M., who himself owned a building and contracting business, after consulting P. and with the consent of the town council, completed the contract. In doing so M. sustained loss.

Held that P. was bound to pay to M. one-half of the loss sustained by M., including one-half of the fee of £75 claimed by M. for having personally superintended the work.

Similarly in *Henderson v. Skinner*, 1990 S.L.T. (Sh.Ct.) 24, where H. and S. were two co-cautioners for a bank loan and H.'s payments to the bank exceeded one-half of the debt by £1,390, H. was entitled to relief against S. for that amount.

Sheriff Principal R. D. Ireland held in that case that the obligation of relief did not depend on agreement but arose *ex lege* ("by law") from the parties' relationship as co-cautioners and applied *pro rata* ("proportionately") in the absence of provision to the contrary.

8–97 In calculating the amount of relief due, any co-cautioner who is insolvent is not counted:

Buchanan v. Main (1900) 3 F. 215: In 1894 by a letter of guarantee Buchanan, Brown, Main and two other persons, all directors of a certain limited company, jointly and severally guaranteed to the Bank of Scotland payment of all sums up to a maximum of £12,500 for which the company might become liable to the bank.

In 1896 Main, who had resigned his office of director, intimated to the bank that he withdrew from the guarantee. The bank thereupon closed the company's current account which was overdrawn. The company then went into liquidation.

Buchanan and Brown paid £4,306 17s. 11d. to the bank under the guarantee, and then brought an action against Main for relief to the extent of one-third, *i.e.* £1,435 12s. 8d. They led evidence to prove that the two other guarantors were insolvent. Main denied that the insolvency of either of the two other guarantors had been proved, and pleaded that he was liable in relief to the extent of only one-fifth of the sum paid by the pursuers.

Held that, whether the two other guarantors were insolvent or not, the pursuers were not bound to bear the whole risk of their insolvency, and that therefore Main was liable in relief to the extent of one-third of the sum paid by the pursuers.

Lord Trayner said (at p. 221): "There were five guarantors all jointly and severally liable. Two of these guarantors, as the pursuers say, and, as I think, have fairly established, are insolvent, in which case the defender must bear with the pursuers the whole claim under the guarantee. But whether the other two guarantors are insolvent or not, I think the same result follows. The pursuers are no more liable than the defender; he must therefore share their burden, with the same rights and the same risk as the pursuers of obtaining relief from the other two guarantors of the amount due by them."

This right of relief does not apply where each of the co-cautioners is bound for a specific part only of the whole debt, as in *Morgan v. Smart* (1872) 10 M. 610 (see 8–148, below). 8–98

(e) **Beneficium Cedendarum Actionum (Right to Assignation)**

A cautioner who has paid the creditor is entitled to obtain from the creditor an assignation of the debt, of any security held for it, and of any diligence done on it, so that he may be in a position to enforce his right of relief against the principal debtor or against co-cautioners. 8–99

This right exists only where the cautioner has made *full* payment: it does not belong to a cautioner who is himself bankrupt, and able to pay only a dividend on the debt: 8–100

Ewart v. Latta (1865) 3 M. (H.L.) 36: Christie, a cautioner, became bankrupt, and L., the trustee in his sequestration, declared a dividend of 7s. 6d. in the £ on Christie's estate. The principal debtor was also bankrupt.

E., the creditor in the cautionary obligation, lodged a claim in Christie's sequestration, and L. required that E., before drawing his dividend, should execute in favour of L. an assignation of securities held by him.

Held (reversing the judgment of the Court of Session) that (i) the cautioner was not entitled, without making full payment, to demand from the creditor an assignation of securities held by the creditor, and (ii) payment of a dividend by the trustee in the cautioner's sequestration was not full payment for that purpose.

The rule as to assignation of securities applies to securities over the principal debtor's estate, not to securities granted to the creditor by a third party: 8–101

Thow's Trustee v. Young, 1910 S.C. 588: Y., M., and T., in security for advances to be made to Y., granted a cash-credit bond to a bank, in which they bound themselves conjunctly and severally to repay to the bank the sums advanced on Y.'s current account.

The bond also contained an assignation in security to the bank by Y. and his brother and three sisters of their interest in the grandfather's trust estate.

Y. received advances and was unable to repay them. The bank called upon M. and T. to pay under the bond. M. was bankrupt, and T. paid the full amount due, receiving from the bank an assignation of its rights against Y. and M., and also of the interest in the grandfather's trust estate.

Some years later, T. died, and his representative claimed relief out of the grandfather's trust estate.

Held that, on a sound construction of the bond, Y.'s brother and sisters were not co-cautioners with T., but had merely conveyed their interest in the trust estate in security of the obligation undertaken by Y., M. and T. to the bank, and that T. was not entitled to relief out of that interest in the trust estate but only out of Y.'s own interest (one-fifth). The mere fact that T. had obtained an assignation of the whole security from the creditor could not alter the substantial rights of the parties.

Lord President Dunedin said (at p. 596): "Nor can Mr Thow's trustee crave in aid the doctrine known as the *beneficium cedendarum actionum*, which, if amplified, means not only the assigning of the right to sue, but also the giving over of any security held by the creditor. Here again I examined the cases and I find that 'security' always means security over the estate of the debtor."

(f) Right to Share in Securities held by Co-Cautioners

8–102 A cautioner is entitled to share in the benefit of any securities granted to any of his co-cautioners over the principal debtor's estate.

8–103 The right does not extend to securities granted to one co-cautioner by a third party:

Scott v. Young, 1909 1 S.L.T. 47 (O.H.): S. and Y. were co-cautioners for M.'s cash credit account with the Bank of Scotland. M. failed to pay interest on the account, and S. and Y. were compelled to make equal payments to the bank.

Later it came to S.'s knowledge that Y. had had an assignation granted to him by M.'s wife of her interest in her father's estate.

Held that S. was not entitled to have one-half of the benefit of that security made over to him by Y.

8–104 According to the decision in *Hamilton & Co. v. Freeth* (1889) 16 R. 1022, it is competent for a cautioner to prove by parole evidence that his co-cautioners have orally agreed that, contrary to the general rule, he has the exclusive benefit of a security obtained from the principal debtor.

VII TERMINATION OF CAUTIONARY OBLIGATIONS

The ways in which a cautionary obligation may be terminated may be considered under two headings: 8–105

(a) termination resulting from extinction of the principal obligation; and

(b) other modes of termination.

(a) Termination Resulting from Extinction of Principal Obligation

Since cautionry is an accessory obligation, it is terminated if the principal obligation is extinguished. The ways in which the principal obligation may be extinguished include: 8–106

(i) discharge;
(ii) novation;
(iii) compensation;
(iv) operation of the rule in *Clayton's Case*; and
(v) prescription.

(i) *Discharge*

The general rule is that if the principal debtor is discharged by the creditor without the cautioner's consent, the cautioner's liability is at an end. There is an exception to this in section 60(1) of the Bankruptcy (Scotland) Act 1985: if the creditor draws a dividend in the sequestration of the principal debtor or assents to the discharge of the bankrupt principal debtor, this does not free the cautioner from his liability. 8–107

There is an illustration of the general rule in *Aitken's Trustees v. Bank of Scotland*, 1944 S.C. 270: 8–108

A father entered into a guarantee, limited to £500, of his son's bank overdraft. The guarantee, which was on a printed form supplied by the bank, authorised the bank to grant the son "any time or other indulgence", and to "compound" with him without discharging the father's liability. At the bank's request, the father lodged the £500 with the bank.

Later the bank brought an action against the son for the whole sum due under the overdraft—about £2,000. The son arranged with another bank to take over the overdraft. About £1,500 was paid to the first bank, which then consented to an unqualified decree of absolvitor being pronounced in its action against the son. The father's consent was not asked.

The first bank then applied the father's £500 to the balance of the overdraft, and the father brought an action against the bank for payment of the £500.

Held that (1) the guarantee had to be construed *contra proferentem* (see 8–65, above), (2) on that construction there had been no "compounding" with the son in the sense of the guarantee, and (3) by its unqualified discharge of the son, the bank had simultaneously extinguished the liability of his father as cautioner.

8–109 A discharge must be distinguished from a *pactum de non petendo* ("agreement not to sue"). A discharge extinguishes the principal obligation and frees the cautioner from liability, whereas in a *pactum de non petendo* the creditor gives up his right to sue the principal debtor but reserves his claim against the cautioner. Such an agreement does not deprive the cautioner of his right of relief against the principal debtor. The cautioner, therefore, if he is required to pay to the creditor, may demand from the creditor an assignation of the debt and may then sue the principal debtor to recover what he has paid. There is an instance of a *pactum de non petendo* in *Muir v. Crawford* (1875) 2 R. (H.L.) 148 (affirming *Crawford v. Muir* (1873) 1 R. 91):

The Scottish Granite Co. Ltd accepted a bill of exchange payable to Cleland of London, by which the company undertook to pay £200 to Cleland on a specified date.

Cleland indorsed the bill to Holmes of London, Holmes indorsed it to Muir of Glasgow, and Muir indorsed it to Crawford of Edinburgh. The object of these indorsations was to give increased security to Crawford who agreed to discount the bill if Holmes and Muir indorsed it.

Crawford discounted the bill, paying the proceeds to Cleland.

The bill was dishonoured when it became due, and all the obligants on the bill were duly notified of the dishonour.

Crawford granted a discharge to the company, reserving his claims against the other obligants. He then sued Muir for the amount of the bill with interest from the date of dishonour.

Held that the discharge had not extinguished the debt, but was merely an agreement not to sue the acceptor, and that the indorser was liable to pay since his right of recourse against the acceptor had not been prejudiced.

Lord Chancellor Cairns said (at p. 149): "There is no doubt that by proper and apt instrument it is competent for the holder of a security of this kind to agree with the principal debtor not to enforce his remedies against the principal debtor; and, if he does that in an instrument, which at the same time reserves his rights against those who are liable in the second degree, there will be no discharge of those persons so liable. . . . If, on looking at the discharge, you find that there is nothing inconsistent in it with a proceeding by the surety afterwards against the principal debtor, then the surety is not in any way discharged."

(ii) *Novation*

The cautioner is liberated where there is novation of the principal debt, *i.e.* where the original principal debt is discharged and a new one substituted for it. **8–110**

(Assignation of the principal debt to a new creditor does not liberate the cautioner.)

(iii) *Compensation*

If the principal debt is extinguished by compensation, the cautioner is liberated. This would occur where the creditor sues the principal debtor and the latter successfully puts forward the defence that a debt due by the pursuer to the defender must be set off against the pursuer's claim. **8–111**

Compensation must, however, be pleaded in an action: a cautioner is not liberated merely because the principal debt might have been extinguished by the plea of compensation if an action had been brought. **8–112**

(iv) *Rule in* Clayton's Case

According to the rule in *Clayton's Case* (which was part of the English case *Devaynes v. Noble* (1816) 1 Mer. 529, 572; 35 E.R. 767, 781), where there is a continuous account such as a current account at a bank, payments into the account extinguish items on the debit side in order of date. If it happens that the cautioner's obligation in connection with such an account is terminated by his giving notice of withdrawal or by an event such as his sequestration, the guarantee crystallises at that point of time and any **8–113** subsequent payments into the account go towards reducing the amount for which the cautioner is liable. The cautioner's liability may thus ultimately disappear, even although the account continues to show as great a debit balance as it did at the time when the guarantee crystallised:

8–114 *Cuthill v. Strachan* (1894) 21 R. 549: Strachan, one of the cautioners for a cash-credit account with a bank, was sequestrated. The balance against the principal debtor, George Cuthill, was then £599. The bank made no claim in the sequestration, and the principal debtor continued to operate on the account until he granted a trust deed for creditors. The bank then closed the account, the balance due by George Cuthill being £615.

William Cuthill, another cautioner, paid £615 to the bank, and then made a claim of relief against Strachan, who had carried through a composition arrangement with his creditors.

In defence, Strachan maintained that the balance due to the bank at the date of his sequestration had been extinguished by subsequent payments by George Cuthill into the bank. The debit balance on the account from day to day had never been reduced below about £550.

Held that the payments into the account were to be appropriated according to the order of the debit items in the account, and that Strachan's cautionary obligation had therefore been extinguished.

8–115 In practice, the termination of a cautionary obligation by the operation of the rule in *Clayton's Case* is avoided by the closing of the principal debtor's existing account and the opening of a new account for him.

(v) *Prescription*

8–116 Where the principal debt has been allowed to prescribe, the cautioner is freed from liability (*e.g. Halyburtons v. Graham* (1735) Mor. 2073).

(b) **Other Modes of Termination**

8–117 A cautionary obligation may be extinguished, without extinction of the principal obligation, in any of the following ways:

(i) by discharge of the cautioner;
(ii) by revocation by the cautioner;

(iii) by death;
(iv) by change in a firm;
(v) by conduct of the creditor; or
(vi) by prescription.

(i) *Discharge of Cautioner*

If the cautioner is expressly discharged by the creditor, he is freed from liability. **8–118**

(ii) *Revocation by Cautioner*

A cautionary obligation may be limited as to time (see 8–75 *et seq.*, above). The cautioner's liability will then be at an end once the period of his guarantee has expired without fault on the part of the principal debtor. **8–119**

The question of revocation can arise if the cautioner wishes to withdraw *before* the fixed period of his guarantee has expired, and it can also arise where the guarantee is a *continuing* one. **8–120**

The rules which apply depend on whether the cautionary obligation is: **8–121**

1. a guarantee for payment of a debt; or
2. a fidelity guarantee.

The effect of revocation, where it is permissible at all, is, of course, to free the cautioner from liability only in respect of future transactions or misconduct: where liability has already been incurred, the cautioner must meet it.

1. **Guarantee for payment of debt**

If the guarantee is for a fixed period, the cautioner is not entitled to withdraw before the expiry of that period unless he "takes the debtor into his own hand", *i.e.* pays the debt to the creditor and himself becomes creditor. **8–122**

If, on the other hand, the guarantee is for an indefinite period, the cautioner is entitled at any time to give notice to the creditor that he will not be responsible for future transactions. **8–123**

In order to free himself from liability for past transactions, the cautioner may, on giving reasonable notice, require the principal debtor to relieve him of all liability already incurred. The principal debtor must then obtain from the creditor and deliver to the cautioner a discharge by the creditor of the cautioner's liability: **8–124**

Doig v. Lawrie (1903) 5 F. 295: In November 1898, by a letter of guarantee addressed to the Bank of Scotland, D. became cautioner for advances made or to be made, not exceeding £6,500, by the bank to L. The letter stated that the guarantee was to remain in force until recalled in writing.

In March 1901, D. intimated to L. that he desired his name to be removed from the guarantee. L., however, failed to make any arrangement with the bank for the release of D., and in August 1901 D. raised an action of relief against L.

Held that L., having been given reasonable notice, was bound to relieve D. of his liability by making payment to the bank of all sums due under the guarantee and obtaining from the bank and delivering to D. a discharge of D.'s liability.

2. **Fidelity guarantee**

8–125 The cautioner may revoke the guarantee for the future if the person whose trustworthiness is being guaranteed becomes guilty of misconduct. It is the duty of the employer to notify the cautioner timeously of the misconduct, and if he fails in this duty, he loses his right to hold the cautioner liable (*Snaddon v. London, Edinburgh and Glasgow Assurance Co. Ltd* (8–55, above)).

8–126 If the employment to which the fidelity guarantee relates is for a fixed period, the cautioner is not entitled to withdraw before the expiry of that period unless there is misconduct.

8–127 If the employment is for an indefinite period, the cautioner may revoke the guarantee for the future by giving reasonable notice of revocation to the creditor. The length of notice which will be considered reasonable depends on the circumstances including the length of notice required to terminate the contract of employment.

(iii) *Death*

8–128 The death of the principal debtor fixes the cautioner's liability: unless the contract of cautionry is to the contrary effect, the cautioner will not be liable for any debt not then due:

Woodfield Finance Trust (Glasgow) Ltd v. Morgan, 1958 S.L.T. (Sh.Ct.) 14: In August 1954 Peter Flaherty rented a television set from a finance company for 139 weeks at a weekly rental of 15s.6d. Two relatives, M. and Festus Flaherty, agreed in writing jointly and severally to guarantee payment of all sums due by Peter Flaherty.

In December 1954 Peter Flaherty died. The rent was then in arrear. Festus Flaherty had disappeared. The finance company sued M. for the arrears due at Peter Flaherty's death and for sums becoming due thereafter.

Held that M. was not liable for sums which had become due after Peter Flaherty's death.

Similarly, the death of the creditor causes the cautioner's obligation to cease to run. Accordingly, in a fidelity guarantee, the employer's death terminates the guarantee, even though the employee is kept on by the deceased's representatives. **8–129**

The death of the cautioner does not affect his existing liability: his estate will be liable to the same extent as the cautioner himself. Further, if the guarantee is a continuing guarantee, the cautioner's representatives will continue to become liable for debts incurred after the cautioner's death unless they withdraw the guarantee; it is not the duty of the creditor to inform them of the guarantee, and so they must be held liable even although they were not aware of the guarantee: **8–130**

British Linen Co. v. Monteith (1858) 20 D. 557: A Court of Session judge, Lord Fullerton, had a current account with a commercial bank. He was allowed a credit of £600 on the account under a cash-credit bond by which McDowall and Monteith, who were truly cautioners, were bound conjunctly and severally along with him.

McDowall died in 1840, Monteith in 1848, and Lord Fullerton in 1853.

In 1854 the bank raised an action against the representatives of McDowall and Monteith for payment, jointly and severally, of £600, which was composed of sums advanced to Lord Fullerton after Monteith's death. The bank did not notify McDowall's or Monteith's representatives of the existence of the bond.

Held that the representatives were liable under the bond.

Lord Deas said (at p. 562): "But it is said there is great hardship in holding representatives liable who may never have heard of the obligation. It may be so. But who is to blame for this? The granter of the obligation, who left no trace of it in his repositories? or the Bank officers, who may or may not have heard of his death? I think the duty lies on the debtor, who binds his representatives, to keep them informed that he has done so, rather than upon the creditor, who receives and relies upon the obligation."

8–131 However, a prudent creditor, on learning of the cautioner's death, would inform the representatives of the guarantee; otherwise he might find himself barred from enforcing the guarantee in court: *e.g.*, in *Caledonian Banking Co. v. Kennedy's Trustees* (1870) 8 M. 862, there were circumstances in which a cautioner's representatives were held to be liberated from the guarantee by transactions between the creditor and the principal debtor.

(iv) *Change in a Firm*

8–132 A cautionary obligation in which a firm is either the creditor or the principal debtor is, in the absence of agreement to the contrary, revoked as to future transactions by any change in the constitution of the firm (Partnership Act 1890, s. 18, re-enacting Mercantile Law Amendment Act Scotland 1856, s. 7, which itself substantially reproduced the common law).

8–133 The change in the constitution of the firm may be the introduction of a new partner or the retiral or death of an existing partner.

(v) *Conduct of Creditor*

8–134 Acts of the creditor which affect the cautioner's liability or his rights of relief terminate the cautionary obligation unless they are done with the cautioner's consent. Such acts are:

1. giving time to the principal debtor;
2. otherwise altering the principal contract;
3. releasing co-cautioners; and
4. giving up securities.

1. **Giving time to principal debtor**

8–135 "Giving time" has a technical meaning: it denotes some act by which the creditor deprives himself of the right to sue the principal debtor when the debt is due, *e.g.* where the creditor takes a bill of exchange payable at a future date in payment of a debt immediately due. By giving time the creditor is postponing the time at which the cautioner may exercise his right of relief against the principal debtor.

8–136 Mere delay on the creditor's part in enforcing payment against the principal debtor does not amount to "giving time": the cautioner is entitled in that case to settle with the creditor and then claim against the principal debtor.

There are instances of giving time in the two following cases: 8–137

(a) *Richardson v. Harvey* (1853) 15 D. 628: R., proprietor of an estate, let two farms to Baird. H., a friend of Baird, by letter guaranteed to R. "full and regular payment of the current year's rent of £373 5s., as it falls due at Martinmas and Whitsunday". 8–138

R., without H.'s knowledge, took two bills from Baird, the one in payment of a balance of the rent which had become due at Martinmas, and the other for the rent which was to become due at Whitsunday. The bills were not payable until dates later than the terms of Martinmas and Whitsunday respectively.

Baird became bankrupt before Whitsunday, and R. brought an action against H. for payment of the balance of the Martinmas rent and for the whole of the Whitsunday rent.

Held that R., by taking the bills from Baird, had freed H. of his cautionary obligation.

Lord President McNeill said (at p. 632): "The broad principle of the matter is, that when a person becomes cautioner for a debt payable at a given time, and especially when it is one with certain rights in the original creditor against the debtor, such as a landlord has against his tenant, if the creditor gives time without concurrence of the cautioner, that liberates the cautioner, because that amounts to an alteration of the contract."

(b) *C. & A. Johnstone v. Duthie* (1892) 19 R. 624: In March 1888 D., a retail grocer in Aberdeen, disposed of his business to Cormack, his brother-in-law, who had been his manager. In April, in order to start Cormack in business, D. granted a letter of guarantee to J., wholesale merchants in Aberdeen, undertaking to see J. duly paid for all goods to be supplied by J. to the order of Cormack. 8–139

J. supplied goods to Cormack until April 1890, when the account was closed.

In September 1890, when there was still a balance due to J. on the account, J., without D.'s knowledge, drew two bills on Cormack, payable at three months from their date, for the outstanding balance.

In November 1890, Cormack became bankrupt, and J. sued D. under the letter of guarantee for the balance.

Held that D. had been liberated by J.'s action in taking the bills.

Lord Adam said (at p. 628): "All transactions under the letter of guarantee came to an end in April 1890.

"The account was closed, and the amount alleged to be due by the defender was then ascertained. . . .

" . . . [*The pursuers*] could not have sued Cormack, the principal debtor, during the currency of these bills, and so they gave him time. . . .

" . . . It is quite settled law that if the creditor gives time to the principal debtor the cautioner is free. Neither is it necessary for the cautioner to shew that he has been thereby *de facto*[5] prejudiced."

8–140 A distinction is made between a cautionary obligation which guarantees a specific transaction and one which is continuing or "general", *i.e.* relates to a course of dealing. In the case of the latter it is less likely that the cautioner will be liberated by arrangements between the creditor and the principal debtor for postponing payment: in particular, the allowance of a period of credit which is in accordance with usage of trade will not free the cautioner:

Stewart, Moir and Muir v. Brown (1871) 9 M. 763: B., a grocer in Glasgow, granted a letter of guarantee to S., muslin manufacturers there, becoming security for goods supplied by S. to Ramsay & Co. of Glasgow.

S. took a bill payable one month after its date from Ramsay & Co. in payment of an account for goods supplied, and later brought an action against B. under the letter of guarantee.

Held that B. had not been liberated, because the taking of the bill had not been at variance with the ordinary custom of merchants.

Drawing the distinction between a cautionary obligation attached to a specific transaction and one attached to a course of dealing, Lord Justice-Clerk Moncreiff said of the latter (at p. 766):

"The cautioner, if there be nothing to the contrary expressed in his obligation, is not presumed to grant it on the faith of any specific conditions, but rather to have contemplated the general usage of trade, and the ordinary credit given among merchants. Where one guarantees all goods which may be furnished to a trader, or all bills which may be discounted by a banker, as a cautioner, he necessarily, by the generality of the obligation, leaves the principal debtor and creditor free to arrange the details of their

[5] "in fact".

transactions as they think fit, provided these are not at variance with the ordinary custom of merchants. This is the principle of a general guarantee, and it has been frequently applied."

Similarly, in *Calder & Co. v. Cruikshank's Trustee* (1889) 17 R. 8–141
74, Cruikshank, whose guarantee related to whisky supplied by distillers to McLaren & Co. over a period of years, was held not to have been liberated by bills taken, without his consent, by the distillers from McLaren & Co. and payable five months after their date.

Lord President Inglis said (at p. 80): "There is a broad distinction taken in all the cases between the guarantee of a particular debt of a certain amount, to be paid at a certain time, and a general guarantee for the price of goods sold or for money advanced or the like.

"In the former case if a creditor innovates or alters the relation of debtor and creditor in any essential point, he liberates the cautioner. In the latter case that result by no means follows. Many general guarantees are intended to extend far beyond the guarantee of a particular debt. This case seems to me to belong to the latter category."

Giving time must be distinguished from a *pactum de non petendo* 8–142
("agreement not to sue"), which preserves the cautioner's right of relief against the principal debtor and therefore does not terminate the cautionary obligation (see 8–109, above).

2. **Otherwise altering the principal contract**

Alteration of the contract between the creditor and the principal 8–143
debtor may adversely affect the cautioner's position, and so, if done without the cautioner's consent, may terminate the cautionary obligation. Giving time is one instance of such an alteration. Another is where the principal debtor materially increases his liability, *e.g.*:

N. G. Napier Ltd v. Crosbie, 1964 S.C. 129: Mrs C., a domestic 8–144
help, entered into a personal credit agreement with N. Ltd, by which, for the purpose of purchasing a television set, she was granted credit facilities up to £200 and undertook to make weekly payments of 17s.6d. to N. Ltd. In security of this contract, N. Ltd entered into a contract of guarantee with Reid.

Shortly afterwards, Mrs C. agreed with N. Ltd to increase her weekly payments to 20s. Reid was not informed of this change.

Held that the increase in the weekly payments was in the circumstances a material alteration of the principal contract, and that since it had been made without the knowledge of the cautioner, he was discharged from the guarantee.

8–145 Similarly, in a fidelity guarantee the cautioner is released if the creditor fails to make the checks on the employee's conduct which were stipulated for in the contract of employment and relied on by the cautioner. An instance is:

Haworth & Co. v. Sickness and Accident Assurance Association Ltd (1891) 18 R. 563: Slater was employed by H. & Co., tea-merchants, as a traveller. An assurance company undertook, in return for payment of a premium, to guarantee H. & Co. against loss by embezzlement on the part of Slater. The assurance company had been informed that there were to be monthly settlements between H. & Co. and Slater, and that, as a check on the accuracy of Slater's accounts, statements were to be sent by H. & Co. direct to customers every three months.

Slater was guilty of embezzlement, and H. & Co. sued the assurance company for £87. It was proved that there had not been monthly settlements between H. & Co. and Slater and that the three-monthly statements for customers had been sent through Slater and not direct to the customers.

Held that as the employer had failed to comply with specified precautions, the assurance company was not liable.

8–146 Where the employee's duties are materially altered, the cautioner is released unless he has been informed of the alteration and has agreed to continue as cautioner:

Bonar v. McDonald (1850) 7 Bell's App. 379; (1847) 9 D. 1537: Bird was appointed teller in the Edinburgh and Leith Bank in 1839, and McD., T. and B. were cautioners for his faithful performance of the duties of teller.

A few months later, Bird was appointed manager of a branch of the bank at Dalkeith, and the cautioners were informed of this and consented to continue as cautioners.

In April 1840, however, an alteration was made in the terms of Bird's appointment: he was to be liable for one-fourth of the losses arising from discounts to customers, and, to reflect this additional possible liability, his salary was to be increased to what was then a large figure (£130 per annum). The cautioners were not informed of this alteration.

A year later Bird was dismissed for various banking irregularities committed by him, especially in connection with a customer Moffat, who became bankrupt.

Bonar, the manager of the bank, brought an action against Bird and his cautioners for the losses incurred by the bank in its business with Moffat.

Held that, although these losses were unconnected with the alteration of April 1840 in Bird's terms of appointment, the cautioners were not liable, since they had not consented to that material alteration.

Lord Mackenzie said (at 9 D. p. 1551): "A person . . . asked to be cautioner for a bank agent might most naturally and reasonably say, 'I am willing to be cautioner for A B if he is to be a mere salaried agent; but if he is to run the risk of loss by discounts, I will have nothing to do with it.' If that be true, however, then on that ground a bank cannot have right to change a cautionry of the one kind into a cautionry of the other, without the consent of the cautioner."

The legal position is different if the fidelity guarantee is separate **8–147**
from the contract of employment and the cautioner is unaware of the terms of that contract: *e.g.* in *Nicolsons v. Burt* (1882) 10 R. 121, a cautioner who had in such circumstances bound himself in general words "for the due and punctual payment of all sums of money collected by" a traveller was held not to have been liberated by the renewal of the traveller's employment for a second period of three years on the expiry of the first three years.

3. **Releasing co-cautioners**

Section 9 of the Mercantile Law Amendment Act Scotland 1856 **8–148**
provides that where there are co-cautioners, a discharge granted by the creditor to any one cautioner without the consent of the other cautioners is to be deemed to be a discharge granted to all the cautioners, unless the cautioner being discharged by the creditor is bankrupt. This applies only where the co-cautioners are bound jointly and severally, each being liable for payment of the full debt: it does not apply where each is bound for a separate sum as in *Morgan v. Smart* (1872) 10 M. 610:

M., an Edinburgh grocer, agreed to sell his stock-in-trade to McDonald provided McDonald found security to the extent of £105.

Two letters of guarantee were handed to M. By one of these Banks became a cautioner for £70, and by the other S. became a cautioner for £35.

Held that the discharge by M. of Banks did not affect the liability of S. for his proportion of the debt.

4. **Giving up securities**

8–149 A cautioner is entitled, on paying the debt, to an assignation of securities held by the creditor (see 8–99 *et seq.*, above); his position is therefore prejudiced if the creditor voluntarily gives up securities. The cautioner is released from his obligation only to the extent of the value of the security which has been given up.

8–150 The same result follows where the creditor fails to take the steps necessary to make his security effectual, *e.g.* fails to record a heritable security in the Register of Sasines.

(vi) *Prescription*

8–151 Formerly the Cautioners Act 1695 provided for the extinction of certain cautionary obligations on the lapse of seven years from the date when they were undertaken. This septennial prescription was abolished, with effect from July 25, 1976, by the Prescription and Limitation (Scotland) Act 1973.

8–152 Under section 6 of the Act of 1973 any cautionary obligation is extinguished on the lapse of five years after "the appropriate date" provided no relevant claim and no acknowledgment of its existence has been made during the five years.

8–153 Difficult questions can arise concerning the date from which the prescriptive period is to run. "The appropriate date" in relation to certain kinds of obligations is specified in Schedule 2 to the Act and in relation to all other kinds of obligation it is the date when the obligation became "enforceable" (1973 Act, s. 6).

8–154 The interpretation of these statutory provisions came before the Inner House of the Court of Session in *Royal Bank of Scotland Ltd v. Brown*, 1982 S.C. 89, and in two Outer House cases—*City of Glasgow District Council v. Excess Insurance Co. Ltd*, 1986 S.L.T. 585 (O.H.), and *City of Glasgow District Council v. Excess Insurance Co. Ltd (No. 2)*, 1990 S.L.T. 225 (O.H.):

8–155 *Royal Bank of Scotland Ltd v. Brown*: On May 23, 1979, a bank raised an action against cautioners who had guaranteed a loan by the bank to a company. The cautioners contended that their obligation had been extinguished under the Act of 1973, since "the appropriate date" was at latest September 1, 1969, when the bank had made a claim in the liquidation of the company.

The bank, on the other hand, maintained that prescription did not start to run until May 27, 1974—the date on which the bank had by letter demanded payment under the guarantee.

Held that (1) "the appropriate date" in relation to cautionary obligations was not to be found in Schedule 2 to the Act: cautionary obligations were neither expressly mentioned in that Schedule nor could they be covered by the category "any obligation to repay the whole, or any part of, a sum of money lent to . . . the debtor under a contract of loan", since "debtor" in that context denoted a principal debtor; and (2) because the guarantee required the cautioner to make full and final payment "on demand" of all sums due to the bank by the company, the cautionary obligation did not become "enforceable" until the date of the demand, *i.e.* May 27, 1974.

The case shows that it is vitally important for banks to ensure that their guarantee forms are so worded as to make a demand for payment a condition precedent to the enforcing of the guarantee.

City of Glasgow District Council v. Excess Insurance Co. Ltd and **8–156** *City of Glasgow District Council v. Excess Insurance Co. Ltd (No. 2)*: Glasgow District Council had engaged a contractor to carry out renovation work on 590 houses at Barrowfield, Glasgow.

In July 1976 a receiver was appointed on the contractor's undertaking, with the result that the building contract was automatically terminated.

In November 1976 the contractor and E. Ltd, an insurance company, granted a performance bond by which they undertook jointly and severally to pay up to £308,748 to the District Council as damages for any default by the contractor.

A second contractor was engaged to complete the work.

In February 1986 the District Council's architect certified the direct loss and damage caused to the District Council as £397,409. The contractor was called upon to make payment of that amount to the District Council but failed to do so.

The District Council therefore claimed £308,748 from E. Ltd, but this action was not raised until June 1986 and the question was whether E. Ltd's obligation had prescribed.

In the first action the District Council conceded that default had occurred in July 1976, when the receiver was appointed. The performance bond was held to be a cautionary obligation, and as more than five years had elapsed since it had become "enforceable", it had prescribed and the action was *dismissed*.

In the second action, it was stated at the hearing that the concession that default had occurred in July 1976 had been wrongly made, and it was submitted that the contractor was not in default until he failed to pay on the architect's certificate issued in February 1986: it was not until that time that the debt had been constituted.

Held that E. Ltd was in the same position as the contractor—not liable to pay until the issue of the architect's certificate—and so the obligation had not prescribed. The result was that the District Council's action for the amount guaranteed (£308,748) was successful.

Further Reading

Gloag and Henderson, *The Law of Scotland*, Chapter 20

David M. Walker, *Principles of Scottish Private Law*, Volume II, Chapter 4.21

W. A. Wilson, *The Scottish Law of Debt*, Chapter 10

The Laws of Scotland: Stair Memorial Encyclopaedia, Volume 3, Title *Cautionary Obligations and Representations as to Credit* by Alistair M. Clark and Sandra M. Eden

Gloag and Irvine, *Law of Rights in Security, Heritable and Moveable, including Cautionary Obligations*, Chapters I and XIX–XXV

Chapter 9

BANKRUPTCY

	Para.
Introduction	9–01
I Insolvency	9–12
(a) Reduction of Gratuitous Alienations	9–17
(i) At Common Law	9–18
(ii) Under Section 34 of the Bankruptcy (Scotland) Act 1985	9–27
(b) Reduction of Fraudulent or Unfair Preferences	9–39
(i) At Common Law	9–42
(1) Payments in cash	9–52
(2) Transactions in the ordinary course of business	9–54
(3) *Nova debita*	9–56
(ii) Under Section 36 of the Bankruptcy (Scotland) Act 1985	9–59
II Sequestration	9–68
(a) Administration of Bankruptcy	9–76
(i) The Accountant in Bankruptcy	9–77
(ii) The Interim Trustee	9–87
(iii) The Permanent Trustee	9–96
(iv) The Commissioners	9–101
(b) Petitions for Sequestration	9–102
(i) Living or Deceased Debtors	9–103
(ii) Other Estates	9–115
(iii) Meaning of "Apparent Insolvency"	9–118
(iv) Jurisdiction	9–119
(v) Concurrent Proceedings	9–121
(vi) Creditor's Oath	9–125
(c) Award of Sequestration	9–126
(i) The Making of the Award	9–127
(ii) "The Date of Sequestration"	9–141
(iii) The Procedure Following the Making of the Award	9–143
(iv) Recall of the Award	9–150
Who may petition for recall?	9–152
Procedure for recall	9–153
Grounds of recall	9–157
Expenses on a recall	9–161
Effect of recall	9–163
(d) Period between Award and Discharge of Interim Trustee	9–164
(i) Removal and Resignation of Interim Trustee	9–167
(ii) Interim Preservation of the Estate	9–172
(iii) Statement of Assets and Liabilities	9–179
(iv) Interim Trustee's Statement and Comments	9–183
(v) Calling of Statutory Meeting	9–188
(vi) Claims for Voting at Statutory Meeting	9–200
(vii) Proceedings at Statutory Meeting	9–203
(viii) Confirmation of Permanent Trustee	9–216
(ix) Discharge of Interim Trustee	9–221
(1) Where the Accountant in Bankruptcy is not the interim trustee	9–222
(2) Where the Accountant in Bankruptcy is the interim trustee	9–230
(e) Conduct of Sequestration by Permanent Trustee	9–235
(i) Replacement of Permanent Trustee	9–235
(ii) Vesting of Estate in Permanent Trustee	9–250
(1) Vesting of estate at date of sequestration	9–252
(2) Vesting after sequestration	9–258
Income	9–260
Acquirenda	9–267
(3) Dealings of debtor after sequestration	9–270
(4) Limitations on vesting	9–272
(iii) Safeguarding of Interests of Creditors	9–278
(1) Gratuitous alienations	9–279
(2) Unfair preferences	9–280
(3) Recalling of order for payment of capital sum on divorce	9–281
(4) Recovery of excessive pension contributions	9–283
(5) Extortionate credit transactions	9–287

	Para.
(iv) Effect of Sequestration on Diligence	9–290
(v) Administration of Estate by Permanent Trustee . .	9–294
(1) Taking possession of estate	9–295
(2) Management and realisation of estate	9–298
(3) Power in relation to debtor's "family home"	9–304
(4) Protection of rights of spouse in "matrimonial home" . . .	9–311
(5) Contractual powers of permanent trustee	9–312
(6) Money received by permanent trustee . .	9–313
(vi) Examination of Debtor .	9–316
(1) Private examination	9–318
(2) Public examination .	9–320
(3) Provisions applicable to both private and public examination .	9–323
(vii) Claims, Distribution and Dividends	9–330
Submission of claims to permanent trustee . . .	9–330
Order of priority in distribution	9–338
Making payments for accounting periods . . .	9–343
Procedure after end of accounting period	9–349
(viii) Discharge of Debtor . . .	9–357
(1) Automatic discharge after three years . . .	9–358
(2) Discharge on composition	9–370
(ix) Discharge of Permanent Trustee	9–379
(1) Where the Accountant in Bankruptcy is not the permanent trustee	9–380
(2) Where the Accountant in Bankruptcy is the permanent trustee	9–384
Unclaimed dividends . .	9–389
(f) Miscellaneous and Supplementary	9–392
(i) Power to Cure Defects in Procedure	9–393
(ii) Arbitration and Compromise	9–405
(iii) Meetings of Creditors and Commissioners	9–407
Meetings of creditors other than the statutory meeting	9–408
All meetings of creditors	9–412
Meetings of commissioners	9–420
(iv) Supplies by Utilities . . .	9–423
(v) The Modified Sequestration Procedure	9–426
Cases to which the Schedule 2 procedure is applicable	9–429
The modifications . . .	9–431
(vi) Summary Administration	9–438
Cases to which the Schedule 2A procedure is applicable	9–443
The modifications . . .	9–444
III Extra-Judicial Settlements	9–449
(a) Private Trust Deed for Creditors	9–450
(i) Trust Deeds Generally . .	9–453
(ii) The Special Features of the Protected Trust Deed . . .	9–471
(b) Extra-Judicial Composition Contract	9–478

INTRODUCTION

9–01 THE term "bankruptcy" has itself no precise technical meaning. It may denote one of three things:

(a) insolvency, *i.e.* a person's inability to pay his debts;

(b) "apparent insolvency," a term with a statutory definition denoting the stage where one of the steps listed in section 7 of the Bankruptcy (Scotland) Act 1985 has been taken; amongst the steps listed are sequestration, granting a trust deed for creditors and failure to pay a duly executed charge for payment of a debt; the general effect is that "apparent insolvency" exists where a person's insolvency has become a matter of public knowledge; or

(c) sequestration, a court process by which the insolvent person's assets are gathered in and sold, the net proceeds (after payment of administration expenses) being then divided, as far as they will go, amongst the creditors, according to their various priorities, in payment or part-payment of the debts due to them.

The principal Act relating to the Scots law of bankruptcy is the Bankruptcy (Scotland) Act 1985, and in this chapter references to sections are to sections of that Act unless the context indicates otherwise. **9–02**

The operation of the Act of 1985 produced some unexpected results, which gave rise to a demand for reform: it had not been foreseen that the payment of public funds for the outlays and remuneration of the trustees in the cases commonly referred to as "small assets" cases (*i.e.* cases where the debtor's assets were unlikely to be sufficient to pay a dividend) would prove so popular; before April 1985 there were under 300 sequestrations a year, but each year thereafter there was a substantial increase until in 1991–92 there were 8,584, about 80 per cent of which were small assets cases; the result was a huge increase in government expenditure to £19.7 million in 1991–92 with an estimate that the expenditure would increase to £50 million by 1993–94 and to over £80 million by 1994–95. The Bankruptcy (Scotland) Act 1993 (referred to in this chapter as "the Act of 1993") was primarily aimed at controlling the public expenditure involved in the system introduced by the Act of 1985. **9–03**

The Acts are supplemented by the Bankruptcy (Scotland) Regulations 1985 (S.I. 1985 No. 1925), the Bankruptcy (Scotland) Amendment Regulations 1993 (S.I. 1993 No. 439) and the Bankruptcy Fees (Scotland) Regulations 1993 (S.I. 1993 No. 486), and references in this chapter to forms and fees prescribed by the Secretary of State are to forms and fees listed in the Schedules to these Regulations. Certain other forms are "prescribed by the Court of Session by Act of Sederunt"; these are set out in the Appendices to the Act of Sederunt (Sheriff Court Bankruptcy Rules) 1996 (S.I. 1996 No. 2507) and in other Acts of Sederunt. **9–04**

Earlier statutes on bankruptcy include two Scots Acts—the Bankruptcy Act 1621 (c. 18), which facilitated the challenge of certain "gratuitous alienations" (gifts) made by an insolvent person, and the Bankruptcy Act 1696 (c. 5), which facilitated the challenge of "fraudulent preferences" (voluntary transactions favouring individual creditors) made by a person who was "notour **9–05** bankrupt" (*i.e.* a person whose insolvency was notorious in the sense of being a matter of public knowledge). These two Acts continued in operation until repealed by the Act of 1985.

9–06 Other earlier Acts on bankruptcy were concerned with the sequestration process. These dated back to a temporary Act of 1772 (12 Geo. III, c. 47) which introduced the process, limiting it to the moveable estate of a debtor. It was re-enacted by an Act of 1782 (23 Geo. III, c. 18) extending the sequestration process to heritable property but restricting it to traders. Later statutes gradually extended the process until the Bankruptcy (Scotland) Act 1856 finally removed all the restrictions on the categories of debtors who might be sequestrated.

9–07 The Bankruptcy (Scotland) Act 1913 consolidated the legislation on sequestration, and, with the Scots Acts of 1621 and 1696 and with some comparatively minor amendments, governed the Scots law of bankruptcy until repealed by the Act of 1985.

9–08 In 1968 the Scottish Law Commission commenced an intensive study of the law of bankruptcy. It was recognised that most of the Bankruptcy (Scotland) Act 1913 had simply re-enacted legislation which had been devised in the early part of the nineteenth century against a social and economic background very different from that of the latter part of the twentieth century. The Act was also open to criticism for its exaggerated emphasis on formal and court procedures, which added to the expense of sequestrations, and for its archaic and complex language. The recommendations made by the Scottish Law Commission were published in their *Report on Bankruptcy and Related Aspects of Insolvency and Liquidation* (Scot. Law Com. No. 68) in February 1982, and with some modifications were enacted as the Bankruptcy (Scotland) Act 1985, entitled "An Act to reform the law of Scotland relating to sequestration and personal insolvency; and for connected purposes".

9–09 Prominent among the reforms, in addition to a general simplification of procedure, were the new supervisory role of the Accountant in Bankruptcy, the appointment of an interim trustee to hold office until the election of the permanent trustee by the creditors, new provisions on gratuitous alienations and unfair preferences replacing the Acts of 1621 and 1696 respectively, the automatic discharge of the debtor after three years and the possibility of having defects in procedure cured by the sheriff rather than by petition to the *nobile officium* of the Court of Session.

Instead of resorting to sequestration, the insolvent and his creditors often in practice prefer to have recourse to a private arrangement, usually a trust deed for creditors. From the standpoint of the creditors such arrangements may save expense (with the result that there will be more funds available to meet the debts due to the creditors), and the debtor has the advantage of avoiding the greater publicity and the statutory disqualifications and disabilities involved in the sequestration process. Private arrangements are described as "extra-judicial", because, unlike sequestration, they are not conducted under "judicial" (*i.e.* court) authority. A major innovation of the Act of 1985 was the introduction of the "protected trust deed", so called because it was protected to a large extent from the possibility of being superseded by a sequestration initiated by creditors who were not parties to the trust deed. It did not prove popular but changes were made by the 1993 Act with a view to increasing its popularity. The Act of 1985 also includes provisions relating to all trust deeds. **9–10**

The topic of bankruptcy is considered in this chapter under the following headings: **9–11**

I. Insolvency;
II. Sequestration; and
III. Extra-judicial settlements.

Registered companies are not subject to sequestration. The appropriate procedures for the winding up of insolvent registered companies are contained in the First and Third Groups of Parts of the Insolvency Act 1986.

The English law of bankruptcy is quite distinct; it is to be found in the Second and Third Groups of Parts of the Insolvency Act 1986.

I INSOLVENCY

Insolvency may be either absolute or practical. **9–12**

A person is absolutely insolvent if his total liabilities exceed his total assets, even though he may be able to meet demands as they are made on him. The common law regards a person who is absolutely insolvent as bound to administer his affairs on behalf of his creditors generally: he is no longer free to make gifts, nor is he entitled to favour one creditor at the expense of other creditors. **9–13**

The principle is described thus in Bell's *Commentaries* (7th ed.), Vol. II, p. 170: "From the moment of insolvency a debtor is bound **9–14** to act as the mere trustee, or rather as the *negotiorum gestor*,[1] of his creditors, who thenceforward have the exclusive interest in his funds. He may, as long as he is permitted, continue his trade, with the intention of making gain for his creditors and for himself; but his funds are no longer his own, which he can be entitled secretly to set apart for his own use, or to give away as caprice or affection may dictate."

Similarly, Lord Dunedin in *Caldwell v. Hamilton*, 1919 S.C.(H.L.) 100, at p. 107, said: "After insolvency a man is truly, *quoad*[2] his property, a trustee for his creditors."

More recently, however, *Nordic Travel Ltd v. Scotprint Ltd*, 1980 S.C. 1, made it clear that the description of the insolvent as being a trustee for his creditors is not to be taken too literally:

In the liquidation of N. Ltd the liquidator attempted to set aside as "fraudulent preferences" certain cash payments which had been made by N. Ltd to S. Ltd, a closely associated company, in respect of debts due by N. Ltd to S. Ltd. Counsel for the liquidator argued that since a person who was absolutely insolvent, and knew it, was a trustee for all his creditors, he would, prima facie ("until the contrary were proved") be in breach of trust even if he merely paid to one of his creditors in cash a debt which was past due and payable.

The court rejected that argument.

Lord President Emslie said (at p. 9): "It is of course the fact that in a number of passages in Bell's Commentaries it is suggested that the doctrine that an insolvent with knowledge of his absolute insolvency is a trustee for all his creditors, is at the root of the common law on fraudulent preferences. When all these passages are read together, however, it is quite evident that the suggestion is not to be taken literally. In particular, nowhere in Bell's Commentaries nor in any other authority or decided case is it for the moment suggested that it is, even prima facie, a breach of trust for an insolvent person who knows of his absolute insolvency to fulfil obligations which are due and prestable and, in particular, to pay in cash debts which are past due. There are no doubt certain acts which, in the interests of all his creditors, such an insolvent person is obliged not to do, but to say that he is, literally, a trustee for his creditors is unwarranted in authority and wholly misleading."

---

1 "manager of affairs".

2 "as regards".

A state of practical insolvency exists where a person either has ceased to pay his debts in the ordinary course of business or cannot pay his debts as they become due, even though his total assets may exceed his total liabilities. What a creditor is primarily concerned with and entitled to in commercial transactions is to receive payment when it is due. Hence the definition of insolvency for the purposes of the Sale of Goods Act 1979 is a definition of practical insolvency: "A person is deemed to be insolvent within the meaning of this Act if he has either ceased to pay his debts in the ordinary course of business, or he cannot pay his debts as they become due" (Sale of Goods Act 1979, s. 61(4), as amended by Bankruptcy (Scotland) Act 1985, s. 75(2) and Sched. 8). **9–15**

Consequences of insolvency are that: **9–16**

(a) gratuitous alienations; and

(b) fraudulent or unfair preferences

may be reduced (*i.e.* set aside).

(a) Reduction of Gratuitous Alienations

Gifts and other gratuitous alienations by an insolvent out of his assets may be reduced either: **9–17**

(i) at common law; or

(ii) under section 34 of the Bankruptcy (Scotland) Act 1985.

(i) *At Common Law*

The underlying principle is the fiduciary position which an insolvent person occupies at common law in relation to his creditors. **9–18**

The challenge may be made by any creditor, whether his debt was incurred before or after the alienation. By the Act of 1985 the permanent trustee, the trustee acting under a protected trust deed and a judicial factor appointed under section 11A of the Judicial Factors (Scotland) Act 1889 on the estate of a deceased person are also given the right to make a challenge at common law (s. 34(8)). **9–19**

The transaction challenged may be any type of alienation, direct or indirect, and whether effected by writing or by simple delivery of money or property. **9–20**

The challenger must prove that: **9–21**

(1) the debtor was absolutely insolvent at the date of the alienation (or was made insolvent by the alienation), and has continued in that state until the date of the challenge;

(2) the alienation was gratuitous, *i.e.* the insolvent received no consideration, in money or money's worth, for it; and

(3) the alienation prejudiced lawful creditors.

9–22 Provided the challenger proves these points, it will be inferred that the alienation was "fraudulent" in the sense that it was unfair to the lawful creditors; it is not essential to prove that the debtor was actively and consciously defrauding his creditors or even, it seems, that he had insolvency in contemplation (*Goudy on the Law of Bankruptcy* (4th ed.), p. 24).

9–23 The following are three instances of reduction of gratuitous alienations at common law:

9–24 (a) *Dobie v. Mitchell* (1854) 17 D. 97: The allegations in this case were that McFarlane, shortly before absconding, had collected various debts which were due to him and had handed over to his sister, without any consideration, £500 which she immediately deposited in a bank; that at that time, to the knowledge of both McFarlane and his sister, D. was a creditor of McFarlane; and that the transaction was a scheme entered into between brother and sister for the purpose of defeating D.'s right to receive payment.

The court held that if these allegations were true the deposit receipt, which was the only title by which the sister held the money, would be reduced.

9–25 (b) *Main v. Fleming's Trustees* (1881) 8 R. 880: From 1865 F. spent large sums in permanently improving an estate which was held by his antenuptial marriage-contract trustees for the benefit of his children. In 1871 F. became to his knowledge insolvent but continued to spend large sums in improving the estate.

Held that the trustee in F.'s sequestration was entitled to a declarator that in so far as the estate had been benefited by F.'s expenditure after his insolvency, the marriage-contract trustees held it on behalf of the trustee in F.'s sequestration.

The effect of F.'s insolvency was explained thus by Lord President Inglis (at p. 886):

"If he had remained solvent nobody could have found any fault with him for increasing the funds in the hands of the trustees, and so increasing the provision in favour of his children. And down to the year 1871 every shilling that he spent on the estate of Keill does go to increase the value of the estate in the hands of these trustees, and so to enlarge the children's provisions. But . . . Mr

Fleming was not entitled to go on expending money in this way after he became insolvent, because that was simply increasing the provision to his children at the expense of his creditors; . . . so far as this expenditure was made after he became insolvent it was at common law an unlawful thing for him to do—a fraud upon his creditors in the technical sense of the term, although I am not at all inclined to suppose that any actual fraud was intended. Still it is what the common law calls a fraud against his creditors, because it is taking the money that ought to have gone to pay them to increase gratuitously the provision in favour of his own children. . . . If the defenders as trustees are *lucrati*[3] by that expenditure, or, in other words, if the value of the children's provisions is, in point of fact, enhanced by the expenditure of that money, then I apprehend to that extent the pursuer, upon the part of the creditors, has a perfectly equitable claim to participate in the trust-estate which is held by them."

(c) *Obers v. Paton's Trustees* (1897) 24 R. 719: P., a Scotsman, **9–26**
after he had been declared bankrupt in France where he carried on business, executed a discharge of legitim at a time when his father was on his deathbed. The effect of the discharge was, on the father's death, to prejudice P.'s creditors by depriving them of several thousand pounds and to benefit to that extent other persons entitled to share the legitim fund (P.'s brothers and sisters).

Although at the time of the discharge P.'s claim to legitim was a mere *spes successionis* ("expectation of succession") which would have been defeated if P. had died before his father, the court held that the discharge could be reduced on behalf of the creditors in P.'s French bankruptcy.

On considering whether P. had had the power to discharge his legitim and so prevent that valuable right from coming into the possession of his creditors, Lord McLaren said (at p. 733):

"There is this difference between a fraud on creditors and fraudulent acts of the ordinary type, that an act may be a fraud on creditors which is perfectly innocent in itself or even laudable if done by a solvent person, because the fraud consists in the violation of the principle that an insolvent is a virtual trustee for his creditors, and is disabled from dealing with his estate so as to defeat or imperil their right to distribution.

[3] "enriched".

" . . . The right of creditors to restoration against fraudulent alienation is independent of statute, and I think that the principle has sufficient strength and consistency to prevail over any device by which an insolvent person seeks to secure a benefit to himself, his relatives, or other favoured persons, by putting away funds which, but for his interference, would be available for the liquidation of his debts."

(ii) *Under Section 34 of the Bankruptcy (Scotland) Act 1985*

9–27 The Bankruptcy Act 1621 had the effect of facilitating the challenge of gratuitous alienations where the recipients were "conjunct or confident" persons. The Act of 1621 was repealed by the Act of 1985 (s. 75(2) and Sched. 8) but revised provisions on gratuitous alienations were included in section 34.

9–28 The challenge may be made by any creditor the debt to whom was incurred on or before the date of sequestration or before the granting of the trust deed or the debtor's death, as the case may be; or it may be made by the permanent trustee, the trustee acting under the trust deed or the judicial factor, as the case may be (s. 34(1)).

9–29 The right to challenge exists where all the three following conditions are fulfilled:

(1) by the alienation any of the debtor's property has been transferred or any claim or right of the debtor has been discharged or renounced;

(2) any of the following has occurred:

(a) his estate has been sequestrated (other than, in the case of a natural person, after his death); or

(b he has granted a trust deed which has become a protected trust deed; or

(c) he has died and within 12 months after his death, his estate has been sequestrated; or

(d) he has died and within 12 months after his death, a judicial factor has been appointed under section 11A of the Judicial Factors (Scotland) Act 1889 to administer his estate and the estate was absolutely insolvent at the date of death; and

(3) the alienation took place on a "relevant day" (s. 34(2)).

9–30 For the purposes of (3), above, the day on which an alienation took place is the day on which the alienation became completely effectual, and the meaning of "relevant day" depends on whether the alienation is in favour of an "associate" of the debtor or in favour of any other person; in the former case the relevant day is a day not earlier than five years before the date of sequestration, the granting of the trust deed or the debtor's death, as the case may be; in the latter case the period is two years before such date (s. 34(3)). The term "associate" is widely defined so as to include husband or wife, specified relatives, in-laws, partners, employees and employers (s. 74).

On a challenge being brought, the court must grant decree of reduction or for restoration of property to the debtor's estate or other appropriate redress, unless the person seeking to uphold the alienation establishes: **9–31**

(1) that immediately, or at any other time, after the alienation the debtor's assets were greater than his liabilities; or

(2) that the alienation was made for adequate consideration; or

(3) that the alienation was in the circumstances a reasonable one for the debtor to make and was either:

(a) a birthday, Christmas or other conventional gift; or

(b) a gift made, for a charitable purpose, to a person who is not an associate of the debtor.

It is further provided that any right or interest of a third party acquired in good faith and for value from the transferee in the alienation is not to be prejudiced by a challenge of the alienation (s. 34(4)).

Section 34(7) expressly preserves the operation of the Married Women's Policies of Assurance (Scotland) Act 1880 by which a policy of assurance taken out by a married man on his own life for the benefit of his wife or children or both is considered to be a trust for her or them, and his creditors have no right to the proceeds of the policy except that if the policy has been taken out in order to defraud creditors or if the bankruptcy occurs within two years of the date of the policy the creditors are entitled to the amount paid as premiums under the policy. The provisions of that Act were extended, by the Married Women's Policies of Assurance (Scotland) (Amendment) Act 1980, to policies taken out by a married woman on her own life for the benefit of her husband or children or both. **9–32**

The permanent trustee must insert in the sederunt book a copy of any decree under section 34 affecting the sequestrated estate (s. 34(9)). **9–33**

9–34 An instance of a successful challenge under section 34(4) resulting in the reduction of dispositions of heritable property is *Short's Trustee v. Chung*, 1991 S.L.T. 472: S. in spring 1986 bought two flats in Glasgow for £1,500 each and sold them in October 1986 to C. for £2,500 each. In May 1987 C. granted two dispositions transferring the flats to his wife "for love, favour and affection".

S. was sequestrated in June 1987, and a valuer for the permanent trustee valued the flats, as at October 1986, at £7,000 and £6,500, respectively. The permanent trustee raised an action against C.'s wife seeking reduction of both the October 1986 and the May 1987 dispositions.

The Lord Ordinary found that the alienations had not been made for adequate consideration and he granted reduction.

C.'s wife reclaimed and submitted that if the remedy of reduction were granted, S.'s estate would benefit by more than the difference in value between the sum paid and the actual market value (namely £8,500) because of the subsequent rise in property prices. She argued that the appropriate remedy was, therefore, to grant decree for payment of £8,500.

The permanent trustee contended that the court did not have a general equitable discretion and that, therefore, reduction was the appropriate remedy.

Held (1) that the general purpose of section 34(4) is to provide that as far as possible any property which has been improperly alienated will be restored to the debtor's estate; (2) that the reference to other appropriate redress is not intended to give the court a general discretion to decide a case on equitable principles but is designed to enable the court to make an appropriate order where reduction or restoration of the property is not an available remedy; and (3) that, as reduction was available in this case, that was the appropriate remedy; and reclaiming motion *refused.*

9–35 Another instance of a successful challenge was *Ahmed's Trustee v. Ahmed (No. 2)*, 1993 S.L.T. 651 (O.H.):

After an assignation by an uncle to his nephew had been in part executed, the nephew got into financial difficulties and the assignation was completed in the name of another nephew.

On the sequestration of the originally intended assignee, his permanent trustee sought and obtained a reduction of the executed assignation and an order that an assignation in favour of the trustee be executed and delivered.

The interpretation of "adequate consideration" was the central point in the two following cases: 9–36

Matheson's Trustee v. Matheson, 1992 S.L.T. 685 (O.H.): A permanent trustee raised an action against a husband and wife concluding for declarator that a disposition of a house by the husband to his wife was reducible as a gratuitous alienation. The wife averred that the alienation had been made for adequate consideration in that between March 1971 and the date of the disposition in August 1986 she had made numerous payments to or on behalf of her husband, amounting to approximately £34,749, which more than cancelled out the value of the house. 9–37

Counsel for the trustee submitted that the giving of "consideration" involved either the discharge of an existing obligation or an exchange of new obligations and that it was not enough simply to aver that there had been a number of past gifts which exceeded in value that of the alienation in question: the payments alleged to have been made by the wife were wholly consistent with a contribution on her part towards the maintenance of the joint home. Moreover, the disposition bore to be granted for "love, favour and affection", and, though such a narrative was not conclusive, it made it all the more necessary that the wife should have given clear notice of how and why she maintained that adequate consideration had been given.

The Lord Ordinary (Marnoch) agreed with these submissions and holding that the wife's pleadings were lacking in specification, excluded her averments from probation.

MacFadyen's Trustee v. MacFadyen, 1994 S.L.T. 1245: This case concerned the disposition of a half share of a dwelling-house made by the bankrupt MacF. to his mother. 9–38

The mother claimed that the disposition had been made for adequate consideration because she had paid the whole purchase price and all the running costs. The house had only been put in the name of her son because part of the purchase price had been funded by a bank loan and the bank had insisted that the title be taken in joint names of mother and son.

Held that "consideration" for the purposes of section 34 meant something which had a patrimonial worth and the disposition could not be said to be in return for any consideration given or in fulfilment of a prior legal obligation of the bankrupt to his mother.

(b) Reduction of Fraudulent or Unfair Preferences

9–39 It is a consequence of the fiduciary relationship in which an insolvent stands towards his creditors as a body that he must not show favour to particular creditors at the expense of other creditors. Transactions which have that effect are referred to as "fraudulent preferences" or "illegal preferences", and may be reduced at common law.

9–40 Fraudulent preferences could formerly be reduced under the Bankruptcy Act 1696 when granted either within six months before, or after, the constitution of "notour bankruptcy". Since the passing of the Act of 1985, the position now is that the common law on fraudulent preferences has been retained, the Act of 1696 has been repealed, the term "notour bankruptcy" has disappeared and there are revised provisions on "unfair preferences" in section 36 of the Act.

9–41 What follows is therefore divided into reduction:

(i) at common law (of "fraudulent preferences"); and

(ii) under section 36 of the Bankruptcy (Scotland) Act 1985 (of "unfair preferences").

(i) *At Common Law*

9–42 The challenge may be made by a prior creditor, *i.e.* a creditor who was already a creditor of the insolvent at the date of the transaction, and perhaps also by a creditor whose debt was contracted after the transaction, although the point is not free from doubt (*Goudy on the Law of Bankruptcy* (4th ed.), p. 42). By the Act of 1985 the permanent trustee, the trustee under a protected trust deed and a judicial factor appointed under section 11A of the Judicial Factors (Scotland) Act 1889 are also given the right to challenge a fraudulent preference at common law (s. 36(6)).

9–43 The underlying principle is that the rights of the creditors become fixed *inter se* ("as among themselves") at the time of the insolvency, and the insolvent must treat all his creditors equally according to their rights as then established: he must not, for instance, voluntarily grant a security to a creditor who is at that time an unsecured creditor.

9–44 The challenger must prove that:

(i) the debtor was absolutely insolvent at the date of the transaction and knew himself to be so;

(ii) the transaction was a voluntary act of the debtor; and

(iii) the transaction was "fraudulent" in the sense that it conferred a preference on one creditor to the prejudice of the others.

The following are two instances of reduction of fraudulent preferences at common law: **9–45**

(1) *Wylie, Stewart & Marshall v. Jervis*, 1913 1 S.L.T. 465 (O.H.): A father had lent money to his son to enable the son to purchase a house. Later the son, knowing himself to be insolvent, transferred the house by an *ex facie* ("apparently") absolute disposition to his father so as to put it beyond the reach of his other creditors. **9–46**

Held that the disposition was reducible at the instance of the other creditors.

(2) *Bank of Scotland v. Faulds* (1870) 7 S.L.R. 619: F., a waggon-builder, when insolvent, entered into an arrangement with his creditors to pay a composition of 7s.6d. in the £ with a condition attached empowering the creditors to make an additional call of 2s.6d. in the £. The additional call was not made and F. was discharged. **9–47**

Between the date of the agreement and the discharge F. made an arrangement with Rowan & Co., iron merchants, his largest creditors, which resulted in his granting to them a promissory note for £1,732 3s.6d, being 2s.6d. in the £ on their claim. Rowan & Co. discounted the note with the Bank of Scotland, and the bank brought an action against F. for the amount of the note.

Held that the transaction constituted an illegal preference and that the bank, as coming in the place of Rowan & Co., could not recover.

It is particularly difficult to prove that the insolvent knew of his insolvency at the date of the transaction, though the courts have readily allowed the debtor's knowledge of his insolvency to be inferred from circumstances. A case in which a challenge failed for lack of evidence on this point is *Macdonald (Logan's Trustee) v. David Logan & Son Ltd* (1903) 11 S.L.T. 32 and 369: **9–48**

In 1898 L. sold his colliery business to L. Ltd. In August 1901 there was a debit balance of £7,460 standing in L. Ltd's books against L., and L. disponed to the company in security of his indebtedness certain superiorities of the value of £2,000. In February 1902 the estates of L. were sequestrated, and the trustee in the sequestration brought an action against the company for reduction of the disposition.

Held that there was no evidence to show that at the date of the disposition sought to be reduced L. knew that he was insolvent; his view of his financial situation, though sanguine, was such as he might not unreasonably have been expected to take.

9–49 It is not, however, essential for the challenger of a fraudulent preference to prove that the favoured *creditor* knew of the debtor's insolvency: the "fraud" does not necessarily involve complicity on the creditor's part; it is inferred from the creditor's acceptance of the *debtor's* fraudulent act. This point was fully explained in *McCowan v. Wright* (1853) 15 D. 494, a case concerned with the reduction of a number of deeds "fraudulently" granted by an insolvent to his brother-in-law in order to give his brother-in-law security for large sums previously advanced by the brother-in-law.

Lord Justice-Clerk Hope said (at p. 498) in considering reduction of securities on the ground of fraud: "It plainly is the act of the debtor which is injurious to the other creditors. His act creates the security. Then the fraud consists in this—that, being insolvent, or in circumstances which must end in hopeless insolvency, he creates that security to the effect of favouring one creditor, and to the prejudice of the rights of his other creditors, by withdrawing all the funds which he can, or which are necessary for the preference, from distribution among the creditors generally, and giving them to the favoured creditor. . . . The creditors are equally injured—the prejudice to them is the same, whether the receiver at the time knew that the security was a fraud against them or not; and if it was a fraud against them to give him that security, it does not become less so, that he did not at the time know that it was a fraud. The character and effect of the debtor's act is not thereby altered."

9–50 A more recent authority on the same point is *Nordic Travel Ltd v. Scotprint Ltd*, 1980 S.C. 1 (see 9–14, above), a case concerned with challenge of a fraudulent preference in the winding up of a registered company.

The court held that N. Ltd, though absolutely insolvent, was entitled to pay, in cash and in the ordinary course of business, debts which were due and payable.

Lord President Emslie said (at p. 14): "The creditor's knowledge of his debtor's absolute insolvency at the time when the debtor performs an act in his favour is quite irrelevant in deciding whether or not the act is a fraudulent preference. If a particular act by an insolvent debtor to his creditor is *per se*[4] unobjectionable and lawful I am unable to see how his creditor's mere knowledge of his insolvency can make it objectionable and unlawful."

Three categories of voluntary acts of the debtor are exempt from challenge unless actual fraud is proved. These are: 9–51

(1) payments in cash;
(2) transactions in the ordinary course of business; and
(3) *nova debita* ("new debts").

The same three categories were exempt from challenge under the Bankruptcy Act 1696, and are included as exemptions in section 36 of the Act of 1985.

(1) Payments in cash

An insolvent who has funds in his hands sufficient to meet a debt which is immediately due is, if he pays that debt in cash, doing no more than he is bound to do. His act is not considered to be a voluntary act, and it is therefore necessarily exempt from challenge. A cheque drawn by the debtor on his bank is regarded as payment in cash in this connection. 9–52

An instance of a payment in cash is *Whatmough's Trustee v. British Linen Bank*, 1934 S.C.(H.L.) 51; 1932 S.C. 525: 9–53

W. was a motor omnibus proprietor whose business was being carried on at a loss. He sold the business, and, knowing himself to be insolvent, paid the cheque for £7,300 representing the price into his bank account which was then overdrawn to the extent of about £8,000. This cheque together with certain securities held by the bank was sufficient to pay off the overdraft. The bank was unaware of W.'s insolvency and no collusion on its part to obtain an illegal preference was shown to have existed.

About a month later W.'s estates were sequestrated, and the trustee sued the bank for £7,300 on the ground that the payment of that amount into the bank account had been an illegal preference both at common law and under the Act of 1696.

Held that the payment of the £7,300, being a payment in cash of an existing debt, made without collusion on the part of the creditor, was not reducible either at common law or under the Act.

The speech of Lord Thankerton in this case (1934 S.C.(H.L.) at pp. 55–65) has a full and authoritative review of the significance of

[4] "of itself".

"payments in cash" as well as of "transactions in the ordinary course of business", and Lord President Clyde's opinion (1932 S.C. at p. 543) is regarded as providing "the clearest summary of settled law on the matter of cash payments of debts by insolvent persons" (*per* Lord President Emslie in *Nordic Travel Ltd v. Scotprint Ltd*, 1980 S.C. 1, at p. 17 (see 9–14 and 9–50, above)).

(2) **Transactions in the ordinary course of business**

9–54 Even where an insolvent is conscious of his insolvency, he remains free at common law to continue in business, and so transactions which are in the ordinary course of that business are protected from challenge. If, however, financial difficulties cause him to depart from the ordinary course of business, the transactions are reducible.

9–55 Questions have arisen in relation to payment by cheque. Where the debtor makes payment by drawing a cheque on his own bank account this is clearly recognised as a transaction in the ordinary course of business. Equally, where, in *Whatmough's Trustee v. British Linen Bank* (9–53, above), the debtor indorsed a cheque to his bank so that the bank might collect the amount of the cheque from the bank on which it had been drawn, there was held to have been a transaction in the ordinary course of business. The position is different where the debtor resorts to negotiating cheques received from his own debtors. For instance, in *Horsburgh v. Ramsay & Co.* (1885) 12 R. 1171, where a boot manufacturer had been carrying on business in financial difficulties, paying his suppliers in cash when he had cash but more often by indorsing to them bills of exchange granted to him by the customers who bought his manufactured goods, such indorsations were held to be reducible under the Act of 1696 on the ground that they were not transactions in the ordinary course of trade. Similarly, in *Carter v. Johnstone* (1886) 13 R. 698, where a bankrupt paid a creditor by indorsing to him cheques on which the bankrupt was named as the payee, the indorsations were held reducible under the Act of 1696 as being neither cash payments nor transactions in the ordinary course of business.

(3) ***Nova debita***

9–56 What is objectionable during insolvency is that the debtor should show favour to one of his existing creditors to the prejudice of his other existing creditors. There is no objection to his contracting new debts and granting to the creditor concerned a right in security or a preference in respect of the new debts, provided the reciprocal obligations (*e.g.* the creditor's obligation to lend money and the debtor's obligation to grant security for the loan) are created simultaneously.

An example of a transaction coming within this third category occurred in *Cowdenbeath Coal Co. Ltd v. Clydesdale Bank Ltd* (1895) 22 R. 682: A merchant obtained an advance from a bank, and on the following day indorsed and delivered to the bank in security of this advance a bill of lading for a cargo of coal. A creditor in an action against the bank sought to have the security set aside on the ground that it was an illegal preference under the Act of 1696. It was, however, proved that the bank had, in making the advance, relied on the bill of lading being delivered to it, and the court accordingly held that the security had been granted for a present advance and not for a prior debt and was therefore not struck at by the Act. **9–57**

Similarly, in *Thomas Montgomery & Sons v. Gallacher*, 1982 S.L.T. 138 (O.H.), a standard security granted by a trader to one of his suppliers, who was becoming restive about the trader's credit-worthiness, was held to be good security to the extent of the value of goods supplied between the date of his undertaking to grant the standard security and the date of sequestration. **9–58**

(ii) *Under Section 36 of the Bankruptcy (Scotland) Act 1985*

The Bankruptcy Act 1696 had the effect of facilitating the challenge of fraudulent preferences if they had been made by the debtor at or after his becoming "notour bankrupt" or in the space of 60 days before notour bankruptcy. The Companies Act 1947 (s. 115) substituted the period of six months before notour bankruptcy for the period of 60 days before notour bankruptcy. The term "notour bankruptcy" came to have a specific statutory definition under section 5 of the Bankruptcy (Scotland) Act 1913. All these provisions were repealed by the Act of 1985 (s. 75(2) and Sched. 7), and replaced by the provisions in section 36 on "unfair preferences". **9–59**

A transaction entered into by a debtor can be challenged as an unfair preference under section 36 if it has the effect of creating a preference in favour of a creditor to the prejudice of the general body of creditors and has been created within six months before: **9–60**

(1) the date of sequestration of the debtor's estate (if he is still alive); or

(2) the granting by him of a trust deed which has become a protected trust deed; or

(3) his death if within 12 months after his death *either*

(a) his estate has been sequestrated; *or*

(b) a judicial factor has been appointed under section 11A of the Judicial Factors (Scotland) Act 1889 to administer his estate and his estate was absolutely insolvent at the date of death (s. 36(1)).

9–61 For the purposes of this provision, the day on which a preference was created is the day on which the preference became completely effectual (s. 36(3)).

9–62 The transactions which are exempt from challenge are modelled on the categories which are exempt from challenge at common law, with one addition. The transactions are:

(1) a transaction in the ordinary course of trade or business;

(2) a payment in cash for a debt which when it was paid had become payable, unless the transaction was collusive with the purpose of prejudicing the general body of creditors;

(3) a transaction whereby the parties undertake reciprocal obligations (whether the performance by the parties of their obligations occurs at the same time or at different times), unless the transaction was collusive with the purpose of prejudicing the general body of creditors; and

(4) the granting of a mandate by a debtor authorising an arrestee to pay over the arrested funds to the arrester where:

(a) there has been a decree for payment or a warrant for summary diligence; *and*

(b) the decree or warrant has been preceded by an arrestment on the dependence of the action or followed by an arrestment in execution (s. 36(2)).

9–63 The addition of (4), above, was made to remove a doubt which had arisen in connection with the Act of 1696. It was a common occurrence for a debtor, after arrestment of his property by a creditor, to grant a mandate for the transfer of the arrested property to the arrester to avoid the expense of furthcoming. The doubt was whether such a mandate was a voluntary act of the debtor (and so open to challenge) or whether the debtor was merely anticipating the inevitable.

The persons who may challenge a transaction under section 36 are: **9–64**

(1) any creditor the debt to whom was incurred on or before the date of sequestration, the granting of the protected trust deed or the debtor's death, as the case may be; or

(2) the permanent trustee, the trustee acting under the protected trust deed, or the judicial factor, as the case may be (s. 36(4)).

On a challenge being successfully brought, the court must grant decree of reduction or for restoration of property to the debtor's estate or other appropriate redress, but any right or interest of a third party acquired in good faith and for value from or through the favoured creditor is not to be prejudiced (s. 36(5)). **9–65**

The permanent trustee must insert in the sederunt book a copy of any decree under section 36 affecting the sequestrated estate (s. 36(7)). **9–66**

An instance of the operation of section 36 is *Balcraig House's Trustee v. Roosevelt Property Services Ltd*, 1994 S.L.T. 1133 (O.H.): **9–67**

B., a partnership, had carried on a hotel business. By an agreement with R. Ltd, which had lent money to B. four years earlier, B. purported to sell certain assets including catering equipment, carpets, curtains and light fittings to R. Ltd though B. retained possession of the items.

In an action by the permanent trustee, the Lord Ordinary (Maclean) held that the transaction was not a sale but an attempt to create security over the property without delivery, and that, even if it was a sale, it could not be said that the transaction was in the ordinary course of the business of a hotelier.

Decree of production and reduction of the agreement was therefore granted.

II SEQUESTRATION

Most of the Bankruptcy (Scotland) Act 1985 is taken up with the details of the process of sequestration. For a general description of the purpose and nature of sequestration, reference may be made to the following three passages: **9–68**

(i) Bell's *Commentaries* (7th ed.), Vol. II, p. 283: "Sequestration may be said to be a judicial process for attaching and rendering litigious the whole estate, heritable and moveable, real and personal, of the bankrupt, wherever situated, in order that it may be **9–69** vested in a trustee elected by the creditors, to be recovered, managed, sold, and divided by him, according to certain rules of distribution."

9–70 (ii) Lord Dunedin in *Caldwell v. Hamilton*, 1919 S.C.(H.L.) 100 (a case in which future instalments of a bankrupt's salary, so far as they exceeded what was required for his reasonable maintenance, were held to vest in the trustee in the sequestration), at p. 107: "The principle of sequestration is that it is a process by which the whole property of a bankrupt person is ingathered by a trustee for the purpose of division *pari passu*[5] among the creditors."

9–71 (iii) Lord Kinnear in *Sinclair v. Edinburgh Parish Council*, 1909 S.C. 1353 (a case in which the word "sequestration" in the context "poinding, sequestration, or diligence whatever" in the Revenue Act 1884 was held to refer to the diligence of sequestration for rent and not to a sequestration under the bankruptcy statutes), at p. 1358: "It is said that sequestration under the Bankruptcy Act is also a diligence. But that is inaccurate. A petition for sequestration is not a diligence, it is an action. . . . It is a totally different thing to say that a trustee who has been confirmed is to have the same rights as if a diligence had been executed and to say that the award of sequestration is itself a diligence. It is in fact the declaration of a Bankruptcy Court that the estates of a bankrupt debtor are set apart for the benefit of his creditors. . . .

" . . . It is a judicial process for rendering litigious the whole estate of the bankrupt in order that no part of it may be carried away by a single creditor for his own benefit, but that the whole may be vested in the trustee, to be administered by him and distributed among the creditors according to certain fixed rules of distribution. Nothing could be more different from a diligence carried out by an individual creditor for his own benefit than a statutory process of that kind."

9–72 A point of terminology should be noted at the outset. It is evident from the passages quoted that sequestration is a process affecting the *estate* of the bankrupt. Therefore, strictly one should not refer to the sequestration of a *person*, but to the sequestration of the *estate of a person*. The former expression, however, is commonly used as a convenient and generally acceptable ellipsis.

---

[5] "equally", "rateably".

The procedure in sequestration lays great emphasis on publicity. Applications and reports to the court are required at several stages. Most steps must be advertised, particularly in the *Edinburgh Gazette*. Entries must be made in public registers—the Register of Inhibitions and Adjudications and the Register of Insolvencies. The interim trustee is appointed by the court, and the permanent trustee, though elected by the creditors, has no title to act without the court's authority, and the conduct of both trustees, as that of the commissioners (creditors or their agents appointed to supervise and advise the permanent trustee), are subject to the supervision of the Accountant in Bankruptcy. **9–73**

Another general aspect of the sequestration procedure which may be mentioned here is the rigidity of the statutory provisions. Formerly, this resulted in an unduly large number of applications to the *nobile officium* ("equitable power") of the Inner House of the Court of Session. An underlying trend of the Act of 1985 is a reduction in formality, and in addition the sheriff now has power under section 63 to cure defects in procedure, so that application to the *nobile officium* is now seldom necessary. **9–74**

The provisions of the Act are outlined below under the following headings: **9–75**

(a) administration of bankruptcy;
(b) petitions for sequestration;
(c) award of sequestration;
(d) period between award and discharge of interim trustee;
(e) conduct of sequestration by permanent trustee; and
(f) miscellaneous and supplementary.

(a) Administration of Bankruptcy

The first seven sections in the Act of 1985 (as amended by the Act of 1993) set out under this heading the general functions of: **9–76**

(i) the Accountant in Bankruptcy;
(ii) the interim trustee;
(iii) the permanent trustee; and
(iv) the commissioners.

(i) *The Accountant in Bankruptcy*

The role of the Accountant of Court was greatly enlarged by the Act of 1985, and when acting in relation to sequestration he took the title of "Accountant in Bankruptcy". The Act of 1993 made **9–77** further fundamental changes in the role of the Accountant in Bankruptcy, and his office is now separate from that of the Accountant of Court.

9–78 The address of the office of the Accountant in Bankruptcy is Strategy House, 3 Cables Wynd, Leith, Edinburgh EH6 6DT.

9–79 The Accountant in Bankruptcy is appointed by the Secretary of State on such terms and conditions as the Secretary of State may, with the approval of the Treasury, decide, and the staff of his office are appointed in the same way. The Secretary of State may appoint a member of the staff to be Depute Accountant in Bankruptcy to exercise all the functions of the Accountant in Bankruptcy at any time when the latter is unable to do so. The remuneration and allowances of the Accountant in Bankruptcy and his staff are decided by the Secretary of State with the approval of the Treasury, as are also arrangements for superannuation, pensions or gratuities (s. 1, as substituted by the Act of 1993, s. 1(1)).

9–80 The Accountant in Bankruptcy has the following general functions in the administration of sequestration and personal insolvency:

(1) the supervision of the performance by interim trustees, permanent trustees and commissioners of their functions under the Act and the investigation of any complaints made against them;

(2) the maintenance of the "Register of Insolvencies", in a form prescribed by the Court of Session, containing particulars of estates which have been sequestrated and trust deeds which have been sent to him for registration;

(3) the preparation of an annual report to be presented to the Secretary of State and the Court of Session; and

(4) such other functions as may from time to time be conferred on him by the Secretary of State (s. 1A(1), as substituted by the Act of 1993, s. 1(1)).

9–81 If it appears to the Accountant in Bankruptcy that an interim trustee, permanent trustee or commissioner has failed without reasonable excuse to perform a duty imposed on him by the Act or by any other statutory or common law rule, he must report the matter to the court, which, after hearing the person concerned, may remove him from office or censure him or make such other order as the circumstances of the case may require (s. 1A(2), as substituted by the Act of 1993, s. 1(1)). Where the court removes an interim trustee from office under this provision, the court must, on the application of the Accountant in Bankruptcy, appoint a new interim trustee (s. 13(1), as substituted by the Act of 1993, Sched. 1, para. 2).

If the Accountant in Bankruptcy has reasonable grounds to suspect that an interim trustee, permanent trustee or commissioner has committed an offence in the performance of his functions under the Act or under any other statutory or common law rule, or that an offence has been committed in relation to a sequestration— **9–82**

(1) by the debtor, in respect of his assets, his dealings with them or his conduct in relation to his business or financial affairs; or

(2) by a person other than the debtor in that person's dealings with the debtor, the interim trustee or the permanent trustee in respect of the debtor's assets, business or financial affairs, the Accountant in Bankruptcy must report the matter to the Lord Advocate (s. 1A(3), as substituted by the Act of 1993, s. 1(1)).

The Accountant in Bankruptcy must make the Register of Insolvencies, at all reasonable times, available for inspection and provide any person, on request, with a certified copy of any entry in the Register (s. 1A(4), as substituted by the Act of 1993, s. 1(1)). **9–83**

Throughout the Act many specific functions not mentioned in section 1 are conferred on the Accountant in Bankruptcy. In addition, he has issued sets of "Notes" for the guidance of interim and permanent trustees. **9–84**

The functions of the Accountant in Bankruptcy, other than those conferred by section 1A of the Act, may be carried out on his behalf by any member of his staff authorised by him to do so. In addition, the Accountant in Bankruptcy may appoint, on such terms and conditions as he considers appropriate, persons whom he considers fit to perform on his behalf any of his functions in a sequestration, giving those persons general or specific directions and paying them fees which he considers appropriate (s. 1B, as substituted by the Act of 1993, s. 1(1)). **9–85**

The Secretary of State may, after consulting the Lord President of the Court of Session, give to the Accountant in Bankruptcy general directions as to the performance of his functions under the Act. These directions may be given for all cases or any class or description of cases, but they must not be given in respect of any particular case (s. 1C, as substituted by the Act of 1993, s. 1(1)). **9–86**

(ii) *The Interim Trustee*

9–87 The introduction of the office of interim trustee was one of the most important reforms recommended by the Scottish Law Commission and adopted in the Act of 1985. In every sequestration there had to be an interim trustee appointed by the court. By the Act of 1993, the court may appoint the Accountant in Bankruptcy to be interim trustee (Act of 1993, s. 2(2)).

9–88 The general functions of an interim trustee are:

(1) to safeguard the debtor's estate pending the appointment of a permanent trustee;

(2) to ascertain the reasons for the debtor's insolvency and the circumstances surrounding it;

(3) to ascertain the state of the debtor's liabilities and assets;

(4) to administer the sequestration process pending the appointment of a permanent trustee; and

(5) whether or not he is still acting in the sequestration, to supply the Accountant in Bankruptcy with such information as the Accountant in Bankruptcy considers necessary to enable him to discharge his functions under the Act (s. 2(4)).

9–89 A petition for sequestration may nominate a person to be interim trustee. The court then, in awarding sequestration, may, if the person nominated satisfies certain conditions, appoint that person to be interim trustee (s. 2, as substituted by the Act of 1993, s. 2).

9–90 The conditions to be satisfied are that the person:

(1) resides within the jurisdiction of the Court of Session;

(2) is qualified to act as an "insolvency practitioner"; and

(3) has given a written undertaking that he will act as interim trustee and, where no permanent trustee is elected, as permanent trustee (s. 2(3), as substituted by the Act of 1993, s. 2).

9–91 The qualifications required for acting as an "insolvency practitioner" are in the Insolvency Act 1986 (ss. 390 to 398) and in subordinate legislation made under that Act, principally the Insolvency Practitioners Regulations 1990 (S.I. 1990 No. 439) and the Insolvency Practitioners (Recognised Professional Bodies) Order 1986 (S.I. 1986 No. 1764). The leading provisions are:

(1) Only an individual can be an insolvency practitioner (s. 390(1)).

(2) He must be authorised to act by either a "recognised professional body" or a "competent authority" (s. 390(2)).

(3) He must provide "caution" ("security") for the proper performance of his functions and this must meet the requirements prescribed in the Regulations (s. 390(3)).

(4) He must not be an undischarged bankrupt or subject to a disqualification order under the Company Directors Disqualification Act 1986 or a patient within the meaning of section 125(1) of the Mental Health (Scotland) Act 1984 (s. 390(4)).

The "recognised professional bodies" for the purposes of (2), above, are the Chartered Association of Certified Accountants, the Insolvency Practitioners Association, the Institute of Chartered Accountants in England and Wales, the Institute of Chartered Accountants in Ireland, the Institute of Chartered Accountants of Scotland, the Law Society and the Law Society of Scotland (Insolvency Practitioners (Recognised Professional Bodies) Order 1986). **9–92**

The "competent authority" for the purposes of (2), above, is the Secretary of State for Trade and Industry (s. 392(2)). **9–93**

Where the court, in awarding sequestration, does not appoint any nominated person to be interim trustee, it must appoint the Accountant in Bankruptcy to be interim trustee (s. 2(2), as substituted by the Act of 1993, s. 2). **9–94**

The provisions so far mentioned apply where the appointment of the interim trustee is made by the court at the time when it awards sequestration. It is also possible for an appointment to be made *before* the award of sequestration: where a petition for sequestration is presented by a creditor or a trustee acting under a trust deed, the court may appoint an interim trustee before sequestration is awarded— **9–95**

(1) if the debtor consents; or

(2) if the trustee acting under the trust deed or any creditor shows cause (s. 2(5), as substituted by the Act of 1993, s. 2).

(iii) *The Permanent Trustee*

In every sequestration there must be a permanent trustee. His general functions are: **9–96**

(1) to recover, manage and realise the debtor's estate, whether situated in Scotland or elsewhere;

(2) to distribute the estate among the debtor's creditors according to their respective entitlements;

(3) to ascertain the reasons for the debtor's insolvency and the circumstances surrounding it;

(4) to ascertain the state of the debtor's liabilities and assets;

(5) to maintain a sederunt book during his term of office for the purpose of providing an accurate record of the sequestration process;

(6) to keep regular accounts of his intromissions with the debtor's estate and make the accounts available for inspection at all reasonable times by the commissioners (if any), the creditors and the debtor; and

(7) whether or not he is still acting in the sequestration, to supply the Accountant in Bankruptcy with such information as the Accountant in Bankruptcy considers necessary to enable him to discharge his functions under the Act (s. 3(1)). This seventh function does not apply where the permanent trustee is the Accountant in Bankruptcy (s. 3(5), added by the Act of 1993, Sched. 1, para. 1).

9–97 The permanent trustee in performing his functions under the Act must have regard to advice offered to him by the commissioners (if any) (s. 3(2)).

9–98 If the permanent trustee has reasonable grounds to suspect that an offence has been committed in relation to the sequestration—

(1) by the debtor, in respect of his assets, his dealings with them or his conduct in relation to his business or financial affairs; or

(2) by a person other than the debtor in that person's dealings with the debtor, the interim trustee or the permanent trustee in respect of the debtor's assets, business or financial affairs,

the permanent trustee must report the matter to the Accountant in Bankruptcy (s. 3(3)). Such a report is absolutely privileged (s. 3(4)).

9–99 A permanent trustee may apply to the sheriff for directions in relation to any particular matter arising in the sequestration (s. 3(6), added by the Act of 1993, Sched. 1, para. 1).

9–100 Where the debtor, a creditor or any other person with an interest is dissatisfied with any act, omission or decision of the permanent trustee, he may apply to the sheriff and the sheriff may then confirm, annul or modify any act or decision of the permanent trustee or may give him directions or make such order as he thinks fit (s. 3(7), added by the Act of 1993, Sched. 1, para. 1).

(iv) *The Commissioners*

Commissioners, whose general functions are to supervise the intromissions of the permanent trustee with the sequestrated estate and to advise him, may be elected in any sequestration other than a sequestration to which the modified procedure in Schedule 2 applies (s. 4). **9–101**

(b) **Petitions for Sequestration**

The sequestration process starts with a petition to the court. The provisions on petitions are in sections 5 to 11. These are outlined below under the headings: **9–102**

(i) living or deceased debtors;
(ii) other estates;
(iii) meaning of "apparent insolvency";
(iv) jurisdiction;
(v) concurrent proceedings; and
(vi) creditor's oath.

(i) *Living or Deceased Debtors*

The leading provision is that any of the following persons may petition for the sequestration of the estate of a living debtor: **9–103**

(1) the debtor, with the concurrence of a "qualified" creditor;
(2) a "qualified" creditor, if the debtor is "apparently insolvent";
(3) the trustee acting under a voluntary trust deed granted by or on behalf of the debtor by which his estate is conveyed to the trustee for the benefit of his creditors generally (referred to in the Act as a "trust deed") (s. 5(2)).

This leading provision became more complex as a result of amendments made by the Act of 1993, one of the main aims of which was to control the circumstances in which a debtor could arrange his own sequestration. The changes in the leading provision are: **9–104**

In (1), above, as an alternative to having the concurrence of a "qualified" creditor, the debtor will be entitled to petition if he satisfies the following conditions: **9–105**

(a) the total amount of his debts (including interest) at the date of presentation of the petition is not less than £1,500;

(b) an award of sequestration has not been made against him in the five years before the presentation of the petition (the aim being to lessen the chance of the debtor abusing the sequestration process by repeatedly applying for sequestration throughout his lifetime); and

(c) the debtor either—

(i) is "apparently insolvent" (but this does not mean in this context merely that he has granted a trust deed or has given notice to his creditors that he has ceased to pay his debts in the ordinary course of business); or

(ii) has granted a trust deed and the trustee has attempted, but failed, to make the trust deed a protected trust deed (s. 5(2B)).

9–106 In (3), above, the trustee may petition only if one or other of the following conditions is satisfied:

(a) that the debtor has failed to comply with—

(i) any obligation imposed on him under the trust deed with which he could reasonably have complied; or

(ii) any instruction or requirement reasonably given to or made of him by the trustee for the purposes of the trust deed; or

(b) that the trustee avers in his petition that it would be in the best interests of the creditors that an award of sequestration be made (s. 5(2C)).

9–107 In the case of a deceased debtor any of the following persons may petition:

(i) an executor or person entitled to be appointed as executor;
(ii) a "qualified" creditor of the deceased debtor;
(iii) the trustee under a trust deed (s. 5(3)).

No change was made in this provision by the Act of 1993.

9–108 The term "qualified creditor" means a creditor to whom, at the date of the presentation of the petition, the debtor owes a debt, liquid or illiquid (but not contingent or future) and whether secured or unsecured, of not less than £1,500 (alterable by statutory instrument). The condition is satisfied if there are two or more creditors to whom, in all, the debtor owes not less than £1,500 (s. 5(4)).

9–109 A petition for the sequestration of a living debtor's estate may be presented at any time by the debtor or by a trustee acting under a trust deed, but by a qualified creditor *only if* the apparent insolvency founded on in the petition was constituted within four months before the petition is presented (s. 8(1)).

A petition for the sequestration of the estate of a deceased debtor may be presented at any time by an executor or a person entitled to be appointed as executor or a trustee acting under a trust deed. A petition may also be presented by a qualified creditor at any time provided the debtor's apparent insolvency was constituted within four months before his death; in any other case the qualified creditor must wait for six months after the debtor's death before presenting the petition (s. 8(3)). **9–110**

The petitioner must, on the day the petition is presented, send a copy of the petition to the Accountant in Bankruptcy (s. 5(6)). **9–111**

Where the petitioner is the debtor, he must lodge with the petition a statement of assets and liabilities, and on the day the petition is presented send the same statement to the Accountant in Bankruptcy (s. 5(6A)). The phrase "statement of assets and liabilities" is defined in the interpretation section as meaning "a document (including a copy of a document) in such form as may be prescribed containing— **9–112**

(1) a list of the debtor's assets and liabilities;

(2) a list of his income and expenditure; and

(3) such other information as may be prescribed" (s. 73, as amended by the Act of 1993).

If the debtor— **9–113**

(1) fails to send to the Accountant in Bankruptcy the statement of assets and liabilities required by section 5(6A); or

(2) fails to disclose any material fact in that statement; or

(3) makes a material misstatement in the statement,

he is guilty of an offence and liable to a fine or imprisonment for up to three months or both (s. 5(9)).

In proceedings for an offence under section 5(9), it is a defence for the accused to show that he had a reasonable excuse for failing to send the statement, failing to disclose a material fact or making a material misstatement (s. 5(10)). **9–114**

(ii) *Other Estates*

In addition to living and deceased individuals, the estates of the following may also be sequestrated: **9–115**

(1) a trust, for debts incurred by the trust;

(2) a partnership, including a dissolved partnership;

(3) a body corporate or an unincorporated body; and

(4) a limited partnership, including a dissolved limited partnership (s. 6(1)).

9–116 A petition for the sequestration of a partnership may be combined with a petition for the sequestration of any of the partners as individuals (s. 6(5)), but this does not result in only one award of sequestration: there must be separate awards for the partnership and for each of the partners who is being sequestrated: *The Royal Bank of Scotland plc v. J. & J. Messenger*, 1991 S.L.T. 492 (O.H.).

9–117 It is not competent to sequestrate a registered company or any other body in respect of which statute provides that sequestration is incompetent (s. 6(2)).

(iii) *Meaning of "Apparent Insolvency"*

9–118 The term "apparent insolvency" is the modern equivalent of the term "notour bankruptcy", which was introduced by the Bankruptcy Act 1696. In outline, the definition of "apparent insolvency", which is in section 7(1) of the Act of 1985, is as follows: a debtor's apparent insolvency is constituted whenever—

(1) his estate is sequestrated or he is adjudged bankrupt in England or Wales or Northern Ireland; or

(2) he gives written notice to his creditors that he has ceased to pay his debts in the ordinary course of business; or

(3) any of the following circumstances occurs:

(a) he grants a trust deed;

(b) after the service on him of a duly executed charge for payment of a debt, the days of charge expire without payment;

(c) after a poinding or seizure of any of his moveable property under a summary warrant for the recovery of rates or taxes, 14 days elapse without payment;

(d) a decree of adjudication of any part of his estate is granted, either for payment or in security;

(e) his effects are sold under a sequestration for rent due by him; or

(f) a receiving order is made against him in England or Wales,

unless it is shown that, at the time when any of these circumstances occurred, the debtor was able and willing to pay his debts as they became due; or

(4) a creditor to whom the debtor owes not less than £750 (which may be altered by statutory instrument) has served on the debtor, by personal service by an officer of court, a demand in the prescribed form requiring him to pay the debt *or* to find security for its payment, and within three weeks after the date of service of the demand the debtor has not *either* complied with the demand *or* intimated to the creditor, by recorded delivery, that he denies that there is a debt or that the sum claimed by the creditor is immediately payable.

(iv) *Jurisdiction*

Both the Court of Session and the sheriff court have jurisdiction in relation to the presentation of a petition for sequestration. The jurisdiction is founded on the debtor's having an established place of business or being habitually resident in Scotland or in the sheriffdom, as the case may be, at any time in the year immediately before the date of presentation of the petition (s. 9(1), (4) and (5)). **9–119**

However, once sequestration is awarded, by the Court of Session or the sheriff, the process becomes in either case a sheriff court process, since section 15(1) of the Act requires the Court of Session to remit the sequestration to such sheriff as it considers appropriate. **9–120**

(v) *Concurrent Proceedings*

It is possible for separate sequestration proceedings or for similar proceedings (including the appointment of a judicial factor, bankruptcy proceedings in England and Wales and Northern Ireland and winding up under the Insolvency Act 1986, the latter being referred to as "analogous remedies") to exist at the same time in respect of the same debtor. **9–121**

To meet such a situation the Act imposes on a petitioner for sequestration and on the debtor or a creditor concurring in the petition the duty to notify the court of the other proceedings as soon as they become aware of them (s. 10(1) and (5)). Failure to comply with that duty makes the petitioner (if he is not the debtor) liable for the expenses of presenting the petition; a debtor who fails to comply is guilty of an offence and liable to a fine (s. 10(2)). **9–122**

Where there are concurrent proceedings in the Scottish courts, the sheriff court to which a second petition is presented may, of its **9–123** own motion or at the instance of the debtor or any creditor or other person having an interest, allow the second petition to proceed or may sist or dismiss it. In addition, the Court of Session has power to direct the sheriff before whom the second petition is pending, or the court before which the first petition is pending, to sist or dismiss the second or first petition, as the case may be, or it may order the petitions to be heard together (s. 10(3)).

9–124 Where there are proceedings for analogous remedies outside Scotland, the Scottish court, on its own motion or at the instance of the debtor or any creditor or other person having an interest, may allow the petition for sequestration to proceed or may sist or dismiss it (s. 10(4)).

(vi) *Creditor's Oath*

9–125 Every creditor who petitions for sequestration or concurs in a petition by a debtor must produce an oath in the prescribed form (s. 11(1)). He must produce along with the oath an account or voucher (according to the nature of the debt) which constitutes prima facie evidence of the debt, and if he is a petitioning creditor he must in addition produce such evidence as is available to him to show the apparent insolvency of the debtor (s. 11(5)).

(c) **Award of Sequestration**

9–126 The provisions of the Act relating to the award may be considered under the following headings:

(i) the making of the award;
(ii) "the date of sequestration";
(iii) the procedure following the making of the award; and
(iv) recall of the award.

(i) *The Making of the Award*

9–127 Where a petition for sequestration is presented by the debtor, the court must award sequestration immediately if the court is satisfied that the Act has been complied with, unless cause is shown why sequestration cannot competently be awarded (s. 12(1)).

9–128 The Act of 1993 introduced a system of summary administration for cases where the aggregate liabilities and aggregate assets of the debtor do not exceed £20,000 and £2,000, respectively (s. 23A and Sched. 2A). The process is initiated by an application to the court for the grant of a certificate for the summary administration of the sequestration of the debtor's estate (s. 23A(1)). In order to enable the Accountant in Bankruptcy to make such an application, section 12(1A) therefore provides that the Accountant in Bankruptcy may, not later than seven days after the date on which sequestration is awarded, apply to the court for the grant of a certificate for the summary administration of the sequestration of the debtor's estate.

Where a petition is presented by a creditor or a trustee acting **9–129** under a trust deed, the court must first grant warrant to cite the debtor to appear before the court on a specified date, which must be not less than six nor more that 14 days after the date of citation, to show cause why sequestration should not be awarded (s. 12(2)).

The warrant must be described with reasonable clarity: if it is set **9–130** out in an inaccurate and confusing manner sequestration will not be awarded: *Scottish & Newcastle Breweries plc v. Mann*, 1989 S.C.L.R. 118 (Sh.Ct.).

The view has been expressed that in the interests of justice the **9–131** court has a discretion to allow a debtor to appear late (*per* Lord Prosser in *The Royal Bank of Scotland plc v. Forbes*, 1988 S.L.T. 73 (O.H.), at p. 76).

If the court is satisfied that the provisions of the Act, including **9–132** the citation of the debtor if he has not appeared, have been complied with, the court must award sequestration unless:

(1) cause is shown why sequestration cannot competently be awarded; or

(2) the debtor forthwith pays or satisfies or produces written evidence of the payment or satisfaction of, or gives *or shows that there is* sufficient security for the payment of, the debt in respect of which he became apparently insolvent and any other debt due by him to the petitioner and any creditor concurring in the petition (s. 12(3) and (3A), as amended by the Act of 1993, s. 4).

The court *must* award sequestration unless one of the two stated **9–133** defences is available, and must do so "forthwith":

Sales Lease Ltd v. Minty, 1993 S.L.T. (Sh.Ct.) 52: S. Ltd petitioned for the sequestration of M. M. objected to the award and the sheriff appointed her to lodge answers.

S. Ltd appealed to the sheriff principal (N. D. MacLeod).

Held that unless (1) or (2), above, applied, there was no justification for withholding the award; the court had no discretion to continue the petition.

The sheriff principal therefore allowed the appeal and granted the petition, stating (at p. 54) that the terms of the Act "could scarcely be more peremptory or enjoin greater dispatch".

9–134 The definition of "security" in the Act is "any security, heritable or moveable, or any right of lien, retention or preference" (s. 73(1)). A standard security, therefore, is within the definition.

9–135 Before the Act of 1993, there were, however, conflicting authorities on whether "sufficient security" in section 12(3) covered pre-existing securities.

9–136 On the one hand, there were cases such as the sheriff court case of *Drybrough & Co. Ltd v. Brown*, 1989 S.C.L.R. 279:

D. Ltd, a company of brewers, petitioned for the sequestration of B., who traded as "The Drookit Dug" in licensed premises in Cupar. B. had granted a standard security over the premises in favour of D. Ltd, and B. had been charged to pay £106,520.

It was argued for B., under section 12(3), that he could give sufficient security, because an up-to-date valuation of the premises might show that the business had a value of £120,000 to £130,000.

Held (by Sheriff J. C. McInnes) that the pre-existing security, even if it were sufficient to cover current indebtedness, was not within the meaning of "sufficient security" in section 12(3).

9–137 Similarly, in *Bank of Scotland v. Mackay*, 1991 S.L.T. 163 (O.H.), Lord Morton of Shuna agreed with Sheriff McInnes.

9–138 On the other hand, there were cases such as *The Royal Bank of Scotland plc v. Forbes*, 1988 S.L.T. 73 (O.H.) in which Lord Prosser held that a pre-existing security was covered and that there should be an inquiry into the existence and validity of the security and its availability for the debt in question.

9–139 The authorities were reviewed by Lord Kirkwood in *National Westminster Bank plc v. W. J. Elrick & Co.*, 1991 S.L.T. 709 (O.H.):

A bank petitioned for the sequestration of E., who had granted standard securities in 1983 over three properties. There was a difference of opinion as to the valuation of the properties: E. averred that the value of the properties exceeded the sum due by E. to the bank, whereas the bank's value was well below that sum.

Held (1) that a completely new security was not always necessary in order to give "sufficient security" within the meaning of section

12(3); it was enough if the court was satisfied that the security was valid, covered the whole of the outstanding debt and would result in the whole debt being paid without undue delay; (2) that the Act envisaged an early decision being taken on whether sequestration should be awarded and that it would not normally be appropriate to hold a proof into the validity, or the value, of a particular security before the court decided whether or not sequestration should be awarded; and (3) that every case had to depend on its own special circumstances, but in the particular circumstances of this case, since the dispute as to the value of the security subjects could only properly be resolved by having a proof and there would be a time-consuming procedure before they could be realised, the three pre-existing standard securities did not constitute "sufficient security" for the purposes of section 12(3), and sequestration *awarded.*

The words in italics ("or show that there is"—see 9–132 above) were added by the Act of 1993 (s. 4) to remove the doubt about pre-existing securities being "sufficient security". **9–140**

(ii) *"The Date of Sequestration"*

In the Act "the date of sequestration", a term of crucial importance for many of the Act's provisions, means: **9–141**

(i) if the petition for sequestration is presented by the debtor, the date on which sequestration is awarded; and

(ii) if the petition is presented by a creditor or a trustee acting under a trust deed, the date on which the court grants warrant (or, where more than one warrant is granted, the first warrant) to cite the debtor to appear (s. 12(4), as amended by the Act of 1993, s. 4).

It is incompetent for a sheriff to alter the date of a sequestration: *Accountant in Bankruptcy v. Allans of Gillock Ltd*, 1991 S.L.T. 765 (O.H.). **9–142**

(iii) *The Procedure Following the Making of the Award*

Immediately after the date of sequestration, the clerk of the court must send a certified copy of the "relevant court order" to the Keeper of the Register of Inhibitions and Adjudications for recording in that register and must send a copy of the order to the **9–143**

Accountant in Bankruptcy (s. 14(1)). The "relevant court order" means:

(1) if the petition has been presented by the debtor, the order awarding sequestration; and

(2) if the petition has been presented by a creditor or the trustee acting under a trust deed, the order granting warrant to cite the debtor to appear (s. 14(5)).

9–144 Recording in the Register of Inhibitions and Adjudications has the effect, as from the date of sequestration, of an inhibition and of a citation in an adjudication of the debtor's heritable estate at the instance of the creditors who have claims accepted in the sequestration (s. 14(2)), *i.e.* the debtor's heritable property becomes "litigious", the consequence being that the debtor is prevented from selling, or otherwise dealing with, the property to the prejudice of the creditors.

9–145 The effect of the recording expires at the end of three years, but the permanent trustee may, if he has not been discharged, renew it by sending a memorandum in a form prescribed by the Court of Session by Act of Sederunt to the Keeper before the end of each subsequent three-year period (s. 14(4), as amended by the Act of 1993, Sched. 1, para. 3). Before the Act of 1993 the permanent trustee had a statutory duty to record a memorandum, but this could involve unnecessary expense if the debtor had no heritable estate or none which could be realised for the benefit of his creditors. As a result of the amendment made by the Act of 1993, the permanent trustee would now be expected to renew the entry only where he still had heritable property vested in him.

9–146 Where the sequestration has been awarded by the Court of Session, that court must remit the sequestration to whichever sheriff court it considers appropriate (s. 15(1)). It may also, on application being made to it, transfer the sequestration from one sheriff to another sheriff (s. 15(2)).

9–147 There are no normal rights of appeal against the award of sequestration. This can be justified by the need to prevent delay such as might result in the disappearance of assets from the debtor's estate. The only right of appeal available is to a petitioning creditor against the court's *refusal to award* sequestration. Any such appeal must be made within 14 days of the making of the court's order (s. 15(3)). The debtor has no right to appeal at all (s. 15(4)).

Where a petition for sequestration has been presented by a creditor or a trustee under a trust deed, the clerk of the court must— 9–148

(1) on the final determination or abandonment of an appeal under section 15(3), or, if there is no appeal, then on the expiry of the 14 days, send a certified copy of an order refusing to award sequestration to the Keeper of the Register of Inhibitions and Adjudications; and

(2) forthwith send a copy of an order awarding or refusing to award sequestration to the Accountant in Bankruptcy (s. 15(5)).

The interim trustee must, as soon as an award of sequestration has been granted, publish in the *Edinburgh Gazette* a notice— 9–149

(1) stating that sequestration of the debtor's estate has been awarded;

(2) inviting submission of claims to him; and

(3) giving other information prescribed by regulations (s. 15(6), as substituted by the Act of 1993, Sched. 1, para. 4). Since the Act of 1993, in order to save expense, it has no longer been necessary to publish a notice in the *London Gazette.*

(iv) *Recall of the Award*

Provision is made for *recall* of an award of sequestration on a petition made to the *Court of Session* under sections 16 and 17. In addition, in the absence of any other remedy, there is the very rare possibility of an action of reduction in the Outer House of the Court of Session (expressly preserved by section 15(4)) or a petition to the *nobile officium* of the Inner House (on which the Act is silent). 9–150

A recall differs from an appeal in the following respects: 9–151

(1) The matter in question in an appeal is whether the court whose decision is being appealed against was entitled to reach its decision in the light of the facts which were then before it. The matter in question in a recall is whether in the light of the facts before the original court *and also* in the light of the facts before the court considering the recall, the original award should be recalled.

(2) As a general principle, an appeal is open only to a party to an action, whereas other parties with an interest may petition for a recall.

(3) The effects of a successful appeal are different from the effects of a successful petition for recall: in the former the court's

order and its consequences would be reversed, whereas in the latter the original order would be considered to be valid until its recall.

Who may petition for recall?

9–152 The persons who may present a petition for the recall of an award are:

(1) the debtor, any creditor or any other person having an interest (even although he may have been the petitioner);

(2) the interim trustee, the permanent trustee or the Accountant in Bankruptcy (s. 16(1)).

Procedure for recall

9–153 The person petitioning for a recall must serve upon the debtor, any person who was a petitioner for the sequestration, the interim trustee or permanent trustee and the Accountant in Bankruptcy, a copy of the petition along with a notice stating that the recipient of the notice may lodge answers to the petition within 14 days of the service of the notice (s. 16(2)).

9–154 At the same time as service is made, the petitioner must publish a notice in the *Edinburgh Gazette* stating that a petition for recall has been presented and that any person having an interest may lodge answers to the petition within 14 days of the publication of the notice (s. 16(3)).

9–155 The time within which the petition must be presented is 10 weeks after the date of the award of sequestration except that it may be presented at any time if it is on one of the grounds mentioned in section 17(1) (s. 16(4), as amended by the Act of 1993, Sched. 1, para. 5) (see 9–158 below).

9–156 Once the court has made its order, the clerk of court must send a certified copy of an order *which recalls an award of sequestration* to the Keeper of the Register of Inhibitions and Adjudications for recording. In addition, he must send a copy of *any order recalling or refusing to recall an award of sequestration* to the Accountant in Bankruptcy and to the permanent trustee (if any) who must insert it in the sederunt book (s. 17(8)).

Grounds of recall

9–157 Section 17(1) confers a wide discretion on the Court of Session: it must be satisfied that in all the circumstances (including those arising after the date of the award) it is appropriate to recall the award (s. 17(1)). This could cover the great variety of situations which may arise in connection with a recall.

9–158 This discretion is, however, limited by the provision in section 16(4) (as amended) that, unless the petition is presented with 10 weeks of the award of sequestration, the ground of the petition must be one of the following:

(1) that the debtor has paid his debts in full or has given sufficient security for their payment; or

(2) a majority in value of the creditors reside in a country other than Scotland and that it is more appropriate for the debtor's estate to be administered in that other country; or

(3) one or more other awards of sequestration have been granted (ss. 16(4) and 17(1)).

9–159 In the case of (3), above, the court may, after appropriate intimation, recall an award other than the award in respect of which the petition is being presented (s. 17(2)).

9–160 The interpretation of section 17(1) when taken along with section 16(4) (as amended) came before the court, seemingly for the first time, in *Martin v. Martin's Trustee*, 1994 S.L.T. 261 (O.H.):

M., who had been sequestrated, presented a petition for recall outside the 10 weeks after the date of the award. His petition had, therefore, to be on one of the grounds mentioned in section 17(1).

M. averred that funds either were available or could be made available and that certain security arrangements could be made by which the creditors either would be paid in full or would have sufficient security for payment.

Counsel for M. argued that the first ground mentioned in section 17(1) ("that the debtor has paid his debts in full or has given sufficient security for their payment") was satisfied. Counsel also emphasised the generality of the opening words of section 17(1).

M.'s petition was dismissed as incompetent.

Lord Clyde (Ordinary) said (at p. 262): "The argument on competency turns upon a construction of the terms of section 17(1)(a). I find that the language of that paragraph is clear and unambiguous. It does not state that the debtor can arrange for payment of the debts or for security, nor does it state that payment can be made or security provided by other means. The situation with which it is dealing is a situation where, to the satisfaction of the court, it is demonstrated that the debtor has paid the debts or has given sufficient security. But that is not what the petitioner in the present petition is claiming that he has done. It was suggested that the language of the paragraph should be so construed as to extend to a situation where the debtor has not made payment but nevertheless is in a position to be able to make it. But that, to my mind, does not meet the plain words of the statute."

In spite of the generality of the opening words of section 17(1), section 16(4) (as amended) required attention to be directed, in this case, to the requirements of the first ground in section 17(1), and M. had not satisfied these requirements.

Expenses on a recall

9–161 On recalling an award of sequestration, the court *must* make provision for the payment of the outlays and remuneration of the interim trustee and permanent trustee by directing that such payment be made out of the debtor's estate or by requiring any person who was a party to the petition for sequestration to pay the whole or part of these outlays and remuneration. The court *may* direct that the expenses of a creditor who was a petitioner, or concurred in the petition, for sequestration be paid out of the debtor's estate, and it *may* make any further order which it considers necessary or reasonable in all the circumstances of the case (s. 17(3)).

9–162 As regards the expenses in the petition for recall itself, the court has a complete discretion to make any order which it thinks fit (s. 17(7)).

Effect of recall

9–163 The general effect of the recall is, so far as practicable, to restore the debtor and any other person affected by the sequestration to the position which he would have been in if the sequestration had not been awarded (s. 17(4)), but this is subject to two exceptions:

(1) The recall does not affect the interruption of prescription caused by the presentation of the petition for sequestration or by the submission of a claim in the sequestration.

(2) The recall does not invalidate any transaction entered into before the recall by the interim trustee or permanent trustee with a person acting in good faith (s. 17(5)).

(d) **Period between Award and Discharge of Interim Trustee**

Under pre-1985 bankruptcy legislation, a considerable time elapsed between the presentation of the petition and the confirmation in office of the trustee; sometimes, where creditors had lost interest, no trustee would be appointed, the sequestration process would never be completed and the bankrupt would not obtain a discharge. One of the most fundamental reforms proposed by the Scottish Law Commission and adopted in the Act of 1985 was to have two trustees—an interim trustee appointed, by the court, early in the sequestration and a permanent trustee, elected by creditors at their "statutory meeting." In the period between the award of sequestration and the creditors' "statutory meeting", therefore, the interim trustee was the key figure. **9–164**

Amongst the changes made by the Act of 1993 were that the Accountant in Bankruptcy could in certain circumstances be appointed as the interim and the permanent trustee and different provisions apply to the "statutory meeting" according to whether the interim trustee is or is not the Accountant in Bankruptcy. **9–165**

The provisions as to the appointment and general functions of the interim trustee are in section 2 (as substituted by the Act of 1993, s. 2) (see 9–88 *et seq.*, above). Provisions as to his resignation, removal and specific functions (which are the working out of the general functions listed in section 2(4)) are outlined below under the following headings: **9–166**

(i) removal and resignation of interim trustee;
(ii) interim preservation of the estate;
(iii) statement of assets and liabilities;
(iv) interim trustee's statement and comments;
(v) calling of statutory meeting;
(vi) claims for voting at statutory meeting;
(vii) proceedings at statutory meeting;
(viii) confirmation of permanent trustee; and
(ix) discharge of interim trustee.

(i) *Removal and Resignation of Interim Trustee*

The provisions as to removal and resignation of the interim trustee are mainly in section 13, as substituted by the Act of 1993 (Sched. 1, para. 2). **9–167**

9–168 As has been seen above (9–81), under section 1A(2), if it appears to the Accountant in Bankruptcy that an interim trustee has failed without reasonable excuse to perform a duty imposed upon him, the Accountant in Bankruptcy must report the matter to the court, and, after hearing the interim trustee, the court *may* remove him from office. If it does so, then it *must*, on the application of the Accountant in Bankruptcy, appoint a new interim trustee (s. 13(1), as substituted by the Act of 1993, Sched. 1, para. 2).

9–169 In addition, where the court is satisfied that an interim trustee—

(1) is for any reason whatsoever unable to act; or

(2) has so conducted himself that he should no longer continue to act in the sequestration,

the court *must* remove him from office and appoint a new interim trustee. The application to the court for its exercise of this power may be made by the debtor, a creditor or the Accountant in Bankruptcy (s. 13(2), as substituted by the Act of 1993, Sched. 1, para. 2). An interim trustee (other than the Accountant in Bankruptcy) may apply to the court for authority to resign office, and if the court is satisfied that one or other of the grounds (1) and (2), above, applies, then the court *must* grant the application (s. 13(3), as substituted by the Act of 1993, Sched. 1, para. 2). Following such a resignation, the court must appoint a new interim trustee (s. 13(4), as substituted by the Act of 1993, Sched. 1, para. 2).

9–170 Where the interim trustee has died, the court must appoint a new interim trustee, on the application of the debtor, a creditor or the Accountant in Bankruptcy (s. 13(5), as substituted by the Act of 1993, Sched. 1, para. 2).

9–171 The interim trustee (other than the Accountant in Bankruptcy) is subject to the same disqualifications as apply to the permanent trustee under section 24(2) (as amended by the Act of 1993, Sched. 1, para. 12), *i.e.* he must not be the debtor, or a person not qualified to act as an insolvency practitioner in relation to the debtor, or hold an interest opposed to the general interests of the creditors, or reside outwith the jurisdiction of the Court of Session or not have given a written undertaking to act as permanent trustee (s. 13(6), as substituted by the Act of 1993, Sched. 1, para. 2).

(ii) *Interim Preservation of the Estate*

The debtor's estate does not vest in the interim trustee. Therefore, what the interim trustee can do to preserve the debtor's estate until the permanent trustee has been elected by the creditors and had his election confirmed by the court takes the form in general of directions to the debtor, *e.g.* as to how the debtor is to conduct his business. **9–172**

The specific provisions as to the interim preservation of the estate are in section 18, as amended by the Act of 1993 (Sched. 1, para. 6). **9–173**

The section first provides that the interim trustee may give general or particular directions to the debtor relating to the management of the debtor's estate (s. 18(1)). The debtor has the right to apply to the court to have an unreasonable direction set aside, and the court will then give such directions to the debtor regarding the management of his estate as the court considers appropriate (s. 18(4)). **9–174**

Secondly, in exercising the general function in section 2(4)(a) of safeguarding the debtor's estate pending the appointment of a permanent trustee, an interim trustee may do any of the following: **9–175**

(1) require the debtor to deliver up to him any money or valuables, or any document relating to the debtor's business or financial affairs, belonging to or in the possession of the debtor or under his control;

(2) place in safe custody anything mentioned in (1), above;

(3) require the debtor to deliver up to him any perishable goods belonging to the debtor or under his control and arrange for the sale or disposal of such goods;

(4) make or cause to be made an inventory or valuation of any property belonging to the debtor;

(5) require the debtor to implement any transaction entered into by the debtor;

(6) effect or maintain insurance policies over the business or property of the debtor;

(7) close down the debtor's business;

(8) carry on any business of the debtor or borrow money in so far as it is necessary for the interim trustee to do so to safeguard the debtor's estate (s. 18(2)).

The court, on the application of the interim trustee, may: **9–176**

(1) on cause shown, grant a warrant authorising the interim trustee to enter the debtor's residence or business premises and to search for and take possession of money, valuables, business or financial documents and perishable goods, if need be by opening shut and lock-fast places; or

(2) make such other order to safeguard the debtor's estate as it thinks appropriate (s. 18(3)).

9–177 The debtor is guilty of an offence if he fails without reasonable excuse to comply with a direction given by the interim trustee or by the court or to comply with requirements as to goods and transactions in (1), (3) and (5), in 9–175, above, or if he obstructs the carrying out of a search warrant (s. 18(5)).

9–178 An instance of the court giving such order "to safeguard the debtor's estate as it thinks appropriate" is *Clark's Trustee, Noter*, 1993 S.L.T. 667 (O.H.); also reported as *Scottish & Newcastle plc, Petitioner*, 1992 S.C.L.R. 540 (O.H.):

The interim trustee averred that a high offer had been received for the debtor's licensed premises conditional on the transfer of the licence and that non-acceptance would have had prejudicial effects.

The court gave authority to the interim trustee to sell the heritage since in the circumstances it was clearly expedient to do so.

(iii) *Statement of Assets and Liabilities*

9–179 Section 19, as substituted by the Act of 1993 (Sched. 1, para. 7), relates to the sending to the interim trustee of a statement of the debtor's assets and liabilities.

9–180 Where the petitioner for sequestration is the debtor, he must, within seven days after the appointment of the interim trustee (where he is not the Accountant in Bankruptcy), send to the interim trustee the statement of assets and liabilities that was lodged with the petition under section 5(6A) (see 9–112, above) (s. 19(1)).

Where the petitioner for sequestration is a creditor or a trustee acting under a trust deed, the debtor must, within seven days after having been notified by the interim trustee of his appointment (as is required by section 2(7), as substituted by the Act of 1993, s. 2), send to the interim trustee a statement of assets and liabilities (s. 19(2)).

9–181 If the debtor—

(1) fails to send the statement of assets and liabilities; or
(2) fails to disclose any material fact in the statement; or
(3) makes a material misstatement in the statement,
he is guilty of an offence and liable to a fine or imprisonment or both (s. 19(4)).

It is a defence for the accused to show that he had a reasonable excuse for his offence (s. 19(4)). **9–182**

(iv) *Interim Trustee's Statement and Comments*

The duties of the interim trustee on receipt of the debtor's statement of assets and liabilities are in section 20, as amended by the Act of 1993 (Sched. 1, para. 8). **9–183**

On receiving the debtor's statement, the interim trustee must, as soon as practicable, prepare a statement of the debtor's affairs so far as he knows them, and must indicate in his statement whether, in his opinion, the debtor's assets are unlikely to be sufficient to pay any dividend whatsoever on the preferred, ordinary and postponed debts (s. 20(1)). **9–184**

The interim trustee must then, not later than four days before the "statutory meeting", send to the Accountant in Bankruptcy— **9–185**
(1) the debtor's statement of assets and liabilities;
(2) a copy of his own statement of the debtor's affairs; and
(3) his own written comments indicating what in his opinion are the causes of the insolvency and as to what extent the conduct of the debtor may have contributed to the insolvency.

The written comments are absolutely privileged (s. 20(3)). This enables the interim trustee to state his suspicions about offences which may have been committed by the debtor. **9–186**

Since the interim trustee may encounter some reluctance on the part of the debtor or others in giving information, he may apply to the sheriff for an order requiring the debtor, the debtor's spouse, or any other person with information to appear before the sheriff for private examination (s. 20(4)). **9–187**

(v) *Calling of Statutory Meeting*

The term "statutory meeting" refers to a meeting of creditors called by the interim trustee under section 21, as amended by the Act of 1993 (Sched. 1, para. 10), or under section 21A, inserted by **9–188** the Act of 1993 (s. 5) (s. 20A, inserted by the Act of 1993 (Sched. 1, para. 9)).

9–189 Section 21 applies where the interim trustee is not the Accountant in Bankruptcy, while section 21A applies where the interim trustee is the Accountant in Bankruptcy.

9–190 Where the interim trustee is not the Accountant in Bankruptcy, he *must* call the statutory meeting to be held within 60 days, or such longer period as the sheriff on cause shown may allow, after the date of the award of sequestration (s. 21(1)). The meeting must be held at the time and place decided by the interim trustee (s. 21(1A)).

9–191 At least seven days' notice of the date, time and place of the meeting must be given by the interim trustee to every creditor known to him and to the Accountant in Bankruptcy, and the notice must invite the creditors to submit claims which have not already been submitted (s. 21(2)).

9–192 The creditors may continue the statutory meeting to a date not later than seven days after the date for which it had first to be called (s. 21(3)). This may give the creditors time to discuss among themselves matters of which they have first become aware at the statutory meeting.

9–193 Where the interim trustee is the Accountant in Bankruptcy, it is not always necessary for the statutory meeting to be held. Initially, the decision as to whether it is to be held rests with the interim trustee, but his decision can be overruled by one quarter in value of the creditors. The time and place for the meeting, if any, are decided by the interim trustee (s. 21A(1)).

9–194 Within 60 days after the date of the sequestration, or such longer period as the sheriff may on cause shown allow, the interim trustee must give notice to every creditor known to him of whether he intends to call the statutory meeting (s. 21A(2)). The notice must be accompanied by a copy of the interim trustee's statement of the debtor's affairs (see 9–184, above), and must inform the creditors, if the interim trustee does not intend to hold the statutory meeting, of the procedure by which they may insist on the calling of the meeting. He must also, if he does not intend to hold the statutory meeting, inform the creditors of whether he intends to apply for the grant of a certificate for the summary administration of the sequestration—a procedure introduced by the Act of 1993 (s. 6(1), inserting s. 23A into the Act of 1985) for cases where the aggregate amount of the debtor's liabilities and assets does not exceed £20,000 and £2,000, respectively (s. 21A(3)).

Within seven days of the giving of the interim trustee's notice, any creditor may request the interim trustee to call the statutory meeting (s. 21A(4)), and where the request is made by not less than one quarter in value of the debtor's creditors, the interim trustee *must* call the statutory meeting not later than 28 days, or such other period as the sheriff may on cause shown allow, after the giving of the notice (s. 21A(5)). **9–195**

Where the interim trustee gives notice that he intends to call the statutory meeting, the meeting must be called not later than 28 days after the giving of the notice (s. 21A(6)). **9–196**

At least seven days before the date fixed for the statutory meeting, the interim trustee must notify every creditor known to him of the date, time and place of the meeting, and must invite the submission of claims which have not already been submitted (s. 21A(7)). **9–197**

The creditors may continue the statutory meeting to a date not later than seven days after the 28 days referred to in section 21A(6) (see 9–196, above) or such longer period as the sheriff may on cause shown allow (s. 21A(8)). **9–198**

It may be that the interim trustee does not call the statutory meeting and also that the seven days during which a creditor may request him to call the meeting have expired. By section 21B, inserted by the Act of 1993 (s. 5), the interim trustee must— **9–199**

(1) forthwith make a report to the sheriff of the circumstances of the sequestration; and

(2) provide to the sheriff a copy of the interim trustee's statement of the debtor's affairs (s. 21B(1)).

In such a case, the court must then appoint the Accountant in Bankruptcy or his nominee as permanent trustee under section 25A (inserted by the Act of 1993 (s. 7)), and the interim trustee may apply to the sheriff for the grant of a certificate for the summary administration of the sequestration under section 23A (inserted by the Act of 1993 (s. 6(1)) (s. 21B(2)).

(vi) *Claims for Voting at Statutory Meeting*

For the purposes of voting at the statutory meeting, a creditor must submit a statement of claim in the prescribed form and an account or voucher (according to the nature of the debt) which constitutes **9–200** prima facie evidence of the debt. The interim trustee may, however, dispense with formalities (s. 22(1)–(3)).

9–201 A creditor who makes a false claim is guilty of an offence unless he shows that he neither knew nor had reason to believe that his claim was false. Similarly, the debtor is guilty of an offence if he knew that a claim was false and failed to report that fact to the interim or permanent trustee (s. 22(5)).

9–202 The submission of a claim bars the effect of the rules relating to limitation of actions in any part of the United Kingdom (s. 22(8)).

(vii) *Proceedings at Statutory Meeting*

9–203 At the beginning of the statutory meeting the interim trustee takes the chair. He decides, for the purposes of voting, on the acceptance or rejection of each creditor's claim. He must invite the creditors to elect one of their number as chairman in his place, but if they decline he remains the chairman throughout the meeting (s. 23(1) and (2)).

9–204 The debtor's statement of assets and liabilities and the interim trustee's statement of the debtor's affairs are then made available for inspection. The interim trustee must answer to the best of his ability any questions, and consider any representations, put to him by the creditors. He then indicates whether, in his opinion, the debtor's assets are unlikely to be sufficient to pay any dividend whatsoever on the preferred, ordinary and postponed debts, and, at or as soon as possible after the statutory meeting, he revises his statement of the debtor's affairs if he decides that revision is necessary (s. 23(3), as amended by the Act of 1993, Sched. 1, para. 11).

9–205 If the interim trustee has revised his statement of the debtor's affairs he must, as soon as possible after the statutory meeting, send a copy of the revised statement to every creditor known to him (s. 23(5), as amended by the Act of 1993, Sched. 1, para. 11).

9–206 After the conclusion of the proceedings in section 23(3) (see 9–204, above), the creditors at the statutory meeting must proceed to the election of the permanent trustee, the provisions for which are in section 24, as amended by the Act of 1993 (Sched. 1, para. 12).

9–207 The following persons are ineligible for election as permanent trustee:

(1) the debtor;

(2) a person who is not qualified to act as an insolvency practitioner or who, though qualified to act as an insolvency practitioner, is not qualified to act as such in relation to the debtor;

(3) a person who holds an interest opposed to the general interests of the creditors;

(4) a person who resides outwith the jurisdiction of the Court of Session;

(5) a person who has not given a written undertaking to act as permanent trustee;

(6) the Accountant in Bankruptcy (s. 24(2)).

The following persons are not entitled to *vote* in the election of **9–208**
the permanent trustee:

(1) anyone acquiring a debt due by the debtor, otherwise than by succession, after the date of sequestration (to discourage a creditor from buying in debts due to other creditors so as to increase his own voting power);

(2) any creditor to the extent that his debt is a postponed debt (s. 24(3)).

In any case where the Accountant in Bankruptcy is the interim **9–209**
trustee and no creditor entitled to vote in the election of the permanent trustee attends the statutory meeting or no permanent trustee is elected, then the Accountant in Bankruptcy must immediately report the proceedings to the sheriff, and the sheriff must appoint the Accountant in Bankruptcy or his nominee as the permanent trustee (s. 24(3A)). Where such a report is made, the Accountant in Bankruptcy may apply to the sheriff for the grant of a certificate for the summary administration of the sequestration—the procedure introduced by the Act of 1993 for cases where the aggregate amount of the debtor's liabilities and assets does not exceed £20,000 and £2,000, respectively, governed by section 23A (inserted by the Act of 1993 (s. 6(1)), Schedule 2 (as amended by the Act of 1993, Sched. 1, para. 30) and Schedule 2A (inserted by the Act of 1993 (s. 6(2)).

In any case where the Accountant in Bankruptcy is not the **9–210**
interim trustee, if no creditor entitled to vote in the election of the permanent trustee attends the statutory meeting or if no permanent trustee is elected, then the interim trustee must immediately notify the Accountant in Bankruptcy and report the proceedings at the meeting to the sheriff, who then appoints the interim trustee as

the permanent trustee (s. 24(4)). Where such a report is made, the interim trustee may apply to the sheriff for the grant of a certificate for the summary administration of the sequestration (s. 24(4A)). The sequestration then follows the modified procedure, the details of which are set out in Schedule 2 to the Act, as amended by the Act of 1993 (Sched. 1, para. 30) (s. 24(5)).

9–211 Only one person can be appointed as permanent trustee: a joint appointment is not competent and will not be confirmed by the court: *Inland Revenue Commissioners v. MacDonald*, 1988 S.L.T. (Sh.Ct.) 7.

9–212 Also at the statutory meeting the creditors (with the same restrictions on voting as in section 24(3), above) may, from among themselves or their mandatories, elect up to five commissioners. Alternatively, the election of commissioners may take place at any later meeting of creditors (s. 30(1)).

The following persons are ineligible:

(1) the debtor;

(2) a person who holds an interest opposed to the general interests of the creditors;

(3) a person who is an associate of the debtor or of the permanent trustee (s. 30(2)).

9–213 A commissioner may resign office at any time (s. 30(3)). He may be removed by the court (on a report made by the Accountant in Bankruptcy under section 1A(2), or by the creditor of whom he is the mandatory recalling the mandate and intimating its recall to the permanent trustee, or on the vote of creditors at a meeting called for the purpose (s. 30(4)).

9–214 There are no commissioners in a sequestration which takes the modified form (Schedule 2).

9–215 Provisions as to holding and procedure at meetings of commissioners are to be found in Schedule 6 to the Act.

(viii) *Confirmation of Permanent Trustee*

9–216 The election by the creditors of the permanent trustee must be confirmed by the court. The provisions are in section 25, as amended by the Act of 1993 (Sched. 1, para. 13). The interim trustee must immediately after the election make a report of the proceedings at the statutory meeting to the sheriff, and the debtor, a creditor, the interim trustee, the permanent trustee or the

Accountant in Bankruptcy may, within four days after the meeting, object to any matter connected with the election (s. 25(1)).

Having made his report under section 25(1), the interim trustee may apply to the sheriff for the grant of a certificate for the summary administration of the sequestration (s. 25(2A)). This would apply where the aggregate amount of the debtor's liabilities and assets does not exceed £20,000 and £2,000, respectively, and the procedure introduced by section 23A of, and Schedule 2A to, the Act would have the effect of modifying the duties of the permanent trustee. **9–217**

If a timeous objection is made under section 25(1), above, to any matter connected with the election, the sheriff must immediately give parties an opportunity to be heard and if he sustains the objection, he must order the interim trustee to arrange a new meeting for the election of a permanent trustee (s. 25(3) and (4)). **9–218**

If there is no timeous objection or if any objection is rejected, the sheriff confirms the election of the permanent trustee, and the sheriff clerk issues to the permanent trustee an act and warrant in a form prescribed by the Court of Session by Act of Sederunt and sends a copy of the act and warrant to the Accountant in Bankruptcy (s. 25(2) and (4)). **9–219**

The permanent trustee must insert a copy of the act and warrant in the sederunt book and, if he is not the same person as the interim trustee, publish a notice in the *Edinburgh Gazette* in the prescribed form stating that he has been confirmed in office as permanent trustee (s. 25(6)). **9–220**

(ix) *Discharge of Interim Trustee*

Before applying for his discharge the interim trustee must follow certain procedure. This differs according to whether: **9–221**

(1) the Accountant in Bankruptcy is not the interim trustee (s. 26, as amended by the Act of 1993 (Sched. 1, para. 14) and s. 27, as amended by the Act of 1993 (Sched. 1, para. 15)); or

(2) the Accountant in Bankruptcy is the interim trustee (s. 26A, inserted by the Act of 1993 (Sched. 1, para. 15)).

(1) **Where the Accountant in Bankruptcy is not the interim trustee**

Where the interim trustee does not himself become the permanent trustee, he must, on confirmation of the permanent trustee in office, hand over to him everything in his possession which relates **9–222** to the sequestration and then cease to act in the sequestration (s. 26(1)).

9–223 Within three months of the confirmation in office of the permanent trustee, the interim trustee must:

(a) submit to the Accountant in Bankruptcy his accounts of his intromissions (if any) with the debtor's estate and a claim for outlays reasonably incurred, and for remuneration for work reasonably undertaken, by him; and

(b) send to the permanent trustee a copy of all the documents in (a), above (s. 26(2)).

9–224 The Accountant in Bankruptcy, on receiving these documents must audit the accounts and fix the amount of outlays and remuneration payable to the interim trustee. A copy of both the audited accounts and the amount of outlays and remuneration is sent to the permanent trustee, who inserts them in the sederunt book. A copy of the amount of outlays and remuneration is also sent to the interim trustee (s. 26(3)).

9–225 Within 14 days after the fixing of the amount of outlays and remuneration payable to the interim trustee, an appeal may be made against it to the sheriff by the interim trustee, the permanent trustee, the debtor or any creditor. The decision of the sheriff is final (s. 26(4)).

9–226 The permanent trustee, on being confirmed in office, must make entries in the sederunt book recording the sequestration process before his confirmation, but he must not include the written comments made by the interim trustee under section 20(2) (indicating what in the interim trustee's opinion are the causes of the insolvency and the extent to which the debtor's conduct may have contributed to the insolvency) (s. 26(5)).

9–227 On receiving his copy of the amount fixed for outlays and remuneration, the interim trustee may apply to the Accountant in Bankruptcy for a certificate of discharge (s. 27(1)). He must give notice of his application to the debtor and to the permanent trustee, and he must inform the debtor that:

(1) written representations concerning the application may be made to the Accountant in Bankruptcy by the debtor himself, the permanent trustee or any creditor within the next 14 days after notification;

(2) the audited accounts of his intromissions (if any) with the debtor's estate are available for inspection at the office of the

interim trustee and that a copy of those accounts has been sent to the permanent trustee for insertion in the sederunt book; and

(3) the grant of a certificate of discharge by the Accountant in Bankruptcy will have the effect of discharging the interim trustee from all liability (other than liability arising from fraud) to the creditors or to the debtor for any act or omission of the interim trustee (s. 27(2)).

On the expiry of the 14 days, the Accountant in Bankruptcy, after considering any representations made to him must grant, or refuse to grant, the certificate of discharge, and must notify, in addition to the interim trustee, the debtor, the permanent trustee and all creditors who have made representations (s. 27(3)). All these parties are allowed a further 14 days after the Accountant in Bankruptcy's decision in which they may appeal to the sheriff, and if the sheriff decides that a certificate of discharge which has been refused should be granted he must order the Accountant in Bankruptcy to grant it (s. 27(4)). The decision of the sheriff is final (s. 27(4A)). **9–228**

On the grant of a certificate of discharge, the permanent trustee makes an appropriate entry in the sederunt book (s. 27(6)). **9–229**

(2) **Where the Accountant in Bankruptcy is the interim trustee**

The provisions of section 26A apply where the Accountant in Bankruptcy has been the interim trustee but some other person becomes the permanent trustee (s. 26A(1)). The procedure is similar to that under (1), above, with some necessary modifications: **9–230**

The Accountant in Bankruptcy submits to the permanent trustee his account of his intromissions (if any) as interim trustee with the debtor's estate, his calculation of his prescribed fees and outlays and a copy of a notice that he has begun the procedure for his discharge, that accounts of his intromissions are available for inspection at an address decided by him and as to the appeal which may be made to the sheriff (s. 26A(3)). **9–231**

The Accountant in Bankruptcy must send to the debtor and to all creditors known to him a copy of his calculation of fees and outlays and the notice referred to in section 26A(3), above (s. 26A(4)). **9–232**

The appeal which may be made to the sheriff (by the permanent trustee, the debtor or any creditor) is against the calculation of fees and outlays or the discharge by the Accountant in Bankruptcy of his actings as interim trustee or both (s. 26A(5)). **9–233**

9–234 If no appeal to the sheriff is made or if such an appeal is refused, the Accountant in Bankruptcy is discharged of all liability (other than any liability arising from fraud) to the creditors or to the debtor for any act or omission in his functions as interim trustee (s. 26A(7)).

(e) Conduct of Sequestration by Permanent Trustee

9–235 The general functions of the permanent trustee as stated in section 3(1) have already been noted (9–96, above). Of the seven general functions listed, the first two summarise the two-way process which he administers—first, recovering, managing and realising the debtor's estate and secondly distributing the estate among the debtor's creditors according to their respective entitlements.

9–236 As has been seen, commissioners may have been elected whose general functions, under section 4, are to supervise the intromissions of the permanent trustee and to advise him. In the provisions which follow the permanent trustee is commonly required to look for authority or supervision to "the commissioners, or if there are no commissioners, the Accountant in Bankruptcy".

9–237 The role of the permanent trustee is outlined under the following headings:

(i) replacement of permanent trustee;
(ii) vesting of estate in permanent trustee;
(iii) safeguarding of interests of creditors;
(iv) effect of sequestration on diligence;
(v) administration of estate by permanent trustee;
(vi) examination of debtor;
(vii) claims, distribution and dividends;
(viii) discharge of debtor; and
(ix) discharge of permanent trustee.

(i) *Replacement of Permanent Trustee*

9–238 Replacement of the permanent trustee may result from his resignation, his death or his removal from office. The provisions are in section 28 (as amended by the Act of 1993 (Sched. 1, para. 17)) and section 29 (as amended by the Act of 1993 (Sched. 1, para. 18)).

9–239 The permanent trustee may apply to the sheriff for authority to resign office, and the sheriff must grant the application if he is satisfied that the permanent trustee—

(1) is for any reason whatsoever unable to act; or

(2) has so conducted himself that he should no longer continue to act in the sequestration (s. 28(1)).

The commissioners, or if there are no commissioners, the Accountant in Bankruptcy, must call a meeting of the creditors to be held not more than 28 days after the permanent trustee's resignation, for the election of a new permanent trustee. However, the sheriff, in granting the permanent trustee's application may impose on the grant the condition that a new permanent trustee be elected; it is then for the resigning permanent trustee himself to call a meeting of the creditors to be held not more than 28 days after the granting of the application. The sheriff has also power to impose such other conditions as he thinks appropriate in granting an application (s. 28(1A) and (2)). **9–240**

Where the commissioners become, or if there are no commissioners the Accountant in Bankruptcy becomes, aware that the permanent trustee has died, they or as the case may be the Accountant in Bankruptcy must as soon as practicable after becoming aware of the death call a meeting of creditors for the election of a new permanent trustee (s. 28(3)). **9–241**

The permanent trustee may be removed from office by the creditors at a meeting called for the purpose if they also elect forthwith a new permanent trustee (s. 29(1)(a)). **9–242**

As has been seen (9–81, above), he may also be removed by the court on a report made to it by the Accountant in Bankruptcy that he has failed without reasonable excuse to perform a duty imposed on him by the Act or by any other statutory or common law rule (s. 1A(2)). **9–243**

An application for removal may also be made under section 29(1)(b) by the Accountant in Bankruptcy, the commissioners or a person representing at least one-quarter in value of the creditors. Such an application must be intimated in the *Edinburgh Gazette* and the permanent trustee must be given an opportunity of being heard (s. 29(2)). The sheriff may order removal, but has the discretion to make any additional or different order as he thinks fit (s. 29(3)). The permanent trustee, the Accountant in Bankruptcy, the commissioners or any creditor may appeal against the sheriff's decision within 14 days after it (s. 29(4)). **9–244**

Where a permanent trustee is unable to act (for any reason other than death) or where he has so conducted himself that he should **9–245** no longer continue to act in the sequestration, an application may be made to the sheriff by a commissioner, the debtor, a creditor or the Accountant in Bankruptcy for a declaration that the office has become vacant and for any order necessary to enable the sequestration to proceed or to safeguard the estate pending the election of a new permanent trustee (s. 29(6)).

9–246 Where the sheriff has removed the permanent trustee or declared the office vacant, the commissioners or, if there are no commissioners, the Accountant in Bankruptcy must call a meeting of creditors, to be held not more than 28 days after the removal or declaration, for the election of a new permanent trustee (s. 29(5) and (6)).

9–247 On any replacement of the permanent trustee, the new permanent trustee may require the former permanent trustee or his representatives to submit accounts for audit to the commissioners or, if there are no commissioners, to the Accountant in Bankruptcy, and the outlays and remuneration payable to the former trustee or his representatives are also fixed by the commissioners or by the Accountant in Bankruptcy (s. 28(6)).

9–248 There is a right of appeal available to the former trustee or his representatives, the new permanent trustee, the debtor or any creditor within the next 14 days against the amount fixed for outlays and remuneration: if the amount was fixed by the commissioners, the appeal is to the Accountant in Bankruptcy and from him to the sheriff, and if the amount was fixed by the Accountant in Bankruptcy the appeal is to the sheriff (s. 28(7)). The decision of the sheriff is final (s. 28(8)).

9–249 Where no new permanent trustee is elected after a resignation, death or removal, the Accountant in Bankruptcy or a person nominated by him may apply to the sheriff for appointment as permanent trustee and the sheriff must make that appointment. The procedure then follows the modified procedure as set out in Schedule 2 (ss. 28(5), 29(8) and 25A).

(ii) *Vesting of Estate in Permanent Trustee*

9–250 A major principle in the sequestration process is that all the debtor's estate, with some limited exceptions, vests in the permanent trustee. The leading provision in the Act is that, subject to specified exceptions, "the whole estate of the debtor shall vest as at the date of sequestration in the permanent trustee for the benefit of the creditors . . . by virtue of the act and warrant issued on confirmation of the permanent trustee's appointment" (s. 31(1)). The "whole estate of the debtor" includes property, wherever situated, and section 426(4) of the Insolvency Act 1986 provides that courts with jurisdiction in relation to insolvency law in any part of the United Kingdom must assist the courts with corresponding jurisdiction in any other part of the United Kingdom. The "whole estate of the debtor" also extends to the capacity to exercise, and to take proceedings for exercising, all powers over any property which might have been exercised by the debtor for his own benefit at or after the date of sequestration (s. 31(8)). In *Cumming's Trustee v. Glenrinnes Farms Ltd*, 1993 S.L.T. 904 (O.H.) this provision enabled the trustee in the sequestration of C., who was a shareholder in G. Ltd, to petition for the winding up of G. Ltd on the "just and equitable" ground (Insolvency Act 1986, s. 122(1)(g), although the trustee was not registered as a member.

In addition to the major principle mentioned, the Act makes **9–251** express special provision for certain related matters. First, there are rules which apply to vesting at the date of sequestration; secondly, there are rules relating to vesting after the date of sequestration and before the debtor's discharge; thirdly, there are provisions on dealings of the debtor after sequestration; and fourthly, there are statutory limitations on vesting.

(1) **Vesting of estate at date of sequestration**

Amongst the matters for which special provision is made are the **9–252** following:

(a) As regards heritable property in Scotland, the act and **9–253** warrant has the same effect as a "decree of adjudication in implement of sale, as well as a decree of adjudication for payment and in security of debt, subject to no legal reversion" (s. 31(1)). The "decree of adjudication in implement of sale" gives the permanent trustee an absolute title. The "decree of adjudication for payment and in security of debt" is normally redeemable by the debtor during "the legal" (*i.e.* 10 years after the decree); hence the words "subject to no legal reversion" are included in order to prevent the debtor from exercising any right of redemption.

(b) The permanent trustee can deal with any heritable property **9–254** vested in him by the act and warrant even where there is a "prior inhibition" (s. 31(2)). The effect of the diligence of inhibition would normally be to prevent the debtor against whom it had been used from dealing with the property, provided the inhibition was prior to the date of sequestration. The provision in the Act makes the permanent trustee's dealing with the property unchallengeable, despite any prior inhibition, but reserves the inhibiting creditor's rights on ranking.

9–255 (c) Where the debtor has an uncompleted title to any heritable estate in Scotland, the permanent trustee may complete title to it either in his own name or in the name of the debtor (s. 31(3)).

9–256 (d) As regards moveable property for which delivery or possession or intimation of its assignation would be required in order to complete title, the Act provides that the property vests in the permanent trustee *as if* at the date of sequestration the permanent trustee had taken delivery or possession of the property or had made intimation of its assignation to him as the case may be (s. 31(4)).

9–257 (e) Any non-vested contingent interest which the debtor has (*e.g.* an interest which vests in the survivor of the debtor and another person) vests in the permanent trustee as if an assignation of that interest had been executed by the debtor and intimation of the assignation made at the date of sequestration (s. 31(5)). If it were not for this provision, a non-vested contingent interest would not form part of the debtor's estate. The result is that if the contingency is not purified until after the debtor's discharge (by the death of the other person before the debtor in the example above), the interest is still vested in the permanent trustee for the benefit of the creditors.

(2) **Vesting after sequestration**

9–258 During the period after the date of sequestration and before the debtor's discharge, the debtor must immediately notify the permanent trustee of any assets acquired by him and of any other substantial change in his financial circumstances. It is an offence for the debtor to fail to comply with this provision (s. 32(7)).

9–259 A distinction is made during this period between *income* received by the debtor after the date of sequestration and *estate* received by him after that date. The latter is usually referred to as *acquirenda* ("after-acquired property").

Income

The general rule is that any income received by the debtor after the date of sequestration and before his discharge, other than income arising from the estate which is vested in the permanent trustee, vests in the debtor (s. 32(1)). **9–260**

However, the permanent trustee may apply to the sheriff for the sheriff, after considering all the circumstances, to decide a suitable amount to allow for— **9–261**

(a) aliment for the debtor; and

(b) the debtor's "relevant obligations";

and if the debtor's income is in excess of the total amount allowed for (a) and (b) the sheriff must fix the amount of the excess and order it to be paid to the permanent trustee (s. 32(2)).

The debtor's "relevant obligations" referred to in (b), above, are: **9–262**

(a) any obligation of aliment owed by the debtor;

(b) any obligation of his to make a periodical allowance to a former spouse;

(c) any obligation of his to pay child support maintenance under the Child Support Act 1991 (s. 32(3)).

Berry's Trustee v. Berry, 1994 G.W.D. 29–1735 is an instance of an application to the sheriff under section 32(1) and (2) to fix a suitable amount to allow for B.'s aliment. B. was claiming social security benefit. **9–263**

A sum of approximately £320,000 was at the credit of an account in B.'s name at a bank in Liechtenstein.

B. claimed that the funds were held in trust for his daughter, although if she predeceased him the funds were to revert to him as the "original donor".

Held that the benefit was sufficient for B.'s aliment and payment of the credit was ordered to be made to B.'s trustee.

B.'s declaration that he was the "original donor" implied that the funds did vest in him under section 32(1). As B. had no "relevant obligations" within section 32(2)(b), it was "suitable" to allow the benefit for his own aliment and to treat the sum at credit of the bank account as an excess of income to be paid to the trustee under section 32(2).

In assessing a suitable allowance under (a) and (b) of section 32(2) the sheriff should balance the interests of the debtor against those of the creditors, giving due weight to each. This was emphasised in *Brown's Trustee v. Brown*, 1995 S.L.T. (Sh.Ct.) 2, by **9–264**

Sheriff Principal N. D. MacLeod in allowing the trustee's appeal against the sheriff's decision because the sheriff had failed to give due weight to the creditors' interests:

In this case, as in many other cases, the income received by the debtor after sequestration was income from employment.

B. and his wife were made bankrupt when B.'s business collapsed owing creditors about £120,000, B.'s wife being a guarantor of the business's debts.

They continued, however, to draw salaries—B. as a lecturer and his wife as a headmistress—and from these they supported themselves and a university student daughter.

The total monthly net income from the salaries was £2,629.51, and the sheriff held that £378.51 of that total was in excess of the amount suitable for the aliment of the couple and their daughter and ordered that amount to be paid to the trustee.

The sheriff principal said that by section 32(2) the sheriff was specifically required to consider all the circumstances, including, in this case, the large amount of debt and how much of it was likely to be met from the sequestrated estate. These were matters which necessarily affected the creditors' interest in the salaries, but the sheriff had made no apparent reference to these matters in reaching his decision.

The case was remitted by the sheriff principal to the sheriff for him to decide the case in the light of the sheriff principal's opinion.

9–265 If there is a change in the debtor's circumstances, an application may be made to the sheriff by the permanent trustee, the debtor or any other interested person (*e.g.* the debtor's spouse) for variation or recall of any order made under section 32(2), above (s. 32(4)).

9–266 Diligence for a pre-sequestration debt is not competent against income vesting in the debtor (s. 32(5)).

Acquirenda

9–267 Any estate which is acquired by the debtor after the date of sequestration and before the debtor's discharge and which would have vested in the permanent trustee if it had been part of the debtor's estate on the date of sequestration vests in the permanent trustee for the benefit of the creditors as at the date of acquisition. Any person holding such estate must, on production to him of a copy of the act and warrant certified by the sheriff clerk, deliver the estate to the permanent trustee (s. 32(6)).

Robinson v. Somerville & Russell, 1997 G.W.D. 11–477 was an action by R., a permanent trustee, against S., solicitors who had paid over £25,000 out of a deceased's estate to the deceased's sequestrated daughter. R. averred that by section 32(6) the proceeds of the daughter's share in her father's estate had vested in R. as *acquirenda.* **9–268**

The action under section 32(6) was dismissed, on the ground that R. had not averred that he had produced a certified copy of his act and warrant to S. R.'s pleadings were also ambiguous and fundamentally deficient in other respects.

Where the debtor learns that he may derive benefit from another estate, he must as soon as practicable after that date inform both the permanent trustee and the person who is administering the other estate. It is an offence for the debtor to fail to comply with this requirement (s. 15(8) and (9)). **9–269**

(3) Dealings of debtor after sequestration

Any dealing of or with the debtor relating to his estate vested in the permanent trustee under section 31 is of no effect in a question with the permanent trustee (s. 32(8)). This general rule, however, does not apply where the person seeking to uphold the dealing establishes: **9–270**

(a) that the permanent trustee has abandoned the property being dealt with to the debtor, or has expressly or impliedly authorised the dealing, or is in some other way personally barred from challenging the dealing; or

(b) that the dealing is—

(i) the performance of an obligation undertaken before the date of sequestration by a person obliged to the debtor in the obligation; or

(ii) the purchase from the debtor of goods for which the purchaser has given value to the debtor or is willing to give value to the permanent trustee; or

(iii) a banking transaction in the ordinary course of business between the banker and the debtor,

and (in each of (i), (ii) and (iii)) that the person dealing with the debtor was, at the time when the dealing occurred, unaware of the sequestration and had at that time no reason to believe that the debtor's estate was the subject of sequestration proceedings (s. 32(9)).

9–271 In *Minhas's Trustee v. Bank of Scotland*, 1990 S.L.T. 23 (O.H.), the question arose of whether in relation to a banking transaction in the ordinary course of business between the banker and the debtor, the "person dealing with the debtor", and whose knowledge was relevant for the purposes of section 32(9), was the bank through its head office or the bank through its teller at the local branch.

Notice of M.'s sequestration had appeared in the *Edinburgh Gazette* on August 1, 1986, and the head office could not establish that it was unaware of the sequestration proceedings, but when M., on August 14, 1986, withdrew £1,540 from his account at the local branch the teller who conducted the transaction was unaware of the sequestration.

Held that the "person dealing with the debtor" was the teller as the employee of the bank transacting in that capacity and not as an individual and that the relevant knowledge was therefore that of the bank through its head office, not that of the individual teller.

It followed that the transaction was not protected by section 32(9) and that the permanent trustee was entitled to payment from the bank of the £1,540.

(4) **Limitations on vesting**

9–272 The following property of the debtor does not vest in the permanent trustee:

(a) property exempted from poinding for the purpose of protecting the debtor and his family; and

(b) property held on trust by the debtor for any other person (s. 33(1)).

9–273 As regards (a), articles which are exempt from poinding are listed in section 16 of the Debtors (Scotland) Act 1987 and include clothing, tools of trade, medical aids, educational materials, toys and 16 items of household furniture and equipment so far as reasonably required for the use in the house of the person residing there or a member of his household.

9–274 As regards (b), the trustee is said to take the debtor's estate *tantum et tale* ("to such an extent and of such quality") as it belonged to the debtor, *i.e.* his right is as great as, but no greater than, the debtor's right. Property held by the debtor in trust is not his own property, and therefore does not vest in the permanent trustee.

The landlord's hypothec is not affected by the vesting of the estate in the permanent trustee (s. 33(2)). **9–275**

Any secured creditor whose right is preferable to the rights of the permanent trustee is not prejudiced by the vesting provisions in sections 31 and 32 (s. 33(3)). **9–276**

An instance is *Berry v. Taylor*, 1993 S.L.T. 718 (O.H.): **9–277**

A wife, in suing her husband for divorce, effected an arrestment on the dependence of the action. Prior to raising an action of furthcoming, the husband was sequestrated.

The wife claimed that she was a secured creditor under section 33(3) and that the arrested fund had not vested in the trustee.

Held that the trustee had to give effect to the preference secured by the arrestment.

(iii) *Safeguarding of Interests of Creditors*

Under this heading come the provisions on: **9–278**

(1) gratuitous alienations;
(2) unfair preferences;
(3) recalling of order for payment of capital sum on divorce;
(4) recovery of excessive pension contributions; and
(5) extortionate credit transactions.

(1) **Gratuitous alienations**

The provisions of section 34 on this subject have been considered already (see 9–27 *et seq*., above). **9–279**

(2) **Unfair preferences**

The provisions of section 36 on this subject have also already been considered (see 9–59 *et seq*., above). **9–280**

(3) **Recalling of order for payment of capital sum on divorce**

Section 35 applies where: **9–281**

(a) a court has made an order for the payment by a debtor of a capital sum or for the transfer of property by him in connection with divorce;

(b) on the date of the order the debtor was absolutely insolvent or was made so by the implementation of the order; and

(c) within five years after the order—

(i) the debtor is sequestrated; or

(ii) he has granted a trust deed which has become a "protected trust deed" (see 9–471 *et seq.*, below); or

(iii) he has died and within 12 months after his death his estate has been sequestrated or a judicial factor has been appointed under section 11A of the Judicial Factors (Scotland) Act 1889 to administer it (s. 35(1)).

9–282 In these circumstances the permanent trustee, the trustee acting under the trust deed or the judicial factor may apply to the court for an order for recall of the order made on divorce and for the repayment to the applicant of the whole or part of any sum already paid or for the return to the applicant of all or part of any property already transferred, or, if the property has been sold, for payment to the applicant of all or part of the proceeds. Before making such an order, the court must have regard to all the circumstances including the financial and other circumstances of the person against whom the order would be made (s. 35(2)).

(4) **Recovery of excessive pension contributions**

9–283 Sections 36A, 36B and 36C were inserted in the Act of 1985 by the Pensions Act 1995 (s. 95(2)). They enable the permanent trustee to apply to the court, where the debtor has within five years before the date of sequestration made excessive contributions to an occupational pension scheme (s. 36A(1) and 36C(4)).

9–284 If, on such an application, the court is satisfied that the making of the excessive contributions has unfairly prejudiced the debtor's creditors, it may make such order as it thinks fit for restoring the position to what it would have been if the excessive contributions had not been made (s. 36A(2)). The court must consider in particular—

(a) whether any of the contributions were made by or on behalf of the debtor for the purpose of putting assets beyond the reach of his creditors or any of them;

(b) whether the total amount of contributions made (including contributions made to any other occupational pension scheme) during the period of five years before the date of sequestration was excessive in view of the debtor's circumstances at the time when they were made; and

(c) whether the level of benefits under the scheme, together with benefits under any other occupational pension scheme to which the debtor is entitled is excessive in all the circumstances of the case (s. 36A(3)).

Amongst the provisions which may be included in the court order are a requirement that the trustees or managers of the scheme pay an amount to the permanent trustee and a reduction of the amount of any benefit to which the debtor (or his spouse, widow, widower or dependant) is entitled under the scheme (s. 36B(1)). **9–285**

The court may, on the application of any person having an interest, review, rescind or vary an order under section 36A (s. 36B(7)). **9–286**

(5) **Extortionate credit transactions**

Section 61 applies where the debtor entered into an "extortionate" credit transaction within not more than three years before the date of sequestration (s. 61(1) and (2)). A transaction is "extortionate" if, in the light of the risk accepted by the person providing the credit, the terms are such as to require grossly exorbitant payments to be made or the transaction in some other way grossly contravenes ordinary principles of fair dealing. The transaction is presumed to be extortionate until the contrary is proved (s. 61(3)). **9–287**

There is a range of orders which the court may make if applied to by the permanent trustee, including setting aside and variation of the transaction (s. 61(2) and (4)). Any sums or property required to be paid or surrendered to the permanent trustee under a section 61 order vest in him (s. 61(5)). **9–288**

Neither the permanent trustee nor the debtor is entitled to make an application under section 139 of the Consumer Credit Act 1974 for the reopening of an extortionate credit agreement (see 5–314 *et seq.*) (s. 61(6)). **9–289**

(iv) *Effect of Sequestration on Diligence*

One benefit of a sequestration is to prevent a "race of diligence", each creditor attempting to attach for himself some property belonging to the debtor towards the payment of his own debt. Two groups of provisions require to be noted, the first relating to the effect of the constitution of apparent insolvency and the second to the effect of the court order awarding sequestration. **9–290**

9–291 First, certain provisions on arrestments and poindings have, by section 75(1) and Schedule 7, Part II, been continued from the Bankruptcy (Scotland) Act 1913, with the substitution of "apparent insolvency" for "notour bankruptcy". The leading provision, derived from section 10 of the Act of 1913, is that all arrestments and poindings executed within 60 days before the *constitution of apparent insolvency*, or within four months after it, rank *pari passu* ("equally", "rateably") as if they had all been executed on the same date.

9–292 The *court order awarding sequestration* takes effect from the *date of sequestration* (9–141, above). In outline the provisions of section 37 are:

(1) The court order has the effect of—

(a) a decree of adjudication of the debtor's heritable estate for payment of his debts, which has been duly recorded in the Register of Inhibitions and Adjudications on that date; and

(b) an arrestment in execution and decree of furthcoming, an arrestment in execution and warrant of sale, and a completed poinding,

in favour of the creditors according to their respective entitlements (s. 37(1)).

(2) An inhibition on the debtor's estate which takes effect within the period of 60 days before the date of sequestration does not create a preference for the inhibitor (s. 37(2)).

(3) No arrestment or poinding executed—

(a) within 60 days before the date of sequestration; or

(b) on or after the date of sequestration,

gives the arrester or poinder a preference (s. 37(4)).

(4) A similar provision to that in (3), above, applies to the diligence of "poinding of the ground" (s. 37(6)).

(5) It is incompetent on or after the date of sequestration for any creditor to raise or insist in an adjudication against the debtor's estate (s. 37(8)).

9–293 The combined effect of these two groups of provisions may be illustrated by *Stewart v. Jarvie*, 1938 S.C. 309, decided under the Act of 1913:

On October 12, 1936, S. brought an action against the Craigelvin Coal and Fireclay Co. for £273, and on October 16 used arrestments which attached the sum of £136. On November 27, notour bankruptcy was constituted against the firm by the expiry of a charge without payment.

Sequestration of the firm's estates was awarded on January 4, 1937.

Held that S.'s arrestments did not give him priority over the creditors claiming in the sequestration.

Lord Fleming said (at p. 312): "It is important to note that, on the one hand, the appellant's arrestment was used within 60 days prior to the constitution of notour bankruptcy, and that, on the other hand, sequestration took place within four months thereafter. . . .

"Applying sections 10 and 104 [*of the Bankruptcy (Scotland) Act 1913*] to the case in hand, the result is that, as at 4th January 1937, the sequestration is to be regarded as equivalent to an arrestment used for behoof of all the creditors equally. And, accordingly, the appellant's claim for a preference over the other creditors must be dealt with on the footing that, in addition to the arrestment which he used on 16th October 1936, there was also used, for behoof of the general body of the creditors, an arrestment on 4th January 1937. . . . The appellant is not entitled to any preference over the other creditors, for his arrestment and their arrestment are equalised under section 10. The appellant is entitled to be ranked on the arrested fund for the amount of his claim, but, equally, all the other creditors are entitled to be ranked thereon *pari passu* with him for the amount of their respective claims."

(v) *Administration of Estate by Permanent Trustee*

The administration of the estate by the permanent trustee is outlined below under the following headings: **9–294**

(1) taking possession of estate;
(2) management and realisation of estate;
(3) power in relation to debtor's "family home";
(4) protection of rights of spouse in "matrimonial home";
(5) contractual powers of permanent trustee; and
(6) money received by permanent trustee.

(1) **Taking possession of estate**

As soon as possible after his confirmation in office the permanent trustee must: **9–295**

(a) take possession of the estate so far as it vests in him and of any document in the debtor's possession or control relating to his assets or his business or financial affairs;

(b) make up and maintain an inventory and valuation of the estate and record it in the sederunt book; and

(c) immediately send a copy of the inventory and valuation to the Accountant in Bankruptcy (s. 38(1)).

9–296 The permanent trustee is entitled to have access to all documents relating to the assets or the business or financial affairs of the debtor sent by the debtor to a third party and in that third party's hands and to make copies of the documents (s. 38(2)).

9–297 The permanent trustee may require delivery to him of any title deed or other document of the debtor, even where a right of lien is claimed over the title deed or document, but delivery does not prejudice any preference to which the holder of the lien is entitled (s. 38(4)).

(2) **Management and realisation of estate**

9–298 As soon as possible after his confirmation in office the permanent trustee must consult with the commissioners or, if there are no commissioners, with the Accountant in Bankruptcy concerning the exercise of his functions of recovering, managing and realising the estate, and he must comply with any general or specific directions given to him by:

(a) the creditors; or

(b) the court, if the commissioners apply to the court for this purpose; or

(c) if there are no commissioners, the Accountant in Bankruptcy (s. 39(1)).

9–299 Perishable goods may be sold by the permanent trustee without complying with directions under (a) or (c), above, if he considers that compliance with such directions would adversely affect the sale (s. 39(6)).

9–300 The permanent trustee may (but if there are commissioners only with the consent of the commissioners, the creditors or the court) do any of the following things if he considers that its doing would be beneficial for the administration of the estate:

(a) carry on any business of the debtor;

(b) bring, defend or continue any legal proceedings relating to the debtor's estate;

(c) create a security over any part of the estate;

(d) where any right, option or other power forms part of the debtor's estate, make payments or incur liabilities with a view to obtaining, for the benefit of the creditors, any property which is the subject of the right, option or power (s. 39(2)).

Any sale of the estate by the permanent trustee may be by either public sale or private bargain (s. 39(3)). 9–301

Special rules apply where a creditor holds a heritable security over any part of the debtor's heritable estate. Either the permanent trustee or the creditor may sell the estate, but the special rules are intended to ensure that the interests of both the secured creditor and the permanent trustee (for the benefit of the other creditors) are sufficiently protected (s. 39(4)). 9–302

Neither the permanent trustee nor an associate of his nor any commissioner is allowed to purchase any of the debtor's estate (s. 39(8)). 9–303

(3) **Power in relation to debtor's "family home"**

The debtor's "family home" vests in the permanent trustee, but the permanent trustee's right to sell it is restricted in the interests of the occupiers. 9–304

The term "family home" means any property in which, on the day immediately before the date of sequestration, the debtor had a right or interest *and* which was occupied at that date as a residence by the debtor and his spouse or by the debtor's spouse or former spouse or by the debtor with a child of the family (of whatever age, and including a grandchild and any person accepted as a child) (s. 40(4)).

Before selling the debtor's family home the permanent trustee must obtain the consent of the debtor's spouse or former spouse who is in occupation of it (whether or not along with the debtor), or of the debtor if the debtor is in occupation with a child of the family. If the permanent trustee is unable to obtain the necessary consent, he requires the authority of the court, and the court may postpone the granting of its authority for a reasonable time of up to 12 months or may impose conditions (s. 40(1), (2) and (4)). 9–305

Before granting authority the court must have regard to "all the circumstances of the case" including the following: 9–306

(a) the needs and financial resources of the debtor's spouse or former spouse;

(b) the needs and financial resources of any child of the family;

(c) the interests of the creditors;

(d) the length of the period during which the family home was used as a residence by any of the persons referred to in (a) or (b) above (s. 40(2)).

9–307 The provisions of section 40 extend to actions for division and sale of the debtor's family home (*e.g.* where husband and wife own equal half shares of the family home) and to actions to obtain vacant possession of the debtor's family home (s. 40(3)).

9–308 *Salmon's Trustee v. Salmon*, 1989 S.L.T. (Sh.Ct.) 49, was seemingly the first case where authority was sought by a permanent trustee under section 40, and Sheriff I. M. Thomson gave full consideration to all the circumstances of the case as required by section 40(2):

The debtor and his wife were equal proprietors of the family home, where they had lived for about 16 years with one child of the family who at the time of sequestration had not completed his schooling.

In 1983 the debtor had set up in business on his own account as a financial consultant. However, he embezzled over £114,000 from in all 12 of his clients, and was sentenced to two years' imprisonment.

The only asset of the debtor was his half share of the family home (about £10,000), and the only asset of his wife was her share in the family home. The amount due to creditors was £60,000 to £70,000.

The permanent trustee raised an action for division and sale against the debtor's wife, and she sought to rely on the protection given to her by section 40.

In addition to considering all of (a), (b), (c) and (d) in section 40(2) and the debtor's lack of co-operation with the permanent trustee, the sheriff in the exercise of his discretion held that the interests of the creditors and the public interest in having the sequestration completed within a reasonable period outweighed other considerations in the circumstances, and granted the decree, postponed for four months. By the expiry of that extended period the debtor would be out of prison and be in agreed employment and the child would not yet have reached the critical pre-examination preparation stage for his "highers".

9–309 Wholly exceptional circumstances led to the refusal of a permanent trustee's application under section 40 in *Gourlay's Trustee v. Gourlay*, 1995 S.L.T. (Sh.Ct.) 7:

The debtor was G. and his wife had refused to consent to the sale of the family home. G.'s wife and their three children opposed the permanent trustee's application, contending that it would be detrimental to G. and to his wife to move out of the family home which they had occupied for 26 years and where one of the children was still dependent on them.

G. (55 years of age) had suffered a stroke, was in poor physical health, required constant attention and supervision and might suffer from another stroke which would prove fatal. His wife (47 years of age) was near to a state of mental breakdown.

Since the stress involved for the debtor in moving would be considerable with potentially fatal results and such a move would be materially detrimental to the health of the debtor's wife, the sheriff (Sheriff J. K. Mitchell) refused the permanent trustee's application, saying (at p. 11): "If ever there was a case in which the application should be refused, it is this application."

McMahon's Trustee v. McMahon, 1997 S.L.T. 1090, decided by **9–310** the Extra Division, is authority for the width of the discretion conferred on the court in imposing conditions on a grant of authority:

McM., the debtor, was owner in common with his wife of their family home. McM.'s trustee brought an action for division and sale and a declaration that the free proceeds should be divided equally between the permanent trustee and McM.'s wife.

McM.'s wife made a counterclaim seeking a declaration that, before a division of the free proceeds was made, she was entitled either to a sum equivalent to half of the increase in value from March 1, 1988 to the date of sale or to a sum equivalent to half the total payments made by her under two standard securities granted by both husband and wife from March 1, 1988 to the date of sale.

The permanent trustee argued that this counterclaim was irrelevant and incompetent, but the sheriff repelled that plea and the trustee appealed against the sheriff's decision.

Held appeal refused and matter remitted to the sheriff for proof. The natural meaning of section 40 was said to entail the wide discretion contended for by McM.'s wife, and complex inquiry might be necessary owing to the width and variety of circumstances to which the section permitted the court to have regard.

(4) **Protection of rights of spouse in "matrimonial home"**

9–311 The debtor's estate may include a "matrimonial home" within the meaning of the Matrimonial Homes (Family Protection) (Scotland) Act 1981, as amended by the Law Reform (Miscellaneous Provisions) (Scotland) Act 1985, which protects the occupancy rights of a "non-entitled" spouse in the family residence. If the debtor was an "entitled" spouse (the house being in his name) it could be that sequestration might be used to defeat his spouse's occupancy rights. By section 41(1) the permanent trustee is under a duty, if he has the necessary knowledge, to inform the non-entitled spouse, within 14 days of the date of the issue of the act and warrant, of the fact that sequestration of the entitled spouse's estate has been awarded and of the right to petition the Court of Session for a recall of the award under section 16 of the Act (9–150 *et seq.*, above). On such a petition the Court of Session may—

(a) recall the sequestration; or

(b) make such order as it thinks appropriate to protect the occupancy rights of the non-entitled spouse,

if it is satisfied that the purpose of the petition for sequestration was wholly or mainly to defeat the occupancy rights of the non-entitled spouse.

(5) **Contractual powers of permanent trustee**

9–312 The permanent trustee has a choice whether to adopt or not to adopt *any contract entered into by the debtor before the date of sequestration.* He may adopt it if he considers that its adoption would be beneficial to the administration of the estate. In some cases he will be barred from adopting the contract because of the express or implied terms of the contract (s. 42(1)).

9–313 For the benefit of the other party to the contract, it is provided that if the permanent trustee receives a written request from the other party, he must, within the next 28 days (or any longer period allowed by application to the court) either adopt or refuse to adopt the contract (s. 42(2)). If the permanent trustee does not give a written reply to the request within the period allowed, he is deemed to have refused to adopt the contract (s. 42(3)).

9–314 The permanent trustee may enter into *any contract* where he considers that this would be beneficial for the administration of the debtor's estate (s. 42(4)).

(6) **Money received by permanent trustee**

All money received by the permanent trustee in the exercise of his functions must be deposited by him in the name of the debtor's estate in an appropriate bank or institution, except that he may retain in his hands at any time not more than £200 (or other prescribed sum) (s. 43). **9–315**

(vi) *Examination of Debtor*

The Act makes provision for both private examination and public examination. It is an important feature of the reforms made in 1985 that public examination before the sheriff, which was regarded as an essential part of sequestration, should become the exception rather than the rule. The investigatory powers of the interim trustee and informal meetings should enable the tracing of the debtor's estate and ascertainment of the causes of his insolvency to be effected at an earlier stage and with much less expense. **9–316**

Section 44 relates to private examination, section 45 to public examination and sections 46 and 47 relate to both types of examination. **9–317**

(1) **Private examination**

The permanent trustee may request: **9–318**

(a) the debtor to appear before him and to give information relating to his assets, his dealings with them or his conduct in relation to his business or financial affairs; or

(b) the debtor's spouse, or any other person who the permanent trustee believes can give such information, to give the information.

It is normally only if he meets with reluctance that the permanent trustee will consider it necessary to apply to the sheriff for a private examination before the sheriff (s. 44(1)). By the sheriff's order not only the debtor but also his spouse and any other relevant person may be required to attend before the sheriff (s. 44(2)). Failure without reasonable excuse to comply with an order is an offence (s. 44(3)). **9–319**

(2) **Public examination**

The permanent trustee *may* (and *must if requested to do so by the Accountant in Banktuptcy or the commissioners (if any) or one-quarter in value of the creditors*) apply to the sheriff for an order for **9–320** the public examination before the sheriff of the debtor, his spouse or any other relevant person. The time for making such an application is at least eight weeks before the end of the first accounting period (which period, by section 52(2), as substituted by the Act of 1993 (Sched. 1, para. 21), is the first six months following the date of sequestration), except that the permanent trustee may, on cause shown, make the application at any time (s. 45(1)).

9–321 When the sheriff makes an order for public examination, the permanent trustee must:

(a) publish in the *Edinburgh Gazette* a notice in the prescribed form and containing prescribed particulars; and

(b) send a copy of that notice to every creditor known to him and (if the person to be examined is the debtor's spouse or some other relevant person) to the debtor, informing the creditor and (where applicable) the debtor of their right to participate in the examination (s. 45(3)).

9–322 Failure without reasonable excuse to comply with an order is an offence (s. 45(4)).

(3) **Provisions applicable to both private and public examination**

9–323 The permanent trustee may apply to the sheriff for a warrant for the debtor to be apprehended and taken to the place of the examination if the court is satisfied that that is necessary in order to secure the attendance of the debtor, his spouse or other relevant person (s. 46(1), as amended by the Act of 1993 (Sched. 1, para. 20)).

9–324 If there is good reason preventing attendance, the sheriff may grant a commission for the examination to be taken by an "examining commissioner" (s. 46(2)).

9–325 The sheriff or the examining commissioner may order the debtor, his spouse or other relevant person to produce for inspection any document in his custody or control, and to deliver the document or a copy of it to the permanent trustee for further examination by him (s. 46(4)).

9–326 The examination, whether before the sheriff or before an examining commissioner, is taken on oath (s. 47(1)).

9–327 The debtor or a relevant person being examined is not excused from answering any question on the ground that the answer may incriminate or tend to incriminate him or on the ground of confidentiality, but the answer is not admissible in evidence in any subsequent criminal proceedings, except where there is a charge of perjury relating to the statement (s. 47(3)).

The debtor's deposition at the examination must be subscribed by himself and by the sheriff (or the examining commissioner) and inserted in the sederunt book (s. 47(5)). **9–328**

The permanent trustee must insert a copy of the record of the examination in the sederunt book and send a copy of the record to the Accountant in Bankruptcy (s. 47(6)). **9–329**

(vii) *Claims, Distribution and Dividends*

Submission of claims to permanent trustee

As has been mentioned (9–200, above), a creditor, for the purpose of voting at the statutory meeting, must submit a claim to the interim trustee (s. 22(1)) and it is the duty of the interim trustee at the beginning of the statutory meeting to accept or reject in whole or in part a creditor's claim to vote at that meeting (s. 23(1)). **9–330**

What has now to be considered is the submission of claims to vote at any meetings of creditors other than the statutory meeting and to draw dividends out of the debtor's estate. These claims are made under section 48 of the Act, but claims already submitted under section 22 (for voting at the statutory meeting) and accepted by the interim trustee are deemed to have been re-submitted under section 48 (for voting at any other creditors' meetings and for drawing dividends) (s. 48(2)). It is for the permanent trustee to decide all claims under section 48. **9–331**

A claim submitted, or deemed to be re-submitted, under section 48 must be in the prescribed form and be accompanied by an account or voucher (according to the nature of the debt) which constitutes prima facie evidence of the debt. The permanent trustee may dispense with formalities, but only with the consent of the commissioners (if any) (s. 48(3)). **9–332**

As with section 22, a creditor and the debtor are guilty of offences where false claims are knowingly made, and the submission of a claim bars the effect of the rules relating to limitation of actions in any part of the United Kingdom (s. 48(7)). **9–333**

The permanent trustee, in order to satisfy himself as to the validity or amount of a claim, may require the creditor to produce **9–334** further evidence or any other person to produce relevant evidence, and if there is refusal or delay on their part to do so the permanent trustee may apply to the sheriff for an order for them to attend before the sheriff for private examination (s. 48(5)).

9–335 A creditor's claim to vote at any creditors' meeting (other than the statutory meeting) is accepted or rejected by the permanent trustee at the beginning of the meeting (s. 49(1)). Where the creditor's claim relates to the drawing of a dividend, the permanent trustee must decide on the claim not later than four weeks before the end of the accounting period in question; he must at the same time decide on the category of debt and the value of any security (s. 49(2)).

9–336 If the permanent trustee rejects a claim, he must immediately notify the creditor giving reasons for the rejection (s. 49(4)).

9–337 The debtor or any creditor, if dissatisfied with the acceptance or rejection of any claim or with the decision on the category of debt or the value of any security, may appeal to the sheriff:

(1) within two weeks of the meeting (in the case of a claim to vote); or

(2) not later than two weeks before the end of the accounting period (in the case of a claim to draw a dividend) (s. 49(6)).

Order of priority in distribution

9–338 The order of priority in distribution is:

(1) the outlays and remuneration of the interim trustee;

(2) the outlays and remuneration of the permanent trustee;

(3) where the debtor is a deceased debtor, deathbed and funeral expenses reasonably incurred and expenses reasonably incurred in administering the deceased's estate;

(4) the expenses reasonably incurred by a creditor who is a petitioner, or concurs in the petition, for sequestration;

(5) preferred debts (excluding any interest which has accrued on them to the date of sequestration);

(6) ordinary debts (*i.e.* debts which are neither secured nor mentioned elsewhere in this list);

(7) interest on—

(a) the preferred debts;

(b) the ordinary debts,

between the date of sequestration and the date of payment of the debt;

(8) any postponed debt (s. 51(1)).

"Preferred debt" means a debt listed in Part I of Schedule 3 to the Act (s. 51(2)). Included in the list are: **9–339**

(a) deductions (such as PAYE) made by the debtor during the 12 months before the date of sequestration and due to the Inland Revenue;

(b) debts (such as VAT referable to the period of six months before the date of sequestration) due to Customs and Excise;

(c) social security contributions which became due from the debtor in the 12 months before the date of sequestration;

(d) contributions to occupational pension schemes; and

(e) remuneration and accrued holiday remuneration due to employees in respect of the four months before the date of sequestration, whether paid by the debtor or by another person (*e.g.* a bank), limited to a prescribed amount per employee (£800 by Bankruptcy (Scotland) Regulations 1985 (S.I. 1985 No. 1925), as amended by S.I. 1986 No. 1914).

"Postponed debt" means: **9–340**

(a) a loan made to the debtor, in consideration of a share of the profits in his business, which is postponed under section 3 of the Partnership Act 1890 to the claims of other creditors;

(b) a loan made to the debtor by the debtor's spouse; and

(c) a gratuitous alienation which has vested in the permanent trustee because he has made a successful challenge of it under section 34 (s. 51(3)).

Any surplus remaining, after payment in full of all the debts mentioned is made over to the debtor; "surplus" does not include any unclaimed dividend (s. 51(5)). **9–341**

The rate of interest referred to in (7), above, is whichever is the greater of: **9–342**

(a) the prescribed rate at the date of sequestration; and

(b) the rate applicable to that debt apart from the sequestration (s. 51(7)).

Making payments for accounting periods

The provisions on this subject are in section 52, as amended by the Act of 1993 (Sched. 1, para. 21). **9–343**

In preparation for distributing the estate, the permanent trustee must make up accounts of his intromissions for each "accounting period" (s. 52(1)). **9–344**

9–345 The first "accounting period" is the period of six months beginning with the date of sequestration. Any subsequent "accounting period" is the period of six months beginning with the end of the previous accounting period, except that a different duration may be agreed by the permanent trustee and the commissioners or, if there are no commissioners, the Accountant in Bankruptcy. If the Accountant in Bankruptcy is the permanent trustee, the decision as to duration is taken by him (s. 52(2)). Different accounting periods may be agreed or decided to be of different durations (s. 52(2A)).

9–346 The permanent trustee is permitted to pay the debts in (1) to (4), above, other than his own remuneration, at any time. He may also pay the preferred debts (listed in Part I of Schedule 3) at any time but only with the consent of the commissioners or, if there are no commissioners, of the Accountant in Bankruptcy (s. 52(4)).

9–347 If the permanent trustee is not ready to pay a dividend for an accounting period or if he considers that it would be inappropriate to pay such a dividend because the expense of doing so would be disproportionate to the amount of the dividend, he may, with the consent of the commissioners or, if there are no commissioners, of the Accountant in Bankruptcy, postpone the payment to a date not later than the time for payment of a dividend for the next accounting period (s. 52(5)).

9–348 Where a creditor submits a claim later than eight weeks before the end of an accounting period but more than eight weeks before the end of the next accounting period, the permanent trustee must, if he accepts the claim and there are funds available, pay the missed dividend along with any dividend payable for the next accounting period (s. 52(9)).

Procedure after end of accounting period

9–349 The provisions are in section 53, as amended by the Act of 1993 (Sched. 1, para. 22).

9–350 *Within two weeks* after the end of an accounting period, the permanent trustee must, in respect of that period, submit to the commissioners or, if there are no commissioners, to the Accountant in Bankruptcy:

(1) his accounts for audit, and, where funds are available after making allowance for contingencies, a scheme of division of the divisible funds; and

(2) a claim for the outlays reasonably incurred by him and for his remuneration.

Where he is submitting these documents to the commissioners, he must send a copy of them to the Accountant in Bankruptcy (s. 53(1)).

Accounts for legal services incurred by the permanent trustee must, before being paid, be submitted for taxation to the auditor of the court, except that, if the commissioners have not decided that an account must be submitted for taxation, the permanent trustee may pay any such account without taxation (s. 53(2) and (2A)). **9–351**

Within six weeks after the end of the accounting period, the commissioners or the Accountant in Bankruptcy, as the case may be, may audit the accounts and must fix the amount of the outlays and remuneration payable to the permanent trustee, who must then make the audited accounts, scheme of division and decision as to his outlays and remuneration available for inspection by the debtor and the creditors (s. 53(3)). **9–352**

Not later than eight weeks after the end of an accounting period, the permanent trustee, the debtor or any creditor may appeal against the amount fixed for the permanent trustee's outlays and remuneration. If the decision was taken by the commissioners, the appeal is to the Accountant in Bankruptcy, and from him to the sheriff; if the decision was that of the Accountant in Bankruptcy, the appeal is to the sheriff. The decision of the sheriff is final (s. 53(6)). **9–353**

On the expiry of the period for appeal or, if an appeal is taken, on the final decision of the appeal, the permanent trustee pays the creditors their dividends in accordance with the scheme of division (s. 53(7)). **9–354**

Any dividend which is not cashed must be deposited by the permanent trustee in an appropriate bank or institution (s. 53(8)). **9–355**

Finally, the permanent trustee inserts in the sederunt book the audited accounts, the scheme of division and the final decision in relation to his outlays and remuneration (s. 53(10)). **9–356**

(viii) *Discharge of Debtor*

One of the major innovations of the Act of 1985 was the provision for the automatic discharge of the debtor on the expiry of three years from the date of sequestration. The possibility that the debtor **9–357** might be discharged as a result of an offer of composition by or on behalf of the debtor to the permanent trustee was carried forward from the Act of 1913, but with a simplified procedure.

(1) **Automatic discharge after three years**

9–358 *Subject to provisions in section 54*, the debtor is discharged on the expiry of three years from the date of sequestration (s. 54(1)). As no application to court or other procedure is involved for this automatic discharge, the debtor, in order that he may have evidence of his discharge, has the right to apply to the Accountant in Bankruptcy for a certificate of discharge in the prescribed form (s. 54(2)).

9–359 An automatic discharge may, however, be deferred for a period of up to two years. For such a deferment, an application must be made to the sheriff by the permanent trustee or any creditor, not later than two years and nine months after the date of sequestration (s. 54(3)).

9–360 The sheriff, on receiving such an application, must order the debtor to lodge in court a declaration that:

(a) he has made a full and fair surrender of his estate and a full disclosure of all claims which he is entitled to make against other persons; and

(b) he has delivered to the interim or permanent trustee every document under his control relating to his estate or his business or financial affairs.

9–361 If the debtor fails to lodge such a declaration in court within 14 days of being required to do so, the sheriff must defer his discharge, without a hearing, for a period of up to two years (s. 54(4)).

9–362 If the debtor lodges the declaration in court within the required period of 14 days, the sheriff fixes a date for a hearing and orders the applicant to notify the debtor and the permanent trustee or (if he has been discharged) the Accountant in Bankruptcy of the date of the hearing. The permanent trustee or the Accountant in Bankruptcy, as the case may be, must then, not later than seven days before the date fixed for the hearing, lodge in court a report upon the debtor's assets and liabilities, his financial and business affairs and his conduct in relation to them and upon the sequestration and his conduct in the course of it (s. 54(5)).

9–363 After considering at the hearing any representations made by the applicant, the debtor or any creditor, the sheriff makes an order either deferring the discharge for up to two years or dismissing the application. The applicant or the debtor may appeal against the sheriff's order within the next 14 days (s. 54(6)).

Nicol's Trustee v. Nicol, 1996 G.W.D. 10–531 gives instances of **9–364**
the circumstances in which the court may defer a discharge:

N.'s trustee, in applying for deferment of N.'s discharge, reported that N. had:

(a) failed to make a full and fair surrender of his estate, and purported to alienate various assets to his girlfriend;

(b) acted as director of two companies contrary to the Company Directors Disqualification Act 1986 and used a restricted company name contrary to the Insolvency Act 1986;

(c) failed to make contributions to the estate during a three months period of employment at a high salary;

(d) acted as a guarantor for his girlfriend; and

(e) failed to disclose an asset of one of the companies to its liquidator.

Held discharge deferred for 18 months. N. had acted with complete disregard for the interests of his and his companies' creditors, and there was something to be said for protecting future creditors for a further period and some benefit in bringing home to N. that he had to take debts seriously.

In *Clydesdale Bank plc v. Davidson*, 1994 S.L.T. 225, the three- **9–365**
year period expired without the application for a deferment of the discharge having been dealt with by the sheriff, though the application had been made timeously. The date of sequestration was January 18, 1989, and an application to defer the discharge was made no later than two years and nine months after the date of sequestration. However, owing to lack of court time, the sheriff did not grant the application until January 30, 1992, deferring the discharge for two years from January 18, 1992.

The debtor appealed to the Court of Session, contending that, in the absence of an interim order deferring his discharge, he had become automatically discharged on the expiry of three years.

The Court refused the appeal.

Lord Justice-Clerk Ross, giving the opinion of the Court, said (at p. 228): "Where an application for deferment has been timeously made and the three-year period has subsequently expired, discharge will not take place automatically until the court has pronounced an order in terms of the subsequent subsections of section 54. It follows that the sheriff was well founded in concluding that the present application was competent."

9–366 Whenever the discharge is deferred, the clerk of the court must send:

(a) a certified copy of the sheriff's order to the Keeper of the Register of Inhibitions and Adjudications for recording; and

(b) a copy of the order to the Accountant in Bankruptcy and (if not discharged) the permanent trustee (s. 54(7)).

9–367 *At any time after a court order deferring his discharge*, the debtor, provided he lodges the required declaration mentioned above, may petition the sheriff for his discharge, and the procedure for a hearing, *etc.*, again comes into operation (s. 54(8)).

9–368 There is also provision for a further deferment of the discharge: the permanent trustee or any creditor may, not later than three months before the end of a period of deferment, apply to the sheriff for a further deferment, making it necessary for the procedure as to the debtor's declaration, a hearing, *etc.*, to be repeated (s. 54(9)).

9–369 The effect of an automatic discharge under section 54 is that the debtor is discharged within the United Kingdom of all debts and obligations contracted by him, or for which he was liable, *at the date of sequestration*, with the following exceptions:

(a) any liability to pay a fine or other penalty due to the Crown or imposed in a district court and any liability under a compensation order;

(b) any liability to forfeiture of a sum of money deposited in court under the Bail etc. (Scotland) Act 1980;

(c) any liability for fraud or breach of trust;

(d) any obligation to pay aliment or any periodical allowance payable on divorce which could not be included in a claim in the sequestration; and

(e) the obligation, imposed on him by section 64, to co-operate with the permanent trustee by executing documents, etc., after the discharge (s. 55(1) and (2)).

(2) **Discharge on composition**

9–370 The discharge of the debtor may be provided for where an offer of a "composition", *i.e.* an offer to pay to each creditor a proportion of his debt, is made to and approved by the permanent trustee. The details are in Schedule 4 to the Act, as amended by the Act of 1993 (Sched. 1, para. 31) (s. 56). Only an outline of them can be given here:

The offer of a composition may be made by or on behalf of the debtor to the permanent trustee at any time after the issue of the act and warrant. The permanent trustee (where he is not the Accountant in Bankruptcy) must submit it, along with a report on it, to the commissioners or, if there are no commissioners, to the Accountant in Bankruptcy. They, or he, as the case may be, if satisfied that the composition would produce a dividend of at least 25p in the £ on the ordinary debts and that the caution or other security specified in the offer is adequate must *recommend* that the offer be placed before the creditors. **9–371**

If there is such a recommendation, the permanent trustee must intimate the recommendation to the debtor, publish a notice in the *Edinburgh Gazette* stating where the offer may be inspected, invite every creditor to accept or reject the offer by completing a prescribed form sent by the permanent trustee and send along with the prescribed form a report summarising the offer and estimating what the dividend would be on the ordinary debts if the offer were accepted. **9–372**

Using the completed prescribed forms returned to him, the permanent trustee decides that the offer has been accepted by the creditors if a majority in number and two-thirds in value of the creditors have accepted it; otherwise he must decide that the offer has been rejected. **9–373**

Where the creditors have accepted the offer, the permanent trustee applies to the sheriff for a hearing to be fixed to consider whether or not to approve the offer. Having examined the documents and heard any representations, the sheriff makes an order approving or refusing to approve the offer. The debtor or any creditor is entitled to appeal against the sheriff's order. **9–374**

If the offer is approved, the permanent trustee, where he is not the Accountant in Bankruptcy, submits his accounts and his claim for outlays and remuneration to the commissioners or, if there are no commissioners, to the Accountant in Bankruptcy. Where the permanent trustee is the Accountant in Bankruptcy, he calculates his fees and outlays in accordance with regulations made by the Secretary of State under section 69A (inserted by the Act of 1993, s. 8). After further procedure similar to that in section 53, above, the permanent trustee lodges with the sheriff clerk a declaration **9–375** that all necessary charges in connection with the sequestration have been provided for, and the bond of caution is lodged with the sheriff clerk by or on behalf of the debtor.

9–376 The sheriff then makes an order discharging the debtor and the permanent trustee. The effect is to re-invest the debtor in his estate as existing at the date of the order, and to convert the claims of creditors in the sequestration into claims for their respective shares in the composition.

9–377 Where, however, it comes to light that there has been, or is likely to be, default in payment of the composition or that for any reason the composition cannot be proceeded with without undue delay or without injustice to the creditors, then any creditor may apply to the *Court of Session* for the recall of the sheriff's order. The effect of a recall is to revive the sequestration.

9–378 A debtor may make two, but not more than two, offers of composition in the course of a sequestration.

(ix) *Discharge of Permanent Trustee*

9–379 The procedure for the discharge of the permanent trustee differs according to whether:

(1) the Accountant in Bankruptcy is not the permanent trustee (s. 57, as amended by the Act of 1993 (Sched. 1, para. 24)); or

(2) the Accountant in Bankruptcy is the permanent trustee (s. 58A, inserted by the Act of 1993 (Sched. 1, para. 26)).

(1) **Where the Accountant in Bankruptcy is not the permanent trustee**

9–380 After the permanent trustee has made a final division of the estate and has inserted his final audited accounts in the sederunt book, he:

(a) must deposit any unclaimed dividends and any unapplied balances in an appropriate bank or institution;

(b) must then send to the Accountant in Bankruptcy the sederunt book, a copy of the audited accounts and a receipt for the deposit of the unclaimed dividends and unapplied balances; and

(c) may at the same time apply to the Accountant in Bankruptcy for a certificate of discharge (s. 57(1)).

9–381 If he makes an application under (c), above, he must notify the debtor and all the creditors of it, informing them of their right to make written representations within the next 14 days and to inspect the sederunt book at the office of the Accountant in Bankruptcy and of the effect of the grant of the certificate of discharge for which he has applied (s. 57(2)).

On the lapse of the 14 days, the Accountant in Bankruptcy, after examining the documents sent to him and considering any representations, must grant or refuse to grant the certificate of discharge (s. 57(3)). The permanent trustee, the debtor or any creditor who has made representations has 14 days in which to appeal against the decision to the sheriff, and if the sheriff decides that a certificate of discharge which has been refused should be granted he must order the Accountant in Bankruptcy to grant it (s. 57(4)). The decision of the sheriff is final (s. 57(4A), inserted by the Act of 1993 (Sched. 1, para. 24)). **9–382**

The grant of a certificate of discharge by the Accountant in Bankruptcy has the effect of discharging the permanent trustee from all liability (other than liability arising from fraud) to the creditors or to the debtor for any act or omission of the permanent trustee (s. 57(5)). **9–383**

(2) Where the Accountant in Bankruptcy is the permanent trustee

The provisions in section 58A apply where the Accountant in Bankruptcy has acted as the permanent trustee (s. 58A(1)). The procedure is similar to that under (1), above, with the substitution of the Accountant in Bankruptcy for the permanent trustee and with some other necessary modifications: **9–384**

After making a final division of the estate, the Accountant in Bankruptcy must enter in the sederunt book a determination of his fees and outlays calculated in accordance with regulations made by the Secretary of State under section 69A (inserted by the Act of 1993, s. 8). **9–385**

He must send to the debtor and to all creditors known to him— **9–386**

(a) a copy of his determination as to fees and outlays; and

(b) a written notice stating that he has commenced proceedings leading to his discharge, that the sederunt book is available for inspection at an address decided by him, and that an appeal may be made to the sheriff against his fees and outlays or against his discharge or both (s. 58A(4)).

Any appeal must be made within 14 days after the issue of the notice, and the decision of the sheriff is final (s. 58A(6)). **9–387**

9–388 If no appeal to the sheriff is made or if such an appeal is refused, the Accountant in Bankruptcy is discharged of all liability (other than any liability arising from fraud) to the creditors or to the debtor for any act or omission in his functions as permanent trustee (s. 58A(7)).

Unclaimed dividends

9–389 The provisions as to unclaimed dividends in section 58 (as amended by the Act of 1993 (Sched. 1, para. 25)) apply, whether the Accountant in Bankruptcy is or is not the permanent trustee.

9–390 Any person, producing evidence of his right, may apply to the Accountant in Bankruptcy to receive his unclaimed dividend, provided the application is made not later than seven years after its deposit (s. 58(1), as amended by the Act of 1993 (Sched. 1, para. 25)). If the Accountant in Bankruptcy is satisfied of the applicant's right to the dividend, he must authorise the appropriate bank or institution to pay to the applicant the amount of the dividend and of any interest which has accrued on it (s. 58(2)).

9–391 *At the expiry of seven years* from the date of deposit of any unclaimed dividend or unapplied balance, the Accountant in Bankruptcy must hand over the deposit receipt or other voucher to the Secretary of State, who is then entitled to payment of the amount of principal and interest due from the bank or institution (s. 58(3), as amended by the Act of 1993 (Sched. 1, para. 25)).

(f) Miscellaneous and Supplementary

9–392 A number of important provisions which have found no home elsewhere in the Act are grouped under this heading in sections 60 to 78. Of special note are:

(i) power to cure defects in procedure (s. 63);
(ii) arbitration and compromise (s. 65);
(iii) meetings of creditors and commissioners (s. 66 and Sched. 6); and
(iv) supplies by utilities (s. 70).

In addition, in Schedule 2 there are the provisions relating to:

(v) the modified sequestration procedure; and
in Schedule 2A (inserted by the Act of 1993 (s. 6(2)) the provisions relating to:
(vi) summary administration.

(i) *Power to Cure Defects in Procedure*

The Act of 1913 made no special provision for cases where there had been a failure to comply with its many formalities such as time limits for submitting notices and holding meetings. The only recourse was to the *nobile officium* of the Inner House of the Court of Session. Because of the expense of petitions to the *nobile officium*, the Scottish Law Commission recommended that the sheriff should have a discretion to remedy a failure to comply with a statutory provision. The Commission recognised, however, that complex situations could arise in bankruptcy, and for these a remit to the Court of Session would be appropriate. The result of these recommendations is section 63 of the Act of 1985. **9–393**

The sheriff may, on the application of any person having an interest— **9–394**

(1) if there has been a failure to comply with any requirement of the Act or any regulations made under it, make an order waiving the failure and, so far as practicable, restoring any person prejudiced by the failure to the position in which he would have been but for the failure;

(2) if for any reason anything required or authorised to be done in, or in connection with, the sequestration process cannot be done, make an order enabling that thing to be done (s. 63(1)).

In any order made under these provisions the sheriff may impose such conditions, including conditions as to expenses, as he thinks fit and may: **9–395**

(1) authorise or dispense with the performance of any act in the sequestration process;

(2) appoint an eligible person as permanent trustee, whether or not in place of an existing trustee;

(3) extend or waive any time limit specified in or under the Act (s. 63(2)).

An application— **9–396**

(1) may at any time be remitted by the sheriff to the Court of Session, of his own accord or on an application by any person having an interest;

(2) must be remitted by the sheriff to the Court of Session, if the Court of Session so directs on an application being made to it by any person having an interest.

This provision applies if the sheriff or the Court of Session, as the case may be, considers that the remit is desirable because of the importance or complexity of the matters raised by the application (s. 63(3)).

9–397 The following are three of the cases which have been successfully brought under section 63:

9–398 (1) *Waverley Vintners Ltd v. Matthew*, 1991 G.W.D. 19–1130 (Sh.Ct.): In a petition presented by W. Ltd for the sequestration of M., the certificate of the sheriff clerk certifying that the charge had been displayed on the walls of court for the days of charge could not be found. The award of sequestration was refused and W. Ltd appealed against that refusal.

Before the appeal was heard, a photostat of the certificate was found in process.

Held, by Sheriff Principal R. A. Bennett, appeal allowed and sequestration awarded.

It had been demonstrated by the copy that the charge had been properly displayed, and the failure to produce the original was a defect in procedure which could be cured under section 63(1).

9–399 (2) *The Royal Bank of Scotland plc v. J. & J. Messenger*, 1991 S.L.T. 492 (O.H.): A partnership and its two partners had been sequestrated by a single award instead of by three separate awards. The permanent trustee sought an order from the sheriff to separate the award into three separate awards, and the sheriff remitted the application to the Court of Session under section 63(3).

Held that the court had power under section 63(1) to waive the failure.

Lord Marnoch had some doubt whether section 63(1) was ever intended to deal with a "failure" quite as radical as the one in this case, but was influenced by the fairly broad terms in which the provisions were expressed.

9–400 (3) *Pattison v. Halliday*, 1991 S.L.T. 645 (O.H.): On October 2, 1986, P. lodged a petition for the sequestration of H. The next day the sheriff granted warrant to cite H. to appear on October 22, 1986, but before that date H. raised proceedings in the Court of Session for the reduction of the Court of Session decree on which the petition for sequestration was founded. The sheriff sisted the sequestration proceedings on October 22, 1986.

On June 12, 1987, the Court of Session action for reduction was dismissed, and there followed a period of negotiation between P. and H. with a view to avoiding a renewal of the sequestration proceedings. The negotiations, however, were unsuccessful, and on

September 1, 1989, P. lodged a motion for the recall of the sist and for an award of sequestration. The motion came before the sheriff on September 6, 1989, and, as it was unopposed, he recalled the sist and awarded sequestration.

By section 12(4) the date of sequestration was the date when the court had granted a warrant under section 12(2), *i.e.* October 3, 1986.

Section 54 provides for a debtor to be automatically discharged *on the expiry of three years from the date of sequestration*, but allows any creditor, *not later than two years and nine months after the date of sequestration*, to apply to the sheriff for a deferment of the discharge. Neither of these time limits could in the circumstances be complied with: as the sequestration had not become effective until September 6, 1989, it could not be completed by October 4, 1989, and a period of more than two years and nine months had already elapsed since the date of sequestration.

P. applied to the sheriff for an order to be made under section 63 to extend the period of three years from the date of sequestration by a further three years.

The sheriff, on account of the importance and complexity of the issues raised, remitted the application to the Court of Session.

Held that the application under section 63 was competent in the circumstances.

Lord Caplan said (at p. 648): "I consider that the statutory objective of s. 63 is to prevent the sensible progress of sequestration from being hampered by irregularities which are purely technical when equitable considerations require otherwise. Paragraph (*b*) of s. 63(1) empowers a court to make an order enabling anything in connection with the sequestration process which is authorised to be done but cannot be done to be done."

On the other hand, in *Whittaker's Trustee v. Whittaker*, 1993 S.C.L.R. 718 (Sh.Ct.) a petition by the trustee to waive the time limit for an application for deferral of an automatic discharge was dismissed. **9–401**

W., the debtor, had been severely injured in an accident as a consequence of which her business failed. She raised an action for damages for her injuries, but her claim had not yet been disposed of by the expiry of the time limit for an application to defer her discharge.

The sheriff principal held that in a section 63 application there was a substantial onus on a trustee to justify a case for deferment and also to comply with the statutory time limit, which was closely linked with an important right of the debtor. The facts that the failure was due to human error, and the possible prejudice to creditors, were outweighed by the facts that the failure was not a trivial one and that continuation of the sequestration would be prejudicial to W.

Sheriff Principal C. G. B. Nicholson said (at p. 725): "I think that it is worth observing that the 1985 Act made a radical change in the law by introducing automatic discharge after three years subject only to the possibility of deferment under section 54(3). That, in my opinion, places a substantial onus on a trustee not only to justify any case for deferment but also to comply with the statutory time limits. It follows, therefore, in my opinion, that a court will often have to scrutinise with care an application for waiver under section 63(1) in order to see if there is a good and sufficient reason for granting it. . . . It does not follow that an application for relief under the section should be lightly granted, far less that its grant should be virtually automatic."

9–402 Similarly, it has been held incompetent to use section 63 to alter the date of sequestration: *Accountant in Bankruptcy v. Allans of Gillock Ltd*, 1991 S.L.T. 765 (O.H.).

9–403 Section 63 does not remove the availablity of an application to the *nobile officium*. A recent instance of a petition to the *nobile officium* is *Wright v. Tennent Caledonian Breweries Ltd*, 1991 S.L.T. 823:

The date of sequestration of W.'s estate was, by section 12(4), the date on which warrant to cite W. had been granted, *i.e.* January 20, 1989, but for a number of reasons the award of sequestration was not made until April 5, 1989.

By section 16(4), a petition for the recall of the award requires to be presented within 10 weeks after the date of sequestration, a time limit with which W. could not comply.

Held that as W. had been deprived of a statutory remedy through an unforeseen circumstance for which the Act made no provision, a petition to the *nobile officium* was competent.

Lord President Hope said (at p. 825): "The problem which has arisen in the present case is that, while the petitioner seeks a recall under the statute, she has been deprived of that remedy because she was unable to meet the statutory time limit for bringing the application. This is due to the unforeseen circumstance, for which the Act makes no provision, that the period between the date of sequestration as defined by section 12(4)(b) and the date when sequestration was in fact awarded was more than 10 weeks. I think that this is the kind of case where the inherent equitable jurisdiction of the Court of Session may be exercised to make good the situation which has occurred."

Wright's case was distinguished in *Brown v. Middlemas of Kelso Ltd*, 1994 S.L.T. 1352: **9–404**

A petition to the *nobile officium* for recall of his sequestration was presented by B. outwith the 10-week period after the date of the award.

The respondents, who were petitioning creditors, contended that no reason had been put forward for failure to comply with the time limit.

Held that it would not be appropriate for the court to exercise its equitable power in the absence of any reasonable explanation for the failure to lodge a petition for recall in due time. There was no *casus improvisus*[6] in the statutory provisions in this case and it would be wrong for the court to extend the operation of the statute beyond what had been enacted by Parliament.

Lord Justice Clerk Ross, delivering the opinion of the Second Division, said that *Wright* had been an exceptional case: after the petition for sequestration had been presented, the debtor had appeared and sought to argue that sequestration should not be awarded. She had been allowed to lodge answers and thereafter a number of agreements had taken place with the result that, by the time when the award of sequestration was made, the 10-week period had elapsed; this was because the date of sequestration in that case was the date on which the court granted warrant to cite the debtor (s. 12(4)(b)).

(ii) *Arbitration and Compromise*

The permanent trustee may (but if there are commissioners only with the consent of the commissioners, the creditors or the court) refer to arbitration any claim or question of whatever nature arising in the course of the sequestration or compromise any claim of whatever nature made against or on behalf of the estate. The decree-arbitral or compromise is binding on the creditors and the debtor (s. 65(1)). **9–405**

[6] "unforeseen occurrence".

9–406 Where there is a reference to arbitration, the Accountant in Bankruptcy may vary any time limit under the Act (s. 65(2)). This provision enables sufficient time to be allowed for the submission to arbitration to be arranged and removes the need to apply to the sheriff under section 63, above, if the statutory time limit were exceeded.

(iii) *Meetings of Creditors and Commissioners*

9–407 The detailed provisions on meetings are in Schedule 6 to the Act. Part I of the Schedule relates to meetings of creditors other than the statutory meeting, Part II to all meetings of creditors and Part III to meetings of commissioners (s. 66).

Meetings of creditors other than the statutory meeting

9–408 The statutory meeting is the only meeting of creditors which *must* be called if the interim trustee is not the Accountant in Bankruptcy (see 9–188 *et seq.*, above), but circumstances may arise which make the calling of other meetings of creditors necessary or desirable.

Schedule 6 provides that the permanent trustee *must* call a meeting of creditors if required to do so by:

(1) order of the court;
(2) one-tenth in number or one-third in value of the creditors;
(3) a commissioner; or
(4) the Accountant in Bankruptcy.

If the permanent trustee does not comply, the Accountant in Bankruptcy may, of his own accord or on the application of any creditor, call a meeting of creditors.

9–409 The permanent trustee, or a commissioner who has given written notice to him, *may* at any time call a meeting of creditors.

9–410 At the commencement of a meeting, the chairman is the permanent trustee, but he must invite the creditors to elect one of their number to be chairman in his place. If no election is made, the permanent trustee remains chairman throughout the meeting.

9–411 An appeal may be made to the sheriff against any resolution of the creditors at a meeting, by the permanent trustee, a creditor or any other person having an interest.

All meetings of creditors

Proceedings at a meeting are not invalidated merely because a notice or other document relating to the calling of the meeting has not reached the creditor before the meeting. **9–412**

Meetings must be held at the place which, in the opinion of the person calling the meeting, is the most convenient for the majority of the creditors. **9–413**

A creditor may authorise in writing any person to represent him at a meeting (referred to in the Act as a "mandatory"). **9–414**

The quorum at any meeting is one creditor. **9–415**

Any question is decided by *a majority in value of the creditors who vote on that question.* **9–416**

The chairman may allow or disallow any objection by a creditor, but any person aggrieved by the chairman's decision has a right of appeal to the sheriff. **9–417**

The chairman, with the consent of a majority in value of the creditors who vote on the matter, *may* adjourn a meeting. He *must* adjourn a meeting if no creditor appears within the first half-hour. **9–418**

A copy of the minutes of every meeting must be sent to the Accountant in Bankruptcy within 14 days of the meeting. **9–419**

Meetings of commissioners

The permanent trustee *may* call a meeting of commissioners at any time, and *must* do so if: **9–420**

(1) required to do so by order of the court; or

(2) requested to do so by the Accountant in Bankruptcy or any commissioner.

If the permanent trustee fails to comply with these provisions, a commissioner may call a meeting of commissioners.

The quorum is one commissioner, and the commissioners may act by a majority present at a meeting. **9–421**

Any matter may be agreed by the commissioners without a meeting if such agreement is unanimous and subsequently recorded in a minute signed by the commissioners. **9–422**

(iv) *Supplies by Utilities*

Prior to the Act of 1985 the suppliers of gas, electricity, water and telephone services were in a position to make the continuing or restoring of these utilities conditional on payment of the arrears **9–423** due to them. They could thus obtain a preference over the other ordinary creditors, especially if the debtor's business was to be carried on or sold as a going concern.

9–424 Section 70 removes the obstacle, both where there is a sequestration and where the debtor has granted a trust deed (whether a "protected" trust deed or not). Where a request is made for one of the utilities by the interim trustee, the permanent trustee or the trustee acting under the trust deed, the supplier:

(1) may make it a condition of the giving of the supply that the person making the request *personally guarantees the payment of the charges for the supply being given*; but

(2) must not make it a condition of the giving of the supply that *any outstanding charges for a supply previously given to the debtor are paid.*

9–425 The request, instead of being actually made by the interim trustee, the permanent trustee or the trustee acting under the trust deed, may be made by or with the concurrence of such person. The request must be for the purposes of any "business" which is or has been carried on by or on behalf of the debtor, but the term "business" is widely defined as meaning "the carrying on of any activity, whether for profit or not" (ss. 70(3) and 73(1)).

(v) *The Modified Sequestration Procedure*

9–426 The Act of 1913 introduced summary sequestration to be available as a speedier process than ordinary sequestration for cases where the debtor's assets did not exceed £300 (a sum for which £4,000 was substituted by the Insolvency Act 1976 (s. 1(1) and Sched. 1)). Summary sequestration did not prove successful, and it was replaced by altogether different provisions for small assets cases in the Act of 1985. The details are in Schedule 2 to the Act, as amended by the Act of 1993 (Sched. 1, para. 30).

9–427 Schedule 2 as introduced by the Act of 1985 had unexpected results: there was a huge increase in the number of sequestrations owing to the provision that where the funds of the debtor's estate were insufficient to meet even the outlays and remuneration of both the interim trustee and the permanent trustee, the outstanding amount was to be paid by the Accountant in Bankruptcy out of public funds.

9–428 The Schedule 2 procedure was radically amended by the Act of 1993: in particular, public funds are no longer available to pay the fees and outlays of private sector trustees; only where there are sufficient assets to pay a dividend to creditors will private sector practitioners be willing to act as interim and permanent trustees.

Cases to which the Schedule 2 procedure is applicable

Schedule 2 procedure does not come into operation where the permanent trustee is elected by the creditors and his election is confirmed by the court. All the instances to which the Schedule 2 procedure applies are cases where the permanent trustee is *appointed* (not *elected*). **9–429**

The instances are where: **9–430**

(1) the Accountant in Bankruptcy is the interim trustee and he does not call the statutory meeting but is appointed as permanent trustee by the court (s. 21B(2), inserted by the Act of 1993 (s. 5), and s. 25A(3), inserted by the Act of 1993 (s. 7));

(2) the Accountant in Bankruptcy applies to the court for a certificate for the summary administration of the sequestration, the certificate is granted and the court appoints the Accountant in Bankruptcy as permanent trustee (s. 23A(4), inserted by the Act of 1993 (s. 6(1)), and s. 25A(3), inserted by the Act of 1993 (s. 7));

(3) the Accountant in Bankruptcy is the interim trustee, no creditor entitled to vote in the election of the permanent trustee attends the statutory meeting (or no permanent trustee is elected) and the court appoints the Accountant in Bankruptcy as the permanent trustee (s. 24(3A), inserted by the Act of 1993 (Sched. 1, para. 12), and s. 25A(3), inserted by the Act of 1993 (s. 7));

(4) the Accountant in Bankruptcy is not the interim trustee, no creditor entitled to vote in the election of the permanent trustee attends the statutory meeting (or no permanent trustee is elected) and the court, on a report by the interim trustee, appoints the interim trustee as the permanent trustee (s. 24(4) and (5));

(5) no permanent trustee is elected to replace a trustee who has resigned or died and the court appoints the Accountant in Bankruptcy to be the permanent trustee (s. 28(5), as substituted by the Act of 1993 (Sched. 1, para. 17)); and

(6) no permanent trustee is elected to replace a trustee who has been removed and the court appoints the Accountant in Bankruptcy to be the permanent trustee (s. 29(8)).

The modifications

9–431 Since the permanent trustee under the Schedule 2 sequestration procedure is not *elected* by the creditors but *appointed* by the sheriff, the provisions in section 25 as to confirmation of the election by the court do not apply: the act and warrant is issued by the sheriff clerk without that preliminary.

9–432 Where the permanent trustee resigns or dies, the court may, on the application of the Accountant in Bankruptcy (or his nominee), appoint the applicant to be the permanent trustee. This is a simplification of the provisions of section 28 on the resignation and death of the permanent trustee.

9–433 Similar provisions apply where the permanent trustee is removed from office. Section 29 is modified for that purpose.

9–434 Section 30, which provides for the election of commissioners, does not apply, and any commissioners already holding office must cease to do so. There is no need for commissioners because of the increased supervision which the Accountant in Bankruptcy exercises under the Schedule 2 procedure.

9–435 Under section 39(2) the permanent trustee has certain powers which he may exercise (to carry on any business of the debtor, etc.) "if there are commissioners only with the consent of the commissioners, the creditors or the court". Under the Schedule 2 procedure, if the permanent trustee is the Accountant in Bankruptcy, no consent is required, and in any other case, the consent of the Acountant in Bankruptcy is required.

9–436 Applications to the sheriff for private and public examinations under sections 44 and 45, respectively, require the consent of the Accountant in Bankruptcy under the Schedule 2 procedure.

9–437 Finally, where the permanent trustee is the Accountant in Bankruptcy, section 53 ("procedure after the end of accounting period") is modified: the Accountant in Bankruptcy prepares accounts and fixes his fees and outlays; these are made available for inspection by the debtor and the creditors, who have a right to appeal to the sheriff; the Accountant in Bankruptcy pays the creditors their dividends and inserts his accounts, the scheme of division and his decision as to remuneration and outlays in the sederunt book. There is no requirement for taxation by the auditor of court.

(vi) *Summary Administration*

The procedure for summary administration of a sequestration was introduced by the Act of 1993 (s. 6, inserting s. 23A and Sched. 2A into the Act of 1985). Its principal effect is to limit the work of the permanent trustee in small assets cases. **9–438**

An application is made to the court for the grant of a certificate for the summary administration of the sequestration, and the court *must* grant such a certificate where it appears to the court that: **9–439**

(1) the aggregate amount of the debtor's liabilities does not exceed £20,000; and

(2) the aggregate amount of the debtor's assets does not exceed £2,000 (s. 23A(1)).

In calculating the aggregate amount of the debtor's liabilities no account is taken of a debt for which a creditor holds a security, and in calculating the aggregate amount of the debtor's assets no account is taken of any of the debtor's heritable property or any property which does not vest in the permanent trustee (s. 23A(2)). Property which does not vest in the permanent trustee is property which is exempt from poinding for the purpose of protecting the debtor and his family and property held on trust by the debtor (s. 33(1)). **9–440**

Where a certificate for summary administration is granted, then: **9–441**

(1) in any case where the application was made by the Accountant in Bankruptcy, the court must appoint the Accountant in Bankruptcy or his nominee as permanent trustee; and

(2) in every case, Schedule 2A (which modifies the duties of the permanent trustee) applies to the sequestration (s. 23A(4)).

Provision is made for the certificate to be withdrawn: the debtor, a creditor, the permanent trustee or the Accountant in Bankruptcy may, at any time, apply to the sheriff to withdraw the certificate for summary administration (s. 23A(5)). An applicant who is not the permanent trustee must send a copy of the application to the permanent trustee, who must then prepare and present to the sheriff a report on all the circumstances of the sequestration (s. 23A(6)). If it appears to the sheriff that it is no longer appropriate for the sequestration to be subject to summary administration, he must withdraw the certificate, and the sequestration then proceeds as if the certificate had not been granted (s. 23A(7)). **9–442**

Cases to which the Schedule 2A procedure is applicable

9–443 The Schedule 2A procedure is applicable where a certificate is applied for and is granted in any of the following cases:

(1) where the petition for sequestration has been presented by the debtor and the Accountant in Bankruptcy, within seven days after the award, applies to the court for the grant of a certificate (s. 12(1A)); since the application is by the Accountant in Bankruptcy, he, or his nominee, will be appointed permanent trustee (see 9–441, above);

(2) where the interim trustee is the Accountant in Bankruptcy and he does not call the statutory meeting and has reported the circumstances to the sheriff, the Accountant in Bankruptcy may apply to the court for the grant of a certificate (s. 21B(1) and (2)); again the Accountant in Bankruptcy or his nominee will be appointed permanent trustee;

(3) where the interim trustee is the Accountant in Bankruptcy and the statutory meeting is called but no creditor attends or no permanent trustee is elected, the Accountant in Bankruptcy, after reporting the proceedings to the sheriff, may apply to the court for the grant of a certificate (s. 24(3B)); the Accountant in Bankruptcy or his nominee will be appointed permanent trustee;

(4) where the Accountant in Bankruptcy is not the interim trustee and the statutory meeting is called but no creditor attends or no permanent trustee is elected, the interim trustee, after notifying the Accountant in Bankruptcy and reporting the proceedings to the sheriff, is appointed by the sheriff as the permanent trustee and he may apply to the sheriff for the grant of a certificate (s. 24(4) and (4A)); and

(5) where the permanent trustee is elected by the statutory meeting, the interim trustee, having reported the proceedings to the sheriff, may apply to the sheriff for the grant of a certificate (s. 25(1) and (2A)).

The modifications

9–444 The leading provision in Schedule 2A is that the permanent trustee must comply with sections 3 and 39 of the Act *only in so far as, in his view, it would be of financial benefit to the estate of the debtor and in the interests of creditors to do so.* Section 3 lists the general functions of the permanent trustee and section 39 deals with his management and realisation of the estate. The effect is that the permanent trustee can limit the amount of work which he would otherwise be required to do (*e.g.* ascertaining the reasons for the debtor's insolvency) if there is to be no financial benefit to the estate or to the interests of the creditors by his fully adhering to the statutory provisions in sections 3 and 39. The words "in his view" indicate that the permanent trustee has a discretion as to the extent to which he should comply with sections 3 and 39.

Until the debtor is discharged, the permanent trustee must require the debtor to give a written account of his current state of affairs at the end of the period of six months from the date of sequestration and at the end of each subsequent period of six months. **9–445**

Where the Accountant in Bankruptcy is not the permanent trustee, the permanent trustee must comply with any general or specific directions given to him by the Accountant in Bankruptcy, whether such directions are general or apply only to a particular case. **9–446**

The permanent trustee must publish in the *Edinburgh Gazette* a notice stating that a certificate for summary sequestration has been granted and that he has been appointed permanent trustee. If the interim trustee has not published a notice in the *Edinburgh Gazette* stating that sequestration has been awarded, inviting submission of claims and giving other prescribed information under section 15(6), the permanent trustee's notice will contain such information. **9–447**

With one exception, Schedule 2, as well as Schedule 2A, applies to summary administration. The exception is where a permanent trustee has resigned or died, no new permanent trustee has been appointed and sheriff has appointed the Accountant in Bankruptcy or his nominee to be permanent trustee. **9–448**

III EXTRA-JUDICIAL SETTLEMENTS

In order to avoid the publicity, formality and expense of sequestration, creditors, as well as the debtor himself, often prefer to enter into some private arrangement which will achieve much the same practical results as sequestration—*pari passu* ("rateable") distribution of the debtor's estate, as far as it will go, among the creditors, and for the debtor the opportunity to make a fresh start free from his crippling burden of debt. **9–449**

The commonest forms of extra-judicial settlements are:
(a) the private trust deed for creditors; and
(b) the extra-judicial composition contract.

(a) **Private Trust Deed for Creditors**

9–450 The debtor may by a trust deed transfer his whole estate to a named trustee for realisation and distribution among his creditors.

9–451 Prior to the Act of 1985, private trust deeds were scarcely affected by bankruptcy legislation. The Act of 1985, though leaving most of the common law untouched, introduced a number of statutory provisions, the most important of which related to the "protected trust deed". Further amendments were made to the provisions on protected trust deeds by the Act of 1993.

9–452 It is appropriate to consider first:
(i) trust deeds generally; and then
(ii) the special features of the protected trust deed.

(i) *Trust Deeds Generally*

9–453 Before the Act of 1985 the trust deed had some major disadvantages:

9–454 (1) The trustee had no act and warrant, but had to complete title to each item in the debtor's estate in the appropriate way in order to prevent it from being attached by the diligence of non-acceding creditors. A trust deed, therefore, did not prevent a "race of diligence", which was one of the desirable effects of a sequestration.

9–455 (2) A non-acceding creditor could challenge the trust deed as an illegal preference.

9–456 (3) A non-acceding creditor could petition for sequestration, which would supersede the trust deed.

9–457 (4) There was no requirement for giving notice, in the *Edinburgh Gazette* or elsewhere, so that creditors might be made aware of the granting of the trust deed.

9–458 The main statutory provisions now applicable to all trust deeds are in Schedule 5, as amended by the Act of 1993 (Sched. 1, para. 32):

9–459 (1) Whatever provision there may, or may not, be in the trust deed for auditing the trustee's accounts and fixing his remuneration, the debtor, the trustee or any creditor may, at any time before the final distribution, have the trustee's accounts audited by and his remuneration fixed by the Accountant in Bankruptcy.

(2) The trustee may cause a notice, in a form prescribed by the Court of Session by Act of Sederunt, to be recorded in the Register of Inhibitions and Adjudications, with the same effect as the recording of letters of inhibition against the debtor; the purpose is to safeguard both the creditors (in that it would prevent the debtor from transferring his heritable property to the prejudice of his creditors) and any person who might transact with the debtor in relation to his heritable property. After final distribution or if the trust deed has otherwise ceased to be operative, the trustee must have a recall of the notice recorded. **9–460**

(3) As in sequestration, the lodging of a claim with a trustee acting under a trust deed bars the effect of the rules relating to limitation of actions in any part of the United Kingdom. **9–461**

(4) The trustee under a trust deed must be qualified as an "insolvency practitioner" (Insolvency Act 1986, s. 388(2)). **9–462**

In the absence of contrary provisions in the trust deed, the trustee's powers and position are governed by the Trusts (Scotland) Acts 1921 and 1961. **9–463**

However, it is usual for the trust deed expressly to confer on the trustee the powers of a permanent trustee in sequestration, and to stipulate that the rights of creditors are to be the same as they would be in a sequestration. **9–464**

A creditor who does not accede to the trust deed is nevertheless entitled to receive from the trustee the same rate of dividend on his debt as the acceding creditors receive, and he may recover his share by direct action against the trustee (*Ogilvie & Son v. Taylor* (1887) 14 R. 399). **9–465**

A non-acceding creditor may sue the debtor for his debt, may obtain a preference for himself by diligence, may challenge the trust deed as a fraudulent preference at common law, and may petition for sequestration. **9–466**

An acceding creditor may also petition for sequestration where the object of the trust deed is being defeated by the action of non-acceding creditors (as in *Campbell and Beck v. Macfarlane* (1862) 24 D. 1097, where non-acceding heritable creditors who had executed a poinding of the ground were about to carry off the moveable estate). A trust deed often expressly confers on the trustee the right to apply for sequestration, but this right can be **9–467** exercised only if certain conditions inserted by the Act of 1993 are satisfied (see 9–106, above).

9–468 On the award of sequestration, the trust deed automatically falls, and the trustee under the trust deed is bound to account to the trustee in the sequestration.

9–469 A trust deed usually provides that the debtor will be discharged of his debts on payment of the dividend which the estate yields. Such a provision does not have the effect of discharging the debtor of a debt due to a non-acceding creditor even where that creditor has received the same rate of dividend as the other creditors (*Ogilvie & Son v. Taylor*, above).

9–470 A trust deed may provide for the appointment of a committee of creditors whose duties would correspond to those of commissioners in sequestration.

(ii) *The Special Features of the Protected Trust Deed*

9–471 The protected trust deed introduced by the Act of 1985 did not prove popular, and the amendments made by the Act of 1993 were intended to enhance its popularity. The principal objection to the procedure was the difficulty in meeting the provision that a protected trust deed required to be acceded to by a majority in number and not less than two-thirds in value of the creditors within four weeks of publication of a notice in the *Edinburgh Gazette*. In order to attain that majority, the creditors had to take an active step. The amendments made by the Act of 1993 have the effect that a creditor, unless he objects to the trust deed, is treated as if he had acceded to the trust deed: inaction on the part of the creditors can therefore allow the necessary majority to be attained. The period has also been increased to five weeks.

9–472 The conditions which must be fulfilled before a trust deed becomes a "protected trust deed" within the meaning of Schedule 5, as amended by the Act of 1993 (Sched. 1, para. 32), are:

(1) The trustee must be a person who would not be disqualified from acting as permanent trustee if the debtor's estate were being sequestrated, *i.e.* he must not be the debtor, he must be an insolvency practitioner qualified to act as such in relation to the debtor, he must not hold an interest opposed to the general interests of the creditors and he must reside within the jurisdiction of the Court of Session (see 9–207, above).

(2) After the trust deed has been delivered to him, the trustee must publish in the *Edinburgh Gazette* a notice containing prescribed information, and within one week after the date of publication of this notice, the trustee must send to every creditor known to him a copy of the trust deed, a copy of the notice and other prescribed information.

(3) Within five weeks from the date of publication of the notice the trustee must not have received written notification from a majority in number and at least one-third in value of the creditors that they object to the trust deed and do not wish to accede to it.

(4) Immediately after the expiry of the five weeks, the trustee must send to the Accountant in Bankruptcy for registration in the Register of Insolvencies a copy of the trust deed with a certificate endorsed on it that it is a true copy and that he has not received the notification of objection mentioned in (3), above.

If these four conditions are fulfilled, the consequences are: **9–473**

(a) a creditor who has been sent a copy of the notice and who has not notified the trustee that he objects to the trust deed is treated as if he had acceded to the trust deed; and

(b) the debtor is not permitted to petition for the sequestration of his estate while the trust deed subsists.

However, a qualified creditor who has not been sent a copy of **9–474** the notice in condition (2), above, or who has notified the trustee of his objection to the trust deed under condition (3), above, has a limited right to present a petition for the debtor's sequestration: if he presents his petition within six weeks after the publication of the notice in condition (2), above, then the court may award sequestration if it considers that to do so would be in the best interests of the creditors; he may also petition at any time provided:

(a) the debtor's apparent insolvency was constituted within four months before the presentation of the petition; and

(b) he avers that the provision for distribution of the estate is unduly prejudicial to a creditor or class of creditors.

Before making an award the court must be satisifed that the averment in (b) is correct.

Not more than 28 days after his final distribution of the estate, **9–475** the trustee must send to the Accountant in Bankruptcy for registration in the Register of Insolvencies:

(1) a statement in the prescribed form indicating how the estate was realised and distributed; and

(2) a certificate to the effect that the distribution was in accordance with the trust deed.

9–476 Where the trustee has obtained a discharge from the creditors who have acceded to the trust deed, he must immediately give notice of the discharge by recorded delivery to every creditor known to him who has not been sent the notice under condition (2) above (at 9–472), or who has notified the trustee of his objection to the trust deed under condition (3) (at 9–472) above. He must also send the notice of discharge to the Accountant in Bankruptcy for registration in the Register of Insolvencies.

9–477 The sending of the notice of discharge to a creditor who was not sent the notice under condition (2) (at 9–472) above, or who notified the trustee of his objection to the trust deed under condition (3), above, makes the discharge binding on that creditor unless he applies to the court, within the next 28 days after the sending of the notice of discharge, and satisfies the court that the intromissions of the trustee with the debtor's estate have been so unduly prejudicial to the creditor's claim that he should not be bound by the discharge. A copy of the court's order to that effect must be sent to the trustee and to the Accountant in Bankruptcy for registration in the Register of Insolvencies.

(b) Extra-Judicial Composition Contract

9–478 This is a private agreement entered into between the debtor and his creditors by which the creditors agree to accept from the debtor a composition, which will be distributed rateably among them, and on payment of which the debtor will usually be discharged. As the debtor is not divested of his property, this type of extra-judicial settlement is more appropriate than the trust deed for the situation where the debtor is in business and it is intended that he should continue his business instead of having it sold and the proceeds distributed.

9–479 The payment of a composition under an extra-judicial composition contract is to be distinguished from the payment of a composition in the course of a sequestration (see 9–370 *et seq.*, above). The former is governed only by the common law (except in so far as the parties to the contract voluntarily incorporate statutory provisions), whereas the latter necessarily involves strict adherence to the Act.

An extra-judicial composition contract is not binding on a creditor who has not acceded to it. Such a creditor may, therefore, use diligence against the debtor's property, and may petition for sequestration. **9–480**

It is an implied condition in any extra-judicial composition contract that all creditors will be treated rateably. If one favoured creditor is to receive an additional instalment, this will constitute an illegal preference (see *Bank of Scotland v. Faulds* (1870) 7 S.L.R. 619 (9–47, above)). **9–481**

If the debtor fails to pay the composition, his original debts revive: **9–482**

Horsefall v. Virtue & Co. (1826) 5 S. 36: V. & Co. entered into an extra-judicial composition contract with their creditors by which they agreed to pay 6s. 6d. in the £ on their debts, in three instalments at six, 12 and 18 months from September 1, 1821. H., a creditor for £500, accordingly received three bills of exchange each for £54 3s. 4d.

V. & Co. duly paid the first two bills, but failed to pay the third.

Held that, in V. & Co.'s sequestration, H. was entitled to lodge a claim for £500 less the amount of the two composition bills which had been paid.

The composition contract may provide security for payment of the composition. A cautioner will be freed from liability if material alteration is made without his consent (as in *Allan, Buckley Allan & Milne v. Pattison* (1893) 21 R. 195, where, on the debtor's failure to pay the first of two instalments of a composition, his creditors took from him a trust deed under which the debtor's estate was realised). **9–483**

Further Reading

Scots Mercantile Law Statutes (reprinted from *The Parliament House Book*) for Bankruptcy (Scotland) Act 1985 (as amended)

Gloag and Henderson, *The Law of Scotland*, Chapter 54

William W. McBryde, *Bankruptcy* (2nd ed., 1995, W. Green/ Sweet & Maxwell)

Alan Adie, *Bankruptcy* (1995, W. Green with the Institute of Chartered Accountants of Scotland)

The Laws of Scotland: Stair Memorial Encyclopaedia, Volume 2, Title *Bankruptcy* by David C. Coull

Scottish Law Commission, *Report on Bankruptcy and Related Aspects of Insolvency and Liquidation* (Scot. Law Com. No. 68) (1982, H.M.S.O.)

CHAPTER 10

ARBITRATION

	Para.
Introduction	10–01
I General Nature of Arbitration	10–09
(a) What Matters may be Referred to Arbitration	10–10
(b) Whether there is a Distinction between Arbitration and Valuation	10–14
(c) The Inherent Characteristics of Arbitration	10–22
(d) The Possible Advantages of Arbitration over Litigation	10–29
(i) Informality	10–30
(ii) Speed	10–32
(iii) Cheapness	10–35
(iv) Privacy	10–38
(v) Expertise	10–39
II Constitution of the Contract of Submission	10–40
(a) The Capacity of the Parties	10–41
(b) The Form of the Contract	10–43
III Scope of the Submission	10–50
(a) The Court's Role in Fixing the Scope of the Submission	10–52
(b) The Assumption that the Arbiter will not Exceed his Jurisdiction	10–56
(c) *Ad Hoc* Submissions and Ancillary Arbitrations	10–60
(i) *Ad Hoc* Submissions	10–61
(ii) Ancillary Arbitrations	10–63
(1) Restricted and ample clauses	10–65
(a) Example of restricted clause	10–66
(b) Examples of ample clause	10–67
(2) Assessing damages	10–69
(3) Incorporation into subcontract	10–71
(4) Termination of the main contract	10–73
(a) Repudiation of the main contract	10–74
(b) Supervening impossibility of performance of the main contract	10–75
(c) Frustration of the main contract	10–76
(5) Date of the arbitration agreement	10–77
(d) The Duration of the Submission	10–80
IV Arbiters and Oversmen	10–88
(a) The Relationship between Arbiters and Oversman	10–93
(b) Appointment	10–106
(i) The Arbitration (Scotland) Act 1894	10–107
(1) Deficiencies in the common law	10–108
(a) Unnamed arbiter	10–108
(b) No implied power to appoint oversman	10–112
(2) The provisions of the Act	10–113
(3) Applications under the Act	10–118
(4) Shortcomings of the Act	10–122
(ii) Section 17 of the Law Reform (Miscellaneous Provisions) (Scotland) Act 1980	10–125
(c) Disqualification	10–127
(d) Remuneration	10–145
V Conduct of the Arbitration	10–151
(a) Formal and Informal Procedure	10–153
(b) The Requirement of Impartiality	10–158
(c) Specific Steps in the Procedure	10–162
(i) Appointment of Clerk	10–162
(ii) Proceedings *Ex Parte*	10–164
(iii) Prorogation of the Submission	10–165
(iv) Applications to Court	10–166
(v) Issue of Award	10–171
VI Challenge of the Award	10–177
(a) Corruption, Bribery or Falsehood	10–184
(b) *Ultra Fines Compromissi*	10–191
(c) Improper Procedure	10–193
(d) Defective Award	10–198
VII Judicial References	10–207

INTRODUCTION

10–01 It is a general rule of the common law that parties to a dispute are entitled to have their dispute settled by litigation (*i.e.* by bringing or defending an action in the courts). In many situations, however, the parties prefer arbitration to litigation and so agree to refer their dispute instead to a person of their own choice (an "arbiter"), whose decision ("decree-arbitral" or "award") they will accept as binding. It is common for there to be two arbiters, one appointed by each party, with the further provision that if the two arbiters disagree the matter will "devolve on" (pass to the decision of) an "oversman" appointed by the parties or by the two arbiters. The agreement of the parties (referred to as the "contract of submission") has the general effect of "ousting" (*i.e.* excluding) the jurisdiction of the courts on the matter referred.[1] A central issue in many arbitration cases is whether the parties have used in their agreement words which, on the court's interpretation, effectively oust the court's jurisdiction in the particular dispute which has arisen.

10–02 This chapter deals with commercial arbitration and not with statutory arbitration. The latter is not based on the agreement of parties but is prescribed by various Acts of Parliament as the means of settling disputes arising out of the statutory provisions. Statutory arbitrations became common from the middle of the nineteenth century for the settlement of disputed claims for compensation where land was required for the large undertakings such as railways (*e.g.* the arbitrations provided for by the Lands Clauses Consolidation (Scotland) Act 1845 and the Railways Clauses Consolidation (Scotland) Act 1845). Other instances of statutory arbitrations include those provided for by the Agricultural Holdings (Scotland) Act 1991 for the settlement of claims between landlord and tenant. The scope of and procedure in such arbitrations depend on the provisions of the particular Act in question.

10–03 The general Scots law of arbitration is almost wholly common law. Such statutory provisions as there are affect only specific aspects of the subject and are to be found in an odd assortment of legislation—the Articles of Regulation of 1695 (which are not an

[1] The jurisdiction of the courts is, however, not wholly ousted (see 10–166 *et seq.*, below).

Act of Parliament but have legislative force), the Arbitration (Scotland) Act 1894, section 3 of the Administration of Justice (Scotland) Act 1972, section 17 of the Law Reform (Miscellaneous Provisions) (Scotland) Act 1980 and the Consumer Arbitration Agreements Act 1988 (which last was wholly repealed by the Arbitration Act 1996 (s. 107 and Sched. 4) and replaced by sections 89 to 91 of that Act (s. 108(3)).

The English law of arbitration is now mainly stated in the **10–04** Arbitration Act 1996 and had a distinct source: its main principles formed Part I of the Arbitration Act 1950 (which consolidated earlier legislation applicable to England), as amended by the Arbitration Act 1979. The leading provision of Part I of the Act of 1950 (re-enacting the provision of the Arbitration Act 1889) was that if any party to an arbitration agreement commenced any legal proceedings in any court against any other party to the agreement, in respect of any matter agreed to be referred, the court *might* make an order staying the proceedings (1950 Act, s. 4(1)). Of the differing approaches to arbitration in the two countries Lord Dunedin said in *Sanderson & Son v. Armour & Co. Ltd*, 1922 S.C. (H.L.) 117, at p. 126:

"The English common law doctrine,—eventually swept away by the Arbitration Act of 1889—that a contract to oust the jurisdiction of the Courts was against public policy and invalid, never obtained in Scotland. In the same way, the right in England pertains to the Court under that Act to apply or not to apply the arbitration clause in its discretion never was the right of the Court in Scotland. If the parties have contracted to arbitrate, to arbitration they must go."

In relation to international commercial arbitration, however, **10–05** there is legislation applicable to Scotland and formerly to England also, namely, Part II of the Arbitration Act 1950 ("Enforcement of Certain Foreign Awards") and the Arbitration Act 1975 which enabled the New York Convention on the Recognition and Enforcement of Foreign Arbitral Awards of 1958 to be given effect in the United Kingdom. The leading provision of the Act of 1975 is to be contrasted with the leading provision of Part I of the Act of 1950 (see 10–04, above): it is to the effect that if any party to an international arbitration agreement commences any legal proceedings in any court against any other party to the agreement, in respect of a matter agreed to be referred, the court *must* make an order staying (or, in Scotland, "sisting") the proceedings, unless the court is satisfied that the arbitration agreement is null and void, inoperative or incapable of being performed or that there is not in fact any dispute between the parties with regard to the matter agreed to be referred (1975 Act, s. 1(1)). As regards English law, the Act of 1975 was repealed by the Arbitration Act 1996 (s. 107(4) and Sched. 4) but section 1(1) of the Act of 1975 is replaced by section 9(4) of the Act of 1996 which provides that the court *must* grant a stay unless satisfied that the arbitration agreement is null and void, inoperative or incapable of being peformed. The Act of 1996 (s. 86(2)) introduced a similar provision to English domestic arbitrations. As regards Scots law, the Act of 1996 preserved the Act of 1975 (1996 Act, s. 108(4)).

10–06 Further legislation on international commercial arbitration, applicable to Scotland only, was introduced by section 66 of, and Schedule 7 to, the Law Reform (Miscellaneous Provisions) (Scotland) Act 1990. The provisions give the force of law in Scotland to "the Model Law", *i.e.* the UNCITRAL Model Law on International Commercial Arbitration as earlier adopted by the United Nations Commission on International Trade Law on June 21, 1985 (1990 Act, s. 66(1)). Schedule 7 sets out the Model Law with certain modifications to adapt it for application in Scotland. It is a fundamental principle of the Model Law that its provisions yield to any contrary provisions in any treaty binding on the state in question (*e.g.* where a provision in the New York Convention is contrary to a provision in Schedule 7, the first-mentioned of these conflicting provisions is applicable). While the scope of the Model Law is primarily international commercial arbitration, the parties to any other arbitration agreement may agree that the Model Law as set out in Schedule 7 will apply to their arbitration (1990 Act, s. 66(4)). Although English law has not adopted the Model Law as a whole, the Act of 1996 includes many provisions which have been influenced by the Model Law.

10–07 The subject-matter of this chapter is confined to non-international arbitrations governed by the law of Scotland and is dealt with under the following headings:

I. General nature of arbitration;
II. Constitution of the contract of submission;
III. Scope of the submission;
IV. Arbiters and oversmen;

V. Conduct of the arbitration;
VI. Challenge of the award.
There is also a brief consideration of:
VII. Judicial references.

Reform of the law of arbitration in Scotland has been considered by the Scottish Advisory Committee on Arbitration Law ("the Dervaird Committee") established by the Lord Advocate in 1986. The first part of the Committee's remit was to consider whether the Model Law should be adopted in Scotland for international commercial arbitrations. In a report of 1989 the Committee decided this question in the affirmative, the Committee's recommendations were accepted by the Lord Advocate and provisions to give effect to them were contained in the Law Reform (Miscellaneous Provisions) (Scotland) Act 1990 (see 10–06, above). The Committee then turned its attention to the second part of its remit, namely, "to examine the operation of the system of arbitration in Scotland in the light of the Model Law and to make recommendations regarding any legislative or other steps which the Committee considers should be taken to improve the system of arbitration in Scotland". The Committee's report of 1996 made recommendations for a statutory framework which would have two main functions: first, to complement, where necessary, terms which the parties have agreed among themselves, and secondly, to ensure fundamental fairness of the arbitral process. The draft Bill, appended to the report, also consolidates earlier statutory provisions on arbitration and includes some new provisions aimed at removing existing uncertainties. **10–08**

I GENERAL NATURE OF ARBITRATION

It is appropriate to look first at the questions of: **10–09**

(a) what matters may be referred to arbitration; and

(b) whether there is a distinction between arbitration and valuation; before considering:

(c) the inherent characteristics of arbitration; and

(d) the possible advantages of arbitration over litigation.

(a) **What Matters may be Referred to Arbitration**

Criminal matters cannot be made the subject of an arbitration. It might be suggested on the authority of *Earl of Kintore v. Union* **10–10**

Bank of Scotland (1863) 1 M. (H.L.) 11; (1861) 24 D. 59 that a criminal matter such as fraud, if incidental to the main question in the submission, could be dealt with in arbitration proceedings. The case concerned a deed by which a truster and trustee, under a voluntary trust for creditors, and the creditors submitted to arbitration "all claims, debts, and demands" against the truster's estate. The Bank were creditors for substantial sums, for which they held documents of debt. The truster, trustee and other parties, alleging fraud, raised an action of reduction of these documents of debt and the court held that their action was excluded by the submission to arbitration. The case is thus restricted to the civil aspect of fraud and is not itself an exception to the proposition that criminal matters cannot be made the subject of an arbitration.

10–11 In general any matter involving civil rights and obligations, whether affecting heritable or moveable property and whether raising questions of fact or law, may be referred to arbitration. It makes no difference whether the court's jurisdiction in the matter is founded on statute or on common law, but in either case the words used must be wide enough to exclude the court's jurisdiction. Thus, in *Roxburgh v. Dinardo*, 1981 S.L.T. 291 (O.H.), where a partnership agreement contained an arbitration clause referring to arbitration "any question, dispute or difference between the parties arising out of this Agreement or relating to the Partnership business", the words were held not wide enough to confer on the arbiter the court's jurisdiction to dissolve the partnership on the "just and equitable" ground (Partnership Act 1890, s. 35(f)).

10–12 However, on grounds of public policy, questions of public rights and of status (*e.g.* as to whether a person is married or divorced) are exceptions to the general rule.

Two cases decided under the workmen's compensation legislation might be taken to suggest that where a question of status is incidental to the determination of another question, an arbiter has power to settle the question of status. However, it seems preferable to regard these cases as applications of particular statutory provisions and not as part of the common law. The Workmen's Compensation Acts of 1906 and 1925 provided that any question as to who was a "dependant" might be settled by arbitration under the Acts, *i.e.* by the sheriff as arbiter. In *Johnstone v. Spencer & Co.*, 1908 S.C. 1015, the question of whether a girl was the illegitimate child of a deceased workman was held to be a question which could competently be decided by the sheriff because it was incidental to deciding whether she was a "dependant". Similarly, in *Turnbull v. Wilsons and Clyde Coal Co. Ltd*, 1935 S.C. 580, it was held competent for the sheriff, as arbiter, to allow proof of the claimant's marriage by habit and repute, this being incidental to determining whether she was a "dependant". Apart from the statutory provision with which these two cases were concerned, there may be no other instance of a question of status being competently referred to arbitration.

An arbiter's power to give a final decision on questions of law **10–13**
arising in an arbitration was to some extent modified by section 3 of the Administration of Justice (Scotland) Act 1972. That section provides that, unless there is an express provision to the contrary in the arbitration agreement, the arbiter or oversman *may*, on the application of a party to the arbitration, at any stage in the arbitration state a case for the opinion of the Court of Session on any question of law arising in the arbitration, and the arbiter or oversman *must* do so if the party applies to the Court of Session and that court directs a case to be stated. The application must be made at a "stage in the arbitration" (*e.g.* after the arbiter has issued proposed findings): it is no longer competent after the arbiter has issued his final award (*Fairlie Yacht Slip Ltd v. Lumsden*, 1977 S.L.T. (Notes) 41). The Rules of Court on appeals by way of stated case (formerly Rules 276–278 of R.C.S. 1965, now Chapter 41, Parts I and II of R.C.S. 1994) must be strictly followed (*Gunac Ltd v. Inverclyde District Council*, 1982 S.L.T. 387, and *John L. Haley Ltd v. Dumfries and Galloway Regional Council*, 1985 S.L.T. 109). The Rules require the arbiter, if he is of the opinion that it is necessary or expedient that the facts should be ascertained before the application is disposed of, to defer further consideration of the application until he has ascertained the facts. It is expressly provided by section 3 that it does not apply to any form of arbitration relating to a trade dispute or to any other arbitration arising from a collective agreement, but in *O'Neill v. Scottish Joint Negotiating Committee for Teaching Staff*, 1987 S.L.T. 648 (O.H.), the Lord Ordinary (Jauncey) held that section 3 would apply to an arbitration concerning a teacher's individual contract of employment which incorporated conditions embodied in a collective agreement: such an arbitration was not an arbitration "*arising from a collective agreement*". It would seem that the arbiter would be

bound to accept as conclusive the opinion of the Court of Session on the question of law submitted to it: see *Mitchell-Gill v. Buchan*, 1921 S.C. 390 (10–170, below). It is not competent to appeal to the House of Lords against the opinion of the Court of Session since such an opinion does not constitute a "judgment" within the meaning of section 40(1) of the Court of Session Act 1988 or an "order or judgment" within the meaning of section 3 of the Appellate Jurisdiction Act 1876 (*John G. McGregor (Contractors) Ltd v. Grampian Regional Council*, 1991 S.C. (H.L.) 1). The Dervaird Committee has recommended that the stated case provisions should be repealed.

(b) **Whether there is a Distinction between Arbitration and Valuation**

10–14 A distinction has been drawn in English law between arbitration proper and valuation, and opinions in some Scottish cases suggest that a similar distinction, though with different effects, exists in Scots law. In this connection an "arbitration proper" has been defined as "the submission of a *lis*,[2] the purpose of which is the determination of an existing dispute", whereas a "valuation" has been defined as "the submission of a *negotium*,[3] the object of which is not the settlement of an existing dispute but the prevention of a dispute; as for instance where parties submit to an arbiter or valuer to assess a claim whose existence is admitted, but which there has been no attempt to adjust, so that the parties cannot in strict language be said to have differed" (Guild, *The Law of Arbitration in Scotland*, p. 3).

10–15 A valuation has been held to require less formality than an arbitration. Several cases relating to agricultural leases illustrate this point, *e.g.*:

10–16 (i) *Nivison v. Howat* (1883) 11 R. 182: At the expiry of a lease two neighbouring farmers were chosen by the outgoing and incoming tenant respectively to value the crop, etc. They agreed on some points, but differed on others, and appointed a third farmer, as oversman, to decide between them.

The oversman issued an award, which the incoming tenant refused to implement on the ground that there had been irregularity in procedure.

---

[2] "dispute".

[3] "matter" (about which parties are negotiating).

Held that in such circumstances no formalities were necessary and that the award was therefore binding.

Lord Young said (at p. 191): "No formalities require to be observed by two farmers in valuing a crop, or by a third who is competently called in to decide where they differ. All the parties here desired or bargained for was the intelligent opinion of two skilled persons, and if they differed then the decision of another skilled man. That is what they have got."

(ii) *Robertson v. Boyd and Winans* (1885) 12 R. 419: An informal sublease of a portion of a farm provided that the rent was to be fixed by valuators. **10–17**

The valuators were appointed by a probative deed, but their award was not in probative form.

Held that, in the circumstances of the case, the award had been homologated.

Lord Young expressed the opinion that neither the nomination of the valuators nor the award required to be in probative form. Lord Young's observation, however, may carry little weight in view of the fact that the other two judges (Lord Craighill and Lord Rutherfurd Clark) would apparently have held that the award, being probative, would not have been binding, had it not been homologated.

(iii) *Gibson v. Fotheringham*, 1914 S.C. 987: In terms of a farm lease the landlord and the outgoing tenant referred certain questions of valuation to two arbiters mutually chosen and their oversman under the declaration that whatever the arbiters or their oversman should "determine . . . by decree or decrees arbitral, interim or final", should be binding on the parties. **10–18**

Held that a formal devolution of the reference upon the oversman was not necessary, and that an award of the oversman would not be invalid merely because it included decisions which had already been arrived at by the arbiters.

Lord Justice-Clerk (John H. A. Macdonald) said (at p. 996): "This is a case of a very ordinary arbitration in which the questions relate to skilled valuation only. There was, therefore, no call for formality of procedure."

(iv) *Cameron v. Nicol*, 1930 S.C. 1: The owner of a farm and the outgoing tenant entered into a submission by which they referred the valuation of certain crops, stock and implements to two arbiters and to an oversman to be appointed by the arbiters to act in the event of their differing in opinion. **10–19**

An award was issued, signed by the two arbiters and the oversman, that did not show on which, if any, of the items being valued the arbiters had differed in their estimate.

Held that the valuation belonged to a class of arbitrations where rigid conformity with formal procedure was not required, and that the award was therefore not invalid merely because it did not show the items on which the arbiters had differed.

Lord Sands said (at p. 15): "The first ground of challenge is that the award is signed by the two arbiters and the oversman indiscriminately, without any indication of how far it represents agreement arrived at by the two arbiters, or a decision by the oversman in regard to a matter about which the arbiters had differed. This objection would be fatal in the case of a formal arbitration to determine a dispute. But that was not the nature of the proceedings here in question. There is here no question of the resolution of matters in dispute, but there is simply a valuation to determine the amount payable in respect of certain things which it had been agreed were to be taken over at an agricultural waygoing. It is well settled that in such valuations the same strictness of form is not required as in an arbitration to determine a dispute, whether as regards heritable or moveable rights of property, or as regards claims of damages."

10–20 (v) *Stewart v. Williamson,* 1910 S.C. (H.L.) 47; 1909 S.C. 1254: The Agricultural Holdings (Scotland) Act 1908 provided that all questions which under a lease were referred to "arbitration" should (in spite of any agreement under the lease providing for a different method of arbitration) be determined by a single arbiter.

The lease in question provided that the tenant should, at the expiry of the lease, leave the sheep stock on the farm to the owners or incoming tenant according to the "valuation" of men mutually chosen, with the power to name an oversman.

Held that the valuation of the sheep stock was referred to arbitration within the meaning of the statutory provision, and therefore fell to be determined by a single arbiter and not by two arbiters as stipulated in the lease.

10–21 A conclusion which may be drawn from such cases is that there is no distinct dividing line in Scots law between arbitration and valuation: rather there is a range of types of arbitration of varying degrees of formality.

(c) The Inherent Characteristics of Arbitration

The arbitration with which this chapter deals is based on contract and has the following inherent characteristics: **10–22**

(i) "The evident and leading object of the contract is to exclude a court of law from the determination of some matter which is in dispute; and to take, in its place, the judgment or award of some private person or persons, selected by the parties to arbitrate between them" (Bell, *Treatise on the Law of Arbitration in Scotland*, p. 20). **10–23**

(ii) The parties bind themselves to abide by the award and to implement it; they have no right to have the matter tried over again in a court of law or to appeal to a court against the award. "It would be a piece of idle curiosity, and nothing more, to ascertain an arbiter's opinion and take his judgment on a disputed matter, if either party could afterwards, at his pleasure, have that judgment reviewed on its merits in a court of law. The forum of the arbiter would then be converted into a mere ante-chamber to the Courts of Law, serving no other purpose except that of creating great extra expense and delay, without any rational or intelligible motive whatsoever" (*op. cit.*, p. 21). By resorting to arbitration the parties have accepted the risk that their arbiter may make a wrong decision. In extreme cases, however, the court would be entitled to interfere with the decision of an arbiter on procedural matters where the decision was unreasonable, making the matter susceptible to judicial review (*Shanks & McEwan (Contractors) Ltd v. Mifflin Construction Ltd*, 1993 S.L.T. 1124 (O.H.)). Once an arbiter has given his answer to a reference, that decision is as good as a decree of the court, with the result that a subsequent court action on the same question is barred (*Farrans v. Roxburgh County Council*, 1969 S.L.T. 35 (O.H.)). On the other hand, a question which has not been included amongst the matters referred may be the subject of a court action (*Crudens v. Tayside Health Board*, 1979 S.C. 142). The conduct of the parties may be such as to amount to waiver of the right to arbitration, but the raising of court proceedings does not necessarily amount to such a waiver (*D. & J. McDougall Ltd v. Argyll and Bute District Council*, 1987 S.L.T. 7 (O.H.)). **10–24**

(iii) Because the arbiter has a judicial role, he must be honest and impartial. "It clearly appears to be an *implied condition* under **10–25** the contract, that [*the parties*] shall only be bound by [*the award*] if it be pronounced with *honesty* and *impartiality* by the arbiter" (Bell, *op. cit.*, p. 22). The element of honesty would seem to be satisfied "wherever the arbiter had conscientiously believed he was doing what was right and just, however much he might have erred in judgment" (Bell, *op. cit.*, p. 23). To satisfy the condition of impartiality, there must be "equal and even-handed procedure towards both parties alike; . . . no hearing of one side only (for example) and refusing to hear the other" (Bell, *op. cit.*, p. 26).

10–26 (iv) There is an implied condition in the contract of submission that the parties will observe fairness of procedure in their relations towards each other. They must "abstain from practising any fraudulent and deceitful devices on the arbiter, for the purpose of thereby impetrating from him an unjust award, pronounced under essential error, so induced" (Bell, *op. cit.*, p. 27).

10–27 (v) The arbiter must keep within the powers which have been conferred upon him: he must observe the conditions imposed on him by the contract of submission, and must not act *ultra fines compromissi* ("beyond the bounds of the submission") or fail to exhaust the submission by not deciding matters referred to him.

10–28 Where there is breach of the conditions mentioned in (iii), (iv), or (v), above, the award can be reduced (*i.e.* set aside by the court).

(d) The Possible Advantages of Arbitration over Litigation

10–29 The parties to an arbitration agreement may regard arbitration as having the following advantages over litigation:

(i) *Informality*

10–30 In an arbitration the parties are free to decide on the degree of formality or may leave that matter to the arbiter's discretion. Strict adherence to court procedures is not required unless the parties so specify.

10–31 The arbiter is, however, bound to do equal justice to both sides (see 10–25, above).

(ii) *Speed*

10–32 In an arbitration the timetable is arranged by the parties and the arbiter, whereas in litigation the case must await its turn in the court timetable. An arbiter's decision may therefore be more speedily obtained.

On the other hand, in some situations arbitration proceedings may be long drawn out: this is especially so in large-scale arbitrations where the arbiters are likely to be well-known professional persons whose services are much in demand and whose commitments prevent them from giving their uninterrupted attention to any one particular arbitration. The case of *Crudens Ltd v. Tayside Health Board*, 1979 S.C. 142, may be referred to as an illustration: **10–33**

C. Ltd had entered into a building contract in 1963 with Tayside Health Board for a new teaching hospital and medical school at Ninewells, Dundee. Several disputes arose and were in 1969 submitted to David M. Doig, F.R.I.C.S., as sole arbiter, acting with the assistance of A. J. Mackenzie Stuart, Q.C., B.A., LL.B., as legal assessor. At the end of the arbitration C. Ltd was awarded £2,313,497, and it is narrated that "the parties . . . spent about 100 days in a very long, expensive and involved arbitration" (*per* Lord Allanbridge (Ordinary) at p. 149). **10–34**

(C. Ltd's subsequent action against the board for damages for loss of use of the money awarded was held to be competent on the ground that that matter had not been referred to the arbiter.)

(iii) *Cheapness*

Litigation is often costly, especially for the unsuccessful party, and an arbitration may prove less expensive. **10–35**

However, a formal arbitration is not necessarily less expensive than litigation: litigants do not pay remuneration to the judge or the clerk of court or a hire-charge for the court room, whereas an arbiter's fee may be substantial and there may also be charges for a legal assessor, for a clerk's services and for suitable accommodation for the hearing. **10–36**

The potential high costs of an arbitration concerning a small matter led to the passing of the Consumer Arbitration Agreements Act 1988—a consumer protection measure applicable to the whole of the United Kingdom. This Act was wholly repealed by the Arbitration Act 1996 (s. 107(2) and Sched. 4) and replaced by sections 89 to 91 of the Act of 1996, which are also applicable to the whole of the United Kingdom. These sections extend the Unfair Terms in Consumer Contracts Regulations 1994 (S.I. 1994 No. 3159) with some modifications to arbitration agreements. The Regulations implemented the E.C. Unfair Terms in Consumer **10–37**

Contracts Directive 1993 and applied to any contract between a consumer (*i.e.* a natural person making a contract for purposes outside his business) and a commercial concern (*i.e.* a seller or supplier who sells goods or supplies goods or services, for business purposes, business including a trade or profession and the activities of any government department or local or public authority). Under the Regulations a contract term is "unfair" and is unenforceable if the term:

(1) has not been individually negotiated;

(2) is contrary to good faith (relevant considerations include the comparative strength of the parties' bargaining positions); and

(3) causes a significant imbalance in the parties' rights and obligations to the detriment of the consumer.

A Schedule to the Regulations gives a long but non-exhaustive list of terms which may be regarded as unfair, and the list includes a term requiring the consumer to take disputes exclusively to arbitration. Whereas the Act of 1988 had given protection to the consumer only where there was an agreement to refer *future differences* to arbitration, the Act of 1996 (s. 89(1)) extends the Regulations to agreements to submit to arbitration *present or future differences*. Further, whereas the Regulations restrict the definition of "consumer" to a *natural* person, the Act of 1996 (s. 90) makes the Regulations applicable also where the consumer is a *legal* person, giving protection, therefore, to a firm or company which obtains goods or services otherwise than for business purposes. The Act of 1996 (s. 91) applies only to claims not exceeding an amount specified by statutory instrument; at present the upper limit is £3,000 (Unfair Arbitration Agreements (Specified Amount) Order 1996 (S.I. 1996 No. 3211).

(iv) *Privacy*

10–38 Most court proceedings take place in public, and may be reported in the press. Parties may wish to keep their disputes from the public gaze: they may, for instance, have been on intimate terms as partners or they may be business organisations wishing to avoid disclosure of financial details.

(v) *Expertise*

10–39 The arbiter chosen may be an expert in a particular line of business, perhaps capable of giving a decision as to the quality of goods by a simple "sniff and look", or well acquainted with the circumstances and terminology of the branch of commerce concerned. The parties may feel more satisfied with such an expert's findings than with a judge's decision.

II CONSTITUTION OF THE CONTRACT OF SUBMISSION

The general law of contract applies to contracts of submission, and only brief notice may be taken here of some points relating to: **10–40**

(a) the capacity of the parties; and
(b) the form of the contract.

(a) The Capacity of the Parties

The parties must have contractual capacity; *e.g.* by the Age of Legal Capacity (Scotland) Act 1991 a person under the age of 16 years cannot enter into a contract of submission and a person over 16 years of age but under 18 years of age, while he may enter into a submission, may, until he reaches the age of 21 years, apply to the court for his action to be set aside on the ground that it is a "prejudicial transaction", *i.e.* a transaction which an adult, exercising reasonable prudence, would not have entered into in the circumstances and which has caused or is likely to cause substantial prejudice to the applicant. **10–41**

A person who is acting in a representative capacity may or may not have authority to refer a matter to arbitration. In some situations there is a statutory provision which will apply: *e.g.* the Bankruptcy (Scotland) Act 1985 (s. 65) provides that the permanent trustee in a sequestration may, with the consent of the commissioners, the creditors or the court, refer to arbitration any claim or question which may arise in the course of the sequestration, and by the Trusts (Scotland) Act 1921 (s. 4) trustees have power to refer all claims connected with the trust estate unless it is at variance with the terms or purposes of the trust. An agent has, as a general rule, no authority to refer a matter to arbitration: he will normally require special authority to do so. Counsel are an exception to the general rule (*Gilfillan v. Brown* (1833) 11 S. 548), but solicitors are not (*Black v. Laidlaw* (1844) 6 D. 1254). Similarly, a partner cannot without the consent of his co-partners enter into an arbitration which will be binding on the firm (*Lumsden v. Gordon* (1728) Mor. 14567). **10–42**

(b) **The Form of the Contract**

10–43 Prior to the Requirements of Writing (Scotland) Act 1995 there were conflicting views as to how the rule relating to the constitution of contracts of submission should be stated:

10–44 On the one hand the rule might be stated as being that submissions were to be regarded as *obligationes literis* ("contracts requiring writing for their constitution") unless they fell into one of a number of categories of exceptions to that rule (Walker and Walker, *The Law of Evidence in Scotland* (2nd ed.), paras. 101–103; Scottish Law Commission, *Memorandum No. 39 ("Constitution and Proof of Voluntary Obligations: Formalities of Constitution and Restrictions on Proof")*, para. 4).

10–45 On the other hand the rule might be stated as being that a contract of submission was not, of itself, one of the *obligationes literis* (though it might be brought into that category by its subject-matter), but fell into the category of contracts which could be proved only by "writ or oath", with the results that writing was in practice required, not as a solemnity, but *in modum probationis* ("by way of proof") and that the writing might be informal (Guild, *The Law of Arbitration in Scotland*, pp. 18–20).

10–46 The law was radically changed by the Requirements of Writing (Scotland) Act 1995. A contract of submission to arbitration is not included in the restricted list of contracts for the constitution of which writing is now required (1995 Act, s. 1(1) and (2)).

10–47 However, the subject-matter of an arbitration may be of such a nature (*e.g.* where it relates to heritable property) or of such importance that it is advisable for the parties to enter into a formal legal document, signed by each party in the presence of one witness (1995 Act, s. 3(1)).

10–48 If the parties have embodied their contract of submission in a formal legal document, then it is advisable that the award also should be of the same nature. In the pre-1995 law it was a requirement that where the contract of submission took the form of a formal deed, the award also had to be of that nature (*Percy v. Meikle*, Nov. 25, 1808, F.C.; *Mclaren v. Aikman*, 1939 S.C. 222).

10–49 In English law the Arbitration Act 1996 applies only to written arbitration agreements (1996 Act, s. 5(1)) and oral agreements to arbitrate are governed by the common law.

III SCOPE OF THE SUBMISSION

It is essential that the parties define the scope of the submission precisely. Otherwise it is likely that the arbitration will at some stage come before the courts—which is just the situation which the parties originally sought to avoid. If the scope of the arbiter's jurisdiction has not been clearly expressed, there may be litigation at the start of the arbitration proceedings: one party, thinking that the matter in dispute is not covered by the contract of submission, may raise an action in court and the other party may then apply for the action to be sisted to await the result of an arbitration; it is also possible that a party may apply to the court for an interdict against an arbiter who is about to deal with matters which have not been referred to him. At the conclusion of an arbitration an action of reduction may be brought to set aside the award if the arbiter has gone *ultra fines compromissi* ("beyond the bounds of the submission") or has failed to exhaust the submission (*i.e.* has failed to decide matters properly referred to him); each of these grounds of reduction is more likely to be open if the contract of submission itself has not been clearly expressed. **10–50**

Some of the principal points which affect the scope of the submission may be considered under the following headings: **10–51**

(a) the court's role in fixing the scope of the submission;

(b) the assumption that the arbiter will not exceed his jurisdiction;

(c) *ad hoc* submissions and ancillary arbitrations; and

(d) the duration of the submission.

(a) The Court's Role in Fixing the Scope of the Submission

The final decision as to the scope of the submission lies with the court. The principle is expressed in such statements as the following: "There must be a dispute between the parties which comes within the terms of the arbitration clause. A question must be truly raised between them which amounts to an arbitral dispute. . . . The court is entitled and bound to see that a question is truly raised. . . . There must, in short, be a real question, and it must be of the kind which the contract between the parties appropriates to the determination of arbiters" (*per* Lord Hunter in *Albyn Housing Society Ltd v. Taylor Woodrow Homes Ltd*, 1985 S.C. 104, at p. 107, **10–52** a case in which the housing society's averments were held to be adequately specific for the limited purpose of proving that there was a dispute which fell within the arbitration clause).

10–53 It is only where there is a dispute that the court can sist the action; for instance, in *Redpath Dorman Long Ltd v. Tarmac Construction Ltd*, 1982 S.C. 14 (O.H.), an action by a subcontractor against the main contractor for payment, since only part of the subcontractor's claim was disputed, the court sisted the action, but only to the extent of allowing the matter in dispute to proceed to arbitration. This case was followed in *Lorne Stewart plc v. Mowlem Scotland Ltd*, 1995 G.W.D. 3–112 (O.H.).

10–54 The arbiter is bound in the first instance to "expiscate" his own jurisdiction, *i.e.* examine the terms of the submission and decide whether or not the particular matter is within his jurisdiction as stated by the parties. Since, however, the leading principle of the law of arbitration is that the court's jurisdiction is ousted only to the extent to which the parties have agreed that it should be ousted, the final decision as to the extent of the arbiter's jurisdiction depends on the interpretation placed by the court on the words used by the parties in their contract of submission. The leading authority Bell states (*op. cit.*, p. 58):

"If an arbiter's judgment as to the construction of the contract of submission itself were exempt from all review, he might exercise, without control, a usurped jurisdiction to any extent over subjects which the parties never intended to submit, and never had submitted to him."

10–55 It is, however, possible for the actings of the parties to extend the scope of a reference beyond the strict terms of the original contract of submission. The principle operating in such a situation is that of personal bar. The court does not readily infer that there has been such an extension; for example, the mere inclusion in the pleadings before the arbiter of questions beyond the scope of the original submission would not take effect as an extension; the consent of both parties is required (*per* Lord President Dunedin in *Miller & Son v. Oliver & Boyd* (1906) 8 F. 390, at pp. 401–402, a case in which the scope of the submission was held not to have been enlarged by the pleadings of the parties before the arbiter).

(b) The Assumption that the Arbiter will not Exceed his Jurisdiction

Until the arbiter has taken some irrevocable step to indicate that he is exceeding his jurisdiction, the court assumes that his final decision will be within his jurisdiction, and so decided cases reveal an unwillingness on the court's part to grant an interdict to prevent an arbitration from proceeding. **10–56**

An instance is *Bennets v. Bennet* (1903) 5 F. 376: A contract of copartnery contained an arbitration clause. In an arbitration under that clause, the parties on one side raised the preliminary objection that while some of the matters referred to the arbiter were admittedly within the reference, others were clearly outside his jurisdiction. The arbiter rejected that preliminary objection, and allowed the parties a proof. **10–57**

The objectors then sought from the court an interdict to prohibit the arbiter from dealing with the matters objected to.

The court *refused* interdict, *holding* that the arbiter had only decided a question of procedure and had done nothing to indicate conclusively that in deciding the merits of the claim he would exceed his jurisdiction.

Lord President Kinross said (at p. 381): "We are bound to assume that he will keep within his powers."

A similar case in the same year was *Moore v. McCosh* (1903) 5 F. 946: In an arbitration under a mining lease the landlord claimed that the arbiter should order the tenant to perform certain works of restoration. The tenant presented to the court a note for interdict against the arbiter proceeding with the reference, on the ground that the order asked for was not within the scope of the arbitration clause in the lease. **10–58**

The court *refused* to interdict the arbiter from proceeding with the reference, since the court could not assume that the arbiter would make an incompetent order.

On similar grounds the court refused in *Wemyss v. Ardrossan Harbour Co.* (1893) 20 R. 500 to reduce an arbiter's interim orders and note of proposed findings. **10–59**

Lord McLaren said (at p. 505): "We can only interfere with the decrees of arbiters by way of reduction when we have a final decree, and can only restrain them from proceeding when the proceedings are outwith the reference.

"This case does not fall under either of these heads. We have here no final decree; everything is open."

(c) *Ad Hoc* Submissions and Ancillary Arbitrations

10–60 A contract of submission may be either an *ad hoc* submission or an ancillary arbitration.

(i) Ad Hoc *Submissions*

10–61 An *ad hoc* (literally, "for this purpose") submission is one entered into by parties who have no pre-existing arrangement for settling disputes. On the occasion of a particular dispute having arisen they agree that it be settled by arbitration, and make a contract of submission which relates only to that dispute.

10–62 The scope of the contract of submission is governed by the terms used by the parties, but since the dispute which it is intended to settle is already in existence, difficulties of interpretation as to the scope of the contract are comparatively unlikely to arise.

(ii) *Ancillary Arbitrations*

10–63 An ancillary arbitration is one founded on an arbitration clause in a contract, the main purpose of which is to deal with some other matter; *e.g.* it is usual to have an arbitration clause in a building contract and in a contract of copartnery.

10–64 Ancillary arbitrations have featured in many decided cases. The points which have been settled by these cases include the following:

(1) **Restricted and ample clauses**

10–65 Arbitration clauses are commonly divided into two varieties—the restricted or limited variety on the one hand and the ample or general or universal variety on the other. The former extends only to disputes which occur during the execution of the principal contract; it is often referred to as being "executorial" of the principal contract (but see the quotation from Lord Rutherfurd Clark's opinion in *Mackay v. Parochial Board of Barry* (1883) 10 R. 1046 (10–67, below)). The other variety of arbitration clause is of wider scope and covers disputes which, though they arise out of the principal contract, do not occur until after its execution. The distinction is described thus by Lord Dunedin in *Sanderson & Son v. Armour & Co. Ltd*, 1922 S.C. (H.L.) 117, at p. 125:

"By the law of Scotland, it has always been possible for the parties in framing the original contract to insert a clause binding themselves to refer future possible disputes to arbitration. This clause may be of two characters. It may be of a limited character, generally known as executory arbitration, providing for the adjustment of disputes concerned with the working out of the contract. But it may also be of a universal character, submitting all disputes which may arise either in the carrying out of the contract or in respect of breach of the contract after the actual execution has been finished. Whether the clause is of the one sort or the other is a matter of construction."

(a) *Example of restricted clause*

An example of the restricted or limited variety of arbitration clause occurs in *Beattie v. Macgregor* (1883) 10 R. 1094: **10–66**

A building contract contained the following clause: "Should any difference arise between the proprietor and any of the contractors in regard to the true meaning of the plans, drawings, or specifications, or the manner in which the work is to be executed, or any matter arising thereout or connected therewith, the same is hereby submitted to the determination of William Hamilton Beattie . . . , whose decision shall be final and binding upon all parties."

Held that this clause applied only to disputes arising during the execution of the contract and did not extend to a dispute concerning the accuracy of the measurements obtained by a contractor after the work had been completed.

The case was one of a series of cases on the interpretation of arbitration clauses in building contracts, and Lord President Inglis observed (at p. 1096):

"I really hope that there will be an end to cases of this class. A very little care in the choice of language would prevent all ambiguity. Let parties only distinctly express themselves so as to mean that the reference is to cover every kind of claim arising out of the contract, and the Court cannot interfere. On the other hand, if they will use language like that in the clause here, let them clearly understand that it is now settled law that such a clause covers only questions which arise during the execution of the contract."

(b) *Examples of ample clause*

10–67 One of the earliest cases giving effect to the ample, general or universal variety of arbitration clause was *Mackay v. Parochial Board of Barry* (1883) 10 R. 1046:

A contract for the introduction of a water supply to Carnoustie included the clause: "Arbiter.—Should any dispute arise as to the true nature, sufficiency, times, or extent of the work intended to be performed under the specification and drawings or as to the works having been duly and properly completed, or as to the construction of these presents, or as to any matter, claim, or obligation whatever arising out of or in connection with the works, the same shall be submitted and referred to the amicable decision, final sentence, and decree-arbitral of Alexander McCulloch . . . ."

McCulloch, who was the local authority's engineer, had power under the contract to alter, add to or modify the specified works during the course of the contract, and any alterations, additions or modifications were to be deemed to be a part of the contract.

Numerous and extensive alterations were made on the works as they proceeded, and McCulloch brought out as due to the contractor for the extra work involved a sum far below what the contractor claimed.

The contractor raised an action against the local authority for an additional payment.

Held that the contractor's claim fell within the arbitration clause.

Lord Rutherfurd Clark said (at p. 1050): "The contracting parties may create a tribunal for settling differences which may occur in the course of executing the works, and which has no other function. But of course they may do more, and extend it to the decision of any claim which may arise out of the contract. In this sense the reference is not less executorial of the contract than when it is confined to the settlement of questions which may arise during the execution of the works."

10–68 Another instance of a general clause—more briefly expressed—occurs in *North British Railway Co. v. Newburgh and North Fife Railway Co.*, 1911 S.C. 710:

An agreement between two railway companies concerning share capital and dividends contained the clause: "All questions which may arise between the parties hereto in relation to this agreement or to the import or meaning thereof or to the carrying out of the same shall be referred to arbitration. . . ."

Held that questions which arose between the parties were questions of the construction of the agreement and therefore had to be determined by the arbiter, even although their determination depended upon the question of *ultra vires* ("beyond the powers" [*conferred by Act of Parliament*]) and even although it involved a point of law.

Lord President Dunedin said (at p. 718): "It has long ago, I think, been settled in the law of Scotland that arbitration clauses in contracts may be of two descriptions. They may be either in the form of what has been called an executory arbitration clause, which is limited to dealing with matters as they arise during the carrying out of the contract. Most of the clauses in the older cases in the books were of that character. But I think it is also perfectly well settled in the law of Scotland that there is nothing wrong in having a general arbitration clause, which may give to the determination of arbiters everything which can be decided either in respect of the carrying out of the contract or in respect of the breach thereof. . . . Now, I have no doubt that on a proper construction of Article Fourteen here it is one of that class of clauses, that is to say, it is not a mere executory clause, but it is a general clause which refers to an arbiter all questions which may properly arise either upon the import and meaning or upon the carrying out of the contract."

(2) **Assessing damages**

An arbiter has no power under an arbitration clause to assess damages unless power to do so is conferred expressly. This point was established by the House of Lords in *Blaikies v. Aberdeen Railway Co.* (1852) 1 Paterson's App. 119; 15 D. (H.L.) 20, and was held to be settled law in later decisions of the Court of Session including *Mackay & Son v. Leven Police Commissioners* (1893) 20 R. 1093: **10–69**

M. & Son entered into a contract for the execution of waterworks for the town of Leven. The contract included an arbitration clause.

M. & Son claimed from the Police Commissioners (i) £1,470 17s. 3d. as the balance due by the Commissioners for the work done under the contract and (ii) £3,255 4s. for loss and damage sustained by M. & Son.

M. & Son brought an action concluding for declarator that the Police Commissioners were bound to join in submitting both claims to the arbiter named in the arbitration clause.

Held that the second claim did not fall within the arbitration clause and that the Police Commissioners were therefore not bound to submit that claim to the arbiters.

It was admitted that the first claim fell within the arbitration clause and the court sisted the action in order that that claim might be submitted to the arbiter.

10–70 An arbitration clause may be so worded as to confer on the arbiter power to decide the question whether liability for damages has been incurred. Assessment of the damages would still remain a matter for the court unless express power to assess the damages were also conferred on the arbiter: *James Scott Ltd v. Apollo Engineering Ltd*, 1993 G.W.D. 29–1796 (O.H.).

(3) **Incorporation into subcontract**

10–71 It is common to find, *e.g.* in building contracts, an arbitration clause incorporated, along with other clauses, from a main contract into a subcontract. The effect of a simple incorporation is to make the arbiter's decision on a dispute between the employer and the main contractor binding on the subcontractor but the clause will not extend to disputes between the main contractor and the subcontractor: special provision to that effect would be required.

10–72 An instance is *Goodwins, Jardine & Co. Ltd v. Brand & Son* (1905) 7 F. 995:

B. & Son were the general contractors with the Caledonian Railway Company for the formation of portions of the Glasgow Central Railway. B. & Son, since they did not do bridge work themselves, entered into a subcontract with G. Ltd for the bridge work.

The subcontract provided that the work was to be executed according to plans and specifications which formed part of the general contract between the Caledonian Railway Company and B. & Son. One of these specifications was an arbitration clause.

The bridge work was made and part of the price was paid, but there was a dispute as to the balance.

In an action by G. Ltd against B. & Son for this balance, B. & Son pleaded that the claim should be submitted to arbitration and the action sisted until the arbiter had given his decision.

Held that the arbitration clause was not incorporated in the subcontract in relation to matters which concerned only the rights *inter se* ("between themselves") of B. & Son and G. Ltd.

Lord President Dunedin said (at p. 1000): "For some purposes there is no doubt that the arbitration clause is incorporated. It is, I think, quite clear that for anything in dispute between the Brands and the Caledonian Railway Company the arbitration clause has effect, and the result arrived at under that arbitration clause is binding on the pursuers. In that respect it is just like all the other clauses in the specification. But the point is not whether it is incorporated at all, but whether it is incorporated in regard to another matter altogether, namely, the dispute about prices between the pursuers and the defenders. That is a matter outside the relations of the defenders and the Caledonian Railway Company. What is binding on the one is not binding on the other. . . . I think the contract incorporated was the contract so far as it existed between the principal contractor and the employer—that is to say, the Brands and the Railway Company—but that you cannot over and above cut out of the provisions of that contract one clause and make it apply *mutatis mutandis*[4] to the rights *inter se* of the principal contractor and the subcontractor—that is, the pursuers and the defenders—in a matter in which the employer never had and never can have any concern."

(4) **Termination of the main contract**

Doubt can arise as to whether an arbitration clause is still operative where the question between the parties is whether the main contract itself of which the arbitration clause forms part has been terminated. Decided cases show that an arbitration clause may be sufficiently wide as to remain operative in such a situation: **10–73**

(a) *Repudiation of the main contract*

The case of *Sanderson & Son v. Armour & Co. Ltd*, 1922 S.C. (H.L.) 117, involved an alleged repudiation of the main contract: **10–74**

S. & Son purchased from A. Ltd a quantity of American eggs which were to be delivered in three instalments. On delivery of the first instalment S. & Son found half of the eggs to be unmerchantable and the remainder to be of inferior quality. On the arrival of the second instalment they proposed to make an examination of the eggs before taking delivery, but A. Ltd refused to allow an

[4] "with the necessary changes having been made", *i.e.* "in corresponding terms".

examination. S. & Son then rescinded the contract on the ground that it had been repudiated by A. Ltd, and brought an action for damages against A. Ltd.

In defence A. Ltd pleaded that the dispute fell to be referred to arbitration under a clause in the contract which provided: "Any dispute on this contract to be settled by arbitration in the usual way."

Held that the question of whether the contract had been repudiated was a question for the arbiter to decide, and the procedure was therefore sisted to enable the dispute to be referred to arbitration.

The Court of Session (1921 S.C. 18) had also held that the dispute fell to be referred to arbitration but on the ground that S. & Son's allegations, if proved, would not have amounted to a repudiation of the contract as a whole by A. Ltd.

(b) *Supervening impossibility of performance of the main contract*

10–75 *James Scott & Sons Ltd v. Del Sel*, 1923 S.C. (H.L.) 37; 1922 S.C. 592, was concerned with contracts which became in part impossible to perform on account of the 1914–18 war:

By 27 contracts made in 1917 jute merchants in Dundee agreed to sell and to ship from Calcutta to Buenos Aires 2,800 bales of jute. Each contract contained provisions relating to late and short shipment attributable to war or "any other unforeseen circumstances", and also an arbitration clause in the following terms: "Any dispute that may arise under this contract to be settled by arbitration in Dundee."

Before all the bales had been shipped, the further export of jute from India to the Argentine was prohibited by an Order in Council of the Governor-General of India. The sellers then intimated to the purchasers that they held the contracts cancelled on the ground that further performance had become impossible.

A controversy arose between the parties, and the purchasers invoked the arbitration clause.

The sellers sought to prevent the arbitration from proceeding, on the ground that the question whether the contracts had been brought to an end was not a dispute arising under the contracts: they argued that the contracts, and with them the arbitration clauses, had been terminated by the Order in Council.

Held on an interpretation of the contracts that the question was a dispute arising under the contracts and that it therefore fell to be decided by arbitration.

Because of the express provisions in the contracts as to war and other unforeseen circumstances the case was not one which raised the general doctrine of frustration.

(c) *Frustration of the main contract*

A case which raised the general doctrine of frustration was *Charles Mauritzen Ltd v. Baltic Shipping Co.*, 1948 S.C. 646 (O.H.): **10–76**

British merchants chartered a Polish ship under a charterparty which provided that the ship should load a cargo of salt for the Faroe Islands at a Spanish port. The charterparty contained a provision that "any dispute arising under this charter" should be referred to arbitration.

On the ship's arrival at the Spanish port the port authorities would not allow loading without a certificate that the ship was running in British service.

The charterers' London agents intimated this to the shipowners' London agents, and also obtained from the Spanish authorities permission for the loading.

Meantime the shipowners' agents, treating the intimation as a claim that the charterparty had been frustrated, had accepted other employment for the ship.

The charterers brought an action of damages for breach of contract.

The shipowners averred that there had been frustration and pleaded the arbitration clause. The charterers contended that this defence was irrelevant since, if there had been frustration, the whole contract including the arbitration clause had been brought to an end.

Held that the question between the parties was a dispute arising under the charterparty and had therefore to be referred to arbitration; and action *sisted.*

The Lord Ordinary (Blades), relying on the English case *Heyman v. Darwins Ltd* [1942] A.C. 356 and on *James Scott & Sons Ltd v. Del Sel* as authorities, said (at p. 650):

"The clause in this charter-party is framed in wide and general terms. . . . The parties are at one in asserting that they entered into a binding contract, there was partial performance of the charter, and now differences have arisen between the parties as to whether the defenders are liable to the pursuers for breach of the charter-party or whether the defenders are discharged from further performance. In my opinion, these are differences which the parties have chosen to refer to arbitration, and, there being no good reason to the contrary, to arbitration they should go."

(5) **Date of the arbitration agreement**

10–77 Where there is an ancillary arbitration, a deed of submission is commonly entered into at the time when a dispute occurs, and in such circumstances the question can arise of whether the arbitration agreement dates from the main contract containing the arbitration clause or from the date of the deed of submission.

Two cases relating to section 3 of the Administration of Justice (Scotland) Act 1972 are to be contrasted. The section provides that "subject to express provision to the contrary in an agreement to refer to arbitration", the arbiter may state a case for the opinion of the Court of Session on any question of law and must do so if so directed by the Court of Session (see 10–13). The statutory provision is declared not to be applicable to "an agreement to refer to arbitration made before the commencement" of the Act. The date of commencement fixed for section 3 of the Act was April 2, 1973 (S.I. 1973 No. 339).

10–78 *Clydebank District Council v. Clink*, 1977 S.C. 147: A local authority had entered into two building contracts in 1966 and 1968 respectively for the erection of houses in a housing scheme. Each contract incorporated the customary arbitration clause.

Disputes arose, an arbiter was appointed, and in March 1974 the parties to the contracts entered into a probative deed of submission identifying their disputes. The arbiter issued a proposed award in June 1976.

The local authority then applied to the arbiter for a case to be stated by him for the opinion of the Court of Session on a question of law. The arbiter rejected that request, and the local authority applied to the Court of Session for an order to direct the arbiter to state a case.

Held that the "agreement to refer to arbitration" was contained in the contracts of 1966 and 1968, and was therefore not one to which the statutory provision applied. The deed of submission was regarded as "purely executorial of the agreement on which it proceeded" (*per* Lord President Emslie at p. 153).

Whatlings (Foundations) Ltd v. Shanks & McEwan (Contractors) Ltd, 1989 S.L.T. 857: A building contract included an arbitration clause. The parties agreed on an arbiter and the disputed matters which were to be remitted to the arbiter. The parties then entered into a formal deed of submission, which included the provision "that section 3 of the Administration of Justice (Scotland) Act 1972 be excluded". **10–79**

After some procedure in the arbitration, W. Ltd, the claimants in the arbitration, asked the arbiter to state a case for the opinion of the Court of Session. The arbiter refused.

W. Ltd then appealed to the Court of Session, arguing that, as the deed of submission postdated the start of the arbitration, it was merely executorial of the parties' agreement in the arbitration clause and so could not have the effect of excluding section 3 of the Act.

Held that the agreement to refer to arbitration was contained both in the arbitration clause and in the deed of submission and that the plain intention of the parties was to amend or vary the arbitration clause by inserting in the deed of submission the express provision that section 3 would not apply to the reference. W. Ltd's appeal was therefore *refused*.

(d) The Duration of the Submission

The duration of the submission is a matter for the parties to decide. **10–80**

Where the submission is a formal deed, it is usual for the arbiter to be given power to decide the dispute "between this and the . . . day of . . . next to come". If the blanks are not filled up, the submission is regarded as lasting (on the authority of Lord Bankton as applied in *Earl of Dunmore v. McInturner* (1829) 7 S. 595) for a year and a day. **10–81**

Where there is no reference to any time-limit the submission lasts for the 20-year prescriptive period. **10–82**

Where the submission expressly fixes a time-limit without conferring on the arbiter power to extend the time, the submission automatically falls on the expiry of the specified time, unless the parties by express agreement or by their actings extend its duration. **10–83**

It is usual practice to confer on the arbiter a power of "prorogation" (*i.e.* a power to extend the duration of the submission). Such **10–84** a power requires to be exercised before the fixed time has expired and before the submission has devolved on the oversman. An arbiter has no implied power of prorogation, except, possibly,[5] in ancillary submissions.

10–85 A case which illustrates several of these points is *Paul v. Henderson* (1867) 5 M. 613:

P. had raised against H. an action for count and reckoning for his intromissions, as P.'s factor, with the rents of certain houses in Linlithgow. Instead of proceeding with the action, the parties agreed to submit the matter to the Accountant of Court as sole arbiter. The submission included a blank time-limit clause and conferred on the arbiter power to prorogate the submission. It bore the date June 29, 1857.

After a great deal of procedure the arbiter finally issued his decree-arbitral on June 27, 1863.

P. then contended that by that date the arbiter's jurisdiction had fallen as a result of his not having duly exercised the power of prorogation conferred on him.

The only prorogation was that dated June 29, 1859, by which the arbiter had extended the duration of the submission to June 29, 1860. Although P. had had ample opportunity to ascertain that fact, he had gone on with his proof without objection.

Held that the submission, though it would otherwise have lapsed on the expiry of a year and a day without prorogation by the arbiter, had been kept in force *rebus ipsis et factis* ("by the circumstances themselves and the actings [*of the parties*]").

10–86 In the absence of agreement to the contrary a submission terminates on the death of either of the parties. It also necessarily terminates on the death of the arbiter.

10–87 A submission also falls if the particular form of arbitration contemplated by the parties becomes impossible, as in *Graham v. Mill* (1904) 6 F. 886 where in a question between an outgoing tenant of a farm and the incoming tenant the phrase "arbitration in common form" was held to mean a valuation by skilled persons who had personally inspected the subjects, and this had become impossible on account of the subjects having been consumed and used.

[5] Irons and Melville, *Law of Arbitration in Scotland*, p. 135.

IV ARBITERS AND OVERSMEN

The parties to a dispute may agree on the nomination of a sole arbiter (*e.g.* as in *Paul v. Henderson* (10–85, above)). **10–88**

Since, however, it is quite possible that the parties, if they are already in disagreement or at least have opposing interests, may fail to agree on the choice of a sole arbiter, it is common for a dispute to be referred to two arbiters, one nominated by each party. In such a situation it is appropriate to have an oversman whose jurisdiction will come into operation only if the two arbiters disagree. The oversman may be nominated by the parties, but the more usual practice is for him to be nominated by the two arbiters. **10–89**

In English law the terms corresponding to "arbiter" and "oversman" are respectively "arbitrator" and "umpire". **10–90**

This fourth part of the chapter deals first with: **10–91**

(a) the relationship between arbiters and oversman,

and then with matters which relate to both arbiters and oversmen:

(b) appointment;

(c) disqualification; and

(d) remuneration.

The powers and duties of arbiters and oversmen can be gathered from Part V, below ("Conduct of the Arbitration"). **10–92**

(a) The Relationship between Arbiters and Oversman

The jurisdiction of the oversman is described as an "ulterior" or "conditional" jurisdiction: the matter must first be considered by the arbiters, and it is only if the arbiters disagree that the jurisdiction of the oversman comes into operation. **10–93**

"Devolution" is the term used to denote the step by which the submission passes from the arbiters to the oversman. **10–94**

It is a common and prudent practice for arbiters who have power to appoint an oversman to do so at the commencement of the arbitration. This avoids the difficulty which may otherwise possibly arise at a later stage when the arbiters, having failed to agree on the subject-matter submitted to them, fail also to agree on the selection of the oversman. This initial appointment of the oversman does not amount to devolution: **10–95**

Brysson v. Mitchell (1823) 2 S. 382: B. and M. entered into a building contract and agreed that all disputes should be settled by two arbiters who had power to appoint an oversman. **10–96**

Before proceeding with an arbitration, the arbiters named an oversman.

The arbiters issued a decree-arbitral against B.

B. raised an action of reduction on the ground that since the arbiters had appointed an oversman they were no longer competent to give a decision.

Held that the oversman had been correctly named by the arbiters, but that as the arbiters had not differed in opinion it was their decision which prevailed, there having been no devolution on the oversman.

10–97 An advantage of an initial appointment of the oversman is that he may sit in at the proceedings before the arbiters and hear the evidence of the witnesses and the arguments of the parties and so be in a position to give a decision without delay should the arbiters disagree. An illustration is *Crawford v. Paterson* (1858) 20 D. 488:

10–98 C. was the tenant of a farm owned by P. Disputes about the repair of fences and water embankments were submitted to two farmers as arbiters or in the event of their disagreeing in opinion to an oversman to be appointed by them.

The arbiters nominated the oversman at an early stage in the proceedings. He inspected the farm along with the arbiters, was present at the subsequent proof, and then heard the arguments put to the arbiters by agents for the parties.

The arbiters differed in opinion and referred the matters in dispute to the oversman.

The oversman issued a draft decree-arbitral, and C. requested to be heard by him. The oversman refused this request, and pronounced his final decree-arbitral.

Held that the fact that the oversman had taken part in the proceedings throughout did not invalidate the arbitration or disqualify the oversman, and that the parties were not entitled to be reheard.

C.'s action of reduction was therefore unsuccessful.

10–99 In selecting the oversman, arbiters must exercise a judicial discretion: they must not make the selection by drawing lots unless they have first decided that all the persons from whom the choice is thus to be made are fit persons for the appointment:

10–100 *Smith v. Liverpool and London and Globe Insurance Co.* (1887) 14 R. 931: S., a shoemaker, incurred a loss of stock in a fire and made claims under an insurance policy.

The claims were referred by S. and the insurance company to two arbiters mutually chosen and in case they differed to an oversman to be chosen by the arbiters before the arbitration proceedings began.

One arbiter suggested Lyon as oversman, and the other arbiter suggested Dowell. Both arbiters stated that they had no objection to either Lyon or Dowell, but each preferred his own nominee. To resolve the difficulty the arbiters drew lots and Lyon was nominated.

The arbiters differed in opinion, and so the submission devolved on Lyon.

S. brought an action of reduction of the deed nominating Lyon and of his decree-arbitral on the grounds (i) that Lyon's nomination had been decided by chance and not by notice and that all that had followed it should be set aside and (ii) that Lyon was personally disqualified because he held shares in the insurance company.

Held that this was not a case in which there had been no choice made by arbiters.

Lord President Inglis said (at p. 937): "It was represented to us by counsel for the pursuer that by the method thus pursued there was a substitution of chance for choice. . . . But I do not think it can be said there was no choice. There was in point of fact a *delectus*,[6] not of one person but of two. Both arbiters were agreed that both the persons suggested by them were equally eligible as oversmen. . . . The element of chance does come in, but to a very limited extent. What was submitted to chance was the choice between two persons acknowledged to be both equally suitable. That is not a good objection to a nomination."

(The court gave decree of reduction on ground (ii).)

Devolution usually takes the form of a minute of devolution signed by the arbiters. In formal arbitrations it would be advisable for the arbiter's signature to be witnessed by one witness (Requirements of Writing (Scotland) Act 1995, s. 3(1)). **10–101**

Where arbiters have power to make part or interim awards, it is open to them to make a partial devolution on the oversman. Thus in *Gibson v. Fotheringham* where the arbiters had power to pronounce "decrees arbitral, interim or final", it was competent for **10–102**

[6] "choice".

them partially to devolve the subject-matter of the reference, while retaining in their own hands the decision of claims which they had not at that time considered and which required further inquiry (such as valuation at a later date).

10–103 Where there is a partial devolution care must be taken to avoid a failure to exhaust the submission, which would invalidate the award:

10–104 *Runciman v. Craigie* (1831) 9 S. 629: Arbiters issued notes of their opinions in a document which was entitled "joint report and interim decree" and which concluded with a clause devolving on the oversman the "determination of these points on which we have differed".

The oversman's award was confined to the points of difference.

Held that the arbiter's notes were not valid as a decree-arbitral and that the oversman's decree-arbitral, since it decided only part of the subject-matter, could not stand by itself; and reduction *granted*.

10–105 In the absence of an express provision enabling arbiters to make part or interim awards difficulties may arise, as in *Taylor Woodrow Construction (Scotland) Ltd v. Sears Investment Trust Ltd*, 1992 S.L.T. 609, and it is doubtful whether arbiters, without express agreement, are entitled to make such awards. The Dervaird Committee has recommended that, in the absence of any express agreement to the contrary by the parties, arbiters should be entitled to make part or interim awards in any arbitration.

(b) **Appointment**

10–106 Statutory provisions to be noted here are:

(i) the Arbitration (Scotland) Act 1894; and

(ii) section 17 of the Law Reform (Miscellaneous Provisions) (Scotland) Act 1980.

(i) *The Arbitration (Scotland) Act 1894*

10–107 This Act was passed mainly to remedy two deficiencies which had become apparent in the common law.

(1) **Deficiencies in the common law**

(a) *Unnamed arbiter*

10–108 It was a principle of the common law that the appointment of an arbiter involved *delectus personae* ("choice of person"). As a result the parties had to make a deliberate selection of a named individual and not merely agree that the arbiter would be the holder of a particular office for the time being or would be named by another person. The courts would not, as a general rule, enforce an arbitration agreement in which the arbiter was not named. There were some exceptions to the general rule (*e.g.* the arbitration agreement would be enforceable if the arbitration was necessary for the purpose of giving effect to another contract).

The common law had the unsatisfactory effect of bringing before the courts matters which the parties had really intended should be settled by arbitration. **10–109**

The defect was particularly noticeable in connection with ancillary arbitrations, as shown in *Tancred, Arrol & Co. v. Steel Co. of Scotland Ltd* (1890) 17 R. (H.L.) 31; (1887) 15 R. 215: **10–110**

An arbitration clause included in a contract for the building of the Forth Railway Bridge stated that any dispute that might arise as to the meaning of the contract was to be referred to "the engineer of the Forth Bridge Railway Company for the time being". **10–111**

Held that the clause was ineffectual because of the absence of *delectus personae*.

Lord Watson said (at p. 36): "It has been settled by a uniform course of judicial decisions, extending over nearly a century, that according to the law of Scotland an agreement to refer future disputes, if and when they shall arise, to the person who shall then be the holder of a certain office is not binding."

(b) *No implied power to appoint oversman*

At common law where there was a reference to two arbiters, one appointed by each side, the two arbiters had no implied power to appoint an oversman: where the arbiters failed to agree, the result was deadlock (*Cochrane v. Guthrie* (1861) 23 D. 865 and *Merry and Cunninghame v. Brown* (1863) 1 M. (H.L.) 14; (1860) 22 D. 1148—both cases relating to an arbitration clause in a mineral lease referring matters in dispute to two persons mutually chosen). **10–112**

(2) **The provisions of the Act**

An agreement to refer to arbitration is no longer invalid or ineffectual merely because the reference is to a person not named, or to a person to be named by another person, or to a person **10–113** merely described as the holder for the time being of any office or appointment (s. 1).

10–114 Where there is an agreement to refer to a single arbiter and one of the parties refuses to concur in the nomination and there is no operative provision for carrying out the reference, then any party to the agreement may apply to the court for an arbiter to be appointed by the court. The arbiter so appointed has the same powers as if he had been duly nominated by all the parties (s. 2).

10–115 Where there is an agreement to refer to two arbiters and one of the parties refuses to name an arbiter and there is no operative provision for carrying out the reference, then the other party may apply to the court for an arbiter to be appointed by the court. The arbiter so appointed has the same powers as if he had been duly nominated by the party refusing (s. 3).

10–116 Unless the agreement to refer provides otherwise, arbiters have power to name an oversman on whom the reference is to be devolved in the event of their differing in opinion. If the arbiters fail to agree in the nomination of an oversman, any party to the agreement may apply to the court for an oversman to be appointed (s. 4).

10–117 The meaning of "the court" in these provisions is normally the sheriff court or the Outer House of the Court of Session, but if any arbiter appointed is a Court of Session judge or if by the terms of the agreement to refer to arbitration an arbiter or oversman to be appointed must be a Court of Session judge, "the court" means the Inner House of the Court of Session (s. 6, as amended by Law Reform (Miscellaneous Provisions) (Scotland) Act 1980, s. 17(4)).

(3) Applications under the Act

10–118 The procedure contemplated by the Act for the exercise of the court's powers of nomination of arbiters and oversmen is of a summary nature. It is suitable for the simple situation where an arbitration is being hindered by the refusal of one of the parties to concur in nominating or to nominate an arbiter.

10–119 It can, however, happen that other matters will require to be decided before the court can exercise a power under the Act. To some extent such other matters can appropriately be decided by the court in the course of an application under the Act of 1894. Where, on the other hand, complex questions are involved, the summary procedure is inappropriate and the questions must be decided in an ordinary action. The following are two illustrations:

(a) *Cooper & Co. v. Jessop Brothers* (1906) 8 F. 714: The case concerned sales of shoddy by J. in Yorkshire to C. in Glasgow. "Contract-notes" contained the condition: "Any dispute arising from this contract to be settled by arbitration here in the usual way." **10–120**

Certain disputes arose concerning the quality of the shoddy supplied. C. nominated an arbiter, J. refused to do so, and C. applied to the court under section 3 of the Act of 1894 craving the court to appoint an arbiter on behalf of J.

C. averred that the contracts had been made in Glasgow and that the usual way of arbitration in the shoddy trade in Glasgow was for each party to nominate an arbiter and for these arbiters to appoint an oversman.

J. averred (i) that there had been no *consensus in idem* ("agreement"), (ii) that, if there was a contract, it was to be found in correspondence and not in the "contract-notes" containing the arbitration clause and it had been made in Yorkshire, and (iii) that there was no shoddy trade in Glasgow and no practice in the shoddy trade either in Glasgow or in Yorkshire with regard to arbitration.

Held that the questions raised in the case could not competently be dealt with in a petition under section 3 of the Act; and process *sisted* in order that they might be decided in an ordinary action.

Lord Low said (at p. 723): "The procedure authorised by the Act was intended to be of a summary nature, and . . . it was not contemplated that an application under the Act should be used for the determination of questions requiring investigation and procedure appropriate to an action in the ordinary Courts."

(b) *United Creameries Co. Ltd v. Boyd & Co.*, 1912 S.C. 617: A contract for the sale of oil by B. & Co. to U. Ltd contained the clause: "Arbitration.—Disputes to be settled by arbitration in Glasgow." **10–121**

A dispute arose. U. Ltd nominated an arbiter, but B. & Co. refused to do so, and U. Ltd presented a petition under the Act of 1894 craving the court to appoint an arbiter. U. Ltd averred that, by a custom of the oil trade in Glasgow, where a contract provided for "arbitration in Glasgow", each party nominated one arbiter and the arbiters named an oversman.

Held that the summary procedure of the Act was inappropriate: an ordinary action was required for proof of the alleged custom.

(4) **Shortcomings of the Act**

10–122 (a) The court has no power to appoint an arbiter unless the parties have agreed to refer to a single arbiter or to two arbiters:

McMillan & Son Ltd v. Rowan & Co. (1903) 5 F 317: A contract relating to the construction by R. & Co. of machinery for M. Ltd contained a clause referring all disputes "to arbitration".

M. Ltd made a claim against R. & Co. for damages for delay. R. & Co. resisted the claim and declined arbitration. M. Ltd presented a petition to the court under the Act of 1894.

Held that as there was neither an agreement to refer to a single arbiter nor an agreement to refer to two arbiters, neither section 2 nor section 3 of the Act applied, and that the court had therefore no power to appoint an arbiter.

10–123 (b) The Act has no provision corresponding to what was formerly section 6 of the Arbitration Act 1950 and was re-enacted by section 15(3) of the Arbitration Act 1996, which is to the effect that in English arbitrations the reference is to be deemed to be to a single arbitrator if no other mode of reference is provided. The Dervaird Committee has recommended that such a provision should be introduced to Scots law. The absence of such a provision in Scots law was regretted by Lord McLaren in *Douglas & Co. v. Stiven* (1900) 2 F. 575:

D. & Co. sold a quantity of timber to S. under a contract which provided that disputes were to be "referred to arbitration in the customary manner of the timber trade".

A dispute arose. D. & Co. raised an action for payment of the price. S. pleaded the arbitration clause and proved that the most usual mode of arbitration in the timber trade was by a reference to two arbiters, one chosen by each party, and by an oversman appointed by the two arbiters.

The court *found* that the parties had had that mode in view, that the reference was therefore equivalent to a reference to unnamed arbiters and was valid under section 1 of the Act of 1894.

With reference to the Arbitration Act 1889, Lord McLaren said (at p. 582): "This question could hardly have arisen if the contract had been made in England, because in the relative English Arbitration Act there is a section to the effect that where no particular mode of arbitration is provided, the reference shall be understood to be to a single arbitrator. Why this useful provision of the English Arbitration Act was not extended to Scotland I have difficulty in understanding."

(c) The Act does not provide a remedy for the situation where the clause of reference names an arbiter and he refuses to act: 10–124

British Westinghouse Electric and Manufacturing Co. Ltd v. Provost of Aberdeen (1906) 14 S.L.T. 391 (O.H.): B. Ltd entered into a contract with the Town Council of Aberdeen to supply an engine for the council's electricity works at Dee Village.

A clause in the contract provided that disputes were to be submitted to William Chamen, electrical engineer for the time being to the Town Council of Glasgow, whom failing to the electrical engineer for the time being.

A dispute arose, and B. Ltd requested in the first instance William Chamen, and then W. W. Leckie, the electrical engineer for the time being, to accept the office of arbiter.

Both refused to act, and B. Ltd applied for an appointment to be made by the court under section 2 of the Act of 1894.

Petition *refused* because it was not warranted by the section upon which it professed to be based.

Lord Dundas said (at p. 391): "It is to be remembered that the jurisdiction of the Court under the Act can only be exercised when the specific condition of matters prescribed in the Act exists. . . . It can not, in my judgment, be properly said that the parties had or have any 'agreement to refer to a single arbiter,' within the meaning of the section, which, as I think, plainly means an arbiter unnamed. What the parties agreed to was to refer to a single arbiter, whom they named, whom failing, to an arbiter whom they sufficiently indicated by description, looking to the remedial provision contained in section 1. In order to bring this petition within the scope of section 2, it would, I apprehend, be necessary to read into the submission clause some further words such as, 'Whom failing, to an arbiter to be named by the parties'—an insertion which would not be in accordance with recognised principles of construction."

(ii) *Section 17 of the Law Reform (Miscellaneous Provisions) (Scotland) Act 1980*

This section enables a Court of Session judge, if in all the circumstances he thinks fit, to accept appointment as arbiter or as oversman under an arbitration agreement where the dispute appears to him to be of a commercial character. It is a condition of 10–125 his accepting appointment that the Lord President of the Court of Session has informed him that, having regard to the state of business in that court, he can be made available to do so. An instance is *Scott Lithgow Ltd v. Secretary of State for Defence*, 1988 S.L.T. 697, in which Lord Jauncey who had been the arbiter stated a case for the Inner House.

10–126 The fees for the judge's services as arbiter or oversman are paid into public funds and are of an amount fixed by statutory instrument. The fees are at present £1,350 on appointment plus £1,350 for each additional day of the hearing (Appointment of Judges as Arbiters (Fees) (Scotland) Order 1993 (S.I. 1993 No. 3125)).

(c) **Disqualification**

10–127 The office of arbiter "is essentially of a judicial character, and requires complete impartiality as one of its inherent attributes. Wherever, therefore, an arbiter is affected by any circumstances having a plain practical tendency to bias him in favour of one of the parties, and so to destroy his impartiality, his acting as arbiter will be open to challenge" (Bell, *op. cit.*, p. 130). The same principle applies to the office of oversman. The Dervaird Committee has recommended that if there are any circumstances which may give rise to justifiable doubts as to the impartiality or independence of an arbiter or oversman, either before appointment or during the course of the arbitration, those circumstances should be disclosed to the parties immediately; failure to disclose would give grounds for a challenge to the continuance of the appointment as arbiter or oversman.

10–128 An instance of a successful challenge of an award on the ground of an arbiter's interest is *Sellar v. Highland Railway Co.*, 1919 S.C. (H.L.) 19; 1918 S.C. 838:

In an arbitration between S., the owner of certain fishings, and a railway company, the arbiters disagreed, and the reference devolved upon the oversman.

After the oversman had issued proposed findings, S. discovered that the arbiter appointed by the railway company held a small quantity of ordinary stock in the company—a fact not known to the directors personally at the time of the appointment.

S. notified the company that he would not regard himself as bound by the award.

Later the oversman issued his final award, and S. brought an action for reduction of the award on the ground of the arbiter's disqualification.

Held that the arbiter's holding of stock was sufficient to disqualify him and that his disqualification vitiated the oversman's award, which therefore fell to be reduced.

A person who is originally qualified to act as arbiter may become **10–129**
disqualified during the course of a contract:

Magistrates of Edinburgh v. Lownie (1903) 5 F. 711: In 1897 the magistrates of Edinburgh entered into a contract with L., a builder, for the mason work of Colinton Mains Hospital. The contract provided that disputes were to be referred to Ormiston, an Edinburgh surveyor.

In May 1898 a question arose under the contract, and was disposed of by Ormiston as arbiter.

In November 1898 Ormiston was elected Dean of Guild and became *ex officio* ("by virtue of his office") a member of the town council.

Another question arose under the contract in July 1902, and L. called upon Ormiston to act as arbiter. The town council craved the court to interdict Ormiston from proceeding with the arbitration on the ground that he was disqualified by virtue of being Dean of Guild and so a member of one of the parties to the dispute.

In November 1902 Ormiston ceased to be Dean of Guild and consequently also ceased to be a member of the town council.

Held that (1) Ormiston's election to the office of Dean of Guild disqualified him from acting as arbiter, (2) this disqualification might be pleaded by the town council, and (3) the disqualification was not removed by Ormiston's ceasing to hold the office of Dean of Guild.

Lord President Kinross said (at p. 714): "It is not suggested . . . that Mr Ormiston would consciously allow his judgment in regard to the question submitted to be affected by his connection with the Town-Council, but what we have to do is to apply the general rule irrespective of the character of particular individuals. That rule is that a man cannot be judge in his own cause, or in the cause of a body of which he is a member. . . . A Dean of Guild might in that capacity or in his capacity of a member of the council acquire information or become imbued with views as to this contract and as to the buildings to which it relates—information or views from the inside—which it would not be desirable that he should have when he came to act as arbiter between parties who should be at arm's length. He might well form views as to this contract while acting as a unit of one of the parties to it which might unconsciously affect his judgment as arbiter. It would, in my view, be contrary to the fundamental rule to which I have referred to allow a party in such a position to act as arbiter."

10–130 The mere existence of a business relationship between the arbiter and one of the parties is not a disqualification:

Johnson v. Lamb, 1981 S.L.T. 300 (O.H.): J. had entered into a contract with Alexander Morrison (Builders) Ltd ("M. Ltd") for the erection of a bungalow. A dispute arose and was submitted to L., as arbiter.

After L. had issued his decree-arbitral, J. raised an action of reduction, averring that, unknown to him at the time when he had entered into the submission, L. was acting as architect for Ross and Cromarty District Council in a school building contract in which M. Ltd were the main contractors.

Held that the "regular business contact" which J. averred to have resulted from this relationship between L. and M. Ltd was not sufficient to disqualify L. from acting as arbiter in the dispute between J. and M. Ltd, because (i) the relationship had nothing to do with the subject-matter of the arbitration, (ii) it was not suggested that L. had any interest whatever in the outcome of the arbitration, and (iii) the relationship was not one in which L. and M. Ltd had a common interest since L. was being employed by the district council in that relationship and not by M. Ltd.

10–131 Where the arbiter's interest is known, it may be waived by the agreement of both parties and it will then be no disqualification. Even a reference to one of the parties has been held valid:

10–132 *Buchan v. Melville* (1902) 4 F. 620: B. entered into a contract to execute the mason-work of two houses belonging to M., who was an architect. The contract included an arbitration clause providing that any dispute was to be referred to M., whose decision would be final and binding on the parties.

B. raised an action against M. for payment for the work, and M. stated the preliminary plea that the action was excluded by the arbitration clause.

Held that the arbitration clause was binding, and cause *sisted* to allow M. to issue his award.

Lord President Kinross said (at p. 623): "I think the conclusion to be deduced from the authorities is, that where an arbiter has an interest in the subject of the reference well known to the parties before they enter into the submission, the award is good notwithstanding this interest; in other words, that it is only a concealed or unknown interest which invalidates an award. If therefore a person chooses to make another with whom he is contracting the final judge of all questions which may arise between them under the contract, it is difficult to see any reason of public policy which should lead to effect being refused to such a contract."

In construction contracts it is common for the parties to agree **10–133** that the arbiter should be the employer's engineer or architect. Though such a person has no immediate financial interest in the matter in dispute, he has an indirect interest and he may also be affected, perhaps unconsciously, by the viewpoint of the employer. The parties' agreement, however, removes the disqualification which would otherwise arise from his office. The following are some instances:

(i) *Scott v. Carluke Local Authority* (1879) 6 R. 616: In a contract **10–134** for the execution of water-works for a local authority the engineer of the local authority was appointed arbiter.

During the progress of the work he made a report to the local authority complaining in strong terms of the manner in which the work was being executed by the contractor.

Held that the engineer was not disqualified from acting as arbiter.

(ii) *Mackay v. Parochial Board of Barry* (1883) 10 R. 1046: A **10–135** contract for the execution of water-works for a local authority named the local authority's engineer as arbiter.

During the execution of the work he complained that some of the contractor's materials were disconform to contract. He also measured the work and brought out as due to the contractor for extra work a sum far below what the contractor claimed.

Held that the engineer was not disqualified from acting as arbiter.

(On this case, see also 10–67, above.)

(iii) *Adams v. Great North of Scotland Railway Co.* (1889) 16 R. **10–136** 843 (affirmed on other points (1890) 18 R. (H.L.) 1): A contract for the making of a railway included an arbitration clause providing that a named person should not be disqualified from acting as arbiter by being or becoming consulting engineer to the railway company.

As consulting engineer that person revised the specifications and schedules upon which the work in dispute was performed.

Held that he was not barred from acting as arbiter.

10–137 (iv) *Halliday v. Duke of Hamilton's Trustees* (1903) 5 F. 800: A contract for the construction of a pier named the employers' engineer as arbiter.

After the pier had been built a question arose as to whether a sum for extra work was due to the contractor. The engineer, in answer to a request by the employers, wrote letters to them giving a detailed opinion to the effect that the greater part of the sum in question was not due to the contractor.

Held that the engineer had not disqualified himself from acting as arbiter.

Lord Justice-Clerk J. H. A. Macdonald said (at p. 808): "In a case where the engineer is named as arbiter, and the contractor comes forward with a claim for a sum of money as being due to him, it is the most natural thing possible for the employers to inquire of their engineer what view he takes of the work done by the contractor and the account rendered by him, because if the engineers are satisfied that the claim is proper, there will not be any need for arbitration, and an engineer who expresses a general opinion, not ultroneously but in answer to his employers, cannot I think be excluded on that account from acting as arbiter. If the employers proceed to arbitration, then the engineer, as arbiter, must receive all competent evidence which the contractor thinks proper to bring before him and give an honest opinion of it. The fact that he has expressed an opinion as an engineer before receiving the evidence does not prevent him from afterwards applying his mind judicially to the questions at issue in the light of the evidence adduced."

10–138 (v) *Scott v. Gerrard*, 1916 S.C. 793: A contract for the execution of the joiner work in connection with the building of a church included an arbitration clause referring disputes to the architect.

After some work had been done the architect declared the contract at an end because of the contractors' delay.

The contractors brought an action against the building committee of the church for payment maintaining that the architect was disqualified from acting as arbiter because any delay in the execution of the work had been due, in part at least, to the fault of the architect and because he had exhibited hostility towards them. They averred that the architect had said that he would "make it hot for them" meaning that he would use his position as architect to their detriment.

Held that there were no averments relevant to infer disqualification of the architect from acting as arbiter.

Lord Salvesen said (at p. 806): "It is not, according to our law, considered against public policy to enforce a clause of reference, though the reference be to the servant or agent of the building owner. It is also alleged by the pursuers that, on one occasion, the architect said that he 'would make it hot for them'; but I should be slow to assume that a casual expression of this kind, possibly uttered in the heat of a discussion, would indicate such a bias as would prevent the architect from acting judicially (so far as his position permits of his doing so) when a reference fell to be made to him. What is to my mind of far more importance is that the cause of the disputes is alleged to have been the personal fault of the architect; but that, according to our decisions, is not sufficient to withdraw from him the jurisdiction which the parties have chosen to confer. I cannot help saying that I think that, in this respect, the law of England is very much more satisfactory than our own. . . . Unfortunately . . . we have no Arbitration Act in Scotland which vests us with any discretion. Unless the arbiter has actually disqualified himself, it is not relevant to consider whether a dispute arises from his own arbitrary or unreasonable conduct, and the Court has no power to extricate the contractor from the difficulties which he has brought upon himself by consenting to be bound by the decision of a person in whom he is presumed to have reposed implicit confidence; but who, in fact, is generally imposed upon him as a condition of his getting the work."

These cases show that the employer's engineer or architect, if agreed to in the arbitration clause, is unlikely to be held to be disqualified from acting as arbiter. If, however, he has placed himself in such a position as to be unable to act judicially in a dispute, he is disqualified from acting as arbiter; an illustration is *Dickson v. Grant* (1870) 8 M. 566: **10–139**

10–140 D., a joiner, contracted with the trustees of a church to execute certain alterations and repairs on the church. A clause of the contract provided that any dispute was to be referred to Coyne, the architect of the works, whose decision was to be final and binding on the parties.

Disputes arose and Coyne often expressed opinions adverse to D. in regard to them.

D. raised an action against the trustees for reduction of the contract or at least of the clause of reference and also for payment of sums which he alleged were due to him by the trustees for joiner work.

The Lord Ordinary allowed a proof and in the course of it Coyne was called as a witness by the trustees and gave evidence which was adverse to D.

Held that Coyne was thereby disqualified from acting as arbiter and that it was therefore for the court to decide the dispute.

Lord Cowan said (at p. 568): "Up to the date when this action was brought, although there had been some conduct on the part of the arbiter not quite so guarded as could have been wished, nothing had occurred to prevent the reference to Mr Coyne from being carried out. . . .

"But there now exists an objection to the carrying out of this reference, which has emerged since the raising of the action. The arbiter has been examined in the course of this case as a witness for the defenders, with reference to the very matters in dispute between the parties. That, I think, is utterly inconsistent with the subsistence of the reference to him. The two positions,—that of witness cited and examined by one of the parties, and that of judge with regard to the same matters between the parties,—are utterly inconsistent. By examining him as witness the party debars himself from resorting to him thereafter as arbiter. The defenders were not obliged to call Mr Coyne as a witness; but having done so, they have by their own act precluded themselves from insisting in the reference to him being gone on with, and from pleading the clause of reference as excluding the Court from dealing with the matters in dispute between them and the pursuer."

10–141 A view to the same general effect was expressed by Lord Kyllachy (Ordinary) in *Aviemore Station Hotel Co. Ltd v. Scott* (1904) 12 S.L.T. 494 (O.H.):

This was an action by A. Ltd against S., contractors and plasterers, for damages for loss caused by alleged defective execution of plaster-work in a hotel building. By the terms of the contract for the plaster-work the architect was to be sole arbiter.

Lord Kyllachy held that the clause of reference did not cover the matters in dispute.

Had his decision been otherwise the second question would have arisen of whether the architect had become disqualified from acting as arbiter. On that second question Lord Kyllachy's opinion was that the architect had become disqualified: the correspondence and the proceedings in an earlier action showed that the architect had committed himself to a particular view and had repeated and insisted upon that view; he had also intervened in the earlier action and placed himself in a position quite inconsistent with his afterwards taking up the office of arbiter.

In *Crawford Brothers v. Commissioners of Northern Lighthouses*, **10–142**
1925 S.C. (H.L.) 22, which concerned certain operations at Cape Wrath lighthouse, the question arose of whether the commissioners' engineer, named as arbiter in the construction contract, could competently deal with matters which involved a conflict of evidence between himself as engineer and the contractors.

The question did not require to be decided because the Commissioners gave an undertaking in the House of Lords that if, in the course of the arbitration, any question of evidence arose which put their engineer in a conflicting position as judge and witness, the matter would be referred to the court for settlement.

Where it cannot be known before the arbitration whether the **10–143**
arbiter would approach the issue with an open mind because of having acted in some other capacity, he is not disqualified from acting as arbiter:

Secretary of State for the Environment v. Grahame House Investments Ltd, 1985 S.C. 201: An arbiter appointed to settle a dispute over the amount of the rent to be fixed for the first floor of an office block had previously been appointed to decide, and had decided, as an independent surveyor acting as an expert, the rent due for a different period for the second floor.

Held that, since it could not be known before the arbitration whether the arbiter would regard the second floor rent as an appropriate comparison, the arbiter was not disqualified.

An arbiter who has issued "proposed findings" may still be able **10–144**
to address the issue with an open mind:

ERDC Construction Ltd v. H. M. Love & Co. (No. 2), 1997 S.L.T. 175: Builders had been appointed by an architect on behalf of the owners to carry out building work on a tenement.

After the work was finished, the builders claimed that because of failures on the part of the architect they were entitled to certain sums in addition to the agreed contract price.

The parties submitted the claim to arbitration. The arbiter issued proposed findings, and the owners then requested the arbiter to state a case under section 3 of the Administration of Justice (Scotland) Act 1972.

After the court had issued its opinion, the arbiter allowed the builders to lodge a minute of amendment changing the basis of their claim.

The owners then requested the arbiter to state a further case in which the main question for the court to answer was whether the arbiter, because he had already issued proposed findings before he allowed the minute of amendment, was prevented from dealing further with the case.

Held that there was nothing to suggest that the arbiter had prejudged the issue or that he would be unable to approach the issue in the amended pleadings with an open mind, even though he would have to reconsider his proposed findings.

(d) **Remuneration**

10–145 The original rule of the common law was that an arbiter or oversman had no legal claim to be remunerated unless he had stipulated for remuneration before he accepted appointment.

10–146 The rule was modified with the passage of time, and by the nineteenth century a condition that the arbiter would be remunerated for his services could be readily implied in an arbitration agreement, especially if the arbiter were a professional man who would be paid in the exercise of his profession for duties similar to those which he was called on to perform as arbiter. An instance was *Henderson v. Paul* (1867) 5 M. 628:

10–147 P. raised an action of count and reckoning against H. The action was taken out of court and referred to Maitland, Accountant of the Court of Session, as arbiter.

Maitland pronounced a decree-arbitral in favour of H., who then raised an action against P. for payment of £31 10s., the amount of the arbiter's fee, which H. had paid.

Held that, though the deed of submission had made no mention of remuneration for the arbiter, the parties had understood that as a professional accountant he was to be remunerated, and that H. was therefore entitled to recover from P. half of the fee which he had paid, *viz.* £15 15s.

Lord Justice-Clerk Patton said (at p. 632): "I think, in point of fact, that the parties conceived that they were going to an accountant on the footing of payment. The presumption, no doubt, is, that an arbiter acts without any right to remuneration; but the presumption is capable of being redargued, and I find what satisfies me, in the facts of the case, that the presumed condition did not hold in this case. The pleadings seem to me strongly to confirm this view—namely, that it was the understanding of parties all along that the arbiter should be paid."

By the time *Macintyre Brothers v. Smith*, 1913 S.C. 129, came to **10–148**
be decided there was no longer even a presumption that an arbiter, if he were a professional man, was acting gratuitously:

A dispute arose out of a contract between M. Brothers and S. for the purchase of a quarry. The dispute was submitted to Cook, a Glasgow solicitor, by a deed of agreement which made no reference to the arbiter's remuneration.

Cook issued a decree-arbitral in which he found S. liable to M. Brothers in a sum which did not include any fee for the arbiter.

Later M. Brothers paid the arbiter a sum of £63, the fee fixed by the Auditor of the Faculty of Procurators in Glasgow as suitable remuneration for his services.

S. refused to pay his share of the arbiter's fee, and M. Brothers brought an action against him for £31 10s.

Held that the arbiter was entitled to remuneration and that S. as one of the parties to the arbitration was liable for half.

Lord Kinnear said (at p. 132): "I think that, in accordance with general practice, the rule must now be assumed that a professional man undertaking the duties of an arbiter is entitled, in the absence of any agreement to the contrary, to be remunerated for his services as arbiter in the same way as he is entitled to receive remuneration for his services in any other professional employment. The general rule is that a request for professional service implies a promise to pay for it; and I do not see why this rule should be the less applicable because the particular service is for the benefit of two parties who are at variance with one another."

10–149 Where the amount of the arbiter's remuneration is not expressly agreed on, he is entitled to charge a reasonable fee for professional work, and this may be based on a scale of fees fixed by the professional body of which he is a member. The case of *Wilkie v. Scottish Aviation Ltd*, 1956 S.C. 198, involved a consideration of the schedule of professional charges of the Royal Institution of Chartered Surveyors:

10–150 W., a chartered surveyor, had been employed professionally as a valuer in arbitration proceedings concerned with the compulsory purchase of Prestwick Airport by the Ministry of Civil Aviation. There was no specific agreement as to his remuneration.

After he had performed his services, W. rendered an account for £3,009 10s. 9d., the scale fee based, in accordance with the schedule of professional charges, on the amount awarded in the arbitration.

His employers refused to pay more than £1,000 and W. brought an action against them for the balance, averring that remuneration on the basis of the schedule was customary and therefore an implied condition of the contract for his services.

Held that W. was entitled to remuneration at the customary rate if he could prove the existence of a custom which was reasonable, certain and notorious, and that accordingly if the schedule were shown to be the basis upon which in practice the profession operated, the court could take the schedule into account but would not be bound rigidly to apply it unless satisfied that the resulting fee were reasonable; and a proof before answer *allowed.*

V CONDUCT OF THE ARBITRATION

10–151 In the conduct of the arbitration the arbiter is always bound to observe those implied conditions of arbitration which are designed for "securing the proper administration of justice" (see the quotation from Lord Watson's speech in *Holmes Oil Co. Ltd v. Pumpherston Oil Co. Ltd* at 10–196, below). The parties may in their agreement to resort to arbitration lay down additional conditions as to the way in which the arbitration is to be conducted; the arbiter is then bound to observe such conditions since his jurisdiction is derived solely from the agreement of the parties. More usually the parties do not expressly specify the procedure which is to be followed, and in that case the arbiter's powers and duties in the conduct of the proceedings depend on what is implied in the arbitration agreement and in other respects on the arbiter's own discretion.

Some description is given in the following paragraphs of: **10–152**
(a) formal and informal procedure;
(b) the requirement of impartiality; and
(c) specific steps in the procedure.

(a) Formal and Informal Procedure

The degree of formality of the procedure varies greatly: at one **10–153** extreme the procedure may be as formal as court procedure and counsel may be instructed to plead the case of each party; at the other extreme the procedure may be very informal, particularly in agricultural and mercantile circles where the arbiter's function often is rather to fix the value of crops, stock or other goods than to decide a dispute.

Where the submission is a formal one, the following are usual **10–154** steps in the procedure. The arbiter fixes a time within which one party must lodge written claims. He then allows a specified time within which the other party must lodge written answers. A "record" (a document setting out both sides of the dispute) may then be made up, "adjusted" and "closed" in much the same way as in a court case. The arbiter then decides what "proof" (*i.e.* evidence) should be allowed. He may wrongly allow or exclude certain evidence, but such errors are part of the risk which the parties have taken in resorting to arbitration and will not be a ground on which the award could be challenged. Sometimes it will be necessary for the arbiter to inspect premises or other property in order to inform himself of the matters in dispute, but inadequacy of inspection is not a ground on which an award may be reduced by the court (*Johnson v. Lamb*, 1981 S.L.T. 300 (O.H.)). The arbiter will almost always allow a hearing to both parties at the conclusion of the proof, and will often issue "proposed findings" so that the parties may have an opportunity to make final "representations" criticising the proposed findings. A further hearing may be allowed for these representations.

In less formal submissions the question is often a practical one to **10–155** be decided by an arbiter chosen for his knowledge and experience of such practical questions, and there may be no objection to the arbiter's dispensing with both a proof and a hearing and deciding the question on the basis of personal inspection only. For examples of informal arbitrations, see the "valuation" cases at 10–16 *et seq.*, above.

10–156 Prior to the Requirements of Writing (Scotland) Act 1995 it was held that where an arbitration is started by a formal probative submission, the award also must be formal and probative:

10–157 *McLaren v. Aikman*, 1939 S.C. 222: McL., the owner of certain heritable property in Melrose, let the property to A. under a lease which gave A. an option to purchase the property at a price to be fixed by arbitration.

A. desired to exercise this option, and the parties referred the price to Hall, an architect, as sole arbiter. The reference was embodied in a formal and probative minute of agreement.

After various procedure the arbiter issued an award in the form of a letter addressed to the firm of solicitors which was acting for both parties. In that document, which was signed by the arbiter but was neither holograph nor attested, the value of the property was put at £1,350.

McL. was satisfied with that figure, but A. made representations to the arbiter against it.

The arbiter later issued a formal and probative decree-arbitral in which he fixed the price at £950.

McL. brought an action against A. for £1,350.

Held that since the submission was a formal one not falling within the category of mercantile and agricultural arbitrations, the award had to be formal and probative, and that the arbiter's first informal valuation was therefore not binding on A.; and action *dismissed.*

(b) The Requirement of Impartiality

10–158 Although the arbiter usually has a wide discretion as to the procedure to be followed, he is in all circumstances subject to the overriding principle of impartiality: he must adhere to "equal and even-handed procedure towards both parties alike" (Bell, *op. cit.*, p. 23).

10–159 The arbiter must not allow to one party what he denies to the other. If, for instance, he is to be accompanied at an inspection of property by one of the parties, he ought to give the other party the opportunity of being present as well. Similarly, if he allows a hearing to one party and not to the other, his award will be open to challenge unless it is in favour of the party not heard. An illustrative case is:

Earl of Dunmore v. McInturner (1835) 13 S. 356: The Earl and McI. entered into a submission referring disputes as to the marches (boundaries) between their lands to arbitration. **10–160**

The oversman inspected the marches in the presence of McI. without intimation of the inspection having been given to the Earl. After the inspection a minute of award was drawn up in McI.'s house in the absence of the Earl or any person representing him. The minute was intimated to the Earl's agent the next day, but the Earl was not warned that if he did not give in objections by a certain day, the decree-arbitral would be extended and executed.

Some two months later without further notice to the Earl the formal decree was made out embodying the words of the minute.

Held that the Earl was entitled to have the decree set aside on the ground that a decree pronounced in such circumstances, with the assistance of the other party and without an opportunity having been given to the Earl to be heard, was "contrary to the principles of fair justice between man and man" (*per* Lord Justice-Clerk Boyle at p. 360).

Similarly, in *Black v. John Williams & Co. (Wishaw) Ltd*, 1924 S.C. (H.L.) 22; 1923 S.C. 510, there had been procedure which Lord President Clyde said (at p. 515) had been "deservedly criticised and might easily have been fatal to the award": **10–161**

B., a plasterer, had contracted with W. Ltd to do certain rough-casting work at their premises. Disputes arose as to whether the work had been properly executed, and McGhie was appointed arbiter.

During the arbitration proceedings the question arose of whether B. had had permission from W. Ltd to use coke breeze instead of granite chips for part of the work.

McGhie requested B. to leave the room when certain witnesses (B.'s son and B.'s foreman) were giving evidence on this point. W., one of the directors of W. Ltd, was present during examination.

The arbiter issued an award in which he found in favour of B. upon the question of the material used but held, upon other grounds, that the work had not been properly executed.

B. brought an action for reduction of the award on the ground that the arbiter had invalidated the proceedings by examining the two witnesses in the presence of one party only.

Held that the arbiter's procedure had been improper but that it did not in the circumstances of the case invalidate the award since B. had suffered no injustice as a result of being excluded during the examination of the witnesses.

Lord Dunedin said (at p. 27): "There are many cases . . . where it has been held that you must not examine witnesses on one side and not on the other, and that you must not examine witnesses without the parties being properly represented. But, after all, those cases, one and all of them, are only illustrations of the general principle that the procedure of the arbiter must not violate the principles of essential justice. How can it be said in this instance that the principles of essential justice have been violated? . . . As a matter of fact, upon this one question whether one material was substituted with the consent of the employers for another, the arbiter decided in favour of the person who is now challenging the award. I think, therefore, that on this matter he fails."

(c) Specific Steps in the Procedure

(i) *Appointment of Clerk*

10–162 Except in very informal proceedings, it is usual for the arbiter to appoint a clerk to take charge of the documents in the case and to act as a channel of communication between the parties and the arbiter.

10–163 If the arbiter is not himself a lawyer but a layman chosen for his technical knowledge and experience, the clerk is often a solicitor, and in practice takes a key role in the proceedings since the arbiter will to a great extent rely on his guidance when a point of law arises in the course of the arbitration.

(ii) *Proceedings* Ex Parte

10–164 In certain circumstances an arbiter is justified in proceeding *ex parte* ("without a party"). This would occur where one party refused to take any further part in the arbitration proceedings, although given full opportunity by the arbiter to do so.

(iii) *Prorogation of the Submission*

Where the submission is subject to a time limit and the fixed duration is about to expire before the proceedings have been concluded, a prorogation is necessary to keep the submission operative. Prorogation may be an act of the parties, but normally it is an act of the arbiter, on whom the parties will have expressly conferred power to prorogate the submission. (See also 10–84 *et seq.*, above.) **10–165**

(iv) *Applications to Court*

Although the parties to an arbitration agreement have the general aim of preventing the intervention of the court in the decision of their dispute, the jurisdiction of the court is not wholly ousted by the agreement. A well-known passage in the speech of Lord Watson in *Hamlyn & Co. v. Talisker Distillery* (1894) 21 R. (H.L.) 21, at p. 25, enlarges on this point: **10–166**

"The jurisdiction of the Court is not wholly ousted by such a contract [*a contract to submit the matter in dispute to arbitration*]. It deprives the Court of jurisdiction to inquire into and decide the merits of the case, while it leaves the Court free to entertain the suit, and to pronounce a decree in conformity with the award of the arbiter. Should the arbitration from any cause prove abortive, the full jurisdiction of the Court will revive, to the effect of enabling it to hear and determine the action upon its merits. When a binding reference is pleaded *in limine*,[7] the proper course to take is either to refer the question in dispute to the arbiter named or to stay procedure until it has been settled by arbitration."

If there is disagreement as to the scope of the arbitration agreement, that is necessarily in the last resort a matter for the court to decide. **10–167**

As is indicated in Lord Watson's speech, there are several occasions when application may be made to court for assistance to enable an arbitration to proceed effectively. Where one party raises an action in respect of a matter which ought to have been submitted to arbitration, the court will sist the action on the application of the other party. It has been the practice to regard **10–168**

---

[7] "as a preliminary plea".

the rule as being that objection to the court's jurisdiction must be made before the closing of the record in the action; otherwise the right to go to arbitration is held to have been waived: *Halliburton Manufacturing and Service Ltd v. Bingham Blades & Partners*, 1984 S.L.T. 388 (O.H.), followed in *Stanley Howard (Construction) Ltd v. Davis*, 1988 S.L.T. (Sh.Ct.) 30 and *Raphael v. Wilcon Homes Northern Ltd*, 1994 S.C.L.R. 940 (O.H.). However, more recently this rule has not been applied by the courts. Instead, it has been said that the correct approach to be adopted by the court where there is no express waiver is to consider the whole history of the litigation to ascertain whether it is inconsistent with an intention to exercise the right to go to arbitration (*Inverclyde (Mearns) Housing Society Ltd v. Lawrence Construction Co. Ltd*, 1989 S.L.T. 815 (O.H.), a case in which a gross delay of several years in the bringing of a sist for arbitration before the court together with other actings (and failure to act) on the part of the defenders indicated an intention to waive the right to insist upon arbitration). The approach in this case was approved by the Second Division case *Presslie v. Cochrane McGregor Group Ltd*, 1996 S.C. 289, in which the circumstances were held not to constitute a waiver of the right to arbitration although the plea to sist an action had been made only after the action had been continued for a lengthy period. Where an arbiter's orders for witnesses to appear or documents to be produced are not complied with, the party desiring the attendance of the witnesses or the production of the documents may apply to court for a warrant for citation. The court may also be applied to for the purpose of enforcing the award by granting "decree conform to it".

10–169 A further instance where the court's jurisdiction was held not to have been ousted is *Mendok B.V. v. Cumberland Maritime Corporation*, 1989 S.L.T. 192 (O.H.): In 1988 M., a Dutch company in liquidation, brought an action against C., an American company which owned a drilling rig in the Cromarty Firth, for payment of a substantial sum for work on the rig done by M. for C. The summons included a warrant for arrestment of the rig on the dependence of the action.

The contract between the parties contained an arbitration clause and there was already an ongoing arbitration which had been started in 1985.

C. sought recall of the arrestment, arguing that, because of the arbitration clause, the action and therefore the warrant to arrest were incompetent.

Lord McDonald refused C.'s motion; if C. wished to avoid prejudice caused by continuance of the arrestment, it seemed that it could offer reasonable caution in exchange for recall of the arrestment.

The parties may expressly agree to be bound by the arbiter's decision on questions of law as well as on questions of fact, but if there is no such express agreement, then, by section 3 of the Administration of Justice (Scotland) Act 1972, a party may apply to the arbiter or to the Court of Session for a case to be stated for the opinion of the Court of Session. (See 10–13, above.) Before the date of that Act stated cases were in Scots law confined to statutory arbitrations, such as those under the Lands Clauses Consolidation (Scotland) Act 1845, the Workmen's Compensation Acts and the Agricultural Holdings (Scotland) Acts. In *Mitchell-Gill v. Buchan*, 1921 S.C. 390, the court held, in relation to a stated case under the Agricultural Holdings (Scotland) Act 1908, that an arbiter was not entitled to disregard the answer given by the court on the question of law. **10–170**

(v) *Issue of Award*

The conduct of an arbitration comes to an end when the award is issued. The arbiter is then said to be "*functus*", an abbreviation of "*functus officio*" ("having performed his role"). The effect is that he no longer has any jurisdiction in connection with the matter in question. **10–171**

An arbiter may have power conferred on him to issue interim and part awards. An interim award is of a tentative nature: it may be altered or recalled. A part award, on the other hand, is a final decision on part of the subject-matter of the submission. **10–172**

An arbiter has power to award expenses without any express power to that effect having been included in the deed of submission (*Ferrier v. Alison* (1845) 4 Bell's App. 161; (1843) 5 D. 456). **10–173**

Interest is due on the amount awarded in a decree-arbitral from the date when it is made. Whether interest is due from any earlier date depends on the terms of the deed of submission: **10–174**

Farrans (Construction) Ltd v. Dunfermline District Council, 1988 S.L.T. 466: F. Ltd were contractors for the building of the **10–175**

Dunfermline sports centre. Disputes which arose between them and the district council were referred to arbitration, but during the course of the arbitration proceedings the parties, by a joint minute lodged on June 30, 1986, informed the arbiter that they had reached agreement on all matters at issue between them with the exception of the general question of whether interest was payable on any of the agreed sums and, if so, for what periods of time and at what rate. These matters were therefore left for the arbiter to decide.

After hearing the parties, the arbiter awarded interest on two of the sums claimed from March 15, 1983 (the date at which he considered that the architect ought to have certified the sums as due), and on two other sums from June 30, 1986 (the date of the lodging of the joint minute settling the principal sums due); he further fixed the rate at 15 per cent on all sums.

The district council appealed to the Court of Session by stated case.

Held (1) that on a proper reading of the deed of submission, the arbiter was expressly empowered to deal with interest, since interest was part of each claim put forward by F. Ltd and there were referred to the arbiter "all and any claims" made by F. Ltd against the district council "upon any ground whatsoever arising out of" the performance of the contract; (2) that the date from which interest should run was June 30, 1986, since it was only at that date that any of the principal sums were due and payable; and (3) that the arbiter had a discretion to award interest at the rate of 15 per cent, that being the rate applicable to a judicial decree at the date of his award (September 5, 1986).

10–176 A contrasting case in *John G. McGregor (Contractors) Ltd v. Grampian Regional Council*, 1991 S.L.T. 136:

Several disputes between the employers and the main contractors in a building contract were referred to arbitration. The deed of appointment of the arbiter did not expressly give him power to award interest, but he awarded interest to the main contractors on the principal sums which he found due to them from the date on which the claims had been lodged in the arbitration.

Held that interest was due only from the date at which the employers came under a legal obligation to pay the principal sums, *i.e.* the date of the arbiter's final decree.

The terms of the deed of submission in *Farrans* were held to be materially different from the terms of the deed of appointment in this case.

Lord Dunpark said (at p. 137): "I have no doubt that an arbiter has an implied power to award interest on sums found due from the date of his final decree until payment but, in the absence of any express agreement that he shall have power to award interest on principal sums prior to that date, I do not consider that such a power may be implied. It was expressly conferred by the deed of submission and the joint minute in *Farrans*, but there is no such agreement in this case."

VI CHALLENGE OF THE AWARD

The parties to an arbitration have voluntarily agreed to take the arbiter's decision instead of a court's decision. In doing so they have taken the risk that the arbiter will err on questions of fact and (subject to the stated case provisions in section 3 of the Administration of Justice (Scotland) Act 1972) on questions of law, and the parties have no right to appeal to the court on the "merits" (substance) of their case. **10–177**

The finality of the arbiter's decision is expressed in memorable, **10–178** but perhaps unduly strong, terms by Lord Jeffrey in *Mitchell v. Cable* (1848) 10 D. 1297, a case in which an award was set aside because the arbiter had considered only proof taken in this country and not proof which ought to have been taken on commission at Bombay. Lord Jeffrey said (at p. 1309):

"On every matter touching the merits of the case, the judgment of the arbiter is beyond our control; and beyond question or cavil. He may believe what nobody else believes, and he may disbelieve what all the world believes. He may overlook or flagrantly misapply the most ordinary principles of law; and there is no appeal for those who have chosen to subject themselves to his despotic power."

Lord Jeffrey then proceeded to explain that, while an arbiter's errors of judgment could not be set right, his decree-arbitral could stand only where he had dealt "*fairly*, that is *equally*, with both parties".

The judicial nature of the arbiter's office which so much qualifies **10–179** the arbiter's "despotic power" was concisely described by Lord

President Clyde in *Mitchell-Gill v. Buchan*, 1921 S.C. 390 (at p. 395):

"When it is said that an arbiter in Scotland is the final judge both of fact and law, it is not implied that he is entitled either to make the facts as he would like them to be, or to make the law what he thinks it ought to be. Like any other judge, he must take the facts as they are presented to him, and the law as it is. Otherwise he would act, not as the parties' judge, but as their oracle; his function would be not judicial but arbitrary; and his award would be given, not according to the principles of justice, but according to the caprice of personal preferences. . . . If it could be proved that, in arriving at his award, an arbiter had invented the facts to suit some view of his own, or had fashioned the law to suit his own ideas, then, however innocent in itself might be the eccentricity which had seduced him into such a travesty of judicial conduct, his behaviour would naturally imply that justice had not been done; he would be guilty of that which Lord Watson in *Adams v. Great North of Scotland Railway Co.* (18 R. (H.L.) 1, at p. 8) described as misconduct; and his award would be reduced."

10–180 The limited grounds on which an arbiter's decree-arbitral may be set aside—by an action of reduction brought in the Court of Session—are considered below under the following headings:

(a) corruption, bribery or falsehood;
(b) *ultra fines compromissi*;
(c) improper procedure; and
(d) defective award.

10–181 Partial reduction is competent but only where one part of the award is open to objection, the other part is valid and the two parts are clearly severable. An instance is *Cox Brothers v. Binning and Son* (1867) 6 M. 161, in which an arbiter superadded an incompetent finding to an award which was already exhaustive of the reference.

10–182 Where an award is partially reduced, but the arbiter had no power to make a part award, the partial reduction may cause the remainder of the award also to be open to reduction on the ground that the arbiter has failed to exhaust the submission.

10–183 In *Miller & Son v. Oliver & Boyd* (1906) 8 F. 390 the question arose of whether an arbiter was *functus* where his award had been reduced on the grounds that it was beyond the arbiter's powers and did not exhaust the reference. Lord Pearson (Ordinary) held that an arbiter in that position was not *functus* and so was not disqualified from again taking up the reference. In the Inner House, however, opinions were reserved on that point; Lord McLaren referred to English law as being undoubtedly to the contrary and was unwilling, unless compelled by principle or authority, to establish a different rule in Scotland from that which had been established and found to work conveniently in England.

(a) Corruption, Bribery or Falsehood

The authority for this ground of reduction is the twenty-fifth Article of the Articles of Regulation of 1695. These Articles were made by Commissioners under the special sanction of an Act of the Scottish Parliament of 1693 (c. 34), and the twenty-fifth of them dealt with the grounds on which an arbiter's award might be challenged. It was in these terms: **10–184**

"That for the cutting off of groundless and expensive pleas and processes in time coming, the Lords of Session sustain no reduction of any decree-arbitral, that shall be pronounced hereafter upon a subscribed submission, at the instance of either of the parties-submitters, upon any cause or reason whatsoever, unless that of corruption, bribery, or falsehood, to be alleged against the judges arbitrators who pronounced the same."

The provision must be viewed in its historical context. Before 1695 the courts of law had come to allow an award to be challenged in court on the grounds of "iniquity" committed by an arbiter or of "enorm lesion" suffered by a party, *i.e.* on the grounds that an arbiter had made a mistake or that a party had suffered undue hardship. The result was that in practically every case an award could be reviewed upon its merits at the discretion of the court—a situation which defeated the main object of the parties in resorting to arbitration. **10–185**

The aim of the twenty-fifth Article was to end the practice of review by the courts: arbiters' awards were to be final and binding on the parties and were no longer to be open to challenge merely because the arbiter had made a mistake or one party had suffered undue hardship. Corruption, bribery and falsehood on the part of the arbiter, however, were to remain grounds on which an award could be challenged in court. **10–186**

If this statutory provision had been given a literal interpretation it would have prevented an award from being set aside on any **10–187** ground other than corruption, bribery or falsehood. Decided cases, however, and particularly the speech of Lord Watson in *Adams v. Great North of Scotland Railway Co.* (1890) 18 R. (H.L.) 1; (1889) 16 R. 843, established that the object for which the provision was made had to be looked to: the provision had never been intended to go beyond the point of putting an end to the practice of review upon the merits; other common law grounds of challenge (see (b) to (d), below) remained available.

10–188 In some cases there were attempts to extend the word "corruption" so as to include "legal corruption" or "constructive corruption", *i.e.* conduct on the part of the arbiter which was mistaken but not strictly corrupt. Lord Watson in *Adams v. Great North of Scotland Railway Co.* protested against this extended meaning of "corruption"; actual corruption was necessary if an award was to be set aside on the ground of the Articles of Regulation: if the arbiter's mistake was innocent, it could not be brought within the term "corruption", though it might lead to reduction of the award on one of the other grounds (b) to (d), below.

10–189 Within a year another appeal to the House of Lords—*Holmes Oil Co. Ltd v. Pumpherston Oil Co. Ltd* (1891) 18 R. (H.L.) 52; (1890) 17 R. 624—provided an opportunity for further observations to the same effect. The decision in that case was that the question raised was one as to the interpretation of the contract—a matter which was within the jurisdiction of the arbiter—and that the arbiter had interpreted the contract in a way which made certain evidence which had been offered irrelevant; there was therefore no ground for reduction on account of the arbiter's refusal to allow the evidence. Lord Watson said (at p. 55):

"I think the only serious argument latterly insisted in by the appellants was founded upon the allegation, not that the arbiter had corruptly given a judgment upon the materials before him, but that there had been misconduct on his part in declining to receive evidence which was tendered to him before he proceeded to dispose of the question submitted.

"Now, I am of opinion that that ground of exception, which may be a good ground of exception to the validity of the award, does not rest at all upon the Regulations of 1695. I think that in so far as regards the conduct of the case, and in so far as regards the jurisdiction of the arbiter to dispose of the case, the Regulations of 1695 make no provision whatever. These rest upon the common law."

Reported cases give few illustrations of what may properly be classed as corruption, bribery or falsehood within the meaning of the Regulations. In *Morisons v. Thomson's Trustees* (1880) 8 R. 147 the court held that it was not corrupt for an arbiter to apply first to one party and then to the other party in the arbitration proceedings for a loan of £1,000 to assist him with his financial difficulties, which were caused by the failure of the City of Glasgow Bank. The arbiter was a mutual friend of both parties, and the court found that there was no ground for supposing that his mind had been influenced one way or the other by each party's refusal to give him the desired loan. **10–190**

(b) *Ultra Fines Compromissi*

An award which is *ultra fines compromissi* ("beyond the bounds of the submission") may be set aside. This follows from the very nature of arbitration, since the parties have agreed to implement the decision of their private judge on certain questions only. Any question which is beyond the bounds of the submission continues to be within the court's jurisdiction, and any attempted decision of such a question by the arbiter has no authority behind it. **10–191**

Where only a part of an award is *ultra fines compromissi*, it may be possible to enforce the award in so far as it is valid, but this will depend on whether the invalid part is severable from the rest of the award or not. This was one of the points which arose in *Miller & Son v. Oliver & Boyd* (1903) 6 F. 77: **10–192**

M., a printer, entered into an agreement with O. & B. by which O. & B. purchased M.'s business. Under an article in the agreement M. was to become an employee of O. & B. at a salary of £150 a year. Other articles of the agreement dealt with the price of goodwill and of the stock, plant, machinery and fittings. There was an arbitration clause naming Ritchie as arbiter.

Disputes arose and the parties referred to Ritchie claims by M. for (1) goodwill, (2) salary, (3) commission, (4) the price of plant and (5) damages for breach of contract and a counter claim by O. & B. for damages for breach of contract.

Ritchie issued an award in which he found O. & B. liable to M. in a lump sum of £618 7s. 11d., and on the parties implementing the award declared them freed of all claims one against the other and ordained each of them to execute and deliver a valid discharge to the other.

M. brought an action for reduction of the award on the ground that it was *ultra vires* ("beyond the powers" [*of the arbiter*]) and that it did not exhaust the reference. O. & B. admitted that the award was *ultra vires* in so far as it ordained the parties to execute mutual discharges but they contended that this order was separable from the rest of the award.

Held that the award fell to be reduced because (1) M.'s claims were not all *ejusdem generis* ("of the same kind") and it was impossible to discover from the face of the award how far the arbiter had considered all M.'s claims, (2) the award did not show how the arbiter had dealt with O. & B.'s counterclaim, and (3) the order for mutual discharges, which was admittedly *ultra vires*, was not separable from the rest of the award.

(c) Improper Procedure

10–193 The parties may specify the procedure which the arbiter is to follow. If he then fails to comply, his award may be challenged.

10–194 More often the procedure is left to the arbiter's discretion, and if so, failure to observe strict court procedure will not be a ground for challenging the award.

10–195 There are, however, in every contract of submission implied conditions of honesty and impartiality, breach of which is a ground of reduction. See 10–25 and 10–158 *et seq.*, above.

10–196 It is under this heading that the supposed cases of "constructive corruption" properly fall, as was made clear by the two House of Lords cases *Adams v. Great North of Scotland Railway Co.* and *Holmes Oil Co. Ltd v. Pumpherston Oil Co. Ltd.* In the latter case Lord Watson said (at 18 R. (H.L.) p. 55):

"The arbiter must confine himself to the jurisdiction which the parties have conferred upon him, and in the conduct of the arbitration before it comes to final judgment he is bound to observe any condition which the parties may have chosen to impose upon him by the deed of submission, and he must also conform to all those rules for securing the proper administration of justice which the law implies in the case of every proceeding before a Court of justice."

10–197 The parties themselves, as well as the arbiter, must refrain from fraudulent and unfair procedure. For example, an award would be set aside if a deliberately false case had been presented to the arbiter.

(d) **Defective Award**

In *Mackenzie v. Girvin* (1840) 3 D. 318 (affirmed (1843) 2 Bell's App. 43), a case relating to a judicial reference, Lord Moncreiff gave a well-known description of the requisites of a valid award. He said (at p. 328) that it was "the established rule and essential principle of the law of Scotland, that, when an award in a judicial reference is clear in its terms, correct in its form, embracing nothing which was not referred, and exhausting all that was referred, it is not competent for this Court to review such an award on its general merits, or to set it aside, or refuse effect to it, on any idea of mere error in judgment in the matters properly within the cognizance of the referee." **10–198**

(i) The first requisite is that the award should be clear in its terms: if it is unintelligible, it will be set aside; if it is merely ambiguous or obscure, the court (but not the arbiter) has the right to interpret it. **10–199**

(ii) Secondly, the award should be correct in its form. What is the proper form depends on circumstances; if, for instance, the arbitration proceedings were started by a formal deed of submission, the award also would require to be in that form (*McLaren v. Aikman*, at 10–157, above); on the other hand, an informal award would be quite sufficient where the reference to arbitration was itself informal. **10–200**

(iii) The award must embrace nothing which was not referred. This point has been considered under the heading "*ultra fines compromissi*" (10–191 *et seq.*, above). **10–201**

(iv) The award must exhaust the submission, *i.e.* it must give a complete decision. The parties have agreed that certain disputes be decided by arbitration, and it is not a proper fulfilment of their agreement if the arbiter decides one question but leaves another question undecided. See *Miller & Son v. Oliver & Boyd* (10–192, above). Another instance of reduction on the ground of failure to exhaust the submission is: **10–202**

Donald v. Shiell's Executrix, 1937 S.C. 52: In an arbitration between the outgoing and the incoming tenants of a farm the questions submitted for the arbiter's decision were (1) what sum should be paid by the incoming tenant to the outgoing tenant for corn crop and various other items, and (2) the sum, "if any", to be paid by the outgoing tenant to the incoming tenant in order to put **10–203** the buildings on the farm into the condition provided for under the conditions of let in favour of the incoming tenant.

The award ordered the incoming tenant to pay certain sums under the first head, but made no mention of items under the second head.

The incoming tenant brought an action for reduction of the award, and was successful on the ground of the omission: it could not be assumed that the arbiter had considered items under the second head and had found nothing to be due for them.

10–204 The mere fact that an arbiter has made no finding as to expenses is not a ground for reducing an award:

Pollich v. Heatley, 1910 S.C. 469: A charterparty provided for claims for demurrage to be settled by arbitration.

After an arbitration in which arbiters found a certain sum due by the shipper to the shipowner as demurrage, the shipowner brought an action to reduce the award on the ground that the arbiters had not exhausted the submission in that they had not dealt with (1) interest and (2) expenses.

Held that (1) the question of interest was not one with which the arbiters had power to deal and (2) the question of expenses was not part of the submission but was merely incidental to the conduct of the arbitration and therefore the fact that the arbiters had made no finding as to expenses was not a ground for reducing their award.

Lord President Dunedin said (at p. 482):

"The matter of expenses is not part of the submission. There may be cases in which special power is given to an arbiter to dispose of expenses, but that really is pleonastic. The matter of expenses is incidental to the conduct of the case, and there is an inherent power in the tribunal to grant them. . . . I do not think it is a case of the submission not having been exhausted; it is merely that no expenses have been awarded."

10–205 According to the early case of *Lord Lovat v. Fraser of Phopachy* (1738) Mor. 625, where there is a submission of certain particulars and also a general submission of all other claims and the arbiter decides only the particulars, his decree-arbitral is not open to reduction on the ground of failure to exhaust the submission provided no claim under the general submission having a connection with any of the particulars decided is left undecided.

10–206 Reduction on the ground of failure to exhaust the submission was described by Lord Maxwell (Ordinary) in *Johnson v. Lamb*,

1981 S.L.T. 300 (at p. 306) as a "somewhat obscure and unsatisfactory" area of law. The following obstacles in the way of reduction on this ground are considered in Lord Maxwell's opinion in that case:

(1) The arbiter cannot be heard as a witness as to the matters on which he reached his decision.

(2) There is doubt as to whether reference may be made to the pleadings in the arbitration or the arbiter's notes.

(3) Where the award expressly bears that the arbiter has heard counsel for the parties on the whole matters submitted to him and that he has reached a decision on the whole matters submitted, there is at least a very strong presumption that the arbiter has in fact considered and determined all matters put before him.

Lord Maxwell's decision in the case was that, even if it were competent to look at the pleadings in the arbitration and the arbiter's notes, the evidence which they provided was wholly unconvincing and insufficient to overcome the presumption described in (3), above.

VII JUDICIAL REFERENCES

By a judicial reference is meant the procedure by which parties to a court action agree to withdraw the decision of the whole or some of the questions raised in the action from the decision of the court and, while still formally leaving the action in court, refer these questions to an arbiter. **10–207**

A judicial reference is started by the lodging with the court of a "minute" stating the agreement of the parties, and the court then, if it thinks fit, "interpones authority to the minute", *i.e.* authorises the judicial reference to proceed. **10–208**

The selection of the judicial referee is a matter for the parties to decide. Like an ordinary arbiter, a judicial referee is not bound by strict court procedure. **10–209**

The scope of the reference is limited to the subject-matter of the action as set out in the "record". **10–210**

The decision of a judicial referee is set out in a report to the court (not an award). The report may be challenged on the same grounds as an award in an ordinary arbitration. The court will either approve of the report and grant "decree conform" (*i.e.* make a court order in conformity with the terms of the report) or set the report aside; the court has no power to amend the report. **10–211**

Further Reading

Gloag and Henderson, *The Law of Scotland*, Chapter 2 (part)

David M. Walker, *Principles of Scottish Private Law*, Volume I, Chapter 1.6

Robert L.C. Hunter, *The Law of Arbitration in Scotland* (1987, T. & T. Clark)

The Laws of Scotland: Stair Memorial Encyclopaedia, Volume 2, Title *Arbitration* by J. A. D. Hope

John Montgomerie Bell, *Treatise on the Law of Arbitration in Scotland* (2nd ed., 1877, T. & T. Clark)

James Campbell Irons and R. D. Melville, *Treatise on the Law of Arbitration in Scotland* (1903, William Green & Sons)

Scottish Advisory Committee on Arbitration Law, *Report to the Lord Advocate on Legislation for Domestic Arbitration in Scotland* (1996, Scottish Courts Administration)

INDEX

APR, 5–49, 5–163n

Acceptance
  buyer's duty, 4–173, 4–202 *et seq.*
  damages for buyer's failure, 4–290 *et seq.*
  time of, 4–207

Acceptance of Bill of Exchange, 6–37 *et seq.*
  for honour *supra* protest, 6–138 *et seq.*

Acceptor of Bill of Exchange, 6-22
  becoming holder, 6–130
  for honour, 6–139 *et seq.*
  liability of, 6–106 *et seq.*

Accommodation Bill, 6–128

Accommodation Party, 6–56

"Account Payee Only"
  on cheque, 6–195

Accountant in Bankruptcy, 9–09, 9–73, 9–77 *et seq.*, 9–382 *et seq.*, 9–475 *et seq.*
  Notes for Guidance in Sequestrations, 9–84

Accountant of Court, 9–77

Accountants, 1–90, 1–141, 2–15, 7–140, 7–142

Accounting
  agent's duty, 1–116
  partner's duty, 2–114 *et seq.*

Accounting Periods (Sequestration), 9–342 *et seq.*

Accounts
  of group of companies, 3–127, 3–153

Acquirenda, 9–258, 9–266 *et seq.*

Act and Warrant, 9–249, 9–252 *et seq.*

Ad Factum Praestandum, 8–87

Ad Hoc Submissions, 10–60 *et seq.*

Advertising (Consumer Credit), 5–154 *et seq.*

Agency, 1–01 *et seq.*, 2–08, 2–36, 2–50 *et seq.*, 4–09, 4–90, 4–324, 8–47
  authority of agent, 1–73 *et seq.*
  capacity, 1–13 *et seq.*
  categories of agent, 1–31 *et seq.*
  commercial agents, 1–47 *et seq.*
  constitution, 1–15 *et seq.*
  duties of agent to principal, 1–103 *et seq.*
  rights of agent against principal, 1–130 *et seq.*
  termination, 1–171 *et seq.*
  third party's rights and liabilities, 1–142 *et seq.*

Agreement to Sell, 4–18 *et seq.*, 4–38

Aircraft
  mortgage of, 7–76

Allonge Attached to Bill of Exchange, 6–64

Alteration of Bill of Exchange, 6–133

Ancillary Arbitrations, 10–63 *et seq.*

Ancillary Credit Businesses, 5–317 *et seq.*

Antecedent Negotiations (Consumer Credit), 5–182 *et seq.*

Apparent Authority, 1–78 *et seq.*, 1–91 *et seq.*, 2–71

"Apparent Insolvency", 9–01, 9–98, 9–291

Applications to Court (Arbitration), 10–166 *et seq.*

Appropriation of Payments, 5–220 *et seq.*

Approval
  sale of goods on, 4–145 *et seq.*

Arbiters, 10–88 *et seq.*
  appointment, 10–106 *et seq.*
  disqualification, 10–127 *et seq.*
  relationship with oversmen, 10–93 *et seq.*
  remuneration, 10–145 *et seq.*

Arbitration, 1–89, 9–404 *et seq.*, 10–01 *et seq.*
  ad hoc submissions, 10–60 *et seq.*

ARBITRATION—*cont.*
advantages over litigation, 10–29 *et seq.*
ancillary, 10–63 *et seq.*
arbiters and oversmen, 10–88 *et seq.*
capacity of parties, 10–41 *et seq.*
challenge of award, 10–177 *et seq.*
characteristics, 10–22 *et seq.*
conduct, 10–151 *et seq.*
constitution of contract, 10–40
distinguished from valuation, 10–14 *et seq.*
duration of submission, 10–80 *et seq.*
form of contract of submission, 10–43 *et seq.*
issue of award, 10–171 *et seq.*
judicial references, 10–207 *et seq.*
matters which may be referred, 10–10 *et seq.*
prorogation of submission, 10–84 *et seq.*, 10–165
scope of submission, 10–50 *et seq.*
stated case, 10–13, 10–77 *et seq.*
statutory, 10–02
ARBITRATION CLAUSE, 2–139, 10–63
ample or general, 10–65, 10–67
effect of termination of main contract, 10–73 *et seq.*
executorial, 10–65
incorporation into subcontract, 10–71 *et seq.*
power to assess damages under, 10–69 *et seq.*
restricted or limited, 10–65 *et seq.*
"ARBITRATOR," 10–90
ARCHITECT, 1–88, 1–111
ARRESTMENT, 2–42
ARRESTMENT OR POINDING
unpaid seller's right, 4–234, 4–275 *et seq.*
ARTICLES OF ASSOCIATION, 3–05, 3–13, 3–21, 3–51, 3–58 *et seq.*, 3–94, 3–130 *et seq.*, 3–249, 3–252, 3–254, 3–262 *et seq.*
alteration, 3–267 *et seq.*
effect, 3–276 *et seq.*
relationship with memorandum, 3–194 *et seq.*
ARTICLES OF REGULATION, 10–03, 10–184 *et seq.*

ASCERTAINED GOODS, 4–131 *et seq.*, 4–299
ASSIGNATION
funds available, 1–179, 6–14
life assurance policy, 6–06
share in partnership, 2–123 *et seq.*, 2–175
ASSIGNATUS UTITUR JURE AUCTORIS, 6–06
ASSIGNMENT OF FUNDS AVAILABLE, 6–99 *et seq.*
"ASSOCIATE" (BANKRUPTCY), 9–30
ASSOCIATION CLAUSE, 3–258 *et seq.*
AUCTION
criminal offences, 4–327 *et seq.*
sale of goods by, 4–311 *et seq.*
AUCTIONEERS, 1–05, 1–38, 1–42 *et seq.*, 1–153, 1–162, 1–169 *et seq.*, 4–90, 4–324
AUDITORS, 3–08
"AUTHORISED INSTITUTION," 6–153
AWARD (ARBITRATION), 10–01
challenge, 10–177 *et seq.*
defective, 10–198 *et seq.*
issue, 10–171 *et seq.*
AWARD OF SEQUESTRATION, 9–126 *et seq.*
making, 9–127 *et seq.*
procedure following, 9–143 *et seq.*
recall, 9–150 *et seq.*

"BACK-LETTER," 7–107, 7–110
BAILMENT, 5–02
BANKER
customer's duty to, 6–175 *et seq.*
definition, 6–152 *et seq.*
duty to customer, 6–159 *et seq.*
protection of collecting, 6–207 *et seq.*
protection of paying, 6–197 *et seq.*
BANKER'S DRAFT, 6–179
BANKRUPTCY, 4–119, 9–01 *et seq.*
(See also INSOLVENCY and SEQUESTRATION)
administration, 9–76 *et seq.*
firm and partners, 2–01, 2–46 *et seq.*, 2–87, 2–136, 2–152, 3–180
insolvency, 9–12 *et seq.*
licensee (consumer credit), 5–144

BANKRUPTCY—*cont.*
principal or agent, 1–191 *et seq.*
sequestration, 9–68 *et seq.*
BARTER, 4–23 *et seq.*, 4–44
BENEFICIUM CEDENDARUM ACTIONUM, 8–80, 8–99 *et seq.*
BENEFICIUM DIVISIONIS, 8–80, 8–89 *et seq.*
BENEFICIUM ORDINIS, 8–80, 8–83 *et seq.*
BILL OF LADING, 4–153, 4–196, 6–12, 7–83, 7–91
BILLS OF EXCHANGE, 4–153, 4–231, 6–01 *et seq.*
acceptance, 6–37 *et seq.*
acceptance for honour *supra* protest, 6–138 *et seq.*
characteristics, 6–14
conflict of laws, 6–145 *et seq.*
damages for dishonour, 6–118
definitions, 6–16 *et seq.*
discharge, 6–125 *et seq.*
functions, 6–08 *et seq.*
holder in due course, 6–47 *et seq.*
in a set, 6–144
issue, 6–40 *et seq.*
liabilities of parties, 6–92 *et seq.*
lost, 6–143
negotiation, 6–62 *et seq.*
payment for honour *supra* protest, 6–141 *et seq.*
presentment for acceptance, 6–70 *et seq.*
presentment for payment, 6–77 *et seq.*
procedure on dishonour, 6–80 *et seq.*
protest, 6–84 *et seq.*
summary diligence, 6–119 *et seq.*
"BLANK" TRANSFER, 7–97, 7–103 *et seq.*
BOARD MEETINGS, 3–42
BONA FIDE, 1–195, 3–271, 3–274
BONAE FIDEI, 4–85
BOTTOMRY, BOND OF, 1–30, 1–70, 7–34 *et seq.*
BOVILL'S ACT, 2–20
BREACH OF CONTRACT OF SALE OF GOODS
actions for, 4–278
BROKERS, 1–36 *et seq.*
BUSINESS NAMES, 2–177 *et seq.*
BUYER'S REMEDIES, 4–116, 4–294 *et seq.*

C.C.C., 3–82
C.I.F., 4–195 *et seq.*
CANCELLATION OF BILL OF EXCHANGE, 6–132
CANVASSING (CONSUMER CREDIT), 5–167 *et seq.*
CAPACITY
in agency, 1–13 *et seq.*
in sale of goods, 4–31 *et seq.*
of cautioner, 8–45 *et seq.*
of parties to arbitration, 10–41 *et seq.*
CAPITAL SUM ON DIVORCE
recalling of order, 9–281 *et seq.*
CARRIERS, 1–30
CATHOLIC AND SECONDARY SECURITIES, 7–119
CAUTIONARY OBLIGATIONS, 2–94, 7–06, 8–01 *et seq.*
constitution and form, 8–36 *et seq.*
definitions, 8–13 *et seq.*
extent of cautioner's liability, 8–61 *et seq.*
general nature, 8–10 *et seq.*
kinds, 8–29 *et seq.*
rights of cautioners, 8–80 *et seq.*
similar obligations, 8–17 *et seq.*
termination, 8–105 *et seq.*
validity, 8–44 *et seq.*
CAUTIONERS, 2–37, 2–52, 8–05 *et seq.* (See also CAUTIONARY OBLIGATIONS)
capacity and authority of, 8–45 *et seq.*
extent of liability, 8–61 *et seq.*
rights, 8–80 *et seq.*
CAUTIONRY, 2–08, 2–50, 2–52, 8–15 (See also CAUTIONARY OBLIGATIONS)
CAVEAT EMPTOR, 4–84 *et seq.*
CEDENT, 2–125, 2–175
CERTIFICATE OF INCORPORATION, 3–75, 3–84, 3–134 *et seq.*
CERTIFICATION OF CHEQUE, 6–179
CHARTERPARTY, 1–71, 1–87, 1–145
CHEQUE CARD, 5–79, 5–87, 5–103

CHEQUES, 6-01 *et seq.*, 6–07, 6–10, 6–22, 6–23, 6–58, 6–99 *et seq.*, 6–124, 6–147 *et seq.*
  banker and customer, 6–150 *et seq.*
  crossed, 6–182 *et seq.*
  forgeries, 6–177
  misuse, 5–224
  precautions in drawing, 6–176
  presentment for payment, 1–179, 6–99 *et seq.*, 6–178 *et seq.*
  protection of bankers, 6–196 *et seq.*
CHURCH CONGREGATION, 1–155
CIRCULARS (CONSUMER CREDIT)
  to minors, 5–171 *et seq.*
CLAYTON'S CASE, RULE IN, 8–113 *et seq.*
CLERK IN ARBITRATION, 10–162 *et seq.*
CLIENT ACCOUNT, 1–62
CLUB, 1–155
CO-CAUTIONERS, 8–57 *et seq.*
  release, 8–148
  right to relief against, 8–96 *et seq.*
  right to share in securities, 8–102 *et seq.*
COLLATERAL REPRESENTATIONS, 4–52 *et seq.*
"COLLECTING BANKER," 6–182
COMMERCIAL AGENTS, 1–47 *et seq.*
COMMISSION
  agent's, 1–75, 1–107, 1–131 *et seq.*, 1–138 *et seq.*
  auctioneer's, 1–45
COMMISSIONERS (SEQUESTRATION), 9–101, 9–212 *et seq.*, 9–236, 9–238 *et seq.*
  meetings, 9–420 *et seq.*
COMPANIES, 2–05 *et seq.*, 2–13, 2–15, 2–32, 2–93, 2–129, 2–176, 3–01 *et seq.*
  articles of association, 3–05, 3–13, 3–21, 3–51, 3–58 *et seq.*, 3–94, 3–130 *et seq.*, 3–249, 3–252, 3–254, 3–262 *et seq.*
  classification, 3–43 *et seq.*
  commencing business, 3–84 *et seq.*
  comparison with partnership, 3–165 *et seq.*
  conversion from limited to unlimited and *vice versa*, 3–67 *et seq.*, 3–113
COMPANIES—*cont.*
  conversion from private to public and *vice versa*, 3–115 *et seq.*
  debentures and debenture stock, 3–34 *et seq.*, 3–181 *et seq.*
  directors, 1–01, 1–17, 3–21 *et seq.*, 3–86 *et seq.*, 3–131, 3–156 *et seq.*, 3–233 *et seq.*
  employees, 3–08, 3–23, 3–25
  holding and subsidary, 3–123 *et seq.*, 3–152 *et seq.*, 3–161
  limited, 2–05 *et seq.*, 2–32, 2–176, 3–45 *et seq.*
  limited by guarantee, 3–18, 3–52 *et seq.*
  meetings, 3–38 *et seq.*
  members, 3–17 *et seq.*, 3–151
  memorandum of association, 3–05, 3–13, 3–21, 3–28, 3–46, 3–50, 3–52 *et seq.*, 3–57, 3–80 *et seq.*, 3–130 *et seq.*, 3–193 *et seq.*
  names, 2–177, 3–82 *et seq.*, 3–199 *et seq.*
  objects, 3–216 *et seq.*
  personality, 3–128 *et seq.*
  private, 2–176, 3–16, 3–43, 3–45, 3–56, 3–63, 3–71 *et seq.*, 3–174, 3–216, 3–245
  public, 3–32, 3–43, 3–45, 3–56, 3–63, 3–71 *et seq.*, 3–174, 3–209, 3–216, 3–246, 3–260
  registered office, 3–210 *et seq.*
  registration, 3–12 *et seq.*, 3–74, 3–129 *et seq.*
  resolutions, 3–39 *et seq.*, 3–110 *et seq.*
  secretary, 3–90, 3–156
  share capital, 3–18, 3–26 *et seq.*, 3–91 *et seq.*, 3–191, 3–244 *et seq.*
  shareholders and stockholders, 3–17 *et seq.*
  ultra vires doctrine, 3–217 *et seq.*
  unlimited, 3–18, 3–61 *et seq.*
COMPANY NOT YET REGISTERED, 1–14, 1–154, 3–15
COMPENSATION, 8–111 *et seq.*
  in partnership, 2–44 *et seq.*
COMPOSITION, 9–357, 9–370 *et seq.*, 9–449, 9–478 *et seq.*
CONDICTIO CAUSA DATA CAUSA NON SECUTA, 4–281
"CONDITION," 4–54 *et seq.*, 4–102

CONDITIONAL SALE AGREEMENT, 4–169, 5–54 *et seq.*
CONFIDENTIAL INFORMATION, 1–129
CONFUSIONE, 6–130
CONSENSUS IN IDEM, 4–46, 10–120
CONSUMER CONTRACT, 4–82
CONSUMER CREDIT, 5–01 *et seq.*
  administration, 5–29 *et seq.*
  agreement control, 5–179 *et seq.*
  aim of legislation, 5–09 *et seq.*
  ancillary credit businesses, 5–317 *et seq.*
  Crowther Report, 5–14 *et seq.*, 5–17, 5–349
  default and termination, 5–230 *et seq.*
  definitions, 5–39 *et seq.*
  Director General of Fair Trading, 5–21, 5–32 *et seq.*, 5–122, 5–125, 5–187, 5–342, 5–356 *et seq.*, 5–363 *et seq.*
  enforcement, 5–285 *et seq.*, 5–362 *et seq.*
  entry and inspection of premises, 5–365 *et seq.*
  entry into credit or hire agreements, 5–180 *et seq.*
  extortionate credit bargains, 5–307 *et seq.*
  form and content of agreements, 5–186 *et seq.*
  judicial control, 5–285 *et seq.*
  licensing of credit and hire business 5–121 *et seq.*
  matters arising during currency of agreement, 5–206 *et seq.*
  meaning, 5–06 *et seq.*
  motor vehicles, 5–384 *et seq.*
  regulated agreement, 5–44 *et seq.*
  security, 5–256 *et seq.*
  trading control, 5–121 *et seq.*
CONSUMER CREDIT AGREEMENT, 4–169, 5–46 *et seq.*
  classification, 5–62 *et seq.*
  early settlement by debtor, 5–244 *et seq.*
"CONSUMER GOODS," 4–375
"CONSUMER HIRE AGREEMENT," 5–51 *et seq.*, 5–55 *et seq.*, 5–218
  financial relief, 5–302
CONSUMER PROTECTION, 4–10 *et seq.*, 4–360 *et seq.*, 10–37
CONSUMER SAFETY, 4–373 *et seq.*
"CONSUMER TRADE PRACTICE," 4–350 *et seq.*
CONTRA PROFERENTEM, 8–65 *et seq.*, 8–108
"COOLING-OFF PERIOD," 5–196 *et seq.*
COPARTNERY
  contract, 2–18, 2–49, 2–97, 2–105, 2–108, 2–129, 2–145
CORPOREAL MOVEABLES
  securities over, 7–75 *et seq.*
CORRUPTION, BRIBERY OR FALSEHOOD (ARBITRATION), 10–184 *et seq.*
COUNCIL ON TRIBUNALS, 1–64, 5–34
COUNTERMAND OF PAYMENT, 6–170
"CREDIT," 5–48
CREDIT BROKERAGE, 4–100, 5–25 *et seq.*, 5–324 *et seq.*
"CREDIT LIMIT," 5–69 *et seq.*
CREDIT REFERENCE AGENCY, 5–337 *et seq.*, 5–349 *et seq.*
CREDIT-BROKER, 4–100, 5–26, 5–327
CREDITORS, 3–192
  duty of disclosure to cautioner, 8–50 *et seq.*
  duty to give information, 5–214 *et seq.*
  duty to give notice, 5–211 *et seq.*
  general or ordinary, 7–02, 7–08
  liability for breaches by supplier, 5–207 *et seq.*
  meetings, 9–407 *et seq.*
  oath (sequestration), 9–125
  "qualified," 9–103 *et seq.*
  safeguarding interests, 9–176, 9–178, 9–277 *et seq.*
  statutory meeting, 9–164 *et seq.*, 9–185
  submission of claims, 9–330 *et seq.*
  trust deed, 9–450 *et seq.*
"CREDIT-TOKEN," 5–99 *et seq.*
  issue of new, 5–226
  misuse, 5–224 *et seq.*
  unsolicited, 5–173
"CREDIT-TOKEN AGREEMENT," 5–99, 5–173
CROSSED CHEQUES, 6–182 *et seq.*

CROWTHER REPORT, 5–14 *et seq.*, 5–17, 5–349
CURATOR BONIS, 2–141, 6–170
CUSTODY, 7–130

DAYS OF GRACE, 6–32
DE FACTO, 3–148, 8–139
"DEALER"
at auction sales, 4–327
DEATH
bank customer, 6–170
cautioner, 8–130 *et seq.*
debtor or hirer (consumer credit), 5–227 *et seq.*, 5–295 *et seq.*
licensee (consumer credit), 5–144
partner, 2–42, 2–87, 2–136 *et seq.*, 2–156, 2–157 *et seq.*
principal debtor, 8–128
principal or agent, 1–187 *et seq.*
DEBENTURE HOLDER, 3–35
DEBENTURES AND DEBENTURE STOCK, 3–34 *et seq.*, 3–181 *et seq.*
DEBT–ADJUSTING (CONSUMER CREDIT), 5–329 *et seq.*
DEBT-COLLECTING (CONSUMER CREDIT), 5–25, 5–335 *et seq.*
DEBT-COUNSELLING (CONSUMER CREDIT), 5–332 *et seq.*
DEBTOR (SEQUESTRATION)
declaration by, 9–360 *et seq.*
discharge, 9–357 *et seq.*
private examination, 9–318 *et seq.*
public examination, 9–320 *et seq.*
"DEBTOR-CREDITOR AGREEMENT," 5–45, 5–91
"DEBTOR-CREDITOR-SUPPLIER AGREEMENT," 5–39, 5–45, 5–89 *et seq.*, 5–207
DECREE-ARBITRAL, 9–405, 10–01
"DECREE CONFORM," 10–168, 10–211
DEFAULT NOTICES (CONSUMER CREDIT), 5–231 *et seq.*
DEL CREDERE AGENTS, 1–46
DELECTUS PERSONAE, 1–193, 2–09, 2–92, 2–95, 2–107, 2–123, 3–175, 10–100, 10–108
DELEGATION, 1–108 *et seq.*, 2–74, 2–82
distinguished from cautionry, 8–22 *et seq.*
DELEGATUS NON POTEST DELEGARE, 1–108
DELICTS
partnership, 2–38 *et seq.*, 2–65 *et seq.*
DELIVERY IN RIGHTS IN SECURITY, 7–08 *et seq.*, 7–80 *et seq.*
actual, 7–82
constructive, 7–86 *et seq.*
symbolical, 7–83 *et seq.*
DELIVERY IN SALE OF GOODS, 4–08, 4–118, 4–137, 4–173 *et seq.*
at distant place, 4–201
buyer's liability for not taking, 4–229 *et seq.*
by instalments, 4–190 *et seq.*
damages for failure, 4–296 *et seq.*
general rules, 4–127 *et seq.*
to carrier, 4–192 *et seq.*
wrong quantity, 4–183 *et seq.*
DELIVERY OF BILL OF EXCHANGE, 6–41, 6–62
DEPOSIT
pre-contract, 1–63
sale of goods, 4–49
DERVAIRD COMMITTEE, 10–08
DESCRIPTION
sale by, 4–72, *et seq.*, 4–148
DEVOLUTION (ARBITRATION), 10–94, 10–101 *et seq.*
DIRECTOR GENERAL OF FAIR TRADING, 1–56, 1–60 *et seq.*, 4–349, 4–352 *et seq.*, 4–388 *et seq.*, 5–21, 5–32 *et seq.*, 5–122, 5–125, 5–187, 5–342, 5–356 *et seq.*, 5–363 *et seq.*
DIRECTORS OF COMPANY, 1–01, 1–17, 3–21 *et seq.*, 3–86 *et seq.*, 3–131, 3–156
disclosure of interests, 3–157
loans, 3–89
meetings, 3–42
powers to bind company, 3–233 *et seq.*
DISCHARGE
bill of exchange, 6–125 *et seq.*
cautioner, 8–118
debtor, 9–357 *et seq.*
interim trustee, 9–221 *et seq.*

DISCHARGE—*cont.*
permanent trustee, 9–379 *et seq.*
principal obligation (cautionry), 8–107 *et seq.*
DISCLOSED PRINCIPAL, 1–143 *et seq.*
DISCONTINUANCE
principal's business, 1–198 *et seq.*
DISCOUNTING (BILL OF EXCHANGE), 6–13
DISHONOUR OF BILL OF EXCHANGE, 6–74 *et seq.*, 6–80 *et seq.*
DISQUALIFICATION
arbiters and oversmen, 10–127 *et seq.*
DISTRIBUTION (SEQUESTRATION)
order of priority, 9–338 *et seq.*
DIVIDENDS (SEQUESTRATION), 9–335, 9–337, 9–341, 9–346 *et seq.*
DOCUMENT OF TITLE, 4–163, 4–165, 7–84
DOCUMENTARY CREDIT, 6–10
DOMINUS, 7–186
DOUBLE RANKING
rule against, 8–72
DRAWEE, 6–21
liability, 6–96 *et seq.*
DRAWER OF BILL OF EXCHANGE, 6–21 *et seq.*
liability, 6–108 *et seq.*

EDINBURGH GAZETTE, 1–176, 3–135, 3–212, 9–73, 9–154, 9–321, 9–372, 9–471
EJUSDEM GENERIS, 10–192
ELECTION
to sue principal or agent, 1–161 *et seq.*
ELECTIVE RESOLUTIONS, 3–112
ENFORCEMENT ORDERS (CONSUMER CREDIT), 5–290 *et seq.*
ENORM LESION, 10–185
EQUITABLE MORTGAGE, 7–97 *et seq.*
EQUITY SHARES, 3–95
ESTATE AGENCY WORK, 1–58, 1–60
ESTATE AGENTS, 1–53 *et seq.*
ESTATE FACTORS, 1–41, 1–53, 1–66 *et seq.*
ESTOPPEL
agency by, 1–19
EX FACIE, 6–124
EX FACIE ABSOLUTE TRANSFER, 7–107, 7–110, 7–112, 7–177, 7–184 *et seq.*
EX LEGE, 8–96
EX PARTE PROCEEDINGS, 10–164
EXAMINATION OF DEBTOR, 9–316 *et seq.*
private, 9–318 *et seq.*
public, 9–320 *et seq.*
EXAMINATION OF GOODS
buyer's right, 4–204 *et seq.*
"EXEMPT AGREEMENT," 5–58 *et seq.*
EXHAUST THE SUBMISSION
failure, 10–202 *et seq.*
EXPENSES
reimbursement, 1–134 *et seq.*
EXPRESS AUTHORITY
of agent, 1–74, 1–78, 1–80
EX-SHIP CONTRACT, 4–200
EXTORTIONATE CREDIT BARGAINS, 5–307 *et seq.*
EXTORTIONATE CREDIT TRANSACTIONS, 9–287 *et seq.*
EXTRA COMMERCIUM, 7–166
EXTRA-JUDICIAL COMPOSITION CONTRACT, 9–478 *et seq.*
EXTRA-JUDICIAL SETTLEMENTS, 9–449 *et seq.*

F.A.S., 4–195, 4–198 *et seq.*
F.O.B., 4–195, 4–197 *et seq.*
FACTORS, 1–36 *et seq.*, 1–139
FACTORY AND COMMISSION, 1–16, 1–196
"FAMILY HOME" (SEQUESTRATION), 9–304 *et seq.*
FICTITIOUS HIRE-PURCHASE TRANSACTION, 7–26
FICTITIOUS LEASE, 7–27
FICTITIOUS SALE, 7–20 *et seq.*
FIDEJUSSIO, 8–07
FIDELITY GUARANTEE, 8–54 *et seq.*, 8–125 *et seq.*, 8–145 *et seq.*
FIDUCIARY DUTY
agent, 1–118 *et seq.*
directors, 3–24 *et seq.*
partners, 2–09, 2–95, 2–113 *et seq.*
promoters, 3–16
FIRM, 2–05, 2–30 *et seq.*
FITNESS OF GOODS
for particular purpose, 4–96 *et seq.*

"Fixed-Sum Credit," 5–64 *et seq.*, 5–67, 5–71, 5–215
Floating Charges, 3–09, 3–181 *et seq.*, 7–10
Foreign Bills of Exchange, 6–08, 6–17 *et seq.*, 6–84
Foreign Principal, 1–147
Fraudulent Misrepresentation
  agent's authority, 1–168
  in partnership, 2–130 *et seq.*
"Fraudulent Preferences," 9–05, 9–39 *et seq.*
  nova debita, 9–56 *et seq.*
  payments in cash, 9–52 *et seq.*
  transactions in ordinary course of business, 9–54 *et seq.*
Frustration
  of agency, 1–185 *et seq.*
Functus, 10–171, 10–183
Functus Officio, 10–171

General Agent, 1–32 *et seq.*, 1–84
Generic Goods, 4–43
Genus Nunquam Perit, 4–43
"Giving Time" (Cautionary Obligation) 8–135 *et seq.*
Goods, Definition, 4–36 *et seq.*
  ascertained, 4–131 *et seq.*
  existing goods, 4–38
  future goods, 4–38
  generic goods, 4–43
  specific goods, 4–39 *et seq.*, 4–131 *et seq.*
  unascertained, 4–123 *et seq.*, 4–148 *et seq.*
Goodwill, 2–01, 2–28 *et seq.*, 2–189 *et seq.*
Gratuitous Alienations
  reduction, 9–17 *et seq.*, 9–279
Gross Returns
  sharing, 2–23 *et seq.*
Guarantee
  company limited by, 3–18, 3–52 *et seq.*
"Guarantor," 8–06

"Hire-Purchase Agreement," 5–52 *et seq.*, 5–55 *et seq.*, 5–71
Holder
  in due course, 6–47 *et seq.*
  of bill of exchange, 6–45 *et seq.*
Holding Companies, 3–123 *et seq.*, 3–152 *et seq.*
  subsidiary company as agent, 3–161
Holding Out, 1–19, 1–89, 2–53, 2–83, 2–86, 2–88 *et seq.*
House Factors, 1–66 *et seq.*
Hypothecs, 7–10, 7–30 *et seq.*
  conventional, 7–34 *et seq.*
  landlord's, 5–255, 7–27, 7–44 *et seq.*
  legal, 7–43 *et seq.*
  maritime, 7–66 *et seq.*
  solicitor's, 7–62 *et seq.*
  superior's, 7–59 *et seq.*
  tacit, 7–43 *et seq.*

Implied Authority
  of agent, 1–74, 1–78, 1–81 *et seq.*
In Limine, 10–166
In Manibus Curiae, 7–54
In Modum Probationis, 10–45
In Re Mercatoria, 8–42 *et seq.*
In Rem Suam, 1–177
In Solidum, 8–32, 8–91, 8–96
In Transitu, 1–25, 4–233n, 4–251
Inchoate Bill of Exchange, 6–43
Incorporeal Moveables
  securities over, 7–93 *et seq.*
Indemnity, Contract of
  distinguished from cautionry, 8–24 *et seq.*
Independent Contractor, 1–11 *et seq.*
Indorsement of Bill of Exchange, 6–62 *et seq.*
  in blank, 6–66
  restrictive, 6–67
  special, 6–66
Indorser of Bill of Exchange, 6-22, 6–62 *et seq.*
  liability, 6–111 *et seq.*
Inhibitions and Adjudications, Register of, 9–73, 9–143 *et seq.*, 9–156, 9–291, 9–366
"Iniquity," 10–185
Inland Bills of Exchange, 6–08, 6–17 *et seq.*, 6–84

INNOCENT MISREPRESENTATION
agent's authority, 1–168
in partnership, 2–130 *et seq.*
INSANITY
partner, 2–141
principal or agent, 1–195 *et seq.*
INSOLVENCIES, REGISTER OF, 9–73, 9–80, 9–83, 9–475 *et seq.*
INSOLVENCY, 4–233, 4–240 *et seq.*, 4–250, 9–01, 9–12 *et seq.*
absolute, 9–12 *et seq.*
practical, 9–12, 9–15
reduction of fraudulent or unfair preferences 9–39 *et seq.*
reduction of gratuitous alienations, 9–18 *et seq.*
"INSOLVENCY PRACTITIONER," 9–90 *et seq.*
INSURABLE INTEREST
company property, 3–143
INSURANCE BROKERS, 1–38
INTER SE, 2–63, 2–95, 9–43, 10–72
INTEREST
bill of exchange, 6–33
seller's right, 4–279, 4–288
INTERIM TRUSTEE (SEQUESTRATION) 9–73, 9–80 *et seq.*, 9–87 *et seq.*, 9–153, 9–164 *et seq.*
appointment, 9–87, 9–89 *et seq.*
discharge, 9–221 *et seq.*
functions, 9–88
preservation of debtor's estate, 9–172 *et seq.*
qualifications, 9–91 *et seq.*
removal and resignation, 9–167 *et seq.*
revised statement, 9–204 *et seq.*
statement of debtor's affairs, 9–183 *et seq.*
INTRA VIRES, 1–24
INVECTA ET ILLATA, 7–27, 7–44, 7–46, 7–56, 7–59
INVESTIGATIONS, DEPARTMENT OF TRADE AND INDUSTRY, 3–154 *et seq.*
ISSUE OF BILL OF EXHANGE, 6–40

JOINT ADVENTURE, 2–16 *et seq.*
JOINT AND SEVERAL LIABILITY
parties to bill of exchange, 6–93
JOINT AND SEVERAL LIABILITY—*cont.*
partners, 2–07, 2–37, 2–52, 2–66, 3–173
JOINT PROPERTY, 2–21 *et seq.*, 2–101
JUDICIAL FACTOR, 2–143 *et seq.*, 2–173, 9–19, 9–29, 9–60
JUDICIAL REFERENCES, 10–207 *et seq.*
JURISDICTION OF ARBITER, 10–50 *et seq.*
JUS AD REM, 4–08, 7–06
JUS CREDITI, 7–186
JUS IN PERSONAM, 7–06, 8–02
JUS IN RE, 4–05, 7–05, 7–19, 8–02
JUS QUAESITUM TERTIO, 2–74
JUS RELICTAE, 2–42
JUS RELICTI, 2–42

LANDLORD'S SEQUESTRATION FOR RENT, 7–54 *et seq.*
LAW AGENT, 1–40, 1–72
LAW COMMISSIONS' REPORT ON SALE AND SUPPLY OF GOODS, 4–02 *et seq.*, 4–10
LAW COMMISSIONS' REPORT ON SALE OF GOODS FORMING PART OF A BULK, 4–04
LEGAL MORTGAGE, 7–97 *et seq.*
LEGITIM, 2–42
LEX FORI, 7–71 *et seq.*
LICENCES (CONSUMER CREDIT), 5–122 *et seq.*
appeals, 5–149 *et seq.*
duty of holder to notify changes, 5–143
group, 5–124, 5–126, 5–133
issue, 5–132 *et seq.*
register of particulars, 5–141 *et seq.*
renewal, variation, suspension and revocation, 5–134 *et seq.*
standard, 5–124 *et seq.*, 5–129 *et seq.*
LICENSING OF CREDIT AND HIRE BUSINESSES, 5–122 *et seq.*
contravention of provisions, 5–147 *et seq.*
LIEN, 1–67, 7–11, 7–14, 7–120 *et seq.*
accountant's, 1–141, 7–140, 7–142
auctioneer's, 1–45, 1–153, 7–152
banker's, 7–155 *et seq.*
bill of exchange, 6–53
general lien, 1–138 *et seq.*, 7–139 *et seq.*, 7–146 *et seq.*

LIEN—*cont.*
house and estate factors', 1–67
maritime, 7–66 *et seq.*
mercantile agent's, 1–37, 1–39, 1–45, 1–138 *et seq.*, 7–150 *et seq.*
need for possession, 7–128 *et seq.*
partner's, 2–132
shares of company, 3–265
solicitor's, 1–140, 7–31, 7–125, 7–157 *et seq.*
special lien, 1–141, 7–139 *et seq.*
stockbroker's, 7–153
unpaid seller, 4–234 *et seq.*, 4–269 *et seq.*
LIMITED COMPANY, 2–05 *et seq.*, 2–32, 2–176, 3–02, 3–45 *et seq.*
conversion to unlimited, 3–67 *et seq.*, 3–113
"LIMITED" (IN COMPANY'S NAME), 3–83
abbreviation, 3–83
exemption from use, 3–60
LIMITED PARTNERSHIP, 2–06, 2–162 *et seq.*, 3–173, 3–177
assignation of share in, 2–175
dissolution, 2–171, 2–175
general and limited partners, 2–163, 2–170, 2–175
management, 2–169 *et seq.*
registration, 2–164 *et seq.*
winding up, 2–172 *et seq.*
"LINKED TRANSACTION" (CONSUMER CREDIT), 5–116 *et seq.*
LIQUIDATION, 2–129, 5–145
LIS, 10–14
LOAN
to a partnership, 2–28 *et seq.*
LUCRATI, 9–25

MANDATE, 1–09 *et seq.*, 1–89, 1–179
letters, 1–16
partners, 2–54 *et seq.*
MANDATORY
duty of care, 1–10
"MARKET OVERT," 4–157
MARKING OF CHEQUE, 6–179
MATERIAL BREACH
contract of sale, 4–116
"MATRIMONIAL HOME"
protection of rights in sequestration, 9–311
MEETINGS
company, 3–38 *et seq.*
creditors, 9–407 *et seq.*
MEMORANDUM OF ASSOCIATION, 3–05, 3–13, 3–21, 3–28, 3–46, 3–50, 3–52 *et seq.*, 3–57, 3–80 *et seq.*, 3–130 *et seq.*, 3–193 *et seq.*
contents, 3–198 *et seq.*
effect, 3–276 *et seq.*
relationship with articles, 3–194 *et seq.*
MENTAL INCAPACITY, 1–196
MERCANTILE AGENT, 1–36 *et seq.*, 1–141, 1–153, 4–163 *et seq.*, 4–324, 7–84
MISLEADING PRICE INDICATIONS, 4–385
"MOCK AUCTION," 4–330 *et seq.*
"MODEL LAW," 10–06, 10–08
MODIFIED SEQUESTRATION PROCEDURE, 9–426 *et seq.*
MOTOR VEHICLES
hire-purchase or conditional sale, 5–384 *et seq.*
"MULTIPLE AGREEMENT" (CONSUMER CREDIT), 5–108 *et seq.*
MUTATIS MUTANDIS, 10–72

N.P., 6–86
NAMED PRINCIPAL, 1–145 *et seq.*
NECESSARIES, 1–100 *et seq.*, 4–31, 4–33
NECESSITY, AGENCY, 1–28 *et seq.*, 1–109
NEGOTIABLE INSTRUMENTS, 6–02, 6–06 *et seq.*, 6–14
restrictions on (consumer credit), 5–279 *et seq.*
NEGOTIATION OF BILL OF EXCHANGE, 6–62 *et seq.*
NEGOTIORUM GESTIO, 1–28 *et seq.*, 1–70, 1–95, 4–156
NEGOTIORUM GESTOR, 9–14
NEGOTIUM, 10–14
NEMO DAT QUOD NON HABET, 4–155
NEW YORK CONVENTION ON ARBITRAL AWARDS, 10–05

NEXUS, 7–05
NOBILE OFFICIUM, 9–09, 9–74, 9–150, 9–393
NON-BUSINESS DAYS, 6–32
"NOT NEGOTIABLE"
  cheques, 6–194
NOTICE OF TERMINATION (CONSUMER CREDIT), 5–249
NOTING OF BILL OF EXCHANGE, 6–86 *et seq.*
"NOTOUR BANKRUPTCY", 9–40, 9–59, 9–291
NOVA DEBITA, 9–51, 9–56 *et seq.*
NOVATION, 8–110

OBITER-DICTUM, 4–77
OBJECTS OF COMPANY, 3–216 *et seq.*
  alteration, 3–238 *et seq.*
OBLIGATIONES LITERIS, 10–44 *et seq.*
ONUS OF PROOF, 1–10, 4–222, 6–54
OPINION
  expressions, 4–52 *et seq.*
OSTENSIBLE AUTHORITY
  agent, 1–78 *et seq.*, 1–91 *et seq.*, 1–166, 1–176
OUSTING JURISDICTION OF COURTS, 10–01, 10–04
OVERSMEN, 10–88 *et seq.*
  appointment, 10–112, 10–116 *et seq.*
  disqualification, 10–127 *et seq.*
  relationship with arbiters, 10–93 *et seq.*
  remuneration, 10–145 *et seq.*

P.L.C., 3–82
P.N. AC, 6–86
P.N.P, 6–86
PACTUM DE NON PETENDO, 8–109, 8–142
PAR VALUE, 3–48, 7–114
PARI PASSU, 3–251, 9–291, 9–449
PARTNERS, 1–01, 1–17, 2–01 *et seq.*, 6–24, 8–48 *et seq.*
  (See also PARTNERSHIP)
  authority to bind firm, 2–54 *et seq.*
  expulsion, 2–105
  general, 2–163, 2–167, 2–170, 2–172, 2–175

PARTNERS—*cont.*
  holding out as, 2–89 *et seq.*
  implied mandate, 2–54 *et seq.*
  incoming, 2–73 *et seq.*, 2–104, 2–175
  liability for firm's debts, 2–06, 2–45, 2–47, 2–50 *et seq.*
  limited, 2–162 *et seq.*
  misapplication of property, 2–71 *et seq.*
  relations with other partners, 2–95 *et seq.*
  relations to outsiders, 2–48 *et seq.*
  remuneration, 2–104
  restrictions on authority, 2–63 *et seq.*
  retired, 1–176, 2–80 *et seq.*, 2–157 *et seq.*
PARTNERSHIP, 2–01 *et seq.*
  (See also PARTNERS)
  assignation of share in, 2–123 *et seq.*, 2–175
  at will, 2–106 *et seq.*
  business names, 2–177 *et seq.*
  comparision with registered company, 3–165 *et seq.*
  constitution, 2–18 *et seq.*
  contracts, 2–35 *et seq.*
  definition, 2–12 *et seq.*
  dissolution, 2–09, 2–133 *et seq.*, 2–171, 2–175
  distribution of assets, 2–161
  fiduciary nature, 2–09, 2–95, 2–113 *et seq.*
  final settlement of accounts, 2–161
  goodwill, 2–01, 2–28 *et seq.*, 2–189 *et seq.*
  holding out, 2–89 *et seq.*
  liability for wrongs, 2–65 *et seq.*
  limited, 2–162 *et seq.*
  management, 2–104, 2–169 *et seq.*, 3–177
  property, 2–41 *et seq.*, 2–98 *et seq.*
  relations among partners, 2–95 *et seq.*
  relations with outsiders, 2–48 *et seq.*
  rescission, 2–130 *et seq.*
  rules for determining existence, 2–20 *et seq.*
  separate persona, 2–30 *et seq.*, 2–44, 2–99, 2–103
  termination, 2–108, 2–126 *et seq.*

PARTNERSHIP—*cont.*
winding up, 2–128, 2–142 *et seq.*, 2–172 *et seq.*
PAWN, 5–266, 7–77
order to deliver, 5–278
realisation, 5–276 *et seq.*
redemption, 5–269 *et seq.*
PAWN-RECEIPTS, 5–267
"PAYING BANKER," 6–182
PAYMENT OF BILL OF EXCHANGE
honour *supra* protest, 6-141 *et seq.*
in due course, 6–127 *et seq.*
PENSION CONTRIBUTIONS (EXCESSIVE), 9–283 *et seq.*
"PER PRO," 6–26
PER SE, 4–222, 9–50
PERMANENT TRUSTEE (SEQUESTRATION), 9–72, 9–80 *et seq.*, 9–96 *et seq.*, 9–153, 9–156, 9–226, 9–235 *et seq.*
accounts of intromissions, 9–344, 9–350 *et seq.*
administration of estate, 9–294 *et seq.*
confirmation, 9–216, 9–219 *et seq.*
contractual powers, 9–312 *et seq.*
discharge, 9–379 *et seq.*
election, 9–206 *et seq.*
replacement, 9–238 *et seq.*
submission of claims, 9–330 *et seq.*
vesting of estate, 9–249 *et seq.*
PERSONA
firm, 2–30 *et seq.*, 2–44, 2–99, 2–103
registered company, 3–128 *et seq.*, 5–145
PERSONAL BAR, 4–158, 6–25, 8–11
by holding out, 1–19, 1–91, 2–83
"PERSONAL CREDIT AGREEMENT," 5–47
PERSONAL LIABILITY
agent, 1–145 *et seq.*
PETITIONS FOR SEQUESTRATION, 9–102 *et seq.*
entities other than individuals, 9–115 *et seq.*
living or deceased debtors, 9–103 *et seq.*
PLEDGE, 4–27 *et seq.*, 5–265 *et seq.*, 7–77 *et seq.*, 7–106, 7–109, 7–111
POLICY OF LIFE INSURANCE
assignation, 6–06
security over, 7–93 *et seq.*
POSSESSION
recovery (consumer credit), 5–241
"POSTPONED DEBT," 9–338, 9–340
POWER OF ATTORNEY, 1–16, 1–196
PRAEPOSITA NEGOTIIS DOMESTICIS, 1–97
PRAEPOSITURA, 1–96, 1–98 *et seq.*
PRAEPOSITUS NEGOTIIS, 1–102
PRAEPOSITUS NEGOTIIS SOCIETATIS, 2–51
PRAESUMPTIO JURIS, 1–147
PRE-EMPTION CLAUSE, 2-112, 3-174
"PREFERRED DEBT," 9–338 *et seq.*
PREMIUMS
apportionment of in partnership, 2–156
PRESCRIPTION
bills of exchange, 6–135
cautionary obligations, 8–116, 8–151 *et seq.*
PRESENTMENT OF BILL OF EXCHANGE
for acceptance, 6–70 *et seq.*
for payment, 6–77 *et seq.*
PRESERVATION OF ESTATE (SEQUESTRATION), 9–172 *et seq.*
PRESUMED AUTHORITY, 1–94 *et seq.*
PRICE, 4–19, 4–23, 4–36, 4–44 *et seq.*, 4–173
action for, 4–287 *et seq.*
PRIMA FACIE, 1–151, 2–26, 3–33, 4–42 *etc.*
PRINCIPAL AND AGENT, 1–01 *et seq.*, 4–90
PRINCIPAL DEBTOR, 8–05
"PRINCIPAL OBLIGANT," 8–06
PRIVATE COMPANY, 2–176, 3–16, 3–43, 3–45, 3–56, 3–63, 3–71 *et seq.*, 3–174, 3–216, 3–245
compared with public company, 3–77 *et seq.*
conversion to public company, 3–115 *et seq.*
deregulation, 3–110 *et seq.*
PRIVATE TRUST DEED FOR CREDITORS, 9–10, 9–80, 9–450 *et seq.*
PRO RATA, 2–07, 2–37, 6–236, 8–89 *et seq.*, 8–96
PRO TANTO, 7–190
PROCURATION, SIGNATURE BY, 6–26
PROCURATORY IN REM SUAM, 1–177 *et seq.*
"PRODUCT"
definition, 4–363
producer, 4–364 *et seq.*

PRODUCT LIABILITY, 4–361 *et seq.*
PROFITS
sharing, 2–25, 2–104, 2–142, 2–157
"PROHIBITION NOTICE," 4–380
PROMISSORY NOTES, 6–01 *et seq.*, 6–07, 6–22, 6–23, 6–225 *et seq.*
delivery, 6–235
joint and several, 6–236
liability of maker, 6–242
payable on demand, 6–237 *et seq.*
presentment for payment, 6–240 *et seq.*
PROMOTERS, 3–14 *et seq.*
PROPERTY AGENTS, 1–53 *et seq.*
PROPERTY DEVELOPMENT BUSINESS, 1–65
PROPERTY IN GOODS
transfer, 4–118 *et seq.*
PROROGATION OF SUBMISSION, 10–84 *et seq.*, 10–165
"PROTECTED GOODS," 5–237 *et seq.*
PROTECTED TRUST DEED, 9–10, 9–19, 9–29, 9–60, 9–281, 9–452, 9–471 *et seq.*
PROTECTION ORDERS (CONSUMER CREDIT), 5–301
PROTEST (BILLS OF EXCHANGE), 6–18, 6–84 *et seq.*
PROUT DE JURE, 4–35
PROXIES, 3–109
PUBLIC COMPANY, 3–43, 3–45, 3–56, 3–63, 3–71 *et seq.*, 3–174, 3–209, 3–216, 3–246, 3–260
authorised minimum capital, 3–32, 3–74, 3–85, 3–91, 3–115, 3–246
compared with private company, 3–77 *et seq.*
conversion to private company, 3–119 *et seq.*
PUNCTUM TEMPORIS, 2–111

"QUALIFIED CREDITOR," 9–103 *et seq.*
QUALITY OF GOODS
implied terms, 4–84 *et seq.*
QUANTUM MERUIT, 1–131
QUOAD, 9–14
QUOTATIONS (CONSUMER CREDIT), 5–174 *et seq.*

"RACE OF DILIGENCE," 9–290
RATIFICATION, 1–20 *et seq.*, 1–109, 1–166, 6–25
RATIO DECIDENDI, 8–08
REAL RIGHT, 7–05, 7–15
REBUS IPSIS ET FACTIS, 10–85
RECEIVERS, 3–09
RECALL OF AWARD OF SEQUESTRATION, 9–150 *et seq.*
effect, 9–163
expenses, 9–161 *et seq.*
grounds, 9–157 *et seq.*
procedure, 9–153 *et seq.*
RECALL OF DISCHARGE (SEQUESTRATION), 9–377
REFEREE IN CASE OF NEED (BILLS OF EXCHANGE)
liability, 6–117
REGISTERED OFFICE (OF COMPANY), 3–210 *et seq.*
REGISTRAR OF COMPANIES, 2–164, 2–167, 3–12, 3–74 *et seq.*, 3–117 *et seq.*, 3–120, 3–129, *et seq.*, 3–211 *et seq.*
REGISTRATION
companies, 3–12 *et seq.*, 3–74, 3–129 *et seq.*
limited partnerships, 2–164 *et seq.*
REGULATED AGREEMENT, 5–06, 5–44 *et seq.*, 7–14, 7–77
cancellation, 5–196 *et seq.*
REI INTERITUS, 1–185
REI INTERVENTUS, 8–43
REJECTION OF GOODS
buyer's right, 4–205 *et seq.*, 4–301 *et seq.*
partial, 4–225 *et seq.*
"RELEVANT COURT ORDER" (SEQUESTRATION), 9–143
"RELEVANT DAY" (BANKRUPTCY), 9–30
RELIEF, RIGHT OF
against agent, 1–117
against co-cautioners, 8–96 *et seq.*
against principal, 1–136 *et seq.*
against principal debtor, 8–92 *et seq.*
among partners, 2–52
prescription, 8–93
REMUNERATION
agent, 1–128, 1–131 *et seq.*

REMUNERATION—*cont.*
arbiters and oversmen, 10–145 *et seq.*
RENUNCIATION OF AGENCY, 1–183 *et seq.*
RENUNCIATION OR WAIVER OF BILL OF EXCHANGE, 6–131
REPRESENTATION AS TO CREDIT, 8–26 *et seq.*
REPUTED OWNER, 4–162
RES PERIT DOMINO, 4–120
RESALE
unpaid seller's right, 4–234, 4–268 *et seq.*
RESERVATION OF RIGHT OF DISPOSAL, 4–149, 4–153
RESOLUTIONS (AT COMPANY MEETINGS), 3–39 *et seq.*, 3–110 *et seq.*
RESOLUTIVE CONDITION, 4–22
RESPONDENTIA, BOND OF, 1–30, 1–70, 7–34 *et seq.*
RESTITUTIO IN INTEGRUM, 2–127
"RESTRICTED-USE CREDIT," 5–79 *et seq.*
RETENTA POSSESSIONE, 7–28
RETENTION, RIGHT OF, 2–132, 4–234 *et seq.*, 4–268, 4–269 *et seq.*, 7–11, 7–120
debt, 7–189 *et seq.*
property title, 7–176 *et seq.*
"RETURN ORDER" (CONSUMER CREDIT), 5–303, 5–305 *et seq.*
REVOCATION
agency, 1–177 *et seq.*
cautionary obligation, 8–119 *et seq.*
RIGHTS IN SECURITY OVER MOVEABLES, 7–01 *et seq.*
corporeal moveables, 7–75 *et seq.*
creditor's power to sell, 7–109 *et seq.*
exceptions to need for possession, 7–30 *et seq.*
founded on possession, 7–11, 7–73 *et seq.*
founded on possesion and implied by law, 7–120 *et seq.*
hypothecs 7–30 *et seq.*
incorporeal moveables, 7–93 *et seq.*
need for possession, 7–15 *et seq.*
pledge, 7–77 *et seq.*
retention of debt, 7–189 *et seq.*
retention on property title, 7–176 *et seq.*
RIGHTS IN SECURITY OVER MOVEABLES—*cont.*
scope, 7–111 *et seq.*
security holder's obligations, 7–113 *et seq.*
statutory charges, 7–32, 7–65
stocks and shares, 7–97 *et seq.*
RISK
passing, 4–120
"ROMALPA" CLAUSE, 4–154, 7–179
"RUNNING-ACCOUNT CREDIT," 5–64 *et seq.*, 5–216 *et seq.*

SALE OF GOODS, 4–01 *et seq.*
acceptance, buyer's duty, 4–173, 4–202 *et seq.*
actions for breach of contract, 4–278 *et seq.*
auction, 4–311 *et seq.*
capacity, 4–31 *et seq.*
definition of contract, 4–18 *et seq.*
delivery, seller's duty, 4–175
description, 4–72 *et seq.*, 4–148
distinguished from barter, 4–23, 4–25
distinguished from security, 4–27 *et seq.*
effects of the contract, 4–117 *et seq.*
examination, buyer's right of, 4–204 *et seq.*
formalities of the contract, 4–35
formation of contract, 4–17 *et seq.*
implied authority, 1–86
implied terms about quality or fitness, 4–84 *et seq.*
performance of the contract, 4–173 *et seq.*
price, 4–19, 4–23, 4–36, 4–44 *et seq.*, 4–173
rejection, buyer's right of, 4–206 *et seq.*
remedies for breach, 4–116
rights of unpaid seller against goods, 4–231 *et seq.*
sample, 4–111 *et seq.*
subject-matter of the contract, 4–36 *et seq.*
terms of the contract, 4–50 *et seq.*
transfer of property, 4–118 *et seq.*
transfer of title, 4–155 *et seq.*
implied authority, 1–86
SAMPLE, SALE BY, 4–111 *et seq.*

SASINE, 7–28
SCOTTISH ADVISORY COMMITTEE ON ARBITRATION LAW (DERVAIRD COMMITTEE), 10–08
SCOTTISH LAW COMMISSION REPORT ON BANKRUPTCY AND RELATED ASPECTS OF INSOLVENCY AND LIQUIDATION, 9–08
SECONDARY AND CATHOLIC SECURITIES, 7–119
SECRET PROFIT, 1–126 *et seq.*
SECURITY
  distinguished from sale, 4–27 *et seq.*
SECURITY HOLDER
  obligations, 7–113 *et seq.*
SELLER'S REMEDIES, 4–286 *et seq.*
SEQUESTRATION, 9–01, 9–68 *et seq.*
  administration, 9–76 *et seq.*
  arbitration and compromise, 9–405 *et seq.*
  award, 9–126 *et seq.*
  concurrent proceedings, 9–121 *et seq.*
  conduct by permanent trustee, 9–235 *et seq.*
  cure of defects in procedure, 9–392 *et seq.*
  date, 9–141
  discharge of debtor, 9–357 *et seq.*
  discharge of interim trustee, 9–221 *et seq.*
  discharge of permanent trustee, 9–379 *et seq.*
  effect on diligence, 9–290 *et seq.*
  examination of debtor, 9–316
  interim preservation of estate, 9–172 *et seq.*
  jurisdiction, 9–119 *et seq.*
  meetings of creditors, 9–408 *et seq.*
  modified procedure, 9–426 *et seq.*
  nature and purpose, 9–68 *et seq.*
  of bank customer, 6–170
  order of priority in distribution, 9–338 *et seq.*
  petitions, 9–102 *et seq.*
  recall of award, 9–150 *et seq.*
  role of interim trustee, 9–164 *et seq.*
  safeguarding interests of creditors, 9–278 *et seq.*
SEQUESTRATION—*cont.*
  statutory meeting of creditors, 9–188 *et seq.*
  submission of claims, 9–330 *et seq.*
  supplies by utilities, 9–423 *et seq.*
SHARE CAPITAL, 3–18, 3–26 *et seq.*, 3–91 *et seq.*, 3–191, 3–244 *et seq.*
  allotment, 3–94 *et seq.*
  alteration, 3–248 *et seq.*
  cancellation, 3–248
  consolidation, 3–248, 3–250
  conversion into stock, 3–248, 3–251
  diminution, 3–248, 3–252
  increase, 3–248, 3–249
  maintenance, 3–103 *et seq.*
  payment 3–97 *et seq.*
  raising, 3–93
  reduction, 3–252
  subdivision, 3–248
  classes, 3–33, 3–253 *et seq.*
  offer to public, 3–93
SHIPBROKERS, 1–17, 1–38, 1–69, 1–87
SHIPMASTER, 1–17, 1–30, 1–33, 1–68 *et seq.*, 1–87
SHIPS
  mortgage, 7–75
SKILL AND CARE
  agent's duty, 1–112 *et seq.*
"SMALL AGREEMENT" (CONSUMER CREDIT), 5–104 *et seq.*
SOLICTOR, 1–33, 1–54, 1–58, 1–72, 1–89 *et seq.*, 1–115, 1–129, 1–140, 1–152, 2–15
SPECIAL AGENT, 1–32 *et seq.*
SPECIAL DAMAGES, 4–280 *et seq.*
SPECIFIC GOODS, 4–39 *et seq.*, 4–131 *et seq.*, 4–263
SPECIFIC IMPLEMENT, 4–280, 4–299 *et seq.*
SPECIFIC PERFORMANCE, 4–299 *et seq.*
SPECIFICATIO, 4–69
STANNARIES, 2–13
STATED CASE (ARBITRATION), 10–13, 10–77 *et seq.*, 10–170
STATUTORY ARBITRATIONS, 10–02
STATUTORY MEETING (SEQUESTRATION), 9–164, 9–188 *et seq.*
  calling, 9–188 *et seq.*
  claims for voting, 9–200 *et seq.*
  proceedings, 9–203 *et seq.*

"STIPULATIONS," 4–54
as to time (in contract), 4–60 *et seq.*
STOCK, 3–20, 3–248, 3–251
STOCK EXCHANGE
members, 2–15
STOCKBROKERS, 1–38 *et seq.*
STOCKS AND SHARES
securities over, 7–97 *et seq.*
STOPPAGE IN TRANSIT, 1–25, 4–234 *et seq.*, 4–240, 4–251 *et seq.*, 4–269 *et seq.*
duration , 4–254 *et seq.*
how effected, 4–265 *et seq.*
SUBCONTRACT, 1–11 *et seq.*
SUBSIDARY COMPANIES, 3–123 *et seq.*, 3–152 *et seq.*
as agent of holding company, 3–161
SUMMARY ADMINISTRATION, 9–438 *et seq.*
SUMMARY DILIGENCE, 5–243, 6–08, 6–84, 6–119 *et seq.*, 6–149, 6–234
SUO ONERE, 2–76
"SUPPLIER" (CONSUMER CREDIT), 5–93
"SURETY," 5–257, 8–06, 8–15 *et seq.*
"SURETYSHIP," 8–06
SURVEYOR, 1–88, 1–111
"SUSPENSION NOTICE," 4–381
SUSPENSIVE CONDITION, 4–21, 4–133

TABLE A (COMPANIES), 3–51, 3–59, 3–131, 3–253, 3–254, 3–264 *et seq.*
TABLE B (COMPANIES), 3–50, 3–81, 3–245
TABLE C (COMPANIES), 3–57, 3–59, 3–81, 3–264
TABLE D (COMPANIES), 3–57, 3–59, 3–80 *et seq.*, 3–209
TABLE E, 3–64, 3–81, 3–264
TABLE F (COMPANIES), 3–50, 3–80, 3–209, 3–246, 3–260
TACIT RELOCATION, 2–106
"TAKE-OVER BID," 3–162 *et seq.*
TANTUM ET TALE, 9–274
TIME ORDERS (CONSUMER CREDIT), 5–297 *et seq.*
TITLE
defective (bills of exchange), 6–57 *et seq.*
TITLE (IN SALE OF GOODS)
implied terms, 4–64 *et seq.*
transfer, 4–155 *et seq.*
"TOTAL CHARGE FOR CREDIT," 5–49
TRADE DESCRIPTIONS, 4–83, 4–336 *et seq.*
TRADING STAMPS, 4–334 *et seq.*
TRADITIONIBUS, NON NUDIS PACTIS, DOMINIA RERUM TRANSFERUNTUR, 7–15
"TRANSFER ORDER" (CONSUMER CREDIT), 5–303 *et seq.*
TRANSFEROR BY DELIVERY (BILLS OF EXCHANGE)
liability, 6–115 *et seq.*
TRUST DEED FOR CREDITORS, 9–450 *et seq.*
"TRUTH-IN-LENDING" PRICIPLE, 5–152

UBERRIMAE FIDEI, 2–130, 8–25
"ULTIMATE LOSS CLAUSE," 8–72 *et seq.*
ULTRA FINES COMPROMISSI, 10–27, 10–50, 10–191 *et seq.*, 10–201
ULTRA VIRES, 1–24, 10–192
ULTRA VIRES DOCTRINE, 3–218 *et seq.*
abolition, 3–228 *et seq.*
"UMPIRE," 10–90
UNCITRAL MODEL LAW ON INTERNATIONAL COMMERCIAL ARBITRATION, 10–06
UNASCERTAINED GOODS, 4–123 *et seq.*, 4–148
UNDERWRITING CONTRACT, 1–178
UNDISCLOSED PRINCIPAL, 1–26, 1–43 *et seq.*, 1–143 *et seq.*, 1–159 *et seq.*
UNFAIR PREFERENCES, 7–100, 9–41, 9–60 *et seq.*, 9–280
UNIVERSITAS, 4–35
UNJUST ENRICHMENT, 1–28, 4–32, 4–156, 4–282
UNLIMITED COMPANY, 3–18, 3–61 *et seq.*
conversion to limited, 3–67 *et seq.*, 3–113
UNNAMED PRINCIPAL, 1–144, 1–156 *et seq.*
UNPAID SELLER, 4–232
rights against goods, 4–231 *et seq.*
"UNRESTRICTED-USE CREDIT," 5–79, 5–82
UNSOLICITED CREDIT-TOKENS, 5–173
UNSOLICITED GOODS, 4–344 *et seq.*
UTITUR JURE AUCTORIS, 6–63

VALUABLE CONSIDERATION
bills of exchange, 6–51 *et seq.*
VALUATION
by third party in sale of goods, 4–47 *et seq.*
distinguished from arbitration, 10–14 *et seq.*
VEIL OF INCORPORATION
lifting, 3–146 *et seq.*
VERGENS AD INOPIAM, 8–93
VESTING OF DEBTOR'S ESTATE (SEQUESTRATION) 9–250 *et seq.*
limitations, 9–272 *et seq.*
VITIUM REALE, 4–155
VOIDABLE TITLE
sale under, 4–159 *et seq.*
VOUCHER (SEQUESTRATION), 9–332

WARRANT TO CARRY BACK, 7–56 *et seq.*
WARRANT TO CITE DEBTOR (SEQUESTRATION), 9–129 *et seq.*
"WARRANTY," 4–55 *et seq.*, 4–58
WARRANTY OF AUTHORITY
breach, 1–45, 1–85, 1–166 *et seq.*, 4–324
WEIGHTS AND MEASURES AUTHORITIES, 1–64, 1–65, 5–363 *et seq.*
"WHITE-BONNET," 4–323
WINDING UP, 2–127, 2–142 *et seq.*, 2–170 *et seq.*, 3–47, 3–53

YOUNGER COMMITTEE ON PRIVACY, 5–349